Core Knowledge®

Teacher Handbook Series
Grade 5

Edited by E. D. Hirsch, Jr.
and Souzanne A. Wright

Core Knowledge® Foundation
Charlottesville, Virginia

Photography Credits

Text Credits

From "The Advantages of Mingling Indians with Whites" by Richard H. Pratt from an extract of the Official Report of the Nineteenth Annual Conference of Charities and Correction (1892), as appeared in *Americanizing the American Indians*, edited by Francis Paul Prucha, Cambridge, MA: Harvard University Press, 1973.

"Sweet Betsy from Pike" from *I Hear America Singing*, adapted from an arrangement by Carl Miller. Used by permission of The Carl S. Miller Irrevocable Trust.

From Bartolomé De Las Casas, *The Devastation of the Indies: A Brief Account*, translated from the Spanish by Herma Briffault. Copyright © 1974 by The Crossroad Publishing Company. Reprinted by permission of The Continuum International Publishing Group.

Published by Core Knowledge® Foundation
Library of Congress Cataloging-in-Publication Data
Grade 5 Teacher Handbook
Edited by E. D. Hirsch, Jr. and Souzanne A. Wright—1st ed.
p. cm.—(The teacher handbook series)

ISBN 1-890517-80-1
2006920266

PRINTED IN CHINA
10 9 8 7 6 5 4 3 2 1

April 2006
First Edition

Requests for permission should be directed to:
Core Knowledge Foundation
801 East High Street
Charlottesville, VA 22902
Telephone: (434) 977-7550
Fax: (434) 977-0021
E-mail: coreknow@coreknowledge.org
Home page: www.coreknowledge.org

This book is dedicated, gratefully,

to

the hard-working Core Knowledge fifth-grade teachers
who have gone for so long without this book.

A Note to Teachers

This book is addressed to, and intended to be read by, Grade 5 teachers. When Core Knowledge was first used in the classroom, some topics in the *Core Knowledge Sequence* sent teachers scrambling to the library. Many teachers spent hours consulting encyclopedias and looking for other reliable sources of information on topics they were asked to teach—topics they had not studied in college or education school. Now, with the development of the *Core Knowledge Teacher Handbooks,* Core Knowledge teachers will have a single, reliable source that gives them not only the background knowledge they need but also valuable teaching tips and review strategies. We hope this handbook will be useful for teachers seeking to build on their foundation of knowledge, whether or not they teach in the growing network of Core Knowledge schools.

If you are interested in learning more about the Core Knowledge curriculum and the work of the Foundation, please contact us for more information: 801 East High Street, Charlottesville, VA 22902; (434) 977-7550; coreknow@coreknowledge.org. On our website (www.coreknowledge.org), you will find an online bookstore, lessons created by teachers in Core Knowledge schools, and other supporting materials developed by the Foundation.

Acknowledgments

This series has depended on the assistance of more than 100 people. Some of those named here already know the depth of our gratitude; others may be surprised to find themselves thanked publicly for the assistance they gave quietly and freely. To all helpers named and unnamed, we are deeply grateful.

Editor-in-Chief of the *Teacher Handbook Series*: E. D. Hirsch, Jr.
Editor and Project Director: Souzanne A. Wright

Core Knowledge Reviewers: Matthew Davis and Cyndi Wells
Resources Coordinator: Rob Hewitt
Assessments Writer: Margarete C. Grove
Expert Reviewer Coordinator: Elizabeth B. Rasmussen

Experts on Subject Matter: Matthew Davis (language arts); Fritz Gritzner (geography); Chris Arndt and Sterling Stuckey (American history); Michael Smith (history and geography—Mesoamerican civilizations); Joseph Miller (history and geography—European exploration); Ann Moyer (history and geography—Renaissance); John Butt (history and geography—England); Matthew Davis (history and geography—Russia); Lucien Ellington (history and geography—Japan); Kristin Onuf (visual arts); Whitney Gatesman and Diane Persellin (music); Wayne Bishop (mathematics); Margaret Saha (science—biology); Lisa Landino (science—chemistry); Louis Bloomfield (science—biographies)

Contributing Editors (across all grades): Matthew Davis; E. D. Hirsch, Jr.; Susan T. Hitchcock; Michael J. Marshall; Elizabeth B. Rasmussen; Charles J. Shields; Souzanne A. Wright

Contributing Editors (specific subject): Sandra Stotsky (language arts); Fritz Gritzner and Sheldon Stern (history and geography); Bruce Cole (visual arts); David Klein (mathematics); Martha Schwartz (science)

Contributing Writers: Mary Epes, Carol Jago, and Mary Yarber (language arts); Michael Chesson, Robert Cole, James Dudley, Fritz Gritzner, Mary Beth Klee, Michael McCahill, and Luther Spoehr (history and geography); Rod Miller (visual arts); David Klein (mathematics); Juliana Adelman, Robert Evans, Roberta Friedman, Steve Lund, Anne Rosenthal, Rick Schwartz, and Stephanie Trelogan (science)

Advisors on Elementary Education: Margarete C. Grove; Debra Mentzer; Elizabeth B. Rasmussen; Cyndi Wells; Souzanne A. Wright

Teachers: Special thanks to the teachers—too many to list here—who have offered their advice and suggestions for improving the *Teacher Handbooks* during focus groups at our national conference.

Development House: Brown Publishing Network, Inc.

Benefactor: The Walton Family Foundation

Contents

Introduction

About These Books

The Core Knowledge Foundation has written this *Teacher Handbook* to help you teach the Core Knowledge curriculum for Grade 5. The handbook is based on the *Core Knowledge Sequence*. The *Teacher Handbook* complements the *Sequence,* so using them together is easy. The *Sequence* outlines the specific topics to be taught in the six subject areas, then the *Teacher Handbook* expands on every topic listed. It's as though the *Sequence* topics are links on a website, and the handbook is the content behind each link.

The *Teacher Handbook* is a rich resource that provides essential background information about language arts, history and geography, visual arts, music, mathematics, and science. It identifies what students should have learned in previous grades and what they will learn in future grades. It defines crucial vocabulary words, points out cross-curricular connections, offers teaching and review suggestions, and lists titles of books and website addresses as resources for you and your class.

IV. Life Cycles and Reproduction

The Big Idea

All organisms go through a series of developmental stages called the life cycle. When maturity is reached, the organism is capable of reproduction.

Remember that each subject you study with students expands their vocabulary and introduces new terms, thus making them better listeners and readers. As you study life cycles and reproduction, use read alouds, independent reading, and discussions to build students' vocabularies.

What Students Should Already Know

Students in Core Knowledge schools should be familiar with

Grade 2

- cycles in nature: life cycles
  - birth, growth, reproduction, death
  - reproduction in animals: egg to egg with a chicken, frog to frog, butterfly to butterfly (metamorphosis)

What Students Need to Learn

- The life cycle and reproduction ❶
  - life cycle: development of an organism from birth to growth, reproduction, death
    - example: growth stages of a human (embryo, fetus, newborn, infancy, childhood, adolescence, adulthood, old age)
  - All living things reproduce themselves; reproduction may be asexual or sexual.
    - examples of asexual reproduction: fission (splitting) of bacteria, spores from mildews, molds, and mushrooms, budding of yeast cells, regeneration and cloning
    - Sexual reproduction requires the joining of special male and female cells, called gametes, to form a fertilized egg.
- Sexual reproduction in animals ❷
  - reproductive organs: testes (sperm) and ovaries (eggs)
  - external fertilization: spawning
  - internal fertilization: birds, mammals
  - development of the embryo: egg, zygote, embryo, growth in uterus, fetus, newborn

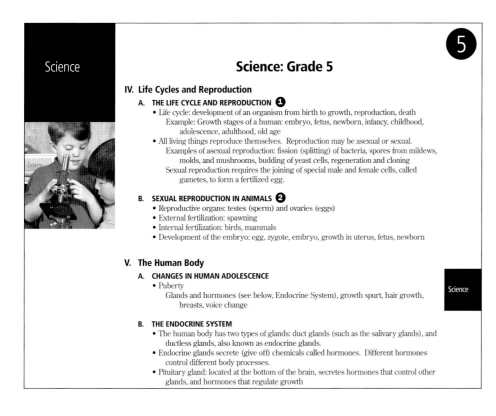

Science: Grade 5

5

IV. Life Cycles and Reproduction

A. THE LIFE CYCLE AND REPRODUCTION ❶
- Life cycle: development of an organism from birth to growth, reproduction, death
  Example: Growth stages of a human: embryo, fetus, newborn, infancy, childhood, adolescence, adulthood, old age
- All living things reproduce themselves. Reproduction may be asexual or sexual.
  Examples of asexual reproduction: fission (splitting) of bacteria, spores from mildews, molds, and mushrooms, budding of yeast cells, regeneration and cloning
  Sexual reproduction requires the joining of special male and female cells, called gametes, to form a fertilized egg.

B. SEXUAL REPRODUCTION IN ANIMALS ❷
- Reproductive organs: testes (sperm) and ovaries (eggs)
- External fertilization: spawning
- Internal fertilization: birds, mammals
- Development of the embryo: egg, zygote, embryo, growth in uterus, fetus, newborn

V. The Human Body

A. CHANGES IN HUMAN ADOLESCENCE
- Puberty
  Glands and hormones (see below, Endocrine System), growth spurt, hair growth, breasts, voice change

B. THE ENDOCRINE SYSTEM
- The human body has two types of glands: duct glands (such as the salivary glands), and ductless glands, also known as endocrine glands.
- Endocrine glands secrete (give off) chemicals called hormones. Different hormones control different body processes.
- Pituitary gland: located at the bottom of the brain, secretes hormones that control other glands, and hormones that regulate growth

Science

In the sections that follow, you will be introduced to the key elements of the handbook, step-by-step. Our purpose is not only to guide you through the handbook, but also to introduce you to some other key resources and help you to teach the Core Knowledge curriculum to your class.

Organization of the Handbook

Both the *Sequence* and the *Teacher Handbook* are divided into six subject areas: language arts, history and geography, visual arts, music, mathematics, and science. Then each of these subjects is divided into sections.

Subject Opener

▶ *Percentage Guidelines*

The first page of every subject includes a brief outline of the subject matter and suggested percentages of time you might choose to allot to teaching each section.

▶ *Introduction*

The introduction to each subject area gives a summary of the topics covered in this subject. Written in essay style, it summarizes upcoming content and often suggests the importance of certain topics to your students.

Sections

Some sections in the handbook can be taught as individual units that last a few weeks; others are better taught by weaving them in throughout the year. Although the *Sequence* and the *Teacher Handbook* have specific sections on reading and mathematics, it is expected that both will be taught on an ongoing basis throughout the year. Most Core Knowledge teachers spend a week or two teaching the material on "Feudal Japan" as a unit. On the other hand, many teachers prefer to spread out the stories and poems in Language Arts and the songs in Music throughout the year. This "stretched-out" approach allows you to combine selected stories, poems, and songs with other units of study. For example, you might teach Renaissance works like *Don Quixote* and *A Midsummer Night's Dream* in tandem with the history and visual arts topics on the Renaissance, or African-American spirituals in connection with the American history topics on slavery, or the Native American legends and trickster stories with the American History section about Native American cultures, and so on. The same strategy will work with the science biographies, which can be paired with the science topics they illustrate; for example, Ernest Just with cells and Carl Linnaeus with "Classifying Living Things."

▶ *Section Opener*

Each section in the *Teacher Handbook* begins in the same way.

• *The Big Idea* contains the central idea of the section.

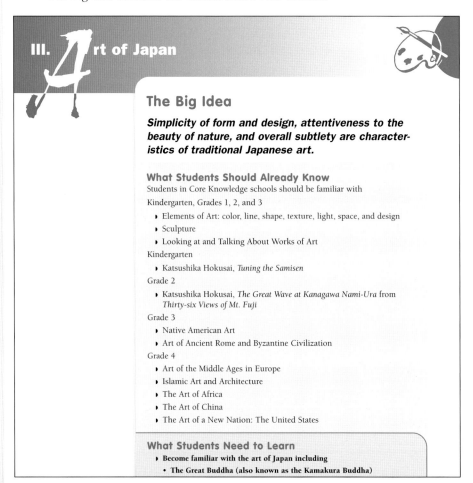

III. Art of Japan

The Big Idea

Simplicity of form and design, attentiveness to the beauty of nature, and overall subtlety are characteristics of traditional Japanese art.

What Students Should Already Know

Students in Core Knowledge schools should be familiar with

Kindergarten, Grades 1, 2, and 3
  ▶ Elements of Art: color, line, shape, texture, light, space, and design
  ▶ Sculpture
  ▶ Looking at and Talking About Works of Art
Kindergarten
  ▶ Katsushika Hokusai, *Tuning the Samisen*
Grade 2
  ▶ Katsushika Hokusai, *The Great Wave at Kanagawa Nami-Ura* from *Thirty-six Views of Mt. Fuji*
Grade 3
  ▶ Native American Art
  ▶ Art of Ancient Rome and Byzantine Civilization
Grade 4
  ▶ Art of the Middle Ages in Europe
  ▶ Islamic Art and Architecture
  ▶ The Art of Africa
  ▶ The Art of China
  ▶ The Art of a New Nation: The United States

What Students Need to Learn
  ▶ Become familiar with the art of Japan including
    • The Great Buddha (also known as the Kamakura Buddha)

• *What Students Should Already Know* outlines what students *should* have learned in previous grades if they have been in Core Knowledge classrooms. You may wish to assess how much of this content they already know and how much they still need to learn.

• *What Students Need to Learn* presents the learning goals for the section, adapted from the bulleted items in the *Core Knowledge Sequence*. Sometimes, the *Sequence* goals are summarized in the handbook, so it's a good idea to compare the handbook learning goals to the *Sequence* as you plan your lessons. Note that if a topic has already been introduced in a previous grade and is a repeated learning goal, it is listed only once under *What Students Should Already Know*.

• *What Students Will Learn in Future Grades* provides a glimpse of topics that Core Knowledge teachers will cover in the grades ahead. You may recognize opportunities for joint projects involving students in different grades. For example, in Core Knowledge schools, students learn about chemical and physical change in Grade 5, then review physical change in Grade 6. Some teachers use this topic as a theme to tie classrooms together, with sixth-grade "experts" helping teach fifth graders. By the same token, your fifth graders, once they have studied the Civil War in detail, may serve as experts for second-grade students learning about the Civil War on a more basic level.

▶ *Vocabulary*

The next two sections list vocabulary words. Core Knowledge is, among other things, an ambitious vocabulary-building program. It is based on the idea that students learning to read need to do more than just sound out words. They also need to recognize the words they are sounding out and rapidly *comprehend* them. Students who are limited by small vocabularies are likely to encounter difficulties in reading comprehension in later grades, even if they have good decoding skills. Consequently, it is almost impossible to overestimate the importance of building vocabulary in the early grades.

III. Art of Japan

Materials

Art Resources 22–24

The Great Buddha of Kamakura

Ryōan-ji Temple Garden

Suzuki Harunobu, *Woman Admiring Plum Blossoms at Night*

Instructional Masters 47–48

Traditional Japanese Art, p. 363

A Japanese Garden, p. 366

instructions to create a simple origami animal, p. 365

gravel, p. 366

small rocks and pebbles, p. 366

cardboard box lids, p. 366

Styrofoam meat trays, p. 367

Vocabulary

Student/Teacher Vocabulary

Buddha: meaning "Enlightened One," the founder of Buddhism (S)

Buddhism: one of the main religions in Japan; the goal of Buddhism is to achieve enlightenment by self-purification (S)

haiku: an unrhymed Japanese poem of three lines of 5, 7, and 5 syllables respectively (T)

landscape garden: a garden that is decorated or developed in an artistic manner (S)

kabuki: a traditional Japanese dramatic form that includes highly stylized singing and dancing (T)

origami: the art of folding paper into decorative objects (T)

Shinto: "way of the gods;" the oldest and largest religion in Japan; emphasizes reverence for family, nature, and the ruling family as direct descendant of the gods (T)

ukiyo-e: "the art of the floating world;" Japanese art (typically woodcuts) that described life around the district of Edo (now Tokyo) (T)

Domain Vocabulary

Art of Japan and associated words:
nirvana, gigantic, enlightenment, personal desires, spiritual, stone, carved, simplicity, elegance, cohesive, culture, subtlety, harmony, serene, perfection, ruling class, calligraphy, paper-art, Korea, China, Edo period, woodcut, prints, rock garden, temple, rocks, sand,

This handbook helps you teach vocabulary in several ways. First, the background information on each topic will enhance your own understanding. Second, each section of the handbook also defines a number of challenging words—unusual words, technical terms, and words that need to be precisely defined. These words are identified with either an (S) or a (T). An (S) means that students should learn this word, so words marked (S) are good candidates for repeated use and explicit vocabulary work. A (T) means that the word is important for teachers to know but not one that students are expected to master. Of course, you always have the option of including (T) words in your instruction, thus exposing students to a richer vocabulary.

▶ *Domain Vocabulary*

The handbook also includes a section called Domain Vocabulary. A domain is simply an area or field of knowledge, such as maps, planets, or Native Americans. Domain Vocabulary is a collection of words you are likely to use while talking about that topic with students. If you were teaching the Grade 5 unit on world geography and discussing great lakes of the world, you might use words like *inland, ocean, navigation, freshwater, salt water, irrigation, trade,* and *recreation.* Sometimes you might use the words often enough that students could eventually add them to their own working vocabularies. Other times, you might use the words only once or twice in passing. This might not be enough for students to master the word, but it will provide a base on which they can build if they encounter the word later.

You don't need to use all the words under Domain Vocabulary; think of them as a bank of words you can draw upon—in large or small amounts—that will enrich your classroom discussions and help your students become better readers because you are strengthening and building their vocabularies. For more details on teaching vocabulary, please refer to the Supplemental Essay on pp. 36–39.

▶ *Materials*

To help you plan your lessons, a list of Instructional Masters, Art Resources, Text Resources, and teaching materials used in the section is found here.

▶ *Cross-curricular Connections*

This section provides suggestions of material from other subject areas that might be incorporated into the current unit of study you are teaching.

blocks and oil paint, p. 367 **large pieces of heavy white paper, p. 367**	brushstrokes, landscape, Edo, Tokyo, city, bridge, water, meditate, kimono, robe, samurai, wood, tea, ceremony, drink, sip, cup, pour, *plus words that describe things in the artworks, e.g., waterfall, pebbles, bridges, Zen, etc.* **Cross-curricular Connections** **History and Geography** World: **Feudal Japan**

▶ *Main Text*

The larger column of text provides you with background information about specific subjects. Since none of us is an expert in all topics, this information is useful as a refresher course on a given topic. The more background you have as a teacher, the better able you will be to guide students' learning.

▶ *Teaching Ideas*

The Core Knowledge Foundation does not require teachers to follow any particular teaching strategy when teaching the topics in the *Sequence*. The teaching ideas in the margins and the cross curricular connections are only *suggestions*.

However, it is worth keeping in mind the ways in which students learn. Students learn through a process of building schemas and connections based upon prior knowledge. Students can build these schemas only through connecting their current experiences with previous ones. In other words, prior knowledge is the base, or foundation, on which new knowledge is constructed.

▶ *Review*

Near the end of each section are suggestions for review and some classroom discussion questions. These review suggestions do not represent a complete Core Knowledge assessment package. You are strongly encouraged to develop or acquire review and assessment materials of your own.

Just a word on assessing students: The purpose of assessment is not to judge students, or to teach to a test, but to guide instruction. The best kind of assessment goes on regularly, not just at the end of a unit or section. Assessments should include initial assessment, monitoring, and summative evaluation.

For an initial assessment, you as the teacher need to evaluate the prior knowledge that students possess and provide the experiences they need to learn more. Monitoring goes on while instruction is taking place; it establishes whether a student is moving toward a goal. This kind of assessment can often be informal and might include noting students' participation in class discussions, observing students as they work on an activity or interact with classmates, journal writing, and keeping portfolios of their work. Summative evaluation happens at the end of the unit or section. It determines whether the student has met the goals and learned the content.

To help gauge your students' level of learning, in addition to the materials offered in this book, you will find summative evaluation materials in the *Pearson Learning/Core Knowledge History & Geography* books and in your basal mathematics and reading programs. Your school may also give various state and national tests. All of these evaluative materials can provide you with data about your students' progress.

III. Art of Japan

More Resources

The titles listed below are offered as a representative sample of materials and not a complete list of everything that is available.

For students —

• *Hokusai: The Man Who Painted a Mountain,* by Deborah Kogan Ray (Frances Foster Books, 2001). Hardcover, 40 pages, ISBN 0374332630.

For teachers —

• *Art of Japan: Wood-Block Color Prints (Art Around the World),* by Carol Finley (Lerner, 1998). Hardcover, 64 pages, ISBN 082252077X.

• Art Print Resources (209 Riverdale Avenue, Yonkers, NY 10705, www.artprintresources.com, or 1-800-501-4278) sells a set of posters of the artworks in the *Sequence* for this grade.

• Art Sense (www.artsense.net) provides an art program using videos and trade books.

• Art to the Core (Davis Publications, www.davis-art.com or 1-800-533-2847). A kit of materials that includes slides of artworks, lessons plans, assessment masters, and vocabulary masters, all keyed to the *Core Knowledge Sequence* for this grade.

• Crizmac (www.crizmac.com) sells a wide range of art education materials.

• *Hokusai: One Hundred Views of Mt. Fuji,* edited by Henry D. Smith (George Braziller, 1999). Paperback, 224 pages, ISBN 080761453X.

• *Japanese Prints: The Art Institute of Chicago,* by James T. Ulak (Abbeville Press, 1995). Hardcover, 320 pages, ISBN 0789206137.

• The Freer Gallery of Art and the Arthur M. Sackler Gallery comprise the National Museum of Asian Art at the Smithsonian Institution in Washington, D.C. Their website, www.asia.si.edu, is a source of images and other information on Japanese art.

▶ *More Resources*

At the end of each section we list some books, websites, and other resources that may be useful to you in teaching the section, including books for students and teachers.

Lesson Plans

You can use the teaching ideas and the background information in the main text of each section to develop lesson plans.

In many cases you may not need to write a lesson plan from scratch: you may be able to borrow or adapt an existing lesson. Every year, veteran Core Knowledge teachers present lesson plans at the Core Knowledge National Conference. Hundreds of these lesson plans are available on our website. The lesson plan web pages also contain links to large collections of lesson plans created by various regional groups dedicated to supporting the teaching of the Core Knowledge curriculum, including the Baltimore Curriculum Project and the Colorado Unit Writing Project.

In addition, there are websites that collect or link to lesson plans that are not written specifically for Core Knowledge schools but might be adapted for your use. Internet search engines like Google.com can be very valuable in locating these.

Supplemental Materials

Supplemental materials that go with the handbook include a set of Instructional Masters, a set of Art Resources, and a set of Text Resources.

• The **Instructional Masters** highlight concepts and information from the curriculum. They can serve as worksheets or be turned into transparencies for introducing, teaching, or reinforcing a topic. These worksheets are meant to supplement the worksheets you create to help your students learn in every subject. We have not included any Instructional Masters for mathematics, because mathematics programs generally come with their own supplementary materials. In the back of the package of Instructional Masters are additional materials for you to use. These include a Venn diagram, T-chart, and K-W-L chart. Instructional Masters are listed under Materials and are reduced and shown next to the topics they support.

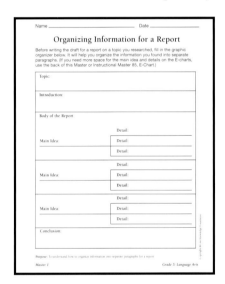

Use Instructional Master 1.

• The **Art Resources** are the works of art listed in the *Sequence,* as well as other important works of art. On the back of each print is a set of Looking Questions to initiate discussion. These same questions are in the main text of the *Teacher Handbook.* Art Resources are listed under Materials, and an icon **⑤** appears in the section of the text they support.

• The **Text Resources** include all of the stories and poems in the second, third, and fourth sections of Language Arts for Grade 5—episodes from *Don Quixote, Little Women (Part First), The Adventures of Tom Sawyer,* and so on, plus three additional Native American trickster tales. There are additional texts in world and American history, visual arts, music, and science. There are lyrics for all the Grade 5 songs listed in the *Sequence* and sheet music is also provided for seven songs. A list of Text Resources appears at the front of the section and then an icon **99** appears in the text.

Developing a Yearlong Plan

Once you are familiar with the *Sequence* topics, you should draw up a yearlong plan. *The Core Knowledge K–8 Guide: A Model Monthly Topic Organizer* (informally known as the "monthly planner") shows one of the many possible ways of arranging the Core Knowledge topics to fit in a school year. The Foundation also has *The Core Knowledge Day-by-Day Planner*, which provides an even more detailed and comprehensive map of topics. You may be able to follow one of these planners more or less exactly, or you may need (or prefer) to develop a customized yearlong plan that indicates when you plan to address the various Core Knowledge topics, when you intend to address state standards, and how and when Core Knowledge topics can be combined to help you meet and exceed state standards.

The Core Knowledge topics are intended to occupy about half of your curriculum, or perhaps a little more. This leaves time to teach material covered in the state standards and add topics of local interest. In many cases Core Knowledge content can be combined with state standards and/or used to enhance state standards. For example, it is often possible to combine a general state standard (e.g., "Learn about significant cultures of the past.") with a specific topic in the *Core Knowledge Sequence* (e.g., Egypt or Mesopotamia). You can find guidelines for state alignments, as well as several completed alignments, on the Core Knowledge website, under "Schools." The Foundation also has consultants who can help you with alignments.

When working on the yearlong plan and during the school year, we strongly encourage you to meet regularly with other fifth-grade teachers. The first year of Core Knowledge teaching can be a daunting experience, with many new topics to master and fit into the school year. But it is much less daunting when teachers are willing to share ideas and work together to identify resources and develop lessons. Research has shown that the Core Knowledge curriculum is most successfully implemented when teachers have common planning time, both before and during the school year. Teachers report that such teamwork helps ease the workload associated with the first year of Core Knowledge teaching and leads to better classroom units, better relations with colleagues, and an enjoyable learning experience for all.

Core Knowledge Resources for Grade 5

This handbook is intended to be a key resource for you as you prepare to teach the topics in the *Core Knowledge Sequence*. However, it is not the only resource at your disposal. Over the past decade, the Foundation has introduced a number of books and other resources to help teachers teach the Core Knowledge curriculum. Except where noted, the following materials can be ordered from the Foundation by visiting our online bookstore or calling our order line: 1-800-238-3233. Some of the materials are also available in bookstores.

• *What Your Fifth Grader Needs to Know*, edited by E. D. Hirsch, Jr. Part of the popular Doubleday series, this book (available in bookstores as well as from the Foundation) contains a brief treatment of the subjects in the *Core Knowledge Sequence* for Grade 5. Although the book's primary audience is parents, Core Knowledge teachers have used it for many years. Overall, you will probably find the handbook is more useful to you than the series book, because the handbook is addressed directly to teachers and addresses issues of pedagogy and review. However, the series book contains much material suitable for reading aloud and can be a valuable secondary source of information.

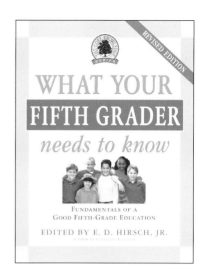

• *Pearson Learning/Core Knowledge History & Geography* series. These are the only official Core Knowledge textbooks for history and geography. The bound book for Grade 5 (also known as level 5; ISBN 0-7690-2972-8) is a richly illustrated, full-color volume intended to be read by students, but also suitable for reading aloud. It covers the following topics: World Lakes; The Maya, Aztec, and Inca Civilizations; The Renaissance; The Reformation; England: Golden Age to Glorious Revolution; The Age of Exploration; Early Russia; Feudal Japan; Westward Expansion Before the Civil War; Westward Expansion After the Civil War; Native Americans: Cultures and Conflicts; and Geography of the United States. The sections on The Renaissance (ISBN 0-7690-5074-3), The Age of Exploration (ISBN 0-7690-5077-8), Westward Expansion Before the Civil War (ISBN 0-7690-5080-8), The Civil War (ISBN 0-7690-5081-6), Westward Expansion After the Civil War (ISBN 0-7690-5082-4), and Native Americans: Cultures and Conflicts (ISBN 0-7690-5084-0) are also available as stand-alone modules. Each section of the bound book also has a matching teacher guide. The teacher guides include discussion guidelines, suggested activities, learning masters, and assessment questions. They are available in classroom sets. Whenever a Pearson unit is available for a topic in this handbook, the unit is listed under *More Resources*. The books are described in more detail on the Core Knowledge website but must be purchased from Pearson Learning: 1-800-321-3106.

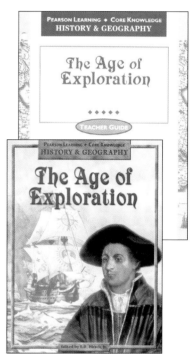

• *Listen, My Children: Poems for Fifth Graders* includes all the poems listed in the *Sequence* for Grade 5.

• *Core Classics* are child-friendly editions of literary classics prepared by the Foundation. Titles for Grade 5 include *Selected Adventures of Sherlock Holmes, Don Quixote, Narrative of the Life of Frederick Douglass,* and *Little Women*.

• *Rats, Bulls, and Flying Machines: A History of the Renaissance and Reformation* is an interdisciplinary history of the period, touching on history, literature, art, and music. A teacher's guide is also available.

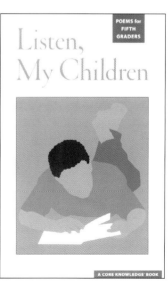

• *Core Knowledge Day-by-Day Planner* is available on individual grade-level CDs as well as workbooks and provides a yearlong plan, weekly plans, and daily plans for Core Knowledge, while allowing plenty of room for state standards and other expectations. Additionally, resources and units are streamlined to ease the daunting task of "fitting it all in" in your first year.

• *The Core Knowledge Music Collection: Grades 3–5* is a multi-CD set that includes works listed in the *Sequence* for Grade 5, such as the Overture from *A Midsummer Night's Dream*.

Note that earnings from the sale of Core Knowledge books and products go to the non-profit Core Knowledge Foundation. E. D. Hirsch, Jr., receives no remuneration for editing the series nor any other remuneration from the Core Knowledge Foundation.

Finding Additional Resources

Although this book and the Core Knowledge publications listed above will help you cover many topics in the *Core Knowledge Sequence,* you will also need to use resources from other publishers.

Your school probably already has a reading program and a mathematics program. Your mathematics program should contain many opportunities for practice to ensure that students master the basic skills they will need to move on to more advanced mathematics. The Foundation can provide you with information on reading and mathematics programs that are widely used in Core Knowledge schools.

In addition, we encourage you to enrich and enliven your teaching by sharing outstanding trade books, both fiction and nonfiction, with students. Using trade books in class is a longstanding Core Knowledge tradition, and one that we hope will continue even now that the Foundation is beginning to offer more resources. You will find lists of book titles and websites at the end of each section of this book, although these are only a sampling of what is available.

The Foundation has also published a book and compiled an online database to help teachers locate additional grade-appropriate books and educational materials. The book is *Books to Build On: A Grade-by-Grade Resource Guide for Parents and Teachers.* Published in 1996, this resource guide lists hundreds of books and resources that will help you teach the topics specified in the *Sequence. Resources to Build On (RTBO)* is an online, searchable database designed to supplement *Books to Build On.* The search engine allows you to search for books relevant for Grade 5, and/or to limit your search by topic. *RTBO* is available, free of charge, on the Core Knowledge website.

Remember to explore your school library and local public libraries as sources for books. Many libraries contain hidden treasures. Ask librarians to carry Core Knowledge books, including *What Your Fifth Grader Needs to Know,* and other books in the series. Search engines and online bookstores can also be tremendously useful when it comes to locating suitable trade books. For example, Amazon.com has an "advanced search" feature that allows you to specify the age level and subject of a book. You can search for books about Abraham Lincoln or the art of Japan or plant structures written for ages 9–12, or titles for young adults that might be suitable for independent reading or reading aloud. Amazon.com also includes published reviews and customer reviews for many books. Search engines like Google.com allow you to find book recommendations from teachers and librarians around the country.

Professional Development

You may have already attended the Core Knowledge "Overview" presentation. This presentation introduces teachers and administrators to the idea of cultural literacy, the nature, aims, and history of the Core Knowledge Foundation, the benefits of implementing the Core Knowledge curriculum, and some of the practical considerations involved in its implementation. If your school has not had an "Overview" session, we strongly recommend that you call the Foundation to schedule one.

After the "Overview" presentation, your next step should be to participate in the Foundation's "Getting Started" workshop to familiarize yourself with the *Core Knowledge Sequence*, the topics it outlines, its unique spiraling nature, and the cross-curricular teaching opportunities it offers. Although you will want to focus most of your attention on fifth grade, we encourage you also to look at other grades, so you can see what students have learned in previous grades and how the curriculum builds on prior learning. You can use the *Sequence* to get an overview of the curriculum for Grade 5, and the *Teacher Handbook* to get more information about specific topics.

A third professional development workshop, "Developing Core Knowledge Lessons and Assessments," focuses on writing lessons and assessments using this handbook and the *Sequence*.

Beyond the Teacher Handbook: Some Additional Strategies for Success

Although this handbook will provide you with the basic knowledge you will need to teach fifth graders the Core Knowledge topics, there are many other things you can do to improve your teaching of Core Knowledge. Here are a few strategies we've learned from successful Core Knowledge teachers and schools over the past decade.

• As you teach the Core Knowledge topics, look for ways in which special area teachers—art, music, and physical education teachers; special education teachers; ESL teachers; media and technology specialists; and so on—can enhance and connect with the topics you are teaching. The most successful Core Knowledge schools are the ones where the curriculum is implemented and supported by all key staffers, where the librarian and media specialists use the *Sequence* as a purchasing guide for books and software, and the physical education teachers enhance the classroom content, for example, by staging "Olympic Games" in conjunction with a unit on Ancient Greece.

• Look for ways to get parents and caregivers involved. Core Knowledge is a popular curriculum with many adults, not only because it is academically rich but also because it is very explicit. If you share the relevant sections of the *Sequence* and/or your yearlong plan with the adults at home, they will know what is happening at school and may be able to help you in various ways. Some may have knowledge of a particular subject that they would be willing to share with the students; others may be willing to talk with students at home about the topics they have been studying at school. The *Sequence* and yearlong plan, when shared, can become a link that enables parents, caregivers, and teachers to work together.

• Look for ways to involve local groups and businesses. They may be able to visit classes to talk about topics that relate to what they do, or they may be able to donate services or materials. One Core Knowledge school in Texas contacted a local tile company when the school was preparing to do a unit on mosaics. The tile company offered them thousands of bits of broken tile. The school got its mosaic materials for free, and the company got a tax write-off! With a little creativity you can accomplish a lot.

• Visit our website, www.coreknowledge.org, which contains a wealth of information about Core Knowledge, as well as lesson plans, Resources to Build On, and other teacher resources.

• Subscribe to our free electronic newsletter. The newsletter includes stories on Core Knowledge schools, articles by E. D. Hirsch, Jr., and other prominent writers, links to useful websites, and announcements of upcoming events. A subscription box is located on our main web page.

• If you don't have an opportunity to share ideas regularly with other teachers at your school—or even if you do—consider subscribing to Core-net, an e-mail newsgroup for Core Knowledge teachers and supporters. For details on how to subscribe, see the Foundation's website.

• Sign up for additional Core Knowledge professional development workshops. In addition to the "Overview," "Getting Started," and "Developing Core Knowledge Lessons and Assessments" workshops mentioned above, the Foundation also offers several other workshops, including "New Teacher Orientation," "Implementation Analysis," "Summer Writing Institutes," and "Core Knowledge Coordinator and Leadership Institutes." For details, see the website.

• Attend the Core Knowledge National Conference. Held each year in the spring, the conference attracts several thousand Core Knowledge teachers who learn about Core Knowledge, attend lectures on topics in the *Sequence,* and share units. Teachers whose units are accepted for presentation get a discounted registration.

• Learn more about the ideas behind Core Knowledge. Two books by E. D. Hirsch, Jr., *Cultural Literacy* and *The Schools We Need & Why We Don't Have Them*, are available in print form and as books-on-tape from Blackstone Audio. Articles by E. D. Hirsch, Jr., can also be found on the Foundation's website.

• Continue to learn more about a subject in order to better teach it. We realize that all 50 states require teachers to take courses regularly to keep their certification. You may want to consider taking courses not only in pedagogy and educational theory, but also in subject areas like history and science.

• Finally, remember that implementing Core Knowledge is not a simple matter of buying materials and following a script. It is an ongoing process, which includes professional development; background reading; individual and group preparation; use of the *Sequence,* the *Teacher Handbook,* and other resources; and the creation of lessons and assessments. Part of the adventure of teaching Core Knowledge consists of finding ways to bring all of these elements together to create successful units. We wish you luck in your own adventure with Core Knowledge, and we hope to see you at conferences and workshops for years to come.

Core Knowledge Foundation
801 East High Street
Charlottesville, VA 22902
Telephone: (434) 977-7550
Ordering line: 1-800-238-3233
Fax: (434) 977-0021
E-mail: coreknow@coreknowledge.org
Home page: www.coreknowledge.org

Language Arts

Percentages beside major topics provide a rough guide for allocating time for Language Arts during the year.

Language Arts in Fifth Grade

The scope of language arts includes all aspects of English. Writing, reading, spelling, grammar, usage, listening, speaking, and the different genres of literature fall under language arts. Continue to follow any required reading programs for skills development as needed. We suggest, however, that more time be spent on the literature recommended in the *Core Knowledge Sequence*, as well as non-fiction readings that cover *Sequence* topics, since students in Grade 5 should have made the transition from "learning to read" to "reading to learn." In Grade 5, students will continue to apply fundamental concepts they learned in previous grades, concentrating on the aspects of spoken and written language that will allow them to become more efficient and independent readers and writers.

Students in Grade 5 will continue to build their spelling and vocabulary skills and to learn more about the conventions of grammar. They will continue to develop research skills and follow the steps of the writing process to produce their own expository and creative written work. As they gain proficiency in writing, Grade 5 students will be given greater responsibility for organizing and revising their own work and for proofreading for errors in spelling, usage, and mechanics.

The poetry, fiction and drama, and speech sections will expand students' exposure to the world of literature. These selections span different periods of time and various cultures, giving students a sense of the diversity and richness of literature throughout the ages. Both classic and modern works with timeless themes and enduring appeal are presented in the *Core Knowledge Sequence*. By listening to and/or independently reading different kinds of poetry, Grade 5 students can strengthen their reading comprehension and build vocabulary, as well as broaden their knowledge of literary techniques and terms such as *alliteration* and *onomatopoeia*.

Fiction selections for Grade 5 focus on Native American myths and legends, classic novels, and drama. Several of these selections connect with and support the history sections on the Renaissance, England, feudal Japan, the Civil War, and Native Americans. Listening to or reading these works of fiction and drama will also help students gain increasing familiarity with the elements and techniques of literature and acquaint them with specific terms such as *metaphor, simile,* and *personification.* Through these selections, students continue to develop reading comprehension potential by learning new vocabulary and by answering specific questions about the story content.

In Grade 5, students will also be introduced to important speeches in American history. They will read Abraham Lincoln's "The Gettysburg Address" and Chief Joseph's "I will fight no more forever," both of which connect to the American history topics for this grade. Reading speeches brings history to life for students and also helps them understand effective rhetorical techniques and different styles of oration.

Finally, students will be exposed to a variety of common English sayings and phrases, learning both their literal and figurative meanings and also

discussing how these sayings and phrases are used in everyday conversation. These are part of cultural literacy. Becoming aware of proverbial sayings and idiomatic expressions is especially useful to students from home environments not dominated by American English, though the experience is pleasurable for native and non-native speakers alike.

Through this curriculum, students in Grade 5 will continue to learn how to convey effectively their own thoughts and ideas using the spoken and written word. Furthermore, reading and listening to poems, stories, plays, speeches, sayings, and phrases will increase their background knowledge and their vocabularies which will in turn help them better comprehend and enjoy works of literature. Building on this core foundation, students in Grade 5 will be better able to read increasingly sophisticated literary and non-fiction works, and to write with clarity and fluency.

I. Writing, Grammar, and Usage

A. Writing and Research

The Big Idea

Students can effectively communicate their ideas, thoughts, and feelings by composing different types of written work.

What Students Should Already Know

Students in Core Knowledge schools should be familiar with

Kindergarten through Grade 4

- producing a variety of types of writing—including reports, summaries, friendly letters, descriptions, stories, and poems—with a coherent structure or story line and making reasonable judgments about what to include based on the purpose and type of composition
- knowing how to use established conventions when writing a friendly letter: heading, salutation (greeting), closing, signature
- organizing writing with a beginning, middle, and end
- writing paragraphs with a topic sentence and supporting examples and details; knowing that each new paragraph is indented
- proceeding through a process of gathering information; organizing thoughts; composing a draft; revising to clarify and refine meaning; proofreading with attention to spelling, grammar, usage, and mechanics; and presenting a final draft
- knowing that writing a report involves
  - gathering information from different sources, such as encyclopedias, magazines, interviews, observations, atlases, and websites, and presenting the information in their own words
  - understanding the audience and purpose of the writing
  - defining a main idea and adhering to it
  - providing an introduction and a conclusion
  - organizing material in separate, coherent paragraphs
  - documenting sources in a bibliography
- knowing that a bibliography is an alphabetical list of sources used to gather information for a report
- knowing that a summary is a short statement of the important ideas in a selection

What Students Need to Learn

- **Writing a research essay involves**
  - **expressing an opinion about a topic.**
  - **gathering evidence from different sources to support an opinion.**
- **Writing an essay that explains a process involves telling how to do something or how something works.**

Materials

**Instructional Masters
1–3, 81, 85**

K-W-S Chart, p. 7

E-Chart, p. 8

Organizing Information for a Report, p. 8

Making a Bibliography, p. 8

Writer's Checklist, pp. 9, 12

writing rubrics, p. 7

individual student journals, pp. 7, 12

sources of information, such as encyclopedias, magazines, atlases, news- papers, or Internet access, p. 7

access to a dictionary, p. 8

class folder for student reports, p. 8

chair or stool for poetry slam, p. 11

class folder or journal for student poems, p. 11

example of a friendly letter, p. 11

overhead projector and transparencies, p. 11

different-colored highlighters, p. 11

editing checklist, 1 per student, p. 12

outside sources about Core Knowledge topics that students collect and bring into the classroom, p. 12

bread, butter, and jelly to make a sandwich, p. 13

basket, p. 13

What Students Need to Learn continued

- giving the steps in the process in chronological, or time, order
- using transitional words and phrases, such as *first*, *next*, and *last*
- ▸ Know how to synthesize information from at least three different sources.
- ▸ Illustrate points with relevant examples.

What Students Will Learn in Future Grades

In Grade 6, students will learn how to write a standard business letter. They will also learn strategies and conventions for writing a persuasive essay, with attention to defining a thesis; supporting the thesis with evidence, examples, and reasoning; distinguishing evidence from opinion; anticipating and answering counterarguments; and maintaining a reasonable tone.

Vocabulary

Student/Teacher Vocabulary

atlas: a book or bound collection of maps (S)

bibliography: an alphabetical list of sources (such as books, magazine articles, and other resources) used to gather information for a report (S)

chronological order: the order in which events or the steps in a process occur (S)

description: a kind of writing that uses specific words and details to describe a person, place, or thing (S)

dictionary: a reference work that provides information about the meanings and uses of words, arranged in alphabetical order (S)

encyclopedia: a reference work containing information on a wide range of subjects in alphabetical order (S)

friendly letter: an informal, personal letter to family members or friends (S)

paragraph: a group of sentences all written about the same idea; in expository writing, a paragraph consists of a topic sentence followed by supporting examples and details that develop the main idea (S)

process explanation: a kind of writing that tells how to do something or how something works (S)

proofread: to read in order to find and correct mistakes in a piece of writing (S)

research essay: an essay that expresses an opinion about a topic and provides evidence from different sources to support this opinion (S)

revision: the process of changing a draft of written work; *revision* literally means "seeing again" (S)

summary: a short statement of the most important ideas in a selection (S)

topic sentence: an initial sentence that states the main idea of a paragraph (S)

Vocabulary continued

Domain Vocabulary

Writing and research and associated words:
report, summarize, heading, greeting, body, closing, address, signature, descriptive, sensory details, adjective, sight, sound, taste, touch, smell, research, researcher, document, documentation, resource, reference work, reference materials, look up, entry, footnote, thesis, main idea, proof, convincing, persuasion, subject, objection, digression, relevant, irrelevant, edit, delete, organization, quotation, quote, paraphrase, sentence, plagiarism, honesty, dishonesty, fairness, magazine, interview, newspaper, journal, book, volume, author, title, publisher, date, observation, Internet, website, World Wide Web, URL, first-hand observation, essay, formal, informal, expository, persuasive, story, story line, plot, character, setting, poem, poetry, outline, outlining, author's purpose, audience, topic, detail, introduction, conclusion, transitional word, time-order word, sequence, sequential, spatial order, reason, example, opinion, grammar, spelling, punctuation, capitalization, mechanics, usage, *plus words students use in their own writing*

At a Glance

The most important ideas for you are:

- Producing original pieces of expository and imaginative writing helps students practice spelling words and using grammar, punctuation, and capitalization correctly. It also teaches students to do research and obtain information from different sources, organize written material in a coherent way, and gain an awareness of the different purposes of the written word.

- Students in Grade 5 should be able to express themselves comfortably in writing, demonstrating their knowledge of the conventions of written language and their ability to spell most words correctly.

- Writing should not be thought of as strictly a language arts subject. The Core Knowledge curriculum offers many exciting topics for writing across the curriculum. Students should be encouraged to write about stories and poems they've read and listened to, as well as about topics they have studied in history, science, art, and music.

What Teachers Need to Know
A. Writing and Research

Background

Providing students with an opportunity to write helps them become better readers and writers. Better writing, in turn, is related to proficiency in underlying skills, such as accurate spelling, handwriting fluency, and knowledge of grammar and punctuation conventions. Spelling needs to be systematically taught within a "word study" curriculum that emphasizes advanced and complex sound-symbol correspondences, syllable conventions, ending rules, morphology (the study of meaningful word parts, like geo- in geology), and word origins.

Learning to research and write a good, well-organized report is important for students at this level. Doing these reports will help students begin to develop the skills that they will use throughout their school years and beyond. It is important for students to learn to look at information critically, to choose information that will help them support their claims, to analyze and correct their own writing, and to complete polished pieces of work.

Writing Stories

Writing their own stories gives students an opportunity to practice writing and enhances their understanding of fiction. First, ask students to remember stories they have recently read at home or in school. Then review elements of fiction: characters, setting, dialogue, and plot (see Section III, "Fiction and Drama," pp. 58–82). Finally, provide students with pencils and lined paper. Encourage them to tap into their imaginations to write their own stories. Provide a few story starters, topic suggestions, or writing rubrics to inspire them. Remind the class that stories should have a clear beginning, middle, and end. After students finish their drafts, encourage them to revise their work for clarity and proofread for correct spelling, grammar, usage, and mechanics.

Writing Reports

There will be many opportunities for students to write reports during the school year. When assigning a report as class work or homework, remind students that a report is writing that presents information about a topic. Explain to students that a report might be about an important event in history, a scientific process, or a well-known musician or artist, among other topics from the *Core Knowledge Sequence*. Reports can be incorporated into the curriculum throughout the school year. Below are steps that you might have students follow. Review them each time you assign a report.

- Choose a topic. Invite students to brainstorm suitable report topics from the materials they are studying in other curriculum areas. Create a cluster, web, or chart on the board to record students' ideas.

- Research information. You may wish to use **Instructional Master 81**, *K-W-S Chart*, when doing research. Provide examples of basic sources of information your class might use, such as encyclopedias, magazines, newspapers, interviews with experts, firsthand observations, atlases, and the Internet. (Be sure to talk with students about how quickly websites change and information is updated. Students should also be aware that some Internet sources are less reliable than others.) Review with students how to use a table of contents and an index of print resources. Discuss ways of recording information that might be useful in writing the report, e.g., jotting notes on a piece of paper or making note cards. Also, remind students to present the information they research in their own words or to cite sources carefully if they use direct quotes. Guide students to synthesize information from at least three different sources when they write reports and research essays.

- Write a draft. Before students write, have them decide on the focus, or main idea, of their reports. They may want to cluster their ideas in the same way that you did when helping students choose a topic. Then make sure they understand how to organize information into separate, coherent paragraphs. Remind students that each new paragraph should be indented. Review the elements of a standard

Teaching Idea

Encourage students to volunteer to read their stories aloud to the class. Scheduling five minutes of "sharing time" after daily journal writing is a good way to structure sharing (and listening) time.

Teaching Idea

Writing can be connected with other subjects in the curriculum. For example, in this grade you might invite students to write a fictional story about the Civil War, a letter to an explorer or an artist, a poem about a plant, or a report on one of the elements studied in science.

Teaching Idea

You may want to discuss plagiarism with students at this point. It is important that students learn how to relay information and express ideas in their own words, rather than copying. Explain that taking other people's work and passing it off as our own is stealing. Point out that sometimes it is preferable to use exact wording, and that, in such cases, it's important to put that wording in quotes and note exactly where it was found.

Teaching Idea

You might want to teach or review report writing early in the school year so that students can develop their report-writing skills further by writing on topics that are in the History and Geography *Sequence* and in the Science *Sequence*.

Teaching Idea

Before students use Instructional Master 1 for their own writing, have them fill it out for a completed research report as a model. This activity should enable students to see the connection between the Instructional Master and the report, and will give them a concrete example to recall while they are constructing their own reports.

Use Instructional Master 1.

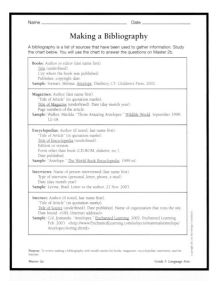

Use Instructional Masters 2a–2c.

report paragraph: a topic sentence that states the main idea, followed by examples and details that develop the main idea. You may wish to use **Instructional Master 85**, *E-Chart,* in conjunction with **Instructional Master 1**, *Organizing Information for a Report.*

Tell students that as they write they should keep in mind the purpose of their report (to inform) and their audience (other students). Also, guide them to provide an introduction that presents their report topic as well as a conclusion that summarizes the information given so that their report has a clear beginning, middle, and end.

• Polish the draft. After students finish their drafts, encourage them to revise their work for clarity. Tell them that their reports should stick to the main idea they are writing about. Have them remove or rewrite any sentences or paragraphs that do not develop the main idea. Encourage them to review the order in which information is presented and make sure the transitions between paragraphs are smooth. Then have students proofread for correct spelling, grammar, usage, and mechanics, using resources such as a dictionary if necessary.

• Finally, ask students to compile and add a bibliography to the end of their reports. Remind them that a bibliography is an alphabetical list of the books, magazine articles, and other resources they used to gather information. Use **Instructional Master 2**, *Making a Bibliography,* to illustrate proper bibliographic format. Point out that a bibliography is organized in alphabetical order by author's last name, and that each entry tells the author, the title, and when, where, and by whom the information was published. Give students opportunities to practice converting information from actual books and magazines into proper bibliographic entries.

• Present the report. Have volunteers read their reports to the class or display them in the classroom, and invite feedback from the class. Once students have completed their final drafts, you can put the reports in a class folder, add them to the students' own portfolios, hang them on the bulletin board, and so on. At times, students might want to illustrate their reports and should be encouraged to do so.

Writing Research Essays

Explain to students that a research essay expresses an opinion on a topic and then provides evidence from different sources to support this opinion. Stress the difference between a report that presents facts about a topic and a research essay that uses facts to support an opinion, or thesis.

Generate a list of topics about which students have an opinion. The list may include opinions on current school issues (uniforms, school lunches) or current events (wars in foreign countries, nutritional information). You may wish to include historical events that have been studied in class (for example, the best general in the Civil War or Thoreau's civil disobedience concerning the Mexican War). Structure your instruction on research essays around these topics of interest. You could begin by having students orally discuss/debate contrasting sides of an issue. Then have students follow the same steps used for the research report to write a short research essay.

Tell students to keep in mind the purpose of their essay, which is to persuade others. They should also think about their audience as they write. Is it other students in the class, parents, or perhaps a historical figure? Also, guide them to provide an introduction that introduces their topic and a conclusion that summarizes the information, so that their research essay has a clear beginning, middle, and end.

As students write the body paragraphs of their essays, help them construct clear and logical arguments by introducing a point and then supporting it with evidence they gathered through their research. Review the need to cite sources in a bibliography and to credit any passages that are direct quotes.

Discuss with students different ways of handling information from sources: they can quote some or all of the source word for word, or they can paraphrase. Use a specific text, and model for students how you might quote it directly in one or more ways. Then model paraphrasing the same ideas or passages.

Help students understand the value of anticipating objections to their thesis. Encourage them to ask questions such as, "If somebody were skeptical about the point I am trying to argue, what kinds of objections would that person be likely to raise? How might I answer those objections?" Help students understand how this way of thinking can sometimes lead them to stronger arguments and even to a good structure for their essay: the paragraphs can be a series of objections and replies to those objections.

Writing Essays That Explain a Process

Inform the class that an essay that explains a process (also called a process explanation) tells how to do something or how something works. Have students follow the steps for writing a report as they write a process explanation. Invite them to brainstorm suitable topics, such as how to make a pizza or how a video game works. Don't neglect topics in other subject areas of the curriculum: how to round a number, how to classify an animal, how to create a simile, etc. Create a cluster, web, or chart on the board or easel to record students' ideas.

Before students begin their drafts, explain that their essays should describe each step in the process in chronological order, or the order in which it occurs. Suggest that they explain one step per paragraph. To make the order of the steps clear, tell them to use transitional words and phrases, such as *first, next, then, finally,* and *last.* Also, direct students to include any background information that their audience might need to know in order to understand the process. Advise them to include definitions of any unfamiliar terms and to list any tools, supplies, or materials that are involved.

To reinforce the importance of detailed directions, take students through the following activity. Divide a piece of paper into four equal squares and number the squares 1, 2, 3, and 4. Tell students that you are going to provide them with four sets of directions, and they are to draw what you tell them in the appropriate square. Give each set of directions slowly to allow students time to follow these directions.

1. Draw a triangle, square, the letter *U,* and two circles.

2. Draw a triangle and square. Put the letter *U* and two circles inside the square.

3. Draw a square that has 1-inch sides. Draw an equilateral triangle with 1-inch sides. Draw the letter *U* inside the lower half of the square. Draw the two circles next to each other on the top half of the square.

4. Draw a square that has 1-inch sides toward the bottom of square number 4. Draw an equilateral triangle with 1-inch sides sitting on top of the square. Inside the square, draw the letter *U* and two circles so that they appear like a smiling face inside the square.

Teaching Idea

Use Instructional Masters 3a–3b, *Writer's Checklist,* to guide students as they write, proofread, and revise reports and other original works. When holding individual writing conferences with each student, give him or her 3 or 4 items on the checklist to focus on. You may also use this Instructional Master to reinforce new lessons in grammar and usage as you teach them.

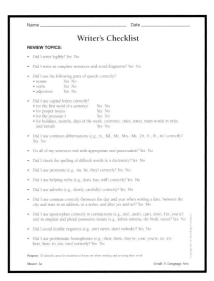

Use Instructional Masters 3a–3b.

I. Writing, Grammar, and Usage
A. Writing and Research

Cross-curricular Teaching Idea

A good way to help students improve their writing and understanding of the American History and Geography and the Science sections in Grade 5 is to ask them to write short summaries about historical events or science topics they learn about throughout the school year.

Teaching Idea

To help students think of a description topic, create a chart on the board with the headings "Art," "History," and "Science." With the class, brainstorm the names of people (for example, Daniel Boone), places (Washington, D.C.), and things (flags, railroad cars, lassos) to which they have been introduced. Write their ideas on the chart. Return to this type of activity often throughout the school year.

Teaching Idea

A simple, nonthreatening way to write a poem is to begin by making a list. Begin with a first line that defines the topic, e.g., "A beach is . . ." Then ask students to make a list of nouns that they associate with the beach: water, waves, beaches, swimmers, children, lifeguards, etc. Next, ask students to think of verbs (one or more for each noun) that go with each of these nouns. Challenge them to think of unusual words: water—glistening; waves—crashing; beaches—shining; swimmers—splashing; children—running; lifeguards—whistling. Finally, see if any of the words rhyme, and arrange the poem to take advantage of any rhymes.

Have students compare all four drawings. Which one is the same for everyone? (number 4) Why? (because the directions were very clear, detailed, and step-by-step) Reread the directions for numbers 1–3 while looking at the picture drawn for number 4. Could the directions describe number 4? (yes) If time permits, allow students the opportunity to draw a simple picture and then write step-by-step directions so a partner can re-create the exact same picture. Apply the experience from this activity to writing out directions for science experiments.

Writing Summaries

Remind the class that a summary is a brief statement of the most important ideas in a selection. Tell them that a summary states only main ideas and important details. Then have students practice writing a summary of a passage of a story, novel (see "Stories," pp. 58–73), play (see "Drama," pp. 74–82), speech (see "Speeches," pp. 83–90), or another selection they have read. Remind them to be concise and to write the main points of the selection in their own words. You might want to assign length limits to ensure conciseness. For example, you might ask that a summary of a 500-word selection be approximately three or four sentences long, or you might give a word limit, e.g., 50–100 words. When they gather information for a report or a research essay, encourage students to take notes in the form of summaries.

Writing Descriptions

Remind the class that a description is a piece of writing that tells about a person, place, or thing. Review with them that a description includes specific details that create a picture in a reader's mind. For example, a description of a flower might include words that tell about its sweet smell, its brightly colored petals, and its smooth, green stem. Read to the class a few examples of strong descriptive writing from grade-appropriate books. Point out the role of sensory language, or of descriptive writing related to the five senses (sight, hearing, taste, touch, and smell).

Provide students with lined paper and pencils and have them write their own short descriptions. You might want to choose a subject from elsewhere in the Core Knowledge curriculum, such as a Mathew Brady photo of a Civil War scene, a Bruegel painting, or a plant. After students finish their drafts, encourage them to revise their work for clarity, and to proofread for correct spelling, grammar, usage, and mechanics. After students finish writing, invite volunteers to share their descriptions with the class.

Writing Poems

Writing their own poems gives students an opportunity to practice writing, express themselves, play with language, and extend their understanding of poetry. First, ask students to remember any poems they have recently listened to or read themselves. Then, review elements of poetry, such as imagery, rhyme, repetition, rhythm, metaphor, simile, personification, onomatopoeia, and alliteration. (See Section II, "Poetry," on pp. 40–57.) Also, review two types of poetry students should have encountered—lyric and narrative—as well as poetic forms such as limericks or list poems.

You may wish to give students additional help in getting started by providing a prompt, a first line, or a theme. For example, you might invite them to write poems modeled on "A Bird Came Down the Walk," by Emily Dickinson. Students could choose an animal and write a poem describing its behavior or an encounter they have had with that animal. Or students could use Ernest Lawrence Thayer's "Casey at the Bat" as a model and describe an experience they have had that is similar. Encourage students to try to make the lines rhyme. Alternatively, write some topics from other curricular areas on the board to get students started.

For suggested poems, see the "Poetry" section of this handbook, pp. 40–57. When discussing poetry, there are several elements you can incorporate, including recollection of information/details from the poem, poetic elements used, and feelings evoked by the poem. There are no right or wrong ways to respond to poetry; encourage students to share their feelings openly and freely.

After reviewing some favorite poems, encourage students to tap their imaginations to write their own poems based on ideas or feelings. When they finish their poems, ask them to revise their work for clarity and to proofread for correct spelling, grammar, usage, and mechanics, allowing for poetic license. Encourage volunteers to read their poems aloud to the class, possibly even modeling "poetry slams," where the author sits on a special chair or stool and shares his or her work with an audience. Reading aloud will allow students to become more fluent readers and will give them more exposure to different examples of poetry. You may wish to keep copies of each student's poems in a folder or journal. Toward the end of the year, you may also want to have students compile a class anthology, arranging poems by subject, theme, or type.

Writing Friendly Letters

Remind the class that a friendly letter is an informal, personal letter written to a friend or a family member. Bring in an example and review the parts of a friendly letter: heading, greeting, body, closing, and signature. Then have students follow this format to write their own friendly letters to a real or imaginary person. Encourage them to revise their letters for clarity and proofread for correct spelling, usage, and mechanics.

Review

Below are some ideas for ongoing assessment and review activities. These are not meant to constitute a comprehensive list.

• Encourage students to plan, practice, and then present a reading of their favorite original pieces of imaginative or expository writing for an audience of other Grade 5 classes.

• To review the components of a paragraph, make transparencies of paragraphs from non-fiction books on topics the class is studying. Using an overhead projector, have the class discuss the purpose of each paragraph. They can also practice identifying the parts of paragraphs—topic sentence, supporting details—and identifying that paragraphs are indented. Create a system of highlighting in different colors so that students can highlight the topic sentence and identify

Teaching Idea

You may wish to reference two websites on poetry: www.giggle poetry.com and www.poetry4kids.com. (See *More Resources*.) Both contain many suggestions for students who are writing poems.

Teaching Idea

Students could be encouraged to write a letter about something that is happening in school. If they have written to a real person, help them correctly address envelopes and then mail their letters. Alternatively, they might be encouraged to write about a subject they have studied, or to imagine themselves as one of the characters they have studied in various subjects. For example, they might be encouraged to write a letter in the voice of Tom Sawyer, or Mistress Mary from *The Secret Garden*. They could also write a letter to an explorer they have studied in history or to an artist or composer they have learned about in art or music class.

The Big Idea in Review

Students can effectively communicate their ideas, thoughts, and feelings by composing different types of written work.

supporting details with another color. This is an excellent way to practice answering questions for reading comprehension as well.

• When working with the class to practice summarizing, you may want to emphasize choosing the most important ideas to include in a summary. This takes time for students to practice. Design a graphic organizer that includes columns labeled *Somebody, Wanted, But,* and *So.* As the class begins to study an event from history or reads a story, use this format for them to locate the most important details of the event to summarize. As students practice using this format, have them also try summarizing without a graphic organizer.

• Have students complete a book report on their favorite book. You may choose to have them complete one book report per grading period. Have students practice their paragraph writing by using the following structure to summarize a book: a topic sentence, supporting details (at least three facts about the topic or story), and a concluding sentence. Also, have students use concrete examples from the book to back up any details, and have them illustrate key points in their reports. Schedule a time for students to share their reports.

• Have students prepare a report on one of the authors studied in this grade. Encourage students to find out the basic facts of the writer's life and to choose another work by the same author to share with the class.

• Incorporate writing into all areas of the curriculum and provide an opportunity to share a variety of writing. For example, when studying poetry, encourage students to write original poems. When studying history topics, provide time to write short reports. When studying science, provide a lab sheet for students to write up experiments, and use this activity to reinforce writing about steps in a process. Have students explain the steps of an experiment using the correct order, and then explain the results.

• Students may practice a variety of different kinds of writing in individual journals. Make sure that each student has a notebook designated only for journal writing. Pose journal questions for students to write about in each subject area. Practice grammar skills and vocabulary development by providing a journal topic at the beginning of the day, and then have students read their entries aloud.

• Have students write a letter to their families, or to a particular family member, at the end of each week, month, or unit of study. Model the format on chart paper using heading, greeting/salutation, body, closing, and signature. Have students prepare for writing each letter by brainstorming three things they learned and would like to discuss. This letter is a great way to communicate with families what has happened in the class during a specific time frame, and it gives students an opportunity to practice writing letters.

• Provide time for individual teacher/student writing conferences. Provide each student with a list of editing points to focus on in his or her own writing, and make sure that students know what is expected when they write a piece to publish in class. You may wish to use **Instructional Masters 3a–3b**, *Writer's Checklist,* as a guide for students. Be sure to point out aspects of writing that the student does well.

• At the end of a unit of study, ask the class to gather sources from outside the classroom about that topic. For example, if you have been studying feudal Japan, have the class bring in magazines from home, books from the school library, printouts from websites, and any other sources that give information about feudal Japan. Then, gather all of the sources into a classroom library and allow

students to practice using sources by asking them to pick at least three to use in a final report about that subject. Be sure to review how to use a source for a report.

• When students are practicing how to write steps in a process, have them start with a simple process, such as how to make a butter and jelly sandwich. Bring in two slices of bread, butter, and a jar of jelly to class. As you make a sandwich, have students list the steps of the process and then write a paragraph explaining how to make the sandwich. Encourage them to use transitional words, such as *first, second, next,* and *last.* After practicing this process, have students choose another task to describe in their writing.

• At the end of a unit of study, prepare slips of paper with topics for research essays for the class. Have students select a piece of paper out of a basket and have them write a research essay on that topic. You may allow students to trade topics. Students must use at least three sources in their reports, and they may also state their opinions, where appropriate. As a review, organize a daily writing workshop with a lesson that addresses an aspect of report writing from the *Core Knowledge Sequence,* and then allow students to work on their essays and apply the lesson of the day.

• You may also ask the following questions after completion of this unit of study:

1. What is a research essay?

   A research essay is an essay that expresses an opinion on a topic and then provides evidence from different sources to support this opinion.

2. What is an essay that explains a process?

   An essay that explains a process is an essay that tells how to do something or how something works.

3. How do you organize an essay that explains a process?

   A process explanation is organized in chronological order; each step in the process is given in the order in which it occurs.

4. Which two types of writing that you learned about should include a bibliography?

   Reports and research essays are two types of writing that should include a bibliography.

More Resources

The titles listed below are offered as a representative sample of materials and not a complete list of everything that is available.

For students —

• *Creative Writing Prompts,* by Laura Layton Strom (Rigby, 2001). A set of blackline masters with more than 50 writing prompts for both narrative and expository writing. A variety of uses. Paperback, 71 pages, ISBN 0763578193.

• *Expository Writing (Writing to Explain),* by Barbara Doherty and Charlotte Jaffe (Educational Impressions, 2002). Paperback, 64 pages, ISBN 1566440998.

• *Key Paragraphs: A Sequential Approach to Teaching Basic Paragraph Writing,* by Barbara Locker-Halmy (Creative Teaching Press, 2002). Paperback, 80 pages, ISBN 1574719084.

• *Scholastic Writer's Desk Reference* (Scholastic, 2001). Covers punctuation, grammar, writing, spelling, and correspondence. Paperback, 312 pages, ISBN 0439216508.

• *The World Book Encyclopedia.* Available in print editions, as an online subscription service, or on CD-ROM for both Windows and Mac. For more information, contact World Book at www.worldbook.com or 1-800-975-3250.

More Resources continued

• *Writers Express: A Handbook for Young Writers, Thinkers, and Learners* (Great Source Education Group, 2002). Also includes a *SkillsBook,* providing editing and proofreading practice, and a *Program Guide* for teachers. To order, contact Great Source at www.greatsource.com or 1-800-289-4490.

• *You Can Write a Report,* by Jennifer Rozines Roy (Enslow, 2003). Hardcover, 64 pages, ISBN 076602086X. See also *You Can Write Speeches and Debates,* part of the same series.

For teachers —

• *Any Child Can Write: An At-Home Guide to Enhancing Your Child's Elementary Education (Fourth Edition),* by Harvey S. Weiner (Oxford University Press, 2003). Paperback, 366 pages, ISBN 0195153162.

• *The Art of Teaching Writing,* by Lucy McCormick Calkins (Heinemann, 1994). Paperback, 540 pages, ISBN 0435088092.

• *Daily Paragraph Editing,* by Sarita Chavez Silverman and Lisa Matthews (Evan-Moor, 2004). Writing across the curriculum. Daily editing assignments with an end-of-the-week writing prompt. Paperback, 176 pages, ISBN 1557999589.

• *The Elements of Style (Fourth Edition),* by William Strunk, Jr., and E. B. White (Pearson Higher Education, 2000). A brief and sensible overview. Paperback, 104 pages, ISBN 020530902X.

• *In Print! 40 Cool Publishing Projects for Kids,* by Joe Rhatigan (Lark Books, 2003). Ideas to spark your imagination. Hardcover, 128 pages, ISBN 1579903592.

• *LETRS (Language Essentials for Teachers of Reading and Spelling),* by Louisa Moats, is a 12-module professional development sequence for teachers of reading available from SOPRIS West, www.sopriswest.com or 1-800-547-6747. Presenter's Packs include a presenter's manual, CD-ROM, and additional resources. Relevant modules for this section are 11 and 12. Topics covered by volume are as follows:

Module 1: The Challenge of Learning to Read

Module 2: The Speech Sounds of English: Phonetics, Phonology, and Phoneme Awareness

Module 3: Spellography: A Road Map to English Orthography

Module 4: The Mighty Word: Building Vocabulary and Oral Language

Module 5: Getting Up to Speed: Developing Fluency

Module 6: Digging for Meaning: Teaching Text Comprehension

Module 7: Teaching Phonics, Word Study, and the Alphabetic Principle

Module 8: Assessment for Prevention and Early Intervention (K–3)

Module 9: Teaching Beginning Spelling and Writing

Module 10: Reading Big Words: Syllabication and Advanced Decoding

Module 11: Writing: A Road to Reading Comprehension

Module 12: Using Assessment to Guide Instruction (3–Adult)

• *Startwrite* is a computer software program that allows you to create individualized handwriting exercises based on children's dictated stories, spelling lists, and more. Fonts include styles similar to Getty-Dubay Italic, D'Nealian, and Zaner-Bloser manuscript and cursive models. Extremely customizable. Both PC and Mac versions are available. To download a free trial, visit their website at www.startwrite.com.

• *Giggle Poetry,* www.gigglepoetry.com, and *Poetry4Kids,* www.poetry4kids.com, are two sites that can provide guidance for students as they are creating their own poems, as well as assistance to teachers in developing lessons and games to teach students about poetry.

The Big Idea

Written English follows certain rules about grammar and usage.

What Students Should Already Know

Students in Core Knowledge schools should be familiar with

Kindergarten through Grade 4

- writing legibly on ruled paper
- understanding the concept of a complete sentence and identifying subject and predicate
- identifying subject and verb and understanding that they must agree
- identifying nouns, verbs, and adjectives (including the articles *a, an,* and *the*) as parts of speech and knowing how they are used
- using the comparative (*-er*) and superlative (*-est*) forms of adjectives
- changing regular verbs from present to past tense using *-ed*
- using the correct present and past tense forms for common irregular verbs
- recognizing singular and plural forms of widely used nouns
- using capital letters for the first word of a sentence, proper nouns, the pronoun *I,* holidays, months, days of the week, countries, cities, states, main words in titles, and initials
- recognizing common abbreviations, such as St., Rd., Mr., Mrs., Ms., Dr., U.S.A., ft., lb., in.
- using end punctuation correctly
- spelling most words correctly or with a highly probable spelling
- using a dictionary to check and correct spelling
- identifying and correcting sentence fragments
- identifying different sentence types:
  - Declarative sentences make a statement.
  - Interrogative sentences ask a question.
  - Imperative sentences give a command.
  - Exclamatory sentences express strong emotion or surprise.
- recognizing that pronouns like *me, he,* or *they* are words that stand for nouns
- recognizing auxiliary (helping) verbs like *does, has,* and *will* that help express action
- recognizing adverbs like *slowly* or *carefully* that describe verbs

Materials

Instructional Master 4
Tracking Down the Antecedent,
p. 23

student dictionary,
pp. 19, 20

large, white easel paper,
pp. 20–25

colored chalk or markers,
pp. 21, 22, 23, 25

index cards, p. 21

clipping file of simple typos
from newspapers and other
published materials, p. 26

word journal for each
student, p. 26

What Students Should Already Know continued

- using a comma
  - between the day and year when writing a date
  - between the city and state in an address
  - in a series and after *yes* and *no*
  - when combining sentences
  - inside quotation marks
- using apostrophes in contractions and in singular and plural possessive nouns
- recognizing and avoiding double negatives
- identifying and correcting run-on sentences
- using conjunctions and interjections
- using quotation marks in dialogue, for titles of poems, songs, short stories, and magazine articles
- using underlining or italics for titles of books

What Students Need to Learn

- **Pronouns must agree with their antecedents in case (nominative, objective, possessive), number, and gender.**
- **Use a colon before a list.**
- **Use commas with an appositive.**

What Students Will Learn in Future Grades

Grade 6

- understand and identify independent and dependent clauses
- write for variety of sentence types by using
  - simple sentences
  - compound sentences
  - complex sentences
  - compound-complex sentences
- learn how to use a semicolon or comma with *and, but,* or *or* to separate the sentences that form a compound sentence
- recognize verbs in active voice and passive voice, and avoid unnecessary use of passive voice
- recognize the following troublesome verbs and how to use them correctly:
  - sit, set
  - rise, raise
  - lie, lay

What Students Will Learn in Future Grades continued

‣ Correctly use the following:

good/well   affect/effect

between/among   who/whom

bring/take   imply/infer

accept/except   principle/principal

fewer/less   their/there/they're

like/as

Vocabulary

Student/Teacher Vocabulary

adjective: a word that describes, or modifies, a noun (S)

adverb: a part of speech that describes, or modifies, a verb (S)

antecedent: the word that a pronoun refers to or replaces in a sentence (S)

appositive: a noun, noun phrase, or pronoun that identifies, renames, or explains another noun or pronoun, e.g., Susan Stuart, *my best friend* (S)

article: a kind of adjective; the words *a, an,* and *the* (S)

auxiliary verb: a verb like *have, is,* or *am* that comes first in a verb phrase and helps form the tense, mood, or voice of the main verb (T)

case: the form of a pronoun that shows how it is used in a sentence; can be nominative, objective, or possessive (T)

declarative sentence: a sentence that makes a statement (S)

double negative: two negative words or phrases in a sentence, such as *don't never* (S)

end punctuation: the punctuation marks that end a sentence—the period, question mark, and exclamation point (S)

exclamatory sentence: a sentence that expresses strong emotion or surprise (S)

imperative sentence: a sentence that gives a command (S)

internal punctuation: punctuation marks used within a sentence, such as commas (S)

interrogative sentence: a sentence that asks a question (S)

morpheme: a meaningful linguistic unit consisting of a word, such as *man,* or a word element, such as *-ed* of *walked,* that cannot be divided into smaller meaningful parts; includes inflectional suffixes and common derivational prefixes, suffixes, and roots (T)

noun: a word that names a person, animal, place, idea, or thing (S)

phonetic spelling: spelling that may not be correct in terms of meeting the conventions of English spelling but captures the sounds in a word. Examples of phonetic spelling include writing *sum* for *some, mi* for *my,* or *bot* for *boat.* This is also sometimes called "invented spelling." (T)

predicate: one of two necessary parts of a sentence; the part that contains the verb (S)

pronoun: a part of speech that stands for, and can be used in place of, a singular or a plural noun, such as *I, me,* or *you* (S)

Vocabulary continued

punctuation: marks such as commas and periods, and the use of those marks (S)

run-on sentence: two or more separate sentences that are written as one (T)

sentence: a group of words that expresses a complete thought (S)

sentence fragment: a phrase that lacks either a subject or a predicate (S)

subject: one of two necessary parts of a sentence; the part that tells whom or what the sentence is about (S)

Domain Vocabulary

Grammar and usage and associated words:
complete sentence, subject-verb agreement, parts of speech, conjunction, interjection, verb, action, auxiliary or helping, singular, plural, nominative case, objective case, possessive, number, gender, contraction, abbreviation, tense, past, present, future, progressive punctuation marks, period, exclamation point, question mark, colon, comma, dash, hyphen, phrase, clause, italic, underline, boldface, capital letter, dialogue, English, language, grammar, usage, mechanics, incomplete, rewrite, combine, edit, proofread, *plus words used or created during grammar work*

At a Glance
The most important ideas for you are:

» Parts of speech that students should know include nouns, pronouns, action verbs, auxiliary verbs, adjectives, adverbs, articles, conjunctions, and interjections.

» Although students develop an innate sense of grammar from hearing spoken language, this does not mean that there is no reason to learn the names of the parts of speech. Knowing the basic parts allows students to talk about sentences and phrases as they read, write, and discuss.

» Students in Grade 5 should understand how to use end punctuation and the following internal punctuation: commas, apostrophes, colons, and quotation marks.

» Although learning the rules of spelling, grammar, and usage can seem tedious, these rules are worth learning because they enable us to communicate more effectively with one another.

» The spelling, grammar, and usage guidelines discussed in this section should be taught in conjunction with the writing assignments discussed in the previous section.

» Instead of treating this section as a discrete unit, you may wish to explain the various points of usage over a longer period of time, as students practice their writing.

» It is seldom adequate to merely explain proper usage. Students should also have repeated opportunities to practice correct usage and to correct improper usage, both in exercises and in their own writing.

What Teachers Need to Know
B. Grammar and Usage

Background

In order for students to write and be understood, they need to master the rules of spelling, grammar, and usage.

In spelling, students should be taught about the variant vowel spelling patterns, six basic syllable types, and common morphemes. Homophones, contractions, abbreviations, and other oddities are also part of the curriculum. This instruction should be grounded in an understanding that English is a "layer cake" language with spellings derived historically from Anglo-Saxon, Latin, Greek, and other languages. Common high-frequency words that are often misspelled should be practiced using multisensory and other visualization techniques, as well as dictation.

By Grade 5, students should use standard spelling. They also need regular practice in grammar and usage to gain mastery. As always, exposure to correct spelling, grammar, and usage can be a powerful aid in gaining mastery. Students should use a student dictionary to check their spelling or use a spell-checker on a word processor.

Students will most likely have already learned some of the rules discussed below, but it is important to review all of the points to be sure that they possess the basic knowledge they will need as a foundation for future study.

Although the basic rules of spelling, grammar, and usage have not always been imaginatively taught in the past, there is no reason why they cannot be taught in a way that is both informative and enjoyable. Well-designed and creative lessons are an important part of the process. Teachers should be mindful that, while providing corrective feedback, they don't overwhelm and discourage the student. Feedback that is constructive and encouraging can mean the difference between mastery and discouragement, either of which can continue into the higher grades.

Practicing Spelling

In earlier grades, students probably have used phonetic spelling. However, by Grade 5, students should be able to spell most words correctly or with a highly probable spelling. Spelling instruction may be included in your reading program. If not, you can teach spelling with a structured, systematic approach to understanding language structure. The tried-and-true method of dictation, where the teacher reads a word, gives a sentence using the word, repeats the word, and then students write down the word, is a key instructional routine. For a more comprehensive background on spelling development and instruction, consult the following resources: *LETRS Modules 2, 3, 7, and 10 (Language Essentials for Teachers of Reading and Spelling); Spelling: Development, Disabilities, and Instruction,* by Louisa Moats; *Spelling by Pattern and Spellography* (Javernick, Rosow, and Moats); as well as *Words Their Way: Word Study for Phonics, Vocabulary, and Spelling Instruction.* (See *More Resources.*)

To learn how to spell words correctly, students need consistent practice. Here are some ideas for you to consider when teaching the conventions and rules of spelling:

• Select five to ten words from a standard vocabulary list for Grade 5 (or perhaps from a specific domain covered by Core Knowledge, e.g., Great Lakes of the World: *lake, sea, depth, freshwater, saltwater, navigable, recreation*). Say each word aloud. Have students write the word on a sheet of lined paper. By Grade 5, students can also select words they want to learn and keep an ongoing list all year long.

• Students should consistently practice associating specific sounds with particular written letters and combinations of letters. Remind them to listen carefully to the individual sounds, or phonemes, that make up each word they want to spell. Suggest that they "sound out" a word they do not know how to spell.

• Provide students with access to a student dictionary. Encourage them to check and correct spellings when they are uncertain about an unfamiliar word.

Teaching About Sentences

Learning how to write good sentences is a skill students need to practice throughout the school year. The following are ideas for you to use with students. Review the following concepts regularly:

• A sentence is a group of words that expresses a complete thought.

• The four sentence types are declarative, interrogative, imperative, and exclamatory.

• A complete sentence has a subject and a predicate.

• Sentence fragments lack either a subject or a predicate.

• Run-on sentences consist of two or more sentences written as one.

• Subjects and verbs must agree in number.

Remind students that the subject tells who or what a sentence is about and the predicate tells about the subject. The following are examples that you can use to review with students. You can create many more of these from material in your basal series and/or books on subjects in the Core Knowledge curriculum.

Tell students that subjects and verbs can be either singular or plural. Tell them that a subject and verb agree in number if they are both singular or both plural. Then write illustrative examples such as these on the board or on easel paper.

Singular	Plural
Timothy has homework.	**Timothy and Don have** homework.
He asks good questions.	**They ask** good questions.

Have volunteers identify the subject in each sentence (*Timothy, Timothy and Don, He, They*) and the singular or plural verb (*has, have, asks, ask*). Then invite students to write several sentences with a singular subject and verb and several more with a plural subject and verb.

Teaching Idea

Hold a spelling bee in your classroom using words from specific domains covered by Core Knowledge. You may also give copies of these words to the physical education teachers, and ask them to have students spell out the words while they are warming up. For example, students can do one jumping jack for each letter of the word *Reconstruction.*

Write some single-clause sentences like the ones below on the board or on easel paper. You might want to add some examples of your own. Make sure that students can identify the subject and predicate. Then have them identify the subject and verb and tell whether each is singular or plural.

Jen skates on the frozen pond.

(subject—Jen; predicate—skates on the frozen pond; simple subject—Jen, singular; verb—skates, singular)

The skaters make figure eights.

(subject—skaters; predicate—make figure eights; simple subject—skaters, plural; verb—make, plural)

A flock of seagulls circles the snack bar.

(subject—flock of seagulls; predicate—circles the snack bar; simple subject—flock, singular; verb—circles, singular)

Remind students that a sentence fragment lacks either a subject or a predicate. Then write some sentence fragments like the ones below on the board or on easel paper. You might want to add some examples of your own. Have volunteers explain how to correct a fragment. Write the corrected sentences in different-colored chalk or colored markers.

One talented pianist at the concert.

(Add a predicate: One talented pianist at the concert played a difficult piece.)

Raised her baton over her head.

(Add a subject: The orchestra conductor raised her baton over her head.)

Remind students that a run-on sentence is two or more sentences written as one. Then write some run-on sentences like the ones below on the board or on easel paper. You might want to add some examples of your own. Have volunteers identify different ways to correct a run-on sentence. Write their responses with different-colored markers or chalk.

The audience clapped wildly the tired musicians sat quietly.

(Possible answers: (a) The audience clapped wildly, but the tired musicians sat quietly. (b) The audience clapped wildly. The tired musicians sat quietly.)

The drummer beat the drums, the violinist played the violin.

(Possible answers: (a) The drummer beat the drums. The violinist played the violin. (b) The drummer beat the drums, and the violinist played the violin. (c) The drummer beat the drums; the violinist played the violin.)

Regularly check students' writing to make sure they avoid or correct fragments and run-on sentences.

Teaching About Parts of Speech

Review the following parts of speech students learned in Grades 2, 3, and 4:

- A noun names a person, animal, place, idea, or thing.
- A pronoun stands for a noun.
- A verb expresses action (and can change tense: run/ran; glides/glided; is/was).
- An auxiliary verb, or helping verb, helps express actions.
- Adjectives describe nouns and pronouns.

Teaching Idea

Write several series of singular and plural subjects and verbs on index cards. Have students work in pairs to match the subjects with the appropriate verbs.

- One kind of adjective is called an article; *a, an,* and *the* are articles.
- Adverbs describe verbs, adjectives, or other adverbs.
- Conjunctions join together words or sentences.
- Interjections express strong thoughts or feelings.

Next, write the sentences below on the board or on easel paper. Have students identify different parts of speech. Using different-colored chalk or markers, write *n* for noun, *v* for verb, and so on above each part of speech. The sentences below are only examples. You will want to come up with more examples of your own (possibly some on subjects studied or taken from stories read in this grade) and repeat this kind of activity throughout the school year.

Tim has bought a new computer.

(Tim—noun, has—helping verb, bought—verb, a—article, new—adjective, computer—noun)

He slowly reads the heavy manual.

(He—pronoun, slowly—adverb, reads—verb, the—article, heavy—adjective, manual—noun)

The strange directions confuse him, but he does not stop.

(the—article, strange—adjective, directions—noun, confuse—verb, him—pronoun, but—conjunction, he—pronoun, does not—helping verb, stop—verb)

Oh! The directions are written in Japanese!

(oh—interjection, the—article, directions—noun, are—helping verb, written—verb, in—preposition, Japanese—noun)

It may be helpful to display a chart reviewing parts of speech students have learned previously so that they may use it as a reference when proofing their own sentences. You can add to this as the year goes on and as you introduce new parts of speech.

Part of Speech	Description	Examples
noun	person, animal, place, thing, or idea	teacher, dog, school, book, classes, gym
pronoun	word that stands for nouns	I, you, him, we, them
action verb	expresses an action	cook, dance, melt, laugh, dig
helping verb	helps express an action	am, is, are, should, will
adjective	describes a noun or pronoun and answers the questions "What kind? Which one? How much? How many?"	three, few, angry, red, some
article	one kind of adjective	a, an, the
adverb	describes a verb and answers the questions "When? Where? How? How often? To what extent?"	suddenly, quickly, daily, calmly, nearly, far, fast
conjunction	word that joins together words or sentences	and, but, or
interjection	expresses strong thoughts or feelings	wow! oh no! my!

Pronoun-Antecedent Agreement

Teach students that pronouns must agree with their antecedents in case, number, and gender. First, explain that an antecedent is the word that a pronoun refers to or replaces in a sentence. Give several sentences in which pronouns replace nouns or noun phrases used earlier. Have students practice identifying the antecedents of the pronouns, that is, the word or phrase to which the pronoun refers.

Sentence: The men went to their house.

Question: What's the antecedent of *their*? Answer: the men.

Sentences: You know Susan? Dave told Bob that he likes her.

Questions: What's the antecedent of *he*? Of *her*? Answers: he (Dave); her (Susan).

You may wish to give some examples of ambiguous antecedents, such as,

The briefcase was on the bus, but now it is not there. (Is the antecedent of *it* the briefcase or the bus?)

Challenge students to rewrite ambiguous sentences more clearly and to identify the various antecedents in a sentence like this:

The detectives told the criminals that they would track them down and arrest them.

What's the antecedent of *they*? Of the first *them*? Of the second *them*? How do students know?

Next, explain that pronouns have three cases: nominative, objective, and possessive. Then tell students when to use each case, as follows. Write the illustrative sentences on the board or on easel paper, highlighting the pronouns and their antecedents with different-colored markers or chalk.

Use the nominative case when a pronoun is a subject.

Karen, Dave, and Theo were bored. *They* **made a pizza.**

Use the objective case when a pronoun is a direct object, an indirect object, or an object of a preposition.

Karen and Dave cut the pizza into wedges. Theo's sister begged *them* **for a slice.**

Use the possessive case when a pronoun shows ownership.

Karen's slice was delicious. *Hers* **had mushrooms and peppers.**

Explain to students that pronouns must agree in number. Tell them that a singular pronoun must agree with a singular antecedent, and a plural pronoun must agree with a plural antecedent. Then write the illustrative sentences below on the board or on easel paper, highlighting the pronouns and their antecedents with different-colored markers or chalk.

Singular

Nominative: I, you, he, she, it

Objective: me, you, him, her, it

Possessive: my, mine, your, yours, his, her, hers, its

Use Instructional Master 4.

Plural

Nominative: we, you, they

Objective: us, you, them

Possessive: our, ours, your, yours, their, theirs

Karen washed *her* pizza cutter. The boys cleaned up *their* mess.

Inform the class that pronouns must agree in gender. Explain that a pronoun and its antecedent may be masculine, feminine, or neuter.

Masculine	**Feminine**	**Neuter**
he, him, his	she, her, hers	it, its

Tell students to use a masculine pronoun when its antecedent is masculine, a feminine pronoun when its antecedent is feminine, and a neuter pronoun when its antecedent is neither masculine nor feminine. Then write the following illustrative sentences on the board or on easel paper. Have students fill in the missing pronoun, and then identify the pronoun's antecedent, its number, its gender, and its case.

Theo put _____ dishes away.

(pronoun—his; antecedent—Theo; number—singular; gender—masculine; case—possessive)

Karen wrapped an extra slice in foil. Then _____ put the slice in the refrigerator.

(pronoun—she; antecedent—Karen; number—singular; gender—feminine; case—nominative)

Theo found a piece of crust and fed _____ to the dog.

(pronoun—it; antecedent—piece; number—singular; gender—neuter; case—objective)

Teaching About Punctuation

First, review the following uses of punctuation students should have learned in Grades 2, 3, and 4:

• Use a period, question mark, or exclamation point to show where a sentence stops.

• Use a comma between the day and year when writing a date, between the city and state in an address, in a series, after *yes* and *no*, before conjunctions that combine sentences, and inside quotation marks in dialogue.

• Use an apostrophe in contractions and in singular and plural possessive nouns.

• Use quotation marks in dialogue and for the titles of poems, songs, short stories, and magazine articles.

• Use underlining or italics for the titles of books.

Give a brief assessment to ascertain whether students have mastered these uses of punctuation. For each type of punctuation, write a few example sentences on the board or on easel paper with the punctuation missing. Have students identify where the missing punctuation belongs.

Teaching Idea

Regularly check students' writing to see that they use punctuation correctly.

Colon

In Grade 5, students should learn that a colon is used before a list. Write examples on the board or on easel paper, highlighting the colons with a different-colored chalk or marker.

The bird-watching group spotted the following birds: hawks, a bald eagle, and a heron.

They brought these items: binoculars, bird guides, a bag lunch, and water.

Commas with an Appositive

In Grade 5, students should continue to review and practice comma skills used in earlier grades. They should also learn that commas are used with an appositive, or a noun or pronoun that renames another noun or pronoun. Write examples on the board or on easel paper, identifying the appositives and highlighting the commas with a different-colored chalk or marker.

The president of the nature club, Vicki Alexander, enjoys bird-watching.

Last month the club visited the Highlands Outdoor Center, a local nature preserve.

In the first sentence, "Vicki Alexander" is an appositive. We say it is placed in apposition to the phrase "the president of the nature club." The appositive renames the president, so we place a comma before and after the appositive.

Help students understand that it is the order of words and the structure of the sentence that determine which phrases are in apposition to which. The first sentence given above could be rewritten:

Vicki Alexander, the president of the nature club, enjoys bird-watching.

In this case, the phrase "the president of the nature club" is placed in apposition to "Vicki Alexander." In the previous sentence, it was the other way around. Give students several examples where the appositives can be reversed and ask them to discuss which sentences would be preferable in various situations. Does one sound better? Why? Help students understand that most sentences can be written in several different ways. Part of becoming a good writer is considering various possibilities in your head before settling on the one that is best in the situation.

Note that appositives are set off by commas only when they rename a preceding noun or noun phrase.

Burnett's book *The Secret Garden* was published in 1911.

At first, you might think *The Secret Garden* should be set off by commas. But Burnett wrote many books. So the phrase *The Secret Garden* does not simply rename "Burnett's book." It specifies which of the several books she wrote is being discussed. This is still an appositive, but it is called a restrictive appositive and is not set off with commas. A restrictive appositive restricts the meaning of an earlier phrase to something more specific. A nonrestrictive appositive renames something that has already been named once before. Here are two more examples:

Shakespeare's play *Hamlet* takes place in Denmark.

Shakespeare's last play, *The Tempest*, takes place on a desert island.

In the first case, *Hamlet* specifies which of Shakespeare's plays is being discussed, so this is not a case of renaming. This is a restrictive appositive and no commas are used. In the second case, there can be only one "last" play, so *The Tempest* simply renames Shakespeare's last play. This is a nonrestrictive appositive, and commas are appropriate.

The Big Idea in Review

Written English follows certain rules about grammar and usage.

Review

Below are some ideas for ongoing assessment and review activities. These are not meant to constitute a comprehensive list.

• Keep a clipping file of simple typos from newspapers and other published materials. Many teachers find it effective to start every day by posting on the board a very brief writing sample with several spelling and grammatical errors (thoughtfully selected to provide practice in those skills that are being taught). Students are expected to copy the writing sample and correct the errors. (This activity also provides an opportunity for handwriting practice.) The teacher then leads the class in a group exercise to discuss and correct the errors. Focus on the concepts that are introduced in Grade 5, such as pronoun-antecedent agreement and the use of commas with an appositive. Be sure that students have an opportunity to review concepts from earlier grades as well. Consider giving students extra credit for examples of published typos they find on their own.

• After thoroughly teaching a bullet point under Grammar and Usage from the *Core Knowledge Sequence,* you can have students review and practice the concept in the context of a literature or grammar lesson. For example, you may choose to practice using pronoun-antecedent agreement by reading a literature passage and identifying pronouns and their antecedents within the text. Then have students practice writing their own sentences using pronouns correctly.

• Have students keep a word journal with pages marked for nouns, verbs, adjectives, adverbs, conjunctions, and interjections. Students can record examples of each part of speech as they read or discover new words. Check their lists for understanding, and encourage students to use their journal as a review tool or when completing creative writing exercises.

• After teaching or reviewing a Grade 5 learning item, ask students to focus on that concept in their writing during the day. For example, they can practice using colons before a list. At the end of the day, have a grammar review where students share examples of their writing from the day and their use of that particular concept. Ask the class to check if the usage was correct.

More Resources

The titles listed below are offered as a representative sample of materials and not a complete list of everything that is available.

For students —

• *Scholastic Writer's Desk Reference* (Scholastic, 2001). Covers punctuation, grammar, writing, spelling, and correspondence. Paperback, 312 pages, ISBN 0439216508.

• *Verbs, Verbs, Verbs: The Trickiest Action-Packed Words in English,* by Marvin Terban (Scholastic, 2002). Paperback, 160 pages, ISBN 043940164X. See also *Building Your Vocabulary,* by the same author.

For teachers —

• *Daily Oral Language (Grades 3–5),* by Gregg O. Byers (Carson-Dellosa, 2001). Thirty-six weeks' worth of daily, two-sentence lessons that teach grammar, punctuation, and usage. Paperback, 96 pages, ISBN 0887246478.

• *Grammar and Punctuation (Grade 5),* by Delana Heidrich (Evan-Moor, 2002). Includes CD-ROM with animated rule charts, printable practice pages, skills review, and record sheet. Paperback with CD-ROM, 112 pages, ISBN 1557998493.

• *LETRS (Language Essentials for Teachers of Reading and Spelling)* is a professional development series authored by Louisa Moats, and available from SOPRIS West, www.sopriswest.com or phone 1-800-547-6747. Modules 3, 7, 10, and 11 can help you teach grammar and usage to Grades 3 and up, and the first nine modules (listed in A. Writing, Grammar, and Usage) provide background information that underlies the recommendations for specific instructional practices. Presenter's Packs include a presenter's manual, CD-ROM, and additional resources.

• *Spelling by Pattern and Spellography* (Javernick, Rosow, and Moats), SOPRIS West. A systematic spelling curriculum for Grades 2–5. Available from SOPRIS West, www.sopriswest.com or phone 1-800-547-6747.

• *Spelling: Development, Disabilities, and Instruction,* by Louisa Moats (York Press, 1995). Paperback, 137 pages, ISBN 0912752408.

• *Words Their Way: Word Study for Phonics, Vocabulary, and Spelling Instruction (3rd edition),* by Donald Bear, Marcia Invernizzi, Shane Templeton, and Francine Johnston (Prentice Hall, 2003). Paperback, 464 pages, ISBN 0131113380.

riting, Grammar, and Usage

C. Vocabulary

The Big Idea

Prefixes and suffixes are word parts that are attached to words and affect word meaning.

What Students Should Already Know

Students in Core Knowledge schools should be familiar with

Kindergarten through Grade 4

- knowing what synonyms and antonyms are and providing synonyms and antonyms for given words
- knowing what homophones are and correct usage of homophones that commonly cause problems (*their, they're, there; your, you're; its, it's; here, hear; to, too, two*)
- knowing that prefixes are word parts that can be attached to the beginning of some words to change the meaning
- knowing that suffixes are word parts that can be attached to the end of some words to change the meaning
- knowing how the following prefixes and suffixes affect word meanings:

    Prefixes:

    re- meaning "again" (as in *reuse, refill*)

    un- meaning "not" (as in *unfriendly, unpleasant*)

    dis- meaning "not" (as in *dishonest, disobey*)

    un- meaning "opposite of" or "reversing action" (as in *untie, unlock*)

    dis- meaning "opposite of" or "reversing action" (as in *disappear, dismount*)

    im-, in- (as in *impossible, incorrect*)

    non- (as in *nonfiction, nonviolent*)

    mis- (as in *misbehave, misspell*)

    en- (as in *enable, endanger*)

    pre- (as in *prehistoric, pregame*)

    Suffixes:

    -er and *-or* (as in *singer, painter, actor*)

    -less (as in *careless, hopeless*)

    -ly (as in *quickly, calmly*)

    -ily, -y (as in *easily, speedily, tricky*)

    -ful (as in *thoughtful, wonderful*)

    -able, -ible (as in *washable, flexible*)

    -ment (as in *agreement, amazement*)

Materials

**Instructional Masters
5–6**
Prefixes, p. 32
Suffixes, p. 34
**dictionaries for students,
pp. 32, 34**
**newspapers, magazines, or
brief excerpts on topics
studied, p. 35**

What Students Need to Learn

▶ **Know how the following prefixes and suffixes affect word meanings:**

Prefixes:

anti- (as in *antisocial, antibacterial*)

co- (as in *coeducation, co-captain*)

fore- (as in *forefather, foresee*)

il-, ir- (as in *illegal, irregular*)

inter- (as in *interstate*)

mid- (as in *midnight, Midwest*)

post- (as in *postseason, postwar*)

semi- (as in *semicircle, semiprecious*)

Suffixes:

-ist (as in *artist, pianist*)

-ish (as in *stylish, foolish*)

-ness (as in *forgiveness, happiness*)

-tion, -sion (as in *relation, extension*)

What Students Will Learn in Future Grades

Grade 6

▶ spelling rules for use of *ie* and *ei;* for adding prefixes and suffixes

▶ commonly misspelled words

▶ the meaning of select Latin and Greek words that form common word roots, as well as examples of English words based on them

Vocabulary

Student/Teacher Vocabulary

antonym: a word that means the opposite of another word (S)

homophone: a word that sounds like another word but is spelled differently and has a different meaning (for example, *buy* and *by*) (S)

prefix: a word part that is attached to the beginning of a word and changes the meaning of that word (S)

suffix: a word part that is attached to the end of a word and changes the meaning of that word (S)

synonym: a word that means just about the same thing as another word (S)

Domain Vocabulary

Vocabulary and associated words:
Greek, Latin, root, syllable, base, addition, add, precede, *plus some of the hundreds of words that are made using the prefixes and suffixes taught, e.g.,* anticommunist, coworker, co-captain, foreordained, foresight, irresponsible, irregular, illegitimate, artist, pianist, scientist, forgiveness, boldness, motion, vision, *etc.*

What Teachers Need to Know
C. Vocabulary

Background

Vocabulary knowledge is very important. It correlates very strongly with reading scores, which means that people who know a lot of words tend also to be good readers.

Vocabulary learning is occurring all the time. Students are constantly building their knowledge of words when they hear speech, when they listen to material read aloud, and when they read independently. Much vocabulary learning is implicit. That is, students learn words by hearing and seeing them multiple times in meaningful contexts. At first, they may have only a vague sense of what the word means—"it's a noun" or "it has something to do with farms"—but, with additional exposures, students develop a fuller and more complete sense of the word's range of meanings and uses. Eventually a word may even pass from receptive vocabulary (words students understand when used by others) into productive vocabulary (words students can use themselves).

Although many of the words we know are learned through implicit vocabulary acquisition, there is also a place in education for explicit vocabulary instruction. In explicit vocabulary instruction, an attempt is made to teach students a particular word or set of words. Explicit vocabulary instruction is most likely to be effective if the student is given some information about the meaning or definition of a word (not necessarily a dictionary explanation, but a simple oral explanation) and also several examples of the word used in different contexts. Several exposures will usually be necessary, and students should have the opportunity not only to see or hear the word but also to interact with the word and use it. For example, if you were teaching the word delicate, you might explain that something delicate is very fragile and easy to break. Then you might give some sentences in which the word is used: "This china is very delicate; please handle it with care." Finally, you might ask students to use the word. For example, you could say, "I'm going to name some things; you tell me if they are delicate or not: a glass, a plastic glass, a flower, a brick," etc. In order to answer questions like this, students have to grasp the meaning of delicate, and each additional exposure helps solidify their understanding of the word.

Instead of choosing words at random for direct vocabulary instruction, consider choosing sets of words related to the topics you are studying. For example, in connection with the Civil War, you might teach words like slavery, abolition, emancipation, fugitive, overseer, assassination, and surrender.

Some other important aspects of vocabulary learning are discussed in the sections that follow.

Teaching About Vocabulary

 ### Synonyms, Antonyms, and Homophones

Review with students what they should have learned in Grades 2, 3, and 4:

- Synonyms are words that have the same or similar meaning (*cold, chilly*).
- Antonyms are words that have the opposite meaning (*hot, cold*).
- Homophones are words that sound alike but are spelled differently and have different meanings.

Homophone	Meaning	Illustrative Sentence
their	belonging to them	The twins wear their new jeans.
they're	they are	They're happy.
there	at that place	Put the presents over there.
your	belonging to you	Your drawing is beautiful.
you're	you are	You're an artist!
its	belonging to it	My cat licks its paw.
it's	it is	It's a gray kitten.
here	at this place	Let's shop here.
hear	to perceive sound	Did you hear the drums?
to	toward, in the direction of	Take this to the principal.
too	also	Do you want cake, too?
two	the number after one	Two crows sit in a tree.

Have students demonstrate their understanding of synonyms and antonyms by supplying examples. Also, have them use each of the homophones listed above in a written sentence to show they understand their meanings.

Once the concept of synonyms and antonyms has been learned, it can be a very useful tool for additional vocabulary instruction. For example, when teaching slavery, you might ask students, "What is the opposite of slavery?" Students may say "freedom" or "liberty." Generally speaking, a student who can supply a synonym and/or antonym for a word can be said to have solid, usable knowledge of the word.

 ### Prefixes and Suffixes

Prefixes are word parts that can be attached to the beginning of some words. Suffixes are word parts that can be attached to the end of some words. A brief review of prefixes (*re-, un-, dis-, im-, in-, non-, mis-, en-, pre-*) and suffixes (*-er* and *-or, -less, -ly, -ily,- y, -ful, -able, -ible, -ment*) introduced in Grades 3 and 4 is recommended.

Teaching prefixes is an important way to help students develop a larger vocabulary. A student who knows the meaning of a common prefix or suffix, and also knows the root word to which the prefix is affixed, can generally guess the meaning of the new compound word. Since a handful of prefixes and suffixes account for a large number of words in English, learning them thoroughly can help students in many different situations in years to come.

I. Writing, Grammar, and Usage
C. Vocabulary

• The prefix *un-* is, statistically, the most important prefix in the English language. It accounts for 26% of all prefixed words. The prefix *un-* means "not," or, in some cases, "the opposite of." When you attach *un-* to the beginning of a word, you reverse the word's meaning and create an antonym for the original word: *unfriendly* means the opposite of friendly, and *uncooperative*, the opposite of cooperative; to *untie* something is the opposite of tying it.

• The prefix *dis-* is the fourth most common prefix in English, accounting for approximately 7% of all prefixed words. It is similar to the prefix *un-* in the sense that it creates a new word with a meaning roughly the opposite of the original word. A *dishonest* person is not honest, and a *disloyal* person is not loyal. To *disappear* undoes what you do when you appear, and *dismounting* is the opposite of mounting.

• The prefix *re-* is the second most common prefix in English. It accounts for roughly 14% of all prefixed words. This prefix means "again." To *reread* is to read again, and to *restate* is to state again.

• The prefixes *im-* and *in-* mean "not." An *impossible* task is not possible, and an *incorrect* answer is not correct. The prefixes *ir-* and *il-* (although not listed in the *Sequence*) generally convey the same meaning: an *illiberal* person is not liberal, and an *irregular* shape is not regular. Taken together, these four prefixes account for roughly 11% of prefixed words in English.

• The prefix *non-* also means "not." A *nonviolent* protest is not violent, and a *noncombatant* is someone who does not fight in combat. The prefix *non-* accounts for about 4% of all prefixed words in English.

• The prefix *mis-* means "bad" or "badly," or "wrong" or "wrongly." If you *misjudge* someone, you judge the person wrongly. If you *misplace* something, you place it badly, so you can't find it again later. To *misspell* is to write the wrong spelling. The prefix *mis-* accounts for about 3% of prefixed words in English.

• The prefix *en-* (sometimes written *em-*) has several related meanings. Often it has to do with putting something in, or going into something. To *encase* something is to put it in a case. To *endanger* someone is to bring the person into danger. To *enslave* someone is to bring the person into a state of slavery. *En-* (and *em-*) is the fifth most common prefix in English, accounting for about 4% of all prefixed words.

• The prefix *pre-* means "earlier than" or "before." A prefix is affixed before a root word. If you *preview* a book, you view it before reading it. If you *premeditate* a crime, you meditate or think about what you plan to do before you do it. Similarly, a *preface* goes before the main part of a book, and a *prelude* goes before, or at the beginning of, a piece of music. *Pre-* prefixed words make up about 3% of all prefixed words in English.

New prefixes for Grade 5 include *anti-*, *co-*, *fore-*, *il-*, *ir-*, *inter-*, *mid-*, *post-*, and *semi-*. It's a good idea to introduce these new prefixes one at a time—one each day or perhaps one each week. For each prefix, give students several examples of words containing the prefix, and use the words in sentences. Then invite students to think of other words that begin with the same prefix. You can find more examples using a dictionary.

Use Instructional Master 5.

- The prefix *anti-* means "against" or "opposed to." Someone who is against slavery is antislavery. This prefix can also mean to prevent or destroy. An anticancer drug fights cancerous cells; an anticorrosive prevents an item from corroding.

- The prefix *co-* means "with" or "together." A coworker is someone you work with, and so is a collaborator. When two people coexist, they manage to live together, even if they don't like each other.

- The prefix *fore-* means "before," "ahead," or "in front." To forewarn someone of something means to warn them beforehand. An old saying says, "Forewarned is forearmed." Your forehead is located in the front of your head.

- The prefixes *il-* and *ir-* mean "not," "in," or "into." If something is illegal, it is not legal. Something that is irrelevant is not relevant. An irregular verb is not regular in its forms.

- The prefix *inter-* means "between" or "among." Interaction means action between two or more things or people. International laws are laws agreed upon among nations. If you intercept a pass in football, it means you move between the quarterback and the receiver and take the ball.

- The prefix *mid-* means "halfway" or "being in the middle." Midway means halfway and midday means the middle of the day. Your midsection is your middle part.

- The prefix *post-* means "after," "subsequent," or "behind." To postpone something is to delay it (put it after other things). A postwar event occurs after a war. A posthumous award is not presented until after the recipient has died.

- The prefix *semi-* can mean "half": a semicircle is half a circle; semiannual is twice a year. The prefix can also mean "partial" or "somewhat." Semiformal is somewhat formal, and semiconscious is partly conscious.

Students are probably already familiar with some of the most common suffixes in the English language, for example, the ending *-s* or *-es* attached to singular nouns to make them plural, e.g., *books, foxes*. They probably also know that the suffix *-ed* is added to verbs to indicate past tense, e.g., he walk*ed* to school. However, a high number of student spelling errors are attributable to the deletion or confusion of past tense and plural endings, and many students need extended, systematic practice to learn to recognize and write these endings.

- The suffix *-er* (or sometimes *-or*) is used to turn a verb into a noun. If someone paints, we say that person is a painter; if you run, you're a runner; if you act, you're an actor.

- The suffix *-less* can be added to mean "without." A hopeless person is without hope, and a clueless person is without a clue.

- The suffix *-ly* is used to make adjectives into adverbs. A quick person runs quickly, and a stern correction is spoken sternly.

- The suffix *-y* is extremely handy for turning nouns or verbs into adjectives. Does your floor creak? Then you have a creaky floor. Does your baby brother make messes? Then he is messy, which is what he's supposed to be!

- The suffix *-ily* (like the suffix *-ly*) can be used to create adverbs like luckily and merrily.

- The suffix *-ful* means "full of." A thoughtful person is full of thoughts and a deceitful person is full of deceit.

- The suffixes *-able* and *-ible* usually convey that something is fit for or worthy of something. Often we use this suffix to make a verb into an adjective. If something can be washed, we say it is washable. If something is worth commending, it is commendable. If something can be drunk, we say it is drinkable. If something can break, it's breakable.

- The suffix *-ment* is often used to change a verb into a noun that describes a state of being. If you and I agree, we are in a state of agreement. If we are amazed, we are in a state of amazement. If we are puzzled, we are in a state of puzzlement.

New suffixes for Grade 5 include -ist, -ish, -ness, -tion, and -sion. New suffixes can be handled in much the same way as new prefixes—introduce them one at a time, rather than all at once. Explain the general meaning of the suffix. Give several examples of words containing the suffix. Use these words in sentences. Think of ways for students to interact with the words, e.g., by asking questions: "Would a pianist tend to have nimble fingers?" "Can you find contentment from the things you own?" Then invite students to think of more words using these suffixes and generate sentences using the words. As you encounter new words that include these suffixes during the year, use these encounters as opportunities to review.

- The suffix *-ist* is used to describe people who hold a certain belief and/or practice a particular profession. For example, an artist is someone who creates art. A socialist is someone who believes in the principles of the economic theory of socialism. This suffix often corresponds with verbs that end in *-ize*, such as: "A doctor who anesthetizes patients before surgery is called an anesthesiologist."

- The suffix *-ish* forms adjectives from nouns and means "characteristic of" or "tending to." Someone from Spain is Spanish, and an adult who acts immaturely is childish. A greenish hue is somewhat green.

- The suffix *-ness* is attached to adjectives and participles and indicates abstract properties such as quality and state. For example, a dark night is sometimes described as darkness; if you are kind to someone, you have shown him or her kindness. Other examples include tenderness, sloppiness, happiness, and tardiness.

- The suffix *-tion* changes action verbs into nouns that express actions. If you react, you have a reaction. When you write down words another person says, or dictates, you are taking dictation.

- The suffix *-sion* works similarly to *-tion*. If something explodes, you will hear an explosion. If you tense up, you experience tension.

Use Instructional Master 6.

The Big Idea in Review

Prefixes and suffixes are word parts that are attached to words and affect word meaning.

Review

Below are some ideas for ongoing assessment and review activities. These are not meant to constitute a comprehensive list.

- Make a class list of the prefixes and suffixes listed in the *Core Knowledge Sequence*. Then, during second readings, encourage students to find these in their texts. Can they guess the meaning of the word if they know the meaning of the prefix or suffix? Check the dictionary for accuracy. (Note: Students need to concentrate

on decoding, building a situation model, and drawing on background knowledge during first readings. Adding more tasks during a first reading is likely to overload the system. This type of activity should always be done after a first reading.)

• As a culminating activity for this section, ask students to read a newspaper, magazine article, or brief excerpt on a topic you have studied. Have them circle any words that have the prefixes or suffixes they have studied.

• Have students create a crossword puzzle using words that have the prefixes and suffixes from this section. Then, when they create the clues for each word, have them use the definition of the prefix or suffix to show understanding.

More Resources

The titles listed below are offered as a representative sample of materials and not a complete list of everything that is available.

For students —

• *Building Your Vocabulary,* by Marvin Terban (Scholastic, 2002). Hardcover, 188 pages, ISBN 0439285615.

• *Scholastic Writer's Desk Reference* (Scholastic, 2001). Covers punctuation, grammar, writing, spelling, and correspondence. Paperback, 312 pages, ISBN 0439216508.

• *Simon & Schuster Thesaurus for Children* (Simon & Schuster, Inc., 2001). Hardcover, 288 pages, ISBN 0689843224.

For teachers —

• *1,001 Affixes and Their Meanings: A Dictionary of Prefixes, Suffixes, and Inflections,* by Raymond G. Laurita (Leonardo Press, 1990). Paperback, 154 pages, ISBN 0914051180. Order online at www.spellingdoctor.com or phone (207) 236-8649.

• *Educators Publishing Service,* www.epsbooks.com or 1-800-225-5750, has a number of publications that help build vocabulary.

• *Prefixes and Suffixes: Systematic Sequential Phonics and Spelling,* by Patricia Cunningham (Carson Dellosa, 2002). Paperback, 192 pages, ISBN 0887246958.

• *Word Parts Dictionary: Standard and Reverse Listings of Prefixes, Suffixes, and Combining Forms,* by Michael J. Sheehan (McFarland & Company, 2000). Library binding, 227 pages, ISBN 0786408197.

• *Word Wall Workbook: Prefixes and Suffixes,* by Karen Sevaly (Teacher's Friend Publications, 1999). This and other vocabulary products are available from Teacher's Friend Publications, www.teachersfriend.com.

• *Words Their Way: Word Study for Phonics, Vocabulary, and Spelling Instruction (3rd edition),* by Donald Bear, Marcia Invernizzi, Shane Templeton, and Francine Johnston (Prentice Hall, 2004). Paperback, 464 pages, ISBN 0131113380.

Supplemental Essay

How to Build Vocabulary

Because a robust vocabulary is essential for successful reading comprehension, it is almost impossible to overstate the importance of building vocabulary in the elementary grades. Students with inadequate vocabularies are likely to begin to encounter difficulties with reading beginning in roughly the fourth grade, as this is when many state and national tests begin testing mostly reading comprehension, as opposed to decoding skills. It is therefore important that teachers remember that reading depends not just on decoding words but also on understanding the meaning of those words. Therefore, beginning in the earliest grades and continuing into the middle years, schools should emphasize vocabulary and knowledge of key subjects as well as decoding skills.

Unfortunately, this does not always happen. In fact, some schools have begun to decrease the amount of time spent on history and science and other subjects in order to increase the amount of time they can spend teaching reading skills (which usually means decoding in the early grades and strategy instruction in Grades 3 and up). This approach is put forward by people with the best intentions, but it is not likely to be successful in the long run, because reading comprehension requires a broad knowledge of words and key subjects. The vocabulary words students would have learned in history and science and the arts include many words they will need to become successful readers.

In order to build vocabulary effectively, it is helpful to know a little about how people learn words. Researchers have established that students learn words gradually, as a result of many exposures. Although a student may say, "I know that word" or "I don't know that word," in fact, knowing a word is not an all-or-nothing matter. There are degrees of word knowledge. For purposes of discussion, experts sometimes refer to four stages:

1. The student has never encountered the word.
2. The student has heard the word but doesn't know what it means.
3. The student has heard the word several times and has some sense of the context in which the word is used, e.g., "It has something to do with food."
4. The student knows the word and can understand it in speech and writing.

Movement from stage 1 to stage 4 is gradual and may require many exposures.

Researchers have also established that students (and people generally) learn a great deal of vocabulary indirectly, without ever being presented with a definition or doing formal vocabulary work. This can be demonstrated mathematically. A college-bound twelfth-grader knows between 60,000 and 100,000 words. Experts disagree on the exact numbers, but even if one uses the lower estimates, it means that the student must have learned more than 3,000, and possibly as many as 5,000 words a year, every year since birth. This is many more words than could be taught explicitly in schools. Vocabulary experts suggest that perhaps 500 words can be explicitly taught in school each year, but probably relatively few schools actually succeed in teaching so many words. It is therefore clear that students learn the great majority of words indirectly, or implicitly, by deducing the meaning of a word based on multiple exposures in different contexts, and not through explicit vocabulary instruction.

Since students learn so many words indirectly, one of the most effective ways of building vocabulary is to increase the amount students read and/or hear; research suggests that this may be a more effective way of increasing vocabulary than any specific, direct instruction technique. In the early grades, when students are learning to read for themselves, they can take in relatively few words and little information through the eye; their primary channel for learning is still the ear. That is why it is crucial that teachers in the early grades provide students with a steady, rich diet of oral language, including many read alouds.

To ensure that students are exposed to a wide range of vocabulary, read alouds and independent readings should include not only fiction but also plenty of nonfiction in areas like history, science, and the arts. Each of these subjects introduces students to words, phrases, and ideas that are less likely to be encountered if read alouds are limited to fiction. *This is a very important point: properly understood, vocabulary instruction is not just an "English" or "Language Arts" topic; it extends across every subject in the curriculum.*

Grade 5 students should have lots of opportunities to read on their own. However, that does not mean that there is no place in the curriculum for reading aloud. Although students should have mastered decoding skills by this point, they will probably still be building fluency and reading comprehension ability. The average student's reading comprehension ability does not "catch up" to listening comprehension ability until roughly Grade 7. Thus, many, perhaps most, students in Grade 5 are likely to understand more when a text is read to them than when they read it themselves—because when the text is read to them, the burden of decoding is lifted from their shoulders and they can focus completely on making sense of what they hear. A good rule of thumb is to save the more difficult texts for reading aloud and use the easier texts for independent reading.

In the past, the most common kind of vocabulary instruction involved giving students lists of words. Teachers would provide matching dictionary definitions or ask students to find dictionary definitions, and then students would memorize the definitions for a quiz. Researchers now believe this kind of instruction is of limited value. Students often have difficulty choosing appropriate meanings from a dictionary and do not always gain the information they need from dictionary-style definitions. Also, students in the early grades are still learning to read and so can make only limited use of dictionaries.

Students need some explanation of what a word means, but they also need to see how the word functions in various contexts. Most dictionaries address the first need, though not always in a way that is clear to young students. Most dictionaries do not illustrate how words are used, because multiple examples of usage would make the dictionary too large for convenient use—and yet examples of usage are precisely what students need.

Instead of just giving dictionary-style definitions, you can explain a new word using words students already know and then give several examples of usage. These examples will help students see, or hear, how the word is used, and how its meaning relates to other words around it. For example, for the word *delicate*, a dictionary is likely to offer as many as seven or eight definitions of various senses, including "requiring careful handling" and "involving matters of a deeply personal nature." This information may not be optimally useful to students. A teacher can do better with just a little effort, for example, by explaining that "something that is delicate is fragile and needs to be handled carefully," then giving several examples of delicate objects (like china and glass) and asking students to name others, and then giving several sample sentences using the word, e.g., "The old newspaper was so delicate, it fell apart in my hands."

Research tells us that a single exposure to a word is usually not enough for students to learn the word. One study found that young readers learn only 5–10% of unknown words from a single exposure; in other words, no better than one word in 10, and possibly as few as one in 20. Another study found that 12 encounters with a word reliably improved comprehension, whereas 4 did not. Both studies point to the same conclusion: vocabulary acquisition depends on multiple exposures to the word.

How can you achieve multiple exposures to words in your classroom? Obviously, frequent reading and reading aloud can help. Some words may appear more than once in a piece of writing. For example, the word *camel* may appear a dozen or more times in the story "How the Camel Got His Hump." You can also achieve repeated exposure by rereading some stories. During the first reading, students may get a general idea of what various words mean; during a second reading, they may be able to develop a more exact idea. A good discussion of a story can also result in several additional uses of the word, and may encourage students to use some of the words themselves. Students are more likely to remember words they have used themselves.

You can also increase the chances of a student being exposed to certain words if you linger on a particular topic for several days or for a few weeks. For example, if you read a series of fictional and non-fiction texts on the Renaissance, you increase the chances that students will get multiple exposures to words like *rebirth, classics, Greek, Latin, humanist, scholar, patron, courtier, Florence,* and *Rome.*

You can also do formal vocabulary work. Although many words are learned indirectly, that does not mean that formal vocabulary work is useless. In fact, it can be very useful, as well as enjoyable. After describing what a word means and giving examples, you can use other tactics to get students actively involved in using the word and give them multiple exposures. Students can be asked to

• relate the new word to words they already know, e.g., given the word *ruby,* relate it to other precious objects like diamonds and gold.

• make up and discuss sentences using the word.

• discuss shades of meaning of the word when used in slightly different contexts, e.g., the difference between "the refrigerator stopped *running* when the power went out," and "the boy went *running* in a race."

• distinguish correct and incorrect examples of usage, e.g., "the army *courageously* charged toward the enemy" vs. "the army *courageously* ran away." When students can distinguish sentences that use a word properly, like the first sentence, from nonsense sentences like the second sentence, they have a functional sense of a word's meaning.

• identify synonyms and/or antonyms for the word; in order to identify a similar or opposite word, students must have some sense of the word's meaning.

- match the word to a picture.

- discuss and define the word along with other words from the same domain, e.g., when defining *rooster*, refer to chickens, chicks, and hens.

- learn the word in conjunction with morphologically related words, e.g., with *elf*, learn *elfin*; with *Europe, European*; with *farm, farmer*.

- make word maps or "word webs" that show relationships between related words.

- discuss meaningful prefixes and suffixes within the word. Twenty prefixes account for 97% of the prefixed words in written English. Teaching key prefixes like *un-, re-, dis-* and *in-, im-, il-, ir-* can help students make sense of scores of words.

An excellent and brief (50-page) summary of vocabulary acquisition and instruction can be found in Steven A. Stahl's *Vocabulary Development* (Brookline Books, 1999), from which some of the insights and suggestions above are drawn.

Another excellent guide to explicit vocabulary instruction is *Bringing Words to Life: Robust Vocabulary Instruction*, by Isabel L. Beck, Margaret G. McKeown, and Linda Kucan (The Guilford Press, 2002).

Two outstanding collections of cognitive research on vocabulary acquisition and instruction are *Vocabulary Instruction: Research to Practice*, edited by James F. Baumann and Edward J. Kame'enui (The Guilford Press, 2004) and *The Nature of Vocabulary Acquisition*, edited by Margaret G. McKeown and Mary E. Curtis (Lawrence Erlbaum Associates, 1987).

II. Poetry

The Big Idea

Listening to poetry or reading poems independently helps students develop an appreciation of the music in the words and enriches vocabulary.

What Students Should Already Know

Students should already be familiar with traditional poems and modern favorites they have heard at home or in school. They should know the terms *line* and *stanza* and should be able to recognize rhyme, rhythm, repetition, imagery, and personification.

What Students Need to Learn

- The poems for this grade, including the ideas they express and some of the memorable words and phrases they contain
- Some poems may
  - use words or phrases that appeal to the senses of sight, hearing, taste, smell, or touch.
  - include similes or metaphors that compare two or more things.
  - contain the same vowel sounds or consonant sounds within words.
  - contain rhyme or follow a strict rhyme scheme.
- Narrative poems
  - tell a story.
  - have characters, settings, plot, and dialogue.
- Lyric poems
  - are short and musical.
  - express the ideas and feelings of one speaker.
- Onomatopoeia is the technique of using words to represent sounds.
- Alliteration is the repetition of initial consonants in a line of poetry.

What Students Will Learn in Future Grades

In future grades, students will read more poems and extend their learning about poetry. In Grade 6, students will learn the terms *meter, iamb, couplet, rhyme scheme,* and *free verse.* They will also continue to look at poems in more detail, asking questions about the poet's use of language and noting the uses of devices such as simile, metaphor, alliteration, etc.

Vocabulary

Student/Teacher Vocabulary

alliteration: the repetition of initial consonants (S)

allusion: a reference to a historical event or custom, a work of literature or art, or a well-known person or place (T)

assonance: the repetition of vowel sounds within words (T)

catalog: a list of people, things, or attributes (T)

consonance: the repetition of consonant sounds within and at the ends of words (T)

couplet: a pair of consecutive lines that rhyme (S)

elegy: a poem that mourns a person's death (T)

free verse: a poem that does not have a regular pattern of rhythm (T)

hyperbole: exaggeration for emphasis (S)

imagery: words or phrases that appeal to the senses of sight, hearing, touch, taste, and smell and help create mental images (S)

internal rhyme: rhyme that occurs within a line of verse (T)

line: a unit of poetry signaled by a visual or typographic break (T)

lyric poem: a short poem that expresses the thoughts and feelings of a single speaker (S)

metaphor: a figure of speech in which a word or phrase used to describe one thing is used to describe a different thing; a resemblance is implied (S)

narrative poem: a poem that tells a story and often contains characters, dialogue, setting, and plot (S)

onomatopoeia: the technique of using words that imitate sounds (S)

parallelism: the use of words, phrases, or sentences that have a similar grammatical structure (T)

personification: a figure of speech in which an animal, object, or idea is given human characteristics (S)

quatrain: a four-line stanza or poem (T)

repetition: the repeating of a sound, word, phrase, or line (T)

rhyme: two or more words that end with the same or similar sounds (T)

rhyme scheme: the pattern of rhymes used in a poem, usually described by using letters of the alphabet to represent each rhyme (e.g., ABBA) (T)

rhythm: a pattern of sound created by the arrangement of stressed and unstressed syllables in words (T)

simile: a figure of speech that directly compares two or more unlike things by using the words *like* or *as* (S)

slant rhyme: rhyme that is not exact, e.g., "heart" and "car" (also known as "off rhyme") (T)

speaker: the person or object whose voice is heard in the poem; the speaker of a poem is not necessarily the poet (T)

stanza: a group of lines that form a section of a poem; stanzas often share a common pattern of meter, rhyme, and number of lines (T)

symbol: a person, place, object, or action that stands for something beyond itself (S)

Materials

Instructional Masters 7–8
Elements of Poetry, p. 44

Be a Poetry Buff, p. 56

audio recordings of poems read by their poets, if possible, p. 44

tape recorder/CD player and audio recording of "John Brown's Body," p. 48

tape recorder/CD player and audio recording of "Battle Hymn of the Republic," p. 48

picture of an eagle, p. 50

individual student journals, p. 51

illustrated version of "A Poison Tree," p. 53

landscape pictures before and after a snowstorm, p. 54

picture of a tiger, p. 55

index cards, p. 56

access to school media center for poetry books, p. 56

chart paper, p. 56

magazines, p. 56

construction paper, p. 56

scissors, p. 56

glue, p. 056

sentence strips, p. 56

Vocabulary continued

Domain Vocabulary

Poetry and associated words:
poet, poetry, poetic, prosody, anthology, bard, nursery rhyme, mood, verse, lyric, lyrical, musical, sensory details, aural, tactile, visual senses, sight, sound, taste, touch, smell, emotions, imagination, content, form, sonnet, ballad, ode, list poem, catalog poem, epic, haiku, cinquain, acrostic, figure of speech, symbolic, patterns, sound device, meter, beat, stress, accent, stressed, unstressed, measure, metrical, foot, meaning, sense, style, connotation, image, compactness, compression, rhythmic, end rhyme, structure, theme, tone, scan, scansion, *plus many words from the poems themselves, including the "Vocabulary" listed within selections in the main text*

Cross-curricular Connections

History and Geography	Music
American: The Civil War	**Songs**
The Civil War	• "Battle Hymn of the Republic"
• Robert E. Lee and General Stonewall Jackson ("Barbara Frietchie")	
• Assassination of Abraham Lincoln by John Wilkes Booth ("O Captain! My Captain!")	

At a Glance

The most important ideas for you are:

▸ Listening to poetry should be a delightful experience, but it can also be a learning experience, as it introduces students to many words and phrases they might not otherwise encounter. Reading poetry can deepen vocabulary and improve students' ability to understand what they read.

▸ Grade 5 is not too early for students to begin learning about some poetic devices such as simile, metaphor, onomatopoeia, and alliteration.

▸ Alliteration and onomatopoeia are sound devices that heighten the musical nature of the words in a poem.

▸ The repetition of initial consonants in a line of poetry is called alliteration.

▸ Onomatopoeia is the technique of using words to represent sounds.

▸ The speaker is the person or object whose voice you hear when you read a poem.

▸ Lyric poems express the thoughts and feelings of a single speaker.

▸ Narrative poems tell a story and feature characters, dialogue, setting, and plot.

At a Glance continued

> Students should have many opportunities to hear poetry, as well as some opportunities to try writing poetry of their own.

> The poems in this section should be the core of the poetry curriculum for this grade. However, you are encouraged to add poems, including more poems by the same authors, poems on similar topics, or poems of your own choosing.

What Teachers Need to Know

A. Poems
B. Terms

Background: Why Study Poetry?

This section offers a selection of poems by favorite writers. The purpose of this section is to help students appreciate the genre of poetry, delight in the play of language, and increase vocabulary. As you teach this section, you may want to read with your class many more grade-appropriate poems by the same poets or different poets.

Although students in Grade 5 should be able to read these poems on their own, you may wish to read some or all of the poems aloud. Listening to poetry helps students develop an awareness of language that will help them become better writers and readers. By listening closely, by repeating certain lines or phrases in a poem, or by reciting poems by heart, students continue to build their vocabulary and to develop an understanding of literary techniques used in poetry and other genres.

In Grade 5, reading aloud can be combined with independent reading by students. Most poems do not give up all their meaning on a first reading; they need to be read at least two or three times. Some of these readings may be done aloud, some may be silent, some may be done by the teacher, and some by one or more students. For example, you might begin by reading a poem aloud to students while they follow along either in a book or by looking at the poem projected onto a screen using an overhead projector. Then you might go through the poem sentence by sentence or stanza by stanza, having individual students read a sentence or stanza. Or you might ask students to all read silently, and to read with a task in mind, e.g., "Find a simile or metaphor," or "Find an adjective that is particularly vivid or descriptive." Then you might conclude with another teacher or student reading. There are many possible combinations of these various kinds of reading.

To encourage students to develop an appreciation for poetry, be sure to give them opportunities to write their own poems. Since students may be intimidated by the prospect of writing a poem from scratch, you may wish to help them get started by providing a topic, some guidelines, a first line, etc. You may wish to draw on the poems that you have read as a class to give students a starting point.

Teaching Idea

Before you begin this section, have students name their favorite poems and poets. Invite volunteers to recite any poems or parts of poems they know by heart.

II. Poetry

Teaching Idea

Give students Instructional Masters 7a–7b, *Elements of Poetry,* before you begin teaching any poems. This graphic organizer lists key elements of a poem that you will discuss with your class (i.e., title, author, characters, setting, and subject). After the discussion of each poem, you can fill it out as a class to help provide continuity to the teaching of poems throughout the year. Please note that the graphic organizer is a tool that can be customized for use throughout the curriculum.

Name _____ Date _____

Elements of Poetry

Title	Barbara Frietchie
Author	John Greenleaf Whittier
Character(s)	Barbara Frietchie, Robert E. Lee, Thomas "Stonewall" Jackson, Confederate soldiers
Setting	Frederick, Maryland, on September 17, 1862
Subject	Barbara Frietchie is a brave elderly woman who flies a Union flag during the Civil War while Confederate troops march into her town.
Literary Elements and Devices	couplets, rhyme scheme, rhythm, alliteration, consonance, assonance, imagery, repetition, symbolism, metaphor

Directions: Review the sample chart with students. Then choose another poem and have students fill in the answers in the appropriate box on Master 7b. If you'd like, you can copy Master 7b and do this exercise for each poem you study.
Purpose: To help students recognize the key elements of a poem, to provide continuity to the teaching of poems throughout the year.

Master 7a   Grade 5: Language Arts

Use Instructional Masters 7a–7b.

Teaching Idea

Before you begin this section, locate recordings of poetry read aloud by the poets themselves. As you introduce each poem, play recorded versions, if possible, so that students can hear the poets' interpretations of their work.

Teaching Poetry

▶ Reading Poetry Aloud

Reading poetry aloud enables students to more immediately experience the music in the words. It also relieves them of the difficulties of decoding the words, freeing them to concentrate on the meanings and sounds. When you read poems, don't be afraid to read them aloud several times. Speak slowly and clearly, pausing when you come to a period or other punctuation, or when the sense of the words requires a pause. Use your voice to emphasize the musical nature of the words, the sense, the speaker's emotion, the poem's rhymes or rhyme scheme, and the rhythm. For purposes of highlighting rhythm, read those poems that have a regular pattern of accented and unaccented syllables, such as "The Arrow and the Song" or "The Eagle," in a singsong manner.

To make characters in narrative poems come alive, try using different voices when you read lines of dialogue. For example, Barbara Frietchie in "Barbara Frietchie" might speak in a fiercely determined older person's voice, and the fans in "Casey at the Bat" might speak with great fervor and enthusiasm.

If necessary, provide additional information that will help students grasp the meaning of the poem, including definitions of difficult words, unfamiliar cultural references, or historical allusions.

▶ Focusing on Meaning

After reading a poem, discuss it, asking questions such as these:

- Who or what is the poem about?
- What happens?
- Where do events take place?
- When do events take place?
- Why do certain events happen?
- What words make the poem rhyme?
- Are there any words or sentences you don't understand?
- Why do you think the poet made particular word choices?
- Which images helped you form a picture in your mind?

Help students paraphrase the events and sentences in the poem in their own words. If a sentence is written in a particularly unusual or poetic word order, work with students to rearrange the words in a more typical English word order. For example, you might take "Mockingly / On coop or kennel he hangs Parian wreaths" (from Emerson's "The Snowstorm") and rewrite it like this: "He mockingly hangs Parian wreaths on coop or kennel." Ask students to identify the antecedents of pronouns. For example, in the sentence just quoted, you might ask, "Who is this 'he' that is hanging wreaths?" If students understand that "he" is "the north wind," they will have a better understanding of the poem and will be in a position to understand that hanging up wreaths is a metaphorical way of describing what the north wind is doing with the snow. For difficult words, like "Parian," you can supply glossaries (many of which are provided in the discussions) or invite students to look up the words in a dictionary.

Once you've gone through the poem and discussed it, read the poem again, inviting students to join in by repeating certain words, phrases, or lines they recall. If the poem is short and relatively simple, you may invite a student to do this reading. Alternatively, you might want to have students read aloud the poems in this section and then discuss the meaning they glean as well as any literary devices they recognize.

Focusing on Literary Devices

One of the pleasures of reading poetry is being able to recognize different literary devices that a poet uses. Some devices—such as alliteration, assonance, consonance, and rhyme—highlight the music of the words. Other devices, such as imagery and metaphor, help convey meaning. As you teach the poems in this section, you may want to point out examples of literary devices.

Grade 5 is an appropriate grade for students to begin looking at poems in more detail, asking questions about the poet's use of language and noting the use of literary devices. You can call attention to these devices as you read. For example, ask questions such as "Which two words have the same /o/ sound?" to help students become aware of assonance; "Which words or phrases appeal to your sense of touch?" to help them recognize imagery; or "What's your favorite line or stanza?" to help them understand a poem's structure. To help students become aware of alliteration ask, "Which words begin with the same letter or sound?" To teach onomatopoeia ask, "Which word sounds like what it describes?"

Literary Device	Definition	Example
alliteration	the repetition of initial consonants	He clasps the crag with crooked hands
allusion	a reference to a historical event or custom, a work of literature or art, or a well-known person or place	"Boanerges" is a biblical allusion to Mark 3:17.
assonance	the repetition of vowel sounds within words	Or a huge blueness in the air
consonance	the repetition of consonant sounds within and at the ends of words	A brick in her back yard
couplet	a pair of consecutive lines that rhyme	What is the opposite of two? A lonely me, a lonely you.
ellipsis	the omission of words that are not necessary for understanding the meaning of a sentence	[What is] well begun is half done.
hyperbole	exaggeration for emphasis	Make a mountain out of a molehill
imagery	words or phrases that appeal to the senses of sight, hearing, touch, taste, and smell and help create mental images	"Then from five thousand throats and more there rose a lusty yell" appeals to the sense of hearing.
internal rhyme	rhyme that occurs within a line of verse	The score stood FOUR to two, with but one inning MORE to play
line	a unit of poetry signaled by a visual or typographic break	He did not know I saw; He bit an angle-worm in halves

Teaching Idea

Create a poetry listening center in your classroom. Record yourself or someone else reading poems. Students will listen to a poem, and then you can ask them to draw and write about the feelings the reading evoked in them.

Teaching Idea

To help students understand these literary devices, refer to works of fiction (pp. 58–82), speeches (pp. 83–90), and sayings and phrases (pp. 91–103) in which these devices are used. Point out examples of imagery, repetition, personification, simile, and so on in novel excerpts, myths, folktales, speeches, proverbs, and idioms. See also Section III, "Fiction and Drama" D. Literary Terms (pp. 58–73).

Literary Device	Definition	Example
metaphor	a figure of speech in which a word or phrase used to describe one thing is used to describe a different thing; a resemblance is implied	"First she is an ancient queen / In pomp and purple veil" compares Narcissa to a queen.
onomatopoeia	the technique of using words that imitate sounds	hoot
parallelism	the use of words, phrases, or sentences that have a similar grammatical structure	The shoemaker singing as he sits on his bench, the hatter singing as he stands
personification	a figure of speech in which an animal, object, or idea is given human characteristics	When the stars threw down their spears, / And watered heaven with their tears
repetition	the repeating of a sound, word, phrase, or line	Heart filled, head filled with glee
rhyme	two or more words that end with the same or similar sounds	oak, spoke
rhythm	a pattern of sound created by the arrangement of stressed and unstressed syllables in words	It FELL to EARTH, I KNEW not WHERE
simile	a figure of speech that directly compares two or more unlike things by using the words *like* or *as*	And like a thunderbolt he falls
slant rhyme	rhyme that is not exact	Crumb, home
stanza	a group of lines that form a section of a poem; stanzas often share a common pattern of meter, rhyme, and number of lines	Small Narcissa sits upon A brick in her back yard And looks at tiger-lilies And shakes her pigtails hard.
symbol	a person, place, object, or action that stands for something else beyond itself	The Union flag in "Barbara Frietchie" is a symbol of patriotism.

Introducing the Poems

When reading each of the following poems, you may use some or all of the information provided to help students understand what the poem is about, what literary devices it contains, and who wrote it. You may wish to preteach some vocabulary if you think not knowing a word might keep students from understanding the poem. However, students in Grade 5 can understand a great deal from context, so you should not need to preteach all of the words listed. Some of the glossaries can be used to deepen your own understanding before you read the poem; others might be used to deepen students' understanding after a first reading. Suggested teaching strategies and activities are also provided.

The Arrow and the Song

Author Information: Henry Wadsworth Longfellow (1807–1882) was born in Portland, Maine. A scholar who knew 10 languages, Longfellow was an esteemed Harvard professor. A beloved poet, his works include "The Song of Hiawatha," "Evangeline," "The Courtship of Miles Standish," "There Was a Little Girl" (a Kindergarten poem in Core Knowledge schools), and "Paul Revere's Ride" (a Grade 4 poem in Core Knowledge schools).

Summary of Content: This lyric poem compares shooting an arrow and singing a song. According to the speaker, both are lost in the air but are found again; the arrow is found in an oak tree, and the song is "found" in the heart of a friend.

Vocabulary: swiftly: quickly; **keen:** sharp, acute

Literary Elements and Devices: rhyme scheme (couplets: AABB AACC DDEE), repetition (It fell to earth, I knew not where), consonance (s<u>w</u>iftly, fle<u>w</u>), assonance (n<u>o</u>t, f<u>o</u>llow), rhythm (I BREATHed a SONG inTO the AIR), alliteration (<u>f</u>ollow, <u>f</u>light), symbol (the lost arrow and the song symbolize something that we believe has been lost and can never be regained) (**1**)

Barbara Frietchie

Author Information: John Greenleaf Whittier (1807–1892) was born in Massachusetts. A self-educated Quaker, he was active in the cause against slavery. Whittier published his first book, *Legends of New England in Prose and Verse*, in 1831. His most popular book, *Snow-Bound*, was published in 1866.

Background: The Civil War inspired Whittier to write this poem. Born in 1766 in Lancaster, Pennsylvania, Barbara Frietchie was a 96-year-old widow when the events described in the poem took place (in 1862). According to the story, Frietchie patriotically displayed a Union flag as Generals Robert E. Lee and Thomas J. "Stonewall" Jackson led 40,000 Confederate soldiers into Frederick, Maryland, on September 17, 1862.

Summary of Content: This narrative poem tells the story of Barbara Frietchie, a brave woman who defiantly flew a Union flag during the Civil War as Confederate troops marched into her town.

Vocabulary: morn: morning; **clustered:** gathered closely together; **spires:** tall, pointed towers, especially of churches; **Frederick:** a city in Maryland, west of Baltimore; **fruited:** filled with fruit; **the garden of the Lord:** the garden of Eden, Paradise, where Adam and Eve first lived; **famished:** very hungry; **rebel:** Confederate; **horde:** crowd; **fourscore years and ten:** 90 (a score equals 20, so four times a score is 80); **hauled:** pulled or dragged; **staff:** the pole that holds a flag; **tread:** heavy step; **slouched hat:** a soft hat with a wide brim; **dust-brown ranks:** Confederate soldiers wearing brown uniforms; **shivered:** broke into pieces; **sash:** the frame in which the glass panes of a window are set; **rent:** tore; **banner:** here, the flag; **royal:** dignified, impressive; **yon:** over there; **o'er:** over; **bier:** a coffin and its stand

Literary Elements and Devices: couplets, rhyme scheme (AA BB CC and so on), rhythm (UP from the MEADows RICH with CORN), alliteration (<u>f</u>orty, <u>f</u>lags; <u>s</u>ilver, <u>s</u>tars), consonance (cluste<u>r</u>ed spi<u>r</u>es of Frede<u>r</u>ick), assonance (r<u>o</u>se, <u>o</u>ld),

Teaching Idea

Before teaching "The Arrow and the Song," ask students if they've ever had an experience in which somebody told them something—a proverb, a saying, a short poem—that they have never forgotten. Tell them that the poem they are going to read is about remembering and forgetting. Help them relate their experiences to the poem's central meaning: a song cannot be lost once it has been sung, because it will always hold special meaning for those who hear or sing it.

Cross-curricular Teaching Idea

Introduce "Barbara Frietchie," "Battle Hymn of the Republic," and "O Captain! My Captain!" when the class studies the Civil War. Students may also enjoy hearing and reading some of the poems from Rosemary and Stephen Vincent Benét's *A Book of Americans*, which includes poems on such Civil War figures as Abraham Lincoln, Ulysses S. Grant, and Robert E. Lee (see *More Resources*).

imagery (forty flags with their crimson bars appeals to the sense of sight, silken scarf appeals to the sense of touch, sounded the tread of marching feet appeals to the sense of hearing), repetition (morn, flag), symbol (the flag represents the Union), characters (Barbara Frietchie, Stonewall Jackson), setting (Frederick, Maryland, on a September morning during the Civil War), dialogue ("Shoot, if you must, this old gray head . . ."), metaphor (the flag is compared to a silk scarf), simile (Fair as the garden of the Lord) ②

Battle Hymn of the Republic

Author Information: American poet and reformer Julia Ward Howe (1819–1910) was active in the antislavery and women's rights movements. She helped her husband, Samuel Gridley Howe, edit the Boston antislavery newspaper *Commonwealth*. Howe also wrote poetry, plays, and articles.

Background: Written at the height of the Civil War, this poem was inspired by a visit to a Union army camp near Washington, D.C. After a picnic with friends, Howe wrote the words in 1861 while staying at the Hotel Willard in Washington. First published in the *Atlantic Monthly* in February 1862, the poem was set to the tune of the folk song "John Brown's Body" and became popular as a marching song for Union troops.

Summary of Content: This poem is a plea to end slavery on the grounds that it is morally wrong and has enraged God.

Vocabulary: hymn: a song of praise or thanksgiving to God; **mine:** my; **trampling:** beating down with the feet; **vintage:** wine; **wrath:** anger; **hath:** archaic form of "has"; **loosed:** set free, released; **watch-fires:** fires kept burning at night by a guard; **circling:** shaped like a circle; **damps:** humid air; **righteous:** moral, without guilt or sin; **sentence:** punishment; **flaring:** flaming up with a bright, wavering light; **sifting:** examining and sorting carefully; **jubilant:** joyful; **transfigures:** changes, alters

Literary Elements and Devices: rhyme scheme (AAAB CCCB and so on), imagery (watch-fires and dews and damps appeal to the sense of touch, sounded forth the trumpet appeals to the sense of hearing, dim and flaring lamps appeals to the sense of sight), alliteration (loosed, lightning), consonance (dim, lamps), assonance (terrible, swift), repetition (marching on), rhythm (HE is TRAMpling OUT the VINtage WHERE the GRAPES of WRATH are STORED), metaphor (the Lord getting ready to unleash His anger is compared to the process of turning mature grapes into wine; the Lord's anger is now fully developed), quatrains, personification (truth marches on), biblical allusions (coming of the Lord refers to the prophesied return of Jesus Christ at the Last Judgment; his terrible swift sword refers to the sword with which Christ will separate the just from the sinners; His righteous sentence refers to the Lord's judgment on those who have not followed the righteous path; sounded forth the trumpet refers to the trumpet that will call humans to Judgment Day; lilies refers to a Christian symbol of innocence and purity; Christ was born across the sea refers to Jesus being born in Bethlehem; He died to make men holy refers to Jesus sacrificing his own life to take away the world's sins) ③

Teaching Idea

When teaching "Battle Hymn of the Republic," consider beginning with the song "John Brown's Body" (which also connects to the U.S. Civil War). There are several versions of the lyrics, all sung to the same tune, and all of which contain the line "John Brown's body lies a-mouldering in the grave." You can find complete lyrics by doing an Internet search for this phrase. Once students are familiar with "John Brown's Body" and its melody, tell them how Julia Ward Howe was inspired by a visit to a Union military camp and wrote new lyrics to the same melody. Next, introduce "Battle Hymn of the Republic." Be sure to take some time to explain the rather complex biblical imagery in Howe's lyrics.

Cross-curricular Teaching Idea

Teach "Battle Hymn of the Republic" during the Music section "Songs," on pp. 000. Have the class listen to an audiotape or CD recording of "Battle Hymn of the Republic" to learn the words and the music. Help students understand that Howe firmly believed the Civil War was just because slavery was against Christian teachings; in her poem, she uses biblical references because she felt that the Union struggle was a holy war.

A Bird Came Down the Walk

Author Information: Emily Dickinson (1830–1886) spent nearly all of her life in the small New England town of Amherst, Massachusetts. During her lifetime, only seven of her poems were published. After Dickinson's death, her sister Lavinia found and rescued more than 1,000 of Dickinson's poems that had been hidden in a box.

Summary of Content: This lyric poem describes the speaker's observations of a bird as it eats a worm, drinks dew, hops sidewise, looks around nervously, and then flies away.

Vocabulary: **angleworm:** an earthworm that could be used by an "angler," or fisherman, as bait; **glanced:** looked; **rapid:** quickly moving; **rowed:** moved as if with oars; **oars:** long poles used to row or steer a boat; **plashless:** without splashing

Literary Elements and Devices: rhyme (saw, raw; grass, pass), quatrains, alliteration (silver, seam), onomatopoeia (plashless), consonance (one, danger), assonance (rowed, home), simile (They looked like frightened beads), imagery (drank a dew appeals to the sense of taste, velvet head appeals to the sense of touch), metaphor (a bird using its wings to fly in the air is compared to a rower using oars to row a boat on the ocean), punctuation (dash highlights important words and breaks up the rhythm), slant or off rhyme (crumb, home; ocean, noon) (4)

Teaching Idea

Teach the two Emily Dickinson poems, "A Bird Came Down the Walk" and "I like to see it lap the miles," together, and consider adding a few other poems to make an "author study" unit. Poems suitable for children include "Nature is what we see," "The morns are meeker than they were," "A narrow fellow in the grass," "There is no frigate like a book," "I'll tell you how the sun rose," "A Word," "Pedigree," "The Hummingbird," "The Snow," and "I'm nobody! Who are you?" Students may also enjoy *The Mouse of Amherst*, by Elizabeth Spires, a novella for children about Emily Dickinson. (See *More Resources*.)

Casey at the Bat

Author Information: Ernest Lawrence Thayer (1863–1940), the son of a prosperous mill owner, graduated from Harvard University. Rather than enter the family business, he became a journalist and took a job writing for the *San Francisco Examiner*, where he composed a poem for each Sunday edition.

Summary of Content: This well-known narrative poem tells the story of a small-town baseball hero who is expected to win the game in the final inning.

Vocabulary: **outlook:** expectation for the future; **died:** stopped (Cooney and Barrows were thrown out at first, so there are two outs. Since only three outs are allowed in a team's "at bat," Casey's turn at bat represented the team's last hope.); **sickly:** nauseating, weak, feeble; **patrons:** supporters, fans; **straggling:** straying; **despair:** hopelessness; **clung:** held on to tightly; **get a whack:** make an attempt to get to the plate; **put up even money:** make a bet that the Mudville team would win; **preceded:** came before (in the batting order); **stricken:** overwhelmed by painful emotion; **multitude:** crowd; **melancholy:** sadness; **wonderment:** surprise; **despised:** hated; **lusty:** strong, powerful, spirited; **dell:** a small, wooded valley; **recoiled:** returned, bounced back, echoed back to; **bearing:** the way in which a person carries or conducts himself or herself; **doffed:** tipped; **writhing:** twisting and turning; **defiance:** bold resistance to an opposing force; **sneer:** a scornful expression created by slightly raising one corner of the upper lip; **hurtling:** moving with great speed; **haughty:** proud; **grandeur:** magnificence; **sturdy:** strong; **unheeded:** not paid attention to; **muffled:** repressed, deadened; **charity:** goodwill, kindness; **visage:** face; **tumult:** noise and commotion of a crowd; **bade:** directed; **spheroid:** round object, in this case a baseball; **fraud:** an act of dishonesty; **stern:** serious; **clenched:** held tightly

Teaching Idea

Invite students familiar with the game of baseball to help explain what happens in "Casey at the Bat." Have them define baseball terms such as *inning*, *single*, *second*, *third*, *pitcher*, *strike*, and so on. As students read the poem, you might want to have them keep score. Make sure students know that a baseball game ends in the bottom of the ninth inning unless the score is still tied, or unless the home team is leading after the "top" of the ninth. Then draw a baseball diamond on the board, and use it to illustrate how base runners and batters fare during the inning. An alternative might be to have pairs of students act as sportscasters calling a game, using details in the poem as a starting point for their commentary.

Literary Elements and Devices: rhyme scheme (AABB CCDD and so on), internal rhyme (score, four, more), quatrains, alliteration (sickly, silence), rhythm (But FLYNN let DRIVE a SINGLE, to the WONderment of ALL), simile (Like the beating of the storm waves), imagery (a lusty yell appeals to the sense of hearing, rubbed his hands with dirt appeals to the sense of touch, and leather-covered sphere appeals to the senses of touch and sight), repetition (mighty Casey), consonance (leather, covered, sphere, hurtling, through, air), assonance (throats, rose), personification (tongues applauded), characters (Casey, Cooney, Barrows, Flynn, Jimmy Blake, the pitcher, the umpire, the fans), dialogue ("Kill the umpire!"), setting (baseball diamond in Mudville), plot, hyperbole (fans at the stadium are a stricken multitude that watch with ten thousand eyes) (5)

The Eagle

Author Information: Alfred, Lord Tennyson (1809–1892) served as England's poet laureate for 42 years. Among his well-known works are "The Charge of the Light Brigade" and *Idylls of the King,* a series of poems about King Arthur.

Summary of Content: The speaker of this lyric poem describes a majestic eagle both from ground level and from the eagle's vantage point.

Vocabulary: clasps: grasps, holds tightly; **crag:** steep, jagged rock that forms rugged cliffs; **ringed:** encircled, surrounded; **azure:** blue; **thunderbolt:** a flash of lightning

Literary Elements and Devices: rhyme scheme (AAA BBB), alliteration (clasps, crag, crooked), consonance (sun, lonely, lands), simile (like a thunderbolt he falls), rhythm (He CLASPS the CRAG with CROOKed HANDS), imagery (wrinkled sea appeals to the senses of touch and sight), personification (the eagle has hands) (5)

I Hear America Singing

Author Information: Walt Whitman (1819–1892), one of the greatest American poets, worked as a carpenter, a printer, a teacher, a journalist, and a nurse during the Civil War. Credited with bringing free verse, or poetry without a regular pattern of rhythm or rhyme, to American audiences, Whitman self-published the first of nine editions of his experimental masterpiece *Leaves of Grass* in 1855.

Summary of Content: This free verse lyric poem celebrates the energy and vitality of mid-19th-century America.

Vocabulary: varied: different; **carols:** songs; **blithe:** carefree and lighthearted; **plank:** a piece of lumber or wood; **beam:** a long piece of timber used as support in construction; **mason:** a person who builds or works with stone or brick; **hatter:** a person who makes or repairs hats; **ploughboy:** a boy who guides a team of animals in plowing; **intermission:** a break from work; **robust:** healthy, vital; **melodious:** pleasant to listen to

Literary Elements and Devices: free verse, catalog (lists of people), repetition (singing), parallelism (The carpenter singing his, The mason singing his), alliteration (singing, sits), metaphor (singing represents the different kinds of work that people do), assonance (strong, songs), consonance (hear, America, varied, carols), imagery (strong melodious songs appeals to the sense of hearing), long lines imitative of those found in the biblical Psalms (6)

Teaching Idea

Before reading "The Eagle," show the class a picture of an eagle and discuss how eagles hunt, where they nest, what they eat, and so forth. Invite students to brainstorm adjectives, similes, and metaphors that describe this awe-inspiring bird of prey. Then read Tennyson's poem.

Teaching Idea

You may wish to teach "The Eagle" along with other poems about animals. Reference *A Child's Treasury of Animal Verse,* by Mark Daniel. (See *More Resources.*)

Teaching Idea

Invite students to add lines to "I Hear America Singing," making a more modern version. For example, they can mention the jobs of their parents, caregivers, or other adults they know: The lawyer singing as she strolls into court, The physician singing as he reads the x-ray.

I like to see it lap the miles

Author Information: This poem is also by Emily Dickinson. See author information on p. 49.

Summary of Content: This lyric poem compares a train to a more familiar mode of transportation at the time: the horse.

Vocabulary: lap: take in, usually a liquid or food; **tanks:** large containers that store water for use by trains powered by steam engines; **prodigious:** amazing, huge, or forceful; **supercilious:** proud; **peer:** look closely; **shanties:** shacks; **quarry:** an open pit from which stone is obtained by cutting, digging, or blasting; **pare:** trim; **Boanerges [bo-ah-NER-jeez]:** a last name meaning "sons of thunder" that Jesus gave to his apostles James and John; **prompter:** more on time; **docile:** obedient; **omnipotent:** all-powerful

Literary Elements and Devices: slant rhyme (up, step; peer, pare), alliteration (<u>h</u>orrid, <u>h</u>ooting), consonance (prompte<u>r</u>, sta<u>r</u>), assonance (Ar<u>ou</u>nd, m<u>ou</u>ntains), punctuation (dash highlights important words and breaks up the rhythm), unconventional capitalization for emphasis (Miles, Roads), extended metaphor (a moving train on its way to a station is compared to a horse going to its stable), simile (neigh like Boanerges), onomatopoeia (hooting), personification (the train laps, licks, feeds, and complains), allusion (Boanerges is a biblical allusion to Mark, chapter 3, verse 17) (7)

I, Too

Author Information: African-American poet Langston Hughes (1902–1967) was one of the most influential writers of the Harlem Renaissance of the 1920s.

Summary of Content: This lyric poem conveys the speaker's feelings about African Americans being treated as second-class citizens and his or her hope that this situation will change.

Literary Elements and Devices: repetition (I, too; When company comes), symbol (the kitchen stands for the second-class status of African Americans), assonance (<u>c</u>ompany, <u>c</u>omes), consonance (darke<u>r</u>, brothe<u>r</u>), enjambment, or the continuation of a syntactic unit from one line to another (Nobody'll dare / Say to me, / "Eat in the kitchen," / Then.) (8)

Incident

Author Information: African-American poet Countee Cullen (1903–1946) began writing poetry when he was 14 years old. Like Langston Hughes, Cullen became a leader of the Harlem Renaissance. A brilliant scholar, Cullen earned a master's degree from Harvard University and later taught in New York City public schools. His first volume of poetry, *Color*, was published in 1925.

Summary of Content: This lyric poem tells about an incident of racial discrimination the speaker experienced as an eight-year-old child in Baltimore, Maryland. NOTE: Be aware that Cullen's poem contains the racial epithet *nigger*. Although the poem is a comment about how unpleasant it is to be called this name, there are some people who feel that this word should not be used in schools, even in situations like this where it is used disapprovingly. If you are uncomfortable teaching the Cullen poem, consider teaching another poem about African-American identity. A good collection of such poems is Arnold Adoff, ed.,

Teaching Idea

You may wish to teach additional Whitman poems as well (see *More Resources*). Some that are suitable for children include "I believe a leaf of grass," "I could turn and live with animals," "Miracles," and "There was a child went forth."

Teaching Idea

Read "I, Too" as a follow-up to the Whitman poem "I Hear America Singing" (p. 50). Explain to students that "I, Too" was written by the African-American poet Langston Hughes in the 1920s in response to Whitman's poem. Have students compare and contrast the messages in these two poems. Help them understand how this poem describes the rigorously segregated world that existed in America, even after the Civil War, indeed, until quite recently. Encourage students to look at the verb tenses; the first half is in the present tense, the second in the future. What is Hughes's speaker predicting about the future?

Teaching Idea

Have students read "Incident" to find evidence that shows that the character was heavily influenced by what happened to him. Have students write in their journals about a time that they felt hurt by the way they were treated by another person. "Incident" can also be taught together with Hughes's poem. To give students a context for the poems by Cullen and Hughes, you might want to have them research the Harlem Renaissance to find out more about what it was, who was associated with it, and why it was significant.

II. Poetry

(See More Resources.)

I Am the Darker Brother: An Anthology of Modern Poems by African Americans. (See *More Resources.*)

Vocabulary: glee: joy; **Baltimorean:** a person who lives in the city of Baltimore; **whit:** the least or smallest bit; **Nigger:** offensive slang for an African-American person

Literary Elements and Devices: rhyme (glee, me; November, remember), repetition (filled), rhythm (Now I was EIGHT and VERy SMALL), quatrains, alliteration (<u>st</u>aring, <u>st</u>raight), consonance (who<u>l</u>e, Ba<u>lt</u>imore), assonance (wh<u>i</u>t, b<u>i</u>gger), enjambment, or the continuation of a syntactic unit from one line to another (but he poked out, / His tongue) ⑨

Jabberwocky

Author Information: Lewis Carroll (1832–1898) was born Charles Lutwidge Dodgson in England. A mathematics professor at Oxford University, he also wrote the children's novels *Alice's Adventures in Wonderland* (1865) and *Through the Looking Glass* (1871).

Background: This poem comes from *Through the Looking Glass* in the "Humpty Dumpty" chapter. The main character, Alice, finds a book in which the poem "Jabberwocky" appears in mirror writing. After she holds the book up to a mirror, she is able to read the poem, but she still doesn't understand it.

Summary of Content: This nonsense narrative poem challenges the reader to decipher the made-up words and find out about the mysterious creature known as the Jabberwock. In the poem, a father warns his son about the Jabberwock and other potential dangers out in the world.

Vocabulary: 'Twas: It was; **foe:** enemy; **hast:** an archaic form of "have"; **thou:** an archaic form of "you"; **slain:** killed; **chortled:** laughed throatily

Literary Elements and Devices: nonsense words (brillig, slithy, toves, gimble), rhyme scheme (ABAB CDCD and so on), repetition ('Twas brillig, and the slithy toves; And the mome raths outgrabe), rhythm (He LEFT it DEAD, and WITH its HEAD), consonance (Satu<u>r</u>day's, wo<u>rk</u>s, ha<u>rd</u>), assonance (tw<u>o</u>, thr<u>ough</u>), onomatopoeia (snicker-snack), imagery (jaws that bite appeals to the sense of touch, and eyes of flame appeals to the sense of sight), internal rhyme (jaws, claws), quatrains, dialogue ("Beware the Jabberwock"), characters (father, son), plot ⑩

Narcissa

Author Information: Gwendolyn Brooks (1917–2000) won the Pulitzer Prize for *Annie Allen.* She was the first African-American poet to win this award. Brooks's poems often focus on the experiences of urban African Americans.

Summary of Content: This narrative poem tells the story of a quiet little girl whose vivid imagination transforms and entertains her while other children play games.

Vocabulary: pomp: magnificent display, splendor; **nightingale:** a brownish European songbird known for singing its beautiful song at night

Literary Elements and Devices: rhyme (ball, all; yard, hard), alliteration (<u>br</u>ick, <u>b</u>ack), consonance (a<u>n</u>, a<u>n</u>cie<u>n</u>t, quee<u>n</u>), assonance (N<u>a</u>rcissa, s<u>i</u>ts), rhythm (And SHAKES her PIGtails HARD), metaphor (Narcissa is compared to

---

Teaching Idea

Help students translate "Jabberwocky," inviting them to tell what they think the nonsense words might mean. Carroll made up the word *chortle* and defined it as "between a chuckle and a snort." It has since entered English as a real word. Students can be asked to draw a jubjub bird or a frumious Bandersnatch, or to guess what they might be.

Teaching Idea

If children enjoy the silliness of "Jabberwocky," introduce them to additional nonsense poems by Lewis Carroll ("Father William," "The Walrus and the Carpenter," "The Crocodile," "Humpty Dumpty's Recitation"), Ogden Nash ("The Panther," "The Llama"), Edward Lear ("The Rhinoceros," "The Pobble Who Has No Toes," "The Table and the Chair," "The Owl and the Pussycat," limericks), or Hillaire Belloc ("The Yak," "The Frog," "Cautionary Tales"). Many of these can be found online. (See *More Resources.*)

Teaching Idea

Read a version of the Greek myth of Narcissus to the class. Explain that the title character in "Narcissa" is an allusion to this myth. Ask students why Brooks might have chosen this name. (Narcissa spends a lot of time thinking about herself.) Have students note what Narcissa compares herself to. Then invite them to write a similar stanza about themselves: First he is [blank]. . . . Soon he is a [blank]. And, next, a [blank].

an ancient queen, a singing wind, and a nightingale), repetition (still), imagery (purple veil appeals to the sense of sight, and singing wind appeals to the sense of hearing), character (Narcissa), setting (Narcissa's backyard)

O Captain! My Captain!

Author Information: This poem is also by Walt Whitman. See author information on p. 50.

Summary of Content: This elegy mourns the death of President Abraham Lincoln in 1865.

Background: This poem was written after President Abraham Lincoln was assassinated by John Wilkes Booth on April 14, 1865, just five days after the end of the Civil War. Booth, who sympathized with the Confederate cause, shot Lincoln while the president and his wife were attending a play at Ford's Theater in Washington, D.C.

Vocabulary: weather'd: survived; **rack:** a mass of high, wind-driven clouds or a storm; **exulting:** feeling joyful; **keel:** the bottom of a ship, often weighted for balance; **vessel:** ship; **trills:** makes a fluttering sound; **swaying mass:** a crowd of people gently moving back and forth; **victor:** the winner in a struggle or contest; **object:** goal or purpose; **mournful:** sad; **tread:** step

Literary Elements and Devices: rhyme (done, won), internal rhyme (The port is near, the bells I hear, the people all exulting), repetition (fallen cold and dead, rise up), alliteration (safe, sound), imagery (bugle trills appeals to the sense of hearing), consonance (While, follow, keel, vessel), assonance (lips, still), rhythm (WHERE on the DECK my CAPtain LIES), extended metaphor (Abraham Lincoln is compared to the captain of a ship; he leads America through difficult times just as a captain pilots a ship through stormy seas), symbol (the storm-tossed ship coming safely into port symbolizes the United States coming through the Civil War intact), onomatopoeia (trills) (12)

A Poison Tree

Author Information: William Blake (1757–1827) was born in London, England. He attended drawing school when he was 10 and began writing poetry at age 12. Blake earned a living as an engraver and illustrator, and he often illustrated his own poems. Blake's works of poetry include *Songs of Innocence* (1789) and *Songs of Experience* (1794).

Summary of Content: This lyric poem describes what happens to the speaker's anger when it is either expressed or suppressed. As the speaker's suppressed anger grows, it poisons both the speaker and the object of his or her anger.

Vocabulary: wrath: anger; **foe:** enemy; **sunned:** warmed; **deceitful:** dishonest; **wiles:** sneaky ways of doing things; **bore:** yielded, produced; **veiled the pole:** shadowed one side of the earth; **outstretched:** stretched out

Literary Elements and Devices: rhyme scheme (AABB CCDD and so on), quatrains, alliteration (sunned, smiles), repetition (wrath, foe), rhythm (IN the MORNing GLAD I SEE), consonance (soft, deceitful), imagery (watered it in fears appeals to the sense of touch, and apple bright appeals to the sense of sight), extended metaphor (the speaker's festering anger is compared to a growing, living tree that eventually poisons all whom it touches) (13)

II. Poetry

Teaching Idea

Invite students to recall a choice they had to make. For example, they might remember making a choice between going to summer camp and going on a family vacation, bringing lunch and eating in the cafeteria, and so on. Have they ever made a decision and later wished they had chosen differently? Introduce "The Road Not Taken" as a description of choosing and then later wishing you had chosen differently. Help them understand that the poem is about a specific choice between two roads, but also about choosing in general.

Teaching Idea

Follow up your reading of "The Road Not Taken" with additional poems by Robert Frost (see *More Resources*).

Teaching Idea

Have students share their impressions or firsthand experiences of a snowstorm. Show pictures of a landscape before and after a snowstorm to help them visualize how it changes. Discuss in particular the sorts of shapes made on buildings and other structures by snowdrifts. You may want to teach "The Snowstorm" during the winter or shortly after a snowstorm, or you may wish to teach it near the end of the year. The slightly archaic language makes this one of the harder poems for this grade. For the same reason, students may benefit from a line-by-line discussion of the poem. Be sure to help students understand the metaphor of the storm as an architect and the final comparison of real architects with the snow-architect.

The Road Not Taken

Author Information: Robert Frost (1874–1963) was an American poet who lived on a farm in New Hampshire. He often wrote about the sights and sounds of rural life in New England. Frost won four Pulitzer Prizes for his poetry and was asked to read a poem at the inauguration of President John F. Kennedy in 1961.

Summary of Content: In this lyric poem, the speaker stands by a fork in the road and contemplates which path to take. The speaker's dilemma symbolizes the many choices one makes in life.

Vocabulary: diverged: branched out, went in different directions; **trodden:** walked on; **hence:** from now

Literary Elements and Devices: rhyme scheme (ABAAB CDCCD and so on), repetition (Two roads diverged), rhythm (In LEAVES no STEP had TRODden BLACK), consonance (yellow, wood), alliteration (first, for), symbol (the roads symbolize the different paths people take in life), imagery (yellow wood appeals to the sense of sight, and grassy appeals to the sense of touch) (14)

The Snowstorm

Author Information: Ralph Waldo Emerson (1803–1882) was born in Boston, Massachusetts. A lecturer, philosopher, and writer, Emerson settled in Concord in 1834 with his second wife and later formed the influential Transcendental Club. Among his writings are *Nature* (1836), *Essays* (1841 and 1844; two volumes), and *The Conduct of Life* (1860). Students who were in Core Knowledge schools in Grade 4 should know his "Concord Hymn."

Summary of Content: This lyric poem portrays what happens to the landscape during a powerful New England snowstorm.

Vocabulary: o'er: over; **alight:** come down and settle; **whited:** made white; **courier:** messenger; **radiant:** giving off heat and light; **tumultuous:** noisy, disorderly; **masonry:** stonework; **quarry:** an open pit from which stone is obtained by cutting, digging, or blasting; **evermore:** forever; **furnished:** supplied; **artificer:** skilled worker; **bastions:** projecting parts of a fortification; **projected:** pushed outward; **windward:** moved in the direction where the wind blows; **stake:** fence pole; **myriad:** many; **savage:** wild, fierce; **naught:** nothing; **proportion:** balance or agreeable relation of parts within a whole; **coop:** shelter for chickens; **kennel:** shelter for dogs; **Parian wreaths:** wreaths that look like they are made of white marble, quarried on the Greek island of Paros; **invests:** covers completely; **maugre [MAW-gur]:** in spite of; **tapering:** narrowed at one end; **turret:** a little tower; **overtops:** rises over; **retiring:** quitting work; **astonished:** very surprised; **mimic:** copy closely; **frolic:** playful

Literary Elements and Devices: rhyme (evermore, door), repetition (farmers, snow), alliteration (tapering, turret), assonance (arrives, driving), consonance (tapering, turrets, overtops, work), rhythm (Hides HILLS and WOODS, the RIVer, and the HEAVen), imagery (radiant fireplace appeals to the sense of touch, and whited air appeals to the sense of sight), personification (the storm is a mason, a carpenter, and an architect), metaphor (the storm's creations are compared to a whole new world created by an architect), enjambment, or the continuation of a syntactic unit from one line to another (Mockingly, / On coop or kennel he hangs Parian wreaths) (15)

Some Opposites

Author Information: Richard Wilbur was born in 1921 in New York City. He won the Pulitzer Prize for *Things of This World* (1956) and *New and Collected Poems* (1988). The recipient of numerous awards and honors, Wilbur has also served as poet laureate of the United States. This poem is an excerpt from a longer work, titled *Opposites*.

Summary of Content: This humorous lyric poem poses a series of questions and answers about opposites.

Vocabulary: riot: a disturbance created by a large number of people; **meditate:** think

Literary Elements and Devices: rhyme (riot, quiet; two, you), repetition (lonely, opposite), alliteration (<u>m</u>inute, <u>m</u>editate), assonance (h<u>u</u>ge, bl<u>u</u>eness), consonance (Wha<u>t</u>, opposi<u>t</u>e, rio<u>t</u>), rhythm (It's LOTS of PEOple KEEPing QUIET), imagery (white reflection on the sea), couplets **16**

The Tyger

Author Information: This poem is also by William Blake. See author information on p. 53.

Summary of Content: The speaker of this lyric poem ponders why a benevolent God would have created such a fearful, violent creature as the tiger.

Vocabulary: tyger: tiger; **immortal:** never dying, godly; **frame:** put together, construct; **symmetry:** balance or agreeable relation of parts within a whole; **deeps:** oceans; **thine:** archaic way of saying "your"; **aspire:** aim for; **seize:** grab; **sinews:** tendons, or taut, strong cords of connective tissue; **thy:** archaic way of saying "your"; **dread:** causing terror or fear; **furnace:** a place where fuel is burned to create heat; **anvil:** a smooth, flat block of steel or iron on which metals are shaped by hammering; **grasp:** a firm hold or grip; **clasp:** hold tightly

Literary Elements and Devices: rhyme (AABB BBDD EEFF and so on), repetition (dare; Tyger! Tyger! burning bright), alliteration (<u>b</u>urning, <u>b</u>right), assonance (f<u>i</u>re, th<u>i</u>ne), consonance (t<u>w</u>ist, sine<u>w</u>s), rhythm (WHEN the STARS threw DOWN their SPEARS), imagery (fire of thine eyes appeals to the sense of sight, and watered heaven with their tears appeals to the sense of touch), symbol (the tiger symbolizes violence and horror), metaphor (God is compared to a blacksmith, and his creative processes are compared to those of a skilled artisan), personification (the stars throw down their spears and cry), quatrains **17**

A Wise Old Owl

Author Information: Edward Hersey Richards (1874–1957) was born in Tamworth, New Hampshire.

Summary of Content: This epigrammatic poem praises the virtue of silence and invites readers to not always be speaking and to sharpen their listening skills and powers of observation.

Literary Elements and Devices: rhyme scheme (AABB), repetition (more, less), alliteration (<u>w</u>hy, <u>w</u>e, <u>w</u>ise), assonance (<u>o</u>ld, <u>o</u>wl, <u>o</u>n, <u>o</u>ak), consonance (o<u>l</u>d, ow<u>l</u>), rhythm (The MORE he SAW the LESS he SPOKE), personification (the owl speaks) **18**

Teaching Idea
The "opposites" printed in the Text Resources are selections. Students may enjoy hearing more selections from the book *Opposites*, by Richard Wilbur. Look for the book at your local library, or order from an online used bookstore.

Teaching Idea
Encourage students to write their own poems posing questions and answers about opposites of commonplace objects: What is the opposite of _____? It is _____.

Teaching Idea
Show the class a picture of a tiger to help them visualize the imagery in "The Tyger." Also, read Blake's "The Lamb" to the class, and have students compare the two poems.

Teaching Idea
Use the example of the owl in "A Wise Old Owl" to call for silence and attention when students are chattering.

Use Instructional Master 8.

The Big Idea in Review

Listening to poetry or reading poems independently helps students develop an appreciation of the music in the words and enriches vocabulary.

Review

Below are some ideas for ongoing assessment and review activities. These are not meant to constitute a comprehensive list.

• As a reinforcing activity for this section, have students write either their own lyric poems about an animal or narrative poems about a sports event. Have them reread "A Wise Old Owl," "The Eagle," "The Tyger," and "A Bird Came Down the Walk" if they write about animals, or "Casey at the Bat" if they write about a sports event. Then invite students to share their poems.

• Review poetry terms by having students play a matching game. Write each poetry term on an index card and create a second deck of cards with examples of onomatopoeia, alliteration, imagery, metaphor, simile, symbol, personification, and other terms taken from poems. Ask students to match the term cards with the example cards.

• Many school media centers have collections of poetry books. Have a poetry scavenger hunt and take the class to the media center to see if they can find any new poems they like. Practice using skills needed to look up poems by favorite authors, and then share findings. Have a poetry day where students can bring in poetry books either from the library or from home. Have students select a poem to read to the class and then explain why they chose it.

• Use poems in this section to practice grammar skills. Select a poem to write on chart paper. Write it out sentence by sentence; then ask students to identify the parts of speech for various words. You may want to label each part of speech a different color. After they identify words, have them suggest another word of the same part of speech that would work in that line and write the word above the one in the poem. Discuss how vocabulary selection can influence the sounds and meaning of a poem.

• Make poetry collages. After reading a poem, provide students with magazines and large pieces of construction paper. Have them make collages and then write about how their collage illustrates their interpretation of the poem. Post these and have students explain their collages to the class.

• Give students many opportunities to write poems while reading the work of various poets. Students may use a poem from this section as a model for writing an original poem. For instance, they might try to write more "opposites." Or they might write a poem about an animal. Write the poems from this section on chart paper and hang them around the room for easy reference.

• Compose group poems based on a poem from this section or from Core Knowledge content for Grade 5. Group students together and have them agree on a topic for a poem. Then pass out sentence strips and have each student write one line for the poem. The group can then manipulate the sentence strips to move lines and check the punctuation of the poem. Groups can type final drafts on the computer, adding color and illustrations. Another variation of this activity that works particularly well is to have the class create a poem using couplets. Have each student write two lines that rhyme, and then the entire class has to assemble the couplets and make sure that the poem flows and makes sense.

More Resources

The titles listed below are offered as a representative sample of materials and not a complete list of everything that is available.

For students —

• *Listen My Children: Poems for Fifth Graders* (Core Knowledge Foundation, 2001). Includes all the poems listed in the *Sequence* for Grade 5.

• *Casey at the Bat: A Ballad of the Republic Sung in the Year 1888*, by Ernest L. Thayer and illustrated by Christopher Bing (Handprint Books, 2000). A Caldecott Honor book. Hardcover, 32 pages, ISBN 1929766009.

• *Corn Chowder*, by James Stevenson (Greenwillow, 2003). Hardcover, 48 pages, ISBN 0060530596.

• *Favorite Poems Old and New*, selected by Helen Ferris (Doubleday Books for Young Readers, 1957). A treasury of more than 700 poems, including many old favorites. A wonderful resource. Hardcover, 598 pages, ISBN 0385076967.

For teachers —

• *A Book of Americans*, by Rosemary and Stephen Vincent Benét (Henry Holt & Company, 1987). Paperback, 114 pages, ISBN 0805002979.

• *A Child's Treasury of Animal Verse*, by Mark Daniel (Dial, 1989). Includes poems by Lewis Carroll; Hillaire Belloc; Edward Lear; Robert Louis Stevenson; Alfred, Lord Tennyson; and others. Hardcover, 16 pages, ISBN 0803706065.

• *I Am the Darker Brother: An Anthology of Modern Poems by African Americans*, edited by Arnold Adoff (Simon Pulse, 1997). Paperback, 192 pages, ISBN 0689808690.

• *The Mouse of Amherst*, by Elizabeth Spires (Farrar, Straus and Giroux, 2001). "The title of this fanciful sliver of a novel is a delectable double entendre, expressing the characters of both Emily Dickinson and Emmaline, a poetry-penning mouse who lodges in the wainscoting of the poet's bedroom" (*Publishers Weekly*). Paperback, 64 pages, ISBN 0374454116.

• Poetry Alive, www.poetryalive.com/products.html. Poetry Alive sells recording and teacher materials to help you bring poetry to life in the classroom.

• *Robert Frost (Poetry for Young People)*, edited by Gary D. Schmidt and illustrated by Henri Sorensen (Sterling Publishing Company, 1994). Hardcover, 48 pages, ISBN 0806906332.

• *Rose, Where Did You Get That Red? Teaching Great Poetry to Children*, by Kenneth Koch (Vintage Books, 1990). Kenneth Koch has inspired even students who "hate" poetry. Here is a teaching method that may inspire you as well. Paperback, 416 pages, ISBN 0679724710.

• *Songs of Innocence and of Experience (Oxford Paperbacks)*, by William Blake (Oxford University Press, 1977). Paperback, 156 pages, ISBN 0192810898.

• *Stopping by Woods on a Snowy Evening*, by Robert Frost and illustrated by Susan Jeffers (Dutton, 2001). Hardcover, 32 pages, ISBN 0525467343.

• American Poems has a brief online biography and the text of 180 poems by Robert Frost, beginning at www.americanpoems.com/poets/robertfrost. See this site also for poems by Walt Whitman and Ogden Nash.

• Poetry Connection, www.poetryconnection.net, has brief biographies and the poetry of Hillaire Belloc and Lewis Carroll.

• The Poetry Lover's Page, www.poetryloverspage.com, contains many links to classic poetry.

• Poetry Teachers.com, www.poetryteachers.com, has suggestions for poetry theater, how to teach poetry, and poetry activities.

The Big Idea

Reading fiction helps students acquire greater reading and language comprehension skills and helps build their vocabulary.

What Students Should Already Know

Students should be familiar with classic stories, legends, and folktales from their language arts instruction in prior grades. They may be acquainted with classic novels from previous classroom experiences or through independent reading. Students should also recognize literary terms introduced in previous grades, such as *author, autobiography, biography, fiction, nonfiction, illustrator, character, hero, heroine, drama, myth, tall tale, limerick, novel, plot,* and *setting.*

What Students Need to Learn

- The plots, major characters, outcomes, and lessons of the stories, myths, and legends for this grade
- Fiction is a narrative that comes from a writer's imagination.
- Stories that are made up are a kind of fiction.
- Stories have characters, a plot, a setting, and dialogue.
- Some stories
  - describe magical people and events that could never happen.
  - describe realistic people and events that could happen.
- A novel
  - is a longer work of fiction.
  - is often divided into sections called chapters.
  - has a more complicated plot than a short story.
  - may focus on one or two main characters.
  - may involve many different characters.
- Nonfiction is a narrative that tells about real people and events.
- Some stories are folktales.
  - Folktales include myths, legends, and trickster tales.
- Literary Terms:
  - Pen name (pseudonym)
  - Literal and figurative language: imagery; metaphor and simile; symbol; personification

What Students Will Learn in Future Grades

In future grades, students will continue to learn about different kinds of stories and to read classic, age-appropriate novels.

Vocabulary

Student/Teacher Vocabulary

autobiography: a person's life story as told by the person himself or herself (S)

characterization: the way an author develops a character through dialogue, narration, or description (T)

characters: the people or animals that take part in the action of a story (T)

conflict: an internal or external struggle that a character faces (T)

dialogue: the words spoken by characters in a story (T)

fantasy: a story that features characters with magical powers and/or impossible events (T)

folktale: an anonymous, traditional story; kinds of folktales include legends, myths, trickster tales, fairy tales, and tall tales (S)

imagery: words or phrases that appeal to the senses of sight, hearing, touch, taste, and smell and help create mental images (S)

legend: a traditional story about the past that may or may not be based on an actual event (S)

metaphor: a figure of speech in which a word or a phrase used to describe one thing is used to describe a different thing; a resemblance is implied (S)

myth: a traditional story, often involving nonhuman beings, that is usually part of a religion and that attempts to describe the origin of their customs or beliefs or to explain mysterious events (S)

narration: the telling of a sequence of events (T)

novel: a longer work of fiction that is often divided into chapters and has a more complicated plot than a short story (T)

pen name: an invented name used by a writer; also known as a pseudonym or *nom de plume* (S)

personification: a figure of speech in which an animal, object, or idea is given human characteristics (S)

plot: the chain of related events in a story (S)

setting: the time and place of the action in a story (S)

simile: a figure of speech that directly compares two or more unlike things by using the words *like* or *as* (S)

symbol: a person, place, object, or action that stands for something else beyond itself (S)

theme: the main idea or message of a story (T)

trickster tale: a story about a character, often a small, skittish animal such as a spider or a rabbit, who outsmarts larger, stronger characters (S)

Domain Vocabulary

Stories and associated words:
narrator, narrative, prose, classic, short story, story, chapter, section, episode, title, satire, satirical, draw conclusions, make generalizations, analyze, predict, prediction, clues, context clues, realistic, magical, tale, genre, mystery, fiction, nonfiction, historical fiction, realistic fiction, biography, memoir, novella, slave narrative, mood, major, minor, flat, static, antagonist, protagonist, foil, time, place, point of view, first-person, third-person, omniscient, limited, internal, external, climax, resolution, description, descriptive, plot twist, surprise ending, author, writer, novelist, dialect, anecdote, exposition, flashback, foreshadowing, irony, ironic, suspense, motivation, *plus words found in the stories themselves, including the "Vocabulary" listed within selections in the main text*

Materials

Instructional Master 9
Story Map, p. 64

story station with a CD or audiocassette player, p. 62

audio recordings of stories, p. 62

student dictionaries, p. 64

***Core Classics* abridged novels, pp. 64, 65, 67, 68, 70**

world map and U.S. map, pp. 64, 70

videocassette or DVD player, p. 64

videotape or DVD of *Little Women*, p. 64

videotape or DVD of *The Secret Garden*, p. 64

videotape or DVD of *Don Quixote*, p. 64

audio recording of *Man of La Mancha*, p. 64

videotape or DVD of *The Adventures of Sherlock Holmes: The Red-Headed League*, p. 70

props for students to use as imaginary newscasters, p. 72

index cards, p. 72

poster board, p. 72

Vocabulary continued

Myths and legends and associated words:
fable, fairy tale, mythology, legendary, hero, parable, oral tradition, folklore, allegory, pourquoi tale, trickster, Anansi, Br'er Rabbit, Coyote, Iktomi

Cross-curricular Connections

History and Geography

World: The Renaissance and the Reformation
• *The Adventures of Don Quixote*

World: Feudal Japan
• "The Samurai's Daughter: A Tale of the Oki Islands"

American: The Civil War
• *Little Women*
• *Narrative of the Life of Frederick Douglass*

American: Native Americans: Culture and Conflicts
• Native American trickster stories

At a Glance
The most important ideas for you are:

▸ Reading or listening to stories helps students understand the elements of stories, while also increasing vocabulary, cultural literacy, and reading comprehension abilities.

▸ Fiction can include novels, stories, folktales, fairy tales, legends, and myths.

▸ Fiction includes characters, dialogue, narration, plot, and setting.

▸ Characters in novels are developed through different characterization techniques.

▸ Characters in novels and other types of fiction often face an internal or external conflict.

▸ Novels and other types of fiction have a theme, or a main message or idea.

▸ Some authors use a pseudonym or pen name. For instance, Samuel Langhorne Clemens wrote under the name Mark Twain.

▸ An autobiography is a work of nonfiction.

▸ Figurative language is language that uses figures of speech such as metaphors, similes, symbols, and personification. Understanding some common figures of speech can help students enjoy and comprehend what they read and hear.

What Teachers Need to Know
A. Stories
C. Myths and Legends
D. Literary Terms

Background: Why Study Classic Novels and Other Stories?

In Grade 5, students are encouraged to become familiar with classic novels such as The Adventures of Tom Sawyer, Don Quixote, Little Women, *and* The Secret Garden. *These works can be read in their original, unabridged form or in adapted versions. If time is tight, excerpts can be substituted for the longer works. The works can be read by students independently, read aloud by teachers, or shared using some combination of these two approaches.*

Studying longer works of fiction helps engage students in the process of reading for pleasure and exposes them to more complex, sophisticated works of literature. Students at this level should be able to read, comprehend, and discuss classic novels; however, they may need assistance with difficult vocabulary, complicated plots, or novels with many different characters. In some cases, teachers may wish to use shorter versions of stories, such as the abridged versions provided in the Text Resources, or the longer abridgments in the Foundation's Core Classics series. The abridged versions and excerpts in the Text Resources are generally quite short and are also useful if there isn't time to teach the entire book or a longer adaptation. They provide a sort of bare minimum, which you are encouraged to move beyond as time permits.

By reading classic novels and other stories in this section, students will develop an awareness of language that will later help them become better writers as well as better readers. In addition, these stories will help students develop an appreciation for fiction from different cultures and time periods. The selections come from Asia, Europe, and North America, yet many of them reflect universal themes and experiences.

Students in Grade 5 are also expected to study myths and legends. The myths and legends in the Sequence have been chosen to connect with history topics. The Native American legends and myths connect with the history section on Native Americans, while the samurai story connects with the section on feudal Japan. These suggestions provide a core collection of readings; you are encouraged to share additional myths and legends with students as well.

Although many of the selections listed for this grade are fictional, students should also have frequent opportunities to read nonfiction, including books about science, history, music, and art. As part of the language arts curriculum, students will study the Narrative of the Life of Frederick Douglass. *Reading Douglass's autobiography not only broadens students' exposure to nonfiction, but also brings American history to life and helps them better understand the issues that divided the nation at the time of the Civil War.*

Teaching Idea

Set aside a time for students to engage in independent silent reading. It is important that the teacher also participate in silent reading as a model during this time, instead of using the time for curriculum planning or other important, but distracting, tasks. Also, encourage students to practice reading independently outside of school for at least 25 minutes daily.

Teaching the Longer Works

The *Sequence* guidelines for this grade include a number of book-length works of fiction. Some of the works are rather long, and others may be difficult for some students in Grade 5 to read in the original. As you plan this section, you will therefore need to think about how you wish to teach each book. Do you have time to teach the book in its original format? Will your students be able to handle the original? Or do you need to rely on an abridgment? How drastically abridged should your abridgment be? How can you strike a balance between abridging to fit the book into a busy schedule and still conveying the essence of the story? Here are some thoughts to bear in mind as you develop your plan.

As far as reading level is concerned, remember that students' listening ability generally outpaces their reading ability until roughly middle school, on average by about two grades. This means that a student who reads at a Grade 5 level may listen at a Grade 7 level. A student who has trouble reading *The Adventures of Tom Sawyer* by himself or herself may not have trouble listening to the story read aloud; you might read it aloud yourself or purchase an audio version for students to listen to.

As far as abridgments are concerned, there are many abridged versions available for some of the titles for this grade, including a series done especially for students in Grade 5 by the Core Knowledge Foundation—the *Core Classics*—and some very short versions and excerpts included in the Text Resources that accompany this book. Teaching an abridgment has its pros and cons. On the pro side, the abridgments are often much shorter than the original and can therefore be taught in less time. Also, most skillful abridgments will give students the basic cultural literacy they need. By reading even a few brief selections from *The Adventures of Tom Sawyer*, students will be able to get a sense of who Tom Sawyer was and when he lived. Even if they do not encounter the story in all its detail, students will be able to recognize and understand references to Tom Sawyer they come across in newspapers and speech. This is valuable in and of itself. On the other hand, because abridgments contain fewer words and often use simpler words than the original, your students will be exposed to fewer words and will have fewer opportunities to build vocabulary—a crucial ingredient in reading comprehension.

For each of the book-length works discussed below, we have provided a very brief abridgment or excerpt in the Text Resources. We think of this as the barebones minimum. These excerpts will give your students basic cultural literacy: they will learn that Don Quixote was a man who imagined he was a daring knight, and that Frederick Douglass was a former slave who became an abolitionist, and so on. Whenever possible, we encourage you to teach a longer version of the story. The *Core Classics* editions are often a good choice. These editions have been prepared by Core Knowledge editors. They are typically much more full than the abridgments provided here and yet shorter and easier to read than the originals. In a few cases, you may wish to be even more ambitious and read the original editions, or parts of them. In the sections below on the individual works, we list several options for each work from which you can choose.

Reading Stories Aloud

Some stories, such as "Adventures of Sherlock Holmes: The Red-Headed League," can be read aloud or offered to students for individual reading. Here are some ideas to consider when reading a story to your Grade 5 class.

- Speak slowly and clearly.
- Mimic actions described in the story.
- Use your voice to emphasize the use of dialogue and the voices of different characters.
- During longer selections, pause occasionally and ask students questions about the characters, plot, and what they think might happen next.
- In some cases you may wish to read a story more than once to make certain students understand it. You can read it aloud once and then ask students to do a second reading on their own, perhaps with a focusing question in mind.
- If there are vocabulary words that students need to know for the story to make sense, you may wish to pre-teach those words; other words can be discussed and explained after the first reading.

These stories need not be clustered together into a single unit; they can be read throughout the school year.

Focusing on Characters and Plot

After students have read or listened to each selection, thoroughly discuss the characters and plot. Ask the class the following types of W questions:

- What happens?
- Who is involved?
- Where do events take place?
- When do events take place?
- Why do certain events happen?

Help students paraphrase the events in the story in their own words.

Focusing on Literary Elements

As students read the stories and novels in this section, point out literary elements such as conflict, theme, or characterization. Before introducing students to the terms for such literary elements, ask questions that will lead students to appreciate these elements. To help them recognize conflict in the plot, for example, ask, "What problems does the main character face?" Ask, "What message do you think the author wants to convey?" to help students identify the theme.

When the class reads *The Adventures of Tom Sawyer* by Mark Twain, introduce the term *pen name*. Explain that Mark Twain is the pen name of Samuel Langhorne Clemens. His pen name was derived from a river pilot's term for safe navigating conditions. (When the river was deep enough for the boat to navigate safely, the crew would call out "mark twain.") As students read the novels and stories in this section, you may also want to introduce or review the terms *literal* and *figurative language*, as well as *imagery, metaphor, simile, symbol*, and *personification* (p. 46), to help students appreciate the use of these literary devices in fiction.

Teaching Idea

After reading a story, ask students to make a list of the main events that occurred in the story. Discuss the lists with the class and make a list of the events on the board. To further review the main aspects of the story and to reinforce the "oral tradition," arrange the class in a large circle. Have students retell the story in the same order each event occurred in the story. Continue circling until the entire story has been retold.

Teaching Idea

Have students make a book jacket for a favorite story or novel. Suggest that they choose a favorite story event or character and then illustrate it. Then have students write a brief summary to entice others to read their book and/or to summarize key information. Display students' work on a bulletin board in your classroom.

Teaching Classic Novels

The following suggestions and activities will help you teach adapted or abridged editions of *The Adventures of Tom Sawyer* by Mark Twain, *Don Quixote* by Miguel de Cervantes, *Little Women* by Louisa May Alcott, and *The Secret Garden* by Frances Hodgson Burnett.

• Make sure students understand that a novel is a longer piece of fiction that is often divided into units called chapters. Before students begin to read, divide each novel into manageable chunks, assigning a certain number of pages or chapters per class period. Allow plenty of class time in which to discuss each reading assignment. Encourage students to ask questions about what they do not understand, and have them answer specific questions about plot, setting, and characters.

• Assist students with difficult vocabulary. Provide them with a student dictionary so that they can look up the meanings of unfamiliar words.

• Have students use **Instructional Master 9,** *Story Map,* to keep track of key elements in the novel as they read. Students can also make a time line of important events.

• Provide students with maps or use classroom maps so that students can identify the diverse geographical settings of these novels: a fictional town near the Mississippi River (*The Adventures of Tom Sawyer*), Spain (*Don Quixote*), New England (*Little Women*), and England (*The Secret Garden*).

• Consider showing students film adaptations of classic novels—not as a replacement for reading but as a supplement. For example, you might show *Little Women,* starring Katharine Hepburn (Turner Home Entertainment, 1933) or Susan Sarandon (Columbia Tristar, 1994); *The Secret Garden* (MGM Warner, 1949; Hallmark, 1987; Warner Home Video, 1993); or *Don Quixote,* starring John Lithgow (Turner Home Entertainment, 2000).

• When your students read *Don Quixote*, play an audio recording of *Man of La Mancha*, the long-running Broadway musical based on the novel.

• Ask students to choose one novel for a short book report.

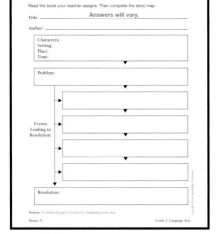

Use Instructional Master 9.

Teaching the Stories

The following information and suggested activities will help you teach each story in this section. Before you read a story aloud or have your students read it independently, be sure to provide any background information necessary to their understanding of the story, and ask them the Before Reading questions. After reading the story, be sure students understand the plot and characters by asking them the After Reading questions.

▶ The Adventures of Tom Sawyer

Author Information: Mark Twain (1835–1910) was born Samuel Langhorne Clemens. He grew up in Hannibal, Missouri, a small town on the Mississippi River. As an adult, Twain worked as a steamboat pilot and traveled quite a bit. He became famous for writing about life on and along the Mississippi River. Mark Twain took his pen name from a nautical term meaning "mark two," or a mark two fathoms deep—water deep enough for a typical boat to navigate.

Background: This story of a young boy named Tom Sawyer is set in St. Petersburg, Missouri, along the Mississippi River, in the 19th century. Full of mischief, Tom gets involved in many adventures, along with his friends Huck Finn and Becky Thatcher. He witnesses a murder, hunts for treasure, and gets lost in a cave for several days. Many of the events in the story actually happened, either to Mark Twain or to his friends, when they were growing up in Missouri in the 1840s.

Before Reading: What kinds of adventures have you and your friends had? Have you ever hunted for a hidden treasure? Did you ever get lost?

Vocabulary: brimming: overflowing; **issued:** came out; **delectable:** highly pleasing; **reposeful:** relaxing; **whitewash:** paintlike liquid used to make a surface white; **surveyed:** looked over, observed; **melancholy:** sadness; **captivity:** confinement, imprisonment; **continent:** large mass of land; **tripping:** skipping with light, quick steps; **expeditions:** journeys; **inspiration:** a moment or event that results in a person having new ideas or actions; **hove:** appeared; **ridicule:** scorn, mockery; **anticipations:** excitement about things that will happen in the future; **melodious:** having a pleasant sound; **whoop:** a happy shout; **intervals:** spaces of time between an event or action; **personating:** imitating ("impersonating"); **slackened:** slowed down; **starboard:** the right side of a ship, looking forward; **ponderously:** slowly and clumsily; **laborious:** long, hard work; **pomp and circumstance:** celebration with much ceremony and fuss; **executing:** carrying out or doing something fully to completion; **chap:** fellow; **wheeled:** changed direction suddenly; **warn't:** "was not"; **druther:** "would rather"; **contemplated:** thought over; **reckon:** suppose, think; **lemme:** "let me"; **reluctance:** not wanting, hesitancy; **alacrity:** quick in response, cheerfulness, readiness; **retired:** no longer active; **jeer:** make fun of or mock; **jew's harp:** a small musical instrument held by the mouth and plucked with a finger; **dilapidated:** decayed, ruined by neglect; **sash:** window frame; **bankrupted:** exhausted, worn out; **philosopher:** person who studies or looks for wisdom; **obliged:** under a duty to do something; **treadmill:** mill worked by a person walking on steps around a wide wheel, was used in prison punishment; **Mont Blanc:** "White Mountain"; **passenger-coaches:** horse-pulled carriages used to carry people; **resign:** quit, stop; **mused:** thought deeply; **substantial:** noticeable, real; **wended:** headed in travel; **rearward:** facing behind or toward the back of something; **balmy:** soothing, mild; **astonishment:** surprise, disbelief; **diluted:** weakened; **tan:** thrash, whip; **splendor:** magnificence, gloriousness; **virtuous:** honest, truthful; **Scriptural:** relating to sacred writing, especially to the Bible; **juvenile:** young person, childish; **pariah:** someone who is hated or rejected by a society; **drunkard:** someone who is frequently drunk or known to be a drunk; **cordially:** sincerely, deeply; **perennial:** constant; **lopped:** cut; **fringed:** frayed; **hogsheads:** a large barrel; **harassed:** bothered or annoyed; **hampered:** disrupted; **hoop-stick:** wooden stick used to control and roll a hoop in a children's game; **refuge:** shelter or protection; **titter:** quiet giggle; **abash:** shame; **hitched:** moved suddenly; **animosity:** hostility, resentment; **rap:** hit, slap; **scuffle:** small fight or struggle; **juncture:** point in time; **vise:** tool with two clamps used to squeeze an object; **borne:** carried, transported; **jubilant:** joyful

After Reading: Describe Tom's relationship with other boys his age. How does Tom trick his friends into whitewashing the fence? How does Tom Sawyer change throughout the story? What oath do Tom and Huck make?

Versions: Complete editions of *Tom Sawyer* fill 150–200 printed pages. Many abridgments and adaptations are also available, including audio versions and adaptations for young children. The selections in the Text Resources include a few of the better-known episodes from the book. **(19)**

The Adventures of Don Quixote

Author Information: Miguel de Cervantes Saavedra (1547–1616) was born in Spain. As a young man, he fought as a soldier in various wars in the Mediterranean. Kidnapped by pirates in 1575, Cervantes was sold as a slave to the Moors. He tried to escape from his enslavement in Algiers several times and was finally ransomed in 1580. Cervantes wrote *The Adventures of Don Quixote* as a satire of popular romantic novels and outdated notions of chivalry. When it was published in 1605, it quickly became very popular.

Background: In this story, a Spanish man named Alonso Quejana is so obsessed with the chivalric lifestyle he has read about in romantic books that he decides to become a knight-errant himself. He adopts the name Don Quixote and roams about Spain on an aging horse, looking for defenseless people to help and getting himself into comical and sometimes pathetic adventures. His assistant is a laborer named Sancho Panza, to whom Quixote has promised the governship of an island in exchange for his services.

Before Reading: How might someone who is chivalrous behave?

Vocabulary: La Mancha: barren, plateau region in south-central Spain; **exploits:** brave adventures or acts; **damsels:** young, unmarried women of high social rank; **chivalry:** customs and spirit of medieval knighthood; **engage:** take part, involve oneself; **wits:** mental ability; **wooings:** romantic attempts to get affection and attention; **fancy:** imagination; **knight-errant:** knight traveling in search of adventures in which he can show his skill and bravery; **visor:** the front, movable piece of a helmet that covers the face; **deficiency:** lack or shortage of something; **quest:** a journey made in search of something or someone; **hack:** a horse worn out from service; **sally:** to leap or rush forward; **clad:** clothed; **improvised:** made up as one goes along; **mounted:** seated or placed; **dubbed:** officially given a title or rank; **steed:** a spirited horse; particularly horses used in war; **valor:** bravery; **turrets:** towers attached to larger structures such as fortresses or castles; **moat:** deep and wide trench, usually filled with water, that surrounds a fortress or a castle; **reined:** stopped or slowed; **swineherd:** person who takes care of swine, or pigs; **humor:** to give in to or agree with; **ill-fitting:** clothing not covering or worn properly; **lass:** young girl; **squire:** male attendant to a knight, one who usually carries the shield or armor for the knight; **knave:** a dishonest or unreliable person; **lance:** a spear; **miser:** a mean person, especially one who is cheap with money; **thrash:** whip or beat; **country bumpkin:** a simple country person lacking in experience; **yonder:** something at a distance but within view; **spurred:** urged a horse to go faster, usually done by the rider kicking the horse's sides; **Briareus:** 100-armed god in Greek mythology; **prevail:** triumph; **miscreant:** criminal or trouble-maker; **brawls:** fights; **absurd:** ridiculous

After Reading: Do you think Don Quixote is really insane or just pretending? Where does Don Quixote get the idea to become a knight-errant? Who is Dulcinea del Toboso? How does Don Quixote go about being dubbed a knight? Who is Sancho Panza? What does Don Quixote think the windmills are?

Versions: Cervantes's novel is nearly 1,000 pages long in some editions. The *Sequence* suggests only selected episodes. Episodes taught should include the ones that are part of cultural literacy, such as the episode where Quixote jousts with the windmills, or the episode in which he frees the galley slaves. These and several other famous episodes are included in the *Core Classics* edition of the novel, which runs 240 pages of large print with illustrations, but which can also be read in part or in selections. A very short version, with just a couple of episodes, is included in the Text Resources. Other abridgments and adaptations are also available. [20]

Little Women

Author Information: Louisa May Alcott (1832–1888) was born in Germantown, Pennsylvania, and grew up near Boston. Although she wrote stories for adult readers as well, she is most well known for her *Little Women* series of books, which were some of the first children's stories to portray children realistically. Alcott based the characters and events in the *Little Women* books on her own experiences and those of her family members and friends. The stories were very popular when first published and continue to be read around the world.

Background: The story is set in a small New England town in the mid-1800s. The March women (sisters Jo, Meg, Beth, and Amy, and their mother) are facing hard times while their father is away fighting with the Union army in the Civil War. In addition to financial hardship and family illnesses, the sisters must deal with the personal challenges of growing up and becoming women.

Before Reading: *Little Women* takes place during the mid-1800s. In what ways do you think life differed for women back then as compared to today? Why do you think it's important to say you're sorry and to accept someone else's apology?

Vocabulary: bridled: showed hostility or resentment; **coaxingly:** soothingly, pleasantly; **fidgety:** unable to be still; **skirmishes:** arguments; **curbing:** controlling, restraining; **repentance:** regret, desire to be forgiven; **assumed:** took upon oneself; **air:** attitude; **tempest:** a violent storm; outrage; **fib:** lie; **cross:** angry or upset; **consumed:** destroyed; **calamity:** disaster; **meekly:** without pride; **abominable:** horrible; **confidential:** private, secret; **gossip:** chatty talk; **virtuous:** having or showing honesty or truthfulness; **crosspatch:** grouch; **good-natured:** pleasant; **spell:** period of time; **bear:** hold, carry; **possession:** ownership, control; **harboring:** sheltering, protecting; **striking out:** heading forward; **terror-stricken:** extremely afraid; **rail:** long piece of wood; **self-possessed:** calm; **bustle:** busy movement or activity; **sensible:** having common sense; **condemning:** declaring wrong or guilty; **temptations:** weaknesses, trials; **remorse:** regret; **humility:** modesty; **reproof:** scolding for an error; **resolution:** determination, resolve; **mend:** sew, fix

After Reading: Why did Amy burn Jo's journal? What was in the journal that was so important to Jo? What happened when Amy followed Jo and Laurie to the river? Why was Jo surprised to learn that her mother used to have a bad temper just like hers?

Versions: The *Sequence* specifies only the first part of the book, through Part I, Chapter XXIII: "Aunt March Settles the Question." This is about 250–300 pages in most editions. If students can't handle that much, they can start at the beginning and read as many chapters as they can. A *Core Classics* edition is available from the Core Knowledge Foundation. Alternatively, use the excerpt provided in the Text Resources. Some adaptations and abridgments are also available. (21)

Cross-curricular Teaching Idea

Introduce the *Narrative of the Life of Frederick Douglass* when your class studies the causes of the Civil War.

Frederick Douglass

Narrative of the Life of Frederick Douglass

Author Information: Born a slave in Maryland, Frederick Douglass (1817–1895) escaped to New Bedford, Massachusetts, when he was 21. An outspoken critic of slavery, he became a popular lecturer and published his autobiography in 1845. In 1847, Douglass officially gained his freedom and settled in Rochester, New York, where he established an antislavery newspaper, the *North Star*. After the Civil War, Douglass served as U.S. Minister to Haiti.

Background: This excerpt is from an autobiography, or the story of a person's life written by that person. In the 1800s, several former slaves who were able to read and write, including Douglass, Harriet Jacobs, and Mary Prince, wrote slave narratives to convince the public about the evils of slavery.

Before Reading: What do you know about slavery in the United States? What do you know about the antislavery movement in the 1800s?

Vocabulary: holdings: legally owned property; **boded ill:** was an omen of trouble; **leased:** granted use of under the terms of a contract; **overseer:** a person who watches over and directs the work of slaves; **deliverance:** rescue; **utterly:** completely; **astonished:** surprised; **forbidden:** not allowed; **unruly:** difficult to discipline or control; **discontented:** unhappy; **reputation:** something a person is known to be or do; **breaking:** weakening or destroying in spirit; **dregs:** the worst part; **unmanageable:** difficult to discipline or control; **tamed:** trained, broke down; **elasticity:** flexibility, ability to bounce back or recover; **languished:** weakened because of neglect or ill use; **intent:** having the mind and will fixed on a certain purpose; **resisted:** fought against, kept from giving in; **contemplated:** thought over; **decidedly:** definitely, certainly; **wretchedness:** terrible condition physically, mentally, and/or spiritually; **strive:** struggle or fight forcefully; **abolition:** the act of doing away with slavery; **brethren:** brothers, or other African Americans who are slaves

After Reading: What kinds of work did Frederick Douglass do? How did he learn to read and write? How was he treated by Mr. Covey? What was the turning point for Douglass? What happened to him after he managed to escape in 1838?

Versions: The selections in the Text Resources represent only a small part of the longer book. The original *Narrative* is not that long—only about 100 pages in most editions—and contains powerful and beautiful writing. However, it also contains some graphic descriptions of whipping and mistreatment of slaves. Douglass intended for these descriptions to shock his readers into more active opposition to slavery. However, some teachers may find them too gruesome for Grade 5. A *Core Classics* edition is available from the Core Knowledge Foundation. Another abridged version is *Escape from Slavery: The Boyhood of Frederick Douglass.* (See *More Resources*.) (56)

The Secret Garden

Author Information: Frances Hodgson Burnett (1849–1924) was born in Manchester, England. After her father died in 1865, the entire family moved to the United States. Burnett's career got under way when her first widely known story appeared in *Scribner's Magazine* in 1872.

Initially, Burnett wrote romance novels that were quite popular during her time, but her most successful work, a children's book called *Little Lord Fauntleroy*, wasn't published until 1886. Mothers were fascinated with it and dressed their sons to look like the book's main character, complete with velvet suits with lace collars. Today, Frances Hodgson Burnett is best known for her children's books, especially *The Secret Garden* (1911).

Background: Ten-year-old Mary Lennox must go to England to live with her uncle after her parents' deaths in India. Early in the story, Mary is depicted as a spoiled, self-centered girl. But story events and circumstances bring about positive changes in her personality and character. Eventually, Mary learns that she has a cousin, Colin, who is bedridden and estranged from his father. Thanks to Mary's friendship, along with the discovery of the secret garden, Colin, too, undergoes a transformation and becomes a healthy, optimistic boy who is reunited with his father.

Before Reading: Is there a special place or room in your house where you like to go to be alone? Who else knows about this special place?

Vocabulary: cholera: disease that affects the intestines; **contrary:** disagreeable, moody; **haughty:** proud, snobbish; **eccentric:** unusual; **moor:** open, bleak land that usually has grasses and sedges for vegetation; **tha':** "thou," you; **indignantly:** angrily, due to something unjust or mean; **thee:** you; **thyself:** yourself; **disdainfully:** filled with scorn; **dawning:** beginning; **sentiment:** feeling or thought; **shrubbery:** bushes; **alighted:** descended from the air or came down to rest; **clod:** pile; **cheeky:** bold in a disrespectful way; **aye:** yes; **fledgling:** young bird; **meddlesome:** nosy; interfering in other people's concerns; **wench:** a young woman; **mantle:** something that covers or envelops; **crocuses:** plants from the iris family that bloom in spring; **jonquils:** yellow or white flowers similar to daffodils; **oft:** often; **absorbed:** thoroughly interested, engrossed; **mignonette:** fragrant, whitish flower; **naught:** nothing; **defiantly:** challengingly; **creepers:** part of a plant that grows up against walls or other plants; **dialect:** a way of expressing oneself; sometimes marks different regions of a country; **missel thrush:** small song bird, usually plain in color with spots

After Reading: What is the setting of Misselthwaite Manor like? For how long has the door to the secret garden been locked? What is so special about the secret garden? Why do you think Mary acts the way she does in the beginning of the story? Who and/or what is responsible for the changes that take place in Mary?

Versions: Most modern editions are about 300 pages. There are many abridgments available. If you can't teach the whole novel or an abridged version, you can use the very short version included in the Text Resources. ㉒

Teaching Idea

Encourage students to read other Sherlock Holmes mysteries. Three additional mysteries are included in the *Core Classics* edition. You may also want to show *The Adventures of Sherlock Holmes: The Red-Headed League* (MPI Home Video, 1985).

Adventures of Sherlock Holmes: The Red-Headed League

Author Information: Sir Arthur Conan Doyle (1859–1930) was born in Edinburgh, Scotland. As a young man, he studied medicine but later turned to writing mystery stories. He published his first Sherlock Holmes story, "A Study in Scarlet," in 1887. After writing more than 50 stories about the fictional sleuth, Doyle wrote a story in which Holmes dies, but he was later forced to resurrect the popular detective due to public demand.

Background: This story is one of many by Doyle in which a fictional detective named Sherlock Holmes solves a mystery. Holmes uses his extraordinary powers of observation and deduction to unearth clues and find solutions to puzzling crimes that stump police. This story is set in London in about 1890 and is narrated by Holmes's friend, Dr. Watson.

Before Reading: Have you ever solved a mystery? What clues helped you figure out what happened?

Vocabulary: lodgings: a place to live; **cordially:** warmly; **bob:** nod, move up and down; **humdrum:** ordinary; **relish:** great enjoyment; **singular:** unique; **recommence:** begin again; **portly:** heavy; **greatcoat:** heavy overcoat; **endeavored:** tried; **deduce:** reach a conclusion by reasoning; **indicated:** shown; **bequest:** something passed on by means of a will; **vacancy:** a spot to be filled; **entitles:** gives a right or claim to; **nominal:** insignificantly small; **eligible:** qualified to be chosen; **fortunate:** lucky; **splendid:** excellent; **tint:** color; **disqualify:** declare unfit or unworthy; **plunged:** moved forcefully; **forfeit:** lose; **hoax:** trick; **tacked:** fastened or attached; **dissolved:** brought to an end; **staggered:** extremely surprised; **prank:** trick; **frankly:** truthfully; **bizarre:** strange, out of the ordinary; **thumped:** beat upon; **capable:** having ability, able; **merit:** worth; **emerged:** came out of; **wild goose chase:** a worthless effort; **forger:** one who creates false stories or things; **cunning:** clever; **massive:** huge; **accomplice:** partner in crime; **glint:** brief flash of light; **gash:** large, deep cut; **rending:** tearing; **gaping:** wide open, as in a yawn; **peeped:** looked; **hauled:** pulled; **blandly:** calmly; **motive:** need or desire; **vanishing:** disappearing; **burrowing:** digging a hole or tunnel

After Reading: What is the Red-Headed League? How does Mr. Jabez Wilson join it? What are his duties? When is the league dissolved? What clues does Holmes use to solve the mystery of the Red-Headed League? What crime do Sherlock Holmes and Dr. Watson help prevent?

Versions: The version presented in the Text Resources is abridged from the original. A somewhat longer abridgment can be found in the *Core Classics* edition. The original, unabridged story is not beyond the capabilities of students in Grade 5, particularly if it is read aloud. **23**

Myths and Legends

The Samurai's Daughter: A Tale of the Oki Islands

Background: This is a legend from Japan.

Before Reading: What do you know or remember about Japan and the samurai?

Cross-curricular Teaching Idea

Introduce "The Samurai's Daughter: A Tale of the Oki Islands" when you teach the class about feudal Japan, the time in which this story takes place. Have students use world maps to locate Japan and the Oki Islands.

Vocabulary: **samurai**: a noble soldier; **offended**: annoyed, upset; **banished**: forced to leave a place; **misfortune**: an unlucky or unfortunate event or series of events; **virtues**: morals or other celebrated traits; **persuade**: convince; **sculling**: propelling a boat using an oar at the stern; **frailer**: weaker; **shrine**: a sacred place; **imploring**: asking desperately, begging; **mumbling**: talking quietly and unclearly; **cursed**: afflicted with evil or bad luck; **sacrifice**: give up something; **laboring**: suffering

After Reading: What is the setting of the story? Why is Oribe sent into exile? Where does he go? Why does Tokoyo travel to the islands? What ceremony does Tokoyo witness? Why does she offer to take the young girl's place? How does Tokoyo kill Yofun -Nushi? What happens to Tokoyo and her father at the end of the story? **26**

▶ The Sun Dance

Background: This is a Native American legend told by the Blackfoot Indians. It is also known as "The Legend of Scar Face." It describes the origin of the Sun Dance, a ceremonial dance that was (and still is) performed as a prayer to the gods.

Before Reading: What Native American legends are you familiar with? (Students should remember legends and stories from earlier grades. Focus on pourquoi tales and other myths that explain the origin of certain events or natural phenomena.)

Vocabulary: **airless**: stuffy; **dyeing**: coloring; **juniper bush**: an evergreen bush; **crowned**: covered the head; **gloss**: shine; **weary**: tired; **bid**: directed; **bundle**: wrap; **edible**: safe to eat; **cooed**: made a murmuring sound like a dove or pigeon; **unearth**: dig up; **consented**: agreed; **peered**: looked with curiosity; **yawning**: gaping; **yearned**: longed for; **traverse**: cross; **her spirit had left for the sandhills**: Feather Woman died; **fast**: stop eating food; **fragile**: delicate; **frantically**: desperately; **felled**: killed; **celebratory**: joyous, festive; **cleanse**: free from dirt; **emerged**: came out of; **bid**: said

After Reading: What happens to Feather Woman after she agrees to marry Morning Star? What is Star Country like? What happens when Feather Woman encounters the cranes? Why is Feather Woman forced to leave Star Country? Whom does Scar Face want to marry? How is Scar Face reunited with his father? What ceremony does this story explain? **27**

Cross-curricular Teaching Idea

Have students read "The Sun Dance" and Native American trickster tales about Coyote, Raven, or Spider when you teach the class about Native American cultures. (See *More Resources*.) There are also three additional Text Resources for this section, including "Coyote Goes to the Land of the Dead," "Raven Returns the Water," and "Turquoise Boy," that you may wish to teach in conjunction with the myths and legends discussed here. **28** **29** **30**

Review

Below are some ideas for ongoing assessment and review activities. These are not meant to constitute a comprehensive list. Keep in mind that the most logical time to review a story is after it has been read. If these stories are to be spread out throughout the year—as we suggest above—then this section is not like certain other units that go a few weeks and end with a unit review. The ideas below should be reviewed with this consideration in mind.

The Big Idea in Review

Reading fiction helps students acquire greater reading and language comprehension skills and helps build their vocabulary.

• As a reinforcing activity throughout the year, give students an opportunity to write their own stories. Remind them to include two or more characters, a setting, dialogue, and a sequence of events. You might want to provide story starters to inspire them, or let them choose from a variety of characters and settings, such as "surly man," "curious young girl," "New York City, 2002," "England, 17th century," and so forth. Then have them share their stories with the class.

• Instruct students to write up a news report about what happened in one of the stories. Model for them the format that would be appropriate for a news story on television. After writing the report, have students act as newscasters and perform the news story for the class.

• Invite students to write a story based on what would happen if one of the characters in the stories they have read met another character, e.g., what would happen if Mary from *The Secret Garden* met Tom Sawyer? Or invite them to write a story about how one of the characters they have read about would behave in the modern world. How would Don Quixote or Tom Sawyer behave in today's world? What about Sherlock Holmes?

• After reading each of these stories, have students write down questions about each story on index cards. Questions may focus on setting, characters, and plot. Have students form two teams and alternate asking each team the questions. Teams win a point for correctly answering the question and another point for identifying the story. The team with the most points wins.

• Have students write about which story or myth character they would like to meet. Then, have students describe why they want to meet that character and how they could spend their time together. Share these papers aloud.

• Have students create a display on poster board for a story they enjoyed reading. The display should include a summary and a description of what the students liked best about the story. Then, invite another Grade 5 class to view the story displays set up as a museum.

More Resources

The titles listed below are offered as a representative sample of materials and not a complete list of everything that is available.

For students —

• *Don Quixote* (*Core Classics* abridged), by Miguel de Cervantes. (Core Knowledge Foundation, 1997).

• *Little Women* (*Core Classics* abridged), by Louisa May Alcott. (Core Knowledge Foundation, 2006).

• *Narrative of the Life of Frederick Douglass* (*Core Classics* abridged), by Frederick Douglass. (Core Knowledge Foundation, 2006).

• *Selected Adventures of Sherlock Holmes* (*Core Classics* abridged), by Sir Arthur Conan Doyle. (Core Knowledge Foundation, 1997).

• *Cricket*, a magazine of fiction for Grades 4 and up, published by Cobblestone Publishing, www.cobble stonepub.com or 1-800-821-0115.

• *Escape from Slavery: The Boyhood of Frederick Douglass in His Own Words*, by Michael McCurdy (Knopf, 1994). Readable for some students, but the events are, not surprisingly, sometimes rough. Paperback, 80 pages, ISBN 0679846514.

• *Len Cabral's Storytelling Book*, by Len Cabral and Mia Manduca (Neal-Schuman Publishers, 1997), includes a Coyote story as well as other grade-appropriate stories. Paperback, 234 pages, ISBN 1555702538.

More Resources continued

• *Mystery! Mystery! for Children*, an audio recording by Jim Weiss (Greathall Productions, www.greathall.com or 1-800-477-6234) includes "The Red-Headed League." *Sherlock Holmes for Children* includes additional mysteries; *Tales from Cultures Far and Near* includes trickster tales.

• *Raven: A Trickster Tale from the Pacific Northwest*, by Gerald McDermott (Harcourt, 1993). One of several Native American tales retold by this author. A Caldecott Honor book. Library binding, 32 pages, ISBN 0152656618.

• *The Samurai's Daughter: A Japanese Legend*, by Robert D. San Souci (Dial Books for Young Readers, 1992). Hardcover, ISBN 0803711352.

For teachers —

• *The Adventures of Sherlock Holmes: The Red-Headed League* (MPI Home Video, 1985).

• *Don Quixote*, starring John Lithgow (Turner Home Entertainment, 2000).

• *Little Women*, starring Katharine Hepburn (Turner Home Entertainment, 1933) or Susan Sarandon (Columbia Tristar, 1994).

• *The Secret Garden* (MGM Warner, 1949; Hallmark, 1987; Warner Home Video, 1993).

III. Fiction and Drama

B. Drama

The Big Idea

Reading Shakespearean drama helps students acquire reading and language comprehension skills and gain an appreciation for different kinds of literature.

What Students Should Already Know

Students may be acquainted with drama in general from previous classroom experiences or through their independent reading.

Grade 1

▸ In drama,

• performers who play different characters are actors and actresses.

• actors and actresses perform on a stage.

• a theater is the building where a play is performed in front of an audience.

• costumes, scenery, and props bring a play to life.

What Students Need to Learn

▸ **A drama is a work of literature that is intended to be performed by actors.**

▸ **A play is usually divided into acts and scenes.**

▸ **An act is a major unit of action in a play.**

▸ **A scene is a smaller part of an act that takes place in one time and place.**

▸ **A drama may be**

• **a tragedy, or a serious story about a heroic character who meets with disaster because of a personal fault or events that cannot be helped.**

• **a comedy, or a humorous story in which everything works out well for the main characters.**

▸ ***A Midsummer Night's Dream* is a comedy by William Shakespeare (1564–1616), a Renaissance English playwright.**

What Students Will Learn in Future Grades

In future grades, students will continue to read and learn about different kinds of drama.

Grade 6

▸ *Julius Caesar* (William Shakespeare)

Vocabulary

Student/Teacher Vocabulary

act: the major unit of action in a play; many traditional plays have five acts (S)

actors: the performers who portray characters in a play (S)

characters: the people or animals that take part in the action of a play (S)

comedy: a humorous story in which everything works out well for the main characters in the end; a comedy often ends with one or more marriages (S)

conflict: an internal or external struggle that a character faces (T)

costumes: the clothes worn on stage by actors and actresses (S)

dialogue: the words spoken by characters in a play (S)

drama: a work of literature that is intended to be performed by actors (S)

monologue: an extended speech by a single character (T)

props: objects used by actors and actresses, such as an umbrella or a map (S)

scene: a subdivision of an act that takes place in a particular time and place (S)

scenery: the painted screens, backdrops, or other materials that show where the action of the play takes place (S)

setting: the time and place of the action in a play (S)

stage: the raised platform in a theater on which a play is performed (S)

stage directions: italicized instructions describing costumes, sound effects, scenery, and lighting, and specifying how actors should move and speak (T)

theater: the building where a play is performed (S)

tragedy: a serious story about a heroic character who meets with disaster because of a personal fault or events that cannot be helped (S)

Domain Vocabulary

Drama and associated words:
Globe Theater, soliloquy, aside, perform, performance, stagecraft, lighting, sound effects, music, script, director, Renaissance, Elizabethan Age, play, humor, humorous, actress, acting, stage crew, Shakespearean, verse drama, blank verse, groundlings, pit, galleries, *plus words from* A Midsummer Night's Dream

Materials

Instructional Masters 10–11
The Globe Theater, p. 78
The Language of Shakespeare, p. 78

pictures of the Globe Theater, pp. 76, 78

condensed or adapted versions of *A Midsummer Night's Dream*, p. 77

audiotape or CD player, pp. 77, 78

audio recording of *A Midsummer Night's Dream*, p. 77

simple props, p. 78

recording of Felix Mendelssohn's *A Midsummer Night's Dream*, p. 78

videocassette or DVD player, p. 78

videotape or DVD of *A Midsummer Night's Dream*, p. 78

hat, p. 78

an example of a Shakespearean tragedy to view or read, p. 81

information about local Shakespearean performances, p. 81

Cross-curricular Connections

History and Geography

World: The Renaissance and the Reformation
World: England from the Golden Age to the Glorious Revolution

Music

Listening and Understanding
• Overture, Scherzo, and Wedding March from *A Midsummer's Night Dream*

> ### At a Glance
>
> The most important ideas for you are:
>
> - Drama is a form of literature that is intended to be performed by actors for an audience in a theater.
> - Plays are divided into acts and scenes. The Romans were the first to divide their plays into acts, and the Roman poet Horace set the number at five. Until the 19th century, the ideal number of acts in a play was five.
> - Drama includes comedies and tragedies.
> - William Shakespeare was one of the finest playwrights of the Elizabethan Age (1558–1603).
> - If possible, students should have an opportunity to participate in and/or attend grade-appropriate dramatic performances as well as study them.

What Teachers Need to Know

B. Drama

Background: Why Study Shakespearean Drama?

In Grade 5, students will be introduced to the dramatic works of William Shakespeare. One of the world's greatest playwrights, Shakespeare wrote comedies and tragedies during the Renaissance that are still performed today. A Midsummer Night's Dream is a fanciful comedy in which love and magic triumph over adversity. The title alludes to the summer solstice, Midsummer Eve (June 23), which in Shakespeare's time was marked by holiday parties and tales of fairies.

Globe Theater

When choosing an edition of the play, you'll find there are many options: full-length, well-annotated versions, adapted or shortened versions, and modern retellings in prose. You'll find some of these options listed in the More Resources list at the end of this section.

Before reading, be sure to introduce and define the terms tragedy, comedy, act, and scene. Also, show students pictures of the Globe Theater so that they can visualize where Shakespeare's plays were performed. Explain that theater was very popular with people of the Elizabethan Age, and, although many theaters at that time allowed only the upper classes to attend, the Globe let in people of all classes. The people who paid the lowest entrance fee stood directly in front of the stage. They were often very boisterous and sometimes threw rotten vegetables at the actors.

Studying Shakespearean drama helps students experience the pleasure of reading great works of literature and understand how the plays come to life when performed on stage. Students at this level should be able to read and generally understand condensed or adapted versions of Shakespeare. However, they may need assistance with understanding difficult vocabulary, following a complicated plot with several twists, comprehending stage directions, and keeping track of many different characters.

Teaching Shakespearean Drama

Teaching Shakespeare in Grade 5 is a challenge, but it can be done. Below, we outline a series of steps that may help you teach *A Midsummer Night's Dream* with success. This is, of course, only one way of approaching the task. You may wish to use some of these ideas but not others.

• Before turning to *A Midsummer Night's Dream*, make sure students understand that a drama, or play, is a work of literature that is intended to be performed for an audience. Introduce the distinction between comedy and tragedy.

• You might want to begin this unit with a very short and simple play—perhaps a modern, one-act play, and preferably a comedy. While teaching the modern play, you can explain about plays, characters, scenes, dialogue, etc. Then, when you turn to Shakespeare, students will already be familiar with the basic conventions of drama and will not have to learn those while wrestling with Shakespeare's language.

• Before attempting to teach *A Midsummer Night's Dream*, read the play at least twice yourself. Get a good school edition, such as the *Oxford School Shakespeare* edition, and use the glosses and footnotes to help you understand difficult parts. If possible, watch a videotape or two of a performance. You want to be teaching with a solid knowledge base.

• Before introducing students to Shakespeare's text, preview *A Midsummer Night's Dream* by reading a short summary of what happens in the play—a prose version like the one in the Text Resources or the one in *Tales from Shakespeare*, by Charles and Mary Lamb. Discuss whether the play is a comedy or a tragedy. How can students tell? Once students have a general sense of where the play is going, they can devote more attention to the language and the speeches.

• Before turning to the text itself, make sure students understand that Shakespeare wrote about 400 years ago. The English language has changed considerably since Shakespeare's time. Therefore, there will be some passages that are hard to understand. Students shouldn't worry about not understanding every single word. Encourage them to raise their hands when they get confused. Tell them that even adults sometimes get confused when watching or listening to Shakespeare.

• Instead of asking students to read the play themselves at first, have them listen to the play on audiotapes and follow along in a printed version. This is much easier than reading Elizabethan language from the page. Audiotapes are widely available in bookstores and online. As you listen, stop every so often to make sure students are following the plot and getting the gist of the speeches. Explain difficult passages as needed.

• If you don't have time to study the whole play, do just selected scenes.

• Don't try to do too much in a given day. Divide the play into chunks and listen to one or two scenes each day to avoid overwhelming students. Allow plenty of class time in which to discuss each section. Encourage students to ask questions about what they do not understand, and have them answer specific questions about plot, setting, and characters.

• Assist students with difficult vocabulary. Using an edition that has glosses and annotations (such as the *Oxford School Shakespeare* edition) will reduce problems with difficult vocabulary.

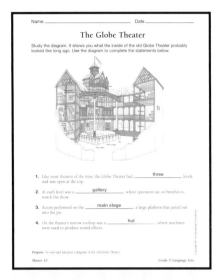

Use Instructional Master 10.

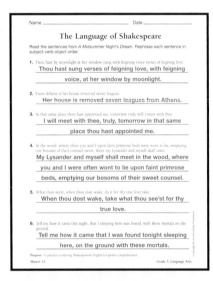

Use Instructional Master 11.

• If students have problems with the word order of Elizabethan English, show them how to rephrase a sentence in subject-verb-object order. Here is an example: original wording: "Thou hast by moonlight at her window sung with feigning voice verses of feigning love." reordered: "Thou hast sung verses of feigning love, with feigning voice, at her window by moonlight."

• Explain to students that Shakespeare sometimes wrote in verse and sometimes in prose, and that he did this to show differences in class. Usually, characters speaking in verse have a high social status.

• While discussing the play, briefly introduce students to iambic pentameter, which was the rhythm typically used by Shakespeare. Each line generally has 10 syllables made up of five clusters of two syllables each. In each cluster, the stress is on the second syllable, like a heartbeat (da-DUM, da-DUM, da-DUM). Read a line aloud as students beat out the rhythm on their desks.

• Once students have listened to the play read by actors and studied it a little, choose one or more scenes and assign students roles. Have students read aloud and/or act out these scenes using simple props.

• To help students visualize the Globe Theater where Shakespeare's plays were performed, use **Instructional Master 10**, *The Globe Theater*, and show them pictures. Explain that this Elizabethan playhouse was built in London in 1599 by Richard and Cuthbert Burbage. The permanent home of Shakespeare's company, the Globe became London's most popular theater.

• After studying the play, play a recording of Felix Mendelssohn's *A Midsummer Night's Dream*. Ask students whether they think the music suits the mood or tone of the play, and why.

• If possible, have students view a live performance of Shakespeare or show them a film adaptation of the play (Warner Home Video, 1935). Again, if you don't have time to watch the whole play, consider watching selected scenes. (The 1999 film version starring Kevin Kline is rated PG-13 and may not be suitable for most students.) (See *More Resources*.)

Introducing the Play

Reading the retelling of the play included in the Text Resources is one way of introducing the play. Another way is to combine this pre-telling strategy with student recitation of some memorable lines.

First, choose a set of memorable lines from the play, including some from each act. Write the lines on slips of paper. For *A Midsummer Night's Dream*, the first few slips might say, "1. Full of vexation come I, with complaint against my child, my daughter Hermia"; "2. I beseech your grace that I may know the worst that may befall me in this case, If I refuse to wed Demetrius." "3. Either to die the death or to abjure for ever the society of men." "4. If thou lovest me then, steal forth thy father's house to-morrow night, and in the wood, a league without the town . . . there will I stay for thee." Make one slip for each member of the class.

Next, ask each student to choose a slip from a hat and prepare a dramatic reading of the line on the slip, guessing how it ought to sound and using his or her voice to express whatever emotions the student thinks the lines were meant to express. Encourage students to "ham it up." After they have recited their lines, tell them these are all lines from a play they will be studying, and that you will be

reading a short story version of the play. Then read a summary of the story, adapted from the one in the Text Resources. As you read the story, pause at appropriate points for the students to read their lines, this time in context. It should go something like this:

First you read: "Once upon a time, in the city of Athens, a young man named Lysander and a young woman named Hermia were deeply in love. They wanted to get married, but Hermia's father, Egeus, would not allow it. Egeus told Hermia it was her duty to marry the man he had chosen, whose name was Demetrius. Egeus dragged Hermia to a hearing in front of Theseus, the Duke of Athens. Egeus turned to the Duke and said . . ."

Then call on the student holding slip #1 to read it, or point to #1 on the board, and the student says his or her line from slip #1: "Full of vexation come I, with complaint against my child, my daughter Hermia."

Then continue: "Egeus asked the Duke to enforce an old law that said a daughter who refused to marry the man her father had chosen could be thrown into a nunnery for the rest of her life, or even put to death. Hermia spoke to the Duke, saying . . ."

Then a student reads slip #2: "I beseech your grace that I may know the worst that may befall me in this case, If I refuse to wed Demetrius."

Continue: "And the Duke replied . . ."

Then a student reads slip #3: "Either to die the death or to abjure for ever the society of men."

Next: "Hermia was saddened by this announcement, but her lover Lysander had an idea. When they were out of the Duke's hearing he whispered to her . . ."

Then a student reads slip #4: "If thou lovest me then, steal forth thy father's house to-morrow night, and in the wood, a league without the town . . . there will I stay for thee."

Continue: "That night Hermia and Lysander snuck out of town, . . ." etc.

This strategy will get the children interested and involved in the play. They will learn the basic plot and be able to participate.

▶ A Midsummer Night's Dream

Author Information: William Shakespeare (1564–1616) was an English playwright, poet, and actor who lived during the Renaissance, specifically during the Elizabethan Age. Many people consider Shakespeare to be the greatest playwright in history. He is often called The Bard of Avon, or simply The Bard. Although Shakespeare was a talented poet, he is most well known for his 38 plays, most of which were performed at the Globe Theater in London.

Background: *A Midsummer Night's Dream* is a comedy of errors set in Athens and the surrounding woods. Hermia loves Lysander, against her father's wishes, but is engaged to marry Demetrius. Her best friend, Helena, loves Demetrius, although this love is unrequited. Oberon, the king of the fairies, decides to improve this unfortunate situation with a "love potion" derived from flowers. But he sends his fairy servant Puck to do the job, and Puck makes things worse by administering the magic potion incorrectly. In the end, Oberon resolves the situation and the couples marry happily.

Teaching Idea
You may also wish to use the biography of William Shakespeare that is included in the Text Resources. ㉕

Before Reading: Have you ever tried to fix a complicated problem, only to make it worse?

Vocabulary: hearing: trial; **vexation:** irritation; **hath:** has; **consent:** permission; **bewitched:** tricked; **impression:** fantasy; **filched:** stolen; **sealing:** joining; **betwixt:** between; **pursue:** chase after; **steal forth:** escape from; **hateth:** hates; **fly:** run away from; **thence:** then; **tradesmen:** workers who practice a specific trade; **melodramatic:** overly emotional or theatrical; **nay:** no; **peach fuzz:** teenage boy's very thin facial hair; *ex tempore:* on the spot, as one goes along; **supernatural:** superhuman; **liquor:** liquid with special properties; **meddling:** annoying, nosy; **tedious:** repetitive and boring; **raven:** large black bird; **mischievous:** naughty; **translated:** changed; **enamored:** in love with; **enthralled:** spellbound; **lair:** den or refuge; **delicacies:** rare or exquisite foods; **nymph:** beautiful and mythical fairy-like being; **divine:** heavenly; **professing:** proclaiming; **superpraise:** flatter; **wooing:** courting; **baffled:** confused; **canker-blossom:** diseased flower; **mortals:** humans; **charms:** spells; **antidote:** remedy, cure; **executed:** killed; **idle gaud:** useless knickknack; **lamentable:** regrettable; **crannied:** having a small nook; **chink:** chip or crack; **loam:** mud-based mixture used for walls; **doth:** does; **sinister:** representative of bad things to come; **mark:** take note; **dole:** sorrow; **mantle:** coat, robe, cloak; **fled:** gone away; **newlyweds:** people recently married; **ministrations:** rituals

After Reading: Why did Hermia and Lysander have to run away? Why did Puck change Bottom's head into that of a donkey? Many people consider Puck to be the main character in this play. Why do you think that is?

Versions: The Text Resources includes a summary of the story, which you can use to introduce students to the play and its plot. This is intended to make the plot and characters clear to students and to serve as preparation for Shakespeare's text, which will be hard for students, but not impossible. Many young students are capable of taking great delight in Shakespeare's plots and language and are able to understand the general meaning, even when not every word is crystal clear. After reading the summary, we encourage you to spend as much time with Shakespeare's text as you can; if you can't read the whole play, try to read and act out selected scenes. The suggestions above provide some guidance for teaching. The bibliography for this section lists several titles that will be helpful to you in introducing students to Shakespeare, including some student-friendly editions of this play. (24)

The Big Idea in Review

Reading Shakespearean drama helps students acquire reading and language comprehension skills and gain an appreciation for different kinds of literature.

Review

Below are some ideas for ongoing assessment and review activities. These are not meant to constitute a comprehensive list.

• As a reinforcing activity for this section, give students an opportunity to memorize, rehearse, and perform their favorite scenes from *A Midsummer Night's Dream* for the class.

• Have students practice writing by creating a scene with characters and an interactive situation. Have students write the scene, practicing with dialogue, quotation marks, and other grammar concepts. They may then perform their original scenes. You may also consider brainstorming a topic for an entire play

with the class, and then group students so that each group can write a short scene for the play. After making sure that the scenes and acts flow smoothly, have the class rehearse and perform their play for another Grade 5 class.

• Choose one of Shakespeare's tragedies (e.g., *Hamlet* or *Macbeth*) for students to view or read in order to compare and contrast a comedy and tragedy. You may wish to share just a summary of one of Shakespeare's tragedies. After they have become familiar with the tragedy, have students write about the similarities and differences between comedies and tragedies and express their opinions about which kind of story they prefer.

• Seek out information from your community about Shakespearean performances. Local theater groups or high school drama clubs may perform Shakespeare's plays. Have a field trip to view one of these productions and then have students write about the experience of seeing the performance.

• After reading the play, have students write a review. Within the review, have them express their opinions about the play, finding examples within the text to support their opinions. Have students share their reviews and then discuss how many liked the play and how many disliked the play.

• You may ask the following questions after completion of this unit of study:

1. What is a tragedy?
   A tragedy is a serious story about a heroic character who meets with disaster because of a personal fault or events that cannot be helped.

2. What is a comedy?
   A comedy is a humorous story in which everything works out well for the main characters.

3. Is *A Midsummer Night's Dream* a tragedy or a comedy? Why?
   It is a comedy because it is humorous and because it has a happy ending.

4. Which character in this play do you like best or would you like to know more about? Why?
   Students' choices will vary.

5. Which act or scene in this play do you like best? Why?
   Students' choices will vary.

More Resources

The titles listed below are offered as a representative sample of materials and not a complete list of everything that is available.

For students —

• *A Midsummer Night's Dream (Oxford School Shakespeare Series),* edited by Roma Gill (Oxford University Press, 2002). Heavily annotated and intended for use by schoolchildren. Paperback, 126 pages, ISBN 0198320213.

• *A Midsummer Night's Dream: For Kids (The Shakespeare Can Be Fun Series),* by Lois Burdett (Firefly Books Ltd, 1997). Paperback, 64 pages, ISBN 1552091244.

• *Shakespeare for Children,* an audio recording by Jim Weiss (Greathall Productions, www.greathall.com or 1-800-477-6234), contains a retelling of *A Midsummer Night's Dream.*

• *Tales from Shakespeare,* by Charles and Mary Lamb (Pearson, 2000). Originally published in 1807, this is a collection of many of Shakespeare's plays told in simple narrative. Paperback, ISBN 0582419417.

More Resources continued

• *William Shakespeare and the Globe*, by Aliki (HarperTrophy, 2000). Honored by the Orbis Pictus Awards program for excellence in children's nonfiction. Paperback, 48 pages, ISBN 0064437221.

For teachers —

• *An Actor on the Elizabethan Stage*, by Stephen Currie (Lucent, 2003). Hardcover, 96 pages, ISBN 1590181743.

• *Irresistible Shakespeare (Grades 5 and Up)*, by Carol Rawlings Miller (Scholastic Professional Books, 2001). Features general information on Shakespeare and a section on *A Midsummer Night's Dream.* Paperback, 80 pages, ISBN 0439098440.

• *A Midsummer Night's Dream.* Warner Home Video, 1935.

• *A Midsummer Night's Dream: A Unit Plan*, by Mary B. Collins (Teacher's Pet Publications, 2000). CD-ROM, 121 pages, ISBN 1583371397.

• *Ready-To-Use Activities for Teaching A Midsummer Night's Dream* (Shakespeare Teacher's Activities Library), by John Wilson Swope (Center for Applied Research in Education, 1996). Paperback, 223 pages, ISBN 087628915.

• *Shakespeare Set Free: Teaching Romeo & Juliet, Macbeth & A Midsummer Night's Dream*, edited by Peggy O'Brien (Washington Square Press, 1993). Be aware that there is a sensual painting on the cover. Paperback, 288 pages, ISBN 0671760467.

• *Shakespeare's Globe*, by Amy Allison (Lucent, 2000). Hardcover, 96 pages, ISBN 1560065265.

• *Starting with Shakespeare: Successfully Introducing Shakespeare to Children*, by Pauline Nelson and Todd Daubert (Teacher Ideas Press, 2000). Includes treatment of *A Midsummer Night's Dream.* Paperback, 217 pages, ISBN 1563087537.

• *Stepping into Shakespeare: Practical Ways of Teaching Shakespeare to Younger Learners (Cambridge School Shakespeare)*, by Rex Gibson (Cambridge University Press, 2000). Spiral-bound, 112 pages, ISBN 0521775574.

• Shakespeare on the Internet, http://shakespeare.palomar.edu, offers links to the writer's life and times, as well as an online edition of Charles and Mary Lamb's *Tales from Shakespeare.*

IV. Speeches

The Big Idea

Reading speeches from American history helps students understand important historical events and gain an appreciation for the art of persuasion.

What Students Should Already Know
Students in Core Knowledge schools should be familiar with

Grade 4

> Speeches
>   • Patrick Henry: "Give me liberty or give me death!"
>   • Sojourner Truth: "Ain't I a woman?"

What Students Need to Learn

 The importance of Abraham Lincoln's Gettysburg Address
 The importance of Chief Joseph's "I will fight no more forever"
 Persuasion
  • **is the art of convincing someone to believe something or to take action.**
  • **uses arguments that are supported by facts and reasons.**
 Persuasive techniques include emotional appeals, logical appeals, ethical appeals, and loaded language.
 Some persuasive speeches include allusions, parallelism, formal language, repetition, and antithesis.

What Students Will Learn in Future Grades
In Grade 7, students will read this speech:

> "Declaration of War on Japan" (Franklin D. Roosevelt)

Vocabulary

Student/Teacher Vocabulary

alliteration: the repetition of initial consonants (S)

allusion: a reference to a historical event or custom, a work of literature or art, or a well-known person or place (T)

antithesis: words or thoughts that have contrasting meaning (T)

argument: an opinion for or against something that is supported by facts, reasons, and examples (T)

emotional appeal: words or ideas that appeal to feelings and emotions (T)

ethical appeal: words or ideas that appeal to values or beliefs or a sense of right and wrong (T)

IV. Speeches

Materials

Instructional Master 83
Venn Diagram, p. 88

newspaper editorials, advertisements, letters to the editor, and other examples of emotional, ethical, or logical appeals, p. 86

map of Pennsylvania, p. 87

videotape recorder and videotapes, p. 89

podium, p. 89

access to school media center for videotapes of speeches, p. 89

Vocabulary continued

formal language: a style of speaking to inform an audience in impersonal terms (T)

idiom: an expression whose meaning differs from the literal meaning of its individual words (T)

imagery: words or phrases that appeal to the senses of sight, hearing, touch, taste, and smell and help create mental images (S)

loaded language: language that is inflated and emotionally charged, and sometimes misleading (T)

logical appeal: words or phrases that appeal to reason or logic (T)

orator: a skilled speaker (T)

parallelism: the use of words, phrases, or sentences that have a similar grammatical structure (T)

persuasion: the art of convincing an audience to adopt an opinion or take a certain action (S)

repetition: the repeating of a sound, word, phrase, or line (T)

rhetoric: the art of communicating ideas (T)

rhetorical question: a question that does not have to be answered (T)

Domain Vocabulary

Speeches and associated words:
oration, oratory, recitation, delivery, elocution, rhetorical, rhetorical device, eloquence, speaker, address, appeal, invocation, invoke, audience, public speaking, communicate, communication, communicator, speech, speak, oral, lecture, lecturer, persuasive, logic, ethics, emotions, Civil War, Battle of Gettysburg, Union, Confederacy, Abraham Lincoln, Chief Joseph, Nez Perce, relocation, *plus words from the speeches themselves*

Cross-curricular Connections

History and Geography

American: The Civil War
The Civil War

• Gettysburg and "The Gettysburg Address"

American: Native Americans: Cultures and Conflicts
Culture and Life

• Great Basin and Plateau American Government Policies (Chief Joseph)

At a Glance

The most important ideas for you are:

- Rhetoric, which dates back to ancient Italy and Greece, is the art of communication.
- Persuasion is the use of argument and rhetorical devices to convince an audience to adopt certain beliefs or to take action.
- Literary devices often found in persuasive speeches include allusions, formal language, antithesis, parallelism, and repetition.
- Reading speeches from American history will give students insight into important historical events and figures and will help them appreciate the art of persuasion.

What Teachers Need to Know

Background: Why Study Speeches?

This section offers two speeches by well-known Americans. The purpose of this section is to help students appreciate rhetoric, or the art of communicating ideas, in the context of American history. Rhetoric, as the art of formal speaking, started in Syracuse and developed in Greece in the 5th century BCE. *When students listen to speeches, they will experience the power of persuasive rhetoric, recognize persuasive techniques such as appeals to emotion, and become familiar with literary techniques used in persuasive speeches, such as allusions, parallelism, and rhetorical questions. As you teach this section, you may want to read other grade-appropriate speeches from American history with your class.*

Students need to have studied the period in which the speeches were given in order to understand them. Out of context, the speeches will not have the same meaning. After reviewing the historical context of the speeches, read the speeches aloud to the class and have students discuss them. Then invite students to read them aloud to practice speaking and listening. Delivering a persuasive speech helps students develop an awareness of language that will help them become better public speakers and persuasive writers. By listening closely, students in Grade 5 learn more about American history, continue to build their vocabulary, and develop an understanding of literary techniques used in persuasive writing.

Reading Speeches Aloud

Reading speeches aloud enables students to more immediately experience the music and persuasive power of words. When you read speeches to students, read them aloud several times. Speak slowly and clearly. Use gestures to punctuate certain passages or important points. Also, use your voice to emphasize the rhythmic nature of the words, the literary elements and devices being employed, and the importance of the message being conveyed.

Cross-curricular Teaching Idea

Before you begin this section, have students share what they already know about Abraham Lincoln and/or Chief Joseph if you have already introduced the related topics in History and Geography. These speeches should be taught in the context of American history lessons. You can return to them several times throughout the lessons.

Teaching Idea

Teach students to write their own short speeches on a topic of interest, and have them deliver their speeches to the class or other large audience.

Focusing on Meaning

After reading a speech, discuss it. Ask questions such as these:

- Who gave the speech?
- Where and when did he or she give it?
- Why did he or she deliver this speech?
- What is the main message in the speech?
- How does the speaker try to convince an audience to accept his or her point of view?
- Do you think the speaker's speech is convincing? Why or why not?
- What do you think were the best parts of the speech?

Then read the speech again, inviting students to join in by repeating certain words, phrases, or lines they recall. If necessary, provide additional information that will help students comprehend the speech, including clarifications of difficult words, unfamiliar cultural references, or historical allusions. Then help students paraphrase the main message of the speech in their own words.

Focusing on Elements in Persuasive Rhetoric

To make a strong argument for or against something, speakers and writers use certain literary devices and persuasive techniques, such as rhetorical questions and emotional appeals. The purpose of these devices is to sway the audience's opinion and give power to the words the speaker or writer uses. As you teach the speeches in this section, you may want to point out examples of these elements.

You do not need to introduce these literary terms or persuasive techniques to your class. However, you can call attention to these devices as you read. For example, ask questions such as, "Which words or phrases appeal to your emotions?" to help them recognize emotional appeals. Ask, "Which words or phrases are said more than once?" to help them identify examples of repetition, or to help them recognize rhetorical questions.

Element	Definition	Example
antithesis	words and thoughts that have contrasting meaning	old men, young men
emotional appeal	words or ideas that appeal to feelings and emotions	The little children are freezing to death.
ethical appeal	words or ideas that appeal to values or beliefs or a sense of right and wrong	It is altogether fitting and proper that we should do this.
formal language	a style of speaking to inform an audience in impersonal terms	consecrate, hallow
loaded language	language that is inflated and emotionally charged, and sometimes misleading	shall not perish from the earth
logical appeal	words or phrases that appeal to reason or logic	It is for us, the living, rather, to be dedicated here to the unfinished work which they who fought here have thus far so nobly advanced.

Introducing the Speeches

When reading the following speeches, you may use some or all of the information provided to help students understand what the speech is about, what literary elements and devices it contains, who gave it, and what reasons the person had for giving the speech. Suggested teaching strategies and activities are also provided.

 ### The Gettysburg Address

Author Information: Abraham Lincoln (1809–1865) was the 16th president of the United States. Born in a log cabin and raised in poverty on the Kentucky and Indiana frontier, he educated himself by reading the Bible, Aesop's fables, *Robinson Crusoe* by Daniel Defoe, and other books. As a young man, he worked as a rail splitter, a storekeeper, and a surveyor. He also practiced law and in 1860 was elected president. After the Civil War broke out in 1861, Lincoln fought to preserve the Union and brought about the emancipation of the slaves in 1863. Just five days after the end of the war in 1865, Lincoln was assassinated by John Wilkes Booth.

Background: After Lincoln won the 1860 presidential election, tension escalated between proslavery states in the South and antislavery states in the North. Seven Southern states seceded from the Union to form the Confederate States of America under President Jefferson Davis. In April 1861, tensions boiled over. War between the states erupted when Confederate troops fired on Union-held Fort Sumter in Charleston, South Carolina. Shortly after Fort Sumter came under Confederate control, four more states joined the Confederacy.

The largest battle of the Civil War was fought in and around Gettsyburg, Pennsylvania. For three days, from July 1 to July 3, 1863, the two armies clashed. Union troops won the bloody Battle of Gettysburg, a turning point of the war, but approximately 28,000 Confederate soldiers and 23,000 Union soldiers were killed or wounded.

On November 19, 1863, President Abraham Lincoln delivered this speech at the dedication of the National Soldiers' Cemetery for Union soldiers at the Gettysburg battlefield. About 15,000 mourners were in attendance. Edward Everett from Massachusetts, the principal orator, had just given a two-hour speech when Lincoln stood to speak. Lincoln's powerful Gettysburg Address lasted only about two minutes. Some people thought the speech was a failure, but Everett and others saw that there was something wonderful about it. Everett told Lincoln, "I should be glad, if I could flatter myself that I came as near to the central idea of the occasion, in two hours, as you did in two minutes." The Gettysburg Address is still seen today as one of the most important speeches in the history of the United States.

After reading the speech with students, help them understand that Lincoln is defining, or redefining, the Civil War as a struggle to see if a nation can really be run on the principle (from the Declaration of Independence) that "all men are created equal." Lincoln is moving his audience toward an understanding of this purpose. Note that many people at the time did not think that this was what the war was about. They thought it was about preserving the Union, not about equality for slaves. Students may be interested to know that the Confederate side also

Cross-curricular Teaching Idea

Have students read the Gettysburg Address when they are studying the Civil War. Encourage them to locate Gettysburg on a state map of Pennsylvania. Also, connect this speech to the poem "O Captain! My Captain!" by Walt Whitman (p. 53.)

Teaching Idea

Invite students to work out the arithmetic of the Gettysburg Address. "Four score and seven" = (4 x 20) + 7 = 87. Take 87 from 1863: 1863 – 87 = 1776. Ask students what happened in 1776.

Teaching Idea

Students may enjoy hearing excerpts from Everett's Gettysburg speech as well. It is too long to read in full, but excerpts might be read aloud. Students may also enjoy listening to another brief but powerful Lincoln speech, his second inaugural address. Both speeches are available online. (See *More Resources.*)

Teaching Idea

Have students use Instructional Master 83, *Venn Diagram,* to compare and contrast the two speeches in terms of style and purpose.

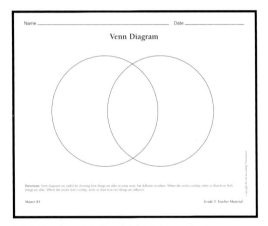

Use Instructional Master 83.

Cross-curricular Teaching Idea

Introduce "I will fight no more forever" when you teach the American History section "Native American Cultures and Conflicts," on pp. 297–313. Encourage students to read other fiction and nonfiction books about Native Americans.

pointed to 1776 as a significant date; they saw their secession from the Union and declaration of independence as exactly parallel to what the colonies had done in 1776. So both sides pointed to 1776, but for different reasons.

Before Reading: What do you know about Abraham Lincoln? What do you know about the Civil War? Why do you think it is important to honor those who give their lives for the good of their country?

Vocabulary: Four score and seven years ago: 87 years ago, or 1776, the year in which the Declaration of Independence was signed; **conceived:** formed or developed; **Liberty:** freedom; **dedicated:** solemnly committed to; **proposition:** suggestion, proposal; **engaged:** involved; **civil:** of citizens; **endure:** carry on despite difficulties; **dedicate:** show to the public for the first time; **fitting:** appropriate; **proper:** correct; **dedicate:** set apart for special use; **consecrate:** declare sacred; **hallow:** set apart as holy; **poor:** inferior, inadequate; **detract:** take away; **note:** notice, pay attention to; **nobly:** honorably; **advanced:** moved forward; **task:** job; **devotion:** dedication, commitment; **measure:** amount, quantity; **resolve:** make a firm decision; **in vain:** without purpose; **perish:** die

Literary Elements and Devices: alliteration (four score, fathers, forth), repetition (of the people, by the people, for the people; dedicate, devotion), antithesis (living, dead; remember, forget), parallelism (we cannot dedicate, we cannot consecrate, we cannot hallow), formal language (devotion, consecrate, hallow), allusion ("All men are created equal" is an allusion to the Declaration of Independence), emotional appeal (We have come to dedicate a portion of that field as a final resting place for those who here gave their lives that that nation might live), ethical appeal (It is altogether fitting and proper that we should do this), logical appeal (The world will little note nor long remember what we say here, but it can never forget what they did here), loaded language (liberty, nobly, perish)

After Reading: How does Abraham Lincoln feel about the Union soldiers who died at the Battle of Gettysburg? According to Lincoln, for what cause did these soldiers die? What emotions does Lincoln appeal to in this speech? **(31)**

I will fight no more forever

Author Information: Chief Joseph (1840–1904) was born in the Wallowa Valley in what is now northeastern Oregon. His tribal name was Hin-mah-too-yah-lat-kekt, or Thunder Rolling Down the Mountain. After succeeding his father as leader of the Wallowa band of Nez Perce in 1871, Chief Joseph refused to allow the U.S. government to force his people from their tribal lands. However, Chief Joseph was unable to resist the government and later died on the Colville Reservation in Washington. According to his doctor, he died of a broken heart.

Background: By the 1860s, whites had begun to settle in the West. Many Native Americans on the Great Plains and in the Pacific Northwest were forced to give up their lands to the U.S. government and were relocated onto reservations. Chief Joseph, leader of the Wallowa band of Nez Perce, resisted being relocated after gold was discovered in Nez Perce territory in the 1860s. However, in 1877,

Chief Joseph and his followers agreed to move onto a reservation in Idaho. After Nez Perce warriors killed a few white settlers, the U.S. Army, under the command of General Oliver O. Howard, pursued the band for three months. To escape to safety, Chief Joseph led 700 people, including 200 warriors, more than 1,400 miles north. After winning many skirmishes and four battles, Chief Joseph was cornered less than 40 miles from the Canadian border. Following a five-day siege in which several prominent chieftains were killed, Chief Joseph made this speech on October 5, 1877, surrendering to Colonel Nelson Miles at Bear Paw Battlefield.

Before Reading: How do you think you might feel if you were forced to leave your home? What was happening to Native Americans at this time?

Literary Elements and Devices: alliteration (<u>s</u>ick, <u>s</u>ad; <u>s</u>un, <u>s</u>tands), repetition (dead, freezing to death), parallelism (Looking Glass is dead. Toohoolhoozote is dead. The old men are all dead.), antithesis (old men, young men), emotional appeal (The little children are freezing to death.), imagery ("freezing to death" appeals to the sense of touch)

After Reading: Why did Chief Joseph surrender? What reasons did Chief Joseph give for making this decision? What emotions does Chief Joseph appeal to in his speech? (32)

Review

Below are some ideas for ongoing assessment and review activities. These are not meant to constitute a comprehensive list.

• Have small groups of students work together to prepare a dramatic reading of either speech. Have students stand before a podium and then record or videotape their presentations.

• Visit the school media center and find an example of a famous speech that you are able to watch on videotape. Discuss with students the differences between hearing the speech, seeing the person, and reading the speech. How does seeing the speech affect the emotional quality? After watching a short segment of a speech, have students write a reaction to what they have heard. Have students complete a Venn diagram comparing a written text of a speech to the one on videotape. How are their reactions different?

• Give students an opportunity to write and give speeches in class. If you have class officers or student body officer elections, encourage students to run for office and give speeches about their positions on school issues. Have the class brainstorm the elements of a good speech.

• Practice summarizing while studying speeches from this section. Speeches provide a good opportunity to listen closely and practice finding the main idea. After hearing both speeches from this section, have students write one or two sentences about the speech's main idea.

The Big Idea in Review

Reading speeches from American history helps students understand important historical events and gain an appreciation for the art of persuasion.

• After reading the speeches from this section, have students write a short "sequel" to the speech. By researching the speeches and the people who gave them, what might that person say next? You may want to find other speeches given by Lincoln or Chief Joseph and have the class listen to those to see if the speaker made any of the same points that they did in their sequel. For example, Lincoln's second inaugural speech could be considered a follow-up speech. (See *More Resources.*)

• You may ask the following questions after completion of this unit of study:

1. What is the main message in Abraham Lincoln's speech?

   The Union army soldiers who died at the Battle of Gettysburg were noble and brave because they gave their lives so that the United States of America could live. The best way to honor these men is to continue fighting for the preservation of the Union and for democracy.

2. Do you think Lincoln's speech is successful? Why or why not?

   Students should tell whether or not they think Lincoln's speech is successful and give reasons to support their answers.

3. What is the main message in Chief Joseph's speech?

   The leader of the Nez Perce will no longer fight the whites because he wants to spare his people from further suffering.

4. Do you think Chief Joseph's speech has emotional appeal? Why or why not?

   Students should tell whether or not they think Chief Joseph's speech has emotional appeal and give reasons to support their answers.

5. Which is your favorite speech in this section? Why do you like it?

   Students' choices will vary.

More Resources

The titles listed below are offered as a representative sample of materials and not a complete list of everything that is available.

For students —

• *The Gettysburg Address*, by Abraham Lincoln and illustrated by Michael McCurdy (Houghton Mifflin, 1995). Striking woodcuts illustrate Lincoln's famous speech. Paperback, ISBN 0395883970.

• *You Can Write Speeches and Debates*, by Jennifer Rozines Roy and Johannah Haney (Enslow, 2003). Hardcover, 64 pages, ISBN 0766020878.

For teachers —

• American Rhetoric, www.americanrhetoric.com, has an archive of over 5,000 text, audio, and video files of major speeches, including an audio recording of Martin Luther King Jr.'s "I Have a Dream" speech.

• *Great Speeches in History* (Naxos Audiobooks, 1996). Dramatic readings of Lincoln's Gettysburg Address, Martin Luther's defense before the Diet of Worms, and others. Audio CD, ISBN 962634083.

• *The World's Great Speeches (Fourth Enlarged Edition)*, selected by Lewis Copeland and others (Dover, 1999). Paperback, 944 pages, ISBN 0486409031.

• The Gettysburg Address as well as the Second Inaugural Address by Abraham Lincoln are available online at The Capitol.net website at www.thecapitol.net/Recommended/lincoln.htm.

V. Sayings and Phrases

The Big Idea

Sayings and phrases are important to study because they are widely used in everyday language and writing, and their meanings are not always immediately clear.

What Students Should Already Know

Students in Core Knowledge schools may have heard sayings and phrases as well as abbreviations used in conversations at home, in school, on television or radio programs, or in cartoons, films, and videotapes. They should have already learned some in previous grades.

What Students Need to Learn

- The meanings and appropriate uses of sayings and phrases
- Proverbs (sayings)
  - are brief statements that express a general truth or observation about life.
  - may have a literal meaning and a figurative meaning.
  - have been passed down orally from one generation to the next.
- Idioms (phrases) are expressions whose meanings differ from the literal meaning of their individual words.
- Proverbs and idioms are commonly used in spoken and written English.

What Students Will Learn in Future Grades

In future grades, students will review and extend their learning about different sayings and phrases and will study their literal and figurative meanings.

Vocabulary

Student/Teacher Vocabulary

allusion: a reference to a historical event or custom, a work of literature or art, or a well-known person or place (T)

antithesis: the arrangement of words and phrases that contrast, e.g., "Ask not what your country can do for you; ask what you can do for your country." (T)

ellipsis: missing words in a sentence or phrase (T)

figurative language: language that uses figures of speech or goes beyond the literal, surface meaning (T)

hyperbole: exaggeration for emphasis (S)

idiom (phrase): an expression whose meaning differs from the literal meaning of its individual words (S)

literal: the exact meaning of a word or series of words (T)

Materials

sentence strips, p. 93

large, white easel paper, pp. 93, 94

colored markers, p. 94

"The Gardener and the Dog" by Aesop, p. 94

recording of "Que Será Será," p. 102

CD/audiocassette player, p. 102

student journals, p. 102

materials to make student books, p. 102

index cards, p. 103

Vocabulary continued

parallelism: the use of words, phrases, or sentences that have a similar grammatical structure (T)

proverb (saying): a short, popular saying, sometimes of unknown authorship (S)

Domain Vocabulary

Sayings and phrases and associated words:
maxim, aphorism, adage, saying, saw, wisdom, wise, proverbial, expression, figure of speech, connotation, denotation, exaggeration, idiomatic, oral, oral tradition, contrast, compare, comparison, metaphor, inference, infer, generalization, generalize, *plus words from the sayings themselves, such as* eureka, molehill, vice versa, mend, *etc.*

At a Glance

The most important ideas for you are:

‣ Proverbs are short, popular folk sayings, sometimes by an unknown author, that express general observations and truths about life.

‣ Idioms are expressions whose meanings do not reflect the meanings of their individual words.

‣ Proverbs and idioms often have both a literal meaning as well as a figurative meaning.

‣ Proverbs and idioms employ such literary devices as repetition, rhyme, and metaphor.

‣ Because proverbs are used frequently in speech and writing, a student who can recognize and understand common proverbs will be better able to understand what he or she reads and hears.

What Teachers Need to Know

Background: The Origins of Proverbs and Idioms

The English language is peppered with familiar sayings and phrases. One kind of familiar expression is called a proverb. Proverbs are short, traditional folk sayings that have been passed along orally from generation to generation or quoted in works of literature and other printed materials. Proverbs usually express general truths based on the experiences and observations of everyday life.

An idiom is a phrase, or a group of words read or spoken as a unit. Idioms have their own meaning apart from the dictionary definitions of the words in the expression. Like proverbs, idioms have also been passed down orally or quoted in literature and other printed text.

Many proverbs and idioms reveal the concerns, interests, and folk beliefs of different peoples in the past. Like the sayings in this section, some proverbs and idioms address familiar customs or commonplace topics such as weather,

medicine, and animal behavior. Invented by ordinary people long ago, these sayings often reflect the wisdom of those who earned their living from the soil or the sea, or who practiced trades and crafts.

While students will primarily study proverbs that originated in the English language, proverbs and idioms exist in most languages, cultures, and countries around the world. In many instances, proverbs and idioms from different cultures express similar ideas. Even though proverbs and idioms may express ideas that derived from a particular craft, belief, or practice that is now obsolete, the wisdom and truth of their meaning still has relevance for students today.

Teaching Proverbs and Idioms

Because proverbs and idioms are widely used in the English language, students in Grade 5 should be introduced to some common ones. Encouraging students to identify familiar proverbs and idioms and learn their meanings will help them better understand and communicate ideas. Students who are learning English as a second language will especially benefit from learning proverbs and idioms, since the meanings of such sayings and phrases often do not derive from the dictionary definitions of their words.

Some proverbial sayings do have literal meanings; that is, they mean exactly what they say. But most proverbs and all idioms have a richer meaning beyond the literal level. To teach proverbs and idioms, you must help students understand the difference between the literal meanings of the words and their implied or figurative meaning.

Focusing on Meaning

As you introduce each of these proverbs and idioms to students, first read it aloud several times. Then have students repeat it. Discuss what the proverb or idiom means on both literal and figurative levels. Provide clear examples to illustrate the meaning of the saying and to show in which situations it would be appropriate to use it. At this point, it should be apparent whether or not students understand the saying.

Reinforcing Understanding

To reinforce students' understanding of the meanings of sayings in this section, watch for opportunities to use them in applicable classroom situations or in connection with any aspects of the curriculum where using them makes sense. Throughout the school year, encourage students to pay attention to the use of proverbs and idioms in conversations at home or in school. Ask them to think about situations when they might use the sayings they have learned.

Recognizing Stylistic Features

Many proverbs and idioms have common stylistic features. As you read them, you may want to point out examples of the literary devices shown in the charts on pp. 45–46 and 86.

Helping your students notice the use of literary devices in proverbs and idioms opens a door to their understanding and appreciation of literature. As you discuss these expressions, you can call attention to the literary devices that make them vivid and easy to remember.

Teaching Idea

Read aloud several of the proverbs and idioms in this section. Then ask students to recall other proverbs or idioms that they have heard. Encourage volunteers to share with the class any proverbs or idioms they may know.

Teaching Idea

Write individual sayings or phrases on sentence strips and provide easel paper to students. Tell them to fold the easel paper in half, copy the saying or phrase at the top of the paper, and then draw and write the literal meaning of it. On the other half of the paper, ask students to write and draw the figurative meaning of the saying or phrase.

Teaching Idea

The idiom "Sit on the fence" does not mean a person literally sits on a fence. It has a figurative meaning, which is that someone refuses to take sides in a debate or disagreement. Learning and understanding the idiom's figurative meaning is the key to being able to use idioms in spoken and written English.

V. Sayings and Phrases

Introducing Sayings and Phrases

When you teach the following expressions, guide students to understand both the literal and figurative meanings. You may also want to use the information about literary devices and origins to enrich students' understanding. At this level, students should be able to recognize such devices as metaphor, rhyme, repetition, and alliteration; understanding of the other devices will come later. Beginning at an early age, students can recognize and use these sayings to enhance their own speaking and writing.

Birthday suit

Meaning: To be wearing your birthday suit means to be naked.

Example: Enrique was just about to step into the bath when he heard the ice-cream truck coming down his street. He was so excited that he ran outside wearing only his birthday suit!

Origin and History: This saying alludes to the way people come into the world when they are born (that is, on their "birth day"): without any clothes on.

Bite the hand that feeds you

Meaning: This idiom means that someone harms or acts ungratefully toward another person or organization that provides help and support.

Example: Julie had outgrown her raincoat, so her grandma surprised her with a brand-new yellow slicker. "Yuck!" said Julie when she opened the package. "I hate yellow!"

"Don't bite the hand that feeds you," cautioned Grandma.

Literary Elements and Devices: metaphor ("bite" represents acting ungrateful or harming someone, and "the hand that feeds you" represents help or support)

Origin and History: The idiom derives from Aesop's fable "The Gardener and the Dog," in which a gardener's dog falls in a well. When the gardener rescues the dog, the dog thinks the gardener is trying to drown him. The dog bites the gardener and is consequently thrown back in the well.

Chip on your shoulder

Meaning: The meaning of this idiom is that a person is angry about something and eager to start a fight.

Example: Juana was worried. "When I said 'good morning' to Dennis today, he yelled at me to leave him alone. Did I do something to make him not like me?"

"Don't worry," Gabe comforted her. "It's not your fault. Dennis just has a chip on his shoulder."

Literary Elements and Devices: allusion, metaphor (the chip represents hard feelings or a grudge)

Origin and History: This idiom alludes to an early 19th-century game played by American boys. A boy would place a chip of wood or stone on his shoulder and then dare another boy to knock it off. If the chip was knocked off, the boys would fight.

Count your blessings.

Meaning: This proverb means that you ought to be thankful for what you have.

Example: Pauline and Nicholas were riding bikes when Pauline lost control and fell. "Now the paint on my bike is scratched!" she complained.

"Count your blessings," replied Nicholas. "At least you weren't hurt."

Literary Elements and Devices: ellipsis ([You should] count your blessings.)

Origin and History: The origin of this proverb is unknown.

Eat crow

Meaning: This idiom means to accept disgrace or humiliation for something arrogant or boastful that one has done or said.

Example: The science fair was coming up and Mariana's class was busy working on their projects. Mariana was busy bragging. "My project is sure to win first prize! It'll be way better than any of yours!" She was so busy talking about her project that she forgot to actually work on it.

On the day of the science fair, Mariana's project was not yet finished, and the grand prize was awarded to Marco.

"You deserved to win, Marco," said Mariana, eating crow. "Your project really was the best."

Literary Elements and Devices: allusion

Origin and History: This idiom alludes to an incident that supposedly occurred during the War of 1812. During an armistice in the war, an American soldier crossed the Niagara River past British lines. While hunting, the soldier shot a crow, but he was caught by a British officer. The officer forced the American soldier to take a bite out of the uncooked crow as punishment for his violation of British territory.

Eleventh hour

Meaning: This idiom means "at the last possible moment."

Example: Kenji wanted to take Erica to the school formal, but he was too shy to ask her. He worried for weeks about what she might say. On the day of the dance, Kenji still hadn't gathered the courage to ask. He was resigned to going to the formal alone. At the eleventh hour, however, he got a phone call; it was Erica, asking him to the dance!

Literary Elements and Devices: allusion

Origin and History: This idiom is a biblical allusion to Matthew 20:9, in which workers hired at the eleventh hour get paid the same amount of money for an hour's work as do those who work for twelve hours.

Eureka!

Meaning: This Greek word (*heureka*) means "I have found it!" This idiom is used to express joy or excitement when a discovery is made or when an answer to a difficult problem or question is found.

Example: It was the first snowfall of the season, and Malik took out his warmest winter clothes. He found his hat, his scarf, and one mitten. "But where is the other mitten?" he wondered. "It does me no good to have only one." He searched and he searched for the missing mitten. Finally, he decided he would need to go out and buy a new pair.

Malik took down his winter coat and put it on. As his arm entered the sleeve, his missing mitten fell out. "Eureka!" he cried. "I have found it!

> **Teaching Idea**
>
> Introduce the saying "Eureka" by telling students the story of Archimedes and the crown of gold. The story is available in many anthologies and also on a recording by storyteller Jim Weiss, *Galileo and the Stargazers.* (See *More Resources.*)

V. Sayings and Phrases

Literary Elements and Devices: allusion

Origin and History: This idiom dates back at least to the 3rd century BCE. There is a famous story about this saying. Hiero, king of Syracuse in ancient Greece, gave a goldsmith 10 pounds of gold to make a magnificent crown. The goldsmith delivered the crown. It was a beautiful piece of work, but the king was suspicious and wondered if it was really solid gold, or if the goldsmith had used some less precious metal for the insides. He asked the mathematician and scientist Archimedes to find a way to determine whether the crown was all gold. Archimedes thought about the problem for days. One day he was thinking about the problem as he prepared to take a bath. His tub was full to the brim, and as he stepped into it, water flowed out upon the stone floor. Archimedes thought, "How much water did I displace? Obviously I displaced a bulk of water equal to the bulk of my body. Now suppose, instead of lowering myself into the tub, I had lowered Hiero's crown into it. The crown would have displaced a bulk of water equal to its own bulk. Now, gold is much denser than silver. Ten pounds of pure gold will not make so great a bulk as seven pounds of gold mixed with three pounds of silver. If Hiero's crown is really pure gold, it will displace the same amount of water as any other 10 pounds of pure gold. But if it is part gold and part silver, it will displace a larger amount. That's the answer!" Then, forgetting about everything else, Archimedes leaped out of the bath and, without getting dressed, ran through the streets to the king's palace shouting, "Eureka!" which in English means, "I have found it!" The crown was tested and found to displace much more water than 10 pounds of pure gold displaced. And so the guilt of the goldsmith was proved beyond a doubt.

Every cloud has a silver lining.

Meaning: This proverb means that there is always hope, even when unfortunate events happen.

Example: Isobel's mother lost her job. "The restaurant went out of business," she moaned. "Now I don't know what I'll do."

"Every cloud has a silver lining," consoled Isobel. "You always wanted to be an artist. Now you'll have more time to paint."

Literary Elements and Devices: metaphor ("cloud" represents a bad situation and "silver lining" represents hope). Ask students, "What do the cloud and the silver lining represent?"

Origin and History: English poet John Milton (1608–1674) used this proverb in his poem "Comus" (1634).

Few and far between

Meaning: The meaning of this idiom is that something is rarely seen or rarely happens.

Example: Deserts are very hot and dry; rainstorms are few and far between.

Literary Elements and Devices: alliteration (few, far). Ask students, "Which two words begin with the same consonant?"

Origin and History: This idiom appeared in "The Pleasures of Hope" (1799), by Scottish poet and journalist Thomas Campbell (1777–1844).

Forty winks

Meaning: This idiom means "a short nap."

Example: It was New Year's Eve and Albert was so tired he could hardly keep his eyes open, but he wanted to be awake for the big fireworks display at midnight. "I'm going to go catch forty winks," he told Minh-Wei. "Make sure I'm up before the fireworks start!"

Origin and History: This idiom has been in use since the 19th century. Its first known appearance was in 1872 in the British humor magazine *Punch*.

The grass is always greener on the other side of the hill.

Meaning: This proverb means that some people feel that what they have is not as good as what other people have.

Example: "You're so lucky!" said Candace to Theo. "I wish I had cool freckles, like you."

"I always envied you because you don't have freckles," answered Theo. "I guess the grass is always greener on the other side of the hill."

Literary Elements and Devices: alliteration (grass, greener)

Origin and History: This proverb can be traced to about 1545 in England.

To kill two birds with one stone

Meaning: This idiom means "do only one thing to accomplish two goals."

Example: Hakim called up his friend, Susan. "It's been so long since we've seen each other. Will you come to my house for dinner tomorrow?"

"Oh, I'd like to," Susan replied, "but my sister is visiting me this week."

"I've always wanted to meet your sister," said Hakim. "Why don't you both come? That way we can kill two birds with one stone."

Literary Elements and Devices: antithesis (two, one), parallelism (two birds, one stone), metaphor (the stone represents one solution or effort, and the two birds represent multiple objectives or goals)

Origin and History: This idiom can be traced to 17th-century England and may refer to the use of a slingshot to kill birds.

Lock, stock, and barrel

Meaning: The idiom refers to the three parts of a flintlock rifle: the lock is the firing mechanism, the stock is the handle, and the barrel is the long, round chamber through which a bullet is fired. The meaning of this idiom is "absolutely everything," or "all the parts."

Example: "At first, Chandra only wanted to sell me half of her baseball card collection, but I offered such a good price that I was able to get the whole set, lock, stock, and barrel."

Literary Elements and Devices: rhyme (lock, stock), metaphor ("lock, stock, and barrel" represents something that is complete or whole; without these three parts, a gun will not operate properly)

Origin and History: This saying can be traced to the 18th century during the settling of the American West.

Make a mountain out of a molehill

Meaning: This idiom means that a person makes a big fuss over something that is not really important.

Example: "You were supposed to meet me at four PM sharp!" screamed Henry. "How dare you be late!"

"Stop making a mountain out of a molehill," replied Edson, calmly. "It's only 4:03. It's not like you were waiting all day!"

Literary Elements and Devices: antithesis (mountain, molehill), hyperbole (being able to make a mountain from a molehill is a gross exaggeration), alliteration (<u>m</u>ake, <u>m</u>ountain, <u>m</u>olehill), metaphor (a mountain represents something important and a molehill represents something trivial)

Origin and History: The origin of this proverb is unknown.

A miss is as good as a mile.

Meaning: This proverb means that a failure is a failure whether you miss your objective by a little or by a whole lot.

Example: Madeline approached Mr. Quinn after class, holding her algebra test. "I missed the answer to number 2 by only one decimal point. Can't I get partial credit?"

"Sorry, Madeline," said Mr. Quinn, "but in math, a miss is as good as a mile."

Literary Elements and Devices: alliteration (<u>m</u>iss, <u>m</u>ile)

Origin and History: This proverb dates back to 1614 in England (An ynche in a misse is as good as an ell). The original proverb meant that an inch in a miss might as well be an ell, or a measurement equivalent to 45 inches. In hunting, carpentry, or other pursuits that demand precision, one can ill afford to miss a target or goal by any amount, even by a measurement as small as an inch.

It's never too late to mend.

Meaning: This proverb means that it is always possible to improve yourself or change for the better.

Example: "I lost several friends because I was too bossy. I guess it's never too late to mend, though. I will try to be a better friend from now on."

Literary Elements and Devices: metaphor ("mend" represents improvement)

Origin and History: This proverb dates to about 1590 in England and is found in the papers of George Clinton, the first governor of New York (1778).

Out of the frying pan and into the fire

Meaning: This idiom is used to describe the experience of trying to get out of a bad situation only to get into an even worse one.

Example: Celina slept through her alarm and was late for school. "I'm going to get in trouble! I'd better write a note saying that I was at Dr. Lee's office this morning."

When she handed her forged note to the teacher, Mrs. Patel raised an eyebrow. "Being late for school is bad enough, but you've jumped out of the frying pan and into the fire: Dr. Lee was here this morning for Career Day."

Literary Elements and Devices: alliteration (<u>f</u>rying, <u>f</u>ire), metaphor (the frying pan represents a bad experience, while the fire represents an even worse experience), antithesis (out, into). Ask students, "Which two words have the opposite meaning?"

Origin and History: This idiom has been used in various forms since the 3rd century CE and is found in Greek (Out of the smoke, into the flame), Russian, and French. It appears in William Shakespeare's plays and in the writings of Sir Thomas More. The idiom derives from cooking practices before electric and gas stoves were invented. As cooks held or suspended a frying pan over an open fire, meats and other foods would often jump from the pan to the fire, where they were burnt to a crisp.

 ## A penny saved is a penny earned.

Meaning: The meaning of this proverb is that saving money instead of spending it is nearly the same as earning money because the end result is the same; you will have additional money in your pocket.

Example: "Mom gave me a dollar to buy a cheeseburger, but a hot dog is only eighty cents. I think I'll get the less expensive lunch; a penny saved is a penny earned!"

Literary Elements and Devices: repetition (penny), parallelism (A penny saved is a penny earned). Ask students, "Which words or phrases follow the same pattern?"

Origin and History: This proverb is found in George Herbert's *Outlandish Proverbs* (1640) and appears in Benjamin Franklin's *Poor Richard's Almanack* (1732–1757).

 ## Read between the lines

Meaning: This idiom means to go past the surface meaning of what someone says or does to find the true meaning.

Example: Lucas was upset. "Every time I ask Dyan to come to the pool with me, she makes up some lame excuse! I can't figure out what's up."

"I think you need to read between the lines," said Sanouk. "Maybe Dyan doesn't know how to swim, and she is ashamed to tell you."

Literary Elements and Devices: metaphor ("between the lines" represents looking beyond the obvious)

Origin and History: This saying may derive from one method of cryptography, or secret writing, in which a coded message made sense only when alternate lines were read.

Sit on the fence

Meaning: This idiom means that a person refuses to take sides, to commit to something, or to make up his or her mind.

Example: "I've had three weeks to decide whether to sign up for the softball team or the drama club, but I'm really sitting on the fence on this one. I just can't make up my mind."

Literary Elements and Devices: metaphor (the fence represents what separates two different points of view)

Origin and History: This idiom has been in use in the United States since the 19th century.

Steal his/her thunder

Meaning: This idiom means that one person takes credit for another's idea or uses it before the other person has an opportunity to do so.

Example: Jamie came home from school with a sad look on his face. "I had a great idea for the fifth-grade fundraiser, and so Maria and I called a meeting of the student council. Before I had a chance to speak, Maria piped up with my idea. She really stole my thunder."

Literary Elements and Devices: metaphor (thunder represents a person's achievement or accomplishment)

Origin and History: In 1709, playwright John Dennis (1657–1734) wrote a tragedy called *Appius and Virginia*. The play was a flop; however, one successful feature of the play was its sound effects, especially a realistic sound of thunderclaps. Later, when Dennis attended a successful performance of *Macbeth* by William Shakespeare, he recognized a close imitation of his sound effects during the witches' scene. Dennis was angry that the show "stole his thunder."

Take the bull by the horns

Meaning: This proverb means that a person stops hesitating and takes action to deal with a difficult situation.

Example: "I'm afraid that Bianca is going to lower our grade on this group project," said Lauren. "I keep suggesting that she help out with the research, but she never does any of the reading."

"Well, you need to take the bull by the horns," answered Daniel. "Tell her that if she doesn't start doing her share of the work, she can't be part of our group, even if she is your best friend."

Literary Elements and Devices: alliteration (<u>b</u>ull, <u>by</u>), metaphor (the bull represents a difficult situation that must be confronted directly)

Origin and History: This proverb derives from the matador's practice of taking a bull by the horns during a bullfight to avoid being tossed. This saying has been in use since the late 19th century when bullfights became a form of international entertainment for tourists, and rodeos became popular in the American West.

Till the cows come home

Meaning: The literal meaning of this idiom refers to the time when cows in the fields return to the barn at the end of a long day. People use this idiom when something is not going to happen for a very long time.

Example: Mom yelled up the stairs, "Lana! Dinner's ready!"

Dad laughed. "You can holler till the cows come home, but she's not coming down. Lana's at soccer practice, remember?"

Literary Elements and Devices: alliteration (<u>c</u>ows, <u>c</u>ome), metaphor ("till the cows come home" represents a long amount of time)

Origin and History: This idiom has been popular since the 19th century. It refers to the way cows take a long time to reach the barn because they often meander and stray on their way home from the fields.

 Time heals all wounds.

Meaning: The meaning of this proverb is that the passage of time helps lessen the hurt of physical and psychological wounds.

Example: "Henry promised he'd let me go to the drag races with his family, but then he took Jaleel. I hate him! I'm never speaking to Henry again!"

"I know you're disappointed," counseled Keisha, "but you'll get over it. Time heals all wounds."

Literary Elements and Devices: hyperbole (time can heal many wounds but not all of them)

Origin and History: English poet Geoffrey Chaucer (c. 1340–1400) used this proverb in 1374. It has been in use in the United States since at least 1830.

 Tom, Dick, and Harry

Meaning: This idiom means "just about anybody," or ordinary, run-of-the-mill types of people.

Example: "When I joined this country club, I was assured that it was exclusive. Now that I've been a member for a while, I realize that it will admit every Tom, Dick, and Harry."

Origin and History: This Victorian idiom incorporates three common English names to signify the ordinary man in the street. The name *Tom* has been the generic name for a jester since the 1400s, and the trio of Tom, Dick, and Harry was associated with buffoons, or clowns, in the 16th century.

 Vice versa

Meaning: This Latin expression means "the same as before but in reverse order."

Example: "Yasmin and I are starting a band. Either I'll be the lead singer and she'll sing backup or vice versa."

Literary Elements and Devices: alliteration (v̲ice, v̲ersa)

Origin and History: The Latin word *vice* means "position," and the Latin word *versa* means "turn." This expression has been in use in English since 1601.

 A watched pot never boils.

Meaning: This proverb cautions a person to be more patient; sometimes when you are very eager for something to happen, it seems to take even longer.

Example: Samuel growled and banged a fist on the computer keyboard. "This website is taking forever to load! Why won't it hurry up?"

"Calm down," answered LeVar, "a watched pot never boils."

Literary Elements and Devices: hyperbole (A watched pot will eventually boil), metaphor (a watched pot represents something that is waited for anxiously)

Origin and History: English novelist Elizabeth Gaskell used this proverb in *Mary Barton* (1848).

Well begun is half done.

Meaning: This proverb means that if you begin a project or task the right way, you are halfway to your goal and will find it easier to finish.

Example: "Have you started writing your book report yet?" asked Su-Lin.

"Not yet," replied Kenneth, "but I have a great outline written. And well begun is half done!"

Literary Elements and Devices: rhyme (begun, done), ellipsis ([What is] well begun is half done), parallelism (Well begun is half done). Ask students, "Which two words end with the same or similar sounds?"

Origin and History: This proverb can be traced back to the Roman poet Horace (65–8 BCE) in *Epistles* (He who has made a beginning, has half done.) It also appears in Middle English sermons in about 1415 and was used by the English writer Oliver Goldsmith in 1775.

▶ **What will be will be.**

Meaning: This proverb means that you cannot change what is going to happen.

Example: Sanjit waited anxiously as the votes for class president were being counted. "If only I had started campaigning sooner, I definitely would win."

"There's no use worrying about it now," said Robert, "the votes are already in. What will be will be."

Literary Elements and Devices: parallelism (What will be will be), repetition (will be), alliteration (what, will). Ask students, "Which words are repeated?"

Origin and History: This proverb was used in "The Knight's Tale" (1390) by English poet Geoffrey Chaucer (c. 1340–1400) and appears in *Heywood's Collection* (1546), a collection of proverbs by John Heywood. It is best known from the popular song "Que Será Será," which is how the proverb is expressed in Spanish.

Teaching Idea
You may wish to play a recording of the song "Que Será Será" for the class.

The Big Idea in Review

Sayings and phrases are important to study because they are widely used in everyday language and writing, and their meanings are not always immediately clear.

Review

Below are some ideas for ongoing assessment and review activities. These are not meant to constitute a comprehensive list.

• As a culminating activity, have small groups of students devise and perform skits in which they use or demonstrate a particular idiom or proverb. For example, one group might have a student briefly close his or her eyes to illustrate "Forty winks."

• Present a saying or phrase to the class and review the meaning. Then have each student write about an experience they have had to which that saying or phrase would apply. This would be a good journal topic.

• Designate a place in the classroom to display the sayings and phrases from this section and encourage students to use them in writing and speaking where appropriate.

• Have students design a cartoon to show the meaning of a saying or phrase.

• Have students create a book of sayings and phrases. The left-hand page can be the literal meaning of the saying. The right-hand page can be the figurative meaning after it is discussed.

• Challenge students to use as many sayings and phrases as possible in a piece of writing and still have the story make sense.

• Play a game of "Win, Lose, or Draw" as a review of all of the sayings and phrases. Write the sayings and phrases on index cards, and have a representative from a team draw one on the board while his or her team tries to guess which is being depicted.

More Resources

The titles listed below are offered as a representative sample of materials and not a complete list of everything that is available.

For students —

• *The Scholastic Dictionary of Idioms*, by Marvin Terban and illustrated by John Devore (Scholastic, 1998). Paperback, 256 pages, ISBN 0590381571.

• *Settler Sayings (Historic Communities)*, by Bobbie Kalman (Crabtree Publications, 1994). Paperback, 32 pages, ISBN 0865055181.

• *There's a Frog in My Throat: 440 Animal Sayings a Little Bird Told Me*, by Loreen Leedy and illustrated by Pat Street (Holiday House, 2003). Hardcover, 48 pages, ISBN 0823417743.

For teachers —

• *Clichés: Over 1500 Phrases Explored and Explained*, by Betty Kirkpatrick (Griffin, 1999). Paperback, 224 pages, ISBN 0312198442.

• *Concise Dictionary of Phrase and Fable*, edited by Elizabeth Knowles (Oxford, 2003). Paperback, 608 pages, ISBN 0192801252.

• *Dictionary of Phrase and Fable*, by E. Cobham Brewer (HarperResource, 2000). Hardcover, 1,326 pages, ISBN 006019653X.

• *Dictionary of Word and Phrase Origins*, by William and Mary Morris (HarperResource, 1988). Hardcover, 688 pages, ISBN 006015862X.

• *Familiar Quotations: A Collection of Passages, Phrases, and Proverbs Traced to Their Sources in Ancient and Modern Literature (17th edition)*, by John Bartlett, and edited by Justin Kaplan (Little, Brown & Company, 2002). Familiarly known as "Bartlett's Quotations." Hardcover, 1,472 pages, ISBN 0316084603.

• *Galileo and the Stargazers*, an audio recording by Jim Weiss (Greathall Productions, www.greathall.com or 1-800-477-6234).

• *Proverbs: Wisdom for Life*. Available from the International Bible Society, 1-800-524-1588.

• *Random House Dictionary of Popular Proverbs and Sayings, (Second Edition)*, by Gregory Y. Titelman (Random House, 2000). Paperback, 480 pages, ISBN 0375705848.

History and Geography

History and Geography in Fifth Grade

WORLD HISTORY AND GEOGRAPHY

From Kindergarten through Grade 3, students focused on learning about the physical characteristics of specific places while expanding their geographic skills and vocabulary. In Grades 4 and 5, students continue to learn and apply geographic skills (Section I) as they move into more abstract concepts, such as longitude and latitude and map projections. Additional landscape features are also introduced.

Section II builds on and expands what students in Core Knowledge schools should have learned in Grade 1 in the American History and Geography section about the Maya, Aztec, and Inca civilizations. In Grade 5, students look at the achievements of these pre-Columbian civilizations in more detail and then at their interactions with the Spanish conquistadors.

Sections III and IV provide a view of European civilization as Europeans began to explore beyond the continent. You might wish to teach Section IV on the Renaissance and the Reformation before you teach Section III in order to show how the Renaissance provided a context for European exploration. In studying Section III, students will be able to plot the parallel explorations and competing goals of the major European Atlantic trading nations—Portugal, Spain, England, France, and the Netherlands. Students will learn why and how the African slave trade became such an important part of the growing trade network with the Americas.

Sections V through VII focus on three specific national cultures from approximately the 1400s until the 1700s—England, Russia, and Japan. The exact time periods are less important than the diverging paths in economic, societal, and political developments that the three cultures took. During these centuries, England became a constitutional monarchy with power resting increasingly in Parliament. However, at about the same time, Russia and Japan saw authority increasingly centralized in the power of the czar and shogun, respectively. While the feudal system had ended in England by 1400, Russia and Japan were embracing it.

Note: *Traditionally the abbreviations AD or BC have been written alongside dates to indicate whether the events in question took place before or after the birth of Jesus. BC means "Before Christ." AD comes from a Latin phrase, "Anno Domini," meaning "Year of the Lord." AD 1000 means one thousand years after the birth of Jesus; 1000 BC means one thousand years before the birth of Jesus. However, scholars increasingly prefer to write 1000 BCE (Before the Common Era) instead of 1000 BC, and 1000 CE (Common Era) instead of AD 1000. Therefore, BCE and CE are used in this book.*

I. World Geography

The Big Idea

Maps and globes are used to show location and other aspects of human and physical geography.

Remember that each subject you study with students expands their vocabulary and introduces new terms, thus making them better listeners and readers. As you study geography, use map work, read alouds, independent reading, and discussions to build students' vocabularies.

What Students Should Already Know

Students in Core Knowledge schools should be familiar with

Kindergarten through Grade 4

- what maps and globes represent and how to use them
- what rivers, lakes, and mountains are and how they are represented on maps and globes
- the location of the Atlantic, Pacific, Indian, and Arctic Oceans, the North and South Poles, and the seven continents
- the name and location of their continent, country, state, and community
- the use of map keys and symbols and directions (east, west, north, south) on a map
- the location of Mexico and Central America; the countries of North America (Canada and the United States); the Equator; Northern and Southern Hemispheres
- the meaning of *peninsula, harbor, bay, island, coast, valley, prairie, desert, oasis, boundary, channel, delta, isthmus, plateau, reservoir,* and *strait*
- the use of scale, an atlas, and online resources
- Canada (French and British heritage; French-speaking Quebec; Rocky Mountains; Hudson Bay, St. Lawrence River, and the Yukon River; division into provinces; major cities including Montreal, Quebec, and Toronto)
- important rivers of the world (terms including *source, mouth, tributary,* and *drainage basin;* Asia's Ob, Yellow or Huang He, Yangtze or Ch'ang, Ganges, and Indus Rivers; Africa's Nile, Niger, and Congo Rivers; South America's Amazon, Parana, and Orinoco Rivers; North America's Mississippi, Mackenzie, and Yukon Rivers; Australia's Murray-Darling River; and Europe's Volga, Danube, and Rhine Rivers)
- measuring distances using map scales
- reading maps and globes using longitude and latitude, coordinates, and degrees
- time zones: Prime Meridian; Greenwich, England; International Date Line
- reading relief maps for elevations and depressions
- major mountain ranges by continent (South America: Andes; North America: Rockies and Appalachians; Asia: Himalayas and Urals; Africa: Atlas Mountains; Europe: Alps)

I. World Geography

Text Resources

(33) *Lake Superior: Biggest, Deepest, Coldest*

Materials

Instructional Masters 12–16

Latitude as Climate Indicator, p. 113

Three Different Map Projections, p. 115

Great Lakes of the World, p. 116

Great Lakes of the Eastern Hemisphere, p. 117

Great Lakes of the Western Hemisphere, p. 118

collection of maps, pp. 111, 120

world map, pp. 111, 120

different-colored markers, p. 113

almanacs, atlases, and globes, p. 119

access to the Internet or the media center, p. 119

"My Country" folder or journal, p. 119

laminated enlargement of each lake, p. 120

dry erase markers, p. 120

index cards, p. 120

What Students Should Already Know continued

- high mountains of the world by continent (Asia: Everest; North America: McKinley; South America: Aconcagua; Europe: Mont Blanc; Africa: Kilimanjaro)

What Students Need to Learn

- **Tropic of Cancer and Tropic of Capricorn: relation to seasons and temperature**
- **Climate zones: Arctic, Tropic, Temperate**
- **Arctic Circle (imaginary lines and boundaries) and Antarctic Circle**
- **From a round globe to a flat map: Mercator, conic, and plane projections**
- **Great Lakes of the World**
  - **Eurasia: Caspian Sea**
  - **Asia: Aral Sea**
  - **Africa: Victoria, Tanganyika, Chad**
  - **North America: Superior, Huron, Michigan**
  - **South America: Maracaibo, Titicaca**

What Students Will Learn in Future Grades

In Grade 6, students will review and extend their learning about geography, including great deserts of the world.

Vocabulary

Student/Teacher Vocabulary

Antarctic Circle: a parallel of latitude approximately 67° south of the Equator, circumscribes the southern frigid zone (S)

Arctic: the region between the North Pole and the Arctic Circle that is geographically bordered by the northern timberlines of North America and Eurasia; characterized by extremely cold weather (S)

Arctic Circle: a parallel of latitude approximately 67° north of the Equator, circumscribes the northern frigid zone (S)

climate: a summary of weather conditions; the general weather patterns, as opposed to the specific conditions on any particular day (S)

conic projection: a type of map in which features on a globe are projected onto a map using a cone-shaped projection (S)

coordinates: a set of numbers used to specify the location of a point on a plane, a map, or a globe (S)

degrees: a unit of measurement used to describe latitude and longitude (S)

globe: a spherical representation of Earth (S)

Greenwich, England: location of the Prime Meridian (0° longitude) (S)

International Date Line (180° Line): a line that marks the difference in time between east and west, largely corresponding to 180° longitude (S)

latitude: a measurement of location north or south of the Equator; measured in degrees (S)

Vocabulary continued

longitude: a measurement of location east or west of the Prime Meridian, measured in degrees (S)

map: a representation, usually on paper, of the whole or part of an area of land (S)

Mercator projection: a type of map in which features on a globe are projected onto a map using a cylinder-shaped projection, which results in a map on which the meridians and parallels of latitude appear as lines crossing at right angles; makes areas far from the Equator appear larger (S)

plane projection: a type of map projection in which the surface of the globe is transferred to a plane; also called an azimuthal projection (S)

Prime Meridian: the meridian of zero degrees (0°) longitude that runs through Greenwich, England, and from which other longitudes are reckoned (S)

Robinson projection: a map projection showing the poles as lines rather than points and more accurately portraying high latitude lands (T)

temperate zone: area between the Tropic of Cancer and the Arctic Circle and between the Tropic of Capricorn and the Antarctic Circle, characterized by moderate climate (S)

temperature: the degree of hotness or coldness in an atmosphere, body, or environment (S)

time zone: geographic area within which the same standard of time is used (S)

Tropic of Cancer: the latitude that is approximately 23.5° north of the Equator and that is the northernmost latitude reached by the overhead sun (S)

Tropic of Capricorn: the latitude that is approximately 23.5° south of the Equator and that is the southernmost latitude reached by the overhead sun (S)

tropics: the region of Earth's surface lying between the Tropic of Cancer and the Tropic of Capricorn (S)

Domain Vocabulary

Maps and related words:
minutes, seconds, north, south, east, west, near, far, grid, locate, location, find, almanac, boundary, halfway, imaginary, perpendicular, right angle, tropical, temperate, torrid, frigid, cold, hot, moderate, sunlight, wet, dry, precipitation, season, rainforest, savanna, plain, grass, climate zone, extreme, polar, ice cap, variation, spring, summer, fall, autumn, winter, time change, hours, clock, day, tomorrow, yesterday, travel, airplane, boat, pictorial, picture, location, place, representation, depiction, projection, accurate, inaccurate, distort, shape, landmass, landform, body of water, ocean, sea, wind, current, size, distance, area, direction, elevation, portable, cone, conic, lines, surface, plane, pole, compass, legend, key, cartographer, mapmaker, grid, geography, intersect, atlas, equinox, solstice

Great lakes and associated words:
freshwater, tide, high tide, low tide, ebb, flood, tidal, recreation, swimming, boat, sail, canoe, drinking, fishing, transportation, shipping, navigable, passenger, freight, shipping, inland, sea, sea level, water, river, continent, outlet, large, largest, diversion, irrigation, cotton, agriculture, saline, salty, explorer, source, system; freshwater, deep, shallow, deepest, freeze, canal, port, saltwater, oil, oil spill, canal, dam, loch, underwater, barge, shore, tanker, steamer, yacht, motorboat, dinghy, tugboat, frigate, paddle, dock, row, reservoir, float, sink, drill, boatman, captain, mast, marine, marina

As a general rule of thumb, when choosing projects to do with your students, they should be well-thought-out and relate directly to the objectives and time allotments outlined in the beginning of each section. Projects have an important place, especially in the early grades when they help reinforce vocabulary and content and don't serve purely as time fillers. Throughout this subject, we have added teaching ideas with fun and purposeful extensions to further students' understanding. Keep in mind that a useful way to engage students in History and Geography topics can be through the use of structured simulations (acting out events).

Cross-curricular Connections

Mathematics

Numbers and Number Sense
• Order and compare numbers

Geometry
• Lines, measuring degrees, angles

At a Glance

The most important ideas for you are:

- Students should recognize the grid pattern that parallels of latitude and meridians of longitude create on a map and globe.
- The land between the Tropic of Cancer and the Tropic of Capricorn (the tropics, in general) has hot weather and little or no change in seasons.
- The polar climate zone, which includes the Arctic and the Antarctic, is typically cold with little precipitation; the tropical zone is typically hot with a great deal of precipitation; and the temperate zone has more variation in temperature and amount of precipitation.
- The International Date Line, at 180° longitude, marks the shift in days between east and west.
- The Arctic Circle and the Antarctic Circle are lines of latitude that demarcate the extreme northern and southern areas of the planet—areas that experience 24 hours of daylight for part of the summer and 24 hours of darkness for part of the winter.
- Maps are representations of Earth that are made using different projections. Each projection distorts various areas of Earth in different ways.
- Lakes may be freshwater or tidal, and are used for recreation, fishing and transportation.

What Teachers Need to Know

Background

The study of geography embraces many topics throughout the Core Knowledge Sequence, including topics in history and science. Geographic knowledge includes a spatial sense of the world; an awareness of the physical processes to which people culturally adapt; a sense of the interactions between humans and their environment; an understanding of the relations between place and culture; and an awareness of the characteristics of specific regions and cultures. In addition to the topics treated in this section, many geographic topics are listed throughout the World History and Geography Sequence in connection with historical topics.

Teaching Idea

Review map-reading skills and concepts from previous grades as needed.

A. Spatial Sense (Working with Maps, Globes, and Other Geographic Tools)

Measuring Distance Using Map Scale

All maps are drawn to scale; that is, they are smaller than the things they represent. Scale is the ratio between the representation and the thing it represents. A map may be drawn so that 1 inch equals 250 miles, or so that 1 inch equals 1 mile. Maps, as well as globes, almost always indicate the scale at which they are drawn.

The scale of a map makes a difference in the amount of detail shown on the map and the kinds of questions that can be asked and answered about what is shown. A large-scale map (i.e., one closest in size to what it represents) will show less area but provide more detail about the area shown than a small-scale map. For example, a road map of a state, with a scale of 1 inch per 10 miles, may show public campgrounds, points of interest, and county roads, whereas a state map in an atlas with a smaller scale of 1 inch per 60 miles may show only major highways and major cities. This difference in detail is a function of the scale of the map.

Longitude and Latitude, Coordinates, and Degrees

Around the center of Earth is an imaginary line called the Equator. It is 0° latitude and is located halfway between the North and South Pole. The Equator divides Earth into Northern and Southern Hemispheres.

Imaginary lines that run parallel to the Equator are called parallels of latitude, or parallels. Latitude is measured north and south of the Equator. The North and South Poles are at 90° N and 90° S, respectively. Any area between the Equator and the North or South Pole is some measurement from 0° to 90° north or south.

The dividing lines for the Eastern and Western Hemispheres are the Prime Meridian (also called the Greenwich meridian) and the 180th meridian. These two imaginary lines are on opposite sides of Earth. The Prime Meridian refers to 0° longitude, an imaginary line that runs from the North Pole to the South Pole going through the Royal Observatory in Greenwich, a suburb of London, England. The International Date Line also runs from the North Pole to the South Pole, generally following the 180th meridian. (It deviates in a few places to avoid dividing Siberia and again to include the Aleutian Islands with Alaska.)

Imaginary lines that measure longitude are called meridians of longitude, or meridians. Longitude is measured east and west from the Prime Meridian, or 0°, at Greenwich, England. The International Date Line marks the difference in time between east and west. When crossing the International Date Line going west, a traveler moves forward to the next day (Tuesday becomes Wednesday). When going east, a traveler goes back one day (Wednesday becomes Tuesday).

Meridians of longitude are not parallel because Earth is a sphere. The widest distance between lines measuring degrees of longitude is at the Equator, and they converge as they approach the poles. You can see this clearly on a globe.

Parallels and meridians intersect on maps and globes in a grid pattern. To find a location on the grid, a person needs to know the coordinates of the location, that is, the point where the latitude and longitude intersect. For example, Washington, D.C., lies at 38°53' N latitude and 77°2' W longitude. If we wanted to say these coordinates out loud, we would say "thirty-eight degrees and

Teaching Idea

To help students see that different maps are useful for different purposes, build a collection of maps of a particular area. (The area could be your own community or one of the countries studied in this grade.) Look for maps with dramatically different scales. Introduce each map and describe its scale. Then ask students which map they would use to locate various things or perform various tasks.

Teaching Idea

On a world map locate countries studied in earlier grades and/or countries being studied in this grade. Using map scale, measure the distance between countries. Students can write word problems comparing distances.

Teaching Idea

Compare the degree symbol used in latitude and longitude and the degree symbol used for temperature. Discuss similarities and differences in their use. (They both show degrees—one shows temperature and one shows locations.)

globe showing latitude and longitude

Teaching Idea

Give students coordinates to locate on the map. After this becomes effortless, ask them questions such as "What city is located near X coordinate, Y coordinate?" Or you might ask them to estimate the coordinates of cities in the United States.

You can play a game called "Wet/Dry." Give students a coordinate and ask them to determine if they would be wet or dry if they were at that coordinate (i.e., would they be on land or in the water).

You can also play "Hot/Cold": have them find a coordinate and say whether they would be hot or cold at that location. This will reinforce the connections between latitude and climate.

You can also play "Twenty Questions." Choose a coordinate and invite students to try to determine where you are by asking questions, e.g., "Is it north of the Equator?" and "Is it west of the Prime Meridian?"

fifty-three minutes north latitude, and seventy-seven degrees and two minutes west longitude." The first set of numbers specifies a latitude north of the Equator, and the second specifies a longitude west of the Prime Meridian. Although the *Sequence* only stipulates that students learn about degrees, you may want to mention minutes as well, since this will enable them to locate places more exactly.

Students need to practice finding coordinates on maps. One way to do this is to have them work with maps of countries you are studying in this grade (e.g., England, Russia, and Japan). Also, activities such as those suggested in the sidebar will help students become familiar with the geographical terms and concepts they are learning.

▶ Tropic of Cancer and Tropic of Capricorn

The area between the Tropic of Cancer (23.5° N latitude) and the Tropic of Capricorn (23.5° S latitude) is known as "the tropics" or "low latitudes." It has the warmest climate on Earth. The Tropic of Cancer is a parallel that measures 23.5° N (or 23°27' N) and runs through Mexico, the Bahamas, Egypt, Saudi Arabia, India, and southern China. The Tropic of Capricorn measures 23.5° S (or 23°27' S), and runs through Australia, Chile, southern Brazil, and northern South Africa. The tropics were so-named because of the particular constellations that the sun was in at the time of their respective solstices, or the time when the sun is the farthest north or south of the Equator. At the time, the sun appeared directly over the Tropic of Cancer during the Northern Hemisphere's summer solstice and directly over the Tropic of Capricorn during the Southern Hemisphere's summer solstice.

Earth rotates on its own axis and at the same time, it revolves around the sun. Earth is tilted at an angle of 23.5°, which means that all locations on Earth do not receive the same amount of direct sunlight. The areas close to the Equator receive the most direct sunlight and, therefore, have the hottest average temperatures year round. As a result, the tropics have no sharply defined seasons. The North and South Poles, the areas farthest away from the Equator—and farthest from the sun— have extreme cold temperatures year round. The polar regions have two defined seasons. Because of the tilt of Earth, polar areas—and the high latitudes in general—have 24 hours of sunlight in the summer and 24 hours of darkness in the winter. The farther a place is from the Equator, the more pronounced the differences will be between summer and winter in terms of length of the days and nights.

Climate Zones: Arctic, Tropical, Temperate

There are three main categories of climate—arctic (also known as polar), tropical, and temperate.

• The arctic climate is often referred to as the polar climate by geographers because the term *polar* makes it clear that the climate includes both the Arctic and Antarctic areas. Polar climates have cool to cold summers and cold to very cold winters. Temperatures average below 32°F year-round on the Antarctic and Greenland ice caps, and drop to well below 0°F during the long, dark winter months. Precipitation is scant, averaging only a few inches each year, and most of it falls in the form of snow. A band of subpolar climate stretches across northern North America and Eurasia. Here, one gets short summers with average temperatures above freezing for two or three months; then the temperature plunges below freezing throughout the remainder of the year. Most of this region receives between 5 and 10 inches of precipitation, with some areas receiving up to 20 inches. Snowfall can occur during any month.

Teaching Idea

Note that latitude is not the only indicator of climate. Elevation and location in relation to landforms and bodies of water, prevailing winds, currents and other phenomena also contribute to climate patterns.

• Tropical climate includes some belts of climate with hot, wet weather year-round and some with hot weather that is dry part of the year and wet part of the year. Areas with wet weather all year are typically rainforests. Rainforests can receive as much as 400 inches of rain annually. Hot areas with alternating wet and dry patterns are savannas, or plains with tall grasses. Savannas receive about 50 inches of precipitation a year. Temperatures average above 68°F throughout the year in the tropics. Tropical rainforests thrive around the Equator in Africa and in South America, Southeast Asia, Indonesia, Borneo, and New Guinea. A large belt of savanna exists north and south of the rainforests in Africa.

• Temperate zones of climate are found in the middle latitudes, between the tropics and the polar areas. In general, temperate climates are characterized by warm to hot summers and cool to cold winters, with variations depending on latitude. Throughout much of these regions, temperatures can rise above 100°F in the summer and drop well below freezing in the winter. The temperate zones experience dramatic changes in seasons, with pronounced periods of spring and fall. Precipitation varies from a few inches in the midlatitude desert regions to more than 100 inches in some areas. Snowfall occurs during winter months in many temperate zone locations. These are regions of considerable variability in both weather and climate. The northeastern and north United States, western Europe, and eastern Asia have temperate climates.

Time Zones

Time zones were developed to bring uniformity to the hours of the day as the sun moves from east to west. Time zones generally follow the rule of one time zone for every 15° of longitude (360° of longitude divided by 15 equals 24 time zones, which correspond with the 24 hours of the day). However, the lines dividing time zones are not perfectly straight. Sometimes they zigzag to avoid dividing countries, states, or metropolitan areas.

To understand why time zones are important, consider this. Imagine there are three cities, City A, City B, and City C. City B is 100 or so miles west of City A, and City C is 100 miles west of City B.

CITY C   CITY B   CITY A

The sun rises first in the easternmost city, which is City A. In actuality, of course, the sun is not "rising"; rather, Earth is rotating. But from our position on Earth, it looks as if the sun is rising. After some time passes and the planet rotates a little more, the sun will rise in City B. Then, after a little more time and a bit more rotation, the sun will come up in City C. If each city based its time completely on its position relative to the sun, then the time would be slightly different in each city, and this could be very confusing. It might be 8:20 in City C, 8:10 in City B, and 8:00 in City C. And if you were on a train halfway between City B and City C, it would be 8:05. To avoid this kind of confusion, people have agreed to divide the globe into 24 time zones, each one hour apart. If City A, City B, and City C are all in the same time zone, this means that the people in these locations have agreed to refer to a particular moment in time as 8:00 AM, even though the actual "solar time" may be a few minutes earlier than that in one of the cities and a few minutes later in another.

As noted earlier, longitude is measured east and west from the Prime Meridian, or 0°, located at Greenwich, England. The 180° line is in the Pacific Ocean; it is

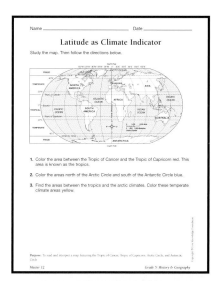

Use Instructional Master 12.

called the International Date Line. The International Date Line marks the difference in time between east and west. (The International Date Line actually zigs and zags from north to south to avoid running directly through settled islands.) When crossing the International Date Line going west, a traveler moves forward to the next day (Tuesday becomes Wednesday). When going east, a traveler goes back one day (Wednesday becomes Tuesday). The International Date Line is a hard concept to explain. At this age it is sufficient that students know the date line exists and understand that it is related to time zones and to the rotation of Earth. They do not need to understand exactly why the IDL was created.

Arctic Circle and Antarctic Circle

The Arctic Circle and the Antarctic Circle are imaginary lines that are drawn around Earth near the North and South Poles. The Arctic Circle is at 66.5° N (or 66°33' N) latitude and the Antarctic Circle is at 66.5° S (or 66°33' S) latitude. The North Pole is within the Arctic Circle; the South Pole is within the Antarctic Circle.

Earth tilts slightly on its axis. As it makes its 365-day orbit around the sun, this tilt causes first the Northern Hemisphere and then the Southern Hemisphere to be tilted toward the sun for a period of months. When this occurs, the polar area of the hemisphere—either the Arctic Circle or the Antarctic Circle—has six months of daylight for 24 hours a day. When the hemisphere is tilted away from the sun, the polar area has 24 hours of darkness per day. This effect lessens further from the poles, with the Arctic and Antarctic Circles experiencing just one day of complete light and dark per year. The circle marks the boundary of 24-hour day or 24-hour night, depending on what time of the year it is in the hemisphere. For the Southern Hemisphere, 24-hour daylight within the Antarctic Circle—and summer—begins on December 22. For the Northern Hemisphere, December 22 marks the beginning of 24-hour night and winter within the Arctic Circle.

From a Round Globe to a Flat Map

Although globes are more accurate models of Earth than flat maps, you can't fold a globe up and take it with you on a trip. Maps—pictorial representations of the location of various places—are a way to make the information on a globe portable.

If Earth were flat, it would be easy to make a map of it on a flat sheet of paper. But Earth is a sphere. This poses certain difficulties for mapmakers and cartographers.

Whenever you transfer information about a spherical planet onto a flat piece of paper, there will be a certain amount of distortion. The act of transferring information from a globe to a flat map is called projection. There are various ways of projecting information from a globe onto a flat page. Each way distorts the original information in a distinctive way.

To understand how projection works, take a long, blank sheet of paper and wrap it around a globe in such a way that the paper touches the globe at the Equator but not at the poles. Now imagine that the globe is made of transparent plastic with the continents and other features drawn on the plastic in a darker color. Also imagine that this transparent globe has a light bulb in the center. If the light bulb were turned on, the light would shine through the transparent orb and the marked parts would cast shadows on the paper. You could trace the shapes cast by the shadows and then unroll the paper to make a rectangular map. In the places where the paper sits right next to the globe, the sizes and shapes of the

Teaching Idea

You may wish to review relief maps with students. Those in Core Knowledge schools studied relief maps in Grade 4.

continents and oceans on your map would be very accurate. However, in those areas where the paper is a long way from the globe, there would be distortion. Thus, the areas around the Equator will be rendered very accurately and the areas near the poles will be distorted and rendered less accurately.

Mercator Projection

In 1569, the cartographer Gerardus Mercator developed a projection scheme that is still widely used today. Mercator projected the globe's features onto a cylinder, in roughly the way described above. The Mercator projection is accurate for the tropics but distorts the areas near the poles (such as Alaska and Greenland), making them look much larger on the resulting map than they are. The shapes of the landmasses are accurate but the sizes and distances between areas are not. Direction, however, is accurate, which is what Europeans moving east and west between Europe and the Americas during the Age of Exploration wanted to know.

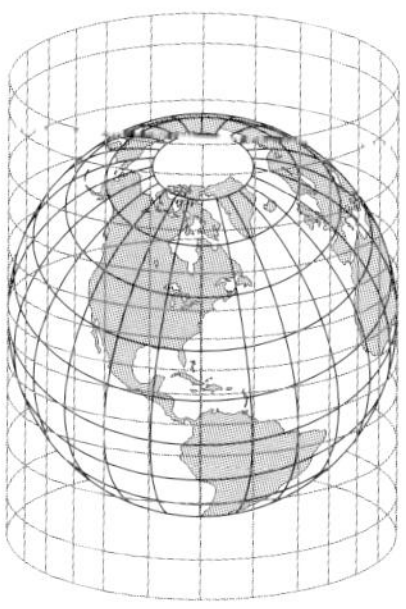

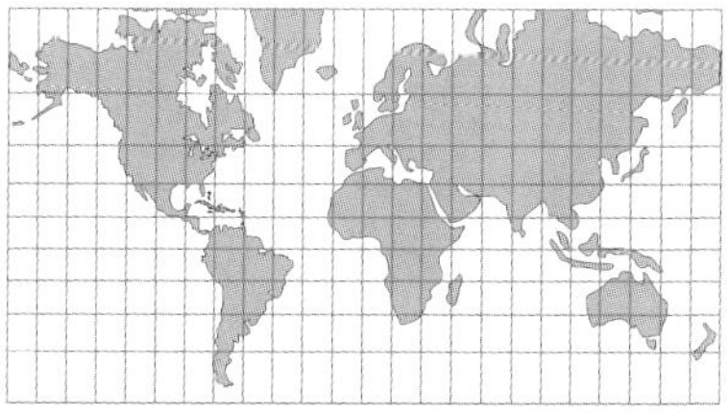

Conic Projection

In a conic projection, a piece of paper is twisted into a cone and placed over the globe so that the circular "top" of the cone touches the globe. Features on the globe are then projected onto the paper. The resulting map is reproduced as a rectangular map with curved parallels and meridians. This is different than the Mercator projection, which has straight lines. A map made using conic projection is most accurate for the areas on the globe that touch the cone. Conic maps are not good for showing large areas, like the whole globe. However, they are good for showing smaller areas, especially smaller areas in the middle latitudes. Direction and distance are also relatively accurate.

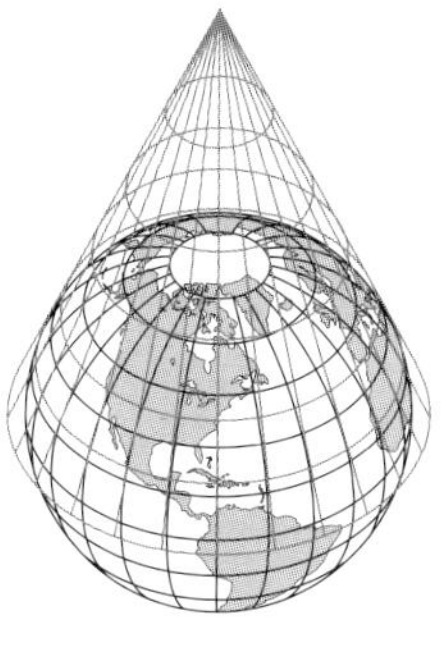

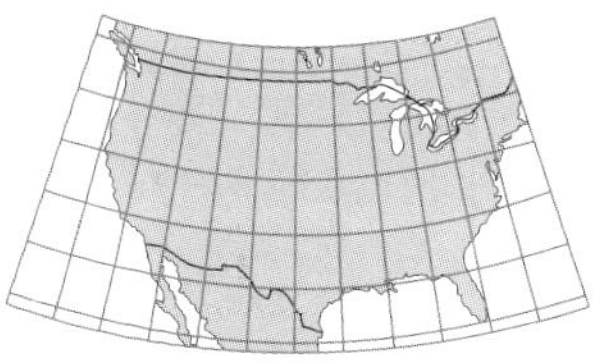

Plane Projection

In a plane projection a flat sheet of paper is placed against the side of globe so that it touches the globe at one point only. (Recall that in a Mercator projection the paper was wrapped around the globe to make a cylinder and made contact with the globe all along the Equator.) Plane projection produces a map that

Teaching Idea

Create an overhead from Instructional Master 13, *Three Different Map Projections*, to illustrate the differences among the Mercator, conic, and Robinson projections.

As you explain the distortions, have students point them out by identifying the continents and oceans where the differences are apparent.

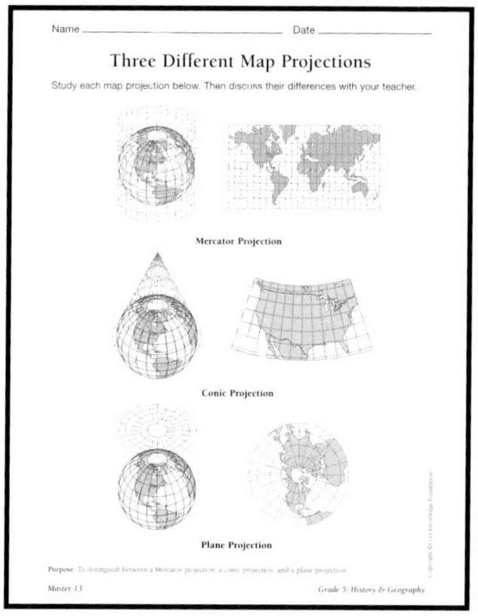

Name ______ Date ______

Three Different Map Projections

Study each map projection below. Then discuss their differences with your teacher.

Mercator Projection

Conic Projection

Plane Projection

Master 13 — Grade 5: History & Geography

Use Instructional Master 13.

I. World Geography

Teaching Idea

Note that the convention of north at the top of maps came about because navigators used a magnetic compass to determine direction. In Grade 4, students in Core Knowledge schools learned about the invention of the compass by the Chinese. Point out compass roses on a variety of maps.

is accurate at the point where it touches, but is less accurate as you move away from the point of contact. The plane projection is also called the azimuthal [AZ-em-MUTH-al] projection. A common form of this projection is a polar projection, in which the North or South Pole is used as the central point of contact.

 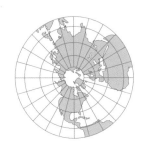

Robinson Projection

The Robinson projection is the most commonly used representation in textbooks. It is called a "compromise projection" because it tries to strike a compromise between some of the other kinds of projection. The goal is to minimize the limitations and distortions inherent in the other schemes while capturing their strengths. In a Robinson projection, the shape and size of continents is somewhat distorted, but less so than with the Mercator projection. The areas around the poles appear somewhat flatter than they are on a globe, but the areas at the eastern and western edges of the projection are fairly accurate. As is the case with conic projections, the parallels and meridians on the resulting map are curved.

B. Great Lakes of the World

Background

A lake is a large inland body of water. A river may feed into a lake and a river may flow out of it. The Great Rift Valley of East Africa has several lakes and rivers running through it. There are lakes on most continents and most of them contain fresh water. Lakes are often important sources of water for irrigation and hydroelectric power, as well as transportation and recreation.

Asia: Caspian Sea and Aral Sea

The Caspian Sea actually lies between Europe and Asia, in the area known as Eurasia. The Caspian borders the countries of Russia, Kazakhstan, Turkmenistan, Iran, and Azerbaijan. It is the world's largest inland sea, spanning 143,000 square miles (370,368 sq. km), and has no natural outlets to the ocean; a canal links the Caspian Sea to the Black Sea. The sea lies 92 feet (28 m) below sea level and is fed by rivers such as the Volga. In recent years, the sea has been shrinking because water is being drawn off the rivers that feed it for use in irrigation. The Caspian Sea is used for fishing, especially in the northern regions, and is an important source of oil and natural gas.

The Aral Sea is bordered by Uzbekistan to the south and Kazakhstan to the north. The Aral Sea was once the world's fourth-largest lake. However, in recent years, it, too, has been shrinking due to diversion of the rivers that feed it to irrigate fields devoted to cotton production. In fact, it has shrunk by more than 40% since the 1960s. This has caused the water in the sea to become highly saline,

---

Name _____ **Date** _____

Great Lakes of the World

Fill in the chart with information about the great lakes of the world.

Name	Lake Superior	Lake Michigan	Lake Huron	Lake Ontario	Lake Erie	Lake Titicaca
Location						
Latitude/ Longitude						
Elevation						
Approximate Surface Area						
Saltwater or Freshwater						
Characteristics						

Master 14a   *Grade 5: History & Geography*

Use Instructional Masters 14a–14b.

Teaching Idea

Before introducing the lakes on each continent, take stock of what students already know about each continent. For example, before talking about Asian lakes, discuss what students already know about Asia.

killing large numbers of fish. The area around the sea is also heavily polluted and the population suffers from high rates of cancer, tuberculosis, and other infectious diseases. The Aral Sea is a good example of how human behavior can cause profound changes in nature. It can be taught as a cautionary tale.

Africa: Victoria, Tanganyika, and Chad

Lake Victoria is the second-largest freshwater lake in the world, second only to Lake Superior in North America. Victoria is the largest lake on the African continent at 26,828 square miles (69,484 sq. km). It borders Tanzania, Uganda, and Kenya in eastern central Africa. It is also known as Victoria Nyanza, its Bantu name. The lake was named after Queen Victoria of Britain by British explorer John Hanning Speke, the first European to reach it. It is the chief source of the Nile River and is in a depression between the Eastern and Western Rift Valleys in East Africa. The lake contains more than 200 species of fish. The completion of the Owens Falls Dam on the Nile raised the level of Lake Victoria and is an important source of hydroelectric power.

Lake Tanganyika [tan-gan-YEEK-ah] is the second-largest freshwater lake on the African continent and is the longest (420 miles or 676 km) and second-deepest (4,700 feet or 1,433 m) lake in the world. It borders Tanzania, the Democratic Republic of the Congo (formerly Zaire), and Burundi. It is also part of the Great Rift Valley system in East Africa. Farmers grow rice and other crops along the shores of the lake. Animals who live around the lake include hippopotamuses and crocodiles.

Lake Chad is a shallow freshwater lake that borders the countries of Chad, Nigeria, Cameroon, and Niger. It has no outlets and is sometimes referred to as a "drowned prairie" because it is extremely shallow, with a large number of islands covered in grasses dotting its surface. In fact, Lake Chad is so shallow that it is in danger of drying up completely! Fishing is an important industry on Lake Chad, and a number of significant archeological discoveries have been made in the surrounding area.

North America: The Great Lakes

Lake Superior is bordered by Canada to the north and east, and the states of Minnesota to the west and Wisconsin and Michigan to the south. It is the largest body of freshwater in the world, with a surface area of 31,700 square miles (82,103 sq. km), and is the largest of the North American Great Lakes. Some 200 rivers drain into the lake and it is a part of the St. Lawrence and Great Lakes Waterway. As such, it is a major transportation route. However, some parts freeze in winter, which limits its transportation season to about eight months. The shores around the lake are sparsely populated and as a result, it is the least polluted of the Great Lakes. The lake is a popular recreation and fishing area. However, the introduction of foreign species, particularly the sea lamprey, as a result of the ships that travel the lake, resulted in a serious decline in native fish populations. Scientists are now attempting to control the growth of foreign fish populations with chemicals that will not affect native species. Henry Wadsworth Longfellow's famous poem "The Song of Hiawatha" begins: "By the shore of Gitche Gumee, / By the shining Big-Sea-Water, / At the doorway of his wigwam, / In the pleasant Summer morning, / Hiawatha stood and waited." The name Gitchee Gumee was derived from a Native American name for the lake, which means something like "big water." (33)

Teaching Idea

Duplicate and distribute one copy to each student of Instructional Masters 15 and 16, *Great Lakes of the Eastern Hemisphere* and *Great Lakes of the Western Hemisphere*. Describe the location of each lake and have students label the correct lake on the map. Then have students, drawing on knowledge from earlier grades and new research, draw and label other important physical features on their maps:

1. important mountain range(s) on each continent
2. highest mountain on each continent
3. important rivers

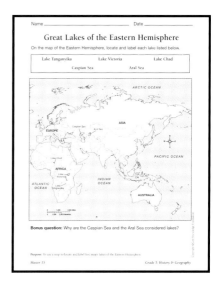

Use Instructional Master 15.

I. World Geography

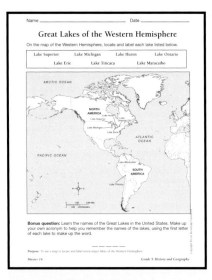

Use Instructional Master 16.

Lake Huron is the second-largest North American Great Lake (23,000 square miles or 59,570 sq. km) and is bordered by Canada to the north and east and the state of Michigan to the south and west. It is also part of the St. Lawrence and Great Lakes Waterway and is connected on its western side to Lake Superior by the St. Mary's River and the Soo Canals, and to Lake Michigan by the Strait of Mackinac. Fishing and lumbering are important economic activities, and the lake is used extensively for commercial transportation. However, as with Lake Superior, areas often freeze in the winter, limiting the shipping season to about eight months.

Lake Michigan is the third-largest Great Lake and the largest freshwater lake located entirely within the United States. The lake covers about 22,300 square miles (57,757 sq. km) and is bordered by Michigan to the north and east, Wisconsin to the west, Illinois to the southwest, and Indiana to the southeast. It is part of the St. Lawrence and Great Lakes Waterway, and the Chicago River links the lake to the Mississippi River and, via the river, the Gulf of Mexico. Chicago and Milwaukee are important ports.

Although the *Sequence* only lists Superior, Huron, and Michigan, you may also wish to teach the other two Great Lakes. They are briefly described below.

Lake Erie is the fourth-largest of the five Great Lakes. It is named for Erie Indians who once lived along its shores. Lake Erie forms the boundary between Canada and the United States (specifically, the states of Michigan, Ohio, Pennsylvania, and New York). It covers 9,910 square miles (25,667 sq. km). The lake lets out at its eastern end through the Niagara River. The water descends at Niagara Falls as part of its journey from Lake Erie to Lake Ontario. During the War of 1812, U.S. commodore Oliver H. Perry defeated a British squadron on Lake Erie and secured the Northwest for the United States. The Erie Canal, which students study in American history for this grade, connects Lake Erie with the Hudson River and the Atlantic Ocean. Today the steel industry depends upon the movement of iron ore and limestone across the Great Lakes to ports on Lake Erie, including Cleveland. The lake became badly polluted in the 1960s but has since improved.

Lake Ontario is the smallest of the Great Lakes. It covers 7,550 square miles (19,554 sq. km) and is fed by water from the Niagara River. The lake was explored by the French but came into British control after the French and Indian War. The name Ontario comes from an Iroquois word meaning either "beautiful lake" or "sparkling water." The climate along the lake's shores is appropriate for fruit growing and the region is a major producer of apples, pears, plums, peaches, and cherries.

South America: Maracaibo and Titicaca

Lake Maracaibo [mare-uh-KAI-bow] is a large body of water in South America and is located in Venezuela. Experts disagree on whether Maracaibo should be considered a sea or a lake because of its connection via a strait to the Gulf of Venezuela on the Caribbean Sea. The water in the southern portion of the lake is fresh, but the part of the lake closer to the ocean is brackish.

The lake contains rich oilfields and is suffering from pollution from oil spills. Fishing is another major industry. A large portion (approximately 12%) of the lake's surface is now covered with a plant called duckweed. Despite efforts by the government to eradicate the weed, it reproduces so rapidly that the cleanup can barely keep pace with the new growth. Although the plant doesn't appear to harm marine life in the lake, it may become a hazard to fishing boats and other vessels that use the lake for transportation.

Lake Titicaca [tee-tee-KAH-kah] is bordered by Peru and Bolivia. It is the largest freshwater lake in South America, and, if Maracaibo is considered a sea, it is the largest lake in South America. Located in the Andes Mountains, it is the world's highest large lake and is an important transportation route between Peru and Bolivia. Located more than 2.37 miles (3.8 km) above sea level, Lake Titicaca is the highest navigable lake in the world. Powered boats steam across the lake carrying passengers and freight. But Lake Titicaca is also home to ancient boats made of reeds by indigenous people called the Uru who predate the Inca. The Uru live in marshlands on platforms also made of reeds they harvest from the lake.

Teaching Idea

Connect Lake Titicaca with students' study of the ancient Inca civilization, a topic introduced in Grade 1 and taught in more depth in this grade.

Review

Below are some ideas for ongoing assessment and review activities. These are not meant to constitute a comprehensive list. Teachers may also refer to the *Pearson Learning/Core Knowledge History & Geography* series for additional information and teaching ideas.

- Assign each student (or pairs or groups of students) a country to study. You can also allow students to select countries that interest them as long as the countries they select represent a variety of continents. As you discuss each geographical concept, have students conduct research to find out how that concept applies to their country. As a starting point, students may use world almanacs to research longitude and latitude information. The CIA website (see *More Resources*) provides the latest maps of the world, along with brief facts and statistics about each region, including populations, languages spoken, and other categories of interest. Students can print out political maps of their countries. After students have completed the subsection "Great Lakes of the World," ask them to label the lakes on a map of their country, if applicable. Students can also conduct research to find other lakes in their country, and then compare the size of the lakes. (This is an excellent math connection.) Have students share their findings, and compare and contrast similarities and differences among the countries. All work can be kept in a "My Country" folder or journal. Also look for opportunities to review geography and map concepts as you study the history topics for this grade, e.g., share maps of Europe during your study of the Renaissance.

- As a culmination of this unit of study, have students write an essay based on the big idea for this section. Post the topic on the board: "Describe in essay form how maps and globes are used to show location and other aspects of human and physical geography." Have students justify their answer with facts learned in this unit of study.

- Have students select one of the climate zones that they found interesting in this unit. Then, have students create a report that would describe a typical day living in that area. For example, they can include what animals live there, what the temperature might be at a certain time of the year, or what you might wear if you are going out on a certain day. Then, have students complete an illustration to include with their report. Share these with the class.

The Big Idea in Review

Maps and globes are used to show location and other aspects of human and physical geography.

• Have students select one of the lakes from this unit and write a report on that lake using at least three outside sources. Remind students about the procedures for using and citing outside sources. Share these aloud.

• Post laminated enlargements of each lake on the wall and have students come forward to share something that they have learned from this unit about one of the lakes. As they come forward, have them share their fact aloud and then write it on the laminated lake with dry erase markers. Share these with another Grade 5 class.

• Make a set of index cards that includes the names and descriptions of the geographical places from this unit. In a center or as a review activity, have pairs of students quiz each other on the location and description of each place. As an extension, you may have students create and share crossword puzzles containing names of places from this section.

• Hang maps on the walls and quiz students on the location of the various lakes that have been studied. Mix in other geographic features they have learned about during their studies as well (e.g., Andes Mountains after studying the Inca civilization).

• You may also ask the following questions after completion of this unit of study.

1. Give the coordinates in degrees of the closest parallel and meridian for your town.
   Answers will vary.

2. What does latitude measure?
   Latitude measures location north or south of the Equator.

3. What does longitude measure?
   Longitude measures location east or west of the Prime Meridian.

4. Locate the Tropic of Cancer and the Tropic of Capricorn on the map.
   Students should indicate the parallel 23.5° N as the Tropic of Cancer and the parallel 23.5° S as the Tropic of Capricorn.

5. Is the North Pole in the Arctic Circle or the Antarctic Circle?
   It's in the Arctic Circle.

6. What would be the typical weather for a day in the tropics?
   The weather on a typical day would be hot and rainy.

7. What are the typical temperature and precipitation patterns in each of the following climate zones: (a) arctic, (b) tropical, and (c) temperate?
   (a) The arctic or polar climate is generally cold and dry. (b) The tropics are generally hot and rainy. (c) The temperate zone has more variation in temperature and precipitation. In general, the winters and summers are milder than in the other climate zones and the precipitation falls as rain and snow.

8. What is the function of the International Date Line?
   The International Date Line marks the shift from one day to the next going east to west, and from one day to the previous going west to east.

9. If it is winter in the Northern Hemisphere, is it 24 hours of day or night within the Antarctic Circle?
   It is 24 hours of day within the Antarctic Circle.

10. Explain why a Mercator projection map would not be very helpful to an Arctic explorer.

Students should identify that the drawback of a Mercator projection is that it distorts the true size of both polar regions.

11. On what continent is Lake Victoria located? Lake Titicaca? Lake Chad?

Lake Victoria is in Africa; Lake Titicaca is in South America; and Lake Chad is in Africa.

More Resources

The titles listed below are offered as a representative sample of materials and not a complete list of everything that is available.

For students —

• *World Lakes,* edited by E. D. Hirsch, Jr. (Pearson Learning, 2002), a unit in the official *Pearson Learning/Core Knowledge History & Geography* series, is available as part of the bound book for Grade 5/Level 5. A teacher's guide is also available. To order, call 1-800-321-3106.

• *Lake Michigan* (*A True Book*), by Ann Armbruster (Children's Press, 1996). Paperback, 48 pages, ISBN 0516261037. Part of a series on the Great Lakes and the St. Lawrence Seaway.

• *Mapping the World,* by Sylvia A. Johnson (Atheneum, 1999). A history of mapmaking. Hardcover, 32 pages, ISBN 0689818130.

• *Paddle-to-the-Sea,* by Holling C. Holling (Houghton Mifflin, 1980). Originally published more than 60 years ago, this is a classic story of a little boy's homemade toy canoe as it journeys along a melting stream through the Great Lakes and out into the Atlantic. Paperback, 64 pages, ISBN 0395292034. Holling's other geography-focused titles include *Minn of the Mississippi, Tree in the Trail,* and *Seabird.*

For teachers —

• *Goode's World Atlas 20th Edition,* edited by John C. Hudson (Rand McNally & Company, 1999). Long a standard reference in classroom libraries. Hardcover, 384 pages, ISBN 0528843362.

• The National Geographic Society, www.national geographic.com/education. Multifeatured website includes a map machine, printable maps, and online adventures, to name a few.

• Nystrom, www.nystromnet.com or 1-800-621-8086, and Rand McNally, www.k12online.com or 1-800-678-7263, both offer a variety of maps and other geography teaching aids. One advantage of choosing a single company from which to purchase maps is that classroom wall maps and student maps will correspond, helping to eliminate confusion over scale, perspective, etc.

• TerraServer, at http://terraserver-usa.com, may be one of the most useful online tools to help students see the relationship between their own home and a topographical map. Zoom in to see aerial or topographic maps of the continental United States up to a resolution of two meters. You can also purchase inexpensive topographical maps from the United States Geological Survey.

• The United States Geological Survey, www.usgs.gov. From the homepage, click on the link for "Students and Teachers" to view a wide range of resources. There is also a comprehensive glossary of terms on this site. To reach it from the "Students and Teachers" page, scroll to the bottom of the column labeled "Explorers" and click on the picture labeled "Glossary," or type in the address http://interactive2.usgs.gov/learningweb/explorer/geoglossary.htm

• The World Factbook, www.cia.gov/cia/publications/factbook, has regularly updated maps and general information about the countries of the world.

The Big Idea

The Maya, Aztec, and Inca had developed large, complex civilizations prior to the arrival of the Spanish.

Remember that each subject you study with students expands their vocabulary and introduces new terms, thus making them better listeners and readers. As you study early civilizations of America, use map work, read alouds, independent reading, and discussions to build students' vocabularies.

The items below refer to content in Grade 5. Use time lines with students to help them sequence and relate events from different periods and groups.

c. 1500 BCE	Earliest known Maya culture
c. 300–900 CE	Peak of Maya civilization
c. 1300s	Beginning of Aztec Empire
c. 1300s	Beginning of Inca Empire
1400s	First cargo of Africans as slaves imported by Portuguese to their colonies
1492	Columbus's first voyage to the Americas
1496	Santo Domingo on Hispaniola founded as first permanent Spanish settlement in Americas
1500s	First cargo of Africans as slaves imported by Spanish to Hispaniola
1513	Balboa discovers the Pacific Ocean

continued on next page

What Students Should Already Know

Students using Core Knowledge should be familiar with

Kindergarten

▸ the voyage of Columbus in 1492
  • Queen Isabella and King Ferdinand of Spain
  • the Niña, Pinta, and Santa Maria
  • Columbus's mistaken identification of "Indies" and "Indians"
  • the idea of what was, for Europeans, a "New World"

Grade 1

▸ Maya, Aztec, and Inca Civilizations
  • The development by the Maya of large population centers in the rainforests of Mexico and Central America
  • The establishment of a vast empire in central Mexico by the Aztec, its capital of Tenochtitlán, and its emperor Moctezuma (Montezuma)
  • The Inca's establishment of a far-ranging empire in the Andes Mountains of Peru and Chile, including Machu Picchu

▸ Columbus

▸ the conquistadors
  • the search for gold and silver

▸ Hernán Cortés and the Aztec

▸ Francisco Pizarro and the Inca

▸ diseases devastate native American population

Grade 2

▸ geography of South America
  • Brazil: largest country in South America, Amazon River, rainforests
  • Peru and Chile: Andes Mountains
  • Locate: Venezuela, Columbia, Ecuador
  • Bolivia: named after Simon Bolivar, "The Liberator"
  • Argentina: the Pampa (also known as the Pampas)
  • Main languages: Spanish and (in Brazil) Portuguese

continued from previous page

1517	Luther initiates Protestant Reformation
1517	Ponce De Leon lands in Florida
1519–22	Magellan circumnavigates the globe
1521	Conquest of the Aztec by Cortés
1531	Conquest of the Inca by Pizarro
1534	Cartier of France explores the St. Lawrence River
1535	Most of central Mexico in Spanish hands
1539–42	De Soto explores North America
1540	Most of Peru under Spanish control
1545–1565	Major silver discoveries in Mexico and Peru
c. 1570	End of era of conquistadors

Text Resources

(34) from *Cortés's Second Letter to Charles V*

(35) *History of the Conquest of Peru*

(36) *Pestilence Strikes*

What Students Need to Learn

▸ Identify and locate Central America and South America on maps and globes
  • Largest countries in South America: Brazil and Argentina
▸ Amazon River
▸ Andes Mountains
▸ The Maya
  • Ancient Maya lived in what is now southern Mexico and parts of Central America; their descendants still live there today.
  • accomplishments as architects and artisans: pyramids and temples
  • development of a system of hieroglyphic writing
  • knowledge of astronomy and mathematics; development of a 365-day calendar; early use of concept of zero
▸ The Aztec
  • A warrior culture, at its height in the 1400s and early 1500s, the Aztec empire covered much of what is now central Mexico.
  • the island city of Tenochtitlán: aqueducts, massive temples, etc.
  • Moctezuma (also spelled Montezuma)
  • ruler-priests; practice of human sacrifice
▸ The Inca
  • ruled an empire stretching along the Pacific coast of South America
  • built great cities (Machu Picchu, Cuzco) high in the Andes, connected by a system of roads
▸ Conquistadors: Cortés and Pizarro
  • advantages of Spanish weaponry (guns and cannons)
  • devastation of native peoples by European diseases

Vocabulary

Student/Teacher Vocabulary

Amazon River: river in South America; the second-longest river in the world (S)

Andes Mountains: a mountain range that runs from north to south along the western coast of South America (S)

Aztec: a warrior culture that dominated central and southern Mexico through force and a tribute system (S)

conquistador: Spanish for *conqueror*, refers particularly to sixteenth-century Spanish explorers who sought to conquer native peoples in Mexico, Central America, and Peru (S)

Hernán Cortés: Spanish conquistador who conquered the Aztec people (S)

hieroglyphs: an ancient system of writing in which pictorial symbols represent words or sounds (S)

Materials

Instructional Masters 17–18, 83

Create a Codex, p. 129

The Civilizations of the Maya, Aztec, and Inca, p. 130

Venn Diagram, p. 135

cardboard, p. 126

self-hardening clay, p. 126

paints, p. 126

pictures of Maya ruins, p. 127

pennies, p. 133

large pieces of white paper for making coloring books, p. 136

materials for a culminating day, including activities for math and physical education, p. 136

Vocabulary continued

Inca: a native people of Peru, established an empire prior to Spanish conquest (S)

isthmus: a narrow strip of land connecting two larger areas of land (S)

Maya: a native people who occupied much of the Yucatán Peninsula in southern Mexico, most of Guatemala, and parts of El Salvador and Honduras (S)

pyramid: massive monument having a rectangular base and four triangular faces culminating in a single apex (S)

temple: building that serves as a site for religious practice (S)

Domain Vocabulary

Geography of Central and South America and associated words:
Caribbean Sea, Pacific Ocean, land bridge, continent, Atlantic Ocean, Pacific Ocean, peak, range, rainforest, tropical, largest, population, square miles, trees, cut, climate, urban, coastal plain, Native Americans, Spanish, Portuguese, language, slaves, grasslands; plateau, pampas, temperate, cattle ranch, river, delta, tributary, navigable, Altiplano, lowlands, fertile, manufacturing, agriculture, Tierra del Fuego, Costa Rica, El Salvador, Guatemala, Honduras, Nicaragua, Panama, Brazil, Venezuela, Argentina, *plus the names of other countries in South and Central America*

Maya and associated words:
Mexico, Yucatán Peninsula, Gulf of Mexico, Caribbean Sea, Central America, Guatemala, El Salvador, Honduras, rainforest, ceremonial center, worship, ball court, marketplace, terrace, archeologist, speculate, guess, Spanish, hacienda, plaza, abandon, epidemic, drought, soil, Toltec, attack, subjugate, force, jungle, gods, warrior, farmer, farm, village, fields, slash-and-burn agriculture, conquer, rulers, kings, Tikal, Coba, Tulum, Uxmal, Uaxactún, Copán, Palenque, Chichen Itza, astronomy, calendar, eclipse, predict, mathematics, zero, ideograph, symbol, religious, myth, priest, noble, collapse, mystery

Aztec and associated words:
Mexico, valley, nomad, nomadic, empire, warrior, culture, dominate, conquer, capture, tribute, tax, payment, labor, city-state, fear, hatred, ruler, emperor, divine, god, subject, advisor, noble, priest, merchant, war chief; farmer, trader, craftworker, slave, capture, gold, silver, Spanish, conqueror, network, trade goods, agricultural, handicrafts, boats, warriors, religion, polytheism, human sacrifice, blood, prisoners of war, ritual, offerings, deity, war, rival, symbol, represent, meaning, transactions, ritual, history, myth, eagle, serpent, snake, beak, perch, cactus, Tenochtitlán, Mexico City, causeway, aqueduct, bridge, canal, canoe, island, garden, agricultural, city, center, palace, plaza, pyramid, temples, market, legend, Quetzalcoatl

Inca and associated words:
South America, Peru, empire, mountain, population, tribute, tax, resettle, royal family, noble, class, priest, military, officials, servant, farmer, merchant, artisan, road, travel, communicate, network, messenger, memorize, recite, rest house, runner, army, march, leader, god, bridge, pass, valleys, river, gorge, ravine, mountain, elevation, highlands, fibers, law, farming, terrace, mountainside, irrigation, land, cultivation, planting, quipu, counting, quantity, knot, string, Machu Picchu, ceremonial center, palace, fort, temple, stonework, stone, rock, cut, altitude, tourist attraction, Cuzco, Lake Titicaca, capital, fort, palace, temple, Atahualpa, Huascar, civil war, llama, alpaca, potato, Quechua

Conquistadors and associated words:
Caribbean, Mexico, Central America, South America, Indies, conquer, conqueror, gold, silver, mine, fortune, wealth, Spanish, Spaniards, monarchy, colonize, colonial, economy, settle, missionary, convert, Christianity, idol, devil, Virgin Mary, church, force, forced labor, slave, slave trade, enslave, farm, hacienda, encomienda, mission, leader, soldier, treasure, pursuit, attack, defeat, slaughter, horse, gun, cannon, shoot, dog, steel, weapon, Malinche, subject, support, allies, tribute system, cruel, mistreat, march, fighting, battles,

Vocabulary continued

Moctezuma, Coronado, Balboa, De Soto, smoke, fire, horses, prophecy, god, prisoner, rebellion, retreat, go back, siege, besiege, surround, Mexico City, capital, New Spain; kidnap, ransom, downfall, collapse, stronghold, fort, defeat, assassinate, disease, sick, illness, sickness, smallpox, measles, immunity, epidemic, slave trade, viceroy, plunder, mestizo, creole, friar, priest, Dominican, Jesuit, expedition, capture, prisoner, colonize, subdue, brave, greedy, ship, Hispaniola, Cuba

An interesting activity while studying the World History and Geography strand this year would be the creation of a world time line including major events. This time line would help students understand the differences from one culture and civilization to another more easily and thus help them make comparisons and contrasts among civilizations.

At a Glance

The most important ideas for you are:

- Students should be able to locate Mexico, Central America, South America, and the major countries, rivers, and mountain chain in South America on maps and globes.
- Mesoamerica is a cultural area that covers central and southern Mexico as well as northern Central America.
- The Maya people constructed large monumental buildings, created a hieroglyphic writing system, designed a 365-day calendar, and developed the concept of zero.
- The Aztec were a warrior culture that dominated central and southern Mexico through force and a tribute system.
- The Inca developed a widespread empire in the Andes Mountains linked by a network of roads.
- Both the Aztec and the Inca empires were conquered by Spanish conquistadors; the Aztec empire was conquered by Cortés, and the Inca empire was defeated by Pizarro.
- The Spanish had an advantage over native Americans because the former had guns, cannons, and horses.
- European diseases killed thousands of native Americans who had no natural immunity against them.

What Teachers Need to Know

Background

In teaching this section, it is important to discuss with students how we know about these ancient civilizations. Among the factors are archaeological findings, ancient artifacts including writings, and writings by European conquistadors, missionaries, and officials.

A. Geography

Central America is part of North America and contains the countries of Belize, Costa Rica, El Salvador, Guatemala, Honduras, Nicaragua, and Panama. It is bordered by the Caribbean Sea to the east and by the Pacific Ocean to the west. To the south is the continent of South America. Central America is an isthmus, or land bridge, which connects the two larger bodies of land.

South America is the fourth-largest continent. To the east is the Atlantic Ocean and to the west, the Pacific Ocean. The Caribbean Sea borders South America to the north. The Andes Mountains range from north to south on the far western side of South America. The northern portion of the continent, including much of Brazil, is covered by tropical rainforest.

Brazil

Brazil covers almost half of the South American continent and is the fifth-largest country in the world. Brazil is so large that it borders all but two (Chile and Ecuador) of the other 12 countries in South America. The word *Brazil* comes from the name of a tree found in the Amazon rainforest. Brazil lies mostly within the tropical zone, so its climate is mainly warm and wet.

Most of the people live in urban areas and about 30 percent of the population lives on the coastal plain, a narrow strip along the Atlantic Ocean. About 700,000 native Americans live within the rainforest, but many others live in cities and urban areas. The overall population is a mix of descendants of Portuguese, native Americans, and Africans. Brazil was conquered by Portugal, unlike most of South America, which was conquered by the Spanish. Its official language is Portuguese.

Argentina

Argentina is the second-largest country in South America. A long, narrow country, Argentina extends east and south of the Andes and south of Paraguay and Uruguay. The Andes form the boundary between Argentina and Chile. The Gran Chaco, a region of low forests and grasslands, dominates Argentina's northern region. The south is a collection of barren plateaus, known as Patagonia. The major economic area of Argentina is the Pampa (also known as the Pampas) in the center of the country. This region of tall grasslands and temperate climate is famous for its cattle ranches. About 70 percent of the population lives in this area.

Most Argentines are descendants of Spanish colonists and Spanish is the official language.

Amazon River

The Amazon River forms at the junction of the Ucayali [OOH-cah-yah-lee] and Marañón [marn-YEOWN] Rivers in northern Peru and empties into the Atlantic Ocean through a delta in northern Brazil. The Amazon is the second-longest river in the world after the Nile, but has the largest volume of water of any river in the world. Hundreds of tributaries feed into it. The Amazon River Basin drains more than 40 percent of South America. With no waterfalls, the river is navigable almost its entire length.

> **Teaching Idea**
>
> Have students work in pairs to create models of the South American continent. They will need cardboard for a base, self-hardening clay, and paints to create their models. Students should include the Andes Mountains; the Amazon, Paraná, and Orinoco Rivers; the Amazon River Basin; and the Pampa, and label all the countries as well.

The Amazon flows through the world's largest rainforest. This rainforest is home to more than 2.5 million species of insects, tens of thousands of plants, and over 1,000 species of birds. In fact, almost half of all of the world's known species can be found in the Amazon. Curious mammals in the Amazon rainforests include the tapir (a hoofed mammal), the nutria (an otterlike creature), the great anteater, and various kinds of monkeys. Insects include large, colorful butterflies. Birds include hummingbirds, toucans, and parrots. A famous reptile dweller is the anaconda, a huge snake that squeezes its victims to death; alligators are also common. Fish include flesh-eating piranhas and the electric eel, capable of discharging a shock up to 650 volts. In recent years environmentalists have grown concerned about threats to the ecosystem posed by logging and deforestation in this rainforest.

The Amazon was named by a Spanish explorer, Francisco de Orellana, who explored the river in 1541 and named it after women warriors he encountered who reminded him of descriptions of the Amazons in ancient Greek mythology.

Andes Mountains

The Andes Mountains are over 5,000 miles (8,047 km) in length, the longest mountain system in the Western Hemisphere. The mountains begin as four ranges in the Caribbean area on the northeastern coast of South America. In Peru and Bolivia, the mountains form two parallel ranges that create a wide plateau known as the Altiplano. The Andes then form a single range that separates Chile from Argentina.

With an average height of 12,500 feet (3,810 m), the Andes are the second-highest mountain range in the world. (The Himalayas are the highest.) The tallest peak in the Western Hemisphere is the Andes' Mount Aconcagua, which rises 22,834 feet (6,960 m) above sea level. Many of the mountains are volcanoes, either active or dormant.

Approximately 50 to 60 percent of Peru's people live in the Altiplano. About a third of the country's population lives in the narrow lowlands between the Andes and the Pacific Ocean. Because the Andes run north to south along the entire length of Chile, most Chileans live in the Central Valley region between the Andes and low coastal mountains. The Central Valley, a fertile area, is home to large cities, manufacturing centers, and agriculture.

The Andes Mountains were the home of the Inca people, whom students in Core Knowledge schools studied in Grade 1 and will study again as part of this unit. Core Knowledge students should also have learned about Mount Aconcagua and the Andes during the Grade 4 geography subsection "Mountains and Mountain Ranges."

B. Maya, Aztec, and Inca Civilizations

The Maya

The Maya are a native people who settled in the rainforest of the Yucatán Peninsula in southeastern Mexico, Belize, much of Guatemala, and parts of El Salvador and Honduras. The dates of their arrival in the area are disputed, but it is generally agreed that their culture reached its apex around 300–900 CE.

> **Teaching Idea**
> Use a search engine to search for pictures of Maya ruins using keywords from this book. Share these pictures with students.

II. Mesoamerican Civilizations

Teaching Idea

The Maya language used glyphs, or symbols, to represent meaning. For example, the glyphs on this page represent days of the month. The Maya month has 20 days, which were called "kins."

Have students make up glyphs to represent a week's worth of days. Working in pairs, students should come up with a name for day 1 by printing their first names, and then combining 2 letters from each name. They should then repeat the process for day 2, and so on. They may use the same letters more than once but not in the same combination. Then have students draw 7 glyphs to represent the 7 days of the week. The glyphs should represent the letters in some way.

Maya glyphs

Teaching Idea

Coordinate instruction with the physical education teacher or on your own class time to simulate "pok-a-tok." Tell students they are going to play a ball game without using their hands or feet. Set up a ring at a right angle to the ground. A player scores when he or she can hit the ball through the ring. You may wish to modify the game after a certain period of time so that it may come to a conclusion. Discuss how challenging this game must have been.

The Maya cultivated maize (corn), beans, and squash. Maya farmers used a variety of farming methods, including what is called the "slash-and-burn" method of farming. Farmers cleared their cornfields by cutting bushes and trees and then allowing the cut plants to dry under the hot sun. After drying was complete, the farmers burned the cuttings and planted corn in the ashes, working around the remaining tree stumps.

The Maya built impressive cities in the midst of the rainforest. The largest buildings—tall temple-pyramids, royal palaces, and ball courts—were concentrated in the city centers. These stone structures required an extensive knowledge of architecture and engineering. Many buildings were covered with hieroglyphs that recounted the history of the city's dynasty and their patron gods. People lived in small houses scattered through the jungle on the outskirts of the city.

The Maya worshipped a variety of gods. Many Maya buildings are decorated with the face of Chac, the Maya rain god. For a society that depended on its harvests, rain was vitally important. Some important Maya myths and traditions are recorded in a sacred book called the *Popul Vuh*.

Most people were farmers who lived in cities or in villages near their fields, while hereditary kings ruled the centers. The principal cities were Tikal, Tuluum, Coba, Uxmal, Kabah, Sayil, Chichen Itza, Labna, Mayapan, Uaxactún, Copán, Bonampak, Palenque, and Río Bec. Many of these sites can be visited today, and they are popular tourist destinations.

The Maya developed advanced systems of astronomy and mathematics. They worked out a calendar of 365 days and could accurately predict eclipses. They also developed the concept of zero, a very important advance in mathematics. Their system of hieroglyphs for writing and keeping records was a complex system of ideographs—symbols representing ideas—that archaeologists have only partly decoded. It has long been one of the great mysteries of linguistics. Maya buildings, especially their temple pyramids, were massive structures built of limestone blocks.

A ball game called pok-a-tok had a prominent role in Maya culture. Players tried to drive a rubber ball through a stone ring set about 30 feet (9 m) in the air, but were not allowed to use their hands or feet. The game had religious significance, with the winners richly rewarded and the losers sometimes offered as sacrifices to the gods.

Sometime about 900 CE, the Maya abandoned many of their ceremonial centers. Experts speculate that an epidemic struck and killed much of the population, a drought occurred, or perhaps the Maya had exhausted the soil and moved on. It is possible that the people simply moved away if the farmers could no longer support a center's population. No one knows for sure what happened.

Although the Maya culture seems to have fallen on hard times, many Maya people survived. By the time the Spanish arrived in the 1500s, the large cities were in ruin and a much smaller population lived scattered throughout the jungle. Some Maya survivors were subjugated by the Spanish conquistador Francisco de Montejo in about 1549.

As you may have noticed, the word *Maya* can be used as a singular and a plural form, and also as an adjective. However, usage differs. Some writers prefer "Mayas" as the plural noun and "Mayan" as an adjective.

The Aztecs

By 1325 CE, the Aztec (who called themselves the Mexica) had moved south to Lake Texcoco [TESH-co-co] in the Valley of Mexico. They were originally a small nomadic group, but their warrior culture enabled them to grow and eventually dominate their neighbors. They established an empire that in time encompassed south and central Mexico. The Aztec ultimately came to dominate 400–500 city-states and over 5,000,000 people. They did not directly govern these other city-states; instead, they established a tribute system. In order to maintain some level of independence, the subjugated peoples paid taxes and labor to the Aztec. The Aztec Empire was similar to a union of city-states, a concept that should be familiar to students from their study of the Greek city-states in Grade 2. This lack of centralized organization, along with the tribute system and the fear that the Aztec engendered among their subjects, created a great hatred of the Aztec. The Spanish were able to capitalize on this hatred when they set out to control the Aztec Empire in the early 1500s.

Part of the fear that these other Indian peoples felt was based on the Aztec religious practice of human sacrifice. Human sacrifice did not originate with the Aztec; it had long been a part of religious practices among the natives of Middle America. However, the Aztec sacrificed on a very large scale. One goal of the wars fought by the Aztec was to capture rivals to use for human sacrifice. Prisoners of war were often killed as ritual offerings to the Aztec deities.

Ritual sacrifices took place atop the great Aztec temple-pyramids. The victim was placed on a stone altar and a priest used a stone knife to cut the still-beating heart from a sacrificial victim. The heart was then presented as an offering to one of the Aztec gods, and the body was pushed down the stairs of the pyramid and dragged away.

Human sacrifice appears to have played a role in each of the Aztec 18 major monthly religious festivals. The Aztec believed that the gods had to be appeased with sacrifices. In particular, they believed constant sacrifices were needed to keep the sun moving.

The Aztec worshipped many gods, including some known earlier to the Maya. Key gods and religious figures included Tlaloc, the rain god, Huitzilopochtli, the war god; and Quetzalcóatl, the "feathered serpent." Religious festivals were based on the Aztec calendar, which had 260 days. The Aztec also had a 365-day solar calendar. This last was derived from the Maya calendar and consisted of 18 months of 20 days and an extra five days.

The Aztec were governed by a king known as a "tlatoani" or "speaker." When the Spanish came, the ruler was Moctezuma II (also spelled Montezuma). Moctezuma lived in a 10-acre palace of 300 rooms that provided private living quarters for the king, offices, workshops, and council halls. Moctezuma also had a zoo and many country retreats.

The ruler was assisted by a council of advisors. Below the advisors was a class of nobles and war chiefs. Most Aztec were farmers, but there were also traders and craftworkers. At the bottom of the social structure were slaves. Slaves were often people captured in battle.

Teaching Idea

Compare and contrast the tribute system with the taxation system we currently have in the United States today. What are the similarities and differences in these systems? Students should recall "no taxation without representation" from Grade 4.

Teaching Idea

Have students follow directions on the Instructional Master 17, *Create a Codex*.

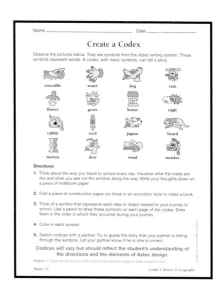

Use Instructional Master 17.

II. Mesoamerican Civilizations

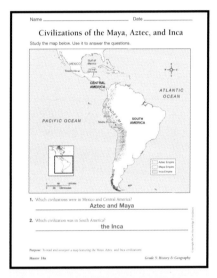

Use Instructional Masters 18a–18c.

Although the Aztec had professional war leaders, armies were made up of all of the able-bodied men available at the time of a campaign. Boys were taught endurance and military skills as part of their schooling. Aztec who took captives and were particularly valorous warriors increased their status in society.

The Aztec were noted for their gold and silver metalwork. Although the chief economic activity of the empire was farming, the empire supported a large and busy network in trade goods—both agricultural products and handcrafts. The Aztec used a system of hieroglyphs to record business transactions, tribute payments, religious rituals, and their history. They recorded information in a special kind of book called a codex.

▶ Tenochtitlán

The center of the Aztec Empire was Tenochtitlán [te-noch-tee-TLAHN]. It was built beginning in 1325 on an island in Lake Texcoco, in the center of what is now Mexico. According to legend, the Mexica would wander until they found an eagle with a serpent in its beak perched on a cactus. There they should settle. Supposedly, they saw this sign on an island in Lake Texcoco. The eagle, snake, and cactus are still symbols of Mexico today; you can find them on the Mexican flag.

Four causeways, or bridges, connected the Aztec capital to the mainland; aqueducts brought fresh water into the city. A network of canals enabled people in canoes to move their goods easily around the city. Islands of mud were anchored to the lake floor and used as gardens and agricultural land. The city was carefully planned and governed. Boatmen paddled around on the canals, transporting merchandise and other items.

By 1519, when the Spanish first saw it, Tenochtitlán was five square miles in size and had a population of more than 300,000. This was larger than most cities in Europe at the time. The city was centered around a large square of palaces and whitewashed pyramids with massive temples atop them. Around this central core were smaller palaces, brick houses, markets, and gardens. One of Cortés's men, Bernal Diaz del Castillo, gave a memorable description of his first glimpse of Tenochtitlán:

> Here we had a clear prospect of the three causeways by which Mexico communicated with the land, and of the aqueduct of Chapultepeque, which supplied the city with the finest water. We were struck with the numbers of canoes, passing to and from the main land, loaded with provisions and merchandise, and we could now perceive, that in this great city, and all the others of that neighbourhood which were built in the water, the houses stood separate from each other, communicating only by small drawbridges, and by boats, and that they were built with terraced tops. We observed also the temples and adoratories of the adjacent cities, built in the form of towers and fortresses, and others on the causeway, all whitewashed, and wonderfully brilliant. The noise and bustle of the market-place below us could be heard almost a league off, and those who had been at Rome and at Constantinople said, that for convenience, regularity, and population, they had never seen the like.

The Inca

Another civilization that grew powerful about the same time as the Aztec is the Inca. By 1525, the Inca had created a vast empire that stretched from what is today northern Ecuador through Peru and into parts of Chile, Bolivia, and Argentina. Their capital was Cuzco, Peru, the original homeland of the Inca in the Andes Mountains.

The Inca began their conquests around 1438. They had a labor tribute system to rule their conquered people. People had to work for the empire under the supervision of imperial bureaucrats and administrators. The Inca also used a complex resettlement policy to govern conquered people. Whole villages were split up and relocated to various villages closer to Cuzco; the conquered were settled among loyal subjects to ensure obedience. Loyal Inca took their place in the conquered villages. This strategy helped ensure that rebellions could not be easily organized and executed.

The leader of the empire was called the "Sapa Inca" and was considered the son of the sun god. Below the royal family came the noble class, which was made up of priests, military leaders, and the men who ran the government. When members of the noble class died, their wives and servants were buried with them. Kings were mummified, sometimes entombed in a seated position, and their bodies were preserved and worshipped in temples. For some ceremonies, commoners were mummified in bundles, their bodies set in the fetal position. A number of ice mummies of children have been found in the Andes. In 1995, a particularly well-preserved mummy of a twelve- to fourteen-year-old girl was found in the Andes. Nicknamed Juanita, her body was frozen intact, allowing for many scientific studies.

The Sapa Inca governed with the help of a complicated network of government employees and civil servants. Especially gifted boys were trained to be civil servants. They learned how to record information on a *quipu* (see p. 132). They also learned religion, governing skills, and math.

An important factor in keeping their vast empire together was the Inca's ability to travel and communicate. The empire had more than 10,000 miles of roads. Suspension bridges made of woven fiber were built where the roads had to pass over river gorges and ravines in the mountains. Messengers, called *chasquis* [CHAWS-kees] or runners, ran in relays over these roads carrying light items, laws, and news of the empire to distant locations. Rest houses were built one day apart on the roads. People in nearby villages provided food for the messengers, as well as new runners to take up the messages.

Since the Inca had no written language, these messengers could not carry a written note, although they often carried quipus that contained important information. Instead, a runner memorized his message, then sprinted to a rest station, where the next runner was ready for his team member's arrival. Without slowing the pace, the first runner recited the message, and, running alongside, the relief runner repeated it. Then the first runner dropped out, and the new messenger continued on. The system was fast! A message could travel 250 miles a day and the 1,250 miles from Quito to Cuzco, the capital, in five days. In an age of automobiles and airplanes, that may not seem especially fast, but it was very fast for the time. In the 1860s, the famous Pony Express riders of the American West were only able to cover about 200 miles a day—and they rode on horseback!

Teaching Idea

Ask students to compare the importance of the Inca road system to that of the Roman Empire, which they learned about in Grade 3 if they were following the *Core Knowledge Sequence*.

mountain bridge in the Andes

Farmers, imperial officials, and the army also used the roads. The army used the roads to march quickly from one area to another to quiet unrest among the Inca's subjects.

Farming was the main economic activity of the Inca. Farmers built terraces on the sides of mountains and used irrigation to put more land under cultivation. One of the most important crops was the potato, of which the Inca grew many varieties. Europeans did not know about potatoes until the Spanish conquered the Inca Empire and took potatoes back to Europe. The Inca also raised llamas and alpacas. They made clothing of the animals' wool, ate the meat, and used the animals as beasts of burden.

As has been noted, the Inca did not have a writing system, but they developed a record-keeping system using quipu [kwee-pu]. A quipu was a rope with 40 or so strings attached. The Inca would tie knots in various places on the string to represent groups of 1, 10, and 100. Quipus were very important record-keeping devices, recording everything from tribute contributions, economic reports, war information, and ceremonial details. Civil servants, village leaders, and important heads of households could communicate with each other and keep records using these quipu.

The Inca were also known for their stone work. They built elaborate walls with gigantic pieces of stone carefully cut and fitted together. Some of these walls are still standing today.

Like the word *Maya*, the word *Inca* is used as a singular and a plural noun, as well as an adjective. You may also encounter "Incas" as the plural and "Incan" as an adjective.

▶ Machu Picchu and Cuzco

Like the Maya and Aztec, the Inca had urban settlement. A fine example of an Inca site is Machu Picchu, with its terraced fields, palaces, fort, fountains, temples, and stonework staircases. Machu Picchu's exact use is unknown, but it may have been a city, fortress, or one of the many country retreats the Inca emperors built throughout the Andes. Located high in the Andes, the city was never found by the conquering Spanish, and thus was not destroyed.

As all roads in Europe led to Rome, so all roads in the Inca Empire led to Cuzco, its capital. According to one Inca creation myth, two Inca heroes emerged from caves and founded the city of Cuzco. A large fort guarded the city of huge palaces and temple compounds.

C. Spanish Conquerors

Background

Beginning in the 1400s, Europeans set forth in a great wave of exploration. (See Section III, "European Exploration, Trade, and the Clash of Cultures," pp. 139–163.) The Portuguese led the way. Later, they were followed by the Spanish, the French, the Dutch, and the English.

Christopher Columbus was funded by the Spanish rulers Ferdinand and Isabella. Columbus landed in the Caribbean, but he incorrectly thought that he was in India. This is why people started calling native peoples "Indians." The Spanish monarchs, Ferdinand and Isabella, sent soldiers, administrators, and colonists to settle these islands. They also sent Catholic missionaries to convert the native people to Christianity.

Another set of men who traveled to the Americas after the initial discoveries of Columbus are known to history as the conquistadors. The word *conquistador* is Spanish for "conqueror." It refers to a Spanish military leader who took part in the conquest of the Americas in the 16th century. The conquistadors were intent on finding and taking the riches of the Indies. They came from many different occupations and were generally not professional soldiers. They sought glory by finding riches, new land, and subjects for the king.

The leader of a group of conquistadors typically signed an agreement with the Spanish government. Spain agreed to recognize the authority of the expedition in exchange for one-fifth of all treasure found. In addition, there was an expectation that any conquered lands would become Spanish colonies. Each member of the expedition would get a share of whatever the expedition took. These shares might consist of gold and silver, or possibly captured native people whom the Spanish seized, in addition to those precious metals.

By 1520, the Spanish had given up their pursuit of treasure on the Caribbean islands and began looking to the mainland. The conquistadors set out from the Caribbean to explore what is present-day Mexico, Central America, and South America. They launched expeditions against the Aztec and Inca empires, and ultimately brought both empires down.

The conquistadors were successful for several reasons. They were brave and daring men driven by a powerful desire for wealth. In some cases they were very clever. In addition, they had horses, guns, and steel weapons, none of which the native people had. There were no horses in the Americas until the Spanish brought them. Also, native populations were decimated by diseases the Spanish brought, diseases for which the natives had no immunity.

The conquistadors gained large amounts of silver and gold by conquering the Aztec and Inca empires, and even more by setting up mines to dig out the huge deposits of silver discovered in Mexico and Peru between 1545 and 1595. The Spanish mine owners made fortunes, as did the Spanish government, because the monarchy received one-fifth of all the silver mined. Silver mining became the basis of the Spanish colonial economy and established the colonies' role as an importer of goods rather than an exporter.

Hernán Cortés and the Aztec

One of the most famous of the conquistadors was Hernán Cortés (also spelled Cortez). Cortés was born in Spain and studied briefly at the University of Salamanca before dropping out. He sailed for the New World in 1504 and took part in the Spanish conquest of Hispaniola (the island which today includes Haiti and the Dominican Republic) and in 1511 helped conquer Cuba. For his services he was given land and a house, along with native slaves for workers. In 1517 and 1518, expeditions returned to Hispaniola with small amounts of gold and big stories about where more was to be found. Cortés decided to go for the gold. He sold or mortgaged all his property and organized an expedition.

In 1519, Cortés left Cuba with 11 ships, about 600 men, and 16 horses. The expedition landed on the coast of the Yucatán Peninsula near what is now Veracruz. Cortés sought to gain control of the wealth of the mighty Aztec Empire (see pp. 129–130). To do this, he made friends with the people along the coast and learned from them of the faraway capital, Tenochtitlán. With the help of an

Teaching Idea

You may wish to teach the Spanish conquest of the Aztec and Inca civilizations as part of the European Exploration section (see pp. 139–163), which comes next in the *Core Knowledge Sequence*.

Teaching Idea

Create a simulation to demonstrate the strong desire for gold that many explorers possessed. While students are out of the room, hide pennies (as a representation of gold coins) around the room and in students' desks. When students come into the classroom, tell them you are an explorer searching for gold. Make a show of looking for some pieces of gold. When you "find gold" in a student's desk, tell them you are claiming it for yourself. The student will probably react, "That's not fair . . . this is mine." Be firm and say, "I am exploring for riches." Proceed to take everything out of the student's desk. (Be sensitive to your students, and try to choose someone who won't cry or become too upset.) Continue to search the room, and tell the students the gold will be only for you and your friends. The students should protest at the injustice of this! Then, stop the simulation, debrief, and tell the students about your simulation. You were being unfair, and this isn't the way you normally act, but this is how the Aztec (conquered by Cortés) or the Inca (conquered by Pizarro) may have perceived exploration.

Aztec woman named Malinche who had been sold as a slave and served as a translator, Cortés persuaded various groups of Aztec subjects to support the Spanish. Gaining allies was not difficult because of the tribute system of the Aztec and because of their cruelty to their subjects. Many city-states welcomed Cortés and his men in the hopes that he would free them from Aztec domination.

Cortés was determined to march to Tenochtitlán and find the gold he sought. When some of his men wavered and wanted to return to Hispaniola, he burned his ships to show them that there would be no going back. Then he turned and marched on Tenochtitlán, fighting battles, enlisting allies, and crossing mountains along the way. Moctezuma was waiting for him. News of the white men, albeit somewhat exaggerated, had traveled quickly. Moctezuma received news of the approach of hundreds of godly creatures whose "magic sticks" (cannons) spit smoke and fire and whose enormous "dogs" (horses) had flat ears and long tongues.

Moctezuma sent gifts of gold, which he hoped would appease the strange white-skinned visitors and make them go away. But the gold only whetted the appetite of Cortés and his men.

Cortés arrived in Tenochtitlán in November of 1519. Moctezuma welcomed him and escorted the Spanish into the city. Cortés asked for gold on behalf of Spanish king. He also demanded that the Aztec remove idols from their pyramids and set up shrines to the Virgin Mary and install Christian images on the pyramids. Moctezuma complied with these requests. Still, Cortés was nervous. After some time, he had his men arrest Moctezuma. Cortés began to rule the city, and reduced Moctezuma to little more than a puppet. Some time later the Spanish massacred some Aztec priests during a festival. This led to increased hostility among the Aztec. They revolted and besieged the Spanish in the palace.

During the siege, Cortés ordered Moctezuma to address his people from a palace balcony. The rebellious Aztec jeered and threw stones at their one-time ruler. Moctezuma died a few days later. The Spanish said that he was killed by a stone thrown by the crowd, but Aztec observers claimed that he was murdered by the Spanish; we may never know the truth.

On the night of July 1, 1520, Cortés decided to try to break out of the city. He and his men were detected and heavy fighting ensued. Over 400 Spaniards and roughly 2,000 of their native American allies were killed, but Cortés and some other leaders managed to escape. This nighttime battle is sometimes referred to as "La Noche Triste," or "the Sorrowful Night."

Instead of retreating, Cortés prepared for a counter-offensive. He ordered his men to build 12 boats for a siege of the city. He also secured more support from the groups that had long been subjects of the Aztec. Then he besieged Tenochtitlán. The fighting lasted for three months, but Cortés ultimately defeated the Aztec. The last Aztec emperor surrendered on August 13, 1521.

Cortés established Mexico City where Tenochtitlán had stood. Mexico City became the center of the Spanish province of New Spain. Cortés went on to conquer central Mexico and the northern area of Central America, but his last years were unhappy. Cortés never received the recognition that he believed he deserved from the Spanish king. He died in Spain in 1547. (34)

Teaching Idea

Students may enjoy listening to some excerpts from primary source documents, such as Cortés's letters to King Charles V of Spain or Bernal Díaz del Castillo's *Conquest of New Spain.* You might also show excerpts from the PBS documentary *Conquistadors* (see *More Resources*).

Francisco Pizarro and the Inca

After the conquest of Mexico, the conquistadors soon turned their attention to the Inca Empire to the south. The expedition against the Inca civilization was led by Francisco Pizarro. Pizarro was born in Spain and came to the New World in 1502, joining an expedition to Colombia in 1509. He accompanied Balboa on the famous expedition that culminated in the discovery of the Pacific Ocean. Pizarro later lived in Panama, and heard of areas to the south that were rich in gold. He began to think about an expedition to South America, and after brief expeditions to Peru in which he saw gold and met some Inca, he soon received Spain's permission to conquer and rule Peru.

Pizarro and his forces sailed to Peru and located the Inca emperor in 1531. A civil war had just been fought over who would lead the empire. Two half-brothers, Atahualpa [a-ta-WAL-pa] and Huascar, had each ruled a part of the empire and had tried to seize the other part. Atahualpa, who had governed the northern region, had won, but the empire had been weakened by the bloody civil war. Pizarro arranged a meeting with the emperor in the town of Cajamarca. Then he prepared an ambush. Pizarro stationed his men in the buildings around the square. Atahualpa came with a large entourage, but his men were unarmed. A Spanish priest stepped forward and asked the Sapa Inca to become a Christian. When he refused, the Spaniards charged out of hiding and began mowing down the unarmed Inca attendants. The Spanish took Atahualpa prisoner and demanded that his followers bring enough gold and silver to fill a room. The Inca people brought the gold and silver, but Atahualpa was executed anyway.

Pizarro captured Cuzco and, with its downfall, the empire began to collapse. Pizarro established a new capital at Lima, near the coast. In 1536, a new Inca emperor, Manco Capac, tried to retake Cuzco but was unsuccessful and retreated to the mountains. Pizarro was later assassinated by friends of a man he had killed. The last Inca emperor, Tupac Amarú, was finally killed by the Spanish in 1572. (35)

Teaching Idea

Use Instructional Master 83, *Venn Diagram,* to compare the explorations of Pizarro and Cortés and/or the Aztec and Inca experiences with the Spanish conquistadors.

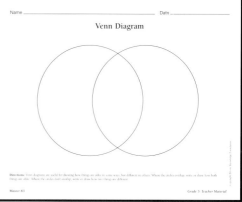

Use Instructional Master 83.

Native Populations Devastated by Disease

The Spanish were able to defeat the Aztec and the Inca not only because they had horses, dogs, guns, and swords, but also because they brought with them germs that made many native Americans sick. Diseases like smallpox and measles were unknown among the natives; therefore, they had no immunity to them.

The first to fall ill from European diseases were the native peoples of the Caribbean islands, who had the initial contact with the Spanish. Between disease and the forced labor policies of the Spanish, the native population on some islands disappeared completely. Some experts believe that in the 1500s and 1600s, anywhere from 50 to 80 percent of the native American population across North and South America died.

In the Caribbean, this meant that there was no longer a cheap supply of forced labor to work the mines and farms that the Spanish established. This need for a new source of labor was the impetus to the beginning of the transatlantic slave trade. A few Africans had been brought to work the mines on Hispaniola, but the need for large numbers of workers spurred the African slave trade. (36)

Review

Below are some ideas for ongoing assessment and review activities. These are not meant to constitute a comprehensive list. Teachers may also refer to the *Pearson Learning/Core Knowledge History & Geography* series for additional information and teaching ideas.

• Since students in Grade 1 also study the Maya, Aztec, and Inca civilizations, have students in Grade 5 create coloring books for the younger students. To make the coloring books, ask students to write one fact about each group at the bottom of large pieces of white paper and to draw an illustration to accompany each fact. Then, arrange a book buddy day where the two classes read together and the younger students color the pages to illustrate the fact about each group. Instruct students to avoid the discussion of human sacrifice with the younger students.

• This section provides an opportunity for students to complete short research reports on any of the three early civilizations. Using the guidelines found in the Language Arts section, provide the class with topics for short reports to write in formal style. Each day of a week, provide a mini-lesson on different aspects of report writing, such as correct paragraph form or bibliographies. Have students share these reports when completed.

• Have students write papers from the point of view of one of the early American civilizations studied in this section. Students should describe what life was like in this civilization and how the members most likely reacted to the European explorers. Students may also turn these papers into interviews between an interviewer and a member of a Maya, Aztec, or Inca civilization.

• Have students work in groups to write a short script demonstrating some aspect of life in one of these groups or an interaction between a group and European explorers. Each group should perform their skits for the class.

• Plan a culminating day for this section and incorporate different subject areas for the students to demonstrate what they have learned about the Maya, Aztec, and Inca civilizations. You may include the physical education teacher so that students can play games from each group, or practice the Inca message-passing system. You can also have students demonstrate what they have learned from these groups, such as math concepts, art and architecture styles, etc. Invite parents and administrators to attend the event.

• You may also ask the following questions after completion of this unit of study.

1. Use the following pairs of words in sentences: Andes Mountains–Argentina, Brazil–Amazon River.
   Possible sentences: The Andes Mountains form the border between Argentina and Chile. The Amazon River drains a large part of the country of Brazil.

2. On a map, locate the countries into which each of the following civilizations extended: Maya, Aztec, and Inca.

Students should be able to identify the following civilizations and countries: Maya: Yucatán Peninsula in southeastern Mexico, Belize, Guatemala, El Salvador, and Honduras; Aztec: Mexico, specifically central and southern; Inca: Ecuador, Peru, Chile, Bolivia, and Argentina.

3. List three accomplishments of the Maya.

Any three: construction of large temples and/or pyramids, development of hieroglyphic writing system, 365-day calendar, concept of zero.

4. How did the tribute system of the Aztec work?

The Aztec allowed conquered peoples to rule themselves as long as they made payments in taxes and labor to the Aztec government.

5. Who was the Aztec emperor at the time of the Spanish conquests?

The emperor was Moctezuma.

6. What was the capital city of the Aztec Empire?

The capital was Tenochtitlán.

7. Who led the Spanish expedition that conquered the Aztec Empire?

Hernán Cortés led the expedition.

8. Who led the Spanish expedition that conquered the Inca Empire?

Francisco Pizarro led the expedition.

9. Why was a road system important to the Inca?

A system of roads allowed officials to send messages quickly back and forth between remote areas and the government in Cuzco. It also made it possible to send troops from one part of the empire to another as they were needed.

10. What advantages did the Spanish have over the Aztec and Inca empires?

The Spanish had guns, cannons, and gunpowder, as well as horses.

11. What was the consequence of native Americans' contracting European diseases like smallpox and measles?

Without a natural immunity, native Americans died by the thousands as a result of contracting European diseases, such as smallpox and measles.

More Resources

The titles listed below are offered as a representative sample of materials and not a complete list of everything that is available.

For students —

• *The Maya, Aztec and Inca Civilizations*, edited by E. D. Hirsch, Jr. (Pearson Learning, 2002), a unit in the official *Pearson Learning/Core Knowledge History & Geography* series, is available as part of the bound book for Grade 5/Level 5. A teacher's guide is also available. To order, call 1-800-321-3106.

• *The Aztecs*, by Jane Shuter (Heinemann, 2002). Paperback, 32 pages, ISBN 1403400245. See also *The Maya*, by the same author. Note that both books deal with human sacrifice, but do not go into great detail.

• *The Inca (New True Books)*, by Stefanie Takacs (Children's Press, 2003). Library binding, 48 pages, ISBN 0516227769. See also *The Maya* and *The Aztec* in this series. Note that the latter two deal with human sacrifice.

• *Sad Night: The Story of an Aztec Victory and a Spanish Loss*, by Sally Mathews (Clarion Books, 2001). Paperback, 40 pages, ISBN 0395630355.

More Resources continued

• *This Place is High: The Andes Mountain of South America,* by Vicki Cobb (Walker, 1993). An introduction to living in the Andean highlands and the history of the Inca. Very thorough. Paperback, ISBN 0802774067.

For teachers —

• *Atlas of Ancient America,* by Michael Coe, Dean Snow, and Elizabeth Benson (Checkmark Books, 1986). "An extensive, well-researched text unites the maps, illustrations, and feature sections so successfully that this book can be recommended as the best available introduction to Native American prehistory." (*Library Journal,* 1987). Includes 56 maps and more than 300 illustrations and photographs. Hardcover, 240 pages, ISBN 0816011990.

• *The Broken Spears: The Aztec Account of the Conquest of Mexico,* by Miguel Leon-Portillo (Beacon Press, 1992). Paperback, 196 pages, 0807055018.

• *Conquistadors,* narrated by Michael Wood (PBS, 2001). Covers Cortés, Pizarro, Cabeza de Vaca, and Orellana. VHS, 240 minutes. You may also wish to review the video *Cortés and Pizarro* (Schlessinger Media, 2000), a 23-minute video designed for students in Grades 5–8. Both are available from Library Video.com, www.library video.com or 1-800-843-3620.

• *The Discovery and Conquest of Mexico: 1517–1521,* by Bernal Díaz del Castillo (Da Capo Press, 2004). Paperback, 512 pages, ISBN 030681319X. See also *The Conquest of New Spain,* by the same author.

• *History of the Conquest of Mexico and History of the Conquest of Peru,* by William Prescott (Cooper Square Press, 2000). Well-known, readable histories of the exploits of Cortés and Pizarro. Paperback, 1330 pages, ISBN 0815410042.

• *In Defense of the Indians,* Bartolomé de las Casas (Northern Illinois University Press, 1992). First published in London in 1556, this bishop's exposure of the cruel treatment of native American slaves at the hands of the Spanish was translated into forty-two languages and led to the abolition of forced labor by the Spanish in 1642. Paperback, 385 pages, ISBN 0875805566.

• *Letters from Mexico,* by Hernan Cortés, translated and edited by Anthony Pagden (Yale University Press, 2001). Paperback, 640 pages, ISBN 0300090943.

• Hernando Cortés on the Web, www.isidore-of-seville .com/cortes, contains links to a number of primary sources.

III. European Exploration, Trade, and the Clash of Cultures

The Big Idea

From the 1400s to the 1600s, Europeans ventured out to explore what was to them the unknown world in an effort to reap the profits of trade and colonization.

Remember that each subject you study with students expands their vocabulary and introduces new terms, thus making them better listeners and readers. As you study European exploration, use map work, read alouds, independent reading, and discussions to build students' vocabularies.

What Students Should Already Know

Students in Core Knowledge schools should be familiar with

Kindergarten

▶ the voyage of Columbus in 1492
  • Queen Isabella and King Ferdinand of Spain
  • the Niña, Pinta, and Santa Maria
  • Columbus's mistaken identification of "Indies" and "Indians"
  • the idea of what was, for Europeans, a "New World"

Grade 1

▶ Columbus
▶ the conquistadors
  • the search for gold and silver
  • Hernán Cortés and the Aztec
  • Francisco Pizarro and the Inca
  • diseases devastate native American population

Grade 3

▶ Early Spanish exploration and settlement
  • settlement of Florida
  • Ponce de León, legend of the Fountain of Youth
  • Hernando de Soto
  • founding of St. Augustine (oldest continuous European settlement in what is now the U.S.)
  • geography: Caribbean Sea, West Indies, Puerto Rico, Cuba, Gulf of Mexico, Mississippi River

▶ Exploration and settlement of the American Southwest
  • early Spanish explorers in the lands that are now the states of Texas, New Mexico, Arizona, and California; missionary settlements (missions), especially in Texas and California
  • Coronado and the legend of the "Seven Cities of Cibola" (of Gold)
  • geography: Grand Canyon and Rio Grande
  • conflicts with Pueblo Indians (1680 revolt led by Popé)

▶ Search for the Northwest Passage
  • Many explorers undertook the perilous, sometimes fatal, voyage to find a short cut across North America to Asia, including

III. European Exploration, Trade, and the Clash of Cultures

The items below refer to content in Grade 5. Use time lines with students to help them sequence and relate events from different periods and groups.

1400s–1750s	European global explorations
1488	Dias sights Cape of Storms/Good Hope
1492	Columbus's first voyage
1494	Treaty of Tordesillas
1497	da Gama rounds Cape of Good Hope; sails to India
1497	Cabot, first European expedition to see North America
1500	Cabral claims Brazil for Portugal
early 1500s	Portuguese control Asian sea trade with Europe
early 1500s	Portuguese seize East African Swahili city-states
1511	Portuguese first Europeans to visit Spice Islands
1513	Balboa reaches the Pacific
1519–1522	Magellan's ships circumnavigate the globe
1519–1522	Cortés conquers the Aztec
1531–1533	Pizarro conquers the Inca
1600	Sugar plantations and the use of African slaves established in Brazil
early 1600s	Control of Spice Islands and other Portuguese holdings shifts to Dutch

continued on next page

What Students Should Already Know continued

- John Cabot and Newfoundland.
- Champlain, "New France" and Quebec.
- Henry Hudson and the Hudson River.
- geography, including "New France," Quebec, Canada, St. Lawrence River, the Great Lakes (Superior, Michigan, Huron, Erie, and Ontario)

What Students Need to Learn

▸ Beginning in the 1400s, Europeans set forth in a great wave of exploration and trade.

▸ European motivations
- Muslims controlled many trade routes.
- Profit through trade in goods such as gold, silver, silks, sugar, and spices
- Spread of Christianity: missionaries, Bartolomé de las Casas speaks out against enslavement and mistreatment of native peoples

▸ Geography of the spice trade
- The Moluccas, also known as the "Spice Islands": part of present-day Indonesia
- Locate the region known as Indochina, the Malay Peninsula, the Philippines.
- Definition of "archipelago"
- "Ring of Fire": earthquakes and volcanic activity

▸ European exploration, trade, and colonization
- Portugal
  - Prince Henry the Navigator, exploration of the West African coast
  - Bartolomeu Dias rounds the Cape of Good Hope.
  - Vasco de Gama: the spice trade with India, exploration of East Africa
  - Portuguese conquest of East African Swahili city-states
  - Pedro Cabral's claiming of Brazil
- Spain
  - Two worlds meet: Christopher Columbus and the Tainos
  - Treaty of Tordesillas between Portugal and Spain
  - Magellan crosses the Pacific; one of his ships returns to Spain, completing the first round-the-world voyage.
  - Vasco Nùñez de Balboa reaches the Pacific.
- England and France
  - Search for the Northwest Passage
  - Colonies in North America and the West Indies

continued from previous page

1604–1610	Champlain, Hudson search for Northwest Passage
1607	First English colony at Jamestown
1608	Quebec founded
1700s	Anglo-French rivalries in India

Text Resources

(37) *Brief Account of the Devastation of the Indies*

(38) *Round Africa to India*

(39) *The Voyage of Columbus*

(40) *Aboard a Slave Ship*

Materials

Instructional Masters 19–22

South Asia, p. 146

Routes of European Explorers, p. 151

The West Indies, p. 159

Triangular Trade Routes, p. 160

spices such as pepper, cloves, nutmeg, and cinnamon, p. 145

atlas or encyclopedia, p. 146

map of the South Atlantic, p. 148

periodicals or access to the Internet for research, p. 161

large blank index cards, p. 161

index cards, p. 161

What Students Need to Learn continued

- Trading posts in India
- Holland (The Netherlands)
  - The Dutch take over Portuguese trade routes and colonies in Africa and the East Indies.
  - The Dutch in South Africa, Cape Town
  - The Dutch in North America: New Netherland, later lost to England
- The sugar trade
  - African slaves on Portuguese sugar plantations on islands off West African coast, such as São Tomé
  - Sugar plantations on Caribbean islands
  - West Indies: Cuba, Puerto Rico, The Bahamas, Dominican Republic, Haiti, Jamaica
- Transatlantic slave trade: the "triangular trade" from Europe to Africa to colonies in the Caribbean and the Americas
  - The "Slave Coast" in West Africa
  - The Middle Passage

Vocabulary

Student/Teacher Vocabulary

archipelago: a series, or string, of many islands (S)

Vasco Núñez de Balboa: a conquistador who explored Central America and discovered the Pacific Ocean (in Peru) (S)

Pedro Alvares Cabral: an explorer who sailed to the east coast of South America and claimed Brazil for Portugal (S)

Bartolomé de las Casas: a former conquistador and owner of an encomienda; de las Casas eventually became a Roman Catholic priest and missionary and preached against the encomienda system and the mistreatment of native peoples by the conquistadors (S)

city-state: a state consisting of a ruling city and the surrounding territory (S)

colony: an area settled by a group of people from another country (i.e., the American colonies were settled by people from Europe) (S)

Christopher Columbus: an explorer who, while searching for a shorter passage to India, made landfall in the Caribbean and claimed land for Spain (S)

Bartolomeu Dias: a Portuguese explorer; he sailed farther south than previous Portuguese explorers and discovered Cape of Good Hope (S)

East Indies: a group of islands in the Indian and Pacific oceans between Asia and Australia (S)

encomienda: a land grant system in which Spanish colonists were given a certain amount of land and the labor of the native people who lived on the land (T)

enslavement: the act of making a person a slave (S)

III. European Exploration, Trade, and the Clash of Cultures

Vocabulary continued

An interesting activity while studying the World History and Geography strand this year would be the creation of a world time line including major events. This time line would help students understand the differences from one culture and civilization to another more easily and thus help them make comparisons and contrasts among civilizations.

exploration: travel for the purpose of discovery (S)

Vasco da Gama: the first European to sail to India; a Portuguese sea captain who opened the spice trade between Asia and Europe (S)

Prince Henry the Navigator: a Portuguese prince who financed explorations of the African coast in the early 1400s; his patronage of sea voyages earned him the nickname "the Navigator" (S)

Indochina: the peninsula in Southeast Asia that lies between China and India; includes the countries of Myanmar, Malaysia, Vietnam, Cambodia, and Laos (S)

Ferdinand Magellan: a Portuguese sea captain who sailed for the Spanish government, Magellan became the first explorer to circumnavigate the globe (S)

Malay Peninsula: the southernmost peninsula in Asia; west Malaysia and southwest Thailand share the area (S)

Middle Passage: a segment of the triangular trade between Africa and the Americas in which enslaved peoples were transported from Africa to the Americas (S)

missionaries: Catholics who were assigned the task of converting the Indians to Christianity (S)

Moluccas ("Spice Islands"): the geographic center of the spice trade; a series of volcanic islands in what is today eastern Indonesia (S)

New Netherland: a Dutch trading post that was the first settlement in the area of present-day New York City; established by Henry Hudson in 1609 (S)

Northwest Passage: a water route, much sought after by explorers, that would enable boats to sail from the Atlantic Ocean through (or around) the American continents to the Pacific Ocean (S)

Philippines: a country made up of some 7,000 islands in the Pacific Ocean off the coast of the Asian continent (S)

plantation: a large farm, usually found in warm climates, where crops such as sugar are grown; plantations often depended on slave labor to function (S)

profit: (n.) income, earnings; (v.) to make money (S)

"Ring of Fire": a series of volcanoes that ring the Pacific Ocean; this area is prone to earthquakes and other volcanic activity (S)

slave: a person who is forced to perform labor in servitude to another (S)

Slave Coast: a section of the west coast of Africa including the modern-day nations of Togo and Benin; many slaves were shipped from forts along this coast to the Americas (S)

spice trade: the dealing in spices that was one of the main motivations of the Age of Exploration; Europeans desired spices from Asia to improve or disguise the taste of their food (S)

Swahili: the name given to the mix of Muslim Arab and African peoples living in trading cities along the east coast of Africa (S)

Tainos: the first native people that Columbus encountered upon reaching the Caribbean islands (S)

trade: buying and selling of goods; commercial transactions (S)

trade routes: passageways, either on land or by sea, that were commonly used for commercial purposes (S)

trading posts: places where goods are traded, often located in strategic places along trade routes (S)

Vocabulary continued

transatlantic slave trade: the traffic in captured Africans who were brought to America and the Caribbean to work as slaves (S)

Treaty of Tordesillas: treaty that divided the Americas between Spain and Portugal (S)

triangular trade: a set of trade routes that linked Africa, the Caribbean and mainland North America, and Europe in a prosperous network that included the slave trade (S)

West Indies: group of islands in the Gulf of Mexico (S)

Domain Vocabulary

Ocean exploration and navigation and related words:
sea, ocean, sail, boat, flagship, wind, knot, direction, landmark, compass, astrolabe, sextant, latitude, star, caravel, ship, galleon, shallow, deep, fast, slow, maneuver, anchor, steer, captain, admiral, crew, mutiny, rudder, deck, warship, cannon, sink, mast, island, landfall, coast, cape, harbor, dock, windward, navigate, circumnavigate, strait, freshwater, river, canal, lock, navigable, waterway, direction, east, west, north, south, aboard, aground, astern, gale, storm, voyage, seaworthy, vessel, aft, fore, stern, hull, seaman, wreck, becalmed

Bodies of water:
Atlantic Ocean, Pacific Ocean, Indian Ocean, Mediterranean Sea, Caribbean Sea, St. Lawrence River, Lake Champlain, Great Lakes, Gulf of St. Lawrence, Lake Ontario, Lake Erie, Lake Huron, Lake Michigan, Lake Superior, Hudson River, Hudson Strait, Hudson Bay, Gulf of Mexico

Places on land:
Asia, Middle East, China, India, Calcutta, Madras, Bombay, Southeast Asia, Africa, Swahili Coast, Kilwa, Mozambique, South Africa, Capetown, Togo, Benin, Niger delta, Senegal, Angola, Europe, Netherlands, Spain, Portugal, France, Great Britain, North America, Canada, Nova Scotia, Quebec, New France, Jamestown, Virginia, Plymouth, Massachusetts, Boston, New York, Manhattan, New Jersey, Albany, New Amsterdam, Mexico, South America, Central America, Antilles, Bahamas, San Salvador, Hispaniola, Cuba, Puerto Rico, Panama, Darién, Virgin Islands, Jamaica, Trinidad and Tobago, Martinique, Guadeloupe, Haiti, Brazil

Groups of people:
European, English, British, French, Dutch, Chinese, Boers, African, Portuguese, Spanish, Spaniard, Bantu, Muslim, Arab, Arawak, native American

Religion and Christianity and related words:
Christianity, Christian, convert, baptize, Roman Catholic, Protestant, priest, bishop, pope, clergy, salvation, soul, Jesuit, church, Bible, teach, heathen, pagan, religion, polytheist, monotheist, God, Jesus, Virgin Mary, saint

Slavery and the slave trade and related words:
bondage, freedom, own, buy, sell, cultivation, slave raider, Africa, black, negro, kidnap, capture, imprison, pen, slave ship, slave trader, transport, chains, chained, import, sell, auction, plantation, mine, climate, planter, master, overseer, agriculture, laborer, heat, hot, soil, profit, plant, harvest, cultivation, runaway, rebellion, indentured servant, contract, term

Trade and trade goods and related words:
buy, sell, barter, trader, route, network, overland, riches, money, profit, economy, power, control, market, import, export, capital, fur trade, monopoly, company, competitor, rival, commercial, joint-stock company, stock, shareholder, share, finance, owner, profit, revenue, invest, investor, grain, fish, cattle, rum, iron, coffee, whale oil, porcelain, pottery, lumber, luxury goods, cloth, silk, jewels, spices, pepper, cloves, nutmeg, cinnamon, furs, sugar, sugar cane, tobacco, rice, indigo, cotton, molasses, guns, textiles, timber

Vocabulary continued

Government and colonies and related words:
power, control, empire, colonist, land grant, claim, title, right, territory, overseas, border, population, establish, government, governance, governor, tax, monarch, king, legislature, negotiate, negotiation, challenge, settler, protect, self-governing, independence, religious toleration, representative government

At a Glance
The most important ideas for you are:

- The European exploration began as a way to wrest control of Asian trade from Muslim merchants and gain its profits, and secondarily, as a way to spread Christianity.

- Students should be able to locate the important centers of European-dominated trade in Asia, the originating location of the sugar plantation culture, and the regions of European colonization in the Americas.

- Students should be able to trace the routes and recognize the discoveries and achievements of the first explorers sailing from Portugal, Spain, the Netherlands, England, and France.

- European countries transported their rivalries overseas and fought one another for trading rights, territory, and the wealth and power they brought.

- The plantation system and slavery grew from origins on the islands off the west African coast.

- The triangular trade linked Africa, the Caribbean and mainland North America, and Europe in a prosperous network that included the slave trade.

- The segment of the triangular trade between Africa and the Americas was known as the Middle Passage and became synonymous with the slave trade.

What Teachers Need to Know

A. Background

The use of time lines is recommended to help students place the people and events they will learn about in this section in the context of their previous studies, especially that of the early exploration and settlement of North America from Grade 3. It is suggested that you examine the Grade 3 guidelines for American history and geography in the *Core Knowledge Sequence* in order to use those topics, which should be familiar to students, as a foundation upon which to build knowledge of the new topics.

European Motivations for Exploration

Beginning in the 1400s, Europeans set forth in a great wave of exploration and trade. They were spurred by the riches brought back from the eastern Mediterranean during the Crusades and the money in their purses from the rise of a money economy. Members of the European middle and upper classes wanted the luxuries that could be found in the East—fine cloth such as silk, jewels, and most of all, spices to improve or disguise the taste of their foods.

Several factors served as motivation for Europeans to engage in exploration for the purpose of developing international trading networks. First, eastern middlemen, mainly Muslims, controlled the overland trade routes from Asia to Europe. Land routes like the Silk Road across the central Asian steppes, which originated in China, ended in the Muslim Middle East. Europeans wanted the power and resulting wealth that would come from controlling trade. Finding all-water routes to Asia and its riches would allow European merchants to cut out Middle Eastern middlemen and reap all the profits of eastern trade.

Some Europeans were also eager to spread Christianity to nonbelievers. Christian teachings had spread from Roman Palestine into parts of North Africa and north and west into Europe. However, the majority of Africa, the Middle East, and the rest of Asia had never heard of Jesus Christ and his message of Christian charity and redemption.

Why did European sailors venture out on the seas at this time and not earlier? The reason is that several nautical inventions—the magnetic compass, the astrolabe, the sextant, and caravels—all came to the Europeans' attention around the same time.

Students should remember from their study of world history and geography in Grade 4 that the Chinese invented the magnetic compass and began using it to find direction in the 1100s. Knowledge of the compass did not reach Europe until the 1200s. The compass enabled sailors to find direction at sea where there were no landmarks. The needle of the compass would point towards magnetic north. The astrolabe and sextant allowed sailors to calculate latitude at sea by sighting stars and measuring angles.

Caravels were longer and shallower ships than had been previously built. The caravels sailed by the Spanish and Portuguese were the result of greatly improved ship designs. Their steering rudder and triangular sails resulted in faster, more maneuverable ships that could sail into, not just with, the wind.

Geography of the Spice Trade

Much of the trade between east and west focused on spices, especially pepper, cloves, nutmeg, and cinnamon. The geographic center of the nutmeg and cloves trade was the Moluccas (also known as the Maluku Islands), a series of volcanic islands in what is today eastern Indonesia. Though mountainous, the islands have rich soil. The Portuguese visited the Moluccas first in 1511, and the Dutch took control of them in the early 1600s. To Europeans, they were known as the Spice Islands.

Three other areas were important in the east-west trading networks: Indochina, the Malay Peninsula, and the Philippines.

Teaching Idea

Ask students if, from their past study of world history, they can think of any peoples who set out to explore other places in pursuit of trade. (Answers might include Islamic traders across North Africa and into West and East Africa; the Chinese under Zheng He during the Ming dynasty; Vikings who were both raiders and traders.)

Ask students what similarities and differences these groups had. (Possible answers might be that the Islamic and European traders attempted to convert the peoples they came in contact with to their religion; the Chinese and Vikings were interested only in trading.)

astrolabe

Teaching Idea

Have students smell the spices pepper, cloves, nutmeg, and cinnamon. To reinforce the importance of spices in early trading, have students find recipes that use the spices listed above. At home, students could smell and/or try food with and without any added spice, and compare the difference.

III. European Exploration, Trade, and the Clash of Cultures

Teaching Idea

Create an overhead from Instructional Master 19, *South Asia*, to orient students to the area of the spice trade. Have students locate each of the important areas in relation to one another: the Moluccas, Indochina, the Malay Peninsula, and the Philippines. Then, have students use an atlas or encyclopedia to find out what nation each area is part of today.

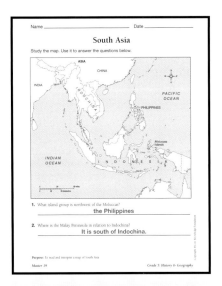

Use Instructional Master 19.

Indochina is the name given to the peninsula in Southeast Asia that lies between China and India. Today, the nations of Myanmar, Malaysia, Thailand, Laos, Cambodia, and Vietnam occupy the peninsula. The French gained control of the eastern part of the peninsula in the 1800s, and in 1887 united Vietnam, Cambodia, and Laos into French Indochina. The French lost control of the area to the Japanese in World War II but later regained control of some areas. The countries of French Indochina all gained their independence in the 1950s.

The Malay Peninsula is the southernmost peninsula in Asia. West Malaysia and southwest Thailand share the area. The island of Singapore lies to its south. To the west are the Andaman Sea (part of the Indian Ocean) and the Strait of Malacca. To the east lie the Gulf of Thailand and the South China Sea. The Portuguese took control of part of the peninsula in 1511 but lost it to the Dutch in the mid-1600s. The British seized sections of the peninsula beginning in 1826.

The Philippines is an archipelago, a series of many islands. The country is made up of some 7,000 islands and lies in the Pacific Ocean off the Asian continent. Because the Philippines are located on the equatorial side of the Tropic of Cancer, its climate is tropical. The islands are mainly volcanic and mountainous. About 1,000 islands are inhabited, but most of the population lives on just 11 of them. The islands are part of the "Ring of Fire," which is a series of volcanoes that ring the Pacific Ocean. Earthquakes are common in this area. The first European to visit the area was Ferdinand Magellan in 1521 on his voyage around the world. He was wounded and killed in a fight there. Based on his voyage, the Spanish later claimed the islands as a colony. They held the islands until Spain's defeat in the Spanish-American War in 1898.

B. European Exploration, Trade, and Colonization

Portugal

Prince Henry the Navigator

The first explorations by Europeans trying to find a sea route to Asia were along the Atlantic, or west, coast of Africa. In the early 1400s, Prince Henry of Portugal, known as Henry the Navigator, sent ships south along the African coast looking for a way around the continent. During his lifetime, his captains explored the coastline as far as modern Sierra Leone, about halfway southward along the continent. Although the prince did not travel with his captains, his patronage of these voyages had an enormous impact on Europe's role in world exploration.

Bartolomeu Dias

Bartolomeu Dias set off from Portugal in 1487 with three ships to find the southern tip of Africa and determine whether an all-water route to India was possible. Dias sailed further south than any previous Portuguese explorer, keeping sight of land to his east. A storm drove him out to sea. When Dias sailed back for the coast he noticed that he was sailing north instead of south and land was now to his west. That meant he had already passed the tip of Africa, and that it should be possible to sail around Africa to India. The crew was unwilling to sail farther, so Dias reversed his course, sailing for home. This time he spotted the Cape of

146 *Grade 5 Handbook*

Good Hope at the juncture of the Indian and Atlantic Oceans. Based on his experiences there, Dias called the cape "Cape of Storms," but later the name was changed to "Cape of Good Hope" because the Portuguese rulers were afraid "Cape of Storms" would scare off additional explorers and traders. Dias later sailed with both da Gama and Cabral, but he was in a subordinate role.

▶ Vasco da Gama

Vasco da Gama was a Portuguese explorer who followed in the footsteps of Dias and became the first European to sail around the southern tip of Africa and all the way to India.

Da Gama sailed from Lisbon, Portugal in July 1497, with four ships. By November he and his men had rounded the Cape of Good Hope and by December they had sailed beyond the point where Dias had turned around. Da Gama hired a pilot on the East African coast at Malindi. This pilot guided the ship to Calicut in India. The expedition arrived in May 1498. Da Gama tried to trade in Calicut but failed to establish a trade relationship or a peace treaty with the local authorities. He and his men took several Hindus on board to bring back to Portugal so that the Portuguese could learn about their customs. Then they set off on the return trip. On March 20, 1499, they rounded the Cape and returned to Portugal in September 1499. In Portugal he was given a hero's welcome and named "Admiral of the Indian Sea."

Three years later, da Gama led 20 ships on a second voyage to Calicut, India, where he established the base of the Portuguese empire in Africa and Asia. He also explored the coast of East Africa. (38)

▶ The Portuguese and the East African Swahili City-States

During his explorations, Da Gama stopped several times along the eastern coast of Africa, known as the Swahili coast. This coastal area was inhabited by a mixture of African, Arab, and Muslim peoples, who communicated using the Swahili language. Swahili evolved from the African Bantu languages and borrowed Arabic and Persian words.

Beginning around the 600s, Muslim Arabs used the seasonal monsoon winds to travel between Arabia and East Africa. By the 800s, Muslim Arabs began settling in these East African cities and marrying native women. It was these Swahili cities like Malindi that da Gama visited at the end of the 15th century. By that time, Muslim religious beliefs, architectural styles, and other cultural influences were evident.

At first, these cities were layover sites for ships going to and from Portugal. Sailing north along the African coast, the ships would stop at one of these cities to take on food and to give sailors a rest before the long trip across the Indian Ocean. The cities served the same purpose for homeward-bound ships.

After a time, the Portuguese government decided to try to take over these city-states. Portugal would then be able to control the trade network that reached between the Indian Ocean and the interior of Africa. The African interior offered such trade goods as iron tools, rhinoceros horn, palm oil, gold from southeastern Africa, and slaves, and in turn it served as a market for such imported goods as Chinese porcelain, Burmese pottery, and Indian cloth.

Teaching Idea

As you teach the various explorers, have students fill in a graphic organizer chart to keep track of the explorers and the facts about them. The categories on the chart may include
• Name
• Nickname
• Host country
• Where he went
• What he is known for
• Other interesting facts
    After studying all the explorers, students may write a paragraph summarizing key facts about the explorers. As an extension of this activity, have students find out about present-day female explorers, such as in space or archeological expeditions.

Teaching Idea

Read *Jambo Means Hello* and *Moja Means One* with the class to share elements of the Swahili language (see *More Resources*). At the end of this section, students can create their own alphabet or number books that summarize key points learned about exploration.

At first, the Portuguese government instructed its sea captains to try negotiating with the rulers of the city-states. If they were unable to reach a settlement, then the ship captains could attack. First, the city of Kilwa (in what is today Tanzania) fell. Soon, the Portuguese had managed to bring the other major east coast trading cities under their control. Over time, as the Portuguese concentrated their trading efforts at Mozambique Island, in the south, closer to the gold they sought, the other cities declined greatly in wealth and importance.

▶ Pedro Cabral Claims Brazil

Pedro Alvares Cabral set out from Portugal for India in March 1500. His mission was to follow the route of da Gama and help consolidate Portuguese power along the route to India, while also introducing Christianity to the peoples he encountered. However, Cabral overshot his course and ended up sailing so far west that he sailed to the east coast of South America. Cabral believed he had landed on an island, which he called "Island of the True Cross." He held a religious service and claimed the land for Portugal. It later became known as Brazil after its forests of dyewoods, also known as brazilwoods.

Cabral eventually reached India and signed a trading agreement between India and Portugal. However, his voyage was plagued with bad weather and bad luck, and only four of his original 13 ships returned to Lisbon in June 1501.

Spain

▶ Christopher Columbus and the Tainos

Students in Core Knowledge schools should have studied Christopher Columbus in earlier grades, but it makes sense to review his voyage again in this grade and place it in the larger context of the Age of Exploration.

Columbus was born in the Italian city of Genoa, but eventually became an explorer for Ferdinand and Isabella, rulers of territories that joined together to form the modern nation of Spain. As a young man, Columbus studied mapmaking and became a sailor. He sailed with the Portuguese along the western coast of Africa in the 1480s. About this time the Portuguese began looking for a route around Africa to India and the Spice Islands. But Columbus had another idea. He believed that Earth was smaller than in fact it is, and he concluded that it should be possible to reach the Indies by sailing west.

In 1484 Columbus presented his idea to the Portuguese king. The king chose not to support the mission. After several years of lobbying, Columbus succeeded in convincing Ferdinand and Isabella to support his expedition.

Columbus sailed with three ships, the Niña, the Pinta, and the Santa Maria. They left in August of 1492. After a stop in the Canary Islands, the ships began sailing west. The crew soon grew nervous at how far they had sailed into unknown territory. In early October, land was finally sighted.

Columbus landed on an island in the Bahamas on October 12, 1492. Columbus promptly renamed the island San Salvador (Saint Salvador) and claimed it for Spain. The first native Americans whom Christopher Columbus met in the New World were the Taino, speakers of the Arawak languages. The Taino were nomadic hunters and gatherers who inhabited several islands in the Caribbean.

Teaching Idea

Use a map of the South Atlantic to show how Cabral ended up in Brazil.

Columbus described his impressions of the people and the land in his journal:

> . . . [T]his people has no religion nor are they idolaters, but very mild and without knowing what evil is, nor how to kill others, nor how to take them, and without arms, and so timorous that from one of our men ten of them fly, although they do sport with them, and ready to believe and knowing that there is a God in heaven, and sure that we have come from heaven; and very ready at any prayer which we tell them to repeat, and they make the sign of the cross.
>
> So your Highness should determine to make them Christians, for I believe that if they begin, in a short time they will have accomplished converting to our holy faith a multitude of towns. Without doubt there are in these lands the greatest quantities of gold, for not without cause do these Indians whom I am bringing say that there are places in these isles where they dig out gold and wear it on their necks, in their ears and on their arms and legs, and the bracelets are very thick.

In December of that year, on an island that Columbus renamed Hispaniola, the Taino helped his crew build a fort, La Navidad, from the lumber of the wrecked Santa Maria. Expecting to return with more ships, supplies, and colonists, Columbus left some of his crewmen on Hispaniola (present-day Haiti and the Dominican Republic) and sailed back to Spain. When he returned to La Navidad a year later, Columbus found that the Taino had killed the sailors in retaliation for the sailors' demands for food, gold, and labor.

These killings, combined with attacks on the Spanish by small groups of Taino and other native peoples on other Caribbean islands, provoked Columbus to use force. As the newly appointed governor of all lands he discovered, Columbus built a second fort on Hispaniola and assigned to it the soldiers who had come on the expedition with him. The soldiers, with their metal armor, guns, and horses, easily subdued the Taino. Columbus then demanded gold from the Taino and ordered that 550 Taino be sent to Spain as slaves. (39)

After two more voyages Columbus was relieved of his post as governor of the new lands because of mismanagement and sent back to Spain. However, the brutal precedent he set in regard to the treatment of native peoples was followed by his successors, who enslaved them by the thousands.

Bartolomé de las Casas Speaks Out

In fewer than ten years, the Spanish had established the *encomienda* system on the islands in the Caribbean. Under encomienda, Spanish colonists were granted a certain amount of land and the labor of the people who lived on it. The system was later transported to Spanish settlements on the mainland. Supposedly, the colonists would pay the native people for their labor and convert them to Christianity. In reality, the natives were either forced to accept Christianity or were given little or no religious instruction, were cruelly treated, and in effect reduced to slaves.

One of those who spoke out against the encomienda system was Bartolomé de las Casas. Las Casas had been a conquistador and owner of an encomienda himself, but he eventually became a Roman Catholic priest. As a missionary in Cuba and South and Central America, and later bishop in Mexico, las Casas sought to protect his native charges by preaching against the encomienda and shaming the consciences of the landowners. (37)

Teaching Idea

Share excerpts from Columbus's log-books with students.

Teaching Idea

Discuss with students what the Taino might have thought about the Spanish and what the Spanish might have thought about the Taino on that momentous morning of October 12, 1492. Ask, "How might they have described one another? What might they have thought about the others' helping or hurting them? Would they even have thought about help or harm?"

Note that the word *Taino* means "gentle ones." One of the early notes that Columbus made in his journal points out that the Taino had no iron weapons.

In his *Short Account of the Destruction of the Indies* (1542), the angry priest denounced the Spanish for mistreating the native peoples:

> Their reason for killing and destroying such an infinite number of souls is that Christians have an ultimate aim, which is to acquire gold, and to swell themselves with riches in a very brief time and thus rise to a high estate disproportionate to their merits. It should be kept in mind that their insatiable greed and ambition, the greatest ever seen in the world, is the cause of their villainies. And also, those lands are so rich and felicitous, the native peoples so meek and patient, so easy to subject, that our Spaniards have no more consideration for them than beasts. And I say this from my own knowledge of the acts I witnessed. But I should not say "than beasts" for, thanks be to God, they have treated beasts with some respect; I should say instead like excrement on the public squares. And thus they have deprived the Indians of their lives and souls, for the millions I mentioned have died without the Faith and without the benefit of sacraments. This is a well-known and proven fact which even the tyrant Governors, themselves killers, know and admit. And never have the Indians in all the Indies committed any act against the Spanish Christians, until those Christians have first and many times committed countless cruel aggressions against them or against neighboring nations. For in the beginning the Indians regarded the Spaniards as angels from Heaven. Only after the Spaniards had used violence against them, killing, robbing, torturing, did the Indians ever rise up against them.

Treaty of Tordesillas

Portugal and Spain took the lead in the exploration of the Americas, and since the two nations were rivals, there was a possibility that they would come into conflict over colonies. To avoid this, in 1493, the pope had established a line of demarcation roughly down the middle of the Atlantic Ocean, dividing the non-European world between Spain and Portugal. Spain was to have the Americas to colonize and Portugal would control Africa and Asia. The following year, the two nations negotiated the Treaty of Tordesillas, which shifted the line of demarcation west. This movement in the imaginary line secured Portugal's claim to Brazil. Essentially, the Spanish and the Portuguese divided up a large portion of the world between them. No consideration was given to the other nations of the world or to the wishes of the native peoples themselves.

Vasco Núñez de Balboa Reaches the Pacific

Vasco Núñez de Balboa was a conquistador who explored Central America. He sailed to the New World from Spain in the early 1500s and spent some time as a planter on the island of Hispaniola. However, he fell into debt and had to sneak off the island, stowing away on a ship along with his dog.

In 1510, in what is today Panama, he founded Santa María de la Antigua del Darién, the first successful settlement on the American mainland. While in Darién, he heard stories about a great sea and a fabulously wealthy kingdom to the south. (This last was probably the Inca empire). Balboa began exploring, hacking his way through jungles and plodding through swamps, occasionally doing battle with native peoples, whom he terrorized with his trained attack dogs. During his explorations in 1513, he became the first European to see the Pacific

Ocean from the Western Hemisphere. He claimed the ocean and its entire coastline for Spain.

Magellan and the Circumnavigation of the Globe

The Portuguese sea captain Ferdinand Magellan, sailing under the Spanish flag, gave the Pacific Ocean its European name. Magellan's expedition became the first to circumnavigate the globe.

Magellan was Portuguese and originally sailed for his native land. He followed the Portuguese trade routes around Africa to the Indies. However, he eventually fell out of favor with the Portuguese king and began to sail for Spain. He convinced the Spanish king that he could reach the Indies by sailing west and then through or around South America.

In September 1519, five ships under his command sailed southwest from Spain. They reached the South American coast in December and sailed south, looking for a passage through South America to the Pacific Ocean. They spent the winter in a settlement along the coast. Magellan had to put down a mutiny by some of his ship captains. He executed one leader and left another to survive on an island. One of his ships was lost in a wreck at sea. When the winter ended in August (remember that the seasons are reversed in the Southern Hemisphere), he sailed on, still searching for a passage.

In October 1520, they at last found a passage—the passage that is now known as the Strait of Magellan. The roughly 350 miles through the passage were extremely difficult, and one of his ships abandoned him and sailed back to Spain. But Magellan pressed on. It is said that he cried for joy when he finally reached the ocean. On entering the Pacific Ocean, Magellan gave it that name because he found it very calm compared to the icy waters he had just crossed.

With three ships out of his original five, Magellan sailed into the Pacific Ocean. He thought it would not take long to reach Asia, but he had no idea of the vastness of the ocean before him. It took six months to reach the Philippines. He and his men barely survived. The ship ran out of water and food. Sailors suffered from scurvy and were reduced to eating rats and pieces of leather. Some men starved to death.

Once Magellan's party reached the Philippines, they began to convert some of the local leaders to Christianity. On the island of Mactan, Magellan was killed in a battle by Chief Lapulapu, the leader of a tribe that resisted the European explorers. Antonio Pigafetta, one of the men on board described the encounter:

> When morning came forty-nine of us leaped into the water up to our thighs, and walked through water for more than two crossbow flights before we could reach the shore. . . . When we reached land, those men [the natives] had formed in three divisions to the number of more than one thousand five hundred persons. When they saw us, they charged down upon us with exceeding loud cries. . . . Recognizing the captain, so many turned upon him that they knocked his helmet off his head twice. . . . An Indian hurled a bamboo spear into the captain's face, but the latter immediately killed him with his lance, which he left in the Indian's body. Then, trying to lay hand on sword, he could draw it out but halfway, because he had been wounded in the arm with a bamboo spear. When the natives saw that, they all hurled themselves upon him. One of

Teaching Idea

Use Magellan's voyage as a way to revisit and reinforce what students learned about the International Date Line and time zones during their study of geography.

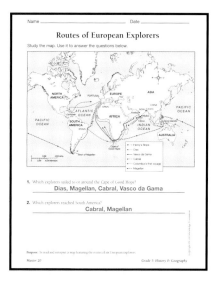

Use Instructional Master 20.

them wounded him on the left leg with a large cutlass, which resembles a scimitar, only being larger. That caused the captain to fall face downward, when immediately they rushed upon him with iron and bamboo spears and with their cutlasses, until they killed our mirror, our light, our comfort, and our true guide. When they wounded him, he turned back many times to see whether we were all in the boats. Thereupon, beholding him dead, we, wounded, retreated, as best we could, to the boats, which were already pulling off.

After this encounter, there were no longer enough men to sail three ships, so one ship was abandoned. The two remaining ships arrived in the Spice Islands in 1521. After loading up with spices, they sailed for home. One ship was captured by the rival Portuguese, so only one ship returned to Spain. This ship had sailed west to Africa, south along the coast, west around the Cape of Good Hope, and northward along the western coast of Africa, reaching Spain in 1522. Despite the loss of four ships and all but 18 men, the spices that the one remaining ship had taken on in the Spice Islands made the voyage a profit for its backers.

Arriving home, the survivors of the journey noticed something interesting. They had kept a careful record of the days they had journeyed, but when they checked the date with locals, they found that their reckoning of what day it was differed by one day from the reckoning of those who had stayed at home. The travelers thought it was Wednesday, but the Europeans who stayed at home said it was Thursday. What had happened was the ship had sailed one rotation around Earth, so that their assessment of time was off by 24 hours. This discovery eventually led to the creation of the International Date Line.

England and France

Search for the Northwest Passage

Although Spain and Portugal led the way in exploration, England and France were not far behind. The English and the French were hopeful that they could find a "Northwest Passage," a water route that would lead them through North America to the Pacific Ocean. Then they could sail to the Spice Islands and grow wealthy.

An early English explorer was John Cabot. Although he was from Venice, Cabot was in the service of the English monarch when he sailed west in 1497. Cabot reached the coast of North America at Newfoundland and possibly sailed as far south as the Chesapeake Bay. Cabot's expedition was the first European expedition to see the North American continent since the Vikings. But Cabot himself did not know this. Like Columbus, he believed he had reached Asia.

When Cabot returned to England, he did not have any spices and silks to show for his journey, but was able to describe scooping codfish out of the water in baskets. Cabot's second expedition in 1498 disappeared, and while he had not located the Northwest Passage, England based its later claim to North American territory on his explorations. When Cabot had first sighted Newfoundland, he had gone ashore and claimed the land for England.

Frenchman Samuel de Champlain searched for a Northwest Passage several times. He explored the St. Lawrence River, northern New York (where he discovered the lake that bears his name), and the Great Lakes Huron and Ontario. From

1603 to 1606, he explored Nova Scotia. In 1608, he founded the settlement of Quebec, which is the oldest city in Canada. His explorations were the basis for French claims to the colony of New France, of which Champlain was governor between 1633 and his death in 1635.

Henry Hudson tried two different routes to Asia. Sailing for the Dutch East India Company in 1609, he first explored along the lower coast of North America around what is now New York and came across the mouth of the river that now bears his name. Thinking this might be the long-sought Northwest Passage, he sailed north on it to what is now Albany. Finding no passage, he returned downstream. His voyage of exploration became the basis for the Netherlands' claim to the area.

In 1610, Hudson, then sailing for his native England, tried a more northerly route. Sailing north and then west around Newfoundland, he found a strait and sailed through it into a huge bay. Both the strait and the bay are now named for him. Once in Hudson Bay, he planned to spend the winter there before going on. When his ship *Discovery* froze in the bay and food ran low, his crew mutinied and put Hudson, his son, and seven others in an open boat with no oars. When spring came, the bay thawed and the crew sailed the *Discovery* back to England, but Hudson, his son, and his loyal crew were never heard from again.

English Colonies in North America

Beginning in the late 1500s, the English attempted to found permanent settlements in North America. However, the first lasting settlement, Jamestown, on the James River in Virginia, was not established until 1607. The next permanent settlement was Plymouth in 1620, in what is today Massachusetts. From these beginnings, the English—partly through independent settlements and partly through acquisition by force of other kingdoms' colonies—had established 13 colonies by the early 1700s. Territories claimed by the English reached south to Florida from what is now the United States–Canadian border and west from the Atlantic Coast to beyond the Appalachians.

Whereas New France and New Spain were both sparsely settled, by 1760 the English colonies had a population of some 2 million, about half of whom were English or of English descent. There were also around 300,000 enslaved Africans in the colonies. Boston—with a population of 20,000—was the largest city in the North American colonies, and second in the British Empire only to London.

English colonies were one of three types: joint-stock, proprietary, or royal. A colony established by a joint-stock company was set up to provide its shareholders with revenue. A joint-stock company was like a modern corporation; members bought shares in it in order to finance an activity, in this case the establishment of a colony.

A proprietary colony was one established by and for the financial benefit of one, two, or a handful of proprietors. The proprietors established the rules for governance, selected the governor, and received the taxes.

In a royal colony, the monarch appointed the governor and often the governor's council of advisors, which was different from the colonial legislature.

Teaching Idea

Here are additional explorers who might be of particular interest depending on your location.

• Giovanni da Verrazano—
Although Italian, he was sailing under the flag of France in 1524 when he discovered New York Harbor and Narragansett Bay. The Verrazano Narrows and the Verrazano Narrows Bridge in New York Harbor are named for him.

• Jacques Cartier—
Searching for the Northwest Passage for his native France, Cartier explored the Gulf of St. Lawrence in 1534 and the St. Lawrence River in 1535 as far as what would become the cities of Quebec and Montreal. He claimed the area for France.

III. European Exploration, Trade, and the Clash of Cultures

Establishment of the Thirteen English Colonies in North America

Virginia

The first permanent English colony was established in North America in 1607 at Jamestown. A joint-stock company named the Virginia Company received a charter from King James I and named the colony Virginia in honor of Queen Elizabeth, the "Virgin Queen." The first settlers were not farmers, but adventurers, interested mostly in searching out goods that would bring substantial prices in trade with England. However, tobacco agriculture was soon introduced to the colony and by 1619, tobacco had become the chief crop. By 1669, Virginia was exporting 15 million pounds of tobacco a year.

Massachusetts Bay

In 1620, a group of Puritans sailed from Holland intending to set up a colony near Jamestown. The Puritans were religious dissenters who believed that the Church of England did not go far enough to remove Roman Catholic practices. As they crossed the Atlantic, they were caught in a storm and ultimately landed at what is now Plymouth, Massachusetts. They named their settlement Plymouth Colony in honor of the English town from which they had set sail. In 1629, a group of English Puritans and merchants formed a partnership called the Massachusetts Bay Company. Its purpose was to establish a colony north of Plymouth that would be both a business venture and an experiment in living according to the Bible and Christian principles. The settlement grew to over 10,000 people by the end of the 1630s.

New Hampshire

New Hampshire was founded in 1623 by Captain John Mason. It came under control of Massachusetts Bay Colony in 1641, but was granted a separate royal charter in 1679. It included the area of what is today Maine.

Maryland

In 1632, Maryland was established as a colony for Roman Catholics seeking refuge from persecution in Protestant England. Maryland was established by a land grant from King Charles I to his friend Lord Baltimore. It was named after the queen, Henrietta Marie. The colony was settled in 1634. It was the first proprietary colony.

Rhode Island

In 1631, Roger Williams arrived in Massachusetts Bay Colony and soon ran afoul of the colony's leaders because of his religious beliefs. Williams advocated religious toleration and fair treatment for Native Americans. In 1635, Williams was banished from Massachusetts Bay Colony. He established a settlement south of Massachusetts Bay Colony in present-day Providence with land he purchased from the Narragansetts.

In 1643, this settlement, along with others in the area, petitioned King Charles I for a charter. It was granted in 1644, and the colony set up its own government that guaranteed self-government and religious freedom.

Teaching Idea

King James did not think much of the chief export from Jamestown. Students may enjoy hearing his famous attack on smoking from his pamphlet, "A Counterblaste to Tobacco." The text is available online.

Teaching Idea

As a round robin activity, ask students to tell you one fact about each of the 13 English colonies. See how many rounds the class can go before running out of information.

Connecticut

Thomas Hooker and fellow dissenters from Massachusetts Bay Colony established Connecticut. In 1636, Hooker and his followers settled in what is now Hartford. In 1639, they and members of several other towns in the area drew up the Fundamental Orders of Connecticut, the first constitution in the English colonies. The colony was granted royal charter in 1662 separate from Massachusetts Bay.

North and South Carolina

The Carolinas were founded by a land grant to a group of eight proprietors in 1663. The colony was named in honor of King Charles II. Rice was introduced into the colony in the 1690s, but the land and climate of the northern part of Carolina were not suitable for rice agriculture. Wealthy men began to buy up land and establish plantations. Slaves from Africa played a large role in the successful cultivation of rice. By 1740, for every European colonist in Carolina, there were two African slaves. Carolina was divided into North and South Carolina in 1729.

New York

The first settlement in the New York area was established by the Dutch in 1609. In 1624, Peter Minuit supposedly purchased Manhattan Island from the Manhattan people for $24 in trade goods. The Dutch named the city New Amsterdam. The success of this trading post drew the attention of the English, who based their claim to the land on John Cabot's voyage in 1497. They captured the city in 1664 and renamed the area New York in honor of the English king's brother, the Duke of York. New Amsterdam was renamed New York City.

New Jersey

New Jersey was named after the Isle of Jersey in the English Channel. The area was part of the New Netherland colony seized by the English. It was given as a proprietary colony to Lord Berkeley and Sir George Carteret, two friends of the Duke of York. The colony was managed as a proprietary colony for the benefit of the two men, but it offered religious toleration and representative government to all who immigrated there.

Pennsylvania

In 1681, William Penn received a land grant from the king to pay off a debt owed to Penn's father. Penn was the sole owner of the huge tract of land. Penn was a member of the Society of Friends, a group familiarly known as the Quakers. Like Puritans, Pilgrims, and Roman Catholics, Quakers were persecuted in England for their religious beliefs. Penn wanted to make Pennsylvania a haven for people of all religions. Because of Quaker belief, slavery was banned, and small farms rather than plantations developed in the colony.

Delaware

The English had occupied the area known today as Delaware since 1664, when they seized it from the original Swedish settlers. In 1682, the Duke of York gave the area to William Penn, who wanted an outlet to the Atlantic for Pennsylvania. The Lower Counties, as they were called, were represented in the Pennsylvania Assembly until 1704, when they were granted their own legislature.

The Lower Counties did not have their own governor, however, and continued to be ruled from Philadelphia.

Georgia

Georgia was the last of the 13 colonies to be established. In 1732, James Oglethorpe and a group of London businessmen received a charter from King George II to set up a colony between South Carolina and Spanish Florida. It was established as a debtors' colony to provide an opportunity for rehabilitation. Attempts at producing silk crops failed and caused economic problems for settlers. In time, plantation-style agriculture, including the use of enslaved Africans, was introduced.

English Colonies in the West Indies

Although the Spanish had been the first Europeans to see and seize the islands of the Caribbean, other countries soon followed them into the region. They took some islands from the native American inhabitants and fought with Spain and with one another for possession of other islands. These conflicts were an outgrowth of the struggle for power among European nations.

The English colonized Saint Kitts, Nevis, and Tortola (part of the British Virgin Islands) and forced Spain out of Jamaica. Today, the British Virgin Islands are a Crown Colony of the United Kingdom and Jamaica is an independent country within the British Commonwealth. Trinidad and Tobago were British colonies, but today they are a single independent country.

French Colonies in North America

One outcome of the interest in finding a Northwest Passage was the French claim to the land that is now Canada and parts of northeastern and upper midwestern sections of the United States. Beginning in 1608, when the settlement of Quebec was founded, the territory claimed by France steadily grew. By 1682, Robert Cavalier, Sieur de La Salle, had claimed all the lands in the Mississippi River valley for France. This colony of New France reached all the way down the center of the continent to the Gulf of Mexico. In 1663, Quebec became its capital.

Despite its size, the European population of New France never reached more than around 2,300 people. The real locus of the colony was in what is today eastern Canada, where the weather is harsher than in the more southerly and temperate Mississippi basin. The French government was more interested in gaining territory and prestige in Europe than in promoting settlement in its faraway colony. France's major concern was protecting New France's lucrative fur trade. France lost the colony to Great Britain in 1763 after the French and Indian War.

French Colonies in the West Indies

Today, all that is left of France's colonies in the West Indies are the islands of Martinique and Guadeloupe, which are now departments of France, or overseas provinces, rather than colonies.

Haiti, part of the island of Hispaniola, came under French rule in 1697. French colonists began importing enslaved Africans to build huge sugar and coffee plantations, which became the basis of a highly prosperous colonial economy. A slave rebellion in 1791 drove out the French and established an independent country in 1804. Core Knowledge students will learn about the revolution, led by

Toussaint L'Ouverture, in Grade 6 as part of the section on Latin American independence.

Trading Posts in India

The Portuguese, thanks to the vision of Prince Henry the Navigator, were the first Europeans to seek trading advantages in India. During the 1500s, they dominated Indian textile trade with Europe. However, over time, the French, English, and Dutch began to encroach on the Portuguese monopoly. The English—later the British—East India Company built trading posts at Calcutta in the northeast, Madras in the south, and Bombay in the west. The French had settlements at Madras and Calcutta. From these posts, by 1700 the British East India Company and the French East India Company had squeezed out their European rivals and were vying for sole control of Indian trade.

Internal Indian politics played into their hands. Southern India was divided into many states, and rival Indian princes sought the help of the two companies in subduing their opponents. In time, both companies gained the approval of their governments to provide troops to Indian rulers in exchange for commercial privileges.

A second influence on the Anglo-French rivalry in India was the Anglo-French rivalry in Europe. Like the English and French colonists in North America, those in India became caught up in their own versions of the English and French wars being fought in Europe—the War of the Austrian Succession (1740–1748) and the Seven Years War (1756–1763; known in North America as the French and Indian War). When the fighting was over in the latter conflict, the French had lost most of their territories in India and were no longer a threat to British power.

Teaching Idea

Draw the parallel between Anglo-French rivalry in India and Anglo-French rivalry in North America. Use this opportunity to review the French and Indian War that students in Core Knowledge schools should have learned about in Grade 4.

Holland (The Netherlands)

Dutch versus Portuguese in Africa and the East Indies

The Portuguese may have been the first to seek out the maritime route to Asia, but inadequate finances, the unprecedented novelty of their enterprise, and aggressive competition from other countries made it difficult for the Portuguese to hold on to their advantage. The Dutch quickly saw the value of the empire that the Portuguese were building in India and beyond.

A small nation of hardworking artisans and merchants in northern Europe, the Dutch set out in the early 1600s to try to dominate trade with Asia. In 1602, a group of merchants founded the Dutch East India Company. By midcentury, backed by warships and force of arms, the company had ousted the Portuguese from their trading centers on the east coast of Africa. The Dutch dominated trade with the Spice Islands and much of the trade with Southeast Asia. They also negotiated trade agreements with China.

Within a century, the Dutch, like the Portuguese before them, had their empire in Asia wrested from them. The French and the English—seeing the riches to be made in Asia—set about challenging the Dutch and each other for control of trade with Asia. (See previous section.)

III. European Exploration, Trade, and the Clash of Cultures

▶ Cape Colony and South Africa

In 1652, the Dutch established a settlement called De Kaap, "The Cape," at the tip of the Cape of Good Hope. The settlement served as a reprovisioning stop for its ships outbound to India and homeward-bound to the Netherlands. This settlement later became known as Cape Town. A few Dutch settled there to grow fruits and vegetables, raise cattle, and provide casks of fresh water to the ships. In time, more settlers and soldiers came to protect the colony from the native Khoikhoi people, who resented Dutch aggression against them, and who were unhappy at the encroachment on their lands.

By the late 1700s, their descendants, the Boers (the Dutch word for farmer) had moved far enough into southern Africa that they came in conflict with black Africans and fought a series of wars against them. In the early 1800s, the British gained control of the Cape Colony and fought intermittent wars throughout the 19th century against their new subjects, the Boers. In 1910, the various Boer colonies were recognized as the Union of South Africa, a self-governing dominion of Great Britain.

▶ New Netherland

The first settlement in the area of present-day New York City was a Dutch trading post established by Henry Hudson in 1609. In 1626, Peter Minuit, acting for the Dutch West India Company, purchased Manhattan Island from the Manhattan people for $24 in trade goods. The Dutch named the city New Amsterdam in honor of the principal city in the Netherlands and turned the settlement into a center for fur trading. The entire Hudson Valley was known as New Netherland.

The success of the Dutch drew the attention of the English, who decided to press their claim to the area. They based their claim on John Cabot's 1497 voyage. In 1664, the English captured the settlement and renamed the entire area New York, in honor of the English king's brother, the Duke of York. New Amsterdam was renamed New York City.

The Duke of York gave the lower portion of New York to two friends, who named it New Jersey after the Isle of Jersey in the English Channel. New Jersey was a proprietary colony managed for the benefit of the two proprietors, but they offered religious tolerance and representative government to all who immigrated there.

C. Trade and Slavery

The Sugar Trade

São Tomé, in the Gulf of Guinea, the Madeira Islands slightly northwest of Morocco, and other islands off the west African coast that the Portuguese explored and colonized became the first centers of sugar agriculture. Likewise, the Spanish introduced sugar cultivation to the Canary Islands, also off the west coast of Africa. Because sugar agriculture is labor-intensive, the Portuguese and Spanish needed large numbers of cheap laborers. Thus the Europeans began to trade with local Muslim merchants and other warlords for captives from the African mainland. The workers were typically captured by political rivals and sold as slaves.

Teaching Idea

For a small nation, the Netherlands was a worldwide commercial power in the 1500s through the 1700s. Have students do research in print and online sources to develop a report about the Netherlands in this time period.

The report could take the form of a written paper, an illustrated history, a model, or a map. Students should conduct their research first and then discuss it with you before choosing their medium.

In the mid-1400s, some 50 years before the transatlantic slave trade began, the Spanish and the Portuguese were buying Africans as slaves to work their sugar plantations on the eastern Atlantic islands. Later, the plantation model was introduced in Spanish colonies in the Caribbean and in the Portuguese colony of Brazil.

Sugar Plantations on the Caribbean Islands

As one historical account states, "The story of sugar in the Caribbean goes hand in hand with the story of slavery." The warm, moist climate and rich soil of the Caribbean islands were well suited to the cultivation of sugar cane. The Spanish knew from their experience on the islands off the African coast that sugar agriculture took vast amounts of labor, which had to be cheap in order to make the plantations profitable. Therefore, they made great efforts to transport enslaved Africans to work these new plantations in the Caribbean. When the English captured islands from the Spanish and colonized other islands on their own, they followed the Spanish example and that of the Portuguese in Brazil. African slaves not only planted the sugar cane and harvested it, but also worked in the mills where the raw cane was crushed and boiled down to make sugar and molasses.

The backers of the southern English colonies on the mainland of North America eventually realized that the climate and soil in parts of the South were suited to the cultivation of labor-intensive crops, such as tobacco, rice, and indigo. After the mid-1600s, the English began acquiring slaves from plantations in the Caribbean. Although relatively poor, the planters on the mainland were able to buy a few cast-off slaves from the West Indies and gradually were able to buy captives direct from Africa as the basis of the economy switched to large plantation farming.

Transatlantic Slave Trade

The first Africans in the English colonies on the mainland arrived at Jamestown not long after 1607. These first Africans are believed to have been treated like English indentured servants, people who contracted to work for a certain period of time and were then released. By the 1680s, however, the terms of service began to change to lifelong servitude. When tobacco cultivation took off in the late 17th century, it was difficult to find enough workers to farm the large plantations that the English were starting in the colony, and buying captured Africans promised a steady supply of labor.

Importing Africans as slaves for the Southern colonies became big business for American merchants and sea captains in the 1700s. Because the climate and terrain of New England were not suitable for large plantation-style farms, slavery did not take a firm hold in New England. However, there were some slaves in those colonies, and the principal merchants trading in slaves resided in Rhode Island. Slavery was less important in the Middle colonies, where most farms were small and tilled by families, although again there were some slaves on farms and in cities, where they worked in houses and as skilled artisans and craftspersons.

Triangular Trade

The slave trade was part of what was known as the "triangular" trade between the Eastern and Western Hemispheres. The triangular trade was so named because the trading networks that comprised it connected three main areas: 1. Africa, 2. the colonies in the Caribbean and on the North American mainland,

Teaching Idea

Create an overhead of Instructional Master 21, *The West Indies*, to help students visualize the location of the islands of the West Indies in relation to the North and South American continents. Point out that the West Indies are divided into four main groups: the Bahamas; the Greater Antilles (Cuba, Hispaniola [Haiti and the Dominican Republic], Jamaica, Puerto Rico); the Lesser Antilles (Leeward and Windward Islands, Trinidad and Tobago, Barbados); and the Netherlands Antilles.

Ask students questions about which island is the largest, which cardinal direction any group is from another and from the mainland, the distance between island groups and the mainland, and so on.

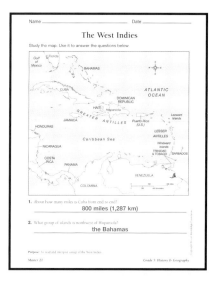

Use Instructional Master 21.

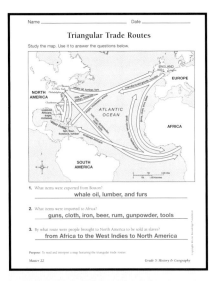

Use Instructional Master 22.

and 3. Europe. As you can see from the map below, goods were transported in different directions, depending on who had what, and who needed what. For example, slaves might be shipped from Africa to the Caribbean and put to work growing sugar cane and making molasses. Then the molasses they produced might be shipped to New England, where it would be made into rum that would be shipped to Africa for sale. Or, slaves might be shipped first to the Caribbean and then onto the southern part of North America. There they would produce a crop like rice, which could be shipped to England.

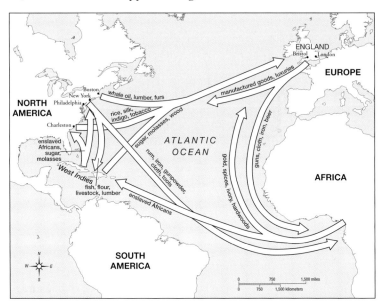

Slaves were shipped from the west coast of Africa. The area affected by the slave trade extended from Senegal to Angola. At different times in the 400-year history of the slave trade, the major areas of exportation shifted from region to region along the coast.

▶ The Middle Passage

The leg of the triangular trade network between Africa and the Americas was known as the Middle Passage. It was during the Middle Passage that Africans were transported in chains to the American colonies. Slave raiders—Africans armed with guns supplied by European slave traders—would kidnap enemies or just hapless men, women, and children who were in "the wrong place at the wrong time," and march them in chains to the coast. There, the Africans would be put into slave factories, or holding pens, until a slave ship came to pick them up.

On board the slave ship, the Africans would be chained together and packed below decks in tight spaces for six to ten weeks with little food and water. They might be allowed on deck in good weather for exercise and fresh air. Sometimes, Africans jumped to their deaths from the railings rather than endure further suffering. If the weather was bad, slaves would be kept below decks for long periods of time. Many caught fatal diseases; others went insane from the dark, claustrophobic, unsanitary conditions. For those who survived, the Middle Passage ended in the Caribbean or in the Southern colonies, where the Africans would be marched off the ship in chains to be examined by prospective buyers and sold at auction. (40)

Review

Below are some ideas for ongoing assessment and review activities. These are not meant to constitute a comprehensive list. Teachers may also refer to the *Pearson Learning/Core Knowledge History & Geography* series for additional information and teaching ideas.

- As a culmination to this section, have students write an essay based on the big idea, "Describe European adventures to the unknown world." Ask, "How did Europeans reap the profits of trade and colonization?" Have students justify their answers with facts learned in this unit of study.

- This section provides an opportunity for students to complete short research reports on any of the explorers from this section. Using the Language Arts section, provide the class with topics for short reports to write in formal style. Each day of a week, provide a mini-lesson on different aspects of report writing, such as correct paragraph form or bibliographies. Share these reports when completed.

- Have students write cause-and-effect papers in which they focus on the effects of exploration on both the explorer's country and the places he traveled. Have students also write about how these explorations impact their lives today.

- Have students write short papers on exploration that is happening today. Students may want to find information on space travel, undersea travel, or scientific advances. They may use periodicals or the Internet for information.

- Ask students to imagine that they are one of the explorers from this section and write a postcard back to their host country to report on the progress of their trip or what they have discovered. Give each student a large blank index card. Students should write their message on one side and then illustrate the other side to show what they have seen on their voyage. Check for correct grammatical form and proper use of addresses.

- To review explorers studied, make cards with the names of explorers, another set with nations they sailed for, and another for significant discoveries. Invite students to work together to line up the cards properly, e.g., "Columbus" with "Spain" and "the Caribbean."

- Have students compare the colonies of Spain, England, France, and the Netherlands. They can present their comparison in a 4-column chart, a 4-circle Venn diagram, or another creative manner.

- You may also ask the following questions after completion of this unit of study.

1. Why did the Portuguese begin to explore along the African coast?
   The Portuguese were looking for an all-water route to Asia so that they could take over control of trade with Asia from Muslim merchants and middlemen. They wanted the profits from this trade. Europeans also wanted to spread Christianity to non-Europeans.

2. Locate the following areas on overhead maps or a globe: (a) the Moluccas (Spice Islands); (b) Indochina; (c) the Malay Peninsula; (d) the Philippines; (e) Cape of Good Hope; (f) Swahili Coast (g) West Indies; (h) São Tomé; (i) Caribbean; (j) Cuba; (k) Hispaniola; (l) Massachusetts; (m) Virginia; (n) Quebec; (o) India.

The Big Idea in Review

From the 1400s to the 1600s, Europeans ventured out to explore what was to them the unknown world in an effort to reap the profits of trade and colonization.

III. European Exploration, Trade, and the Clash of Cultures

3. Locate the routes of the following explorers on an overhead map or globe: (a) Bartolomeu Dias; (b) Vasco da Gama; (c) Pedro Cabral; (d) Ferdinand Magellan; (e) Vasco Nùñez de Balboa; (f) John Cabot; (g) Samuel de Champlain; (h) Henry Hudson.

4. What were some of the European countries involved in the Age of Exploration? Where are some colonies that each one set up?

   Major players included Spain, Portugal, England, France, and The Netherlands. Students should be able to identify at least one place colonized by each nation.

5. Explain the importance of each of the following: (a) Prince Henry the Navigator; (b) Bartolomeu Dias; (c) Vasco da Gama; (d) Pedro Cabral; (e) Ferdinand Magellan; (f) Vasco Nùñez de Balboa; (g) John Cabot; (h) Samuel de Champlain (i) Bartolomé de las Casas.

   (a) Prince Henry the Navigator supported voyages of exploration; (b) Bartolomeu Dias sighted Cape of Storms/Good Hope at tip of Africa; (c) Vasco da Gama was the first European to sail around Africa to India; (d) Pedro Cabral claimed Brazil for Portugal; (e) Ferdinand Magellan's expedition was the first to circumnavigate the globe; (f) Vasco Nùñez de Balboa was the first European to see the Pacific; (g) John Cabot led the first European expedition to see the North American mainland, forming the basis for English claims; (h) Samuel de Champlain explored the area of St. Lawrence, forming the basis for French claims; (i) Bartolomé de las Casas was a priest who spoke out against the encomienda system.

6. What was the Treaty of Tordesillas?

   The Treaty of the Tordesillas was a treaty in which the Spanish and Portuguese divided the new world between themselves.

7. What was the Northwest Passage, and why were so many explorers trying to find it?

   The Northwest Passage was a hoped-for water route through or around North America. Explorers were eager to find it so they could get to the East Indies by sailing west.

8. Why was the plantation system exported from the islands off the African coast to the Caribbean islands?

   Both areas were suited to growing sugar cane, which requires moist, fertile soil. The Spanish and Portuguese who settled on the islands off the African coast found that by purchasing enslaved Africans, they could get large numbers of workers cheaply and that it cost little to feed and clothe them. It was then easy to take the same system to the Caribbean.

9. What was the "Middle Passage"?

   The Middle Passage is a name for the journey from Africa to the Americas endured by millions of enslaved Africans.

10. Identify some of the goods that flowed along the segments of the triangular trade network.

    In the Caribbean, slaves from Africa were exchanged for sugar and molasses, which were shipped to England for supplies or to mainland North America for grain, fish, cattle, and lumber if the ship was going back to the Caribbean. Ships from Africa going directly to North America unloaded slaves and took on rum and iron for Africa. Ships leaving North America for Europe carried whale oil, lumber, iron, tobacco, rice, indigo, furs, meat, fish, grain, and rum, depending on where the ship originated in the colonies. Ships from Europe to the colonies transported textiles, horses, and hardware.

More Resources

The titles listed below are offered as a representative sample of materials and not a complete list of everything that is available.

For students —

• *The Age of Exploration,* edited by E. D. Hirsch, Jr. (Pearson Learning, 2002), a unit in the official *Pearson Learning/Core Knowledge History & Geography* series, is available as part of the bound book for Grade 5/Level 5 and also as a stand-alone module. A teacher's guide is also available. To order, call 1-800-321-3106.

• *The Age of Discovery, 1492 to 1815 (World Atlas of the Past, Volume 3),* by John Haywood (Oxford University Press, 1999). Hardcover, 64 pages, ISBN 0195214439.

• *Around the World in a Hundred Years: From Henry the Navigator to Magellan,* by Jean Fritz and illustrated by Anthony Bacon Venti (Putnam Juvenile, 1998). Paperback, 128 pages, ISBN 0698116380.

• *Calliope,* a magazine of world history for Grades 4 and up, published by Cobblestone Publishing, www.cobblestonepub.com or 1-800-821-0115.

• *Exploration and Conquest: The Americas after Columbus (1500–1620),* by Betsy and Giulio Maestro (Mulberry Books, 1994). ISBN 0688092683.

• *The First Americans: Prehistory–1600,* by Joy Hakim (Oxford University Press, 2002). Book 1 in the highly acclaimed series, *A History of US.* Paperback, 177 pages, ISBN 0195153200. See also *Making Thirteen Colonies: 1600–1740,* by the same author.

• *Follow the Dream: The Story of Christopher Columbus,* by Peter Sis (Knopf, 2003). Winner of the New York Times Best Illustrated Children's Book Award. Hardcover, 40 pages, ISBN 0679806288.

• *Jambo Means Hello: Swahili Alphabet Book,* by Muriel L. Feelings, and illustrated by Tom Feelings (Puffin Books, 1981). Paperback, 56 pages, ISBN 0140546529. See also *Moja Means One: Swahili Counting Book,* by the same author and illustrator.

For teachers —

• *Atlas of Ancient America,* by Michael Coe, Dean Snow, and Elizabeth Benson (Checkmark Books, 1986). "An extensive, well-researched text unites the maps, illustrations, and feature sections so successfully that this book can be recommended as the best available introduction to Native American prehistory" (*Library Journal,* 1987). Includes 56 maps and more than 300 illustrations and photographs. Hardcover, 240 pages, ISBN 0816011990.

• *The Atlas of North American Exploration: From the Norse Voyages to the Race to the Pole,* by William H. Goetzmann and Glyndwr Williams (University of Oklahoma Press, 1998). A survey atlas intended for the general reader. Each two-page spread focuses on a particular explorer and includes selections from original journals. Paperback, 224 pages, ISBN 080613058X.

• *In Defense of the Indians,* Bartolomé de las Casas (Northern Illinois University Press, 1992). First published in London in 1556, this bishop's exposure of the cruel treatment of native American slaves at the hands of the Spanish was translated into forty-two languages and led to the abolition of forced labor by the Spanish in 1642. Paperback, 385 pages, ISBN 0875805566.

• *The Life of Christopher Columbus from His Own Letters and Journals, and Other Documents of His Time,* by Edward Everett Hale. First published in 1891, this is currently available in paperback (Indypublish.com, 2002, 144 pages, ISBN 140431573X); as an ebook through amazon.com; or online through the University of Virginia etext at http://etext.lib.virginia.edu/toc/modeng/public/HalLife.html.

• The Journal of Christopher Columbus for 1492 (3 August–21 October) is available at www.historyguide.org/earlymod/columbus.html. This site also contains a number of additional references and web links.

The Big Idea

The Renaissance was a time of great artistic and literary achievement; the Reformation was a religious movement that divided the Western Church.

Remember that each subject you study with students expands their vocabulary and introduces new terms, thus making them better listeners and readers. As you study the Renaissance and the Reformation, use map work, read alouds, independent reading, and discussions to build students' vocabularies.

The items below refer to content in Grade 5. Use time lines with students to help them sequence and relate events from different periods and groups.

1300s	Rise of towns and money economy
c. 1400	Beginning of Italian Renaissance
1400s	Network of trade routes within Europe and between Europe and Asia and the Middle East
1400s	Venice, important international trading city, controlled trade route between Europe, the Middle East, and the rest of Asia
1400s–1700s	Florence governed by the Medici
1440s	Invention (in Europe) of movable type by Gutenberg
1452–1519	Leonardo da Vinci
1475–1564	Michelangelo
c. 1500	Peak of Renaissance

continued on next page

What Students Should Already Know

Students in Core Knowledge schools should be familiar with

Grade 2

Ancient Greece

- geography: Mediterranean Sea, Aegean Sea, Crete
- Sparta
- Persian Wars: Marathon and Thermopylae
- Athens as city-state: the beginnings of democracy
- Olympic games
- worship of gods and goddesses
- great thinkers: Socrates, Plato, and Aristotle
- Alexander the Great

Grade 3

Ancient Rome

- Geography of the Mediterranean region
  - Mediterranean Sea, Aegean Sea, and Adriatic Sea
  - Greece, Italy (peninsula), France, Spain
  - Strait of Gibraltar, Atlantic Ocean
  - North Africa, Asia Minor (peninsula), Turkey
  - Bosporus (strait), Black Sea, Istanbul (Constantinople)
  - Red Sea, Persian Gulf, Indian Ocean
- The background to the founding and growth of Rome including
  - the definitions of BC/AD and BCE/CE
  - the legend of Romulus and Remus
  - Latin as the language of Rome
  - the worship of deities based on Greek religion
  - the Republic: Senate, Patricians, Plebeians
  - the Punic Wars: Carthage, Hannibal
- The Empire
  - Julius Caesar (defeats Pompey and becomes dictator; "Veni, vidi, vici"—"I came, I saw, I conquered"; associated with Cleopatra of Egypt; assassinated in the Senate by Brutus)
  - Augustus Caesar
  - Life in the Roman Empire (the Forum; the Colosseum; roads, bridges, and aqueducts)

continued from previous page

1513	**The Prince, published 1532**
1517	**Luther's 95 Theses**
1528	**The Book of the Courtier**
1541	**Calvin establishes theocracy in Geneva**
1543	**Copernicus's theory of sun-centered universe published**
mid 1500s–1600s	**Counter-Reformation**
1609	**Galileo invents astronomical telescope**
1632	**Galileo publishes in support of Copernicus's theory**

Text Resources

41 from *The Book of the Courtier*

42 from *The Prince*

43 *Martin Luther's* 95 Theses

What Students Should Already Know continued

- eruption of Mt. Vesuvius and the destruction of Pompeii
- persecution of Christians
▸ The decline and fall of Rome
  - corrupt emperors
  - civil wars
  - the sacking of Rome by the Visigoths in 410 CE
▸ The rise of the Eastern Roman, or Byzantine, Empire
  - Constantine, the first Christian emperor
  - Constantinople merges diverse influences and cultures as the seat of the empire
  - Emperor Justinian and his code of laws

Grade 4

Europe in the Middle Ages

▸ Geography related to the development of Western Europe
  - Rivers: Danube, Rhine, Rhone, and Oder
  - Mountains: Alps, Pyrenees
  - Iberian Peninsula: Spain and Portugal, proximity to North Africa
  - France: the region known as Normandy
  - Mediterranean Sea, North Sea, Baltic Sea
  - British Isles: England, Ireland, Scotland, Wales; the English Channel
▸ Background related to Europe in the Middle Ages
  - Beginning about 200 CE, nomadic, warlike tribes moving into Western Europe, attacking the western Roman Empire; city of Rome sacked by Visigoths in 410 CE; The Huns: Attila the Hun
  - Peoples settling in old Roman Empire including Vandals (cf. English word "vandalism"), Franks in Gaul (now France), Angles (in England: cf. "Angle-land"), and Saxons
  - The "Middle Ages" are generally dated from about 450 to 1400 CE. Approximately the first three centuries after the fall of Rome (476 CE) are sometimes called the "Dark Ages."
▸ Development in history of the Christian Church
  - Growing power of the pope (Bishop of Rome)
  - Arguments among Christians leading to the split between Roman Catholic Church and Eastern Orthodox Church
  - Conversion of many Germanic peoples to Christianity
  - Rise of monasteries and preservation of classical learning

IV. The Renaissance and the Reformation

Materials

Instructional Master 23
Renaissance Italy, p. 176

materials needed for a Renaissance Fair, p. 172

drawing paper, p. 174

set of letter stamps, p. 178

access to a local artist or art teacher, p. 186

access to research about Italian cities, p. 186

index cards, p. 186

class library of picture books about Italy, the Renaissance, and the Reformation, p. 186

paper figure template, p. 186

tag board, p. 186

construction paper, p. 186

yarn, p. 186

fabric pieces, p. 186

What Students Should Already Know continued

- Charlemagne (temporarily unites the western Roman Empire; crowned Emperor by the pope in 800 CE; idea of a united "Holy Roman Empire"; his love and encouragement of learning)
- Aspects of feudalism including life on a manor, castles; lords, vassals, knights, freedmen, serfs; code of chivalry; knights, squires, and pages
- The Norman Conquest: location of the region called Normandy; William the Conqueror and the Battle of Hastings, 1066
- Growth of towns as centers of commerce; guilds, and apprentices; the weakening of feudal ties
- England in the Middle Ages
  - Henry II (beginnings of trial by jury; murder of Thomas Becket in Canterbury Cathedral; Eleanor of Aquitaine)
  - Significance of the Magna Carta, King John, 1215
  - Parliament and the beginnings of representative government
  - The Hundred Years' War and Joan of Arc
  - The Black Death sweeps across Europe

The Spread of Islam and the "Holy Wars"

- The origins of Islam, including
  - Muhammad (the "last prophet"), Allah, Qur'an (Koran), jihad, sacred city of Mecca (Makkah), and mosques
  - "Five Pillars" of Islam (declaration of faith; prayer five times daily facing toward Mecca; fasting during Ramadan; helping the needy; pilgrimage to Mecca)
  - Uniting of Arab peoples to spread Islam in northern Africa, through the eastern Roman empire, and as far west as Spain
  - Ottoman Turks conquer region around the Mediterranean; in 1453, Constantinople becomes Istanbul
  - The first Muslims were Arabs, but today diverse people around the world are Muslims.
  - The development of Islamic civilization, including its contributions to science and mathematics (Ibn Sina or Avicenna), Arabic numerals), translation and preservation of Greek and Roman writings, Islamic cities as thriving centers of art and learning (such as Cordoba, Spain)
- Wars between Muslims and Christians, including the location and importance of the Holy Land, the Crusades, Salah al-Din (Saladin) and Richard the Lion-Hearted, and the growing trade and cultural exchange between east and west that resulted

An interesting activity while studying the World History and Geography strand this year would be the creation of a world time line including major events. This time line would help students understand the differences from one culture and civilization to another more easily and thus help them make comparisons and contrasts among civilizations.

What Students Need to Learn

The Renaissance

▸ Islamic scholars translate Greek works and so help preserve classical civilization.

▸ A "rebirth" of ideas from ancient Greece and Rome

▸ New trade and new wealth

▸ Italian cities: Venice, Florence, Rome

▸ Patrons of the arts and learning

- The Medici family and Florence

- The popes and Rome

▸ Leonardo da Vinci, Michelangelo

▸ Renaissance ideals and values as embodied in

- *The Courtier* by Castiglione: the "Renaissance man"

- *The Prince* by Machiavelli: real-world politics

The Reformation

▸ Gutenberg's printing press made the Bible widely available.

▸ The Protestant Reformation

- Martin Luther and the 95 Theses

- John Calvin

▸ The Counter-Reformation

▸ Copernicus and Galileo: Conflicts between science and the church

- Ptolemaic (Earth-centered) vs. sun-centered models of the universe

Vocabulary

Student/Teacher Vocabulary

95 Theses: a document that Martin Luther nailed to the door of All Saint's Church in Wittenberg, Germany, in 1517; usually identified as the beginning of the Reformation (S)

John Calvin: a French theologian who was converted to the ideas of the Reformation and established Calvinism (S)

city-state: a self-governing state consisting of a city and surrounding territory (S)

classical: relating to the culture or civilization of ancient Greece or Rome (S)

Nicolas Copernicus: a Polish astronomer who rejected Ptolemy's theory that the sun and planets revolved around Earth (S)

Counter-Reformation: the Roman Catholic Church's efforts to reform the church and stop the spread of the Reformation (S)

courtier: one who attends, or serves at, a royal court (S)

Crusades: invasions of the Middle East by European Christians from the 11th to 13th century and beyond (S)

Vocabulary continued

Leonardo da Vinci: a painter, sculptor, architect, engineer, naturalist and inventor; Leonardo created such works as *The Last Supper* and *Mona Lisa* (S)

Florence: a central Italian city that dominated trade during the Renaissance and was an important center of the arts (S)

Galileo: a scientist and inventor, Galileo invented a telescope that allowed him to observe the heavens and confirm Copernicus's conclusions that Earth and other planets revolved around the sun (S)

Johann Gutenberg: first printer in Europe to combine printing press and use of movable type to make books (S)

indulgence: the pardoning of punishment for a sin by the Roman Catholic Church (S)

Martin Luther: a priest and professor whose *95 Theses* initiated the Protestant Reformation (S)

Medici family: a wealthy family that rose to power in Florence in the 1300s and supported many great artists of the Renaissance (S)

movable type: a process for printing in which individual letters are arranged in rows on a wooden frame; the letters are then inked and a sheet of paper pressed over the letters. After printing, the letters could be removed from the frame and reset to form a new page. (T)

patron: a wealthy supporter of an artist or a writer (S)

pope: leader of the Roman Catholic Church (S)

printing press: invention by Gutenberg which produced printed copies of writing (S)

Ptolemaic theory: the theory that Earth was stationary and at the center of the universe; also known as geocentric theory (S)

Reformation: 16th-century religious movement which objected to some Roman Catholic doctrines and practices and led to the establishment of Protestant denominations, including Lutheran, Reformed, and Anglican (S)

Renaissance: a period in European history from about 1400 to 1650, marked by a revival of classical influence on the arts and literature, as well as the beginning of modern science (S)

Rome: a city in central Italy that was the center of the Roman Empire and, later, of the Roman Catholic Church (S)

transubstantiation: the Roman Catholic doctrine that the bread and wine in the Eucharist changes in "substance" into the body and blood of Christ (T)

Venice: a city of more than 100 small islands on the northeastern coast of Italy (S)

Domain Vocabulary

The Renaissance and associated words:
rebirth, revival, classics, learning, text, Greek, Roman, Latin, Medieval, Gothic, Islamic, scholar, humanist, humanism, manuscript, preserve, study, edit, philosopher, architect, architecture, build, sculptor, painter, engineer, inventor, science, religion, writings, world-view, beauty, style, art, masterpiece, thinker, inquiry, intellectual, philosophy, revival, middle class, market, banking, money, economy, commerce, merchant, patron, Italy, Genoa, Pisa, Milan, Genoa, Ferrara, city-state, republic, duchy, duke, papal, commission, fresco, painting, sculpture, court, dynasty, wealth, banking, commerce, rulers, academy, scholars, Plato, Aristotle, Homer, Cicero, Virgil, church, altarpiece, dome, columns, portrait, Raphael, Michelangelo, Boccaccio, Erasmus, Dante, Machiavelli, Shakespeare, Cervantes, machiavellian, Castiglione, "Renaissance man," sketch, invention, last supper, oil-tempura paint, plaster, light, shade, anatomy, form, figure, pieta, Madonna, Virgin

Vocabulary continued

Mary, Jesus, statue, David, Moses, Adam, creation, God, chapel, Sistine Chapel, author, diplomat, sprezzatura, attend, serve, manual, well-rounded, diplomat, ruler, cynical, power politics, ends, means, ruthless, morality

The printing press and associated words:
books, reproduce, reproduction, copy, by hand, slow, monks, manuscript, illuminated, copying error, Chinese, printing, printer, letterpress, font, typeface, typesetting, ink, proof, correct, blocks, system, letters, lead, molten, arrange, set, row, frame, spell, words, page, print, sheet, bind, affordable, cheaper, Bible, Latin, vernacular

The Reformation, Counter-Reformation, and associated words:
church, afterlife, mass, Heaven, Hell, Purgatory, hierarchy, parish, congregation, community, clergy, bishop, prelate, priest, parish, diocese, archbishop; cardinal, abbot, cathedral, Peter, Petrine, Paul, Pauline, tenet, dogma, belief, theology, authority, papacy, papal, pontiff, supremacy, excommunication, sacrament, baptism, Eucharist, poverty, chastity, Bible, scripture, New Testament, Old Testament, epistles, gospel, university, Wittenberg, Protestant, reform, reformed, practice, Wycliffe, Zwingli, liturgy, sin, confess, confession, penance, absolution, forgiveness, reparation, pilgrimage, remission, pardon, punishment, indulgence, Tetzel, money, sell, thesis/theses, debate, protest, nail, door, papal bull, Vatican, retract, refuse, recant, excommunicate, prince, Germany, war, Protestant, Lutheran, north, Catholic, south, salvation, damnation, faith, works, France, French, theologian, convert, systematize, preacher, influence, Geneva, government, predestination, election, damnation, omniscient, corruption, Calvinism, Huguenot, Presbyterians, Puritan, reform, spread, council, Trent, ban, education, doctrine, monastery, monastic order, monk, friar, founded, Jesuit, Spanish, Ignatius Loyola, saint, heretic, heresy, schism, division, Christendom, diet, orthodox, heterodox, apostle, apostolic, sola scriptura, "priesthood of all believers," preacher, doctrine, crucifix, transubstantiation, altar, sacrifice, ordain, devout, denomination, translate, brethren, minister, pastor, millenarian, missionary, pulpit, sermon, trinity, venial sin, mortal sin, deadly sin, Sabbath, Sunday, Satan, devil, belief

Copernicus and Galileo and associated words:
scientist, philosopher, mathematician, test, prove, theory, disprove, reject, planets, Earth, Sun, Jupiter, moon, revolve, center, universe, geocentric, heliocentric, eclipse, solar, orbit, Ptolemy, astronomer, unmoving, publish, telescope, observe uproar, controversy, church, conflict, teachings, Inquisition, recant, punish, scientific revolution: observe, study, data, hypothesis, test, predict, confirm, deny, experiment, suppositions, conclusion, verify

Cross-curricular Connections

Language Arts

Fiction and Drama

Stories

• Episodes from *Don Quixote* (Miguel de Cervantes)

Drama

• *A Midsummer Night's Dream* (William Shakespeare)

Music

Listening and Understanding

Musical Connections

• Music of the Renaissance

• Mendelssohn's *A Midsummer Night's Dream*

Songs

• "Greensleeves"

Visual Arts

Art of the Renaissance

Science

Science Biographies

• Galileo Galilei

At a Glance

The most important ideas for you are:

- The Renaissance was characterized by a renewed interest in writers, works, and ideas from the Greek and Roman past and a desire for wealth and the opportunity to gain that wealth through trade. The Renaissance largely overlapped with the Age of Exploration; they both partook of the same curiosity about the world.

- The Renaissance was marked by an interest in the physical world, which was manifested in art, in scientific observation and investigation, and in exploration.

- Michelangelo's and Leonardo da Vinci's art and Copernicus's and Galileo's scientific studies exemplify the Renaissance interest in the physical world.

- Renaissance ideals of a courtier and a prince are exemplified in the writings of Castiglione and Machiavelli.

- The invention of movable type by Gutenberg (in the West) made possible widespread literacy in vernacular languages and aided the adoption of Protestant religions.

- The Protestant Reformation and the Catholic Counter-Reformation were reactions to the abuses that had developed in the Catholic Church.

- The Protestant Reformation was both a religious and political revolution against the authority of the Roman Catholic Church and the pope.

What Teachers Need to Know

A. The Renaissance

Background

The Renaissance, which began in Italy and eventually spread to other parts of Europe, is usually said to have lasted from about 1400 to 1650. The word Renaissance *means "rebirth." This period saw a rebirth of interest in ancient Greece and Rome and a rediscovery of Greek and Roman works. It was a time of great artistic creativity in literature, painting, sculpture, and architecture. Scholars studied Greek authors who had been lost or forgotten for many years; writers created new works of literature; political theorists set forth new ideas about government; architects built gorgeous churches based on the classical models; and painters created beautiful new works, sometimes blending Christian and classical themes.*

Perhaps no passage expresses the spirit of the Renaissance and its love affair with the classical world as well as the following passage from Nicolo Machiavelli, in which the Renaissance writer describes how he spent his evenings:

The evening being come, I return home and go to my study; at the entrance I pull off my peasant-clothes, covered with dust and dirt, and put on my noble court dress, and thus becomingly re-clothed I pass into the ancient courts of the men of old, where, being lovingly received by them, I am fed with that food which is mine alone; where I do not hesitate to speak with them, and to ask for the reason of their actions, and they in their benignity answer me; and for four hours I feel no weariness, I forget every trouble, poverty does not dismay, death does not terrify me; I am possessed entirely by those great men.

This feeling of being tremendously drawn to the thinkers of ancient Greece and Rome was typical of many of the great artists and scholars of the Renaissance.

Preserving Classical Civilization

The two great civilizations of classical antiquity were ancient Greece and ancient Rome. Ancient Greece gave the world the poetry of Homer; the plays of Sophocles, Euripides, and Aeschylus; the histories of Herodotus and Thucydides; and the philosophical writings of Plato and Aristotle. The Greeks also produced beautiful sculptures and striking buildings like the Parthenon in Athens.

The Romans borrowed many ideas and techniques from the Greeks. They copied Greek statues and buildings, and created new structures like the Pantheon. They also created literary masterpieces of their own, including poetry by Virgil, Ovid, and Horace, and speeches by Cicero.

After the fall of Rome, some of the artistic and literary creations of classical culture survived, but others were lost. During the Middle Ages, Western Europe was broken up into small regions with economies based on agricultural labor. In most places there was little time for education and the arts. For the most part, only a few monks in monasteries had exposure to classical literature, and many of them knew Latin but not Greek. Although some Latin texts were still read (notably Virgil and Ovid), very few people were able to read Greek.

Some of the most significant advances in scholarship made during the Middle Ages were made by Islamic scholars. During the 600s and 700s, Muslims spread their religion across North Africa into the Iberian Peninsula, through the Middle East, and into the lands of the Byzantine Empire. Some of these areas had previously been conquered and governed by Alexander the Great, who exposed them to Hellenistic Greek culture and then by the Romans. The Muslim conquerors eventually came into possession of various Greek and Roman manuscripts. Rather than destroy these works, Muslim scholars carefully preserved them, translating them into Arabic, studying them, and in some cases building on ideas set down by the ancient writers in their own works. The Muslims were particularly interested in philosophic and scientific works. (Students who were in Core Knowledge schools in Grade 4 should have learned about significant Muslim contributions to learning during the Middle Ages, including Arabic numbers and algebra, as well as the achievements of particular scholars such as Ibn Sina, known in Europe as Avicenna.)

Jewish scholars in Muslim-held areas such as Spain and Egypt also studied and used Greco-Roman writings. One of the best known of the Jewish scholars was Maimonides, who lived in Cordoba, Spain, and Cairo, Egypt. Maimonides was a doctor and philosopher who tried to reconcile science and religion in his writings.

It was mainly through the efforts of these scholars that the works of the Greeks and Romans were preserved for later Europeans. Although artists and scholars were working in any number of Muslim cities (Baghdad, Constantinople, Timbuktu, Damascus, and Cairo, for example), the cities of Andalusia in southern Spain were especially rich centers of scientific work and artistic development. Scholars working in these cities translated works that had originally been written in Greek out of Arabic and into Latin. Over time, these Latin translations began to be studied at European universities that sprang up in the late Middle Ages, and Greek began to be studied again as well.

The Humanists

As European scholars learned more about the writings of the ancient Greeks and Romans, interest in the ancient world increased. Some people began to wish they could read Plato, Aristotle, and other classical authors in the original Greek. Others rummaged through monasteries looking for manuscripts of forgotten classical works. These scholars became known as humanists because they devoted their lives to studying the humanities and sought to find a balance between thinking about human virtues and actively participating in life. This focus on studying how to reform human culture and actively engaging in life's pursuits was an important hallmark of the humanist movement.

The humanists wanted to recover lost texts and establish the best text of a particular book by comparing various surviving copies. They wanted to study the classical writers and learn to write in an elegant classical style. Machiavelli, in the quotation cited on p. 171, gave voice to the mind of the humanist scholar.

One of the earliest and most important of the humanists was the Italian poet Francesco Petrarch. Petrarch was born in 1304 not far from Florence. He was a dedicated student of Latin literature and a talented poet. Petrarch wrote part of an epic poem in Latin on the Second Punic War (an episode from Roman history). Petrarch also commissioned the first translation of Homer's *Iliad* from Greek into Latin and wrote about the lives of famous people from the ancient world. He visited monasteries, searching for lost classical manuscripts. One of his greatest finds was a set of previously unknown letters by the Roman orator Cicero. In one of his most famous works, Petrarch imagines himself speaking with Saint Augustine, the great Latin writer and church father.

It was Petrarch as much as anyone who created the idea of the Renaissance as a historical period. He held that history could be divided into three ages: 1. the classical era, which Petrarch loved and admired; 2. the "Dark Ages," which he detested and saw as an age in which learning and the classics were forgotten or neglected; and 3. an age that later became known as the Renaissance, or rebirth of learning, which he encouraged. For Petrarch, this third age would be a period when classical works and ideals were rediscovered and the "darkness" lifted.

Teaching Idea

At the beginning of the section, begin work on a Renaissance Fair as a class project. Working in pairs and small groups, students should choose a topic to present as an illustrated oral report, model, picture, or performance. Possible topics include
• Food
• Music
• Clothing
• Architecture
• Paintings
• Sculpture
• Science

Although Petrarch's scheme was grossly unfair to the Medieval period, it outlined a way of looking at the world that most Renaissance humanists came to share.

Another great Italian humanist was Leon Battista Alberti (1404–1472). Born in Florence and given a good education, at age twenty he wrote a comedy in Latin that was so completely in the classical style that many people believed it was a classical piece that had been rediscovered. Later Battisti wrote an important treatise on art that helped Renaissance painters learn how to give an impression of depth on a flat surface. Alberti was also a talented architect who worked on many churches and buildings in the classical style in Florence and Rome. Because he was a master of so many arts, Alberti was later known as a "Renaissance Man."

Leonardo da Vinci

Perhaps the most famous "Renaissance Man" was Leonardo da Vinci. Leonardo was a painter, sculptor, architect, engineer, naturalist, and inventor. He filled notebook after notebook with sketches and notes for inventions, including a robot, a calculator, and a flying machine that looks much like a modern helicopter.

Leonardo was born in Vinci, a town in Tuscany that is near Florence. The name Leonardo da Vinci actually means "Leonardo from Vinci." As a young man, Leonardo was apprenticed to a painter named Andrea del Verrocchio in Florence. He created a number of promising paintings during this time. Later he went to work for the duke of Milan, whom he served as an engineer and painter. It was in Milan that Leonardo began to fill many of his famous notebooks. He also painted one of his most famous paintings, *The Last Supper,* which shows Jesus and his apostles. Leonardo used an experimental technique for this painting, oil-tempera paint applied to dry plaster, rather than using the traditional fresco method of applying pigments to plaster while the plaster was still wet. Unfortunately the experiment was not a success, and the painting has deteriorated over the years.

Around 1500 Leonardo returned to Florence. It was there that he painted another famous masterpiece, *Mona Lisa.* The dreamy quality of the portrait of *Mona Lisa* resulted from Leonardo's use of subtle gradations of light and shade. (For more information about *Mona Lisa* and *The Last Supper,* see the Visual Arts section, pp. 327–349.)

Leonardo was also interested in anatomy and believed that the human form, as well as animal figures, should be drawn as realistically as possible. For this reason, he studied cadavers and made numerous sketches of human anatomy in order to understand how muscles and bones work. In his last years, he was engaged with scientific studies rather than painting.

Michelangelo

Michelangelo Buonarroti (1475–1564) was a preeminent sculptor, painter, and architect of the Renaissance. He grew up in Florence and was apprenticed to a well-known Florentine painter. As a young man, he was supported by the most powerful man in Florence, Lorenzo de' Medici. Michelangelo was allowed to spend time in the Medici sculpture garden, which contained a number of fragments of Roman sculptures. As an adult he worked in Florence, Rome, and Bologna.

Teaching Idea

Find pictures of great works by Leonardo and Michelangelo in art books or online and share them with students. In cases where the works are based on stories from mythology, begin by telling the story. Then show the work, and ask if students can tell what part of the story is depicted.

Cross-curricular Teaching Idea

The information on Leonardo da Vinci and Michelangelo provides a good opportunity to reinforce topics from the Visual Arts section, such as the influence of classical sculpture and architecture, and the inventiveness of Renaissance artists, such as their development of linear perspective.

Cross-curricular Teaching Idea

Explain that Michelangelo spent four years painting the ceiling of the Sistine Chapel. Contrary to popular myth, he most likely did not paint while lying on his back on scaffolding. However, he did stand on scaffolding and had to paint overhead, often bending back to reach the ceiling. Talk about what it must have been like to do this—how tired his arm must have gotten; how the paint must have run down his arm, probably splattering onto his face. Ask students to try it out. You might do this in class, but it would probably be a better homework assignment.

Give each student a piece of drawing paper and tell them to take it home and tape it as far over their heads as they can reach. They should ask an older sibling, parent, or a caregiver to time them for 10 minutes. Then the students should try drawing with a marker or crayon—not paint—for 10 minutes straight. When the other person calls time, students should untape their pictures and write a brief paragraph describing what it was like painting, how they felt, and what they think of Michelangelo. Display their artwork on the ceiling of the class.

Among his sculptures are the following:

• His *Pietà* in St. Peter's Basilica in Rome. A pieta is a statue of the Virgin Mary mourning over the dead body of Jesus.

• A colossal statue of David, the young Hebrew boy who used his slingshot to defeat the hulking giant Goliath in the Old Testament. Michelangelo carved this statue from a gigantic piece of marble that another sculptor had begun working on and then abandoned.

• A statue of the Hebrew leader Moses, which he carved for the tomb of Pope Julius II. Julius II had been a supporter and patron of Michelangelo before his death.

Among his best-known frescoes are the following:

• *The Creation of Adam* on the ceiling of the Sistine Chapel in Rome. This is one of several paintings based on episodes from the book of Genesis in the Bible that Michelangelo painted in the Sistine Chapel, an important meeting place for cardinals and high church officials in Rome.

• *The Last Judgment*, also in the Sistine Chapel, but done many years later, in a somewhat different style. Christ is in the center passing judgment; the saved souls rise, while the damned sink down.

In addition, Michelangelo wrote poetry and worked as an architect. His most important work in architecture was the design of the great dome on St. Peter's. (See more information about Michelangelo in the Visual Arts section, pp. 337, 339–340.)

Patrons and Patronage

It takes a lot of time and money to carve a block of marble into a statue or paint the ceiling of the Sistine Chapel. Many of the great artistic and literary achievements of the Renaissance might never have occurred if there had not been wealthy people willing to commission works and subsidize artists. Fortunately, there were a number of wealthy people in Italy who were eager to be patrons, or supporters, of the arts.

In order to understand where the great patrons of the Renaissance came from, it is important to know a little about politics and economics during the late Middle Ages and early Renaissance. At this time Italy was not a unified nation but a collection of independent city-states. Among the most important of these city-states were Venice, Florence, Rome, Milan, Genoa, Ferrara, and Naples. These city-states competed with one another, and a number of them eventually grew wealthy from trade. Ships from Italian city-states controlled much of the commerce in the Mediterranean. They transported goods back and forth from the Middle East and sold goods to the rest of Europe. (It was this Italian dominance of trade that the Portuguese and Spaniards set out to break with their voyages of exploration.) Gradually some men in these Italian city-states began to acquire large fortunes. Bankers and merchants often did especially well. Some of these wealthy men eventually emerged as patrons of the artists and humanists.

Florence and the Medici

The most famous of the patrons were the Medici [MED-uh-chee] family of Florence. Florence is located on the Arno River in central Italy. The city flourished from the 1300s to the 1700s and dominated the region. Florence was a republic and an important center of commerce and the arts. Among its trade

goods were wool, silks, and tapestries. Artists who worked in Florence included Leonardo da Vinci, Raphael, and Michelangelo. Petrarch, Boccaccio, Dante, and Machiavelli were some of its famous writers.

The Medici were among the greatest patrons of the arts. The dynasty was founded in Florence in the 1300s and achieved its wealth through banking and commerce. The early Medici controlled Florence from behind the scenes by making sure that people sympathetic to the family occupied all key offices. In later years, members of the family became queens, cardinals, and popes. Three of the most important members of the family are listed below:

• Cosimo de' Medici (1389–1464) is often regarded as the founder of the political dynasty. He carried on the family business and ruled Florence by seeing that friends of the family were elected to all key offices. He also became a major patron of scholarship and the arts and collected rare books and manuscripts. He set up an academy of learned scholars based on the ancient Academy founded by Plato. At this academy, the humanist scholar Marsilio Ficino taught the works of Plato. At the same time there was a renewed interest in teaching ancient Greek, a language which had been virtually unknown in Western Europe for hundreds of years. Cosimo also supported master artists including Ghiberti and Donatello.

• Lorenzo de' Medici (1449–1492) was Cosimo's grandson. He was known as Lorenzo the Magnificent. He was a powerful leader who is credited with making Florence one of the most beautiful cities in Europe. Among the artists whose work he commissioned to adorn Florence were Donatello, Botticelli, Michelangelo, and Verrocchio—the master for whom Leonardo da Vinci was an apprentice. Lorenzo started a school of sculpture where Michelangelo studied as a young boy. He supported an important library, as well as a number of great humanist scholars, including Ficino, Pico della Mirandola, and the poet Politian. In fact, Lorenzo was a poet himself. It was Pico della Mirandola who suggested Lorenzo invite the Dominican monk Savonarola to preach in Florence. Savonarola surprised everybody by launching into a series of attacks of the Medici and their expensive tastes. He said Florentines had gone too far in the direction of classical culture and were forgetting about their duties as Christians. (Eventually Savonarola attracted such a following that he was able to take over the city for awhile. He attempted to turn Florence into a model of Christian piety, and he established a democratic government. But his dominance was short-lived.)

• Giovanni di Lorenzo de' Medici (1475–1521), the son of Lorenzo, is better known to history as Pope Leo X. He was educated by humanist scholars associated with his father, including Pico della Mirandola. As was often the custom with second sons, he entered the church as a young boy. He advanced through the ranks until he was elected pope in 1513. As pope, he spent lavishly and made Rome grander than it had ever been before, accelerating the construction of Saint Peter's Cathedral (with financial support from the sale of indulgences), stocking the Vatican library with valuable books, and commissioning artists to decorate churches and other buildings. Leo X was also a patron of artists. Michelangelo did some famous sculptures for the tombs of some members of the Medici family in what is known as the Medici Chapel in Florence. But Leo's special favorite was Raphael. Leo had Raphael work on St. Peter's in Rome and the Sistine Chapel. Leo X played an important role in religious history as well. He was pope at the time Luther posted his 95 Theses, and he signed the papal bull that excommunicated the German priest in 1521.

Teaching Idea

To help students understand the extent of territory that city-states ruled in the Renaissance, create an overhead of Instructional Master 23, *Renaissance Italy*. Begin by asking students what they think the term *city-state* means. Do they think that it means just the city itself? Does a *city-state* mean the city plus some additional land around it, or lands hundreds of miles away?

Use the overhead to show the extent of the territory that Venice, Florence, Milan, Genoa, and Siena controlled.

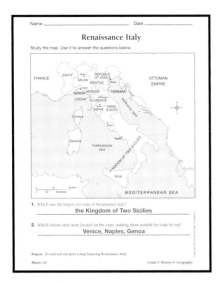

Use Instructional Master 23.

Rome and the Popes

Rome, on the Tiber River in central Italy, was once the center of the Roman Empire, but it had been sacked by the Visigoths, the Vandals, overshadowed by events in other parts of Europe, and torn by internal strife. By the time of the Renaissance, however, the city was once again an important center of culture. As the seat of the Roman Catholic Church, it was not only a spiritual center but also the temporal center of the Papal States, a large area of central Italy that the papacy had acquired over time through treaties and donations of land.

Many of the popes during the Renaissance were patrons of the arts, and artists flocked to Rome to serve them. Leo X, described above, was only one of many popes who commissioned artists to beautify the city. Many of the most elegant palaces and churches in Rome date to the Renaissance. One of the most notable is St. Peter's Basilica, the central church of Roman Catholicism. The huge dome, columns, and colonnades showcase Greek and Roman influences.

Venice

Venice is located on the northeastern coast of Italy at the northern tip of the Adriatic Sea. Today, the city sits on 120 small islands in the lagoon of Venice. A causeway, or bridge, links the city to the Italian mainland and more than 150 canals connect the islands to one another. People can travel from place to place in small boats called gondolas.

In the 1400s, Venice controlled many trade routes. It established trading centers around the eastern Mediterranean, the Aegean Sea, and the Black Sea. Merchants did not own ships but rather leased them from the government. The city government also built and maintained a fleet of warships to protect its interests.

Venice contains many beautiful Renaissance palaces, and was the home of one of the most famous artists of the Renaissance, the painter Titian.

Renaissance Ideals and Values

Castiglione

Baldassare Castiglione was the author of a widely influential work of the Renaissance, *The Book of the Courtier*. A courtier is one who attends, or serves at, a royal court. Castiglione himself was an Italian courtier and diplomat who for a time served at the court of King Henry VII of England.

Published in 1528, Castiglione's book was a manual about how to be a successful courtier. In it, he paints a portrait of what a courtier should know and how he or she should act. Above all, a courtier, or "Renaissance man," should be well-rounded, able to do many things, from playing a musical instrument to reciting a sonnet to competing in a sport. The ideal female courtier should also be reserved, gracious, and above all, beautiful. One word that is often associated with the court and courtiers is *sprezzatura*, which means the art of making everything look easy. (41)

Machiavelli

If Castiglione's book influenced the ordinary courtier of the Renaissance, Niccolo Machiavelli's *The Prince* set the standard for those who wished to rule. Macchiavelli was a diplomat who spent most of his life in Florence. Florentine

politics during the Renaissance were famously dangerous—not unlike the politics of the Mafia in the modern world. There were many wars and feuds. Politicians used bribery, intimidation, and even murder to get power, and leadership changed hands frequently. The Medici were only one of several powerful and ruthless families involved in Florentine politics. Machiavelli moved in this world and was several times in and out of power, and once even thrown in jail and tortured.

Based on his experiences, Machiavelli wrote a book about how a prince ought to behave if he wanted to gain power and preserve the peace in a state. (He dedicated this book to one of the Medici.) Machiavelli was one of the first to argue that being a good person is not necessarily the best way to be a good prince and to hold the state together in dangerous times. Machiavelli wrote that "it is necessary for a prince wishing to hold his own to know how to do wrong, and to make use of it or not according to necessity."

Machiavelli asked whether it was better for a prince to be loved or feared. He answered that the best thing would be to be both loved and feared, but, if a prince had to choose one or the other, it would be better to be feared.

The following brief excerpt gives some taste of the arguments Machiavelli puts forward in *The Prince*:

> Therefore it is unnecessary for a prince to have all the good qualities I have enumerated, but it is very necessary to appear to have them. And I shall dare to say this also, that to have them and always to observe them is injurious, and that to appear to have them is useful; to appear merciful, faithful, humane, religious, upright, and to be so, but with a mind so framed that should you require not to be so, you may be able and know how to change to the opposite.

> And you have to understand this, that a prince, especially a new one, cannot observe all those things for which men are esteemed, being often forced, in order to maintain the state, to act contrary to faith, friendship, humanity, and religion. Therefore it is necessary for him to have a mind ready to turn itself accordingly as the winds and variations of fortune force it, yet, as I have said above, not to diverge from the good if he can avoid doing so, but, if compelled, then to know how to set about it.

> For this reason a prince ought to take care that he never lets anything slip from his lips that is not replete with the above-named five qualities, that he may appear to him who sees and hears him altogether merciful, faithful, humane, upright, and religious. There is nothing more necessary to appear to have than this last quality, inasmuch as men judge generally more by the eye than by the hand, because it belongs to everybody to see you, to few to come in touch with you. Every one sees what you appear to be, few really know what you are, and those few dare not oppose themselves to the opinion of the many, who have the majesty of the state to defend them; and in the actions of all men, and especially of princes, which is not prudent to challenge, one judges by the result.

Many people over the years have taken a dim view of Machiavelli and have implied that he undermines morality by suggesting that "the ends justify the means." It has also been asserted that Machiavelli provides a license for rulers to

Niccolo Machiavelli

Teaching Idea

Read excerpts from *The Prince* to students and invite them to discuss the text. (42)

IV. The Renaissance and the Reformation

Gutenberg's printing press

think of themselves as "above the law" and not subject to the same rules as everybody else. The word *Machiavellian* has entered our language to describe someone who is full of trickery and deceit and will do anything to get to the top. Defenders of Machiavelli say he was just being realistic about what was needed to keep order and that his advice made sense in the dangerous world of Italian Renaissance politics.

Discuss that the term *Machiavellian* has come to mean "deceitful" and "expedient." Machiavelli wrote *The Prince* after a brief imprisonment by the Medici. The theory set forth in the book is contrary to Machiavelli's other works and to the deeds of his own life. His purpose in writing *The Prince* has been the subject of much debate. Ask students what they think the purpose behind *The Prince* could have been and discuss the purpose for other writings from this time period.

B. The Reformation

Gutenberg's Printing Press and the Bible

Prior to the 1400s in Europe, any books that were reproduced, including the Bible, were copied by hand. (In Grade 4, students in Core Knowledge schools should have learned that monks copied manuscripts of the early Greeks and Romans and in this way helped preserve the knowledge of the ancients.) One problem with this system was that it was slow; it could take years to make one copy. There was also the possibility of introducing errors into works. A monk could make an error in copying a verse of the Bible in the year 600 and that same error would continue to be made in copies in the year 1400—if some other error had not taken its place by then.

The ability to make many exact copies of the same work quickly and at a reasonable cost did not appear in Europe until the 1400s. As early as the 700s, as students should have learned in Grade 4, the Chinese had developed a system of printing with blocks of type. They did not develop movable type until the 1040s. In the 1440s, Johann Gutenberg developed a system for making individual letters out of molten metal. Once the individual letters had been cast, they were arranged in rows on a wooden frame to spell the letters of the words on an entire page, or on several pages at once. The type was then inked and a sheet of paper pressed over the letters. Once enough copies had been printed in his way, letters could be removed from the frame, and a new page or set of pages could be set from the type and printed. In this way, the type could be reused, but it also meant that many sheets could be printed from the same frame of type. It only needed to be re-inked as the ink came off on the printed sheets. While the first books printed by this process were very expensive, in time the cost was greatly reduced, so that books became affordable for middle-class Europeans. The development of printing spurred the development of literacy.

Whereas in the Middle Ages the vast majority of people were illiterate, from 1500 on the percentage of people who could read and write began to grow. During the Middle Ages most important documents were written in Latin. Although the Bible was originally written in Hebrew and Aramaic (Old Testament) and Greek (New Testament), it was generally read in Latin. During the age of printing, Latin continued to be an important language. Presses produced editions of classical works edited by humanist scholars, as well as new works written in Latin. However, printers also begin to print works in the vernacular (the language

actually spoken in a particular place). In response to a growing demand for these books, English printers produced books in English, German printers produced books in German, etc.

The Protestant Reformation

 ### Background

During the Middle Ages, the Church was the single largest and most important organization in western Europe. The Church provided stability in the face of political upheavals and economic hardships. This stability was evident both in its organization and in its message: life on Earth might be brutally hard, but it was the means to a joyful life in heaven. The Church taught that life on Earth was a time of divine testing and preparation for life after death.

Because of the central position of the Church in the West, the pope, the head of the Church, became a powerful secular as well as religious figure. As the Christian church grew during the Roman Empire, it developed a structure and a hierarchy. At the local level was the parish, a congregation of worshippers within a local community who were looked after by a priest. Many parishes made up a diocese, which was overseen by a bishop. Several dioceses were then combined into a province, which was overseen by an archbishop. Above the archbishops was a layer of cardinals who not only supervised the lower ranks, but who were advisers to the pope. In 1059, cardinals gained the power to elect new popes. At the head of the Church was the pope, who was also known as the Bishop of Rome.

The pope derived his power through the doctrine of Petrine Supremacy. This tenet of the Church said that the pope was the direct successor of St. Peter, the first Bishop of Rome. Because he possessed (or claimed to possess) that authority, the pope could claim to be God's spokesman on earth. Based on this concept, ambitious popes extended their authority to claim papal supremacy over secular rulers. Wielding political influence and the threat of excommunication—withholding the sacraments from an individual—various popes enforced and enlarged the power of the Church.

Papal power grew gradually during the Early Middle Ages. The height of papal power occurred during the reign of Pope Innocent III, from 1198 to 1216. Pope Innocent III had the Holy Roman Emperor Otto replaced and forced King John of England to become a vassal of the pope. However, the popes suffered some serious setbacks in the 14th century. From 1309–1377, the papacy relocated to Avignon in France. Then, from 1378 to 1417, there were actually rival popes, each claiming to be the head of the Church, and each denouncing the other. This was a serious blow to the prestige of the papacy.

After the schism was healed in 1417, the popes, now back in Rome, set about restoring the power of the papacy and rebuilding the city of Rome. They wanted to build new churches and redesign old ones. They were eager to hire the great artists of the day—men like Leonardo, Michelangelo, and Raphael—to paint frescos. Of course, all of this was going to cost money, and the Church looked for ways to raise more money. The church tried to tax believers in other countries, but the rulers of those countries were trying to raise money themselves and did not want to see their subjects' money sent out of the country and to Rome—particularly since the Church generally did not pay taxes on its properties.

Resentment against papal fundraising was acute in some parts of Northern Europe. As a result, the Church had to develop creative ways of raising money. One of those creative ways evolved into the selling of indulgences, a practice which would lead to the Protestant Reformation.

In the past, historians have sometimes depicted the late Medieval Church as deeply corrupt and ripe for the Reformation that struck in the 1500s. However, more recent scholars believe this was not in fact the case. They argue that, in the centuries before the Reformation, the Church was in many ways quite strong, and in some ways it was actually gaining strength. This is not to say that there were no abuses. It was widely known that some priests were not well trained or well educated, that some monks were more interested in hunting than praying, that some friars actually seduced the women whose sins they were supposed to be forgiving, and that some popes and cardinals lived a life of luxury rather than a life of piety. Improprieties of this sort were noted in poems like Geoffrey Chaucer's *Canterbury Tales* (circa 1390s), and there were periodic efforts to curb these abuses and reform the Church from 1000 on. Even the Protestant Reformation began as a call for reform within the Church. Only later did it lead to the creation of a new Church.

Anticipations of the Reformation

The Protestant Reformation began as an attempt to reform certain beliefs and practices within the Roman Catholic Church and ended with the founding of various Protestant denominations and the division of European Christianity.

Although Martin Luther is usually credited with starting the Reformation, there had been other attempts at reform prior to Luther's time. One important early reformer was the English theologian John Wycliffe (died 1384), sometimes called "the morning star of the Reformation." In disputes between the English king and the pope, Wycliffe sided with the English king. Wycliffe also believed that all Christians should have access to the Bible in their native language. He therefore initiated a translation of the Bible into English. Wycliffe questioned other accepted ideas, including the idea of transubstantiation. This idea held that the bread offered to the people during the Eucharist (or communion) was transformed into the actual body of Christ. Wycliffe's ideas and writings were condemned, but Luther and other Protestant reformers would advance similar ideas many decades later.

Martin Luther and the 95 Theses

Martin Luther (1483–1546) was an Augustinian monk who later became a professor of Bible studies at the University of Wittenberg in Germany. Based on his close study of the Bible (especially the epistles of St. Paul), he concluded that man is justified by faith alone—not by works. The key Biblical text for Luther was Paul's statement: "For we hold that a man is justified by faith apart from works of law" (Romans 3:28). In other words, a person cannot obtain salvation by going on pilgrimages or performing other good works; salvation can only be obtained through faith in Jesus Christ. This idea eventually brought Luther into conflict with the Church. In order to understand why this happened, one must know a little about the Church's doctrines concerning sin and the forgiveness of sins.

Martin Luther

According to Church teachings of the time, a person could confess his or her sins to a priest in the sacrament of penance and then receive absolution, or forgiveness, from the priest in God's name. The priest assigned prayers for the lay person to say as penance, that is, as an act of reparation. If the person was truly penitent, and said the required prayers, the sins would be forgiven and the person would have an opportunity to go to heaven in the afterlife.

However, if a person died without having gained forgiveness for all of his or her sins, that person's soul would be sent to a place called purgatory before it would be allowed to enter heaven. In purgatory a soul could work off sins accumulated during life.

The Church taught that good works, such as making a pilgrimage to a holy place or saying special prayers, could remove some or all of this additional punishment that would otherwise have to be worked off in purgatory. The Church called this remission, or pardoning, of punishment an indulgence. The Church insisted that an indulgence would only work if the sinner was truly sincere in his or her repentance.

Originally, there was no idea that forgiveness could be bought or sold. However, by the time Martin Luther became a professor at Wittenberg, indulgences were being bought and sold, sometimes by rather unscrupulous salesmen. One of these salesman, a man named Johann Tetzel, sold indulgences in a town near Wittenburg. Some of the funds raised by the sale of these indulgences were to go to the rebuilding of St. Peter's Basilica in Rome, one of the great architectural achievements of the Renaissance. Tetzel said people could gain an indulgence, not by being truly repentant, doing good works, and by saying prayers, but simply by paying money for a printed indulgence. Tetzel also claimed his indulgences were so powerful they could get not only the sinner, but also his or her relatives out of purgatory. He even had a little jingle he used to sell his indulgences: "As soon as the coin in the coffer rings, the soul out of purgatory springs."

Tetzel's extreme sales tactics angered Martin Luther and prompted him to write out 95 Theses, or points of debate. In them Luther protested against indulgences and other Church practices. Luther nailed his 95 Theses to the door of All Saint's Church in Wittenberg in 1517.

Among Luther's teachings were the following:

• Salvation comes through faith in Jesus Christ alone. You cannot buy your way into heaven with indulgences, or work your way to heaven by good works.

• The Bible contains all the guidance that anyone needs in matters of faith.

• Individuals are responsible for their own salvation. The power of the priest and of the sacraments that formed the core of the doctrine of the Catholic Church could be dispensed with. To Luther, every individual's spiritual status was as high as that of a priest. He believed in "the priesthood of all believers." The head of a parish still conducted church services as before and served as the group's leader, but he did so because that was his job, just as other members of the church had jobs and worked for a living. Every person held a great spiritual responsibility, as great as that which had formerly been ascribed to priests.

• The pope has no political authority over church organizations or property within nations; the rulers of the nations should govern churches within their boundaries.

• The longstanding policy of clerical celibacy was unwarranted. Priests should be allowed to marry. (Luther himself married. However, in the Roman Catholic Church the requirement of priestly celibacy continues to this day.)

• The church service was to be performed not in Latin but in a language the people could understand.

• There was no transubstantiation, or transformation of bread and wine into Christ's actual body and blood, in the Eucharist.

• Only a handful of the traditional sacraments of the Church had a genuinely biblical basis.

• Nunneries and monasteries should be closed.

Because of his emphasis on the Bible as the central element of faith, Luther translated the Scriptures into German. One reason that his ideas created so much interest and spread so widely is that he wrote in German, not Latin. Another reason was the development of the printing press. Many historians believe that without Gutenberg's invention of movable type decades before the Reformation, Luther's revolt against the Church would have failed from lack of popular support. (43)

Luther's ideas spread rapidly. The pope sent a papal bull (a special order) ordering Luther to retract his views. Luther refused—and even burned the papal bull in defiance. Luther wrote more pamphlets and added to his list of complaints about the pope and the Church. The pope gave Luther opportunities to recant his statements. When Luther refused, the pope excommunicated him. Luther was declared an outlaw, but one of the local princes protected Luther and kept him from getting arrested for heresy. Over the next 18 years, Luther published several more works denying additional church teachings.

Because Luther questioned the authority of the pope and suggested that the ruler of a territory should lead the church in that territory, his ideas attracted the support of a number of princes in northern Germany. These princes were only too happy to seize church property and declare themselves heads of new, local Christian churches that were independent of Rome. Eventually war broke out between Luther's supporters and supporters of the pope. There was also an uprising among the peasants. Luther condemned this uprising, and it was put down with brutal force. By the time the wars and bloodshed ended in 1555, Germany had suffered through a series of terrible religious and political wars. Many thousands of people had died, and the area was divided between Protestants (those who protested against Rome, including Lutherans and some other groups) and Catholics (those who remained loyal to the pope and rejected Luther's ideas). In general, Protestantism was stronger in the north and Catholicism had more favor in the south.

John Calvin

Another important religious reformer was the French theologian John Calvin. Having been converted to the ideas of the Reformation in the early 1530s, he wrote a book, *Institutes of the Christian Religion*. Written in 1536, the book attempted to systematize the ideas of the Reformation. By then, Calvin had been forced to leave Paris because of his beliefs. He was invited to Geneva to help establish the Reformation there, but his ideas about how Christians should live

John Calvin

were too harsh and again he had to flee. However, in 1541, he was asked to return to Geneva, where this time he was able to establish a model government based on religious principles. Calvin ordered that stained glass windows, altars, and similar "distractions" be removed from churches. Dancing, fancy clothes, games, and other worldly "pleasures" were banned. According to Calvin, living a moral life was serious business.

Among the important teachings of Calvin are the following:

• Like Luther, Calvin believed Christians are saved through faith alone, not works.

• Like Luther, Calvin believed that the Bible was the only reliable source of God's teaching.

• Like Luther, Calvin rejected the authority of the pope.

• Calvin rejected the doctrine of transubstantiation.

• Calvin also believed in predestination, that God decrees that certain people—the elect—will be saved and others will be sent to hell. (By contrast, the Catholic Church teaches that through free will, people make their own choice for salvation or damnation.) Calvin argued that the Bible said God was all-powerful and all-knowing. If God is all-knowing, he must know who will be saved and who will be damned. And if he knows who goes to heaven and who goes to hell, then how can people have free will?

• People must constantly strive to be good, and worldly success was an indication that a person was one of the elect (was saved).

• Fancy church decorations, like pictures of saints and the Virgin Mary, statues, elaborate altars, and stained glass windows (all very popular in Catholic churches) were corruptions of pure, genuine, simple Christianity. Calvin based his argument on the Ten Commandments, one of which is a prohibition of "graven images." Since statues and other decorations were "graven images," Calvin judged them to be improper.

• Calvin also protested against some rituals that had become traditional in the Church, against fancy priestly garments, and against observation of countless saints' days. In each case he pointed to the conduct of the earliest Christians and argued that many rituals, garments, and festivals had been added to the Church many years after the time of Jesus. Calvin wanted to reform the Church so as to return to the simplicity of the early Christians.

Calvin was an effective preacher and his influence was felt across Europe. Calvinism, as his religious thought became known, spread to France (by the Huguenots), the Netherlands, Scotland (by John Knox and the Presbyterians), and England (by the Puritans). The Puritans, who ultimately settled Massachusetts Bay Colony, had their roots in Calvinism. Many Christians in America today are partly or wholly Calvinist in their views.

The Counter-Reformation

The Counter-Reformation, or Catholic Reformation, was the Roman Catholic Church's own effort to reform the Church and stop the spread of the Reformation. Recognizing that there were some problems with the Church and its policies, the pope convened the Council of Trent, a committee of important churchmen that

Teaching Idea

Point out that what Calvin established in Geneva was a theocracy, a government based on religious doctrine. Students in Core Knowledge schools should be familiar with this concept, though not the term, from their study of the Plymouth and Massachusetts Bay colonies in Grade 3.

met several times between 1545 and 1563. Among the reforms that resulted from this meeting of cardinals and the pope were the following:

• Many of the theological teachings of Luther and Calvin, such as predestination, were explicitly rejected.

• The Protestant principle that faith should be based wholly on the scriptures—"sola scriptura"—was rejected. The Catholic Church reaffirmed the value of the Bible but insisted that tradition and scholarly work were also important.

• The practice of selling indulgences was banned.

• Higher educational standards for priests were established.

• Moral standards for the clergy were reiterated.

• The authority of the papacy was reaffirmed.

• Various doctrines about the Bible, the sacraments, transubstantiation (the Roman Catholic doctrine that the bread and wine in the Eucharist changes into the body and blood of Christ) and the Mass were affirmed and clarified.

The administrative structure and doctrines of the Roman Catholic Church as they are today are, in large part, the result of the reforms decreed by this council.

Another lasting effect of the Counter Reformation was the founding of a new monastic order, the Society of Jesus, better known as the Jesuits, by a Spanish priest, St. Ignatius Loyola (1491–1556). The Jesuits took on the role of soldiers of the Church. Jesuits took the lead in reinvigorating the education of priests and of intellectual inquiry. Fearless Jesuits sailed to the New World to convert Native Americans. Jesuit scholars played a leading role at the Council of Trent.

Copernicus and Galileo: Scientific Questioning

While many of the scientific theories of the ancient Greeks and Romans stood the test of time—such as Galen's belief that the arteries carried blood and not air—some theories were not grounded in demonstrable facts. As scientists, philosophers, and mathematicians of the Renaissance attempted to test and prove these older theories using new scientific and mathematical tools, many of the theories were disproved and discarded. However, whether all the planets and the sun revolved around Earth or Earth revolved around the sun became a heated controversy during the Renaissance.

Until the 1500s, the most influential theory on the movement of the planets was that of Ptolemy, a Greco-Egyptian mathematician, astronomer, and geographer who lived in the 100s CE. He claimed that Earth was stationary and at the center of the universe, and that all the planets and the stars revolved around it. This view was generally accepted by Christians because it put Earth, God's "greatest creation," at the center of the universe, which was considered unmoving and perfect, and also because it seemed to accurately describe what we see in the skies every day: when the sun "rises" and "sets" each day, it certainly seems like the sun is moving and Earth is standing still.

Even before astronomical telescopes were invented, Nicolaus Copernicus used mathematics to try to prove or disprove the Ptolemaic theory. Copernicus, a Polish astronomer, could not prove the truth of Ptolemy's theory. In fact, Copernicus argued that the geocentric theory (which held that Earth was at the

center) was actually less likely than the heliocentric theory (which held that the sun was at the center). At the request of Pope Clement VII, he published his findings in 1543, but his book raised little controversy.

Some 50 years after Copernicus published his findings, in 1609, the Italian inventor Galileo heard about a telescope that had been invented in the Netherlands. Galileo built a telescope of his own and began to study the heavens. He quickly made a series of important discoveries. He discovered that the surface of the moon was not flat but pockmarked with craters. He also observed that there were many more stars in the sky than could be seen with the naked eye. Finally, he observed several of the moons of Jupiter and noticed that these moons appeared to be orbiting Jupiter. If that were true, then it must mean that not everything in the universe was going around Earth. Eventually, Galileo came to the same conclusion as Copernicus: the sun, not Earth, was at the center of the universe.

In 1632, Galileo published a book in support of the heliocentric theory. Copernicus had previously written in support of the heliocentric theory, but he had been moderate in his claims. Galileo was bolder. Although his book was written in the form of a dialogue, in which each speaker gets a chance to state his case, he gave the strongest arguments to the spokesman for the heliocentric views, and he put some of the then-pope's own views into the mouth of the book's most rigid geocentric believer. Also, his book appeared at a time when Europe was involved in religious wars between Protestants and Catholics. At this time, the Catholic Church was very sensitive to any questioning of its authority, having been stung by the questioning of Luther and other Protestants. For all of these reasons, Galileo's book created an uproar among other scholars and the Church's hierarchy for questioning both the ancients' view of the world and, seemingly, the Church's teachings. Galileo insisted his ideas were not necessarily in conflict with religious truth. He said his work investigated "how the heavens go," whereas the Church taught "how to go to heaven." He was summoned before the Inquisition, a Roman Catholic court organized to detect and defeat heretical ideas, and told to recant his views or be punished. He chose to recant. Supposedly, as he left the court after having recanted, Galileo murmured to himself, "But it [Earth] does move."

The discoveries of Copernicus and Galileo were early episodes in what would later be called the scientific revolution. Beginning in the 1600s, those interested in understanding how nature worked set about the careful observation and study of natural laws, including those that governed human development and activity. Rather than simply accepting what Aristotle and other ancient writers had deduced the Bible said, scientists gathered data, established hypotheses, performed experiments to test their suppositions, and drew conclusions. Then they repeated the process to verify their conclusions. In the years following the discoveries of Copernicus and Galileo, important discoveries were made in various fields, including botany, physics, optics, and medicine. The work of Copernicus, Galileo, and other scientists of the time continues to be carried on and advanced by modern scientists.

Teaching Idea

Core Knowledge students should be familiar with Copernicus and astronomy from their studies in Grade 3. You may wish to review the content.

Cross-curricular Teaching Idea

You may wish to teach the science biography on Galileo in conjunction with this section.

The Big Idea in Review

The Renaissance was a time of great artistic and literary achievement; the Reformation was a religious movement that divided the Western Church.

Review

Below are some ideas for ongoing assessment and review activities. These are not meant to constitute a comprehensive list. Teachers may also refer to the *Pearson Learning/Core Knowledge History & Geography* series for additional information and teaching ideas.

• This section provides an opportunity for students to complete short research reports on any of the historical figures of the Renaissance and Reformation. Using the Language Arts section, provide the class with topics for short reports to write in formal style. Each day of a week, provide a mini-lesson on different aspects of report writing, such as correct paragraph form or bibliographies. Share these reports when completed.

• Have students research some of the artistic works of Leonardo or Michelangelo and then invite an artist or art teacher to class to demonstrate some of the techniques, such as sculpting or painting. Give students an opportunity to practice the artistic techniques, and arrange an art show for the school to view.

• Have students create travel brochures about Venice, Florence, or Rome. Give students an opportunity to research these cities and find examples of buildings or museums that were built during the Renaissance that people can visit today. Also include museums where people can see works of Leonardo or Michelangelo. Post these in the classroom.

• Create a class time line of Renaissance events by giving students index cards. Have students write a summary of an event that happened on a certain date and draw pictures to illustrate what happened during that event. Use the dates at the beginning of the chapter as a guide, and give students extra index cards to use as they discover other dates.

• With help from the school media specialist or local librarian, compile a class library of picture books about the important cities in Italy during the Renaissance and the Reformation. There are many beautiful books on the art from this period. Have students select a book to read and then give a book report to the class about what they learned. Have students use a book report format to write up a summary of the book.

• Have students create paper figures for the Renaissance. Give each student a template to cut out a body from tag board. Have students use construction paper, markers, yarn, and bits of fabric to create a paper figure representing a notable person from this section. Then, have students write a short biography to accompany their paper figure, including the name and accomplishments of each Renaissance or Reformation person. Post these in the room.

• You may also ask the following questions after completion of this unit of study.

1. What does the term *Renaissance* mean?
   The term Renaissance *means "rebirth."*

2. What was the Renaissance a rebirth of?
   The Renaissance was a renewed interest in the works of the ancient Greeks and Romans.

3. What were some Italian cities that played an important part in the Renaissance?

   Students may name Florence, Rome, Venice, or other cities.

4. Name one work that each of the following men is noted for:
   (a) Castiglione; (b) Machiavelli; (c) Michelangelo; (d) Leonardo da Vinci.

   *(a) Castiglione: **The Book of the Courtier**; (b) Machiavelli: **The Prince**; (c) Michelangelo: **David, Moses, Pietá**, ceiling of the **Sistine Chapel, Last Judgment**; (d) Leonardo da Vinci: **Last Supper, Mona Lisa**, inventions and scientific studies.*

5. Who were the Medici, and why were they important during the Renaissance?

   The Medici were a wealthy family originally based in Florence; they were patrons of many important Renaissance artists.

6. Why was the invention of movable type by Johann Gutenberg important?

   The invention of movable type made it possible to print numerous copies of books relatively quickly and inexpensively.

7. What were the 95 Theses and why did they matter?

   The 95 Theses were a document written by Martin Luther against the sale of indulgences. They helped set off the Reformation.

8. What was the difference between the Protestant Reformation and the Catholic Reformation, or Counter-Reformation?

   The Protestant Reformation began as an attempt to reform the Catholic Church from within but ended by creating differing religious groups and viewpoints, whereas the Counter-Reformation made changes, or reforms, within the Catholic Church.

9. Why was the work of Copernicus and Galileo controversial?

   Up until the work of Copernicus and Galileo, people had accepted the Ptolemaic system, which said that Earth was stationary and at the center of the universe. This fit well with the teaching of the Catholic Church that the heavens were perfect and unchanging. First Copernicus and later Galileo said that the sun was at the center of the universe and that Earth and the other planets and the stars moved around it.

More Resources

The titles listed below are offered as a representative sample of materials and not a complete list of everything that is available. Teachers may also refer to the *Pearson Learning/Core Knowledge History & Geography* series for additional information and teaching ideas.

For students —

• *Rats, Bulls, and Flying Machines: A History of the Renaissance and Reformation,* by Deborah Mazzotta Prum (Core Knowledge Foundation, 1999). An interdisciplinary history of the period, touching on history, literature, art, and music. A teacher's guide is also available. To order, call 1-800-238-3233.

• *The Reformation,* edited by E. D. Hirsch, Jr. (Pearson Learning, 2002), and *The Renaissance,* edited by E. D. Hirsch, Jr. (Pearson Learning, 2002), two units in the official *Pearson Learning/Core Knowledge History & Geography* series, available as part of the bound books for Grade 5/Level 5. A teacher's guide is also available for each unit. To order, call 1-800-321-3106.

• *The Age of Discovery, 1492 to 1815 (World Atlas of the Past, Volume 3),* by John Haywood (Oxford University Press, 1999). Hardcover, 64 pages, ISBN 0195214439.

More Resources continued

• *The Court (Life in the Renaissance),* by Kathryn Hinds (Benchmark Books, 2004). Library binding, 80 pages, ISBN 0761416765. See also *The Countryside,* in this same series.

• *Florence: Playing with Art,* by Maria S. DeSalvia Baldini (Mandragora Publishing, 1995). Hardcover, 45 pages, ISBN 8885957129.

• *Johann Gutenberg and the Amazing Printing Press,* by Bruce Koscielniak (Houghton Mifflin, 2003). Hardcover, 29 pages, ISBN 0618263519.

• *Leonardo: Beautiful Dreamer,* by Robert Byrd (Dutton, 2003). A detailed and interestingly illustrated biography of Leonardo. Hardcover, ISBN 0525470336.

• *Leonardo Da Vinci,* by Diane Stanley (Morrow Junior Books, 1996). Hardcover, ISBN 0688104371.

• *Renaissance Town (Inside Story),* by Jacqueline Morley (Peter Bedrick Books, 2001). Hardcover, 48 pages, ISBN 0872262766.

• *William Shakespeare and the Globe,* by Aliki (Harper Trophy, 2000). Honored by the Orbis Pictus Awards program for excellence in children's nonfiction. Paperback, 48 pages, ISBN 0064437221.

For teachers —

• *The Foundations of Early Modern Europe, 1460–1559* (2nd edition), by Eugene F. Rice and Anthony Grafton (W.W. Norton & Company, 1994). Paperback, ISBN 0393963047.

• *A History of Christianity, Volume 2: Reformation to the Present,* by Kenneth Scott Latourette (Harper SanFrancisco, 1975). A very readable, yet scholarly, history of Christianity. Paperback, 928 pages, ISBN 0060649534.

V. England from the Golden Age to the Glorious Revolution

The Big Idea

The 1500s and 1600s were a time of English expansion abroad and consolidation of Parliamentary power at home.

Remember that each subject you study with students expands their vocabulary and introduces new terms, thus making them better listeners and readers. As you study England from the Golden Age to the Glorious Revolution, use map work, read alouds, independent reading, and discussions to build students' vocabularies.

The items below refer to content in Grade 5. Use time lines with students to help them sequence and relate events from different periods and groups.

1509–1547	Reign of Henry VIII
1517	Luther posts 95 Theses
1533	Henry VIII marries Anne Boleyn and his marriage to Catherine of Aragon is annulled
1534	Church of England separates from Church of Rome
1534	Act of Supremacy
1547–1553	Reign of Edward VI
1553–1558	Reign of Mary I ("Bloody Mary")
1558–1603	Reign of Elizabeth I
1577–1580	Circumnavigation of globe by Sir Francis Drake
1587	Settlement on Roanoke Island; Lost Colony

continued on next page

What Students Should Already Know
Students in Core Knowledge schools should be familiar with

Grade 1

▶ English settlers
  • story of the Lost Colony; Sir Walter Raleigh; Virginia Dare
  • Virginia; Jamestown; Captain John Smith; Pocahontas and Powhatan
  • Slavery, plantations in Southern colonies
  • Massachusetts; Pilgrims, Mayflower, Thanksgiving Day, Massachusetts Bay Colony, the Puritans

Grade 3

▶ the search for the Northwest Passage
  • John Cabot: Newfoundland
  • Champlain: "New France," Quebec
  • Henry Hudson: the Hudson River

▶ geography
  • "New France" and Quebec; Canada, St. Lawrence River; The Great Lakes: Superior, Michigan, Huron, Erie, Ontario

▶ the thirteen colonies
  • Differences in climate and agriculture among the three colonial regions
  • Location of the thirteen colonies and important cities, such as Philadelphia, Boston, New York, Charleston
  • Southern colonies: Virginia (especially the story of Jamestown); Maryland, South Carolina, Georgia; the founders of these colonies, their reliance on slavery; the Middle Passage
  • New England colonies: Massachusetts (especially Pilgrims and Puritans), New Hampshire, Connecticut, Rhode Island; development of maritime economy and the influence of religion
  • Middle Atlantic colonies: New York, New Jersey, Pennsylvania, Delaware; the Dutch in New York, Penn and the Quakers in Pennsylvania

V. England from the Golden Age to the Glorious Revolution

continued from previous page

1588	Spanish Armada defeated
1588–1613	Shakespeare's plays
1603–1625	Reign of James I
1607–1732	Establishment of 13 permanent English colonies in North America
1611	Printing of King James Bible
1625–1649	Reign of Charles I
1640–1653	Long Parliament
1642–1649	English Civil War
1645	Cromwell chosen to lead Roundheads
1649	Execution of Charles I
1649–1660	Puritan Commonwealth
1653	Cromwell becomes Lord Protector
1655	England placed under military rule
1660	Restoration, King Charles II
1685–1688	Reign of James II
1688–1689	Glorious Revolution
1689	English Bill of Rights

What Students Should Already Know continued

Grade 4

> • England in the Middle Ages
>   • Henry II; beginnings of trial by jury, murder of Thomas Becket in Canterbury Cathedral, Eleanor of Aquitaine
>   • Magna Carta, King John, 1215
>   • Parliament, beginning of representative government
>   • The Hundred Years' War, Joan of Arc
>   • The Black Death sweeps across Europe

What Students Need to Learn

> • **Henry VIII and the Church of England**
> • **Elizabeth I**
> • **British naval dominance**
>   • **defeat of the Spanish Armada**
>   • **Sir Francis Drake**
>   • **British exploration and North American settlements**
> • **The English Revolution**
>   • **King Charles I, Puritans and Parliament**
>   • **Civil War: Cavaliers and Roundheads**
>   • **Execution of Charles I**
>   • **Oliver Cromwell and the Puritan regime**
>   • **The Restoration (1660): Charles II restored to the English throne and many Puritans leave England for America**
> • **The "Glorious Revolution" (also called the Bloodless Revolution)**
>   • **King James II replaced by William and Mary**
>   • **Bill of Rights: Parliament limits the power of the monarchy**

Vocabulary

Student/Teacher Vocabulary

Catholicism: one of the three major branches of Christianity; during the fourth century CE, became the official religion of the Roman Empire; the Bishop of Rome (the pope) is the ultimate earthly authority and voice of the Catholic Church. (T)

Cavaliers: supporters of Charles I during the English Civil War (S)

Charles I: an English monarch who reigned from 1625 to 1649; Charles I believed in the absolute authority of the monarchy. His disregard for Parliament led to civil war and eventually to his execution by Oliver Cromwell and the Roundheads. (S)

Charles II: son of Charles I, he took power after Cromwell died; Charles II reigned during the period known as the Restoration. (S)

Church of England: official church of England; the Church rejected papal authority and became independent from Rome in 1534 because the pope would not annul King Henry VIII's marriage to Catherine of Aragon (S)

Vocabulary continued

civil war: a war between opposing groups of citizens of the same country (S)

commonwealth: a nation, state, or other political unit united by compact or tacit agreement of the people for the common good (S)

Oliver Cromwell: a Puritan and leader of the New Model Army, which seized control of Parliament and executed Charles I (S)

Sir Francis Drake: a sea captain who led the first English expedition to circumnavigate the globe (S)

Elizabeth I: daughter of Henry VIII; she reigned for 45 years, during which time England experienced relative stability and prosperity (S)

English Bill of Rights: 1689 English law that imposed limits on the monarchy (S)

exploration: travel for the purpose of discovery (S)

Glorious Revolution: revolution in which English Parliament forced James II off the throne and replaced him with William and Mary (S)

Henry VIII: the monarch who established the independence of the Church of England from Rome when the pope would not annul his marriage to Catharine of Aragon (S)

James II: the monarch who was in power prior to the Glorious Revolution; attempted to assert Roman Catholic influence over a largely Protestant population and was forced into exile (S)

monarchy: undivided rule by a single person (S)

Parliament: the legislative body in England, consisting of two houses, the House of Commons and the House of Lords (S)

Protestantism: one of the three major branches of Christianity; formed during the Reformation based on the work of Martin Luther and John Calvin. Its followers reject papal authority and believe in the supremacy of the written word of the Bible and the faith of individual practitioners rather than the power of priests. (T)

Puritans: people who, influenced by Calvinist religious ideas, believed the reformation of the Church of England under Elizabeth I did not go far enough to practice or preach a rigorous moral code of conduct (S)

Restoration: period beginning in 1660 with the return of the Stuart kings under Charles II (S)

Roundheads: supporters of Parliament against the king in the English Civil War (S)

Spanish Armada: great fleet sent in 1588 by Catholic Spain against Protestant England (S)

William and Mary: Protestant rulers of England who were invited by Parliament in 1688 to take the throne from James II; installed during the Glorious Revolution (S)

Domain Vocabulary

England in the Golden Age and associated words:
Tudor, Stuart, father, son, grandson, grandfather, daughter, heir, throne, reign, prince, widow, king, queen, monarch, Renaissance, Reformation, Wycliffe, clergy, prelate, excommunicate, worship, separatist, purify, Pilgrim, Mayflower, Bible, charter, preacher, sermon, bishop, archbishop, Anglican, Presbyterian, religion, head, pope, supreme, supremacy, Rome, feudal, papal, sovereignty, Luther, Calvin, defender, faith, overthrow, Spain, annul, annulment, marriage, marry, courtier, separate, divorce, established church, persecution, opposition, doctrine, ceremony, Canterbury, London, Book of Common Prayer, article, execute, punish, "Bloody Mary," burn, stake, stabilize, settle, conflict, ritual, liturgy, belief, practice, Elizabethan, Shakespeare, play, tragedy, comedy, settlement, tempt, compromise, peace, reign, prosperity, territory, power, wealth, armada, ship, flotilla, artillery, defeat, sink, pirate, piracy, raid, broadside, fire, collide, anchor, storm, coast, Ireland,

Materials
Instructional Masters 24, 83

Tudor and Stuart Family Tree, p. 194

Venn Diagram, p. 199

resource materials for an Elizabethan Day, p. 196

index cards, p. 203

poster board, p. 203

list of important historical figures from this section, enough to assign one to each student in class, p. 203

An interesting activity while studying the World History and Geography strand this year would be the creation of a world time line including major events. This time line would help students understand the differences from one culture and civilization to another more easily and thus help them make comparisons and contrasts among civilizations.

Vocabulary continued

drown, ashore, invade, admiral, "sea dog," expedition circumnavigate, globe, settlement, strait, Magellan, Pacific, gold, silver, knight, governor, colonist, Roanoke Island, coast, North Carolina, Indian, kill, fight, trace, Croatoan Island, inland, Jamestown, proprietor, charter, Georgia, colony, seaboard, restriction, belief, divine right, God, govern, Parliament, convene, right, Magna Carta, finance, tax, dismiss, rule, money, subject, revolt, Laud, impose, hierarchy, Scotland, Long Parliament, advisor, arrest, trial, execution, bill, approval, House of Commons, House of Lords, opposition, opponent, interregnum, aristocrat, New Model Army, discipline, organization, surrender, control, Rump Parliament, republic, treason, guilty, murder, Whitehall, scaffold, decapitation, executioner, martyr, commonwealth, Barebones Parliament, Lord Protector, military rule, dictator, retaliation, invasion, land, confiscate, persecute, ideal, moral, godly, believer, Sunday, observance, colonization, trade, hold, office, emigrate, restrict, diplomatic, abdicate, bloodshed, declaration, flee, exile, Whig, Jacobite, threat, hereditary right, limitation, Bill of Rights, consent, petition, government, standing army, excessive, bail, fine, cruel, unusual punishment, amend, strengthen, preserve, law, limited philosophy, John Locke, social contract, natural law, limitation, influence, leader, American Revolution

Cross-curricular Connections

Language Arts

Fiction and Drama

Drama

- *A Midsummer Night's Dream* (William Shakespeare)

Music

Listening and Understanding

Musical Connections

- *A Midsummer Night's Dream* (Felix Mendelssohn)

Songs

- "Greensleeves"

At a Glance

The most important ideas for you are:

- Henry VIII established the independence of the Church of England when he could not get his way with the Roman Catholic Church.

- Much of English history and politics during this period turns on religious questions. The key debates were whether England should be Catholic or Protestant, and whether the Church of England had been sufficiently reformed and purified of Catholic ideas and practices.

- The reign of Elizabeth I was a time of expansion abroad and peace and prosperity at home.

- Charles I's need for money brought him into conflict with Parliament; this conflict deteriorated into a civil war.

- The English Civil War pitted supporters of Charles I, known as Cavaliers, against supporters of greater Parliamentary control, known as Roundheads.

> **At a Glance** continued
>
> ▸ Whatever advantages Charles I had at the beginning of the Civil War, he could not overcome Oliver Cromwell's leadership of the rebel army.
>
> ▸ During the late 1640s and 1650s England was ruled as a republic, or commonwealth, with no king.
>
> ▸ Cromwell's Commonwealth could not survive after his death and at the Restoration, in 1660, Charles II was invited to take the throne.
>
> ▸ The Glorious Revolution removed James II from the English throne in favor of Mary and William of Orange from the Netherlands, who agreed to the English Bill of Rights.

What Teachers Need to Know

A. England in the Golden Age

Background

The two centuries from 1500 to 1700 were a particularly eventful time in the history of England. The nation struggled over religion, vacillated between Catholicism and Protestantism, defeated an invasion by Spain, became a sea power, embarked on worldwide colonization, fought a civil war, executed a king, transformed itself into a republic, restored the monarchy, drove a king from the throne on account of his Catholicism, and finally emerged as a parliamentary government with strong checks on the power of the monarch. An understanding of this period of English history is particularly important for Americans, because American politics of the Revolutionary era were based on issues and disagreements in the mother country.

The House of Tudor

Members of the House of Tudor were a family of Welsh descent that ruled England from 1485 until 1603. The first Tudor was Henry VII, who ruled from 1485 to 1509. He was the father of Henry VIII and the grandfather of Queen Elizabeth. Henry VII took control of the monarchy after defeating Richard III in the War of the Roses (so-named because a red rose and a white rose were the symbols of the houses of Lancaster and York, respectively). The reign of the Tudors ended when Elizabeth, who did not have any children, died in 1603.

▶ Henry VIII and the Church of England

By the time of the Renaissance, the Roman Catholic Church was the dominant religion in Europe. The head of the Church was the pope in Rome, who for a time wielded great power in Europe, and could even control heads of state. As monarchs in the 15th and 16th centuries shaped nation-states from their assorted feudal domains, they saw papal power as a threat to their new sovereignty.

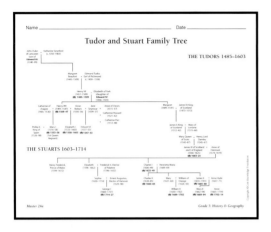

Use Instructional Masters 24a–24b.

Henry VIII of England had not begun his monarchy expecting to overthrow the Roman Catholic Church in England. In 1521, Henry had published a work attacking the errors of Martin Luther's teachings. For this, Henry had been given the title "Defender of the Faith" by a grateful pope. However, Henry's personal concerns eventually led him to abandon his staunch support of the Church.

In 1509, he had married Catherine of Aragon, the daughter of Ferdinand and Isabella of Spain and the widow of his older brother Arthur. All their sons died in infancy. Only a daughter, Mary, born in 1516, survived. This worried Henry VIII. He was eager to have a male heir. Although a daughter could accede to the throne, Henry's concern was that a daughter would probably get married, at which point her property would transfer to her husband's control. If that happened, England might become part of the husband's kingdom.

By the late 1520s, Henry had convinced himself that that they had failed to have a son because Catherine had first been married to Henry's older brother. Henry asked the pope for an annulment because of Catherine's first marriage. By this time, Henry wanted to marry Anne Boleyn, a courtier.

The pope refused to annul the marriage for political as much as ecclesiastical reasons. The pope did not want to antagonize Catherine's nephew, the Holy Roman Emperor. Not to be denied, in 1529 Henry began taking steps to have Parliament declare the church in England separate from the church directed from Rome by the pope. Henry proceeded to marry Anne Boleyn and had his marriage to Catherine annulled in 1533. Their daughter Elizabeth was born the same year. The following year, Henry had Parliament pass the Act of Supremacy, which made the monarch the head of the Church of England (later known as the Anglican Church).

To build support among powerful Catholics, Henry had Parliament confiscate church lands (e.g., monasteries, nunneries, etc.) and sold the lands, most of which were bought by members of the gentry class who wanted to own property.

In Europe at this time, people within a country were expected to practice the religion that their government approved. To do otherwise was to risk fines, imprisonment, and even death. All English subjects were expected to remain loyal to the Church of England, with Henry at its head, because the Church was the "official" or established church of the country. Henry VIII demanded that all Englishmen take an oath of allegiance to him as the head of the new church. Some people, including Sir Thomas More, the Lord Chancellor of England, remained loyal to the pope and refused to swear the oath. More was one of several executed for refusing the oath.

By 1539, Henry had launched a series of persecutions of English Catholics on the one hand and of extreme Protestants on the other hand. The former objected to the Church because of the break with Rome. The latter objected because they felt that Henry had not gone far enough in his break with Rome. Although Henry VIII had rejected papal authority, the Church at this point was still very similar to the Catholic Church in its doctrines, ceremonies, and hierarchy. Protestants, influenced by the ideas of John Calvin (see section on the Reformation, pp. 178–185) thought Henry's reformation had not gone nearly far enough.

In addition to initiating the English Reformation, Henry VIII is famous for his series of six wives. After Catherine of Aragon (1509–1533) and Anne Boleyn (1533–1536), came Jane Seymour (1536–1537), Anne of Cleves (1540),

Catherine Howard (1540–1542), and Catherine Parr (1543–1547). A well-known rhyme describes the fate of each wife:

Divorced, beheaded, died

Divorced, beheaded, survived.

Protestant or Catholic?

When Henry VIII died, it was unclear whether England would ultimately become a solidly Protestant country or revert to Catholicism. Henry's son with Jane Seymour, Edward VI, became king in 1547 when he was only nine years old. Although Henry had older children, Edward was next in line for the succession because he was a male. Edward's chief advisers were Protestant, and during Edward's reign, England became more solidly Protestant, introducing changes in doctrine, liturgy, and ceremonies. During Edward's brief rule, the *Book of Common Prayer*, a book of prayers, and *Forty-Two Articles of Religion*, the official statement of the articles of belief of the Church of England, were published. However, Edward VI lived for only a few years. He died of tuberculosis in 1553.

In 1553 Mary I ascended to the throne. She was the daughter of Henry VIII and his first wife, Catherine of Aragon. Mary had been raised a Catholic and she attempted to return England to Catholicism. She dissolved the Church of England, married a Spanish (Catholic) prince, and had many Protestants executed or severely punished, earning herself the name "Bloody Mary." Several hundred Protestants were burned at the stake during the last years of her reign, which ended in 1558.

Elizabeth I

When Mary died in 1558, she was replaced by Elizabeth I. The only child of Henry VIII and Anne Boleyn, Elizabeth was 25 when she ascended the throne. To stabilize the nation, one of her first acts was to settle the conflict between Catholics and Anglicans. A moderate Protestant, she reinstated the Church of England, but kept the hierarchy of bishops and archbishops as it was in the Catholic Church and also much of the Catholic Church's ritual. However, the *Thirty-Nine Articles of Faith* (outlining a Protestant creed) replaced previous creeds and became the official statement of religious beliefs and practice. She also reinstated the *Book of Common Prayer*, which Mary had withdrawn, and English replaced Latin as the language of the Church. Under the Elizabethan Settlement, as it was called, Elizabeth attempted to reach a compromise with Catholics in order to maintain peace, but a stipulation was that they had to accept the monarch as head of the Church in England. Catholicism went underground. At the same time, some Puritans, influenced by the ideas of John Calvin, grumbled that the Church was insufficiently reformed, but peace was preserved.

During Elizabeth I's 45 year reign, England enjoyed prosperity and peace for much of the time. The exception was conflict with Spain, a Catholic power that refused to accept Elizabeth as queen, since the pope did not recognize the annulment that had allowed Elizabeth's mother to marry Henry VIII. But at home, agricultural production increased, trade grew, villages became towns, and towns became cities. The arts, especially, reaped the benefit of good times and the financial support of the queen, who loved music, dancing, and theater performances.

Queen Elizabeth I

Cross-curricular Teaching Idea

Introduce or review Shakespeare when you begin the study of the Elizabethan period. You may also wish to have students listen to Elizabethan music during the course of study.

V. England from the Golden Age to the Glorious Revolution

Teaching Idea

Stage an Elizabethan Day. Have groups of students do research to find out what kind of clothes the Elizabethans wore, what they ate, what music they listened to, and what they read. Have the groups plan a class event to showcase this information. It could be an event in which students wear costumes, prepare easy-to-make simulated Elizabethan dishes, play tapes of Elizabethan music, etc. Or if there is less time and fewer resources, the "event" could be oral presentations of illustrated reports about Elizabethan times.

Although most people expected Elizabeth to marry, she never did. She was known as the Virgin Queen and liked to say that she was "married to England."

The period during which Elizabeth I reigned is sometimes called the Elizabethan Age in recognition of the impact that Elizabeth had on her nation. The term *Elizabethan* is used as a noun to designate a person who lived during that time, e.g., "Elizabethans became used to warnings that the Spanish were about to invade." It is also used as an adjective: "Elizabethan poets were highly inventive in their use of imagery." The Elizabethan Age is especially noted for its output of excellent literature. Elizabeth was a great patron of the arts. Elizabethan playwrights and poets included William Shakespeare, Ben Jonson, Christopher Marlowe, Sir Phillip Sidney, and Edmund Spenser.

England's Naval Dominance

It was actually Henry VIII who started England on the road to naval supremacy. Although he strengthened the navy, it was Elizabeth who used it to expand England's territory, power, and wealth.

Defeat of the Spanish Armada

Before her death in 1558, Queen Mary I had been married to Philip II, the king of Spain, a staunchly Catholic country. Philip continued to rule in Spain after Mary was succeeded by Elizabeth. Philip and the Spanish refused to accept the annulment of Henry's first marriage. They believed Henry had done a great wrong by setting aside Catherine of Aragon, and also by breaking with Rome. In 1588, Philip sent an armada, a huge fleet of ships, to battle against and possibly invade England. He had the pope's blessing to conquer the island and bring it back to the "old religion." The flotilla of 130 ships carried some 29,000 men and 2,400 pieces of artillery. Philip wanted to end attacks from the pirates Elizabeth was supporting (like Sir Francis Drake, see below) and remove her from the throne, not only because of her Protestantism but because she was supporting Spain's enemies in Europe. Spain had been trying to stamp out Protestantism in the area known as the Low Countries (Belgium and the Netherlands), which it controlled. England had been supporting the reformers.

Sir Francis Drake made a surprise raid on part of the fleet before it left its Spanish port and destroyed 30 ships. The Spanish had large, clumsy ships, whereas the English had developed smaller, faster vessels. Rather than fight broadside, the traditional method of naval warfare, the small English ships moved in, fired quickly, and sailed off before the slower Spanish galleons could turn and pursue them. At night, the Spanish ships had to be on the lookout for fire ships. The English would set empty ships afire and set their sails to collide with anchored Spanish ships. Drake destroyed many tons of supplies that were intended for the invasion of England. He joked that he had "singed the beard" of the Spanish king.

The biggest help the English received against the Spanish Armada was from nature. A huge storm blew the Spanish fleet off course. Many ships were forced onto the rocky coast of Ireland, where English soldiers shot the half-drowned sailors and soldiers as they dragged themselves ashore. What was left of the fleet turned home to Spain, and Philip gave up all idea of invading England. To the English, their victory seemed to be an indication that God smiled on their

religion and their nation. They said the defeat of the Armada was due to providence, or God's supervision, and they called the wind that drove the Spanish Armada to its defeat the "Protestant Wind."

Just before the defeat of the Armada, Queen Elizabeth made a speech to her English soldiers gathered at Tillbury. Here are the most famous lines:

> I know I have the body of a weak, feeble woman; but I have the heart and stomach of a king—and of a king of England too, and think foul scorn that Parma or Spain, or any prince of Europe, should dare to invade the borders of my realm; to which, rather than any dishonour should grow by me, I myself will take up arms—I myself will be your general, judge, and rewarder of every one of your virtues in the field.

Sir Francis Drake

England called its sea captains admirals. But to England's enemies, the sea captains were called "sea dogs," or pirates. One of the most famous was Francis Drake. Drake was born into a strong Protestant family and apprenticed on a ship at age 13. In 1577, Drake sailed west on a voyage sponsored by Queen Elizabeth. The goal was to become the first English expedition to circumnavigate the globe. But Elizabeth mentioned another purpose when she told Drake, "I would gladly be revenged on the King of Spain for divers injuries that I have received." (Recall that the Spanish viewed Elizabeth as an illegitimate child, the product of an invalid second marriage and the head of a heretical church.) Along the way, Drake left behind two ships, lost another two of his five ships, and had to put down a plot against him. He sailed through the Straits of Magellan and into the Pacific Ocean, where he did battle with terrible storms. He raided Spanish ships and settlements along the way and explored the Pacific coast of North America, including the San Francisco area. He sailed north all the way to Vancouver, hoping to find the Northwest Passage. Then he sailed across the Pacific to the Philippines, on to the Spice Islands, then around the tip of Africa and back to England. When he returned to England in 1580, his ship *Golden Hind* was filled with Spanish gold and silver. For his service in behalf of England, Elizabeth knighted him. As Sir Francis Drake, he was an admiral of the fleet that routed the Spanish Armada in 1588.

English Exploration and Settlements in North America

During the reign of Elizabeth I, the English attempted their first permanent settlement in North America. In 1587, Sir Walter Raleigh sponsored an expedition to America to establish a settlement of 100 English men, women, and children. He appointed John White governor.

The colonists settled on Roanoke Island off the coast of North Carolina. White reluctantly returned to England for supplies. Several people—colonists and some of the local native people—had already been killed as a result of fighting between the two groups. When White arrived in England, he found a country braced for an invasion by the Spanish Armada at any moment. No large ships were allowed to leave England. It was not until 1590 that White could return to Roanoke.

When he arrived, he found no trace of the settlement or the colonists. A fort stood where the houses had been and carved on a nearby tree were the letters c-r-o-a-t-o-a-n. White thought that this meant that the colonists had either moved to Croatoan Island or had gone inland to the Croatoan Indians. These people had

Teaching Idea

Students may be confused by the use of the term *England* sometimes and *Great Britain* at other times, so you will want to clarify this.

In 1707, Scotland was legally joined to England and Wales by the Act of Union. The term *Great Britain* is used after that date to refer to the larger entity. Prior to 1707, *England* is the proper term. Even after 1707, *England* is the correct term if referring simply to that nation, such as the English midlands or the south coast of England. Wales had been joined with England in 1536 under Henry VIII.

Teaching Idea

Make a geography connection by sharing with students some of the names of places (cities, towns, counties, states) in the United States that are named after English kings, queens, and nobles, e.g., Virginia (named for the Virgin Queen, Elizabeth I), Jamestown (named for James I), Charleston, Williamsburg, etc.

V. England from the Golden Age to the Glorious Revolution

been friendly to the colonists when they first arrived. White was never able to search for the colonists, however, because storms intervened, and he returned to England without knowing what had happened.

Between 1607, when Jamestown was founded, and 1732, when a group of proprietors were given a charter for Georgia, the English established thirteen colonies along the eastern seaboard of North America. All but Georgia were founded during the time of Elizabeth I's immediate successor, James I, and the Glorious Revolution. You can read more about these colonies on pp. 154–156 of this book.

B. From the English Revolution to the Glorious Revolution

Background

While Elizabeth managed to quiet religious conflict during her long reign, it resurfaced after her death. Childless, she acknowledged James VI of Scotland, the son of her deceased cousin Mary, Queen of Scots, as the legitimate heir to the English throne.

Upon Elizabeth's death in 1603, James also became James I of England. Although he was a Presbyterian, he supported the Church of England, and supervised a translation of the Bible that is still much cited and read today, the King James Bible (1611). James also attempted to ease some of the restrictions against Catholics. This only worsened the conflict. However, his greatest problem with his new subjects was not religion, but his belief in the divine right of kings. This philosophy had been embraced by the French and Austrian monarchies. According to this theory, the monarch received from God his or her right to govern and, therefore, answered only to God, not the governed. Any opposition to the monarch was opposition to God.

Unfortunately for James, Parliament had evolved a number of rights of its own since the Magna Carta was signed in 1215, including control of the nation's finances. When James called Parliament into session to ask for new taxes, it refused. He then dismissed Parliament and ruled without it, which he was able to do so long as he had no need for new taxes.

The English Revolution

When James died in 1625, his son became King Charles I (1625–1649). Like his father, Charles believed in the absolute authority of the monarchy. The stage was set for a series of confrontations between king and Parliament. Religion also entered into the disputes.

▶ King Charles I, Puritans, and Parliament

By 1628, Charles I had already held and dismissed two sessions of Parliament that had refused to grant him all the money he had requested to pay for his foreign wars. Before Parliament would grant Charles his money in 1628, the members forced him to sign the Petition of Right, in which he agreed that only Parliament could levy new taxes.

Charles dismissed Parliament and did not call it back into session until 1640. By then, he had angered his subjects in Scotland and needed money to put down their revolt. Under the guidance of William Laud, Archbishop of Canterbury and head of the Anglican Church, Charles had tried to impose the *Book of Common Prayer* and the hierarchy of bishops and archbishops on Presbyterian Scotland. This led to war with Scotland. However, Laud had also attempted to clamp down on religious dissenters in England, notably Puritans. For example, he had the Puritan pamphleteer William Prynne thrown in jail and even had Prynne's ears chopped off. Many of the Puritans who came to America in the 1620s and '30s were fleeing from Laud and his regulations.

When Charles called Parliament into session, his opponents in Parliament seized the opportunity to stage their own revolt against him. The king and the Long Parliament, as it came to be known (it met irregularly from 1640 to 1653), goaded each other in a series of escalating actions. Parliament had several of Charles's advisors, including Archbishop Laud, arrested, tried, and executed. Charles had little choice but to make peace with Scotland. Parliament forced Charles to agree that Parliament could not be dismissed without its consent, that only Parliament could approve new taxes, and that Parliament must be called into session every three years.

By 1641, the Puritans had gained enough power to force passage of a bill requiring Parliament's approval of the king's advisors. In retaliation, Charles marched into the House of Commons at the head of a group of soldiers to arrest the leaders of the opposition. They escaped, but the political rivalry had turned into civil war.

Civil War: Cavaliers and Roundheads

The English Civil War lasted from 1642 to 1649. The followers of the king were known as Cavaliers, meaning gallant gentlemen. His opponents were known as Roundheads. The name came from the men's habit of cropping their hair close to their heads, rather than wearing their hair in the long, flowing style of the aristocrats who supported the king.

For the first two years of the war, the king and his forces were successful. However, in 1645, the Roundheads chose Oliver Cromwell, a Puritan, as their general. Cromwell turned the forces supporting the dissidents in Parliament into the New Model Army, a highly disciplined and efficient military organization that believed that God supported it and that it fought with divine help. By 1646, Charles had surrendered, but the civil war was not over.

Cromwell's supporters seized control of Parliament by ousting the majority of members who wanted a monarchy limited by constitutional guarantees for the rights of the people and Parliament. Cromwell installed the Rump Parliament, 100 members who agreed with his idea of eliminating the monarchy in favor of a republic. Another round of fighting broke out. Though Cromwell's supporters were in the minority, they controlled the army and within a few months had defeated the supporters of the king.

Execution of Charles I

Cromwell had Charles tried for treason. The verdict was guilty, and on January 30, 1649, a sentence of immediate execution was handed down to that "tyrant, traitor, murderer, and public enemy." He was taken to his own Palace of

Cavaliers and Roundheads

Whitehall, where a scaffold had been erected outside a second-floor window. Crowds braved the bitter January weather to watch the decapitation from nearby rooftops, marveling at the doomed king's courage as he knelt by the executioner's block. It is said that Charles called himself "a martyr of the people," forgave his enemies, and gave the signal himself for the executioner to strike. It is also said that he wore two shirts on the day of his execution in order to be sure he didn't shiver and appear to be nervous. When his head was chopped off, many in the crowd groaned in disbelief.

The execution of the king was a shock to the English and to others as well. No European monarch had ever been tried and executed by his or her own people. The precedent was now established that a ruler who attempted to exercise absolute power without the consent of the governed could be punished.

Oliver Cromwell and the Puritan Regime

With the Rump Parliament in power, the monarchy, the Church of England, and the House of Lords were abolished and a Commonwealth was established based on Cromwell's idea for a republic. Opposition to Cromwell continued, however. In 1653, he dismissed the Rump Parliament, called a new Parliament (the Barebones Parliament), and assumed the title of Lord Protector. By 1655, he had dissolved Parliament again and placed England under military rule with himself as dictator.

Charles I's son, also named Charles, and his supporters invaded England from bases in Scotland and Ireland but with little effect. In retaliation, Cromwell led his own invasion of Ireland in 1649 and 1650. By the time the fighting was over, as many as a third of the Irish people had been killed and as much as two-thirds of Irish lands were confiscated from their Roman Catholic owners and given to Cromwell's English Protestant, often Puritan, supporters. While Cromwell supported a policy of religious toleration for Jews and all Protestants except Anglicans, he persecuted Roman Catholics.

The Commonwealth was based on Puritan ideals. Like Calvin in Geneva, Cromwell sought to establish a moral, godly community of believers. Sunday was a day of prayerful observance, to be used only for religious services. Because reading the Bible was important to one's duty of examining one's conscience continually, Cromwell supported public education for girls as well as boys. Theaters and taverns were closed as distractions and obstacles to godliness. Dancing, gambling, maypole dancing, and other traditional festive activities were also prohibited.

The Restoration, 1660

Cromwell died in 1658 and it was soon apparent that without him, the harsh regulations of the Commonwealth could not hold the English public's loyalty. In 1660, a new Parliament, with the support of the army, asked Charles I's son to return and be crowned Charles II (1660–1685). This marks the beginning of a period in English history known as the Restoration. During the Restoration, England expanded its power and wealth through colonization and the development of international trade.

Under the religious settlement that ended the Puritan regime, the Church of England was reinstated and a series of laws passed between 1661 and 1665 limiting the activities of Puritans and Roman Catholics. They were allowed to practice

their religions, but could not hold membership in town corporations, which meant that they could not hold any local public office. A later law barred them from holding public office on the national level. The restrictions lasted until the early 1800s. As a result of these laws and the change in life in England, Puritans again emigrated as they had in the early 1600s. Many Puritans emigrated to Massachusetts during these years.

With the Restoration, the Puritan restrictions against the theater, dancing, gambling, and similar activities were lifted. Charles II was less interested in the politics of kingship than in living its good life, and was known as "The Merry Monarch." He was notorious for his leisure activities, including riding, sailing, drinking, and cavorting with mistresses. More diplomatic than his father, he had better relations with Parliament for most of his reign, though there was some suspicion that Charles was secretly a Roman Catholic. Charles had no child to succeed him, and in 1681 Parliament tried to a pass a law to keep his brother James, Duke of York, a Catholic, from succeeding him. Many Protestants feared that if James succeeded to the throne, he would try to bring Catholicism back. Charles dealt with this by dissolving Parliament and ruling without it until his death in 1685.

James II and the "Glorious Revolution"

When James II assumed the throne of England in 1685, he was a Roman Catholic monarch of a Protestant nation. When he married his second wife, he had converted from Protestantism to Catholicism, but his two daughters from his first marriage had been raised as Protestants. The eldest, Mary, was married to William III, Prince of Orange, in the Netherlands. The English expected that when James died, his daughter Mary would succeed to the throne. This would mean they would only have to endure a Catholic monarch for a short while. However, in 1688, James and his second wife had a son who automatically became first in line for the throne, thus assuring the continuation of a Roman Catholic monarchy.

Whether the monarch was Roman Catholic or not would have mattered less if James had not set about trying to restore Roman Catholic influence in England. He issued two declarations allowing freedom of worship for non-Anglican Protestants and Catholics. He also appointed Catholics to a number of high government and military posts. There was also concern that James would attempt to lessen the power of Parliament.

In 1688, Parliament, fearing the worst, invited Mary and her husband, William of Orange, to rule England. In the face of English hostility and the army that accompanied William and Mary, James fled to France. This became known as the Glorious Revolution, or Bloodless Revolution, because it was accomplished very easily, with no bloodshed. Of course, not everyone thought it was so glorious. The supporters of James, known as Jacobites (from the Latin form of James, Jacobus), tried several times to invade England and put James (or, later, his heirs) back on the throne. But they were never successful.

Bill of Rights: Parliament Limits the Power of the Monarchy

Before Parliament allowed William and Mary to be crowned, the new monarchs had to accept certain limitations on the power of the monarchy. In 1689,

Teaching Idea

Students in Core Knowledge schools should have learned about the Magna Carta and the beginnings of Parliament in the Grade 4 World History and Geography section "England in the Middle Ages." Ask them to explain the significance of each as a way to introduce later steps in the development of England's unwritten constitution.

Great Britain's form of government is a constitutional monarchy; that is, the actions of the monarch are limited by a series of laws and precedents set over the centuries. These serve as an unwritten constitution. Great Britain has no single document similar to the United States Constitution.

V. England from the Golden Age to the Glorious Revolution

Teaching Idea

Compare the English Bill of Rights to the Bill of Rights that accompanies the U.S. Constitution. Students in Core Knowledge schools should have studied this in-depth in the Grade 4 American History and Geography section "Making a Constitutional Government."

William and Mary

The Big Idea in Review

The 1500s and 1600s were a time of English expansion abroad and consolidation of Parliamentary power at home.

Parliament passed and William and Mary accepted what has become known as the English Bill of Rights. Among its provisions are the following:

- The suspension of laws by the monarchy "without the consent of Parliament is illegal."

- "That levying money for . . . the use of the Crown . . . without grant of Parliament . . . is illegal."

- That the people have the right to petition the government and "prosecutions for such petitioning are illegal."

- "That the raising or keeping a standing army within the kingdom in time of peace, unless it be with consent of Parliament is against [the] law."

- "That excessive bail ought not to be required, nor excessive fines imposed, nor cruel and unusual punishment inflicted."

- "That . . . for the amending, strengthening and preserving of the laws, [sessions of] Parliaments ought to be held frequently."

The Glorious Revolution and the English Bill of Rights were important landmarks on the road to limited monarchy. Several important philosophical ideas that were used to justify the Revolution and write the Bill of Rights came from the contemporary philosopher John Locke, whose ideas on natural law and the limitations of governmental power profoundly influenced the leaders of the American Revolution ninety years later.

Review

Below are some ideas for ongoing assessment and review activities. These are not meant to constitute a comprehensive list. Teachers may also refer to the *Pearson Learning/Core Knowledge History & Geography* series for additional information and teaching ideas.

- Have students play "Who/What Am I . . . ?" Students should work in pairs to create four questions and answers using a statement of what a person did or what an event was, followed by the question "Who am I?" or "What am I?" Combine pairs into groups of four to ask each other their questions.

- As a culmination to this unit of study, have students write an essay based on the big idea, "Describe English expansion abroad, consolidation of Parliamentary power at home, and how these two factors changed England." Make sure students justify their answers with facts learned in this section.

- This section provides an opportunity for students to complete short research reports on any of the historical figures of England from the Golden Age to the Glorious Revolution. Using the Language Arts section, provide the class with topics for short reports to write in formal style. Each day of a week, provide a mini-lesson on different aspects of report writing, such as correct paragraph form or bibliographies. Share these reports when completed.

• Have students write a newspaper article describing one of the events or people from this section, such as the defeat of the Spanish Armada or one of the rulers of England. Students should use the "who, what, when, where, and how" model to write their articles. After writing their articles, they should draw an illustration to serve as a "picture" of the subject.

• Divide the class into groups and ask each group to come up with five questions to review the material from this section. They must write their questions on index cards and also provide the answers. When completed, have groups stand and ask the questions to the class, providing correct answers when needed.

• Have students create portraits of important figures from this period in history. Brainstorm enough important figures from this unit for each student to choose one person. Then, have students draw a picture of that person on poster board and include a biographical sketch at the bottom. Post these in the hallway and have a gallery tour where visitors are able to come through the gallery and hear explanations of each person's accomplishments.

• You may also ask the following questions after completion of this unit of study.

1. Why did Henry VIII have the Church of England reject the pope and break from Rome?

   Henry wanted to have his marriage to Catherine of Aragon annulled because they had not had a son. When the pope refused to grant the annulment, Henry had Parliament declare that he as monarch was the head of the Church of England.

2. Why was the defeat of the Spanish Armada important?

   The defeat of the Spanish Armada ended any threat to Protestant England from Catholic Spain.

3. Who was the ruler of England when the Spanish Armada was defeated and Shakespeare began writing his plays?

   Queen Elizabeth I was the ruler.

4. Who was Sir Francis Drake and why is he remembered?

   Drake was a sea captain and pirate. He was the first Englishman to circumnavigate the globe. He also played a key role in the defeat of the Spanish Armada.

5. Why did Charles I have to call Parliament into session?

   Parliament needed to approve Charles's requests for money.

6. Over what issue did the English Civil War begin?

   Charles believed in exercising greater authority than Parliament was willing to allow a monarch. Parliament wanted more authority for itself.

7. What were the supporters of the King called during the English Civil War? What were the supporters of Parliament called?

   Cavaliers supported Charles I and Roundheads supported Parliament.

8. Why was the selection of Oliver Cromwell to lead the Roundheads significant?

   Until the appointment of Cromwell, Charles's forces had the advantage on the battlefield. Cromwell disciplined the Roundhead army and turned it into the New Model Army, a well-trained and efficient army that defeated the royalist forces.

9. What was restored at the Restoration?

   The monarchy was restored after several years of republican government.

10. Why was James II removed in favor of William and Mary?

    Parliament feared that James was going to reinstate the Roman Catholic Church in England.

11. Why is the English Bill of Rights important?

    The English Bill of Rights imposed limits on what the monarchy could do in favor of Parliament and set standards for the power of Parliament.

More Resources

The titles listed below are offered as a representative sample of materials and not a complete list of everything that is available.

For students —

• *England: Golden Age to Glorious Revolution*, edited by E. D. Hirsch, Jr. (Pearson Learning, 2002), a unit in the official *Pearson Learning/Core Knowledge History & Geography series,* is available as part of the bound book for Grade 5/Level 5. A teacher's guide is also available. To order, call 1-800-321-3106.

• *Don't Know Much About the Kings and Queens of England*, by Ken Davis (Harper Collins Publishers, 2002). Hardcover, 48 pages, ISBN 0060286113.

• *Good Queen Bess: The Story of Elizabeth I of England*, by Diane Stanley (Harper Collins, 2001). Hardcover, 40 pages, ISBN 0688179614.

• *The Queen's Pirate: Queen Elizabeth and Sir Francis Drake*, an audio recording by Jim Weiss (Greathall Productions, www.greathall.com or 1-800-477-6234) fits well with this unit.

• *Shakespeare's London: A Guide to Elizabethan London*, by Julie Ferris (Kingfisher, 2000). Hardcover, 32 pages, ISBN 0753452340.

For teachers —

• *The Life of Elizabeth I*, by Alison Weir (Ballantine, 1999). Paperback, 560 pages, ISBN 0345425502. Weir is also the author of numerous other books on English history, including *The Six Wives of Henry VIII.*

• *This Realm of England, 1399–1688 (History of England)*, by Lacey Baldwin Smith (Houghton Mifflin, 2000). A standard textbook on this era. Paperback, 400 pages, ISBN 0618001026.

• *Two Treatises of Government*, by John Locke (Tuttle Publishing, 1994). Originally published in 1690, this and other writings by Locke had an influence on both the French and American revolutions. Paperback, 384 pages, ISBN 0460873563.

VI. Russia: Early Growth and Expansion

The Big Idea

Much of Russia's history dealt with the expansion of territory abroad and the extension of autocratic rule at home.

Remember that each subject you study with students expands their vocabulary and introduces new terms, thus making them better listeners and readers. As you study Russia, use map work, read alouds, independent reading, and discussions to build students' vocabularies.

The items below refer to content in Grade 5. Use time lines with students to help them sequence and relate events from different periods and groups.

1453	Byzantine Empire falls to Ottoman Turks
1453	Moscow declares itself the "Third Rome"
1462–1505	Reign of Ivan the Great
1477	Ivan the Great takes title *czar*
1480	Ivan the Great declares Russia free of Mongol rule
1500s	Conquest of much of Siberia by Russians
1533–1584	Reign of Ivan the Terrible
1533–1584	Beginning of feudalism in Russia
1689–1725	Reign of Peter the Great
1700–1721	Russia defeats Sweden to become power in Baltic Sea
1712	St. Petersburg becomes capital

continued on next page

What Students Should Already Know

Students in Core Knowledge schools should be familiar with

Grade 3

- important rivers of the world
  - Volga River
- Ancient Rome
  - Julius Caesar, Augustus Caesar
- Eastern Roman Empire: Byzantine Civilization
  - the rise of the Eastern Roman, or Byzantine, Empire
  - Constantine, the first Christian emperor
  - Constantinople (now called Istanbul) merges diverse influences and cultures as the seat of the empire
  - Emperor Justinian and his code of laws
- the Vikings
  - originated in an area now called Scandinavia (Sweden, Denmark, Norway)
  - also called Norsemen
  - skilled sailors and shipbuilders as well as traders; sometimes raiders of European coastal areas
  - Eric the Red; Leif Ericson, also known as Leif "the Lucky"
  - earliest Europeans in North America
  - locations of Greenland, the mainland of Canada, and Newfoundland

Grade 4

- mountains and mountain ranges
  - Ural Mountains
- Europe in the Middle Ages
  - Arguments among Christians: split into Roman Catholic Church and Eastern Orthodox Church
  - Feudalism, serfs
  - Baltic Sea
- China
  - The Mongols

VI. Russia: Early Growth and Expansion

continued from previous page

1762–1796	Reign of Catherine the Great
1772, 1793, 1795	Partitions of Poland
1773–1775	Peasant revolt under Pugachev
1789–1799	French Revolution
1861	Emancipation of Russian serfs
1905	Opening of Trans-Siberian Railroad
1917	Bolshevik Revolution
1918	Capital moves to Moscow

Text Resources

(44) *Peter the Great*

What Students Need to Learn

- Russia as successor to Byzantine Empire: Moscow as new center of Eastern Orthodox Church and of Byzantine culture (after the fall of Constantinople in 1453)
- Ivan III (the Great), czar (from the Latin "Caesar")
- Ivan IV (the Terrible)
- Peter the Great: modernizing and "westernizing" Russia
- Catherine the Great
  - Reforms of Peter and Catherine make life harder for peasants
- Moscow and St. Petersburg
- Ural Mountains, Siberia, vegetation, steppes
- Volga and Don Rivers
- Black, Caspian, and Baltic Seas
- Search for a warm-water port

What Students Will Learn in Future Grades

In Grade 7, students will learn about the Russian Revolution.

Vocabulary

Student/Teacher Vocabulary

autocratic: adjective describing a despotic ruler, one who rules alone (T)

Baltic Sea: arm of the Atlantic Ocean; bordered by Sweden, Finland, Russia, Estonia, Latvia, Lithuania, Poland, Germany, and Denmark (S)

Black Sea: an inland sea that lies between Asia and Europe and is bordered by Turkey, Bulgaria, Romania, Ukraine, Georgia, and Russia (S)

boyars: the Russian aristocracy that headed the civil and military administration of the country (T)

Byzantine Empire: the eastern part of the Roman Empire; mostly composed of the Balkan Peninsula and Asia Minor; collapsed when Constantinople fell to the Ottoman Turks in 1453 (S)

canal: a human-made waterway that connects rivers, lakes, or other bodies of water (S)

Caspian Sea: one of the great lakes of the world; located in Eurasia (S)

Catherine the Great: ruler of Russia from 1762 until 1796, oversaw a great expansion of Russian territory (S)

Cyrillic: the Russian alphabet, named after the monk who invented it (Cyril) (T)

czar: term derived from the Roman title "Caesar," used by the emperors of Russia until the 1917 revolution (S)

Don River: river which flows through southwest European Russia in a southerly direction and empties into the Sea of Azov (S)

Vocabulary continued

Eastern Orthodox Church: body of churches originating from the church of the Byzantine Empire; acknowledges the superiority of the patriarch of Constantinople (S)

heresy: adherence to religious views contrary to the views of the established church (T)

Ivan III: the Grand Prince of Moscow and ruler until 1505, also known as Ivan the Great (S)

Ivan IV: ruler of Russia from 1533 to 1584, also known as Ivan the Terrible because of his cruelty (S)

kremlin: Russian word meaning "walled center of a city"; in Moscow the Kremlin is the central area of the city, housing the offices of the Russian government (S)

modernize: to update, bring up to current standards (S)

Moscow: the capital of modern Russia (S)

orthodox: from the Greek words for "correct" and "belief," describes correct or mainstream views, especially in religion; the Christian Church in the East is known as the Orthodox Church (T)

peasant: a person who pays rent to a landowner in order to farm the land (S)

Peter the Great: ruler of Russia from 1689 to 1725; Peter was fascinated by Western culture and modernized Russia (S)

reform: to make changes in order to correct abuses or injustices (S)

serf: a person who is tied by law to the land and the owner of the land and cannot move to another place (S)

Siberia: a vast region in Asian Russia that makes up most of the land area of Russia (S)

St. Petersburg: city on the Gulf of Finland built by Peter the Great, once the capital of Russia, known as Peter's "Window on the West" (S)

steppe: a broad, open, treeless plain usually found in southeastern Europe or Asia (S)

taiga: a belt of forestland just south of the tundra (S)

tribute: a payment made to another ruler or country by subject peoples (S)

tundra: a treeless plain in the far north where only the smallest of plants can survive the winds and extreme temperatures (S)

tyrant: an absolute ruler, unrestrained by a constitution or laws (S)

Ural Mountains: low mountains that form part of the border between Europe and Asia (S)

Volga River: the longest river in Europe; the principal water transportation route in Russia, linked by canals to a network of other rivers (S)

westernize: to make one's country or land more like the nations of Western Europe (S)

Domain Vocabulary

Russian history and related words:
Mongol, nomad, warrior, invade, conquer, ruler, pay, tribute, prince, land, title, power, peninsula, tradition, culture, trade route, capital, trade, network, connect, influence, Greek, monk, Cyril, Methodius, alphabet, Russian, Slavic, language, translate, Bible, God, church, convert, patriarch, emperor, icon, Jesus, Mary, saint, ban, excommunicate, priest, marry, schism, division, break, branch, Catholic, Vladimir, Viking, state, Hagia Sophia, baptism, orthodox, commercial, state, city-state, adopt, read, write, architecture, music, art, czar, tsar, czarist, monarch, divine right, authority, absolute, absolutist, "Third Rome," spiritual, Ivan the Great, reign, control, annex, Poles, Lithuanian, government, centralize,

Materials

Instructional Masters 25–28

Czars of Russia (1613–1917), p. 211

Russia, p. 214

Vegetation Zones in Russia, p. 215

Black, Caspian, and Baltic Seas, p. 216

books showing European fashions in the early 1700s, p. 212

poster paper, p. 212

pictures of Moscow and St. Petersburg, p. 214

atlases, geography books, almanacs, and other references that contain maps, p. 216

a list of review questions from this section to use for bingo questions, p. 217

a list of answers to the review questions on chart paper, or overheads for students to use on bingo cards, p. 217

bingo template card for each student, p. 217

markers to use to play bingo, p. 217

Internet access, p. 217

construction paper for each student, p. 217

glue, p. 217

index cards, p. 217

Vocabulary continued

An interesting activity while studying the World History and Geography strand this year would be the creation of a world time line including major events. This time line would help students understand the differences from one culture and civilization to another more easily and thus help them make comparisons and contrasts among civilizations.

influence, splendor, ceremony, symbol, double eagle, Ivan the Terrible, expand, border, Swede, Pole, assembly, convene, autocrat, autocratic, hereditary, aristocracy, treason, seize, military, peasant, nobility, noble, feudal, Oprichniki, guard, traitor, secret police, Peter the Great, fascinate, curiosity, information, visit, shipyard, university, art gallery, Parliament, shipbuilding, medicine, manufacturing, education, expert, transform, beard, tax, shave, coat, clothing, style, navy, army, westernize, Slavophile, conscription, equip, weaponry, train, officer, development, mining, international, trading, reform, rank, efficient, system, oversee, agriculture, Senate, governor, province, service, requirement, position, secure, warm-water port, land, move, capital, learn, adopt, culture, Catherine the Great, German, duke, alliance, freedom, marriage, husband, plot, conspirator, expand, territory, Ottoman Turks, serf, serfdom, agriculture, ownership, revolt, Pugachev, French Revolution, Romanov, peasant, bind, land, chattel, landowner, slave, status, emancipation, right, payment, land, crop, animal, continent, capital, seat, Russian Orthodox Church, Russian Revolution, Kremlin, palace, museum, boulevard, city, rename, Russification, Lenin, border, mineral, forests, mining, lumbering, industry, vast, north, south, west, east, indigenous, extreme, winter, tundra, settle, labor camps, climate, temperatures, taiga, forest, pine, fir, oak, birch, steppe, plains, fertile, empty, delta, route, canals, network, European, Asian, links, important transportation route, sea level, flow, strait, continent

Names of places and bodies of water:
Dnieper River, Moscow River, Don River, Gulf of Finland, Pacific Ocean, Atlantic Ocean, Sea of Azov, North Sea, Arctic Ocean, Arctic Circle, Asia, Europe, Russia, Ukraine, Turkey, Bulgaria, Romania, Georgia, Odessa, Azerbaijan, Iran, Turkmenistan, Kazakhstan, Estonia, Latvia, Lithuania, Germany, Denmark, Middle East, Asia, Greece, Poland, Sweden, Prussia, Western Europe, Alaska, Mongolia, Manchuria, China, Asia Minor, Leningrad, Kiev, Constantinople

Cross-curricular Connections

Language Arts

Writing, Grammar, and Usage
• Writing reports

Music

Listening and Understanding
Composers and Their Music

• *Pictures at an Exhibition*, Modest Mussorgsky

At a Glance

The most important ideas for you are:

▶ Students should be able to locate important places and geographical features in Russia.

▶ Russia has a long tradition of rule by autocrats. During the years when England was moving towards balanced and constitutional government, Russia remained an autocratic state.

▶ Moscow declared itself successor to the Byzantine Empire when the Ottoman Turks captured Constantinople.

- Ivan III (the Great) and Ivan IV (the Terrible) expanded Russian territory and the authority of the czars.

- Peter the Great sought to modernize and westernize Russia in order to enable it to compete with European nations for trade, territory, and prestige.

- The desire to find a warm-water port was one factor that encouraged Russian expansion.

- Catherine the Great, while once interested in reforming certain abuses of Russian government, became as autocratic as her predecessors after a peasant revolt and the French Revolution.

- The lives of peasants worsened under Peter and Catherine.

What Teachers Need to Know

A. History and Culture

Byzantine Influence in Russia

Teaching Idea

You may want to teach section B, "Geography," before "History and Culture."

The rise of Russia is closely related to the history of the Byzantine Empire, which students in Core Knowledge schools should have encountered in Grades 3 and 4. For a thousand years after the fall of the Roman Empire in the west, the Eastern or Byzantine Empire continued to build on ancient Greek and Roman traditions and culture. For example, Byzantine architects used the Roman dome to build magnificent churches, such as Hagia Sophia in the Byzantine capital of Constantinople (now called Istanbul). Byzantine artists also created beautiful mosaics and icons. Students in Core Knowledge schools should have studied Hagia Sophia and Byzantine mosaics as part of the art curriculum for Grade 3. However, they may not be acquainted with icons, which are special pictures of Jesus, Mary, and the saints. Icons are meant to help Christians during worship and meditation.

Constantinople was a great religious center, home of the Eastern Orthodox Church, which had split with the Roman Catholic Church in 1054. Constantinople was also the center of a vast trading network that connected Europe with the Middle East and Asia. Trade brought the Byzantine Empire great riches as well as new cultural influences.

The influence of the Byzantine Empire in Russia dates at least to the 860s, when the Byzantine Emperor sent two monks to convert the Slavic people of Eastern Europe to Orthodox Christianity. At the time, the Slavs were pagans who worshipped many gods. The two monks sent to convert them were two brothers named Cyril and Methodius. Cyril and Methodius invented a new alphabet, called the Cyrillic alphabet after Cyril. The Cyrillic alphabet was loosely based on the Greek alphabet. Cyril and Methodius then taught the Slavs to read and write using the Cyrillic alphabet so that they could read the Bible.

A little more than a century later, Christianity began to spread around Slavic and Russian territories, but many people remained pagans. Once such person was Prince Vladimir, the ruler of the city-state of Kiev, which would become the first Russian state. According to legend, the prince sent emissaries to investigate the major monotheistic religions of his day: Eastern Orthodox Christianity, Roman Catholic Christianity, Judaism, and Islam. When his emissaries visited Constantinople and saw Hagia Sophia, they were astonished and overwhelmed by the beauty of the church, its dome, and its mosaics. Surely, they thought, this is the house of the true God. Vladimir selected Orthodox Christianity as his own religion, and decided it would also be the religion of his people. It is also possible that he may have been influenced to convert to Christianity by the economic and political advantages of an alliance with Byzantium, as well as in order to get approval to marry the Byzantine emperor's sister. He ordered the old pagan idols thrown into the Dnieper River and conducted mass baptisms in the same river.

Adoption of Eastern Orthodox Christianity had a number of benefits for the Russians. It strengthened the commercial ties between Russia and the Byzantine Empire and also provided the basis for the development of a national identity among the various Russian city-states by giving them something in common. Over time, princes of the various city-states adopted the written language of the empire, as well as its architecture, music, and art. Like the Byzantine emperor, the Russian czars (also spelled tsars) would claim jurisdiction over the church in Russia, thus strengthening their own power. Similar to the monarchs of western Europe, the Russian czars also came to believe in the theory of the divine right of kings—that they ruled as the representative of God on Earth, and as such, their authority was absolute.

Moscow as the Third Rome

Over time Kiev became less important and Moscow, to the north, became more important. Moscow became the headquarters of the Russian church. When the Byzantine Empire fell to the Turks in 1453, the rulers of Moscow announced that Moscow was "The Third Rome." Rome had been the capital city of Christianity and so the "spiritual center of the world," but then the popes and the Roman Catholic church had fallen into heresy and false belief. After 1054, when the Orthodox Church split with the Roman Catholic Church, Constantinople had become the new "spiritual center of the world," the "Second Rome." When Constantinople fell to the Turks in 1453, the Russians thought Moscow was poised to take its place and become the latest spiritual center of the world, the "Third Rome."

The Czars

Ivan III

Beginning in 1236, Mongols, nomadic warriors from Central Asia, had invaded and conquered large parts of Russia. Students in Core Knowledge schools should have learned about the Mongols in the Grade 4 section on China. The same people who swept south to conquer China swept north to conquer large parts of Russia. In return for acknowledging the Mongols as their rulers and paying tribute to them, the princes of the various states were allowed to keep their lands and titles. The Mongols remained in power until 1480 when Ivan III declared Russia free of Mongol rule.

Ivan III, also known as Ivan the Great, had come to power as the Grand Prince of Moscow in 1462. During his reign of 43 years, he extended Moscow's control over a large area, annexing land from other city-states and from the Poles, Lithuanians, and Mongols.

The government was centralized and Ivan asserted his influence over the church. He surrounded himself with the splendor and ceremony befitting an emperor and adopted as the symbol of the czar the Byzantine symbol of the double eagle. Ivan's reign laid the foundation for the later Russian state.

Ivan IV

Ivan IV, also known as Ivan the Terrible, reigned from 1533 to 1584. He greatly expanded Russia's borders, extending Russian rule throughout the Volga River Basin to the Caspian Sea and pushing across the Ural Mountains into Siberia. His attempt to win a foothold on the Baltic Sea was less successful. The Swedes and Poles defeated the Russian forces.

Ivan earned his nickname because of his cruelty. He was initially called "Ivan the Terrible" because he terrified his enemies, but later he also began to terrify his own people. Indeed, he became one of history's most famous examples of the paranoid tyrant. Convinced that enemies and intrigue surrounded him, Ivan IV was suspicious of everyone. He established the Oprichniki, a group of special guards, to search out traitors among his subjects. They acted like secret police and wore black uniforms. These policemen could throw people in jail or torture them on the slightest suspicion of disloyalty. Ivan the Terrible also had a terrible temper. One day in a fit of anger, he hit his eldest son so hard that he killed him.

Ivan also established the Zemski Sobor, or land assembly, to act as an advisory body to the czar. It was the first national assembly of Russians ever convened. However, Ivan IV was even more autocratic than Ivan III had been. In an effort to rid himself of any threat from the boyars, who were hereditary aristocrats, he had many of them accused of treason. He then seized their lands and divided the lands among a new class of landholders that he created. In return for land, these men owed the czar military service when he asked for assistance. The service was to be performed by peasants supplied by the new nobility. In effect, Ivan created a feudal system in Russia.

Peter the Great

Peter the Great ruled Russia from 1689 to 1725. Like his predecessors, Peter was an autocratic ruler. Unlike them, he was fascinated by western Europe, its culture, its sciences, and its growing industries.

Only 17 when he became czar, Peter had an immense curiosity about people, ideas, and things. His appetite for information matched his size. He was 6 feet 9 inches tall and weighed close to 300 pounds. As a young man, he spent time in the German Quarter of Moscow, where not only Germans but also Scottish, English, and Dutch artisans lived. Although previous czars had been generally suspicious of foreigners, some had been allowed to settle in special zones of the city, but their contact with Russians was limited to people the czars trusted.

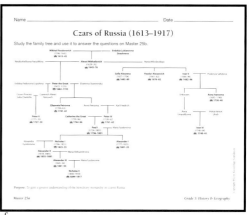

Use Instructional Master 25a–25b.

VI. Russia: Early Growth and Expansion

Peter the Great visiting Europe

Teaching Idea

Peter the Great's trip to western Europe included many fascinating adventures. Students may enjoy learning more about Peter's experiences, including his travels in England and Holland, his work as a carpenter, his studies in dentistry, his purchases while abroad, and his attempts to travel incognito.

Teaching Idea

Have pairs of students create posters advertising either of Peter's decrees: that men must be beardless or that Russians—except for peasants—must wear western European-style clothes. Posters should contain the gist of the decree and some slogan to promote compliance. The message could rely on what will happen if a person fails to obey or could tout some benefit such as a beardless man will be cooler in summer. Illustrations could be optional.

You may want to provide students with books that show what western Europeans were wearing in the early 1700s.

Wanting to see for himself, Peter took two trips to western Europe during 1697 and 1698, and during 1716 and 1717. Among the places he visited were shipyards, universities, art galleries, and the British Parliament. He was an eager student and learned about shipbuilding, medicine, military science, manufacturing, and the educational systems of the countries he visited. He returned to Russia with a group of European experts that he had hired to help him transform Russia. 44

Modernizing and Westernizing Russia

When Peter returned from his first European tour, he set about changing how Russians looked and what they did for a living. Peter decreed that Russian men were henceforth to be beardless, because that was the fashion in western Europe. Men found wearing beards were at risk of having them shaved off on the spot. A man could get around the decree by paying a tax for a beard license. Peter also decreed that the long coats of Russian men were to be shortened and that everyone above the rank of peasant was to adopt western clothing.

Peter established a navy and modernized the army. No longer would the czar have to depend on peasant soldiers supplied by the nobility. He established a standing army by introducing conscription (forced service) and equipped it with new weaponry from the west. He also established military-technical schools and required that the sons of the nobility be sent to train as officers. Peter used government subsidies to encourage the development of manufacturing, shipbuilding, mining industries, and international trading companies.

In part to make the government more efficient, and in part to further lessen the influence of the nobility, Peter introduced reforms into the government. He established a committee system to run government operations. Each committee had eleven members who were to oversee a particular area, such as agriculture and foreign affairs, similar to our government departments. To strengthen his position, the czar personally appointed many officials, including the members of the new advisory body of nobles, called the Senate, and the governors of provinces.

Peter built on the idea of the service nobility, initiated by earlier czars. According to this concept, service to the state was a requirement for admission to the nobility. Peter established the Table of Ranks, which listed 14 civil and military ranks, covering all positions in the government and military. As one advanced up the ranks and reached a certain level, one automatically became a noble. As more men entered the nobility, the old landed aristocracy—the boyars—became a smaller percentage of the nobility. Through this maneuver, Peter continued to lessen the influence of the boyars.

Search for a Warm-Water Port

One of Peter's great ambitions, as it had been for previous czars, was to secure a warm-water port for trade. Most Russian ports were located in the far north and froze up for part of the year. By increasing the amount of Russia's international trade, Peter believed he would also increase its wealth and power. His first efforts were aimed at wresting territory on the Mediterranean from the Ottoman Turks, as Ivan IV had tried to do, but Peter was unsuccessful in finding allies and abandoned the idea.

Peter then set his sights on land along the Baltic Sea. He declared war on Sweden in 1700 and ultimately won his warm-water port. He built St. Petersburg on the Gulf of Finland, an arm of the Baltic, and moved the capital there from Moscow. His new city was as grand as any capital in western Europe. It is called Peter's "Window on the West," not only because it was a port that allowed Peter to trade with the west year-round, but also because the city was built in the European style, with canals and stately palaces like the ones Peter had seen on his trips to western Europe. Peter encouraged western Europeans to come to Petersburg and required many Russians nobles to build houses in his new capital.

Ever since Peter the Great, Russians have often found themselves divided between two groups. One group, the so-called "westernizers," has argued, in the tradition of Peter the Great, that Russia needs to be more like the countries of western Europe. On the other side are the "Slavophiles," who think Russia is better than western Europe and should stick to its traditional Slavic ways. For the most part, the westernizers have gravitated to St. Petersburg, with its European style, while Slavophiles have preferred Moscow, built in the old Russian style.

Catherine the Great

Catherine the Great was actually not Russian, but German. She was chosen to marry Peter, Duke of Holstein, a grandson of Peter the Great. As Czar Peter III, the Duke initiated a series of policies that angered powerful nobles. He entered into an alliance with Prussia, a long-time rival, expanded religious freedom, and closed down the secret police. Catherine and the czar were not well suited for each other and theirs was an unhappy marriage. Catherine—who had become thoroughly Russian after almost twenty years in Russia—joined in a plot against Peter. The conspirators removed him from the throne and made Catherine sole ruler.

Catherine greatly expanded Russian territory, adding more of the Baltic region and Ukraine. She also warred against the Ottoman Turks and seized portions of their empire. When European powers partitioned Poland in 1772, 1793, and 1795, she gained the largest part for Russia. It was during her reign that Russian exploration and colonization of Alaska began.

Like Peter the Great, Catherine was interested in the west. When she began her reign, she intended to make a number of reforms to ease the life of serfs (peasants), promote education, and limit land acquisitions by nobles. However, the peasant revolt led by Pugachev [POO-ga-chov] between 1773 and 1775 and the French Revolution soon caused Catherine to become as autocratic as earlier czars. The peasant uprising was a bloody and brutal revolt that resulted in the death of thousands of wealthy Russian landowners, priests of the Russian Orthodox Church, and merchants. Not wishing to antagonize the nobility, Catherine increased the privileges of the nobility and decreased the freedom of peasants.

▶ Reforms of Peter and Catherine and the Peasants

The reforms of Peter and Catherine had little effect on the peasants—except to bind them to the land as serfs. By the time of Peter, many peasants already had no personal freedom of movement. A peasant family could not decide to move from one landed estate to another because the second landowner offered better working terms.

Catherine the Great

Teaching Idea

Compare the lives of peasants in Russia, slaves in the colonies, and serfs in the Middle Ages. What made serfdom in Russia different?

History and Geography: World   **213**

During Peter's reign, peasants became chattel, the property of the landholders on whose estate they worked. They could, therefore, be bought and sold. After the peasant uprising during Catherine's reign, she allowed the nobles to continue the process of turning peasants into serfs. The word *serf* is from the Latin word for slave; however, the status of the serf was somewhere in between that of a slave and a free person. Serfs were the property of nobles, yet they had certain rights. They were required to give certain payments to and perform specific services for their owner. On the other hand, a serf was usually given a house, a plot of land on which to grow crops, and some animals. Serfs were required to give some of what they grew to their noblemen masters. In addition, serfs were required to work the noble's land.

Serfdom—the agricultural system based on the ownership of serfs—had existed in Russia for centuries. In western Europe, the actual bonding of the peasant to the soil had largely ended by the 1400s and 1500s. By contrast, in Russia, serfdom was gaining strength. In the 1700s, during the reign of Peter and Catherine, while the Industrial Revolution was getting underway in Great Britain, the restrictive powers of serfdom reached their height. Serfdom was not abolished in Russia until 1861—four years before the United States abolished slavery.

B. Geography

Background

Russia stretches across two continents, Europe and Asia. Much of the early history of Russia occurred in the European section as people there traded with the Vikings, Byzantines, and later western Europeans.

Cities

▶ Moscow

Moscow is located in west central Russia—European Russia—on the Moscow River and is the capital of modern Russia. Ivan IV made it the capital of Russia in the 1400s, and it also became the seat of the Russian Orthodox Church. Peter the Great transferred the capital from Moscow to the new city of St. Petersburg in 1712. The capital was returned to Moscow in 1918 during the Russian Revolution.

Today, Moscow is the largest city in Russia (with a metropolitan area population of over 13 million), an important inland port, and the seat of Russia's government. The Kremlin, meaning walled center of a city, is the heart of Moscow. Here the czars built their palaces, Communist leaders reviewed thousands of soldiers marching through Red Square, and today, the national government uses a former palace for the legislature. The Kremlin is also the site of St. Basil's Cathedral, once the center of the Russian Orthodox Church and now a national museum. St. Basil's is built in the traditional Russian style, with several onion domes reaching up to the sky. From the Kremlin, wide boulevards extend through the city in all directions. A person from Moscow is called a Muscovite.

▶ St. Petersburg

St. Petersburg is Russia's second-largest city (population 5 million) and is located in northwestern European Russia on the Gulf of Finland. Peter the Great built it in the western European style, with canals and glittering palaces, after

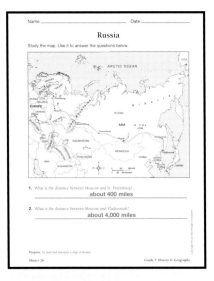

Name _____ Date _____

Russia

Study the map. Use it to answer the questions below.

1. What is the distance between Moscow and St. Petersburg?
   about 400 miles

2. What is the distance between Moscow and Vladivostok?
   about 4,000 miles

Purpose: To read and interpret a map of Russia
Master 26   Grade 5: History & Geography

Use Instructional Master 26.

defeating Sweden and gaining the land. As the onetime capital of Russia, the city has a number of examples of czarist palaces and Russian Orthodox Churches. The city was named in honor of St. Peter, not Peter the Great. In 1914, at the outbreak of World War I, it was renamed Petrograd to "russify" the Germanic original name. After the Russian Revolution, the name was changed once again to Leningrad in honor of V. I. Lenin, the architect of the Soviet Russian state. It was renamed St. Petersburg in 1991 after the collapse of the Soviet government.

Ural Mountains

The Urals are low mountains that form part of the border between Europe and Asia. The Urals extend for about 1,500 miles (2,414 km) north to south through Russia from the Kara Sea to Kazakhstan. Mount Narodnaya is the highest peak at 6,217 feet (1,895 m). The mountains are rich in minerals and forests, and as a result, mining and lumbering are important industries.

Siberia

Siberia is a vast region in Asian Russia that makes up most of the land area of Russia and northern Kazakhstan. It is bordered on the north by the Arctic Ocean and on the south by Mongolia and Manchuria, a region of China. To the west are the Ural Mountains and to the east is the Pacific Ocean.

There were indigenous people in the area before Russians and Ukrainians began moving into the edges of Siberia in the 1200s. By the end of the 1500s, Russia had conquered much of the region, but because of its extreme cold in the winter, few people settled there. However, both the czars and Communist leaders used Siberia to rid themselves of political opponents and criminals. Under the Communist leaders Lenin and Stalin, millions of people were sent to forced labor camps in Siberia, where many of them died. The forced labor camps, known as gulags, were described in the works of the Nobel Prize-winning Russian author Alexander Solzhenitsyn (*The Gulag Archipelago; One Day in the Life of Ivan Denisovich*) and other survivors. Forced labor camps were not closed until 1991.

Vegetation Zones

Russia is so large that it has a number of climate and vegetation zones that lie in parallel belts running from east to west across the region. The far north is tundra, a treeless plain where only the smallest of plants can survive the winds and extreme temperatures.

South of the tundra is the taiga, a belt of forestland. In all, 4,000,000 square miles (10,359,952 sq. km) of Russia are forest—about half its land area. Depending on how far north a forest stand is, it can include various kinds of trees, such as pines, firs, cedars, aspens, oaks, and birches.

South of the taiga are the steppes. The steppes are broad, open plains similar to the Great Plains in North America and the Pampa in South America, both of which students should have learned about in previous grades. The steppes provided a natural pathway into Russia for nomadic peoples from the east, south, and west, including the Mongols. The steppes have fertile soil and were and continue to be an important agricultural area for Russia.

Teaching Idea

Talk about labor camps in Russia and prisons in the U.S. as a deterrent to criminal behavior. Do these systems work to change behavior—why or why not?

Teaching Idea

Assign each student one of the vegetation regions noted in the text. Have students do research and create a 2-page report about the region's vegetation and climate. At least 1 page should be a written report, and the other page can be an illustration—drawn, clipped from a magazine, or downloaded from a website.

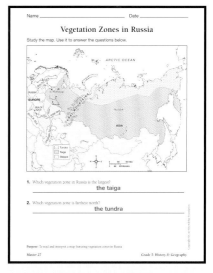

Use Instructional Master 27.

History and Geography: World　**215**

Rivers

Volga River

The Volga River rises in the Valdai Hills near Moscow, wanders south, and empties through a delta into the Caspian Sea. The Volga is the longest river in Europe and to Russians it has been known through history as "Mother Volga." It is the principal water transportation route in Russia and is linked by canals to a network of other rivers. The Volga is an important source of hydroelectric power and irrigation. The river was immortalized in Igor Stravinsky's "Song of the Volga Boatmen" and Ilya Repin's painting of the Volga boatmen. Its shores are dotted with old monasteries and churches.

Don River

The Don River flows through southwest European Russia in a general southerly direction and empties into the Sea of Azov, which is connected to the Black Sea. A canal links the Don to the Volga, some 65 miles away. The Don has been and continues to be an important transportation route in European Russia. The area along the Don was also the homeland of the Cossacks, a people famous for their bravery and horsemanship.

Black, Caspian, and Baltic Seas

The Black, Caspian, and Baltic Seas are seas that border areas of European Russia.

The Black Sea lies between Asia and Europe and is bordered by Turkey, Bulgaria, Romania, Ukraine, Georgia, and Russia. Like the Mediterranean, the Black Sea was an important waterway in ancient commerce. Today, the Rhine-Danube Canal links the Black Sea to the North Sea. Odessa is an important Russian port on the Black Sea.

The Caspian Sea actually lies between Europe and Asia, bordering the countries of Russia, Kazakhstan, Turkmenistan, Iran, and Azerbaijan. It is the world's largest inland sea, spanning 143,000 square miles (370,368 sq. km). Because it has no natural outlets to an ocean, it has no tides. A canal links the Caspian Sea to the Black Sea. The sea lies 92 feet (28 m) below sea level and is fed by rivers such as the Volga. In recent years, the sea has been shrinking because water is being drawn off the rivers that feed it for use in irrigation. The Caspian Sea is used for fishing, especially in the northern regions, and is an important source of oil and natural gas.

The Baltic Sea is an arm of the Atlantic Ocean and is bordered by Sweden, Finland, Russia, Estonia, Latvia, Lithuania, Poland, Germany, and Denmark. It is connected to the North Sea through several straits and the Kiel Canal. During the 1300s, the Baltic was an important center of international trade because of the Hanseatic League of northern European trading cities. In the 1400s and 1500s, the European trading networks that developed south along the coast of Africa to India and west to the Americas supplanted the Baltic's importance. One reason Peter the Great chose the site that was to become St. Petersburg was that it afforded access to the Baltic. St. Petersburg was an important port for Russia beginning in the 1700s and 1800s, and it still is today.

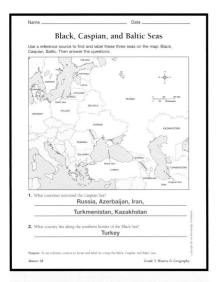

Use Instructional Master 28.

Review

Below are some ideas for ongoing assessment and review activities. These are not meant to constitute a comprehensive list. Teachers may also refer to the *Pearson Learning/Core Knowledge History & Geography* series for additional information and teaching ideas.

• As a culmination to this section, have students answer the question based on the big idea, "Describe Russia's expansion of territory abroad while extending autocratic rule at home." Have students justify their answer with facts learned in this section.

• This section provides an opportunity for students to complete short research reports on historical figures of Russia. Using the Language Arts section, provide the class with topics for short reports to write in formal style. Each day of a week, provide a mini-lesson on different aspects of report writing, such as correct paragraph form or bibliographies. Share these reports when completed.

• Have students select one of the rulers of Russia to describe in a short paper in class. Make sure that students include a section in their papers about whether or not they felt that this ruler was effective. They must include their opinion and then use examples from history to support their opinions. Share these aloud and discuss as a class what makes an effective and fair ruler of a country. You may wish to discuss other countries and governments as a review.

• Have students play bingo to review the information from this section. Before playing, prepare a list of questions about information from this unit, and then list the answers to the questions on a piece of chart paper or on an overhead transparency. The answers should be names of people, places, and terms from this section. Pass out a blank bingo card template to each student. Show students the list of answers and have them choose enough answers to fill their cards in any order they would like. Then, ask the students the prepared questions. When students hear a question asked that matches an answer on their card, they may cover the answer with a marker. If students call bingo, make sure they can refer to the spaces on their cards and define the answers that are found there.

• Provide an opportunity for students to download pictures of Russia from the Internet. Give students pieces of construction paper and ask them to make collages to summarize what they have learned about Russia. Students should glue their pictures to the construction paper and write a summary of their collages to explain why each picture selected illustrates something that they learned about Russia and its rulers. Share these with the class, and post them in the classroom.

• Have students select one of the historical figures from this section and write an acrostic poem using the letters of that person's name. For each line, students should write a historical fact that they have learned about that person.

• Have students select one of the historical figures from this section and write several facts about that person on an index card. Have students take turns reading what they have written on their card. Classmates should guess which historical figure is being described.

• Compare and contrast the czars of Russia with the monarchs of England. Then, compare the system of government in these countries in the past to the present-day form of rule. You may even want to go one step further and compare these rulers with the President of the United States. Then students can write a paragraph explaining the system they would like to live under, and justify their answer with facts learned from these sections.

• You may also ask the following questions after completion of this unit of study.

1. Locate the following places on an overhead map or globe: (a) Moscow; (b) St. Petersburg; (c) Ural Mountains; (d) Volga River; (e) Don River; (f) Black Sea; (g) Caspian Sea; (h) Baltic Sea.

2. What were the rulers of old Russia called?

   They were called czars.

3. Why did Moscow consider itself the successor of the Byzantine Empire?

   Russian leaders declared Moscow "The Third Rome" because the Eastern Orthodox Church had established its center there. Later, Ivan III married the niece of the last Byzantine emperor and took the title czar, *meaning Caesar.*

4. How did both Ivan III and Ivan IV expand Russian territory?

   Ivan III annexed land from other city-states and from the Poles, Lithuanians, and Mongols. Ivan IV extended Russian rule throughout the Volga River Basin to the Caspian Sea and across the Ural Mountains into Siberia.

5. How did Peter the Great modernize and westernize Russia?

   Peter ordered beards to be shaved and Russians (other than peasants) to wear western-style clothes; established a navy; modernized the army by turning it into a standing, or full-time, army equipped with modern weapons; established military-technical schools and required the sons of the nobility be sent to them to train as officers; encouraged the development of manufacturing, shipbuilding, mining industries, and international trading companies through subsidies.

6. Where did Peter the Great finally establish his warm-water port?

   Peter was able to defeat Sweden to gain enough territory to build a city, St. Petersburg, on the Gulf of Finland, an arm of the Baltic Sea.

7. Why did Catherine end her plans to carry out reforms in Russian society and government?

   The peasant revolt and the French Revolution showed what could happen if tight control was loosened over subjects who were unhappy and angry over conditions.

8. How did conditions for peasants worsen under Peter and Catherine?

   More peasants became serfs, that is, they became the possession of the landholder on whose land they lived and worked. They could be bought and sold like possessions.

More Resources

The titles listed below are offered as a representative sample of materials and not a complete list of everything that is available.

For students —

• *Early Russia,* edited by E. D. Hirsch, Jr. (Pearson Learning, 2002), a unit in the official *Pearson Learning/Core Knowledge History & Geography* series, is available as part of the bound book for Grade 5/Level 5. A teacher's guide is also available. To order, call 1-800-321-3106.

• *Moscow (Cities of the World),* by Deborah Kent (Children's Press, 2000). This book provides an engaging introduction to the history, culture, daily life, food, and people of Moscow. Pages 19–24 relate directly to this unit of study. Library binding, 64 pages, ISBN 0516211935. See also *St. Petersburg,* by the same author and in this same series.

• *Peter the Great,* Diane Stanley (Aladdin, 1992). Honored by the Golden Kite Award committee for excellence in children's nonfiction. Paperback, 32 pages, ISBN 068971548X.

• *Russia in Pictures (Visual Geography Series),* by Heron Marquez (Lerner Publications, 2003). Pages 20–27 relate directly to this unit. Hardcover, 80 pages, ISBN 0822509377.

• *Russian Folk Tales,* retold by James Riordan (Oxford University Press, 2000). Hardcover, 96 pages, ISBN 0192745360.

For teachers —

• *Catherine the Great,* by Henri Troyat (Plume, 1994). Paperback, 377 pages, ISBN 0452011205. Troyat is also the author of two other books on Russian leaders, *Ivan the Terrible* and *Peter the Great.*

• *A History of Russia to 1855 (Seventh Edition),* by Nicholas V. Riasanovsky (Oxford University Press, 2004). Paperback, 340 pages, ISBN 0195153928.

• *The Icon and the Axe: An Interpretive History of Russian Culture,* by James Billington (Vintage, 1970). Paperback, 880 pages, ISBN 0394708466.

• *Land of the Firebird: The Beauty of Old Russia (Thirteenth Edition),* by Suzanne Massie (Hearttree Press, 1980). Paperback, 493 pages, ISBN 096441841X.

• *Peter the Great,* by Robert K. Massie (Ballantine Books, 1981). Paperback, 928 pages, ISBN 0345298063.

• *Peter the Great: A Biography,* by Lindsey Hughes (Yale University Press, 2004). Paperback, 285 pages, ISBN 030010300X.

• *Rise of Russia (Great Ages of Man),* by Robert Wallace (Time-Life Books, 1967). Out of print but widely available; eminently readable and generously illustrated. Hardcover, ISBN 0809403536.

• *Russia Under the Old Regime (Second Edition),* by Richard Pipes (Penguin, 1997). Paperback, 384 pages, ISBN 0140247688.

• *St. Petersburg: Russia's Window to the Future, The First Three Centuries,* by Arthur L. George with Elena George (Taylor Trade Publishing, 2003). Hardcover, 512 pages, ISBN 1589790170.

• Visual Geography Series, www.vgsbooks.com, is the companion website to the book *Russia in Pictures,* listed in resources for students.

VII. Feudal Japan

The Big Idea

Japan's island location and geography resulted in its unique culture and history.

Remember that each subject you study with students expands their vocabulary and introduces new terms, thus making them better listeners and readers. As you study Japan, use map work, read alouds, independent reading, and discussions to build students' vocabularies.

The items below refer to content in Grade 5. Use time lines with students to help them sequence and relate events from different periods and groups.

500s	Buddhism carried to Japan from China by missionaries
700s	Imperial family claims descent from female sun deity
1100s	Minamoto Yoritomo takes title of hereditary shogun
1100s	Beginning of feudal society in Japan
1200s	Sects of Buddhism developing, including Zen
1603–1867	Tokugawa Shogunate
1603–1867	Japan closed to virtually all outsiders
1854	Admiral Perry and United States warship open Japan to United States
1868	Edo renamed as Tokyo and made capital of Japan
later 1800s	Shinto divided into State Shinto and Sect Shinto

continued on next page

What Students Should Already Know

Students in Core Knowledge schools should be familiar with

Grade 2

- Buddhism
  - Prince Siddhartha becomes Buddha, "the Enlightened One"
  - Buddhism begins as an outgrowth of Hinduism in India, and then spreads through many countries in Asia
  - King Asoka (also spelled Ashoka)
- geography of Japan
  - location in relation to continental Asia, "land of the rising sun"
  - a country made up of islands, four major islands
  - Pacific Ocean, the Sea of Japan
  - Mt. Fuji
  - Tokyo
- Japanese culture
  - Japanese flag
  - big modern cities, centers of industry and business
  - origami as representative of traditional Japanese crafts
  - the kimono as representative of traditional Japanese clothing

What Students Need to Learn

- **Emperor as nominal leader, but real power in the hands of shogun**
- **Samurai, code of Bushido**
- **Rigid class system in feudal Japanese society**
- **Japan closed to outsiders**
- **Religion**
  - **Buddhism: the four Noble Truths and the Eightfold Path, Nirvana**
  - **Shinto: reverence for ancestors, reverence for nature, *kami***
- **Pacific Ocean, Sea of Japan**
- **Four main islands: Hokkaido, Honshu (largest), Shikoku, Kyushu**
- **Tokyo**
- **Typhoons, earthquakes**
- **Pacific Rim**

Vocabulary

Student/Teacher Vocabulary

archipelago: a series, or string, of many islands (S)

Buddhism: one of main religions in Japan; the goal of Buddhism is to achieve enlightenment by self-purification (S)

code of Bushido: a code of ethics followed by the samurai; samurai were to be frugal, incorruptible, brave, self-sacrificing, loyal to their lords, and above all, courageous (Bushido: way of the warrior) (S)

daimyo: Japanese feudal lords who were large landholders (T)

earthquake: shaking or turbulence caused by underground plate movement (S)

Eightfold Path: the means of achieving nirvana in Buddhism by living a life that embraces right views, right aspirations, right speech, right conduct, right livelihood, right effort, right mindfulness, and right contemplation (S)

emperor: the ruler of Japan (S)

feudalism: in Japan, a system based on status in society, land ownership, and labor, with the shogun at the top, followed by daimyo, samurai, lesser soldiers, peasants, artisans, and merchants (S)

Four Noble Truths: the principles of Buddhism:
1. Pain, suffering, and sorrow are natural components of life.
2. Desire is the cause of suffering.
3. Achieving nirvana—overcoming desire—is the only way to end suffering.
4. Achieving nirvana is possible by following the Eightfold Path. (T)

Hokkaido: the second-largest island of Japan, sparsely inhabited because of its harsh climate and terrain (S)

Honshu: one of the islands that make up the nation of Japan; the most densely populated island and home to the capital, Tokyo (S)

kami: forces of nature worshiped in Shinto (S)

Kyushu: one of the islands that make up the nation of Japan; heavily populated, it is home to the major port city of Nagasaki (S)

nirvana: in Buddhism, the state of overcoming desire and reaching enlightenment (S)

Pacific Rim: a term used to describe nations in Asia and North and South America that border the Pacific Ocean (S)

Ring of Fire: a series of volcanoes that ring the Pacific Ocean; this area is prone to earthquakes and other volcanic activity (S)

samurai: a soldier-noble in feudal Japan (S)

Sea of Japan: a body of water located between the west coast of the Japanese islands and the east coast of China (S)

Shikoku: the smallest of the four major Japanese islands (S)

Shinto: one of main religions in Japan; Shinto involves worship of natural forces and until 1945 regarded the Emperor as a descendant of the sun goddess (T)

shogun: a great general or military governor ruling feudal Japan (T)

Tokyo: the capital city of Japan and its largest city, with a population of approximately 12 million people, originally known as Edo (S)

tsunami: a great sea wave produced by submarine Earth movement or volcanic eruption (S)

continued from previous page

| 1923 | **Highly destructive earthquake in Japan** |
| 1945 | **End of World War II; State Shinto banned** |

Text Resources
(45) *The Code of the Samurai*
(46) *Tsunamis*

Materials
Instructional Masters 29, 83
Venn Diagram, p. 224
Japan, p. 227
names of levels of feudal society in Japan on slips of paper, enough for each student in class, p. 229
basket, p. 229
classroom collection of fiction dedicated to this unit, p. 229
local university professor or high school teacher who can talk about feudal Japan, p. 229

VII. Feudal Japan

An interesting activity while studying the World History and Geography strand this year would be the creation of a world time line including major events. This time line would help students understand the differences from one culture and civilization to another more easily and thus help them make comparisons and contrasts among civilizations.

Vocabulary continued

typhoon: a tropical hurricane that forms over the western Pacific Ocean, particularly in the South China Sea to the south of Japan (S)

Domain Vocabulary

Feudal Japan and associated words:
Japanese, general, military, commander, soldier, emperor, imperial, family, title, hereditary, Shogunate, dynasty, ruler, faction, regent, feudal, vassal, lord, landholder, army, noble, peasant, artisan, merchant, farmer, castle, administrator, trade, knight, position, serve, armor, sword, code, ethics, incorruptible, brave, self-sacrificing, loyal, courageous, ritual suicide, honor, dishonor, Zen Buddhism, Buddha, Buddhist, monk, monastery, self-discipline, self-restraint, poverty, suffering, meditation, enlightenment, enlightened, pain, suffering, sorrow, nirvana, overcome, desire, aspiration, conduct, livelihood, mindfulness, contemplation, teaching, art, architecture, government, isolation, isolationist, foreigners, missionary, abroad, Matthew Perry, navy, Edo, treaty, trade, modernization, industrialization, westernize, adopt, absolute, ruler, class, sect, ritual, ceremony, self-understanding, nature, reverence, rain, shrine, bridge, water, rock garden, worship, prayer, imperial, descend, deity, divide, emperor worship, religious, loyalty, obedience, patriotism, Nippon, pagoda, origami, rising sun

Geography of Japan and associated words:
island, mountaintop, sea level, Japan, India, China, Tibet, Korea, Sri Lanka, industry, electronics, automobiles, Pacific Ocean, Guam, Philippines, New Zealand, volcano; Sea of Japan, warm, current, tropical, archipelago, mountainous, terrain, barren, rocky, forest, climate, capital, Osaka, Yokohama, Kobe, Hiroshima, Kyoto, population density, populated, coal, deposit, industry, Nagasaki, Mt. Fuji, rice paddy, staple, fishing, crop, terrace, commerce, finance, bullet train, Tokyo Bay, Edo, bombing, atomic bomb, World War II, rebuild, hurricane, South China Sea, landslide, flood; tectonic, eruption, Pacific Rim

Cross-curricular Connections

Language Arts	Visual Arts	Music
Fiction and Drama	**Art of Japan**	**Songs**
Myths and Legends	• The Great Buddha (Kamakura Buddha)	• "Sakura"
• "A Tale of the Oki Islands" (also known as "The Samurai's Daughter")	• Landscape gardens	

At a Glance

The most important ideas for you are:

- Japan is a nation of around 3,500 islands, but the majority of the population lives on the four islands of Hokkaido, Honshu, Shikoku, and Kyushu.
- Because of its location in the Ring of Fire and in the western Pacific, Japan is subject to typhoons and earthquakes.
- *The Pacific Rim* is a term used to describe countries in Asia and North and South America that border the Pacific Ocean.
- From the time of the Kamakura Shogunate, the emperors ruled in name only; the real power was held by the shoguns or members of powerful families ruling in the shogun's name.
- Japan from the 1100s on was a feudal society headed by the shogun or by those ruling in the shogun's name.
- Samurai, soldier-nobles, owed allegiance to daimyos, higher lords who were large landholders and direct vassals of the shogun.
- A samurai's conduct was dictated by the code of Bushido.
- The Tokugawa Shogunate closed Japan to most outsiders to hold onto their power.
- Buddhism and Shinto are two important religions in Japanese history.

What Teachers Need to Know

A. History and Culture

Background

Students in Core Knowledge schools should have studied modern Japan in Grade 2; this unit focuses on feudal Japan, the age of the samurai and the shoguns.

Emperor and the Shogun

The title of *shogun* [SHOW-gun], or general, was first bestowed on military commanders in the 700s who were asked to recruit soldiers for some specific campaign. Once the campaign was over, the title of shogun reverted back to the emperor. The temporary shogun was always a member of the imperial family.

However, in the late 1100s, the shogun Minamoto Yoritomo maneuvered to make the title of shogun permanent and hereditary, meaning that it would remain in his family generation after generation. This was the beginning of the Kamakura Shogunate [kah-mah-KOOR-ah SHOW-gun-it]. A shogunate in Japan is like a dynasty in China. The term refers to both the rulers and the period during which they ruled.

Teaching Idea

You may want to teach section B, "Geography," before beginning "History and Culture."

Teaching Idea

Discuss with students what types of honors/names remain in families for generations. Ask if they think it is good for a country to have a lot of hereditary titles, or if they think people should earn their titles themselves.

VII. Feudal Japan

Teaching Idea

Have students do research on the Internet and in print sources to find out what position the emperor has in Japanese life today. They should use their information as the basis for a short report on the modern Japanese emperor.

Teaching Idea

Students in Core Knowledge schools should have studied European feudalism in Grade 4. Ask them to describe what they learned about feudalism in Europe. Use a Venn diagram to chart the similarities and differences between the two forms of feudalism.

samurai

At the time, Japan was beset with rival factions, and a strong military power was needed to keep the warring parties in check. The emperor was a child and Yoritomo conspired with the regent (the official who rules when a child occupies a hereditary office) to abolish the emperor's right to choose his own shogun. Without this power, the emperor was at the mercy of the shogun because the shogun controlled the military. In practice, the emperor became ruler in name only and the shogun, or members of powerful families ruling in the name of the shogun, held the real power through the military. This continued through three dynasties of shoguns. In the 1800s, Japan moved beyond its feudal society and began to modernize.

Feudal Japanese Society

Like Europe, Japan developed a feudal society; however, Japanese feudalism developed later than in Europe. In the 1100s through the 1300s, when feudalism was strengthening its hold on Japan, its influence in Europe was lessening through the development of stronger national states, the development of towns and cities, and the growth and spread of commerce. As students may know from their study of European feudalism in Grade 4, feudalism was a political and military system based on a concept of reciprocal self-defense.

The Japanese feudal system can be imagined as a large pyramid:

• At the top of Japanese feudal society was the shogun.

• Below the shogun were the vassal lords, known as daimyo [DIME-yo]. The daimyo were large landholders who held their estates at the pleasure of the shogun. They controlled the armies that were to provide military service to the shogun when required.

• The armies were made up of samurai [SA-moo-rye] and lesser soldiers. The samurai were minor nobles and held their land under the authority of the daimyo.

• Peasants were the next rank in feudal society. As in Europe, they were the majority of the population, and it was their labor that made possible the functioning of the rest of the society.

• Below the peasants were the artisans.

• At the bottom of society were the merchants. As buyers and sellers of others' goods, they had little status. Japanese society valued the creators—farmers and artisans—above those who merely sold and traded.

The ranks changed over time, however. By the 1600s, the samurai became less important as war became less important. Samurai moved from small estates to castle towns and became administrators. At the same time, the status of artisans and merchants rose as towns and cities developed, and trade became more important to the Japanese economy.

▶ Samurai: Code of Bushido

The samurai were the soldier-nobles of feudal Japan, similar to the knights of feudal European society. Their position was hereditary and they served a daimyo in return for land. Below the samurai were foot soldiers.

The samurai dressed in armor made of strips of steel held together by silk cords. More colorful and less bulky than European armor, it provided greater flexibility, yet ample protection against an enemy's sword.

The samurai developed a code of ethics known as Bushido, the way of the warrior. According to Bushido, samurai were to be frugal, incorruptible, brave, self-sacrificing, loyal to their lords, and above all, courageous. It was considered better to commit ritual suicide than to live in dishonor. In time, Zen Buddhism influenced the samurai code, and self-discipline and self-restraint became two important virtues for samurai to master. ㊺

Japan Closed to Outsiders

From 1603 to 1867, the Tokugawa Shogunate ruled Japan. Early in the dynasty, the shogun closed off Japan from most of the rest of the world and reasserted feudal control, which had been loosening. In the 1500s, the first European traders and missionaries had visited the island nation and brought with them new ideas. Fearing that further contact would weaken their hold on the government and the people, the Tokugawa banned virtually all foreigners. One Dutch ship was allowed to land at Nagasaki once a year to trade.

The ban was not limited to Europeans. Only a few Chinese a year were allowed to enter Japan for trading purposes. In addition, the Japanese themselves were not allowed to travel abroad for any reason.

This isolation ended when Commodore Matthew Perry of the United States Navy sailed into Edo (Tokyo) Bay in 1853 and forced the Tokugawa to sign a treaty allowing trade with the United States the next year. Other countries followed and by 1867, a group of lords removed the Tokugawa shogun and set Japan on a path to modernization and industrialization.

Religion

 ### Buddhism

Buddhism originated with the thinking of Siddhartha Gautama in the late sixth century BCE. A son of a wealthy Hindu family in India, Gautama lived in luxury behind palace walls, shielded from poverty and human suffering. One day while out riding, he came across a sick man, a poor man, and a dead man. For the first time, he saw what it meant to be human. He gave up his life of privilege and began six years of wandering while he looked for an answer to life. After sitting under a tree meditating for 48 days, he suddenly received enlightenment, that is, he understood the answer.

Taking the name Buddha, meaning "Enlightened One," he began to teach others the Four Noble Truths and the Eightfold Path. The Four Noble Truths are

1. Pain, suffering, and sorrow are natural components of life.

2. Desire is the cause of suffering.

3. Achieving nirvana—overcoming desire—is the only way to end suffering.

4. Achieving nirvana is possible by following the Eightfold Path.

The Eightfold Path to nirvana means living a life that embraces "right views, right aspirations, right speech, right conduct, right livelihood, right effort, right mindfulness, and right contemplation."

Buddha's followers spread his teachings throughout India and to what are now the nations of China, Tibet, Korea, Japan, and Sri Lanka. Buddhism reached Japan from Korea around 552 CE. The emissaries of the Korean king who

Teaching Idea

Research groups that have codes of ethics, and compare Bushido to these other codes. Restate the "code of ethics" for the class, and possibly develop a code of ethics for the class during this unit of study.

Teaching Idea

Teach students about samurai by reading fictional samurai stories. See *More Resources* for suggestions.

Teaching Idea

If Japan or any nation wanted to isolate itself today from outside influences, what would it have to do? Discuss with students the difficulty of implementing such a policy today. Talk about how very few sources of information there were in the 1600s, and how many there are now.

VII. Feudal Japan

Shinto shrine

commended Buddhism to the Japanese also brought with them Chinese writing and ideas about the arts, architecture, and government. The Japanese adopted some of these ideas. In the 1200s, several sects, or offshoots, of Buddhism developed. One major sect was Zen Buddhism. The word *zen* means "meditation" and this is the central element of Zen Buddhism. Rituals and ceremonies are considered useless. Meditation is one important exercise Zen Buddhists use in their attempt to achieve Satori, or self-understanding. Zen became particularly popular among the samurai. Today, less than 10 percent of Japan's population are adherents of Zen, but Zen Buddhism has attracted followers in the west as well.

Shinto

Shinto is the original religion of the Japanese. It did not have a name until Buddhism arrived and people wanted to distinguish the two. Shinto means the way of the *kami*, which are the forces of nature; for example, typhoons, rain, sunlight, earthquakes, a growing flower. A reverence for nature is a major element of this religion.

Early Shinto had no shrines. After the arrival of Buddhism, the Japanese began to build simple shrines in beautiful natural settings in which to worship the kami. These shrines typically have a gateway, called a *torii*, marking the entrance, and a basin for washing hands before entering the oratory, known as a *haiden*. The haiden is where a visitor will make an offering and pray. There are no rituals in Shinto—other than washing one's hands before entering a shrine with an offering—and no ceremonies other than reciting prayers. The most important building in the shrine is the *honden*, a sanctuary where an important religious symbol called *shintai* is kept. The shintai is generally a mirror but it could also be a sword, a wooden symbol, or another object. Only the main priest is allowed to enter the honden; all others are forbidden to enter or see the shintai.

By the 700s, the imperial family was claiming that it had descended from the female sun deity, Amaterasu [AH-ma-tah-rah-su], in order to legitimize its role and its power. In the later 1800s, Shinto was divided into State Shinto, which involved worship of the emperor as divine, and Sect, or religious, Shinto. Because the emperor was considered to be a god, he was to be given complete loyalty and obedience. Government ministers manipulated State Shinto in order to develop a sense of national identity, or patriotism, among the Japanese and gain support for the government's new industrial and military policies. State Shinto was banned after World War II, when the emperor renounced any claim to divinity.

An important aspect of Shinto is ancestor worship. Followers believe that a person continues to play a role in the family and community after their death. In some Shinto households, an altar called a *tamaya* is built to honor deceased relatives.

Buddhism and Shinto are not seen as incompatible religions: The majority of modern Japanese—about 84 percent—practice both Buddhism and Shinto.

B. Geography

Pacific Ocean and Sea of Japan

The Pacific is the largest and deepest of the four oceans, extending over about a third of the surface of Earth. The Pacific reaches from the Arctic to Antarctica

and separates North and South America from Asia and Australia. Thousands of islands dot the ocean's surface from the Bering Strait to the South China Sea and beyond to the southeast. These include the islands of Oceania, such as Guam and the Marshalls, as well as Japan, the Philippines, and New Zealand. The Ring of Fire is a series of volcanoes that ring the ocean.

The Sea of Japan lies between the west coast of Japan and the east coast of China and North and South Korea. The warm Japanese current, which originates in tropical waters, divides around the islands and part of it flows north through the Sea of Japan.

Four Main Islands

Japan is an archipelago, that is, a chain of islands. About 3,500 islands make up the nation of Japan. The islands are the crests of mountaintops that rise above sea level. Most of the islands are barren and rocky with no inhabitants.

The four largest islands are Hokkaido, Honshu, Shikoku, and Kyushu. Honshu is the largest, with about 60 percent of the land area of Japan. None of the islands is more than 200 miles wide.

Hokkaido is the second-largest island, but is sparsely inhabited because of its mountainous terrain, great stands of forests, and harsh winter climate. The majority of Japanese live on the island of Honshu. This is an area of heavy industrial development. Tokyo, the nation's capital, is located on Honshu, as are other major cities, including Osaka, Yokahama, Kobe, Hiroshima, and Kyoto.

Kyushu is also heavily populated. The island has coal deposits, which helped it become an early center for industry. Nagasaki is a major port city. It was hit by an atomic bomb late in World War II, but it has been rebuilt. People on Shikoku, the smallest of the large islands, live mostly along the northern coast in industrial areas.

Less than 20 percent of Japan is suited to agriculture because Japan is so mountainous and so heavily forested. As a result, the ancient Japanese learned to farm rice, their staple crop, in small paddies on the sides of terraced mountains. Beginning in the late 1800s, wealthy Japanese, with the help of the government, began a program to industrialize the country. While World War II destroyed much of the country's industry and infrastructure, Japan rebuilt and is today a leading exporter of electronics, automobiles, and other manufactured goods.

 Tokyo

Tokyo, on the island of Honshu, is the capital of Japan and its largest city with around 30 million people in the metropolitan area. Nearly 25 percent of Japan's population lives in the Tokyo metropolitan area. Tokyo is also a center of commerce, industry, finance, and education. There are more than 100 colleges and universities in the city. The high-speed bullet trains, which can travel over 150 miles per hour, link Tokyo with other cities on the island of Honshu. The city sits at the head of Tokyo Bay, Japan's busiest port.

Originally known as Edo, Tokyo was established in the 1100s. In 1868, it was renamed Tokyo and became the capital of the Japanese Empire. Devastated by earthquakes and the bombing of World War II, the city has been rebuilt several times, making it very modern in appearance.

Teaching Idea

Because students using the *Core Knowledge Sequence* learned about Japan in Grade 2, begin by asking them what they know about the location and geography of Japan.

Create an overhead of Instructional Master 29, *Japan*, to help students locate the island nation in relation to the Asian continent. Have them identify those nations in terms of direction from Japan.

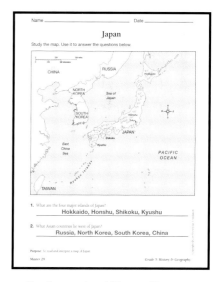

Use Instructional Master 29.

VII. Feudal Japan

Typhoons and Earthquakes

A typhoon is a tropical hurricane that forms over the western Pacific Ocean, particularly in the South China Sea to the south of Japan. Typhoons can be so severe that they result in landslides and floods. ㊻

Japan, as noted above, is part of the Ring of Fire, an area of active tectonic movement. *Tectonic* refers to changes in the structure of Earth's surface resulting from the movement of plates. Because of its location, Japan regularly experiences earthquakes and occasional volcanic eruptions. Experts who measure Earth's activity have found that there are 7,500 earthquakes a year in Japan, of which 1,500 are strong enough for people to be aware of them. About every two years, an earthquake occurs that causes major damage and loss of life. One of the worst was in 1923 when 140,000 people in Tokyo were killed.

The Pacific Rim

The Pacific Rim refers to those countries in Asia and North and South America that ring the Pacific Ocean. They include

- in North America: Canada, the United States, Mexico, El Salvador, Honduras, Nicaragua, Costa Rica, Panama
- in South America: Colombia, Ecuador, Peru, Chile
- Australia
- in Asia: China, Russia, Japan, Korea, Taiwan, Singapore, Hong Kong

These countries have strong trading ties with one another and by the 1970s, trade goods flowing among them had outpaced transatlantic trade. By 2020, the Pacific Rim nations expect to have created a free-trade zone around the Pacific similar to the North American Free Trade Association that links Canada, the United States, and Mexico.

The Big Idea in Review

Japan's island location and geography resulted in its unique culture and history.

Review

Below are some ideas for ongoing assessment and review activities. These are not meant to constitute a comprehensive list. Teachers may also refer to the *Pearson Learning/Core Knowledge History & Geography* series for additional information and teaching ideas.

- As a culmination to this section, have students write a report based on the big idea, "Describe how the geography of Japan had an impact on its culture and history." Have students justify their answers with facts learned in this section.

- This section provides an opportunity for students to complete short research reports on feudal Japan. Using the Language Arts section, provide the class with topics for short reports to write in formal style. Each day of a week, provide a mini-lesson on different aspects of report writing, such as correct paragraph form or bibliographies. Share these reports when completed.

- Have students write Japanese haiku to illustrate an idea they have learned about feudal Japan from this section. A haiku is unrhymed Japanese poetry with three lines. The first line has five syllables, the second line has seven syllables,

and the last line has five syllables. Have students illustrate their poems and post them in class.

• Write the names of the levels of feudal society in Japan on slips of paper and put them in a basket. Have students select a slip of paper from the basket and then write a paragraph to describe what kind of life they would lead in Japan if they were members of that class. What rights and privileges would they enjoy? Have them share their descriptions with the class.

• Ask the media specialist at your school or the local librarian to assemble a classroom collection of fiction related to this period of time. Have these books available for students to read while you study feudal Japan, and have students use references from their books in class discussion.

• Research local universities or high schools to see if a historian can come to the class and discuss feudal Japan. After the classroom visit, have students write a letter to the speaker illustrating something that they learned from the talk.

• You may also ask the following questions after completion of this unit of study.

1. What does it mean to say that Japan is an archipelago?

   An archipelago is a series, or string, of many islands. Japan is made up of about 3,500 islands, but most people live on four islands—Hokkaido, Honshu, Shikoku, and Kyushu.

2. Where is Tokyo, the capital of Japan, located?

   Tokyo is on Honshu, the largest of the islands.

3. How does Japan's location have an influence on the number of earthquakes and occurrence of typhoons?

   Japan is located in the Ring of Fire, an area of tectonic plate activity, that is, where there is frequent movement of Earth's crust, causing earthquakes. The western Pacific where Japan is located is an area that experiences typhoons, or tropical hurricanes.

4. Who ruled in Japan after the Kamakura Shogunate came to power—the emperor or the shogun?

   The real power was held by the shogun.

5. What were the levels of feudal society in Japan?

   At the top was the shogun, then the daimyos (the higher landed nobles), samurai (lesser landed nobles and soldiers), peasants, artisans, and merchants. The ranks changed as war become less important and trade grew.

6. What was the code of Bushido?

   The code of Bushido told samurai how they were to act. They were to be frugal, incorruptible, brave, self-sacrificing, loyal to their lord, and courageous.

7. Why did the Tokugawa Shogunate close Japan to outsiders and forbid the Japanese to travel outside Japan?

   The Tokugawa were afraid that the new ideas that foreigners would bring would weaken the control of the shogunate over the Japanese people.

8. What is Shinto?

   Shinto is a Japanese religion that involves reverence for nature.

9. According to Buddhism, what must a person do to attain the state of nirvana?

   The person must overcome desire by following the Eightfold Path.

More Resources

The titles listed below are offered as a representative sample of materials and not a complete list of everything that is available.

For students —

• *Feudal Japan*, edited by E. D. Hirsch, Jr. (Pearson Learning, 2002), a unit in the official *Pearson Learning/Core Knowledge History & Geography* series, is available as part of the bound book for Grade 5/Level 5. A teacher's guide is also available. To order, call 1-800-321-3106.

• *Japan (Enchantment of the World)*, by Anne Heinrichs (Children's Press, 1998). Library binding, 143 pages, ISBN 0516206494.

• *Japanese Children's Favorite Stories*, compiled by Florence Sakade (Tuttle, 2003). Hardcover, 108 pages, ISBN 0804834490.

• *The Samurai's Daughter: A Japanese Legend*, by Robert D. San Souci (Dial Books for Young Readers, 1992). Hardcover, ISBN 0803711352.

• *Shipwrecked! The True Adventures of a Japanese Boy*, by Rhoda Blumberg (Harper Trophy, 2003). Follow the story of 14-year-old Manjiro, whose adventures brought him to a place of influence in Japan's reacceptance of foreign trade. Paperback, 80 pages, ISBN 068817485X. See also *Commodore Perry in the Land of the Shogun*, by the same author. Both titles may offer some opportunities for reading aloud.

• *Three Samurai Cats: A Story from Japan*, by Eric A. Kimmel (Holiday House, 2003). Library binding, 32 pages, ISBN 0823417425.

For teachers —

• *Japan: A Global Studies Handbook*, by Lucien Ellington (ABC-CLIO, 2002). An introduction to Japan's history, culture, economics, and society. Written by one of the expert reviewers for the Core Knowledge curriculum, this book draws on the author's experience in leading teacher institutes on Japan in more than 20 states. Contains an extensive resource section. Hardcover, 307 pages, ISBN 1576072711.

• Japanese Consulate offices typically offer a variety of materials for loan, including videos. To find the Japanese Consulate nearest you, go to www.japanatlanta.org/cgofj.html, or phone the Japanese Embassy in Washington, DC at 202-238-6700.

• Asia for Educators at http://afe.easia.columbia.edu, contains several multimedia units on medieval Japan.

• Student Activity: The Making of a Class Carp Streamer. Lesson plan available online from SPICE (Stanford Program on International and Cross-Cultural Education), at http://spice.stanford.edu/lp/carp/index.html.

History and Geography in Fifth Grade

AMERICAN HISTORY AND GEOGRAPHY

In Grade 5, students continue the chronological study of United States history begun in Grade 3. They pick up with westward expansion. Because of the importance of geography to an understanding of how the United States was settled, you might want to teach Section IV on geography before beginning the rest of the topics. In Section IV, students will learn about the ways that the nation can be divided by region, what states are in each region, and something about the climate and characteristics of each region. In Grade 5, students should also learn the capitals of the 50 states.

In Section I, students briefly review some people and events they encountered in earlier grades, such as Daniel Boone and the Lewis and Clark expedition. Then they look at pioneers, Native-American resistance, the influence of the concept of Manifest Destiny, and how this idea propelled the nation into the Mexican-American War. The second part of Section I describes expansion after the Civil War. Among the topics students will explore are the influence of the Homestead Act, the impact of the transcontinental railroad, the rise and fall of the cattle business on the Texas plains, the myth of the Wild West versus its reality, and the significance of the frontier and its end. Although it is possible to teach the Westward Expansion section as a single unit, either before or after the Civil War, the best approach may be to teach it as two separate units, one before the Civil War and one after.

Section II discusses the Civil War. The first part looks at the events and issues that led up to the Civil War. Students who were in Core Knowledge schools learned about some of these in earlier grades, but the topics are expanded for Grade 5. The second part focuses on the war itself. The battles covered have been chosen because of their impact or significance on political events. The third part of the section brings students up to 1877 and the end of Reconstruction. Students will explore the conflict between Presidential and Radical Reconstruction and the resulting impeachment of President Andrew Johnson.

Section III looks at how the United States dealt with Native Americans on the Plains. It complements the topics in Section I; however, in Section I, the primary emphasis is on the settlers. In Section III, the main emphasis is on the Native Americans and how they were affected by the influx of settlers. First, students look at the cultures of some of the peoples who lived in the path of frontier settlement in the latter part of the 19th century. Then students learn what happened to these peoples—forced removal to reservations, the breakdown of tribal life, and loss of population through disease, starvation, and wars.

Note: Traditionally the abbreviations AD or BC have been written alongside dates to indicate whether the events in question took place before or after the birth of Jesus. BC means "Before Christ." AD comes from a Latin phrase, "Anno Domini" meaning "Year of the Lord." AD 1000 means one thousand years after the birth of Jesus; 1000 BC means one thousand years before the birth of Jesus. However, scholars increasingly prefer to write 1000 BCE (Before the Common Era) instead of 1000 BC, and 1000 CE (Common Era) instead of AD 1000. Therefore, BCE and CE are used in this book.

I. estward Expansion

The Big Idea

Throughout the 1800s, Americans moved west, settling lands previously occupied by Native Americans.

Remember that each subject you study with students expands their vocabulary and introduces new terms, thus making them better listeners and readers. As you study historical people and events, use read alouds, independent reading, and discussions to build students' vocabularies.

The items below refer to content in Grade 5. Use time lines with students to help them sequence and relate events from different periods and groups.

1775	Wilderness Road
1803	Louisiana Purchase
1804–1806	Lewis and Clark's expedition
1805–1806	Pike's exploration of Southwest
1807	Steamboat invented
1811	Battle of Tippecanoe
1820s–1830s	Heyday of Mountain Men
1821–1880	Santa Fe Trail
1825	Opening of Erie Canal
1835–1842	Second Seminole War
1836	Battle at the Alamo
	Republic of Texas
1840s–1850s	Height of travel on Oregon Trail
1845	Annexation of Texas

continued on next page

What Students Should Already Know

Students in Core Knowledge schools should be familiar with

Kindergarten

▸ Native American Peoples, Past and Present

  • representative peoples in all eight culture regions in what is today the United States (Pacific Northwest: Kwakiutl, Chinook; Plateau: Nez Perce; Great Basin: Shoshone, Ute; Southwest: Dine [Navajo], Hopi, Apache; Plains: Blackfoot, Comanche, Crow, Kiowa, Dakota, Cheyenne, Arapaho, Lakota [Sioux]; Northeast: Huron, Iroquois; Eastern Woodlands: Cherokee, Seminole, Delaware, Susquehanna, Mohican, Massachusett, Wampanoag, Powhatan)

Grade 1

▸ The Earliest People

  • hunters who historians believe either wandered over Beringia, a land bridge linking Asia and North America, or found a coastal route to North America

  • the shift from hunting to farming in places

  • the gradual development of towns and cities in places

▸ Early Exploration of the American West

  • Daniel Boone and the Wilderness Road, the Louisiana Purchase

  • the explorations of Lewis and Clark and their Native American guide Sacagawea

  • the geography of the Appalachians, Rocky Mountains, and Mississippi River

Grade 2

▸ Pioneers Head West

  • new means of travel (Robert Fulton and the invention of the steamboat, Erie Canal, railroads and the transcontinental railroad)

  • routes west (wagon trains on the Oregon Trail)

  • the Pony Express

▸ Native Americans

  • Sequoyah and the Cherokee alphabet

  • forced removal to reservations and the Trail of Tears

  • displacement from their homes and ways of life by the railroads (the "iron horse")

  • the effects of near extermination of the buffalo on Plains Native Americans

continued from previous page

1846–1847	Mexican-American War
1847	Move of Mormons to Great Salt Lake Basin
1848	Gold found in California
1849	California gold rush
1850s–1880s	Age of the "Wild West"
1850s–1890	Plains Wars
1862	Homestead Act
mid 1860s–1880s	Era of cattle drives on the Great Plains
1867	Purchase of Alaska
1869	First transcontinental railroad
1890	Closing of the frontier

Text Resources

What Students Should Already Know continued
Grade 4

❯ early presidents and politics, including the Louisiana Purchase; Jackson's Indian removal policies

What Students Need to Learn

Westward Expansion Before the Civil War

❯ **Early exploration of the West**
  - **Daniel Boone, Cumberland Gap, Wilderness Trail**
  - **Lewis and Clark, Sacagawea**
  - **"Mountain Men," fur trade**
  - **Zebulon Pike and Pikes Peak**

❯ **Pioneers**
  - **Getting there in wagon trains, flatboats, steamboats**
  - **Many pioneers set out from St. Louis (where the Missouri and Mississippi Rivers meet).**
  - **Land routes: Santa Fe and Oregon Trails**
  - **Mormons (Latter-day Saints) settle in Utah, Brigham Young, Great Salt Lake**
  - **Gold Rush, '49ers**

❯ **Geography**
  - **Erie Canal connecting the Hudson River and Lake Erie**
  - **Rivers: James, Hudson, St. Lawrence, Mississippi, Missouri, Ohio, Columbia, Rio Grande**
  - **Appalachian and Rocky Mountains**
  - **Great Plains stretching from Canada to Mexico**
  - **Continental Divide and the flow of rivers: east of Rockies to the Arctic or Atlantic Oceans, west of Rockies to the Pacific Ocean**

❯ **Indian resistance**
  - **More and more settlers move onto Native American lands, treaties made and broken**
  - **Tecumseh (Shawnee): attempts to unite tribes in defending their land**
  - **Battle of Tippecanoe**
  - **Osceola, Seminole leader**

❯ **"Manifest Destiny" and conflict with Mexico**
  - **The meaning of "Manifest Destiny"**
  - **Early settlement of Texas: Stephen Austin**
  - **General Antonio Lopez de Santa Anna**
  - **Battle of the Alamo ("Remember the Alamo"), Davy Crockett, Jim Bowie**

I. Westward Expansion

Materials

Instructional Masters 30–33

Important Physical Features of the United States, p. 242

The Lewis and Clark Expedition, p. 244

Going West, p. 247

Cattle Drives and Railroads, p. 256

atlases and other resources with a current map of the United States, pp. 244, 260

Sacagawea dollar, p. 245

index cards, pp. 259, 260

access to school media center, p. 260

books of historical fiction that address topics from this section, p. 260

What Students Need to Learn continued

 ▶ The Mexican War (also known as the Mexican-American War)
   • General Zachary Taylor ("Old Rough and Ready")
   • Some Americans strongly oppose the war, Henry David Thoreau's "Civil Disobedience"
   • Mexican lands ceded to the United States (California, Nevada, Utah, parts of Colorado, New Mexico, Arizona)

Westward Expansion After the Civil War

 ▶ Homestead Act (1862); many thousands of Americans and immigrants start farms in the West
 ▶ "Go west, young man." (Horace Greeley's advice)
 ▶ Railroads, transcontinental railroad links east and west, immigrant labor
 ▶ Cowboys and cattle drives
 ▶ The "Wild West," reality versus legend: Billy the Kid, Jesse James, Annie Oakley, Buffalo Bill
 ▶ "Buffalo Soldiers," African-American troops in the West
 ▶ U.S. purchases Alaska from Russia, "Seward's folly"
 ▶ 1890: the closing of the American frontier (as acknowledged in the U.S. Census), the symbolic significance of the frontier

What Students Will Learn in Future Grades

In Grade 6, students will learn about American history of the late-nineteenth and early-twentieth century, including immigration and industrialism.

Vocabulary

Student/Teacher Vocabulary

Alamo: a mission-fortress built by Spanish priests in San Antonio; the Alamo was the site of the most memorable battle of the Texas Revolution against Mexico (S)

Appalachian Mountains: the oldest mountain chain in North America; stretches from Newfoundland to central Alabama (S)

buffalo soldiers: a regiment of African-American soldiers formed after the Civil War to fight in the western U.S. against Native Americans (S)

cattle drive: an operation in which a group of cattle (cows, bulls, steers) are herded from one place to another (S)

cede: to remove or give up (S)

Continental Divide: a series of mountain ridges extending from Alaska to Mexico that form the watershed of North America; most of it runs along peaks of the Rocky Mountains and is often called the Great Divide in the United States (S)

cowboy: a man who tends cattle or horses (S)

Vocabulary continued

Cumberland Gap: one of the few passes in the Appalachian Mountains that allowed for westbound travel; located in Kentucky (S)

Erie Canal: the canal that joined the Atlantic Ocean to Lake Erie and to the Great Lakes beyond; opened in 1825 (S)

flatboat: a boat with a flat bottom, used to carry heavy cargo (S)

'49ers: a nickname for miners who went to California during the gold rush of 1849 (S)

frontier: a minimally settled or developed territory; the border line (or border zone) between settled and unsettled areas (S)

Great Plains: the plateau that slopes downward from the Rockies and stretches south to north from Mexico up into Canada (S)

Great Salt Lake: a large, shallow body of salt water in northwestern Utah; area where the Mormons finally settled (S)

gold rush: a rush to an area of newly discovered gold (S)

Homestead Act: an act passed by Congress during the Civil War that encouraged people to settle in the Plains (S)

Manifest Destiny: the belief that God had given the United States a clear right to extend its authority across the continent, and that the nation was destined to do so (S)

Mexican-American War: the war between Mexico and the United States in order to determine where the southwestern boundary between Texas and Mexico lay (S)

Mormons: members of the Church of Jesus Christ of Latter-day Saints (S)

mountain men: the name given to trappers who were lured west by the profits of the fur trade (S)

Oregon Trail: the major nineteenth century overland route from various cities on the Missouri extending to the western United States through the Rockies to Oregon (S)

pioneers: group of people first to settle in an area (S)

Rocky Mountains: the mountain range that extends for more than 3,000 miles from Alaska to New Mexico (S)

Santa Fe Trail: a major trade route connecting Independence Missouri, and Santa Fe, New Mexico; used in 1821 until the opening of the railroad line (S)

steamboat: a major advance in transportation in the 1800s because it could travel upstream against river currents; so-named because it is powered by a steam engine; used for transportation of people and goods (S)

transcontinental railroad: railroad route that ran from Nebraska to California (S)

treaty: a written agreement between two parties (S)

wagon train: a long chain of wagons; during westward expansion, many people traveled west in a wagon train (S)

Wilderness Trail: the wagon road blazed by Daniel Boone that ran from Virginia through the Cumberland Gap and into the Ohio River Valley (S)

"Wild West": the western United States during its settlement period; characterized by roughness and lawlessness (S)

As a general rule of thumb, when choosing projects to do with your students, they should be well-thought-out and relate directly to the unit objectives and time allotments outlined in the beginning of each section. Projects have an important place, especially in the early grades when they help reinforce vocabulary and content and don't serve purely as time fillers. Throughout this subject, we have added teaching ideas with fun and purposeful extensions to further student's understanding. Keep in mind that a useful way to engage students in History and Geography topics can be through the use of structured simulations (acting out events).

Vocabulary continued

Domain Vocabulary

Early exploration of the West and associated words:
Rockies, natural barrier, Alleghenies, Blue Ridge, Great Smokies, White Mountains, peak, plains, gorge, desert, plateau, vegetation, trail, path, rut, rutted, ford, overland, ox, oxen, trudge, blaze, wagon, wagon train, pack animal, Prairie Schooner, National Road, California Trail, Pony Express, stage, fresh horse, saddle, saddlebag, train, engine, steam engine, track, railroad, locomotive, station, freight train, passenger train, arrive, depart, Union Pacific, Central Pacific, Promontory Point, coastal plain, freight, bridge, construction, interior, wasteland, "The Great Desert," Old Northwest, Old Southwest, Oregon Country, Louisiana Territory, Canada, Mexico, France, Spain, Great Britain, Scotland, Great Salt Lake Basin, Spanish Florida, Everglades, Indian Territory, Republic of Texas, *plus the names of the 50 U.S. states,* Albany, New York, Pittsburgh, Baltimore, Cincinnati, Richmond, New Orleans, St. Louis, Omaha, San Francisco, St. Joseph (Missouri), Council Bluffs, Independence, Sacramento, Nauvoo (Illinois)

Pioneers and associated words:
Daniel Boone, Thomas Jefferson, DeWitt Clinton, Lewis and Clark, Sacagawea, Corps of Discovery, Napoleon, James Monroe, Zebulon Pike, James Watt, Robert Fulton, Joseph Smith, Brigham Young, John Sutter, James Marshall, Andrew Jackson, William Henry Harrison, Stephen Austin, Horace Greeley, Billy the Kid, Pat Garrett, Jesse James, Buffalo Bill Cody, Annie Oakley, William Seward, Santa Anna, Sam Houston, Davy Crockett, Jim Bowie, James K. Polk, Zachary Taylor, Henry David Thoreau, settlers, farmers, pioneers, traders, trappers, naturalists, guides, interpreters, soldiers, generals, frontiersmen, woodsmen, cowpokes, vaqueros, cattle rustlers, trail bosses, sheriffs, outlaws, train robbers, gangs, outlaws, circus performers, buffalo hunters, Pony Express riders, scouts, sharpshooters, French Canadians, immigrants, Irish immigrants, Chinese immigrants, Latter-day Saints, Native Americans (also see below), Americans, free blacks, slaves, governors, "war hawks," presidents, czars, passengers, engineers, conductors, workers, citizens, founders, consumers, leaders, inventors

Geography and associated words:
Rockies, natural barrier, Alleghenies, Blue Ridge, Great Smokies, White Mountains, Atlantic Ocean, Pacific Ocean, Great Lakes, Lake Erie, Lake Champlain, Chesapeake Bay, Gulf of Mexico, Mississippi River, Missouri River, Hudson River, Ohio River, Potomac River, Red River, Colorado River, Columbia River, Rio Grande, Arkansas River, American River, Allegheny River, Monongahela River, navigation, navigable, navigate, tributary, port, boat, canoe, raft, barge, paddle, source, upstream, downstream, river valley, canoe, flatbed boat, shallows, falls, rapids, Clermont, canal, Canal Era, locks, fill, empty, link, connect, engineering, elevation

Native American resistance and associated words:
Tecumseh, Tenskwatawa (the Prophet), Sequoyah, Sacagawea, Sitting Bull, Geronimo, Chief Joseph, Osceola, Cherokee, write, oral tradition, syllabary, characters, syllables, alphabet, Five Civilized Tribes (nations), Shoshone, Cherokee, Choctaw, Chickasaw, Creek, Mohawk, Seminole, Shawnee, Indian Territory, lawsuit, court, appeal, Indian Removal Act, Supreme Court, uphold, cruel, inhumane, massacre, decimated, buffalo, bison, hunt, hide, extinct, nonrecognition, sovereign, honor, promise, reservation, Bureau of Indian Affairs, sustain, survive, corruption, Dawes Act, parcels, property, ownership, assimilate, adapt, horse, spirit world

Manifest Destiny and associated words:
explore, blaze, trade, purchase, buy, sell, barter, build, collect, pan (for gold), recognize, refuse, force, move, displace, relocate, enforce, declare, attack, fight, invade, resist, defeat, win, lose, ambush, besiege, die, survive, surrender, renounce, hunt, farm, settle,

Vocabulary continued

annex, ban, trap, round up, drive (cattle), lasso, stampede, sentence, hang, escape, rob, kill, disband, irrigate, boundary, border, inland, territory, telegraph, colony, independence, wilderness, market, amendment, Constitution, Senate, Supreme Court, expedition, territory, military, mineral, prisoner, fur trade, adventurous, beaver, monopoly, profit, trading post, trade goods, trade route, beaver, overtrapping, buckskin, winter, village, canvas, sod, revelation, tablet, prosperous, sawmill, fortune, rich, conflict, skirmish, battle, misunderstanding, epidemic, negotiate, land, uncivilized, Christianity, land, legal, lawsuits, trek, traditional, allied, swampy, casualties, truce, continent, destiny, settlement, rebellion, mission, fortress, cannon, folk hero, Bowie knife, annexation, compromise, campaign issue, opposition, civil disobedience, industries, labor, spike, longhorns, unbranded, mavericks, market, lariat, chaps, open-range, ranch, railhead, meat-packing factory, chuck wagon, herd, lawless, romanticized, reward, regiment, respect, courage, integrated, segregation, "Seward's Folly," forest, timbering, contiguous

Mexican-American War and associated words:
War of 1812, Mexican-American War, Compromise of 1850, Civil War, First Seminole War, swampy, Second Seminole War, Battle of Tippecanoe, Texas Revolution, Battle of San Jacinto, Republic of Texas, Battle of the Alamo, Treaty of Guadalupe Hidalgo, Homestead Act

Cross-curricular Connections

Language Arts

Fiction and Drama

Poems

• "I like to see it lap the miles" (railroads)

Stories

• *The Adventures of Tom Sawyer* (Mark Twain)

Sayings and Phrases

• Eureka! (gold rush)

• Lock, stock, and barrel (gold rush)

• Take the bull by the horns (cowboys)

• Till the cows come home (cowboys)

Visual Arts

American Art: Nineteenth-Century United States

Music

Songs

• "Git Along Little Dogies"

• "Shenandoah"

• "Sweet Betsy from Pike"

I. Westward Expansion

At a Glance

The most important ideas for you are:

- Students should be able to locate some physical features that have been important in the development of the United States.

- A variety of people helped to open up the West to settlement.

- Even before railroads made travel west easier, people wanting a better life were willing to undergo the hardship of going to the far West by wagon train.

- The opening of the West to settlement resulted in a series of broken treaties with Native Americans and much bloodshed.

- The concept of "Manifest Destiny" was used to justify acquisitions of territory by the United States from the 1850s onward.

- Annexation of Texas gave the United States additional territory, fueled the controversy over slavery, and provided a pretext for war with Mexico.

- The West, with its cowboys and outlaws, has a special place in the American imagination. Images of the "Wild West" are part fact and part fiction.

- The final settling of the continental United States took only twenty-five years after the Civil War, for by 1890 the frontier was gone.

What Teachers Need to Know

Guidelines for the study of westward expansion are divided into two parts, with part A focusing on the decades before the Civil War, and part B focusing on the years after the Civil War. Teachers may wish to plan a single section on westward expansion, or divide the material so that part B becomes a section taught after the Civil War. See Section II of American History and Geography for Grade 5, beginning on page 264.

Background

A frontier is defined as the border between settled territory and wilderness. When teaching about the West in American history, however, it is important to note that frontier meant the edge of white settlement adjoining Native American territory, and that Native Americans were settled beyond the frontier. Where the frontier was and what constituted the American West shifted as the nation's boundaries moved west and southwest.

In addition, the line of settlement was not a steady progression across the country from east to west. The far West (California, Oregon, and Washington) was settled before the middle of the country. For many years the interior of the nation was considered a barren wasteland; people called this area "the Great Desert."

Originally, the frontier was anything to the west of the Atlantic coastal plain. The first English colonists had settled along the coast. By the time of the American Revolution, the frontier line had moved generally west to the Appalachian Mountains. After independence, people began to push inland into the newly acquired lands of the Old Northwest Territory and the Old Southwest. The new United States had received these lands as a result of the peace treaty ending the Revolutionary War. The Old Northwest would become the states of Ohio, Indiana, Illinois, Michigan, and Wisconsin. The Old Southwest was the area south of the Ohio River and would become the states of Tennessee, Kentucky, Alabama, and Mississippi. (Notice that the Old Northwest is not the same as the area we consider the Northwest today; nor is the Old Southwest the same as the modern Southwest.)

By 1803, when the United States, under Thomas Jefferson, bought the Louisiana Territory from France, the frontier had moved west to the Mississippi River as more and more people moved inland. By that time, Kentucky, Tennessee, and Ohio had large enough populations that they asked for and were granted statehood. The Louisiana Purchase opened up an area west of the Mississippi as far as the Canadian border to the north, the British Territory of Oregon in the northwest, and Spanish lands in the far west, including the present-day states of California, New Mexico, Arizona, Texas, Colorado, Nevada, Utah, Oklahoma, Kansas, and Wyoming.

The United States acquired the Oregon Territory (Oregon, Washington, Idaho, and parts of Montana and Wyoming) as a result of a treaty with the British in 1846. It was not until the Treaty of Guadalupe Hidalgo, which ended the Mexican-American War (1848), that the Mexican lands in the west became United States territories. The former Mexican-held area of Texas also joined the Union in 1845.

A. Westward Expansion Before the Civil War

Geography

 Rivers

North America is crisscrossed by a network of rivers. These rivers were important for the initial settlement of the continent (many early towns sprang up along the banks of rivers) and also for the later expansion of the United States to the west. The chart below presents basic information on some important North American rivers.

River	Source	Drainage Area	Empties into	Interesting Facts
James	Botetourt County, Virginia	Virginia	Chesapeake Bay	• The lower part of the river is near the site of Jamestown, the first permanent English colony on North American mainland. • Important as navigable waterway for Richmond, capital of the Confederacy

frontier cabin, 1700s

I. Westward Expansion

Teaching Idea

Students in Core Knowledge schools should have studied rivers in detail in Grade 3. They should also have studied ancient civilizations that sprang up along the banks of rivers, e.g., Mesopotamia, Egypt, and India, in earlier grades. Before discussing American rivers, review what students know about rivers and why they are important for people and settlements. Then work with students to recreate a chart similar to the one shown to the right as you discuss specific rivers.

Teaching Idea

If there is a river near you that played a role in westward expansion, you may wish to add it to this unit of study.

River	Source	Drainage Area	Empties into	Interesting Facts
Hudson	Adirondack Mountains, part of the Appalachian chain, in northern New York State	New York	Atlantic Ocean at New York City	• Explored in 1609 by Henry Hudson, for whom it is named • Navigable to Albany, the state capital • Linked by the Erie Canal to the Great Lakes in 1825
St. Lawrence	Lake Ontario	Forms 120 miles of U.S.-Canadian border	Gulf of St. Lawrence	• One of the largest rivers in Canada • Part of the St. Lawrence-Great Lakes Seaway
Mississippi	Lake Itasca, Minnesota	Minnesota, Wisconsin, Iowa, Illinois, Missouri, Kentucky, Arkansas, Tennessee, Mississippi, Louisiana	Gulf of Mexico	• Longest river in North America, 2,348 miles • Has more than 250 tributaries; two major tributaries, the Ohio and Missouri Rivers • Explored by the Spaniard De Soto in 1541; Frenchman La Salle in 1682 • Control of the Mississippi an important reason for the Louisiana Purchase
Missouri	Formed in Rockies by the Jefferson, Madison, and Gallatin Rivers	Montana, North Dakota, South Dakota, Nebraska, Iowa, Missouri	Empties into Mississippi, 17 miles north of St. Louis	• One of two major tributaries of the Mississippi • Seen by Frenchmen Marquette and Joliet in 1673 • Explored by Lewis and Clark
Ohio	Formed at Pittsburgh, Pennsylvania, by the Allegheny and Monongahela Rivers	Pennsylvania, Ohio, West Virginia, Indiana, Kentucky, Illinois	Mississippi River at Cairo, Illinois	• One of two major tributaries of the Mississippi • Navigable its whole length • From 1783 to opening of Erie Canal in 1825, principal route west
Columbia	Rocky Mountains in British Columbia	British Columbia, Washington, Oregon	Pacific Ocean at Cape Disappointment, Washington	• Followed by Lewis and Clark to the Pacific Ocean • Many rapids and dams • Source of irrigation and hydroelectric power today
Rio Grande	Rocky Mountains in southwest Colorado	Colorado, New Mexico, Texas, Mexico	Gulf of Mexico	• Name means "large river" • Name in Mexico is Rio Grande del Norte, meaning "large river to the north" • Forms two-thirds of border between United States and Mexico • Shallow river used for irrigation today

River	Source	Drainage area	Empties into	Interesting Facts
Colorado River	Rocky Mountains in Colorado	Wyoming, Colorado, Utah, New Mexico, Nevada, Arizona, and California	Gulf of California in Mexico	• In Arizona, forms 17 miles of border between U.S. and Mexico • Known as the "Lifeline of the Southwest" • The Hoover Dam (formerly known as the Boulder Dam), completed in 1936, was a unique engineering project that allows the river to be used for irrigation, power, tourist recreation, flood control, and navigation.

 ## Erie Canal, Hudson River, Lake Erie

Although rivers were an important means of travel, some rivers were not navigable, or not navigable beyond a certain point, and others came close to but did not connect to important bodies of water. To overcome these limitations, Americans built canals that connected rivers, lakes, and other bodies of water. The most famous of these canals was the Erie Canal.

In 1811, DeWitt Clinton, the governor of New York, proposed building a canal linking the Hudson River (near Albany) with the Great Lakes. This would open up a natural route to the West. Albany was near the limits of navigation on the Hudson River above New York City. In 1825, when the Erie Canal opened, it joined the Atlantic Ocean to Lake Erie and to the Great Lakes beyond.

The Erie Canal was the largest public works project of its time, employing thousands of workers to dig a 300-mile canal. The canal was 40 feet wide and four feet deep. In addition to the digging of the canal, the construction of canal locks was an important engineering achievement. A canal lock is the part of a canal that has sets of doors in the front and back. Canal locks are necessary to accommodate changes in elevation. When a boat comes into the lock, the doors shut behind it. Then water comes in or goes out of the lock depending on whether the land is going uphill or down. When the water inside the lock has risen or fallen to the level of the water outside the lock, the front doors open, and the boat moves on.

Canal boats had no motors or sails. Mules or horses that walked along a path on the bank of the canal pulled the boats.

When Dewitt Clinton proposed the Erie Canal, many people laughed at the idea and said it would never work. No canal that long had yet been built. But Clinton had the last laugh. In 1825, the first canal boat made its way from Buffalo to New York City. It carried a barrel of water from Lake Erie, and Governor Clinton dumped the water into the Atlantic Ocean to show that these two bodies of water were now connected.

Aside from rushing people and goods westward, the canal helped New York City dominate other Eastern seaboard ports, such as Philadelphia, Baltimore, and Boston; all these lacked direct links to the West. Before the canal was built, New York was less important than the other cities noted. After the canal was built, New York rose to become the largest and most important city in the United States. The canal also dramatically cut the cost of transporting goods. For example, shipping between New York City and Buffalo dropped from $100 a ton to $10 a ton.

Cross-curricular Teaching Idea

Students in Core Knowledge schools should have learned "The Erie Canal" song in Grade 2. You may wish to review this song, as it gives a good feel for what it was like to travel along the Erie Canal. Other songs from the Grade 2 *Sequence* that are relevant for westward expansion include "Casey Jones," "Buffalo Gals," "Home on the Range," "John Henry," and "Old Dan Tucker."

Erie Canal

I. Westward Expansion

Teaching Idea

Create an overhead of Instructional Master 30a, *Important Physical Features of the United States*. Have students state one fact they have learned about each feature shown. For example, "James River: The first permanent English colony in North America was founded along the James River."

The purpose is to help students create mental maps of events and the physical settings in which they occurred or which contributed to their happening. Provide an example, such as how the flatness of the Great Plains made open-range ranching possible until farmers began to fence in their acreage.

Return to this map and this connection-building activity throughout the study of this section.

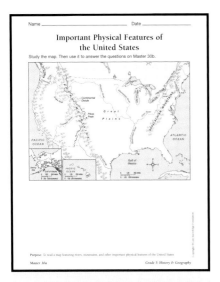

Use Instructional Masters 30a–30b.

The success of the Erie Canal stimulated a boom in canal building. Among the most important were the Champlain Canal, connecting Lake Champlain and the Hudson River, the Chesapeake Canal, the Ohio Canal (which was never completed but was meant to connect Pittsburgh and the Ohio River to the Potomac River and the Atlantic Ocean), and the Miami and Erie Canals in Ohio, which connected Lake Erie to the Ohio River at Cincinnati. Canal building continued for many years until canals were gradually replaced by railroads.

Appalachian Mountains

The Appalachian Mountains are the oldest mountain chain in North America and stretch from Newfoundland to central Alabama. They are about 1,800 miles (2,897 km) long and range from 120 to 375 miles (193 to 604 km) wide. The highest peak is Mount Mitchell in North Carolina, named for Maria Mitchell, a 19th-century astronomer. It rises 6,684 feet (2,037 m) above sea level. The Appalachians are divided into various ranges, such as the White Mountains in Maine and New Hampshire; the Alleghenies in Pennsylvania, Maryland, and Virginia; the Blue Ridge Mountains in Pennsylvania, Maryland, West Virginia, Virginia, North Carolina, South Carolina, and Georgia; and the Great Smokies in North Carolina and Tennessee. Major rivers that flow through the mountains are the Hudson, Delaware, Susquehanna, Potomac, and Tennessee. The mountains are rich in iron and coal deposits, but proved a barrier to westward movement in the colonial era until Daniel Boone blazed the Wilderness Trail, also known as the Wilderness Road, through the Cumberland Gap in 1775. Further north, settlers traveled down the Ohio River on keelboats to get through the mountains.

Rocky Mountains and Continental Divide

The Rocky Mountains extend for more than 3,000 miles from Alaska to New Mexico. The highest point in North America is Mount McKinley in Alaska. It rises 20,320 feet (6,194 m) above sea level. The major ranges of the Rocky Mountains are the Southern, Central, and Northern Rockies in the contiguous United States, the Brooks Range in Alaska, and the Canadian Rockies. The Rocky Mountains were more formidable barriers to travel than the Appalachians because the Rockies are in general more than twice as tall as the Appalachians. The major pass through the Rockies for travelers in the nineteenth century was South Pass in Wyoming. The Oregon Trail took this route.

Of major topographical interest is the Continental Divide that runs north and south through the mountains. Rivers to the east of this long, high crest flow to the east toward the Arctic or Atlantic Oceans, and rivers to the west of the divide flow toward the Pacific on the west. Lewis and Clark, whom students should have studied in earlier grades and will study again this year, crossed the Continental Divide in 1805 as part of their voyage of discovery.

Great Plains

The Great Plains stretch south to north from Mexico into Canada roughly along the 98th parallel. The plains are a plateau, or high flat land, that slopes downward from the Rockies. The plains vary in width from 300–700 miles (483–1,127 km) and cover all or part of the following states: Montana, Wyoming, Colorado, New Mexico, North and South Dakota, Nebraska, Kansas, Oklahoma, and Texas.

The area experiences hot summers and cold winters. Rainfall is typically only about 20 inches a year, but some parts may also have heavy snows. Natural

vegetation is typically short grasses; however, the rich soil in some areas makes the region a major grain producer. Before the Civil War, the Great Plains were settled by whites who moved there in larger numbers after the war.

Early Exploration of the West

 ### Daniel Boone, Cumberland Gap, Wilderness Trail

Daniel Boone was born in Pennsylvania in 1734. As a boy he hunted animals, first with a spear and later with a gun. He became a crack shot and is said to have shot his first bear at age 12. Boone took part in the French and Indian War in 1755.

For many of his adult years, Boone was a "long hunter." He would hunt alone in the woods, hundreds of miles from white civilization, for months at a time. One of his hunting trips lasted 18 months.

In 1769, Boone and some others passed through the Cumberland Gap in the Appalachian Mountains into Kentucky. They found a land filled with buffalo, deer, and wild turkeys, as well as meadows perfect for farming. Boone was separated from his party and spent the winter of 1769–70 in a cave.

In 1775, Boone began working for the Transylvania Company, which wanted to establish a colony called Transylvania in the frontier areas of Virginia and North Carolina. The scheme collapsed, but not before Boone had blazed the Wilderness Road in 1775. This wagon road, which was often nothing more than a wide place in the forest, ran from Virginia through the Cumberland Gap and into the Ohio River Valley.

The Appalachian Mountains had long been a natural barrier to westbound travel, but the Wilderness Road allowed settlers to travel through the mountains more easily. Settlers moved along it into what would become the states of Kentucky and Tennessee. The road was a main route west in the southeastern states until the National Road was completed in 1837. The Wilderness Road, which eventually became part of U.S. Highway 25, is still around today.

After blazing the Wilderness Road, Daniel Boone continued to hunt and explore. During the Revolutionary War he was taken prisoner by the Shawnee. He so impressed his captors with his great skills as a hunter and woodsman that he was accepted as a member of a Native American family. Eventually, however, Boone returned to his original family.

After several more years in sparsely settled Kentucky, Boone went west to Missouri in a dugout canoe. When someone asked him why he was leaving Kentucky, Boone allegedly replied: "Too crowded." He lived in Missouri for the rest of his life, dying in 1820 at the age of 85.

Boone published his memoirs, *The Adventures of Colonel Daniel Boone,* in 1784. In them he describes his explorations and his many encounters with Native Americans. After his death, Boone was romanticized and marketed as an American hero, a man who lived close to nature, fought Native Americans, and helped "win the West." His genuine adventures have been supplemented and embellished with numerous additional stories. (47)

 ### Lewis and Clark

In 1800, France, under Napoleon Bonaparte, had acquired the Louisiana Territory from Spain. Napoleon was interested in rebuilding France's holdings in North America. In 1802, Americans were banned from using the port of New

Teaching Idea

Students may enjoy learning more about Daniel Boone and some of his adventures. In addition to Boone's autobiography, many biographies are available.

Teaching Idea

Students may enjoy listening to poems about key figures involved in westward expansion. A number of poems are included in Stephen and Rosemary Benet's *Book of Americans* (see *More Resources*). Poetic profiles in the book include "Lewis and Clark," "Zachary Taylor," "Daniel Boone," "Sam Houston," "Westward Wagons," "Clipper Ships and Captains," "Jesse James," and "P. T. Barnum."

I. Westward Expansion

Teaching Idea

Begin the lesson by asking students what they know about Lewis and Clark and Sacagawea. Students should have studied the expedition in Grade 1 if they were in a Core Knowledge school.

Create an overhead from Instructional Master 31, *The Lewis and Clark Expedition*. Have students trace the route of the Corps of Discovery to and from the Pacific. You may also have them use atlases or other print resources with maps to label the states that were created from the Louisiana Purchase.

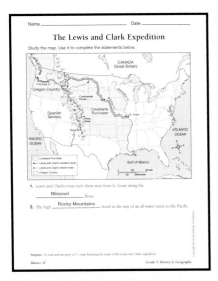

Use Instructional Master 31.

Teaching Idea

Students may enjoy listening to selected episodes from the journey of Lewis and Clark. There are a number of good books on the journey from which you might read sections aloud, e.g., Rhonda Blumberg, *The Incredible Journey of Lewis and Clark;* and John Bakeless, *The Journals of Lewis and Clark.* (See More Resources.)

Orleans at the mouth of the Mississippi. This meant closing the major route by which settlers in the Midwest and South shipped their goods to market.

Thomas Jefferson, president of the United States at the time, sent James Monroe and Robert Livingston to France with an offer to buy New Orleans. Although his political opponents argued for war, Jefferson preferred to avoid a fight. Napoleon agreed to sell not only New Orleans but also the entire Louisiana Territory. The price was $15 million.

By 1803, Napoleon had abandoned his dream of an empire in North America. He had lost the colony of Santo Domingo because of a revolt begun by Pierre Toussaint L'Ouverture and other enslaved Africans. Napoleon worried that the United States might someday try to take Louisiana by force. In that event, he would not be able to deploy troops to America to defend the territory. Most of all, Napoleon was about to go war with much of Europe and needed money. For all these reasons, he decided it would be wiser to sell all of Louisiana than to try to keep it.

Although President Jefferson had initiated the offer to buy New Orleans, he was not sure that the United States Constitution allowed him to acquire new territory for the nation or to grant citizenship to the 50,000 or more inhabitants of Louisiana. Jefferson believed that an amendment to the U.S. Constitution was needed. His advisers, however, warned him that it would take time to ratify a constitutional amendment and that Napoleon could change his mind if he had to wait. In the end, Jefferson decided to do what he believed the majority of Americans wanted. He sent the treaty approving the purchase of the Louisiana Territory to the Senate for ratification. Thus, the United States acquired land that more than doubled the nation's size. The Louisiana Territory stretched from the Mississippi River to the Rocky Mountains and from the Canadian border to the Gulf of Mexico.

Once the American flag was raised over New Orleans, Jefferson was eager to find out what exactly the United States had purchased. He appointed his private secretary, Meriwether Lewis, to lead an expedition into the territory. A former military man and naturalist, Lewis had a great deal of experience in the West (Old Northwest). His co-leader, William Clark, was also a soldier who had seen action in the West and who had experience dealing with Native Americans. Together, they signed up 48 men for their Corps of Discovery, and in the spring of 1804, they left St. Louis and set off up the Missouri River.

By the fall of that year, the Corps had reached what is today North Dakota. They wintered in a fort they built and named Fort Mandan after the local Native Americans. Among the Mandan, Lewis and Clark met a French Canadian trader named Toussaint Charbonneau and his Shoshone wife, Sacagawea. Lewis and Clark decided to take them on as guides and interpreters.

In April, the expedition and its new members continued their journey northwest, reaching the Rockies and, eventually, the Great Falls in Montana. Carrying their canoes and boats through the mountains was difficult work, but by late summer, the Corps had crossed the Continental Divide in what is now Montana. After sailing down the Columbia River, they reached the Pacific by November. There, they built Fort Clatsop and spent the winter of 1805–06. When spring arrived, the Corps began their return trip home. By September 1806, two years after leaving St. Louis, the Corps was back home. ㊾

Jefferson had given Lewis and Clark specific instructions about what the expedition should accomplish. The men were to look for a water route that

connected the Upper Mississippi with the Pacific Ocean, to map the region they explored, to establish contact with the Native Americans in the area, and to take notes about and collect specimens of the plants, animals, and minerals they found. These would be sent to Washington for further study. The Corps discovered that the Rockies stood in the way of an all-water route to the Pacific. The expedition did, however, establish official relations with many Native Americans bands. The most valuable information brought back from the expedition was the notes, drawings, and specimens that documented the trip. The Lewis and Clark expedition stimulated interest in the West and brought thousands of settlers into the territory.

Sacagawea

Sacagawea was a young Shoshone woman who was the wife of a French Canadian trader, Toussaint Charbonneau. She had been kidnapped as a child by another tribe, the Hidatsa, and sold to a Mandan who later traded her to Charbonneau. Charbonneau signed on with Lewis and Clark as an interpreter and guide during the winter of 1805 to 1806, along with his wife Sacagawea and her baby. She proved to be of great help in enlisting the aid of Native Americans when the Corps reached the Upper Missouri River. In late summer, the Corps crossed paths with Sacagawea's band, the Shoshone, and her brother Cameahwait. Sacagawea persuaded the Shoshone to provide horses for the expedition and to guide the Corps through the mountains of Idaho.

 ## Zebulon Pike and Pikes Peak

Lewis and Clark were not the only explorers that President Jefferson commissioned. From 1805 to 1806, Lieutenant Zebulon Pike was sent to explore the sources of the Mississippi, Red, and Arkansas Rivers. When his expedition reached Colorado, they attempted to climb the mountain (Pikes Peak) that was later named after him. Pike and his men moved south into New Mexico and were taken prisoner by the Spanish. They were returned to the United States, bringing with them much important information about the Spanish territory.

 ## "Mountain Men" and the Fur Trade

"Mountain Men" was the name given to trappers who were lured west by the profits of the fur trade. They moved into Oregon Country, the huge, barely charted area beyond the Rockies, where the forests and mountains were home to beaver and other fur-bearing animals. These men opened the way for later settlers. Today, this area includes the states of Oregon, Washington, Idaho, parts of the states of Wyoming and Montana, and southwestern Canada.

The fur trade was an important industry in the first 200 years of European settlement in North America. The French and their Indian allies had dominated the trade in the old Northwest Territory. The trade attracted adventurous frontiersmen who trapped beaver and traded with the Native Americans.

At first, the British had a monopoly on the fur trade in Oregon Country, but by the 1820s, U.S. companies were competing for the enormous profits to be made from the fur trade. Originally the British and the Americans set up trading posts where Native Americans and a few non-Native American trappers would come to sell or barter their furs. Then two U.S. businessmen hit upon the idea of an annual rendezvous, or fair, where Native Americans and trappers could bring their furs and sell them to traders for guns, knives, whiskey, cloth, and similar trade goods.

Teaching Idea

Have students work in groups of three or four to create quiz questions about the Lewis and Clark expedition. Then you could have teams take turns quizzing each other.

Teaching Idea

Bring in a Sacagawea dollar during your study of Sacagawea and Lewis and Clark.

Teaching Idea

Use the overhead for Instructional Master 31, *The Lewis and Clark Expedition*, to have students locate the following: the route Zebulon Pike took; Pikes Peak; the Oregon Country.

Have students label the states that Pike explored and that once were called Oregon Country. Students should note some overlap with the Louisiana Territory.

[Answers: Pike's route: Missouri, Kansas, Colorado, New Mexico, Texas, Louisiana. Oregon Country: Oregon, Washington, Idaho, Wyoming, Montana]

I. Westward Expansion

Teaching Idea

Students may enjoy learning about the exploits of one or more of the mountain men. Some interesting characters for further study include Jedediah Smith, Jim Bridger, and James Beckwourth. A web search for these names, or for "mountain men," will turn up many resources.

The rendezvous took place at a designated site in Wyoming. From the 1820s until the late 1830s, beaver was the most important trade commodity. Beaver hats were in style in the East and in Europe. By the late 1830s, however, styles had changed and the beaver had all but disappeared due to overtrapping. The life of the mountain man was ending.

But by then the mountain men had gained a reputation as wild and colorful characters. To Easterners, they were romantic figures, dressed in buckskin, with long hair, roaming the forests at will and answering to no man. But the life of mountain men was hard. They lived off the land, finding food where they could— animals, plants, nuts. In the spring, summer, and fall, they hunted and trapped on their own, but they often wintered in Native American villages. If a trapper fell and broke a leg, was mauled by a bear, or slipped and fell into a river, he could die. No one would know because he was alone in the forests.

Pioneers

 ### Flatboats and Steamboats

Both native-born Americans and immigrants (who began to come in greater numbers after 1820) wanted to make a better life for themselves. But in the early 1800s, the coastal plain was becoming crowded, there was little land left to buy, and there were a limited number of jobs. To own land and to make a living, people were forced to move to less settled areas.

The first people to move into the land beyond the mountains traveled either down the rivers or overland through the valleys and gaps between mountains. Going downstream was the easiest way to travel, and people used canoes, rafts, and flatboats to carry passengers and freight. Overland, people used wagons and pack animals to carry them along dirt roads and mountain trails—both of which were little more than tracks that became muddy in the rainy season and treacherously rutted in the winter.

The transportation revolution of the early 1800s greatly spurred the movement of people inland. In the 1760s, James Watt of Scotland invented the first practical steam engine. In 1807, Robert Fulton used a steam engine to power his boat, the *Clermont*, up the Hudson River from New York to Albany. He covered the 150 miles in 32 hours, averaging a little under 5 miles per hour—slow by modern standards, but much faster than a canoe or flatboat could have covered the same distance. His was the first commercially successful steamboat company. By 1811, the steamboat *New Orleans* was plying up and down the Mississippi, carrying passengers and freight. Steamboats, being fast and large, could carry many passengers and much cargo. They could also navigate upstream against the current.

The steamboat helped ignite the transportation revolution, but without canals, its ability to travel the inland waterways would have been severely hampered. The canal era began in 1825 when the Erie Canal was opened. The canals were the best routes of transportation available, especially for heavy, bulky cargoes, such as coal, timber, and stone. In the 1850s, there was a boom in railroad building, offering faster, longer distance travel than steamboats. Still, many passengers found travel by canal boat smoother, less tiring, and less dangerous than land travel.

 ### Wagon Trains

Before the transcontinental railroads and regional rail lines were built, linking all parts of the country, people went west by wagon. The wagons, called

prairie schooners, were small, four-wheeled vehicles with canvas tops and wooden bodies. They were light enough so that they would not sink easily into the soft prairie sod. Teams of oxen, rather than horses, often pulled the wagons. Horses were faster but not as strong or hardy as oxen.

Some pioneers, including women, traveled west alone. Others traveled in small groups, either on foot or on horseback. The most common arrangement was for several families to travel together in an organized wagon train. An experienced leader, or an elected head assisted by guides, would take command of the group.

Land Routes: Santa Fe Trail and Oregon Trail

Between 1840 and 1860, more than 250,000 people went west. Most settlers went to the Oregon Territory and California. The most famous route was the Oregon Trail, which began in Independence, Missouri, and crossed 2,000 miles of plains, mountains, and rivers. In southern Idaho, the trail diverged. Those wanting to go to California followed the California Trail through northern Nevada into California's Sacramento Valley. The ruts cut by thousands of wagon wheels can still be seen along parts of the Oregon Trail. (50)

The even older Santa Fe Trail went from Independence, Missouri, to the former Spanish capital of Santa Fe. It was first used in 1821 and continued as a major trade route until 1880, when a railroad line was opened. The trail was relatively short—780 miles—on open plains across Kansas and up the Arkansas River or across the desert. The Santa Fe Trail, unlike the Oregon Trail, was basically a trade route.

Mormons: Brigham Young, Salt Lake City

The Mormons are members of the Church of Jesus Christ of Latter-day Saints. The church was founded in 1830 by Joseph Smith, who claimed to have received revelations from God on golden tablets. The teachings, known as the Book of Mormon, became the basis of the Mormon faith. Mormons believe the Bible and the Book of Mormon are the "Word of God" and that the president of the church is a prophet of God. One of their most publicized practices was the practice of polygamy, having more than one spouse at a time.

Smith and his followers moved from their original home in New York State to Ohio because they were attacked for their religious beliefs. After again being persecuted, they moved to Missouri, but controversy and resistance followed them and they were forced to move a third time. In 1844, after settling in Nauvoo, Illinois, conflict again broke out and Smith was killed. Under the leadership of Brigham Young in 1847, the Mormons moved far west to the Great Salt Lake Basin in what is now Utah. At the time, the area was part of Mexico. (51)

Considered unsuitable for agriculture, the area was passed over by other pioneers, but the Mormons irrigated the desert and established farms. They built a prosperous community and in 1849, after the Mexican-American War, they formed the state of Deseret with Young as governor. The same year, the people of Deseret petitioned the United States Congress for admission as a state. Congress, however, was in the midst of the controversy over whether to allow the spread of slavery into the territories and denied the request (see "The Civil War: Causes, Conflicts, and Consequences," on pp. 264–296). Congress also had a problem with the Mormon practice of polygamy. The following year, the Compromise of 1850 was worked out and Deseret was recognized as the Utah Territory. However, Utah did not become a state until 1896, after the Mormons had banned polygamy.

Teaching Idea

Create an overhead of Instructional Master 32, *Going West*. Have students identify the states through which each trail passed. If necessary, have students use the map on Instructional Master 31, *The Lewis and Clark Expedition.*

Have students relate the areas that the trails passed through to the Louisiana Territory and to Zebulon Pike's explorations. What do students notice?

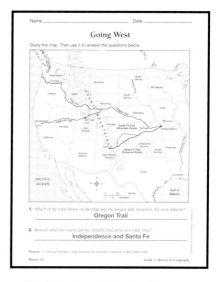

Use Instructional Master 32.

Teaching Idea

Share with students a book or shorter narrative about traveling west by wagon. One classic title is Francis Parkman's *The Oregon Trail.* (See *More Resources.*)

I. Westward Expansion

Teaching Idea

Students may enjoy hearing excerpts from letters and autobiographies of people who participated in the gold rush of 1849. One well-known set of documents is a series of letters by William Swain written to his wife Sabrina Swain and his brother George Swain. Another interesting document is the memoirs of Luzena Stanley Wilson. Excerpts from both the Swain and the Wilson materials can be found online. (See *More Resources*.)

Cross-curricular Teaching Idea

Have students do research on the California gold rush or another factor that influenced westward expansion. Suggest that they use online and print resources. Their final products could take the form of written or oral reports with accompanying artwork illustrating something learned from the research. Have students submit a bibliography (formal or informal) of the material they consulted to create their project and written report.

Teaching Idea

Tell students that many sports teams' names are based on historical events. Find out the names of professional sports teams and see how many relate to history of the area (e.g., the San Francisco '49ers' name comes from the gold rush of '49).

Gold Rush and the '49ers

In January 1848, John Sutter hired James Marshall to build a sawmill on the American River, which ran through Sutter's property near Sacramento, California. As he worked, Marshall noticed in the riverbed shiny flakes that looked golden in the light. When he examined them more closely, he saw they were gold. Though the two men tried to hide Marshall's discovery, word got out and the rush to find gold was soon on. (52)

Californians took to the rivers and streams looking for gold. Much of it was easily found in streams and riverbeds by panning. Miners literally used pans with small holes poked through their bottoms. They let the water flow through the holes, and the heavy gold sank to the bottom of the pans.

By the following summer, 100,000 people arrived in California—not just from the east coast of the United States but from Europe and much of the Pacific Basin, especially China, as well. Most came overland by horse and wagon train, but many came by boat. Some sailed around Cape Horn at the tip of South America and up the coast, while others sailed to Panama, trekked overland, and took a ship again from the west coast of Central America.

The '49ers, as the miners were called, were an enterprising group of men and women. Most miners were young men who expected to make their fortune and then return home. Some family men brought their wives and children along, expecting to stay. Single women, hoping to find gold or to earn money cooking or doing laundry for the miners, traveled to California as well. Some free blacks came, as well as some southerners who brought their slaves to mine for them. Even though few miners found a substantial amount of gold, many stayed for the climate and the rich farmland.

Native American Resistance

From the beginning, the new United States' dealings with Native Americans resulted in a string of conflicts, misunderstandings, epidemics, skirmishes, wars, broken treaties, and unfulfilled promises. At first, the federal government recognized Native Americans as sovereign nations and negotiated treaties with them for their land. Sometimes these treaties were freely negotiated, and other times they were the result of wars. The Treaty of Greenville (1795) is an example of a treaty that was forced on the Native Americans as a result of war. The treaty, by which the native peoples of the Old Northwest (Ohio, Illinois, Wisconsin, Michigan) gave up most of their lands, was an outcome of the Battle of Fallen Timbers (1794). The Treaty deprived Natives of claims to roughly two-thirds of the land of modern-day Ohio. Federal troops under General Anthony Wayne defeated a force of Shawnee, Miami, Ottawa, Potawatomi, Ojibwa, Fox, and Sauk near what is today Toledo, Ohio. Later, the War of 1812 would break the back of Native resistance in the rest of the region.

As more settlers pushed the frontier back by moving west and south from the original thirteen states, they came in contact with more Native Americans. Many European Americans considered the Native Americans uncivilized, and saw them as obstacles standing in the way of settlers' ambitions. The settlers continued to push the Native Americans westward. Sometimes the army tried to prevent settlers from encroaching on Native American lands, but at other times the army

fought against the Native Americans. The conflict over land in the Southeast is an example.

The Native American nations of the southeastern United States—the Cherokee, Creek, Choctaw, Chickasaw, and Seminole—became known as the "Five Civilized Tribes" due to their adoption of constitutions, laws, and other aspects of culture deemed to be "civilized." The Cherokee in particular adopted European American ways by becoming farmers and converting to Christianity. However, as the frontier moved south and west, settlers covered the tribal lands in the Carolinas, Georgia, Alabama, Mississippi, and Florida.

In 1830, President Andrew Jackson supported passage of the Indian Removal Act, which gave him the power to force the Native Americans of the Southeast to move to what was known as the Indian Territory, now part of the state of Oklahoma. The Choctaw left first, followed by the Creek and the Chickasaw. The last to leave were the Seminole after the Second Seminole War (1835–1842). (48)

The Cherokee chose legal means rather than warfare to resist removal. In two lawsuits that went all the way to the Supreme Court, Cherokee rights to their lands were upheld. But President Jackson and the state of Georgia ignored both decisions, and seeing the inevitable, some 2,000 Cherokee agreed to move. By 1838, some 14,000 still remained in the Southeast. Jackson was no longer president, but his successor, Martin Van Buren, decided to enforce the move. The Cherokees' forced march to the Indian Territory became known as the "Trail of Tears." The four-month trek took place in winter and it is estimated that about 4,000 men, women, and children died along the way. The cost of the removal was subtracted from the money to be paid to the Cherokee for their lands, so they were left with $3 million.

The Cherokee and the other nations removed to Indian Territory were promised that this land would remain theirs forever. "Forever" lasted a generation. First, they lost part of their land to other Native American peoples whom the federal government resettled in the Territory in 1866. As the West filled up, there was pressure on the government to open Native American lands. In 1889, the Creek and the Seminole sold 50,000 acres to the United States for white settlement. By 1907, there were more whites than Native Americans in the Territory, and in that year, it was made part of the new state of Oklahoma.

Tecumseh and the Battle of Tippecanoe

In the first decade of the 1800s, the states and territories bordering the frontier believed that the British in Canada were aiding Native Americans who were attacking frontier settlements. Beginning around 1811, Tecumseh, a Shawnee chief, and his brother Tenskwatawa, tried to unite native peoples east of the Mississippi in a giant confederacy. The two men believed that if the Native American nations banded together and refused to sell land to Americans, they could hold back American settlement.

Tenskwatawa was known as the Prophet because he claimed to have entered the spirit world, communicated with the "Master of Life," and returned to Earth with knowledge of how Native Americans should live. He said they had to renounce dependence on American trade goods and return to their traditional ways of living and hunting. Here are some of the things he told his people:

. . . But now those things of the white men have corrupted us, and made us weak and needful. Our men forgot how to hunt without noisy guns. Our women don't want to make fire without steel, or cook without iron, or sew without metal awls and needles, or fish without steel hooks. Some look in those mirrors all the time, and no longer teach their daughters to make leather or render bear oil. We learned to need the white men's goods, and so now a People who never had to beg for anything must beg for everything! . . . Many of us now crave liquor. . . . There are drunkards in almost every family. . . . We were fools to take all these things that weakened us. We did not need them then, but we believe we need them now. We turned our backs on the old ways. Instead of thanking the Great Spirit for all we used to have, we turned to the white men and asked them for more. So now we depend upon the very people who destroy us! This is our weakness! . . . And that is why Our Creator purified me and sent me down to you full of the shinning [sic] power, to make you what you were before! . . . Do not eat any food that is raised or cooked by a white person. It is not good for us. Eat not their bread made of wheat, for Our Creator gave us corn for our bread. Eat not the meat of their filthy swine, nor of their chicken fowls, nor the beef of their cattle, which are tame and thus have no spirit in them. Their foods will seem to fill your empty belly, but this deceives you for food without spirit does not nourish you. . . . There are two kinds of white men. There are the Americans, and there are the others. You may give your hand in friendship to the French, or the Spaniards, or the British. But the Americans are not like those. The Americans come from the slime of the sea, with mud and weeds in their claws, and they are a kind of crayfish serpent whose claws grab in our earth and take it from us. . . . That is what the Creator instructed me to tell you.

General William Henry Harrison, governor of the Indiana Territory, was concerned about the growing influence of Tecumseh and the Prophet. In 1811, Harrison led 1,000 soldiers to the Shawnee village on Tippecanoe Creek, near what is now Lafayette, Indiana. Tecumseh was not there, but Tenskwatawa was. Although Tecumseh had warned of the dangers of engaging the military in fighting, Tenskwatawa still attacked Harrison's force at night. Before attacking, Tenskwatawa gave an impassioned speech in which he promised his troops that the white man's bullets could not hurt them. Fighting was fierce and neither side won a decisive victory, although Harrison burned the Native American village and declared that the Americans had won.

Harrison also claimed that his men had found British weapons in the Native American camp. This sent shockwaves around the country. For many years settlers who lived near the frontier had claimed that the British were arming the Native Americans from bases in Canada and encouraging the native peoples to attack American settlers. Now Harrison had given them a "smoking gun" that seemed to prove what they had long suspected. The "war hawks" used Harrison's claim to press for a war with Great Britain. This was one of the reasons for the War of 1812.

Tenskwatawa lost most of his supporters after the Battle of Tippecanoe, but Tecumseh continued the struggle. During the War of 1812, Tecumseh allied with the British. When he died while fighting in Canada, so did his dream of a Native American alliance.

Tecumseh's significance in the struggle of Native Americans against land-hungry American settlers can be seen in the following statement:

> I am a Shawnee. My forefathers were warriors. Their son is a warrior. From them I take only my existence, from my tribe I take nothing. I am the maker of my own fortune, and Oh! that I could make that of my Red people, and of my country, as great as the conceptions of my mind, when I think of the Spirit that rules the universe. I would not them come to Governor Harrison to ask him to tear up the treaty [of 1809], and to obliterate the landmark, but I would say to him: "Sir, you have liberty to return to your own country."

> The Being within, communing with past ages, tells me that once, nor until lately, there was no Whiteman on this continent, that it then all belonged to the Great Spirit that made them to keep it, to traverse it, to enjoy its productions, and to fill it with the same race, once a happy race; since made miserable by the White people, who are never contented but always encroaching.

> The way, and the only way, to check and to stop this evil, is for all the Redmen to unite in claiming a common and equal right in the land, as it was at first and should be yet; for it was never divided, but belongs to all for the use of each. That no part has a right to sell, even to each other, much less to strangers—those who want all and will not do with less. The White people have no right to take the land from the Indians, because they had it first, it is theirs. . . there cannot be two occupations in the same place. The first excludes all others. It is not so in hunting or traveling, for there is same ground will serve many. . . but the camp is stationary. . . . It belongs to the first who sits down on his blanket or skins, which he has thrown upon the ground, and till he leaves it, no other has a right.

William Henry Harrison went from his "victory" at Tippecanoe to fight in the War of 1812. He was made a brigadier general and later promoted to major general. After the war, he ran for and was elected to the Ohio legislature and later to Congress. He also served as United States minister to Colombia. A popular military figure, even more than 20 years later, he won the Whig nomination for President in 1840. He and his Vice Presidential running mate, John Tyler, campaigned on the slogan of "Tippecanoe and Tyler, too!" At his inauguration in March 1841, Harrison caught a cold and developed pneumonia. He died a month later.

Tecumseh

Osceola, Seminole Leader

Before his election to the presidency, Andrew Jackson had a long record of fighting the Native Americans of the Southeast. In the First Seminole War, Jackson invaded Spanish Florida in an effort to end Seminole raids into the United States. Weakened by war and in need of money, Spain sold Florida to the United States. By the 1830s, the Seminole had been forced south to live in the Everglades, a swampy area.

When the Seminole were told they had to leave Florida and resettle in Oklahoma, Chief Osceola and his supporters refused. It is said that Osceola stabbed the treaty with a dagger and declared: "This is the only treaty I will make with the white man!" By 1835, the Second Seminole War was underway. For two years Osceola and his warriors foiled successive American campaigns to destroy the Seminole. They did this even though they were outnumbered. Hiding in the

Teaching Idea

Students may enjoy looking at portraits of Osceola by George Catlin and Robert J. Curtis. Images can be located online.

Everglades, Osceola and his warriors fought a guerilla war, luring the army into traps and ambushes and inflicting high casualties on soldiers fighting in a terrain for which they had no training. In 1837, Osceola arranged to meet the commander of the U.S. troops under a flag of truce. Despite the truce, he was taken prisoner. Although Osceola was imprisoned, the Seminole continued to fight until 1842, by which time most of the Seminole had been killed. Over 4,000 were deported to Oklahoma. The Second Seminole War cost the United States more than $30 million.

Manifest Destiny: Texas and Conflict with Mexico

The term manifest destiny was coined in the 1840s. The phrase appeared in an editorial in the United States Magazine and Democratic Review in 1845. The editorial said that the United States had a "manifest destiny to overspread the continent allotted by Providence." *Manifest* means "clear or obvious"; *destiny* means "something that is bound to happen," and *Providence* refers to God's oversight of the world. The writer meant that God had given the United States a clear right to extend its authority across the continent, and that the nation was destined to do so. This idea was popular with many Americans during the 1840s and 1850s. They had seen their country growing and concluded it was destined to continue growing until it covered the whole continent. "Manifest Destiny" was an expression of pride in the young, growing nation, but it was also a way of justifying the displacement of native peoples and supporting other land-hungry actions of the 1800s.

Early Settlement of Texas: Stephen Austin

The settlement and annexation of Texas can be seen as an example of America pursuing its "manifest destiny." Mexico had won its independence from Spain in 1821. During the 1820s, small numbers of Americans began moving into the Mexican province of Texas from the southeast to raise cotton and sugar on plantations.

In 1821, Stephen Austin was given permission by the newly installed Mexican government to establish settlements in East Texas. In 1822, he and 300 families entered Texas. More immigrants followed. In less than a decade, there were 25,000 Americans, including many slaves, in Texas. The settlers far outnumbered the 4,000 Mexicans living there. Concerned about the growing imbalance, the Mexican government banned all further settlement by Americans and all further importation of slaves.

Texans—transplanted Americans and native Mexicans—asked several times for autonomy. They declared that they needed slaves to work their plantations and wanted to rid themselves of Mexican government in general. Austin was jailed by the new Mexican dictator, General Antonio Lopez de Santa Anna, for delivering the most recent request for autonomy, and the Texans rebelled. Santa Anna had seized control of the Mexican government in 1834 and declared himself president.

Battle of the Alamo

The Texas Revolution ended almost as quickly as it had begun. The fighting lasted from late 1835 to April 1836.

The most memorable battle of the revolution was the Battle of the Alamo. The Alamo was a mission-fortress built by Spanish priests in San Antonio. About

1,500 to 2,000 Mexican troops besieged the fort defended by fewer than 200 Texans. The siege began in February 1836 and ended twelve days later when Mexican cannons blew huge holes through the walls. Mexican soldiers entered the fort through the gaps in the walls, and all 182 Texans as well as 1,500 Mexican soldiers died during the heroic defense.

The defense of the Alamo was led by William B. Travis. When Santa Anna demanded that he surrender, Travis is said to have replied, "The enemy has demanded my surrender. I have answered their demand with a single cannon shot. I shall never surrender."

Among the other defenders who died during the siege of the Alamo were Davy Crockett and Jim Bowie, who had shared leadership of the men with Travis until falling ill. Both Crockett and Bowie were well-known frontiersmen, and both have become folk heroes. Crockett was from Tennessee. He had fought with Andrew Jackson during the Indian Wars in the southeast and had served in Congress from 1827 to 1835. Crockett was an expert rifleman. At the Alamo, it is said that Crockett's marksmanship killed five successive Mexican gunners who were manning a cannon hundreds of yards from the Alamo walls. Jim Bowie was born in Kentucky and spent most of his life in Louisiana before moving to Texas. He or his brother invented the Bowie knife, which is used for hunting.

During the Battle of the Alamo, Mexican and American Texans proclaimed their independence. Two months after the Battle of the Alamo, Texan troops led by General Sam Houston charged into battle during the Battle of San Jacinto crying "Remember the Alamo!" The slogan emerged as a reminder of the defeat and as an inspiration to continue the fight. The Texans defeated Santa Anna in that battle and secured their independence, later electing the hero of the Battle of San Jacinto, Sam Houston, as their first president. (53)

Teaching Idea

Today, the Alamo is in the center of bustling downtown San Antonio. Have students do library or Internet research on the Alamo and the settlement of Texas.

Have students share the information they learn and compile the reports in a class book about the settling of Texas.

the Alamo

The Mexican-American War

Although Mexico had not recognized Texas's declaration of independence, Texas asked for annexation by the United States. The United States initially refused for two reasons. First, annexation would surely mean war with Mexico, and second, Texas would be a slave state. The United States was still trying to reach a compromise over the issue of slavery. By 1844, however, the clamor to admit Texas was growing and it became a major campaign issue in the presidential election that year.

James K. Polk ran on a platform of annexation against the incumbent President John Tyler and won. Early in 1845, the United States annexed Texas. The Mexican-American War was fought to determine where the southwestern boundary between Texas and Mexico lay. When United States troops under General Zachary Taylor moved across the boundary, they were attacked. The United States responded with a declaration of war.

Zachary Taylor led an army across the Rio Grande into Mexico. He won a victory at the Battle of Monterrey in September of 1846. Santa Anna marched north to meet Taylor's army but was defeated at the battle of Buena Vista in February of 1847. Meanwhile, another American army under the command of Winfield Scott landed on the Mexican coast, near Veracruz. Scott won battles at Veracruz and Chapultepec and eventually occupied Mexico City.

The war lasted from May 1846 to September 1848. Under the Treaty of Guadalupe Hidalgo (1848), which ended the war, Mexico ceded to the United States all or part of what became the following states: California, Nevada, Utah, Colorado, Wyoming, New Mexico, and Arizona.

General Zachary Taylor was known to his soldiers as "Old Rough and Ready." He was a soldier for forty years, fighting in the War of 1812, subduing Native Americans in the Midwest, and defeating the Seminole in the Second Seminole War in Florida. He became a national hero after his defeat of General Santa Anna in the Mexican-American War.

Taylor was nominated as the Whig candidate for President in 1848 and won. Although it was his success that added large tracts of land to the United States, he opposed the expansion of slavery into any territory seeking admission to state-hood. He died after only sixteen months in office.

Opposition to the War

Opposition to the war was strong among some Americans. Southerners and Westerners felt they would benefit from a larger United States and supported the war. Many Northerners, on the other hand, opposed the war on moral grounds; they opposed the addition of more slave states to the Union. One of those who was against the war was Henry David Thoreau. In his "Essay on the Duty of Civil Disobedience," Thoreau asked whether a man had the right to disobey a law or government he felt was wrong. He concluded that there was such a right:

> Must the citizen ever for a moment, or in the least degree, resign his conscience to the legislator? Why has every man a conscience, then? I think that we should be men first, and subjects afterward. It is not desirable to cultivate a respect for the law, so much as for the right. The only obligation which I have a right to assume is to do at any time what I think right.

Thoreau went on to explain his opposition to a government more concerned, in his eyes, with conquest than justice. (54)

> The government itself, which is only the mode which the people have chosen to execute their will, is equally liable to be abused and perverted before the people can act through it. Witness the present Mexican war, the work of comparatively a few individuals using the standing government as their tool; for, in the outset, the people would not have consented to this measure.

Thoreau had actually declined to pay his taxes, and spent one night in prison. Was he ashamed of this? On the contrary, Thoreau wrote: "Under a government which imprisons any unjustly, the true place for a just man is . . . a prison."

Thoreau's opposition did little to affect the war, though his ideas about civil disobedience would influence the thinking of others, including Gandhi and Martin Luther King, Jr., who chose nonviolent resistance, such as going to jail, rather than cooperation with unjust laws.

B. Westward Expansion After the Civil War

Homestead Act of 1862

Settlement of the Great Plains—the land between the Mississippi and the Rockies—did not take place to any great degree until after the Civil War. During the War, Congress passed the Homestead Act in 1862, which encouraged people

to settle in the Plains. The government announced it would give 160 acres of land to any citizen or immigrant who was willing to farm it for five years. Land could also be bought for $1.25 an acre after six months of living on it. Before this law was passed, people had either bypassed the Great Plains in favor of the fertile Northwest or were lured to California by the get-rich-quick tales of the gold rush. But the Homestead Act changed that. In the next 40 years, the U.S. government gave away 80 million acres of land under the act.

In the late 1800s, largely because of the Homestead Act, many thousands of white Americans, as well as many freed slaves (known as Exodusters) and European immigrants, relocated to the Great Plains. These settlers established farms and ranches on the plains. Because trees were scarce on the Great Plains, many settlers built "sod houses" by cutting and piling up blocks of grass and turf. Farmers battled with great swarms of grasshoppers and other insects that devoured their crops. They raised windmills to bring water up from below the earth's surface, and they used a new invention called "barbed wire" to help fence in their livestock.

Life on the Great Plains was hard. Some parts of the plains were fertile and received enough water for successful farming, but other parts suffered occasional droughts, which made farming impossible and led to blinding dust storms. When these droughts struck, they drove farmers out of business.

 ### "Go West, young man!"—Horace Greeley

Horace Greeley was the founder and editor of the *New York Tribune,* an influential newspaper during the mid-1800s. In 1851, he wrote an article advising young men how to make their fortune. He said the following:

> If you have no family or friends to aid you . . . turn your face to the great West and there build up your home and fortune.

In time, this advice was boiled down to "Go West, young man!" Thousands of young men and women did just that.

Railroads

Railroads had several advantages over roads, rivers, and canals. Railroads were dependable, cheap, and convenient. The first railroads were built in British coal mines, but in 1831, the Mohawk and Hudson line was inaugurated between Albany and Schenectady, New York. In 1853, when the Baltimore and Ohio Railroad reached Wheeling, West Virginia, it achieved what the Erie Canal had done years earlier—it crossed the Appalachians to join east and west. A rail network spread quickly across the Northeast and the upper Midwest in the 1840s. The 1850s were the great railroad-building years in the Southeast.

By 1861, some 300,000 miles of railroad track had been laid down in the United States. The Midwest was the focus of much of this track laying, making it easier for people to travel there from the East. As a result, land in the Midwest became more expensive as more and more settlers arrived. The fast, cheap transportation the railroads provided allowed for goods, such as wheat and corn, to be easily shipped to the Northeast for sale. Manufactured items, such as farm tools from the Northeast, could, in turn, be shipped to consumers in the Midwest. Over time, larger, faster, and more powerful engines pulling heavier cars required tracks made from stronger iron, and eventually steel rails. Coal powered the

I. Westward Expansion

Teaching Idea

Create an overhead and copies for each student of Instructional Master 33, *Cattle Drives and Railroads*. Have students locate and name each railroad on the map. They should identify the states through which each runs. It may be helpful to have students label the states on their maps first and then identify the various routes.

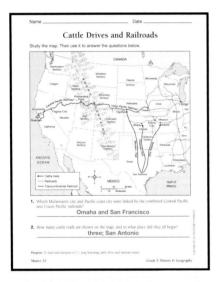

Use Instructional Master 33.

Teaching Idea

Use the overhead you created from Instructional Master 33, *Cattle Drives and Railroads*. Have students identify the railroads that served each cattle trail.

Cross-curricular Teaching Idea

Collaborate with the music teacher to teach the students "Git Along Little Dogies" while you are teaching about cattle drives.

steam engines, and iron and steel were used in the construction of railroads, bridges, and engines. The demands of the emerging railroad business were an enormous stimulus for such industries after the Civil War.

The Transcontinental Railroad

Construction of the transcontinental railroad began in 1862. The route ran from Nebraska to California. The Union Pacific built west from Nebraska, and the Central Pacific built east from California. Irish immigrants did much of the work on the eastern section, which consisted of largely flat and gently rolling plains until it reached the Rocky Mountains. Chinese immigrants did most of the labor on the western portion, and it was rugged, dangerous work that took them over and through mountains and across gorges and desert.

The federal government paid the two companies for each mile of track laid, with higher payments for work in the mountains. The two competing railroads continued building east and west until they met in 1869 at Promontory Point, Utah. The completion of the railroad was marked by a final golden spike being driven into the ground. By the 1890s, four more transcontinental railroads had been built joining East and West across more northern and southern routes. These railroads made it easier than ever before to move across the continent.

Cowboys and Cattle Drives

By 1860, Texas longhorns—cattle—numbered 3 to 4 million on the open range in Texas. Open range means that the land was unfenced. Much of the Plains was owned by the federal government and no one lived on or worked it. Most of the cattle were descended from cattle brought to Mexico by the Spanish. Mexico, at one time, had included Texas. The longhorns on the Plains were unbranded, which meant that no one owned them. Seeing a potential business in these mavericks, as they were called, Americans in Texas began to round them up and drive them to market. Mexican *vaqueros*, the Spanish word for cowboys, taught the Americans how to rope, brand, and drive cattle. Many words associated with ranching are Spanish in origin, such as lariat (a rope to tie a horse), chaps (leather leggings worn over pants to protect the legs), and lasso (a long rope with a sliding noose, used to catch horses or cattle).

Open-range cattle ranching had begun on the Texas Plains in the 1840s and 1850s and by the end of the Civil War had moved up through the northern Plains. Initially, ranchers in Texas had driven their herds to New Orleans for sale. After the Civil War, however, with the coming of railroads linking the Plains with the Midwest, ranchers began to drive their herds to railheads in Kansas, Missouri, and Nebraska. From there, the cattle were shipped to meat-packing factories in Chicago, and then sent to the growing cities of the Northeast.

Depending on where the cattle drive started and where it was to end, cowboys could be on the trail for as long as two months. It is estimated that some 30,000 cowboys, several thousand of whom were African American, drove cattle north over the Sedalia, Chisholm, Western, and Goodnight-Loving trails.

A rancher would hire eight or ten cowboys to herd his 2,000 or 3,000 head of cattle to market. There was always a trail boss and a cook and helper who rode in the chuck wagon. The cowboys had specific jobs. Two would ride point—out

in front of the herd. Two would ride drag—at the back to round up and urge lagging cattle to keep up with the herd. Two would ride swing (left side of the herd), and two would ride flank (right side). Their jobs were to move the herd along and to keep it from veering off course.

The worst thing that could happen on a cattle drive was a stampede. When a stampede occurred, the herd took off at a run. Cattle herds were nervous and anything could set them off—a gunshot, a bolt of lightning, a clap of thunder, or a loud yell. That's one reason cowboys sometimes sang—music soothed the cattle. To stop a stampede, several cowboys would work their horses to force the cattle to run in a wide circle. As more and more cattle were added to the circle, the sheer size of the herd forced it to slow its pace.

By 1890, not only had the frontier closed, but open-range ranching had ended as well. The federal government had encouraged the opening of the Plains to farmers with the passage of the Homestead Act in 1862. Farmers and sheep ranchers built fences and dammed streams and rivers, blocking the free access of cattle to grazing land and water. Under these new conditions, cattle could no longer survive in large numbers on the open range. In the future, cattlemen would raise cattle on fenced-in properties called ranches.

The "Wild West"

From the 1850s through the 1880s, the West was—in different places and at different times—lawless, brutal, and deadly. Many of the early settlers in the West were unmarried men, and some western towns were hotbeds for drinking, gambling, brawling, and prostitution. But as more people came, especially men with families, law and order soon followed. Mining camps run by vigilante committees became respectable towns and, eventually, cities. As the open range disappeared, so did the long-haul cattle drive and the freewheeling life of the cowboy.

But the Wild West has lived on in dime novels and the Wild West Shows of the nineteenth century, and in movies, radio, and television shows in the twentieth century. The sheer brutality of life on the Plains became romanticized over the years. It began with newspapermen sending stories about the exploits of Billy the Kid and the James Gang to their eastern papers. Curious Easterners flocked to see Buffalo Bill's *Wild West*, featuring Annie Oakley shooting her rifle from the back of a horse and Native Americans dressed in buckskin chanting war songs. Some of the people in these shows have entered into the popular imagination and become part of cultural literacy.

Outlaws

Billy the Kid (William H. Bonney)
- cattle rustler and murderer in New Mexico
- caught, tried, and sentenced to hang, but escaped, killing two guards
- killed by Sheriff Pat Garrett

Jesse James
- with his brother Frank, led an outlaw gang known as the James Gang
- bank and train robber, murderer
- Arkansas, Texas, Colorado
- killed by one of his own gang for the reward

Teaching Idea

Students may enjoy listening to you read "The Spelling Bee at Angels" by Bret Harte. This comical poem tells of a cowboy spelling bee, which ends with a shoot-out. The poem is available on the Internet. (See *More Resources*.)

Teaching Idea

Students may enjoy listening to ballads and songs about the West, such as the ballad "Jesse James." Lyrics can be found online or in *Songs of the Great American West* by Irwin Silber. (See *More Resources*.)

I. Westward Expansion

Annie Oakley

Teaching Idea

Students may enjoy looking at posters from Buffalo Bill's Wild West shows. These posters are available online.

Teaching Idea

You may wish to check out a number of interesting websites on the buffalo soldiers. (See **More Resources**.)

Teaching Idea

Students may be interested to know that, in addition to the buffalo soldiers, who came west to fight, some African Americans moved west to farm. Many were motivated by the terror waged against former slaves by the Ku Klux Klan and other groups. These settlers were known as Exodusters, after the biblical story of the Jews' exodus from Egypt.

Teaching Idea

Ask students if they or anyone they know has ever bought anything that they thought was foolish. Relate their personal experience to what William Seward experienced when purchasing Alaska. Conduct research to see what the average price of an acre in Alaska is today. Looking back, was it really a waste of money?

Wild West Show Entertainers

Buffalo Bill (William F. Cody)

- former professional buffalo hunter, Pony Express rider, and Union scout during the Civil War
- His Wild West Show featured Native Americans such as Sitting Bull, as well as trick riders and sharpshooters like Annie Oakley.
- His show started in 1883 and toured the United States and Europe for decades. The show featured a stage-coach robbery and lots of gunfights. Audiences of up to 20,000 attended. Even Queen Victoria of England saw the show.

Annie Oakley

- Born Phoebe Ann Oakley Moses, she learned to shoot at age 9.
- At age 15 she entered a shooting contest against well-known marksman Frank E. Butler. Annie won the match and later married Butler.
- Known as "Little Sure Shot" for her height and her skill with a gun, she could hit a dime tossed in the air from 90 feet away and shoot five or six bullets through a playing card tossed in the air before it hit the ground.
- sharpshooter with Buffalo Bill's *Wild West Show* from 1885 to 1902
- The musical *Annie Get Your Gun,* with music by Irving Berlin, including the famous songs "There's No Business Like Show Business" and "Anything You Can Do," was loosely based on the life of Annie Oakley. **55**

Buffalo Soldiers

During the Civil War, African-American units were formed within the Union Army. (See next section.) After the Civil War, the United States Congress authorized the creation of six regiments of African-American soldiers. The 24th and 25th Infantries and the 9th and 10th Cavalries were sent west to fight in the Plains Wars (See Section III, "Native Americans: Cultures and Conflicts," pp. 297–313). The Native Americans, whom they fought, may have named these African Americans "buffalo soldiers" out of respect for their courage. Fourteen buffalo soldiers won the Congressional Medal of Honor. The black units were disbanded in 1952, and the soldiers integrated into the rest of the army after the federal government banned segregation in the armed forces.

"Seward's Folly"

In 1867, Czar Alexander of Russia was looking to raise money and offered to sell Alaska to the United States. While Native Americans had lived on the land for thousands of years, the Russians were the first Europeans to the area and had established a settlement there in 1784. Secretary of State William Seward immediately agreed to the purchase price of $7.2 million, or about 2 cents an acre. Most Americans considered it a waste of money and jeeringly referred to it as "Seward's Folly" and "Seward's Ice Box." However, when gold was found in 1880, the deal no longer seemed so foolish. The gold soon ran out, but many miners stayed to earn a living by fishing, farming in the southern part of the territory, or timbering in the dense forests. Today Alaska is still sparsely populated but is the home of important oil reserves.

1890: The Closing of the Frontier

In 1890, the U.S. Census declared the frontier closed. The frontier had ceased to exist as a clearly defined line between settled and unsettled areas. Only pockets of frontier remained. The continental United States was either divided into states or organized as territories on their way to statehood. Between 1864 and 1912, thirteen states were admitted to the Union, making the contiguous United States complete. A process that had begun with the founding of St. Augustine in 1565 had ended.

Many historians have argued that the frontier experience had transformed Europeans into Americans and defined what it meant to be an American.

Review

Below are some ideas for ongoing assessment and review activities. These are not meant to constitute a comprehensive list. Teachers may also refer to the *Pearson Learning/Core Knowledge History & Geography* series for additional information and teaching ideas.

• This section provides an opportunity for students to complete short research reports on Daniel Boone, Lewis and Clark, Sacagawea, Tecumseh, or other important figures during early exploration of the West. Using the Language Arts section, provide the class with topics for short reports to write in formal style. Each day of a week, provide a mini-lesson on different aspects of report writing, such as correct paragraph form or bibliographies. Share these reports when completed.

• So many events and people are named in this section that a good way to review the information is to have students do one of the following:

Have students create crossword puzzles with at least 12 clues about people and events from this section, and then exchange them with each other. Check for accuracy.

Play "Who/What Am I?" Have teams of two create five identifications. Then pair teams together and have them take turns asking their identification questions.

• Have students write up interviews with prominent people from this section. Divide students into pairs and have them research important events from a person's life. Then, have them write up questions on index cards to ask that historical figure. Have the pairs take turns conducting their interview in front of the class, with one person playing the role of the interviewer and the other the role of the prominent person. After the interview, discuss if the information presented is accurate and make corrections accordingly.

• In order to have a balanced and well-rounded understanding of this period, students should be able to understand how events looked from the perspective of white Americans and also from the perspective of Native Americans. Have students write a paper from a point of view not their own. What would it be like to have the settlers come onto their land if they were Native American? Have students practice using examples from history to support their point of view. Share these papers aloud.

The Big Idea in Review

Throughout the 1800s, Americans moved west, settling lands previously occupied by Native Americans.

I. Westward Expansion

• Have students review the importance and historical impact of U.S. physical features. On index cards, write the name of a physical feature and place the cards in a container. Possible physical features could include: James River, Hudson River, Erie Canal, Mississippi River, Missouri River, Ohio River, Columbia River, Rio Grande, Rocky Mountains, Cumberland Gap, and the Appalachians. Have students take turns pulling out a card, reading the name aloud, and locating the place on a map. Next, fellow students must think of an interesting statement about that place in relation to its importance to westward expansion. For example, if the card with "Cumberland Gap" is pulled out of the container, a response might be, "The Cumberland Gap is an important pass through the Appalachian Mountains, and it helped people move west to the first line of the frontier."

• Have the class visit the school media center and find works of fiction that address this time in American history. You may want to have the school media specialist help you compile a library of titles that tell stories about the people and places from this section. Assign a book report for the works of historical fiction and have students share their books with the class.

• Have students write poems to depict events or describe people from this section. They can choose a type of poetry based on the study of poems in Language Arts and then brainstorm a list of people and places that would make good topics for poems, such as seeing a sunset from a wagon train. Have students illustrate their poems and post these for other classes to enjoy.

• Have students write up short skits to depict historieal events from this section. They can use situations such as the first time someone rode on a train or a conversation about moving west. Students can also use their papers written from another point of view to build a skit. Have them perform these for the class.

• Have students create concentration games with names and facts about the historical figures and events studied in this section. They can use different-colored index cards for people, places, and events.

• As a culminating activity, have students tell the story of a family's journey across the west. Students can work in pairs or small groups to write a historical-fiction story or play about the journey. They should describe the family, where they started and ended their journey, what they took with them and what they had to leave behind, their reason(s) for traveling west, what they encountered along the way, and if they felt the trip was worth it or not. Students can share this information as a play, as an oral report, or in another creative manner as long as they include historical facts to support their selections.

• You may also ask the following questions after completion of this unit of study.

1. How did each of the following help to open the West: (a) Lewis and Clark, (b) Zebulon Pike, (c) Mountain men?

   (a) Lewis and Clark explored Louisiana Purchase; (b) Pike explored Spanish territory; (c) Mountain men blazed trails into Oregon Country.

2. Who was Sacagawea?

   Sacagawea was a Shoshone woman who helped Lewis and Clark on their journey of exploration.

3. How did the concept of "Manifest Destiny" affect United States policy toward Native Americans?

   The idea of "Manifest Destiny" encouraged Americans to keep moving west, because it suggested that it was their destiny to dominate the continent. Students should recognize that the settlers' pursuit of "destiny" had terrible consequences for native peoples.

4. How did Texas help cause the Mexican-American War?

   Texas won its war of independence from Mexico and then eventually was annexed by the United States. Mexico never recognized Texas's independence. When American troops crossed a disputed boundary in Texas, Mexico declared war.

5. Where is the Erie Canal located?

   The Erie Canal is in New York State.

6. What happened at the Alamo?

   During the Mexican-American War a small group of Texans died defending the Alamo from an attack by the Mexican Army.

7. Why did the '49ers go to California?

   They hoped to strike it rich by finding gold.

8. What was a cowboy's job?

   A cowboy was responsible for driving cattle to railheads.

9. What was important about the transcontinental railroad?

   It was the first railroad to link the east and west coasts.

10. Who were the "buffalo soldiers"?

    Buffalo soldiers were African Americans who fought in the Indian Wars in the West after the Civil War.

More Resources

The titles listed below are offered as a representative sample of materials and not a complete list of everything that is available.

For students —

• *Westward Expansion Before the Civil War* and *Westward Expansion After the Civil War,* edited by E. D. Hirsch, Jr. (Pearson Learning, 2002), two units in the official *Pearson Learning/Core Knowledge History & Geography* series, are available as part of the bound books for Grade 5/Level 5 and also as stand-alone modules. A teacher's guide is also available for each unit. To order, call 1-800-321-3106.

• *Along the Santa Fe Trail: Marion Russell's Own Story,* by Marion Russell, adapted by Ginger Wadsworth (Albert Whitman & Company, 1993). Library binding, ISBN 0807502952.

• *Battle of the Alamo (Cornerstones of Freedom),* by Andrew Santella (Children's Press, 1997). Library binding, 32 pages, ISBN 0516202936. See also *Voices of the Alamo,* by Sherry Garland and illustrated by Ronald Himler (Pelican, 2004). Hardcover, 40 pages, ISBN 1589802225.

• *A Book of Americans,* by Rosemary and Stephen Vincent Benét (Henry Holt & Company, 1987). Paperback, 114 pages, ISBN 0805002979.

More Resources continued

• *By the Great Horn Spoon!*, by Sid Fleishman (Little Brown, 1988). Light fiction. Paperback, 193 pages, ISBN 0316286125.

• *Cowboys of the Wild West*, by Russell Freedman (Clarion, 1990). Paperback, 112 pages, ISBN 0395548004. One of several relevant titles by Freedman.

• *Daniel Boone and the Cumberland Gap (Cornerstones of Freedom, Second Series)*, by Andrew Santella. For more detail and a more difficult read, see *Daniel Boone: Beyond the Mountains (Great Explorations)*, by Patricia Calvert (Benchmark Books, 2002).

• *Daniel Boone: Wilderness Scout*, by Stewart Edward White (Kessinger, 2003). A reprint of a 1926 biography for young people. Paperback, 312 pages, ISBN 0766170357.

• *Facing West: A Story of the Oregon Trail (Once Upon America Series)*, by Kathleen Kudlinski (Puffin, 1996). Paperback, 58 pages, ISBN 0140369147.

• *50 American Heroes Every Kid Should Meet*, by Dennis Denenberg and Lorraine Roscoe (The Millbrook Press, 2002). Contains a profile of Tecumseh. Paperback, 128 pages, ISBN 0761316450.

• *Following the Great Herds: The Plains Indians and the American Buffalo (Library of the Westward Expansion)*, by Ryan P. Randolph (PowerKids Press, 2003). Written for younger children, but very informative with lots of photos and illustrations. Library binding, 24 pages, ISBN 0823962962. Other titles in this series include *The Oregon Trail, Frontier Women Who Helped Shape the American West, Lewis and Clark's Voyage of Discovery, The Quest for California's Gold, The Santa Fe Trail*, and *The Transcontinental Railroad*.

• *Frontier Fort: Fort Life on the Upper Mississippi, 1826*, by Megan O'Hara (Capstone Press, 1998). Library binding, 32 pages, ISBN 1560657243.

• *Going to School in Pioneer Times*, by Kerry A. Graves (Blue Earth Books, 2002). Includes quotations from primary sources, games, activities, special events, and crafts. Library binding, 32 pages, ISBN 0736808043.

• *Hurry Freedom: African Americans in Gold Rush California*, by Jerry Stanley (Crown, 2000). Honored by the Orbis Pictus Awards program for excellence in children's nonfiction. Hardcover, 96 pages, ISBN B0001PBYBS.

• *Indian Chiefs*, by Russell Freedman (Holiday House, 1992). Paperback, ISBN 0823409716.

• *The Ledgerbook of Thomas Blue Eagle*, by Jewel H. Grutman and Gay Matthaei (Lickle Publishing, 1994). Fictional account of Native Americans going to the Carlisle School. Hardcover, 72 pages, ISBN 1565660633. Available directly from Lickle Publishing, www.lickle publishing.com or 1-866-454-2553.

• *Lewis and Clark: Explorers of the American West*, by Steven Kroll (Holiday House, 1996). Paperback, 32 pages, ISBN 0823412733.

• *The Little House on the Prairie series*, by Laura Ingalls Wilder and illustrated by Garth Williams (Harper Trophy, 1989). Paperback, nine-volume boxed set, ISBN 0064400409.

• *A Picture Book of Sacagawea*, by David Adler (Holiday House, 2001). Paperback, ISBN 0823416658. See also *A Picture Book of Davy Crockett*, by the same author.

• *Reconstructing America (1865–1890)*, by Joy Hakim (Oxford, 2002). Book 7 of the popular series *A History of Us*. Paperback, 160 pages, ISBN 0195153324.

• *Sacagawea*, by Judith St. George (Philomel, 1997). Hardcover, 128 pages, ISBN 0399231617.

• *The Santa Fe Trail (We The People)*, by Jean F. Blashfield (Compass Point, 2000). Straightforward, easy-to-read text with good illustrations. Library binding, 48 pages, ISBN 0756500478. See also in this series *The Transcontinental Railroad; The Oregon Trail;* and *The Lewis and Clark Expedition*.

• *Ten Mile Day and the Building of the Transcontinental Railroad*, by Mary Ann Fraser (Henry Holt, 1996). Paperback, 40 pages, ISBN 0805047034.

• *Travel in the Early Days (Historic Communities)*, by Bobbie Kalman and Kate Calder (Crabtree Publishing, 2000). Paperback, 32 pages, ISBN 086505472X. See also *Pioneer Recipes*, by Bobbie Kalman and Lynda Hale in this same series.

For teachers —

• *The American West: An Illustrated History*, by Liz Sonnenborn (Fair Street, 2002). Hardcover, 144 pages, ISBN 0439219701.

More Resources continued

• *Children of the Wild West,* by Russell Freedman (Clarion, 1990). Paperback, 112 pages, ISBN 0395547857.

• *The Food Journal of Lewis & Clark: Recipes for an Expedition,* by Mary Gunderson (History Cooks, 2002). Paperback, 176 pages, ISBN 0972039104.

• *Frontier Living: An Illustrated Guide to Pioneer Life in America,* by Edwin Tunis (Lyons Press, 2000). Paperback, 168 pages, ISBN 158574137X.

• *The Incredible Journey of Lewis and Clark,* by Rhonda Blumberg (HarperTrophy, 1995). Paperback, 144 pages, ISBN 0688144217.

• *The Journals of Lewis and Clark,* by John Bakeless (Signet Classics, 2002). Paperback, 384 pages, ISBN 0451528344.

• *The Journals of Lewis and Clark,* edited by Bernard DeVoto (Mariner Books, 1997). Paperback, 576 pages, ISBN 0395859964.

• *Land of Enchantment: Memoirs of Marian Russell along the Santa Fe Trail,* as dictated to Mrs. Hal Russell (University of New Mexico Press, 1985). Paperback, ISBN 0826308058.

• "Lewis and Clark and the Language of Discovery," in *Smithsonian in Your Classroom, Fall 2003.* Available electronically in Adobe Acrobat .pdf format at educate.si.edu or in print form by requesting a copy in an e-mail to educate@si.edu.

• *Lewis and Clark: Voyage of Discovery,* by Stephen Ambrose with photography from Sam Abell (National Geographic, 2002). Hardcover, 256 pages, ISBN 0792264738.

• *Life of David Crockett: An Autobiography,* by David Crockett (Kessinger Publications, 2003). Paperback, 444 pages, ISBN 076616182X. An online (and searchable) text/facsimile of the 1865 edition of this book can be found at the University of Michigan's Making of America website at www.hti.umich.edu/m/moagrp.

• *My Father, Daniel Boone: The Draper Interviews with Nathan Boone,* (University Press of Kentucky, 1999). Biographical information supplied by the frontiersman's son, Nathan, in 1851. Hardcover, 192 pages, ISBN 0813121035.

• *The Oregon Trail (National Geographic Adventure Classics),* by Francis Parkman (National Geographic, 2002). Paperback, 320 pages, ISBN 0792266404.

• *The West (A PBS Documentary),* produced by Ken Burns (Warner Home Video, 2003). 5 DVDs, 750 minutes, ASIN B0000A02Y5.

• *Words West: Voices of Young Pioneers,* by Ginger Wadsworth (Clarion Books, 2003). Hardcover, 193 pages, ISBN 0618234756.

• "Jesse James" and background information, both from Irwin Silber's *Songs of the Great American West,* can be found online at http://www.fortunecity.com/tinpan/parton/2/jesse1.html

• "Buffalo Soldiers and Indian Wars," www.buffalo soldier.net, is an interesting source of information. You may also wish to take a look at www.buffalosoldiers.net.

• "Diaries, Memoirs, Letters and Reports Along The Trails West," at www.over-land.com/diaries.html, has links to a number of original writings.

• The Memoirs of Luzena Stanley Wilson can be found on the PBS website at www.pbs.org/weta/thewest/resources/archives/three/luzena.htm. The site also has two of William Swain's letters, as well as information on Kit Carson, Daniel Boone and other pioneers of westward expansion. Search from the home page.

• "The Spelling Bee at Angels," a poem by Bret Harte can be found online at http://whitewolf.newcastle.edu.au/words/authors/H/HarteBret/verse/completepoetical/spellingbee.html

II. The Civil War: Causes, Conflicts, Consequences

The Big Idea

Slavery, the Civil War, and Reconstruction occupied much of the United States' attention and energy in the mid-19th century.

Remember that each subject you study with students expands their vocabulary and introduces new terms, thus making them better listeners and readers. As you study historical people and events, use read alouds, independent reading, and discussions to build students' vocabularies.

The items below refer to content in Grade 5. Use time lines with students to help them sequence and relate events from different periods and groups.

1739	Stono Uprising
1767	Mason-Dixon Line surveyed
1787	Three-Fifths Compromise in the Constitution
1800	Gabriel Prosser Conspiracy
1820	Compromise of 1820
1822	Denmark Vesey Conspiracy
1831	Nat Turner Rebellion
1850	Compromise of 1850
1852	*Uncle Tom's Cabin*
1854	Kansas-Nebraska Act
1857	Dred Scott decision
1858	Lincoln-Douglas debates
1859	John Brown's raid

continued on next page

What Students Should Already Know

Students in Core Knowledge schools should be familiar with

Kindergarten

▸ some people were not free, slavery in early America

▸ Abraham Lincoln: humble origins, "Honest Abe"

Grade 1 and 2

▸ slavery in ancient Egypt, Greece, Rome

Grade 2

▸ the Civil War: the controversy over slavery, Harriet Tubman and the "underground railroad," Northern versus Southern states (Yankees and Rebels), Generals Ulysses S. Grant and Robert E. Lee, Clara Barton ("Angel of the Battlefield" and founder of the American Red Cross), President Abraham Lincoln and keeping the Union together, Emancipation Proclamation and the end of slavery

▸ civil rights: Jackie Robinson and the integration of major league baseball; Rosa Parks and the bus boycott in Montgomery, Alabama; Martin Luther King, Jr., and the dream of equal rights for all

▸ symbols and figures: Lincoln Memorial

Grade 3

▸ slavery in the Southern colonies, including economic reasons that the Southern colonies came to rely on slavery (slave labor on large plantations); the difference between indentured servant and slave (slaves as property); the Middle Passage

Grade 4

▸ abolitionists

What Students Need to Learn

Toward the Civil War

▸ Abolitionists: William Lloyd Garrison and *The Liberator*, Frederick Douglass

▸ Slave life and rebellions

▸ Industrial North versus agricultural South

▸ Mason-Dixon Line

▸ Controversy over whether to allow slavery in territories and new states

  • Missouri Compromise of 1820

  • Dred Scott decision allows slavery in the territories

▸ Importance of Harriet Beecher Stowe's *Uncle Tom's Cabin*

▸ John Brown and Harper's Ferry raid

continued from previous page

1860	Election of Lincoln
1860	South Carolina secedes
1861–1865	Civil War
1861	Confederate States of America established
1861	Fort Sumter falls
1861	First Battle of Bull Run
1862	Battle of *Monitor* and *Virginia*
1862	Battle of Antietam Creek
1863	Emancipation Proclamation
1863	Gettysburg Address
1864	Sherman's "March to the Sea"
1864	Reelection of Lincoln
1865	Freedmen's Bureau
1865	Fall of Richmond
1865	Surrender at Appomattox
1865	Assassination of Lincoln
1868	Johnson impeached
1868	Radical Reconstruction
1877	Compromise of 1877 ends Reconstruction

What Students Need to Learn continued

▸ Lincoln: "A house divided against itself cannot stand."
  • Lincoln-Douglas debates
  • Lincoln elected president, Southern states secede

The Civil War

▸ Fort Sumter
▸ Confederacy and Jefferson Davis
▸ Yankees and Rebels, Blue and Gray
▸ First Battle of Bull Run
▸ Robert E. Lee and Ulysses S. Grant
▸ General Stonewall Jackson
▸ Ironclad ships, battle between USS *Monitor* and CSS *Virginia* (formerly the USS *Merrimack*)
▸ Battle of Antietam Creek
▸ The Emancipation Proclamation
▸ Gettysburg and the Gettysburg Address
▸ African-American troops, Massachusetts Regiment led by Colonel Shaw
▸ Sherman's march to the sea and the burning of Atlanta
▸ Lincoln reelected, concluding words of the Second Inaugural Address ("With malice toward none, with charity for all . . .")
▸ Fall of Richmond (Confederate capital) to Union forces
▸ Surrender at Appomattox
▸ Assassination of Lincoln by John Wilkes Booth

Reconstruction

▸ The South in ruins
▸ Struggle for control of the South, Radical Republicans vs. Andrew Johnson, impeachment proceedings against Johnson
▸ Carpetbaggers and scalawags
▸ Freedmen's Bureau, "40 acres and a mule"
▸ 13th, 14th, 15th Amendments to the Constitution
▸ Black Codes, the Ku Klux Klan, "vigilante justice"
▸ End of Reconstruction, the Compromise of 1877, all federal troops removed from the South

What Students Will Learn in Future Grades

In Grade 6, students will learn about reform movements, including

▸ Ida B. Wells: campaign against lynching
▸ Booker T. Washington: Tuskegee Institute, Atlanta Exposition Address
▸ W. E. B. DuBois and the founding of the NAACP

In Grade 8, students will learn about the civil rights movement.

II. The Civil War: Causes, Conflicts, Consequences

Text Resources

Vocabulary

Student/Teacher Vocabulary

abolitionist: a reformer who favored the ending—sometimes the immediate ending—of slavery (S)

agricultural: related to farming and the cultivation of plants and livestock for sale (S)

Appomattox Court House: the town in Virginia where Confederate forces surrendered, ending the Civil War (S)

Battle of Antietam Creek: decisive Civil War battle that resulted in a victory for the Union and the issuance of the Emancipation Proclamation by President Lincoln (S)

Battle of Gettysburg: a major battle that was a turning point in the Civil War; Confederate forces attempting to invade the North were turned back by the Union Army (S)

Black Codes: laws created by Southern legislation in an attempt to reimpose some of the restrictions of slavery (S)

carpetbagger: a disparaging nickname given by ex-Confederates to Northerners who came south during Reconstruction (S)

Confederacy: the nation formed by eleven southern U.S. states that seceded from the Union in 1860 and 1861 (S)

***Dred Scott* decision:** the 1854 decision by the Supreme Court that declared that slaves were property, not citizens, and that the Missouri Compromise was unconstitutional (S)

Emancipation Proclamation: the declaration issued by President Lincoln in 1863 that proclaimed freedom for all slaves in those states or parts of states still under the control of the Confederacy (S)

Fifteenth Amendment: known as the suffrage amendment; gave African-American males the right to vote (S)

54th Massachusetts Regiment: one of the most notable of the African-American military units (S)

First Battle of Bull Run: first battle of the Civil War, fought along Bull Run Creek near Manassas Junction, Virginia (S)

Fort Sumter: a federal military base in Charleston Harbor, South Carolina; the site of the first shots fired in the Civil War (S)

"40 acres and a mule": a term used after the Civil War to describe some former slaves' expectation that they would receive 40 acres and a mule (S)

Fourteenth Amendment: amendment that prohibits states from denying any citizen "life, liberty, or property, without due process of law" and equal protection under the law; a portion of the amendment is known as the equal protection clause (S)

Freedmen's Bureau: a division of U.S. Department of War; established to look after the welfare of freed slaves. Agents of the bureau provided food for the former slaves, helped them find housing and employment, and established schools for African-American children and adults. (S)

Gettysburg Address: the address by Abraham Lincoln at the dedication of a national cemetery on the site of the Battle of Gettysburg (S)

Harper's Ferry: a town in northern Virginia (now northeast West Virginia) that was the scene of John Brown's rebellion and brief seizure of the U.S. arsenal in 1859 (S)

impeachment: a charge against a person in public office for misconduct; a guilty verdict could result in the person being removed from office (S)

Vocabulary continued

industrial: relating to industry, or the manufacture of goods and services for sale (S)

Ku Klux Klan: a secret society advocating white supremacy (S)

The Liberator: an abolitionist newspaper published by William Lloyd Garrison, an influential white abolitionist (S)

Mason-Dixon Line: a line established in the 1760s to settle a border dispute between Pennsylvania and Maryland; considered the dividing line between free and slave states up to the Civil War (S)

Missouri Compromise: an agreement in which Missouri entered the Union as a slave state, while Maine entered as a free state (S)

USS *Monitor*: a Union ironclad ship involved in battle with the Confederate ship CSS *Virginia* (S)

popular sovereignty: a doctrine which held that people had the right to determine for themselves by voting if they wanted to extend slavery to their territory (S)

Radical Republicans: a group of Congressional Republicans who believed that the South should be reconstructed after the Civil War and wanted to guarantee the rights of freed slaves (S)

rebels: the nickname given to members of the Confederacy by members of the Union during the Civil War (S)

Reconstruction: the period immediately following the Civil War; also, the procedures by which the states that had seceded were reorganized and reincorporated into the Union (S)

scalawags: a disparaging nickname given by ex-Confederates to the Southerners who sympathized with the Northerners after the Civil War (S)

secede: to formally withdraw from an organization, association, or federation (S)

Second Inaugural Address: a speech by President Lincoln upon his inauguration for a second term as president; in the speech he spoke of what should happen to make the Union whole again (S)

Thirteenth Amendment: the amendment that outlawed slavery in the United States (S)

Uncle Tom's Cabin: the novel by Harriet Beecher Stowe that brought home to thousands of Americans the terrors and brutality of slavery (S)

Union: a name used to refer to the states that did not secede during the Civil War (S)

vigilante justice: a lawless and brutal means through which white supremacy groups enforced their beliefs that African Americans are inferior to whites (S)

CSS *Virginia*: a Confederate ship, previously known as USS *Merrimack*, involved in battle with the Union Ship USS *Monitor* (S)

Yankees: a nickname given to members of the Union by members of the Confederacy during the Civil War (S)

Domain Vocabulary

Pre-civil war and associated words:
abolition, slavery, antislavery, proslavery, enslaved, bondsman, servitude, abolish, justify, controversy, debate, racism, brutality, plantation, planter, farm, cotton, rice, tobacco, indigo, agriculture, slaveholder, master, overseer, slaver, cruel, whip, flog, chattel, property, African-American, negro, field hand, house slave, slave quarters, slave auction, liberate, emancipate, insurrection, river, Canada, "downriver," three-fifths clause, free state, slave state, balance, fugitive, runaway, spirituals, Exodus, Moses, Promised Land, bondage,

Materials

Instructional Masters 34–36, 82–84

Slave Rebellions, p. 272

The United States of America and the Confederate States of America, p. 279

The Civil War, 1861–1865, p. 281

Venn Diagram, pp. 280, 281

Time Line, p. 287

T-Chart, p. 288

a picture of a Southern plantation and a picture of a bustling Northern town, p. 274

wall map or overhead of a map of United States, p. 274

ruler p. 274

poster board, pp. 276, 293

colored markers or paints, pp. 276, 293

pictures of the *Monitor* and the *Virginia*, p. 282

journals, p. 285

examples of original sources from this section, such as the 13th, 14th, or 15th amendments of the Constitution or Lincoln's speeches, p. 293

Vocabulary continued

escape, slave catcher, dogs, scent, moss, tree, star, publish, Quakers, freedom, conductors, stations, stops, safe houses, compromise, unconstitutional, justice, scout, spy, rebellion, weapons, arsenal, fort, militia, plot, seize, fanatic, capital, conspiracy, troops, trial, hanging, balance of power, capture, vote, frontier, poverty, log cabin, attorney, legislator, honesty, nominate, Republican, Democrat, secession, states' rights, election, independence

Civil War and associated words:
open fire, shell, shelling, bombard, surrender, firing, president, gentleman, border state, advantage, disadvantage, natural resource, rail system, mills, factories, navy, sailor, ship, blockade, army, soldier, troops, artillery, cavalry, infantry, ammunition, regiment, officer, private, colonel, general, brigadier, lieutenant, captain, commander, cannon, cannonballs, rifle, musket, gunner, cemetery, immigrant, boundary, refuse, camp, encamp, besiege, capture, rout, battlefield, salute, obey, morale, ambush, bloody, gunfire, fort, flank, outflank, brave, bravery, heroism, wound, wounded, deserter, bayonet, capture, military, outnumbered, enlist, West Point, hero, traitor, Yank, Reb, federal, civilian, nurse, advance, march, attack, counterattack, invade, defend, retreat, battle, win, lose, draw, defeat, charge, split, cut off, burn, destroy, demoralize, infrastructure, supplies, reinforcements, ironclad, warship, victory, reelect, inauguration, declare, decree, symbolic, passage, ratify, speech, white flag, terms, tyrant, play, shoot, assassination, freemen

Reconstruction and associated words:
ruined, decimated, reunite, rebuild, punish, forgive, blame, economy, debt, creditor, inflation, loyalty, Constitution, amendment, suffrage, radical, harsh, lenient, plan, veto, districts, civil rights, order, martial law, restrictions, override, impeach, wrongdoing, corruption, acquit, work, wages, vote, voting, amnesty, readmit, freedman, unreconstructed, terror, beating, Klansman, cross burning, racist, supremacy, postbellum, forbid, slave code, curfew, lawful, arrest, fine, unemployed, victim, abduct, hanging, lynching, troops, withdrawal, end

Cross-curricular Connections

Language Arts

Fiction and Drama

Poetry

- "Battle Hymn of the Republic" by Julia Ward Howe
- "O Captain! My Captain" by Walt Whitman (assassination of Lincoln)
- "Barbara Freitchie" ("Stonewall" Jackson)

Stories

- *Narrative of the Life of Frederick Douglass* (Frederick Douglass)

Speeches

- Gettysburg Address (Abraham Lincoln)

Visual Arts

American Art: Nineteenth-Century United States

- Mathew Brady's photographs of the Civil War
- "The Shaw Memorial" by Augustus Saint-Gaudens

Music

American Musical Traditions (Spirituals)

Songs

- "Battle Hymn of the Republic"
- "Shenandoah"

At a Glance

The most important ideas for you are:

- A series of compromises over several decades attempted to avert open confrontation over slavery between the North and South.

- Sectional tension over slavery increased as the United States acquired more territory in the mid-1800s and abolitionists and other opponents of slavery became more outspoken.

- Both sides expected the Civil War to be short and each expected to win easily.

- From the time of the first military engagement until fall 1864, the war went so badly for the Union that some Northerners wanted to negotiate peace.

- When Lincoln issued the Emancipation Proclamation, he effectively changed the focus of the fight from merely preserving the Union to preserving the Union while also ending slavery.

- Bull Run, Antietam, and Gettysburg were key battles in the war.

- Robert E. Lee was the most important general for the South, and Ulysses S. Grant was the most important general for the North.

- Sherman's march to the sea effectively cut the South in half.

- The Union forces won major battles each time Confederate forces invaded the North.

- Lee surrendered to Grant at Appomattox.

- Lincoln's assassination shortly after the surrender led to conflicts about Reconstruction.

- Andrew Johnson and Radical Republicans in Congress clashed over who would oversee the reconstruction of the South; Johnson lost.

- A political compromise ended Reconstruction.

What Teachers Need to Know

A. Toward the Civil War

Abolitionists

There had been calls for the abolition of slavery since before there had been a United States. The first formal abolitionist organization was formed in 1787 when a group of free African Americans met in Philadelphia and founded the Free African Society to work for the end of slavery.

Although the U.S. Constitution ended the foreign slave trade in 1808, the inter- and intrastate slave trade continued, and by the 1830s, slavery had become entrenched in the Southern states. As the practice of slavery grew, ordinary people (many of them slaves or former slaves) actively opposed it, giving voice to what became known as the abolitionist movement.

Being an abolitionist—especially an outspoken activist—was dangerous. Those who supported slavery often used violence to try to silence critics. They burned the homes and offices of abolitionists, ran abolitionists out of town, and even murdered some.

Frederick Douglass

Among the most notable abolitionists was Frederick Douglass. Douglass was an escaped slave who wrote an autobiography describing his life as a slave and who later published the abolitionist newspaper *North Star*. Born on a plantation in Maryland, he was sold to a new owner and sent to Baltimore. While there, the wife of the owner began teaching him how to read but had to stop when her husband discovered what she was doing and forbade her from teaching Douglass any more. Douglass was very disappointed that his reading instruction stopped, but he felt fortunate to discover the value of reading by listening to his owner's arguments against teaching him. Douglass, now determined to gain these skills, continued to learn to read and write the letters of the alphabet by asking neighborhood boys to help him and sometimes by tricking children into teaching him. At 21, while working in a Baltimore shipyard, he was able to pass himself off as a sailor and get a job on a ship. He landed in New Bedford, Massachusetts. An articulate and powerful writer and speaker, by 1845 Douglass was an important figure in the antislavery movement, writing and lecturing about the inhumanity of slavery. His autobiography, *Narrative of the Life of Frederick Douglass*, was published in London, and he traveled there to speak out against slavery in the British Empire. (56)

Douglass was not alone on the abolitionists' lecture circuit; those who joined him included Sojourner Truth, a former slave, and Harriet Tubman, a former slave and conductor on the Underground Railroad. Students learned about both of these women in earlier grades.

William Lloyd Garrison

Influential white abolitionists included William Lloyd Garrison, who published *The Liberator*, another abolitionist newspaper. Garrison had begun the paper in 1831 in Boston, a center of the antislavery movement. Garrison's aim was the immediate end to slavery—without compensating any slaveholder for the loss of his so-called property.

Garrison actually advocated that the North should secede from the South. When people pointed out that slavery was protected by the Constitution, Garrison said that any document that supported slavery ought to be burned, even the Constitution. In 1854 he actually did burn a copy of the Constitution, calling out "So perish all compromises with tyranny!" Garrison's extreme views led to disagreements between him and others, including Frederick Douglass. But Garrison was unapologetic. He wrote:

> To those who find fault with his harsh language he makes reply: I will be as harsh as truth, and as uncompromising as justice. On this subject, I do not wish to think, or to speak, or write, with moderation. No! no! Tell a man whose house is on fire to give a moderate alarm; tell him to moderately rescue his wife from the hands of the ravisher; tell the mother to gradually extricate her babe from the fire into which it has fallen; – but urge me not to use moderation in a cause like the present. I am

Teaching Idea

In addition to Frederick Douglass, there are many interesting people associated with the antislavery movement. You may wish to have students do research in print and online sources to find out about other prominent abolitionists such as David Walker, Charlotte Forten, Angelina and Sarah Grimké, and F. E. W. Harper.

Cross-curricular Teaching Idea

The *Narrative of the Life of Frederick Douglass* is included in the Language Arts section for this grade. It would make sense to teach this work while you are studying the pre-Civil War era.

in earnest – I will not equivocate – I will not excuse – I will not retreat a single inch – AND I WILL BE HEARD.

Garrison's attacks on slavery made him unpopular in the South. The state of Georgia offered a reward for his arrest and conviction, and he received numerous death threats. Even many in the North did not approve of his views. On one occasion a Boston mob looped a rope around his neck, as if threatening to hang him, and paraded him through the streets.

After the emancipation of the slaves, Garrison continued to work for reform in areas such as temperance and women's rights.

Slave Life

The first Africans to be enslaved in the Americas in the early 1500s were brought by the Spanish to the Caribbean to work on farms and in mines. The first Africans in the English colonies on the mainland arrived at Jamestown not long after 1607. The status of these first Africans is believed to have been indentured servants—people who contracted to work for a certain period of time and then were released to work for themselves. The status of Africans changed gradually over the years, and by the 1680s the term of service had changed to lifelong enslavement. By then, it was difficult to find enough workers to farm the large tobacco plantations that white colonists were starting in Jamestown, and captured Africans seemed to promise a steady supply of labor.

In the 1700s, importing Africans as slaves for the Southern colonies became big business for white merchants and sea captains. The climate and terrain of New England were not suitable for large plantation-style farms. Slavery, therefore, did not become the basis for the economy in New England, although there were some slaves in those colonies. New York, for example, had the most slaves of any colony north of Maryland, with over 10,000 slaves, almost 20% of the total population, in the mid-1700s. Most of these slaves lived in New York City. Slavery was less important in the Middle Colonies as well. There, most farms were small and tilled by families, although there were slaves on both farms and in cities, where they worked in houses and as skilled artisans and craftworkers.

The situation was quite different in the South where there were many farms that ranged in size from small, with simple homes, to large, elaborate plantations. While most Southerners did not own any slaves at all, the vast majority who owned small farms had fewer than 20 slaves. Only a few farms were large enough to be considered plantations with crops—tobacco, indigo, and later, cotton—that required large numbers of workers. Most plantations had anywhere from 50 to 200 slaves. The plantation system, which the Spanish and Portuguese had developed on islands in the Atlantic, and which had also been established in British colonies in the Caribbean, was adopted to address Southern colonists' need for workers on these large farms.

The owners of the plantations lived in large, well-furnished houses separate from their slaves. The latter lived in the slave quarters, a cluster of small cabins—shacks, really—with a few sticks of furniture, straw for mattresses, a cooking pot, and little else. The slaves often worked in the fields from sunup to sundown.

Slaves had little time to themselves to care for their families or tend their own gardens to supplement the food rations they were given by their owners. Enslaved Africans were not paid for their work, so they could not buy extra food, clothes, or other necessities. Everything they had was given to them by their owners.

Cross-curricular
Teaching Idea
Teach the spirituals listed under "American Musical Traditions" in the *Sequence* while studying about slavery and slave life.

Teaching Idea

Students learned about slave life in earlier grades. This section delves into how slaves reacted to their inhumane conditions. Review with students what they know or remember about slave life. Make sure they understand that slavery has existed in many civilizations and was not a uniquely American phenomenon. Make sure they also understand the distinctive race-based nature of American slavery. Although there were some free blacks and some white indentured servants, the vast majority of slaves in the United States were black, and the slave system was maintained by and for the benefit of a white elite. Ask students how they might feel if they had been slaves. What might they have done about their situations? Use this as a lead-in to the discussion of slave uprisings.

Teaching Idea

Use Instructional Master 34a–34b, *Slave Rebellions*, when discussing each uprising.

Use Instructional Masters 34a–34b.

However, in some areas of the South in particular, slaves were able to establish a trade network to gain cash and goods in exchange for their personal crops and craft goods.

Slaves could not leave the plantation without permission, and by the early 1800s laws were established that prohibited slaves from learning to read and write. About the only thing they could do that their owners did not interfere in was go to church—as long as it was a Christian service. Slave owners discouraged the practice of religions that slaves had known in Africa, but slaves did retain some aspects of their African culture in their religious practice. Slaves also embraced biblical stories about freedom, particularly the story of Moses leading the Israelites out of slavery in Egypt.

Slave Rebellions

Enslaved African Americans found many ways to resist slavery. They broke tools, lost or misplaced them, worked slowly, and on occasion burned down a slaveholder's property. Many slaves also attempted to escape from their owners, and others staged rebellions.

As early as 1658, African slaves joined with Native American slaves in Hartford, Connecticut, to burn the homes of their owners. Five years later, African slaves and European indentured servants were caught as they attempted a rebellion. Each time a slave uprising took place or a planned uprising was exposed by a spy, new, tougher slave codes were passed. Among the regulations might be the banning of meetings of more than two slaves at a time and the adoption of slave curfews. A curfew was the time by which all slaves had to be on their plantation or, if an urban slave, at his or her owner's house.

There are four slave uprisings that stand out, however, for the number of enslaved people involved and the havoc they created in their areas.

Stono Uprising

- September 9, 1739
- Along the Stono River near Charleston, South Carolina
- Under the leadership of a man named Jemmy, 20 slaves stole weapons from an arsenal and set out for a fort near St. Augustine in Spanish Florida to join a group of slaves who had escaped from South Carolina and Georgia plantations. The men killed people and burned plantations as they went. They were eventually caught and killed by South Carolina militia.

Gabriel Prosser Conspiracy

- August 30, 1800
- Henrico County, Virginia
- Gabriel Prosser and about 1,000 armed slaves marched on Richmond to seize the state capital and kill all whites except Quakers, Methodists, and French. Roads were impassable because of a huge thunderstorm on the night prearranged for the march; in addition, the conspiracy was revealed by two slaves and 600 troops were sent to disperse the rebels; Prosser and 34 others were tried and hanged.

Denmark Vesey Conspiracy

- May 1822

- Charleston, South Carolina

- Denmark Vesey, a former slave who had bought his freedom, and an unknown number of slaves and free blacks plotted to seize Charleston.

- Plot revealed by informant; Vesey and 34 others executed

Nat Turner Rebellion

- August 21 to late October, 1831

- Southampton County, Virginia

- Nat Turner and seven others were joined by slaves as they went from plantation to plantation, gathering a force of about 60 people in all. Through a vision, Turner became convinced he was to kill whites who enslaved African Americans; for two months he and his men moved around the area, freeing slaves and killing plantation owners, as well as their wives and children. They killed about 60 people.

- Turner was captured and hanged, and there was a terrible backlash. Many slaves and free Africans who had nothing to do with the rebellion were beaten and murdered by vindictive white mobs. The Virginia legislature actually considered abolishing slavery but decided instead to impose restrictive new laws to keep slaves under control.

Industrial North versus Agricultural South

The Civil War, or the War Between the States as it was known in the South, arose out of social, political, and economic differences between the Northern states, where slavery had gradually been abandoned, and the Southern states, where slavery had become both an economic system and a way of life—even though most white Southerners did not own slaves.

In reality, there were very few large plantations in the South and many small farms. The large plantations had anywhere from 20 to 200 slaves and raised tobacco or cotton. The crop depended on whether the plantation was located in Virginia, Kentucky, Tennessee, and North Carolina, where tobacco was the chief crop, or in the Deep South, where cotton was king. Small farmers typically raised their own food and a small cash crop like tobacco or cotton; usually, they owned few, if any, slaves. There were few wealthy small farmers. However, the rich planter with a large plantation worked by hundreds of slaves became the ideal to which many poor Southern whites aspired. This ideal took hold in their imaginations and explains why so many poor Southerners were willing to fight for an institution from which they did not directly benefit. Southern intellectuals developed certain arguments to justify the continued use of human beings as slaves. One argument said that slavery was essential to the Southern economy, which was based on the cultivation of cotton, a very labor-intensive crop. These same white Southerners pointed to the abuse of workers in Northern mills and factories and claimed that slavery was actually preferable to working in such a mill. Slavery, they said, ensured that slaves had food, clothing, and shelter, regardless of whether they were healthy and able to work or too ill or too old to work. Some Southerners made religious arguments and claimed that certain Bible passages seemed to sanction slavery. Another argument used was the racist argument that black people were inherently inferior to whites and needed to be taken care of, like small children.

Teaching Idea

The information about slave rebellions is set up using the journalistic format of when, where, who, what, and how, or the outcome. The "why" in each case was to escape and/or end slavery.

Explain that news reporters answer these questions about an event as they write their articles. Then have students imagine they are reporters. They are to choose one of the uprisings and write a news report about it answering the "5 W's and the how." Talk with students about whether they are covering "the story" as a modern reporter might cover it, or as a 19th-century newspaper reporter might have covered it. How might the coverage differ if the paper reporting the story was a Northern abolitionist paper? A Southern proslavery paper?

Teaching Idea

Discuss with students the ethical dilemmas posed by a slave rebellion. Students should see the inherent violence in the tyranny of slavery and discuss the general abuse of slaves. Is it permissible to use violence to resist an unjust institution or law? Make sure students understand that the active, violent rebellions described here go one step beyond the civil disobedience practiced by Thoreau during the Mexican-American War (see p. 254).

II. The Civil War: Causes, Conflicts, Consequences

Teaching Idea

Show the class a picture of a Southern plantation and a picture of a bustling Northern town. Have them write a description comparing and contrasting the scenes. How was the South different from the North? What type of people would live in each place? Have students share their thoughts aloud.

Teaching Idea

Students may enjoy learning a little more about the factories and mills of the North, such as the mills in Lowell, Massachusetts. Web searches for "Lowell mills" and related terms will turn up interesting descriptions and primary source documents.

Teaching Idea

Explain that the "Deep South" was the name given to the states of Georgia, Alabama, Louisiana, and Mississippi. This is the area where the phrase "King Cotton" originated, meaning that cotton was the chief crop and drove not only the economy but also social and political patterns. You could also review the importance of Eli Whitney and his invention of the cotton gin in making cotton a profitable crop.

Teaching Idea

On a wall map of the United States (or an overhead of a map of the United States such as Instructional Master 35, *The United States of America and the Confederate States of America*), place a ruler straight across from the southern border of Pennsylvania into the Atlantic Ocean. Ask what students notice about New Jersey. (The southern portion is actually below the Mason-Dixon Line.)

The North by this time had become the center of American industry. Northern farms were small for the most part and had little potential for great wealth; they could not grow cotton or tobacco or other large-scale cash crops. However, certain parts of the North were well suited to the development of industry, and the Industrial Revolution that had begun in Great Britain had quickly taken hold in the Northeast. The North had reserves of coal to produce power for factory machines, and it had an abundance of people to run the machines. Men and women were moving away from farms, and thousands of immigrants were entering the country every year. By 1860, almost all the industry in the nation, most of the banking and financial centers, most of the rail lines, and most of the coal, iron, and gold reserves in the nation were located in the North.

Mason-Dixon Line

The Mason-Dixon Line was established in the 1760s to settle a boundary dispute between the Penns of Pennsylvania and the Calverts of Maryland. These families were descendants of the original proprietors of the two colonies. The line became the boundary between western Pennsylvania and Virginia in 1779. The Mason-Dixon Line, along with the Ohio River further to the west, was considered the dividing line between free and slave states up to the Civil War.

The line was named after the two English men who conducted the land survey, Charles Mason and Jeremiah Dixon.

Slavery in Territories and New States

Beginning with the Declaration of Independence, when the delegates to the Second Continental Congress removed references to King George's part in the slave trade in order to mollify Southern slaveholders, the United States made compromises over slavery. These compromises did not solve the controversy over slavery, but only prolonged it and raised the stakes each time a new compromise was reached. Among the compromises were the following:

• In 1787, the Constitutional Convention compromised and agreed to count every five enslaved Africans and African Americans as three free men for purposes of determining representation in the House. This is known as the three-fifths clause. The new Constitution did mandate an end to the importation of slaves by 1808 but did not abolish slavery or end the internal slave trade.

• In 1820, the Missouri Compromise enabled Missouri to enter the Union as a slave state as long as Maine entered as a free state. In addition, it declared that any new states created from the Louisiana Purchase above the 36th parallel would be free. The Missouri Compromise ensured the balance between free and slave states, but set the stage for future conflicts over the entrance of new states into the Union.

• The Compromise of 1850 kept the balance of slave and free states by allowing California to enter the Union as a free state and the Utah and New Mexico territories to decide for themselves through popular sovereignty if they would enter as free or slave states. Congress also abolished the slave trade in the District of Columbia and passed a Fugitive Slave Act, which required the return of escaped slaves to their owners.

• The Kansas-Nebraska Act of 1854 took up the issue of slavery in lands above the 36th parallel and overturned the Missouri Compromise. The new law allowed voters in the two territories to determine for themselves whether the states should be free or slave. Nebraskans voted to become a free state, but bloody fighting broke out in Kansas as pro- and antislavery factions fought each other for power and the outcome of the vote. The fighting was so widespread that Kansas became known as "Bleeding Kansas."

Dred Scott Decision

Dred Scott was a slave whose owner, an army doctor, had taken him from Missouri (a slave state) to live in Illinois (a free state). After two years in Illinois, Scott and his owner moved to the Wisconsin Territory to live for two years before returning to Missouri. According to the terms of the Missouri Compromise of 1820, slavery was banned in the Wisconsin Territory. When Scott's owner took him back to Missouri, Scott sued for his freedom on the grounds that he had lived in a territory where slavery was expressly forbidden and had therefore ceased to be a slave. The lawsuit, known formally as *Dred Scott v. Sandford*, made its way to the Supreme Court.

In 1857, seven of the nine justices ruled in favor of Scott's owner. (It should be noted that five of the seven were Southerners.) Chief Justice Roger B. Taney of Maryland wrote the majority ruling. First, Taney wrote, Scott had no right to sue because he was not a citizen. The Constitution did not recognize slaves as citizens. Even if he could have sued, that Scott had once lived in a free state was of no consequence; as a slave, he was the property of his owner. As such, Congress could not deprive an owner of his property. Third, and of the greatest consequence to the nation, the justices ruled that the Missouri Compromise was unconstitutional. The justices found that the right to own a slave was a property right and Congress under the Fifth Amendment could not interfere with a person's property rights.

As a result of the decision in the *Dred Scott* case, slavery was allowed in all new territories and, therefore, new states. The South was jubilant; the North was outraged.

Uncle Tom's Cabin

Sometimes, books can change history. *Uncle Tom's Cabin,* by Harriet Beecher Stowe, is one book that did. Stowe was born into a New England family that was opposed to slavery. She moved to Cincinnati, Ohio, as a young woman, where she saw firsthand what slavery was like. She was moved in particular by a scene she witnessed in which a slave husband and wife were separated and sold to different buyers.

Stowe became a writer. Around that time, the Fugitive Slave Act was passed in 1850, outraging abolitionists. Stowe's sister-in-law challenged her to "write something that would make this whole nation feel what an accursed thing slavery is!" In 1852, Stowe published *Uncle Tom's Cabin,* which sold more than 300,000 copies in its first year and more than 3 million copies before the outbreak of the Civil War. The novel describes the life of the gentle slave Tom who eventually dies at the hands of a brutal overseer named Simon Legree. Although somewhat melodramatic, the novel brought home to thousands of Americans the terrors and brutality of slavery. The novel greatly boosted the antislavery movement and created alarm in the South where Southerners felt maligned by the brutal depiction of slavery. Abraham Lincoln paid tribute to the impact of the novel when, during the Civil War, he characterized Stowe as "the little woman who caused this big war."

During the years since Stowe's novel was published, the term "Uncle Tom" has taken on a life of its own. In the book, Tom accepts the great suffering that comes upon him, in part because of his strong Christian faith. Among African Americans today, the phrase "Uncle Tom" is sometimes used to attack a black person who is perceived as being too accepting of an inferior position in society and too eager to please whites in positions of authority.

John Brown and Harpers Ferry

Today, John Brown would be called an extremist. He believed in the use of force to further his cause—in this case, the end of slavery. And he was willing to die to achieve his goals.

Brown claimed he was a devout Christian and believed slavery was a terrible sin. He met and corresponded with the abolitionist Frederick Douglass. Douglass described Brown as a true friend of the black man: "Though a white gentleman, he is in sympathy a black man, and as deeply interested in our cause, as though his own soul had been pierced with the iron of slavery."

In the 1850s, Brown participated in the bloodshed in the Kansas Territory over the fight to ban slavery. He and his sons were involved in the killing of five settlers who held proslavery beliefs. Brown soon returned to the East and hatched a plot to establish a nation of free African Americans in Virginia. His plan was to take over the federal arsenal at Harpers Ferry, a town in northern Virginia (now northeast West Virginia), and call for slaves to stage an uprising with the weapons from the arsenal.

On the night of October 16, 1859, with about 18 supporters, including five Africans, Brown raided the arsenal at Harpers Ferry and took hostages, but no additional slaves joined him and the anticipated uprising never happened.

However, news of his seizure of the arsenal spread and soon the building was surrounded by a company of Marines that included a contingent led by Robert E. Lee. By morning, the raiders were either dead or captured. Brown was tried for treason and hanged.

While Southerners mostly felt Brown got what he deserved, his death stirred more antislavery feeling in the North. Brown's conviction of his righteousness caused many Northerners to see him as a martyr. In his speech to the court at his trial, Brown said:

> I believe that to have interfered as I have done, as I have always freely admitted I have done, in behalf of his despised poor, I did not wrong but right. Now, if it is deemed necessary that I should forfeit my life for the furtherance of the ends of justice, and mingle my blood further with the blood of my children and with the blood of millions in this slave country whose rights are disregarded by wicked, cruel, and unjust enactments, I say let it be done. (57)

John Brown

Brown also issued an ominous warning about the future: "I, John Brown, am now quite certain that the crimes of this guilty land will never be purged away but with blood."

Brown was remembered in a popular song of the era, "John Brown's Body." A version current during the Civil War went like this:

John Brown's body lies a-moulderin' in the grave,

John Brown's body lies a-moulderin' in the grave,

John Brown's body lies a-moulderin' in the grave,

But his soul goes marching on.

CHORUS:

Glory! Glory! Hallelujah!

Glory! Glory! Hallelujah!

Glory! Glory! Hallelujah!

His soul goes marching on.

He captured Harper's Ferry with his nineteen men so true;

He frightened old Virginia 'til she trembled through and through.

They hanged him for a traitor, themselves the traitor's crew,

His soul goes marching on.

During the Civil War, Julia Ward Howe took the melody from "John Brown's Body" and wrote new lyrics to create her "Battle Hymn of the Republic."

Abraham Lincoln

Abraham Lincoln was born in poverty on the Kentucky frontier and grew up in a log cabin that his father had built. There was no mandatory public education at the time. Children were expected to work in the family business, whether it was a farm or a store. As a boy, Lincoln taught himself to read and write by fire-light at the end of his long workdays on the farm. He read the Bible, *Aesop's Fables, Robinson Crusoe,* and (later) Shakespeare's plays. Lincoln grew to be tall (as an adult he stood about 6'4") and strong. He was a rail splitter and a champion wrestler in his youth.

At age 22, he moved to New Salem, Illinois, also a frontier area. He taught himself the law while supporting himself by working in a store, as a surveyor, and as postmaster. In time, Lincoln became a much-respected attorney in the state. He also earned a reputation for honesty: he was known as "honest Abe."

Lincoln was first elected to public office in 1834 when his district sent him to the state legislature. He served there until 1841. Lincoln ran successfully for the U.S. House of Representatives in 1846, but was turned out of office in the next election because of his opposition to the Mexican-American War. Although defeated in his Senate bid in 1858 against Democrat Stephen A. Douglas, Lincoln's oratorical skills and his opposition to the expansion of slavery won him attention from the new national Republican Party, which nominated him for president in 1860.

In his speech to the Illinois State Republican Convention, which nominated him to face Douglas in the 1858 Senate race, Lincoln said:

A house divided against itself cannot stand. I believe this [federal] government cannot endure permanently half slave and half free. I do not expect the Union to be dissolved; I do not expect the house to fall; but I do expect it will cease to be divided. It will become all one thing, or all the other. (59)

Lincoln-Douglas Debates

During the campaign for a United States Senate seat from Illinois, Lincoln and the incumbent Stephen A. Douglas met in seven debates. One of the most important issues they debated was whether Douglas supported the *Dred Scott* decision or whether he supported the doctrine of popular sovereignty. The latter meant that the people had the right to determine for themselves by voting if they wanted to extend slavery to their territory. This had been the basis of the Compromise of 1850 and the Kansas-Nebraska Act. Douglas had proposed this solution himself in the Kansas-Nebraska Act.

By asking Douglas this question, Lincoln placed him on the spot. Douglas still supported the idea of popular sovereignty, but the Democratic Party, many of whose supporters were Southerners, had come out in favor of the decision in the *Dred Scott* case. Douglas formulated what has become known as the Freeport Doctrine. He hedged and said that if the people so wished, a territorial legislature could discourage slavery by failing to pass laws that recognized the right of slave ownership. Thus, acting on the will of the people, the legislature would subvert the decision in *Dred Scott*. (58)

Douglas succeeded in the short term. He won reelection to the Senate. But Southerners called the Freeport Doctrine "the Freeport Heresy." The long-term future of a Democratic Party that could satisfy both Northerners and Southerners was in question. The debates also catapulted Lincoln to national fame and set the stage for his presidential run in 1860.

Election of Lincoln as President

The issue of slavery divided the nation in the election of 1860. Lincoln was selected as the candidate of the new Republican Party, which pledged to stop the spread of slavery. He ran against three opponents. Neither the Republican Party nor Lincoln himself promised to abolish slavery. The Democratic Party had split into Northern and Southern factions and supported two different candidates. A fourth party, the Constitutional Party, campaigned on a platform to uphold the Union and the Constitution. The vote was largely split along regional lines. Even though Lincoln captured less than 40 percent of the popular vote, the sectional split of the country allowed him to receive more than enough electoral votes to win the election.

Southern States Secede

South Carolina had threatened to secede if Lincoln was elected. In November 1860, a few weeks after the election, South Carolina made good on its word and passed an ordinance of secession in December of 1860. By spring 1861, eleven states had joined to form the Confederate States of America. (The western part of Virginia refused to follow the rest of the state out of the Union, and in 1863 it joined the Union as the state of West Virginia.) The eleven states of the Confederacy were Alabama, Arkansas, Florida, Georgia, Louisiana, Mississippi, North Carolina, South Carolina, Tennessee, Texas, and Virginia.

The Union included the states of the Northeast and Midwest and the western territories: Connecticut, Illinois, Indiana, Iowa, Kansas, Maine, Massachusetts, Minnesota, New Hampshire, New Jersey, New York, Ohio, Pennsylvania, Rhode Island, Vermont, and Wisconsin; Indian Territory; and the Colorado, Dakota, Nebraska, New Mexico, Nevada, Utah, and Washington Territories.

Delaware, Kentucky, Maryland, Missouri, and West Virginia were known as border states. They remained loyal to the Union even though they were slaveholding states.

B. The Civil War

When the Southern states seceded in 1861, Lincoln declared their act unconstitutional. He threatened to use force if necessary to protect United States property, enforce United States laws, and return the Southern states to the Union. Preservation of the Union continued to be his primary goal throughout the war. (Later he added emancipation of slaves.) Lincoln viewed the war as a rebellion by the Southern states.

Southerners took a very different view. They saw the creation of the Confederacy in 1861 as exactly analogous to the American Revolution of 1776. In both cases, a set of states seceded from a larger government and exercised their right to declare independence. The Southerners believed they were resisting the tyranny of Lincoln and the North, and preserving states' rights, just as the colonies had resisted the tyranny of King George III and the British Parliament in 1776.

Fort Sumter

Lincoln's resolve was soon tested. Fort Sumter was a federal military base in Charleston Harbor, South Carolina. When South Carolina seceded, the fort's commander, Major Robert Anderson, was ordered to surrender the fort. He refused and the Confederates cut off the fort by firing on a ship sent with additional troops and provisions. Lincoln ordered another supply ship be sent to resupply the fort. The Confederates again opened fire on the ship and the fort and eventually forced Anderson to surrender. Lincoln declared that the shelling of Fort Sumter was an act of rebellion against the U.S. government. The Civil War had begun.

An eyewitness to the events was Mary Chesnut, whose husband was the negotiator for the Confederate side. The following is her account of the evening of April 12, 1861, when the war began:

> I do not pretend to go to sleep. How can I? If Anderson does not accept terms at four, the orders are, he shall be fired upon. I count four, St. Michael's bells chime out and I begin to hope. At half-past four the heavy booming of a cannon. I sprang out of bed, and on my knees prostrate I prayed as I never prayed before.

> . . . I knew my husband was rowing about in a boat somewhere in that dark bay, and that the shells were roofing it over, bursting toward the fort. If Anderson was obstinate, Colonel Chesnut was to order the fort on one side to open fire. Certainly fire had begun. The regular roar of the cannon, there it was. And who could tell what each volley accomplished of death and destruction?

Teaching Idea

Create an overhead from Instructional Master 35, *The United States of America and the Confederate States of America*, and duplicate one copy per student. Have students do research to label the states that remained in the Union, those that seceded, and those known as "border states." After students have completed their own maps, use the overhead to repeat the activity as a whole group exercise.

Alternatively, read aloud the state names to students and have them decide in which category they fit and where they are on the map. Have students label the states and complete the map key. This is also a good exercise in forming mental maps of the Union and the Confederacy.

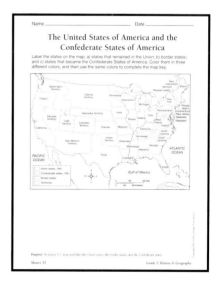

Use Instructional Master 35.

Cross-curricular Teaching Idea

Go to the Internet and find examples of Civil War music and photographs to help the facts of the Civil War come to life. (See *More Resources*.) In addition, "Battle Hymn of the Republic" from the Grade 5 music *Sequence* lends itself well to this unit of study. You may also wish to review songs from Grade 2, including "Follow the Drinking Gourd" and "When Johnny Comes Marching Home."

Teaching Idea

Use Instructional Master 83, *Venn Diagram*, with students to compare and contrast the Union and the Confederacy.

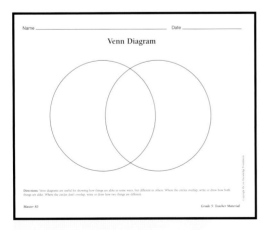

Name _____ Date _____

Venn Diagram

Directions: Venn diagrams are useful for showing how things are alike in some ways, but different in others. Where the circles overlap, write or draw how both things are alike. Where the circles don't overlap, write or draw how two things are different.

Master 83   Grade 5: Teacher Material

Use Instructional Master 83.

Jefferson Davis

Even before the first guns had been fired, representatives for the secessionist states had met in Montgomery, Alabama in February 1861 and formed the Confederate States of America (CSA). It was eventually decided that Richmond, Virginia, would be the capital. Jefferson Davis was elected president.

Davis had represented Mississippi for several terms in the United States Senate and had been the secretary of war under Franklin Pierce. When Mississippi seceded, he had resigned from the Senate. It was his direct order that launched the attack against Fort Sumter.

Davis was a West Point graduate who had gained national fame as a hero in the Mexican-American War. His prestige was an asset to the Confederacy. But as a leader, Davis was high-handed and divisive, feuding throughout the war with Southern governors over military, fiscal, and political affairs.

The Union and Confederacy

The Union had many advantages over the Confederacy. The North had a larger population than the South. The Union also had an industrial economy, whereas the Confederacy had an economy based on agriculture. The Union had most of the natural resources, like coal, iron, and gold, and also a well-developed rail system. Most of the financial centers were in the North, which made borrowing money to fight the war difficult for the South. The Union had a small navy, but the Confederacy had to resort to using private ships because it had no naval vessels. While some believed the South had the better officers, the North had twice as many soldiers.

Yankees and Rebels, Blue and Gray

"Yankee" and "Rebel" are nicknames that the Northerners and Southerners gave each other shortly after the start of the Civil War. The Northerners were called "Yankees" and the Southerners, "Rebels." Sometimes these nicknames were shortened even further to "Yanks" and "Rebs."

At the beginning of the war, each soldier wore whatever uniform he had from his state's militia, so soldiers were wearing uniforms that didn't match. For example, some uniforms were blue or gray, while others were black or red. As the war dragged on, that changed. The soldiers of the Union Army wore blue uniforms and the soldiers of the Confederate Army wore gray. Today, that's how many people remember the two sides—the North wore blue, and the South wore gray.

First Battle of Bull Run

Neither side—North or South—had a realistic view of what it would take to fight the war in terms of time and resources. Each side thought the war would be short and easily won. The outcome of the first engagement of the war greatly bolstered Confederate confidence and jolted the Union into a realization of how hard it would be to defeat the South.

The first battle was fought in July along Bull Run Creek near Manassas Junction, Virginia, just 20 miles from Washington. Many civilians rode out from Washington thinking to spend an interesting afternoon watching the Confederates get a good thrashing. Some even brought picnics to eat while they watched the confrontation. Instead, the Confederates fought tenaciously and ulti-

mately overwhelmed the Union forces, who retreated willy-nilly back to Washington. It was anything but an orderly retreat as the raw troops sprinted back to safety, leaving the civilians to hurry back as best they could. Fortunately for the Union, the surprised and elated Confederates, who were also untrained, disorganized, and exhausted, were not in a position to press their advantage and pursue the fleeing soldiers.

The Battle of Bull Run is also known as the Battle of Manassas. The Confederates often named battles according to nearby towns. The Union troops often referred to them according to nearby geographical features, like rivers and creeks.

 ## Ulysses S. Grant and Robert E. Lee

Although the Union had the advantage because of the size of its army, both sides had excellent leadership. The start of the war went badly for the Union, both on the western front along the Mississippi and in the east. Union generals in the east had opportunities to strike at the Confederate army, but the generals often hesitated. Lincoln became particularly upset with General George McClellan. After McClellan hesitated to attack several times, Lincoln relieved him of his command.

The first victories for the Union came in 1862 under General Ulysses S. Grant. Grant captured Fort Donelson in Tennessee. When the Confederates in the fort inquired about terms of surrender, Grant replied that no terms but "unconditional surrender" would be accepted. People began to refer to him as "Unconditional Surrender" Grant.

In the same year, Admiral Farragut scored a major victory for the Union when his squadron of ships defeated the Confederate defenses in New Orleans and took the city. This victory secured the lower Mississippi River for the Union and was a major blow to the Confederacy. Another turning point in the war occurred in 1863, when Grant defeated the Confederate troops in Vicksburg, Mississippi. Grant's victories there and in Tennessee gave the Union control of the Mississippi River, split the Confederacy, and effectively ended the war in the west. Union control of the Mississippi River cut off the flow of much-needed supplies and reinforcements from Texas and Arkansas to the rest of the Confederacy. In 1864, Lincoln consolidated command of all the Union armies under Grant.

Grant moved to the eastern front and began a long, punishing attack on the Confederate Army of Northern Virginia, a force led by Robert E. Lee. By April 1865 Grant's men had worn down and defeated the Confederates. Grant accepted Lee's surrender in the little town of Appomattox Court House, Virginia. Grant went on to become the eighteenth president of the United States in 1872.

Grant and Lee are often compared, as they had lived two strikingly different lives prior to becoming rival generals in the last years of the Civil War. Grant was born on a small Ohio farm, whereas Robert E. Lee was born on a large plantation in northern Virginia. (Lee's plantation was seized by Union forces and became the site of Arlington National Cemetery.) Grant was a mediocre student at the U.S. Military Academy at West Point and had an undistinguished military career before the Civil War. He had failed in business and was rumored to be a heavy drinker. Lee also graduated from West Point but was at the top of his class. He

Teaching Idea

Create an overhead of Instructional Master 36, *The Civil War, 1861–1865*, to help students understand where some important battles took place.

Point out that many battles were also fought in the Mississippi Valley. There, General Grant earned his reputation as a tough fighter; this is why Lincoln chose him to command the entire Union Army.

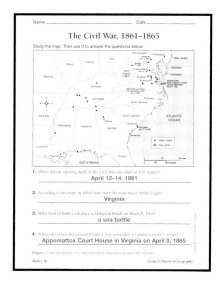

Use Instructional Master 36.

Teaching Idea

Use Instructional Master 83, *Venn Diagram*, with students to compare and contrast Grant and Lee.

had a highly successful military career. He served with distinction in the Mexican-American War, was superintendent of West Point for a period in the 1850s, and was in command of the troops at Harpers Ferry that captured John Brown.

At the beginning of the war, Lincoln asked Lee to assume command of the Union forces, but Lee refused out of loyalty to his home state, Virginia. He instead accepted a command in the Confederate army. Lee scored a number of important victories, but faced with dwindling resources, his army was unable to withstand the larger, better-equipped Union army.

General Stonewall Jackson

General Thomas Jackson was given the nickname "Stonewall" because of his actions in the First Battle of Bull Run. During the battle, a Confederate soldier noted that Jackson and his men were "standing like a stone wall." The nickname stuck: for the rest of the war Jackson was known as "Stonewall Jackson."

Considered by many to be General Lee's most able general, Jackson orchestrated Confederate victories in the Shenandoah Valley campaign. He led his forces brilliantly at the Second Battle of Bull Run, and at the battles at Antietam and Fredericksburg. He was wounded in 1863 during the battle of Chancellorsville and died eight days later.

Battle of the USS *Monitor* and the CSS *Virginia*

The Union had a great advantage in the naval war and used its advantage to blockade Confederate ports. But in March 1862, the Confederacy struck back. The CSS *Virginia* steamed out of its port at Hampton Roads, Virginia, and attacked and sunk several Union ships. The *Virginia* was no ordinary ship. It had originally been a Union ship called the *Merrimack,* but the Confederates had plated its sides with iron. Now Union cannonballs bounced harmlessly off its sides.

The Confederates hoped to sail their ironclad ship up the Potomac, sinking Union ships, and possibly even shelling Washington, D.C. The Confederate hopes were short lived, however. The next day a Union ironclad ship called the *Monitor* steamed out to meet the *Virginia.* The *Monitor* had a distinctive design, with a small, rotating turret on top of the main body of the ship. The battle between the two ironclads was a draw, as neither ship was able to harm its adversary. But the Southern threat had been countered, and the era of wooden warships had come to a sudden end. (60)

Battle of Antietam Creek

In September 1862, Lee started to move his troops north toward Washington. In a fierce battle, Lee's forces were driven back at Antietam Creek, Maryland, by a Union army under General George B. McClellan.

Antietam was the bloodiest single-day battle of the war—almost 23,000 men were killed or wounded. More than 8,000 died in a single cornfield. When the day began, the field was full of tall, ripe corn. By the end of the day, cannons, rifles, and charging troops had decimated the corn so that "every stalk of corn in the northern and greater part of the field was cut as closely as could have been done with a knife."

Cross-curricular Teaching Idea

"Stonewall" Jackson is described in "Barbara Freitchie," listed in the poetry selections for this grade. You may wish to teach this poem in conjunction with your discussion of Jackson and the battles in the east.

battle between the Monitor *and the* Virginia

Teaching Idea

Share pictures of the *Monitor* and the *Virginia* with students. Point out the *Monitor*'s design, with the rotating gun turret. Note that the idea of a rotating gun turret would be important in the development of both ships and tanks.

Although the Union forces suffered higher casualties, Antietam was considered a victory for the Union because it halted Lee's invasion of the North. The war in the east had been going badly for the Union up to this point, and this victory was important for several reasons. First, it saved Washington, D.C., the capital of the Union. Second, it kept Great Britain and France from recognizing or assisting the Confederacy, and, third, it provided the opportunity that Lincoln had been looking for to issue the Emancipation Proclamation. He had not wanted to issue it while the Union had been losing and have it appear an act of desperation.

▶ The Emancipation Proclamation

During the early years of the Civil War, Lincoln was eager to issue an Emancipation Proclamation freeing slaves, but he hesitated to do so for fear that his action might harm the Union cause. Emancipating the slaves was an idea opposed by many Northern workers who feared competition from newly freed—and jobless—slaves. Lincoln was also concerned that the border states would leave the Union if slave owners there were deprived of their slaves. On the plus side, however, Lincoln believed that an Emancipation Proclamation would win over Europeans who had already abolished slavery, especially the British. It was important to Lincoln that the British not trade with the South. If the South could sell its cotton to the British, it could gain money and buy supplies to help with the war effort.

Abolitionists had lobbied for the end of slavery since the early 1800s, and as the war continued, more Northerners began to see the need for emancipation. In addition to humanitarian concerns, they were moved by a desire to punish the South for secession.

Finally, in September 1862, after Lee was stopped at Antietam, Lincoln issued the Emancipation Proclamation. The proclamation was to go into effect on January 1, 1863. There is often confusion about what the Emancipation Proclamation actually did. The document promised to free all slaves in those states or parts of states still under the control of the Confederacy on January 1, 1863. Since the Union did not control most areas of the Confederacy, there was no practical effect on the lives of slaves in those states. The document also did not affect slaves in border states or in states or areas of states under the control of the Union army. (Lincoln did not want to drive the border states into an alliance with the South.) In those areas, slaves were still enslaved. Therefore, the Emancipation Proclamation actually set no one free.

The importance of the Emancipation Proclamation was symbolic. It changed and broadened the goals of the Civil War. What had begun as merely a struggle to preserve the Union was now also a quest to free the slaves. In 1865, enslaved African Americans were finally freed through passage and ratification of the Thirteenth Amendment (see p. 290).

Gettysburg

In the summer of 1863, Lee invaded the North again, for what would be the last time. Lee began to move northward in June in the hope that a successful invasion of the North would convince the Union to end the war. He reached Pennsylvania by July 1 and met Union forces under General George S. Meade near the town of Gettysburg.

Teaching Idea

Use the Internet to locate photographs and other images of key battles as well as soldiers' recollections. These can be found using search engines.

Teaching Idea

You will want to use an overhead of Instructional Master 36, *The Civil War 1861–1865*, frequently in this section to help students visualize where the action was taking place. You may also want to keep a graphic organizer or time line that lists names, dates, and outcomes of key events.

Teaching Idea

Have the class brainstorm a list of the symbols of America, as these have been studied in Core Knowledge schools since Kindergarten. Expand the list to include symbolic documents such as the Emancipation Proclamation. Continue adding to the list throughout the school year.

The battle raged for three days. Union forces had a tactical advantage in occupying higher ground. Lee, in an effort to dislodge the Union forces, sent General George Pickett and an army of 15,000 men across a mile of open ground. Pickett's charge was a disaster. Union gunners cut down the courageous charging Confederates. Pickett's division alone lost almost 3,000 men. After the charge, when Lee ordered Pickett to reassemble his division to prepare for a possible Union counterattack, Pickett replied, "General Lee, I have no division now." Lee regretted the decision to order Pickett's charge for the rest of his life. After three days of attacks and counterattacks, with the Confederates making no headway, Lee turned his army southward on July 4. The Confederates had lost about a quarter of their forces in the field; about an equal number of Union soldiers were killed, amounting to more than 20,000 dead on each side.

The Battle of Gettysburg was the turning point of the war in the east. Lee never again threatened Union territory. Unfortunately for the Union side, Meade failed to pursue the gravely weakened Lee. Through his military genius, Lee was able to continue the war for two more years and inflict terrible casualties on Union forces. This was despite being badly outnumbered and suffering from critical shortages of materials.

Gettysburg Address

Later that year, on November 19, 1863, President Lincoln journeyed to Gettysburg to dedicate a national cemetery for the war dead buried there. Lincoln was not the featured speaker. Edward Everett, a well-known orator of the time, spoke for more than two hours. Lincoln's speech lasted about two minutes. In the speech, Lincoln spoke of his grief for the dead, the principles for which they died, and the need to maintain those principles. Among its famous lines are the following:

Four score [twenty years times four] and seven years ago our fathers brought forth on this continent, a new nation, conceived in liberty, and dedicated to the proposition that all men are created equal. . . .

It is for us the living, rather, to be dedicated here to the unfinished work which they who fought here have thus far so nobly advanced. It is rather for us to be here dedicated to the great task remaining before us—that from these honored dead we take increased devotion to that cause for which they gave the last full measure of devotion—that we here highly resolve that these dead shall not have died in vain—that this nation, under God, shall have a new birth of freedom—and that government of the people, by the people, for the people, shall not perish from the earth.

Although Lincoln's speech is now recognized as one of the most important in American history, it received little attention that day and in subsequent news reports. Everett, however, recognized its significance. In a note to Lincoln he wrote, "I should be glad if I could flatter myself that I came as near to the central idea of the occasion, in two hours, as you did in two minutes."

54th Massachusetts Regiment

When the Civil War began, there was no thought given to enlisting free African Americans. However, after a string of Union losses in 1862, Congress passed a law allowing African Americans—freemen and escaped slaves—to become soldiers in the Union army. By war's end, 186,000 African Americans had

Teaching Idea

Work with students to paraphrase the Gettysburg Address to help them understand the depth of Lincoln's beliefs and his feelings toward his country and the soldiers who died for it. Read the first part of the Declaration of Independence to students, and point out how Lincoln carefully linked his brief speech to the central tenets of that document. Invite students to read parts of the speech out loud and possibly even memorize brief passages. (See "Speeches," on pp. 83–90 and Text Resource 31.)

served in 150 all-black regiments and 30,000 more African Americans had seen service in the navy. The first African-American regiment was led by Thomas Wentworth Higginson. All told, about 13 percent of the Union army was composed of men of color. This number does not count the African-American men and women who served as cooks, laborers, and carpenters for the army. Some 37,000 African-American soldiers died for the Union during the war. Twenty African-American soldiers were awarded the Congressional Medal of Honor, and between 75 and 100 were commissioned as officers.

One of the most notable of the African-American regiments was the 54th Massachusetts under Colonel Robert Gould Shaw, a white officer. White officers commanded units of African-American soldiers. The 54th led the assault on Fort Wagner at Charleston, South Carolina in 1863. According to one account,

> Advancing through the cover of darkness along a narrow strip of beach, they [the 54th] were raked by ferocious rifle and cannon fire from the fort. They pressed on and scaled the parapets in desperate hand-to-hand fighting. White regiments arrived to bolster the Union force, but the men were too few and the enemy fire too fierce.

The assault failed, and 300 soldiers of the 54th died in the attack. Four soldiers were awarded medals for their bravery, including the first Congressional Medal of Honor awarded to an African American.

Sherman's March to the Sea

As Lee had taken the war to the North, Union General William Tecumseh Sherman took the war to the heart of the South. Sherman (named after the famous Native American warrior) was promoted often to replace Grant as Grant took on greater responsibilities for the Union army. In 1864, Sherman and his force of 60,000 soldiers invaded Georgia from Tennessee, captured and burned Atlanta, marched to the coast where they captured Savannah, and then wheeled north. They engaged the Confederate army of General Joseph E. Johnston in a running fight until Johnston surrendered near Durham, North Carolina. Sherman's campaign effectively split the Confederacy.

Sherman's advance through Georgia to Savannah is known as Sherman's "march to the sea." In an effort to destroy supply sources for the Confederate army, Sherman had his army destroy everything in its path. The men tore up railroads, burned houses, and destroyed crops. This was one of the first instances of the kind of war sometimes called "total war," in which an effort is made not only to destroy the enemy's armies, but to destroy the infrastructure and morale of the society at large. Sherman's attacks demoralized the civilian population and inspired much hatred among Southerners.

The End of the War

▶ Reelection of Lincoln

Sherman's successful invasion of the South greatly improved Lincoln's chances for reelection as president in 1864. The Democrats had chosen as their

Mathew Brady took many photographs
of the Civil War. Have students do
research about Brady in print or online
sources. Note that many of Brady's photographs are graphic representations of
war and may not be appropriate for students. You may wish to select several
images beforehand and allow students
to choose from those. (You may also
use Art Resource 19, Brady's photograph *Battery at Attention*. See the discussion in the Visual Arts section
"American Art: Nineteenth-Century
United States" on pp. 350–360.) Have
students choose a photograph and copy
it from a book or download it from the
Internet. Then have students write a
paragraph describing what they see in
the photo. Encourage them to describe
as many details as possible.

When Grant's troops heard that Lee had
surrendered, they began to cheer. Grant
is said to have silenced them with the
words, "The war is over. The rebels are
our countrymen again."

Ask students whether they think that
Lincoln would have agreed with Grant.
What about the Radical Republicans?
Ask students to provide evidence to
support their opinions.

*Lee surrendering to Grant
at Appomattox*

286   *Grade 5 Handbook*

candidate General George B. McClellan, whom Lincoln had fired. McClellan cam-
paigned on a platform to end the war through peace negotiations. Many
Northerners were weary of a war that the Union seemed unable to win, and
McClellan was willing to allow slavery to continue if the war could be ended.

However, once Sherman had split the Confederacy, and other Union generals, including Grant, began destroying Confederate forces, it began to appear to
be only a matter of time until the South capitulated. Although the election was
close, Lincoln was reelected. With ultimate victory in mind, Lincoln spoke of
what should happen to make the Union whole again. In his Second Inaugural
Address, he said

> With malice toward none, with charity for all, with firmness in the right as
> God gives us to see the right, let us strive on to finish the work we are in,
> to bind up the nation's wounds, to care for him who shall have borne the
> battle and for his widow and orphan, to do all which may achieve and cher-
> ish a just and lasting peace among ourselves and with all nations. (61)

Fall of Richmond to Union Forces

Richmond was the capital of the Confederacy. In the first two years of the war,
battles had been fought to take the city, but the Union forces had always failed due
to the timidity of McClellan and other Union generals. In May 1864, Grant—now
in command of the Union army—moved aggressively to take Richmond. He
pushed Lee and his army ahead of him and by August, Lee had been forced back
to Petersburg, not far from Richmond. For nine months, Grant besieged Lee's army
at Petersburg. Finally, on April 2, 1865, when Grant launched an attack, Lee abandoned Petersburg. Later that day, the Union army marched into Richmond.

Surrender at Appomattox

Even though Jefferson Davis had left Richmond with what was left of the
Confederate government, once the capital had fallen it was only a matter of days
until the Confederacy collapsed. Lee and his army had retreated across Virginia to
the little town of Appomattox Court House, Virginia, where they were trapped by
Union forces. On April 9, Lee said to his fellow officers, "There is nothing left for
me but to go and see General Grant, and I had rather die a thousand deaths." Lee
raised the white flag, Grant and Lee agreed to surrender terms, and the Civil War
was effectively over.

The surrender terms were generous:

• Officers and enlisted men could go free.

• Rifles had to be surrendered, but officers could keep their side arms (pis-
tols and swords).

• Any soldier who had a horse could keep it, as it would be needed for
plowing.

Assassination of Lincoln

On April 14, 1865, less than a week after Lee's surrender, Lincoln and his wife
Mary attended a comedy at Ford's Theater in Washington. When Lincoln arrived,
the play was already in progress. One of the actors saw the presidential party
arrive and began to applaud. The audience looked up to the balcony where the
Lincolns were seated, saw the president, and took up the clapping. The orchestra
struck up "Hail to the Chief," and Lincoln acknowledged the salute. The president took his seat in the state box and the play continued.

During the third act, a young actor named John Wilkes Booth gained entrance to the presidential box with a note. He waited until laughter filled the theater and then moved toward the President. He drew out a pistol, shot the President once, and leaped from the balcony down to the stage. Breaking his leg as he fell, John shouted, "Sic semper tyrannis," meaning "Thus, always to tyrants," the motto of Virginia. Booth was a Confederate supporter and saw Lincoln as a tyrant who had not allowed the South to secede from the Union. He had planned his assassination of Lincoln as a counterblow to Lee's surrender days earlier. In the screaming and confusion that followed, Booth got away. He was later traced to a barn in Virginia. What happened next is unclear. He either shot himself or was shot by his pursuers. **62**

Lincoln died of his wounds the following morning, April 15, 1865.

C. Reconstruction

The South in Ruins

When Lee surrendered to Grant, the South lay in ruins. Unlike the North, where there was little direct impact from battles except in central Pennsylvania (Gettysburg) and Maryland (Antietam), little of the South had escaped the fighting. Grant had battered first the Mississippi Valley and then Virginia, and Sherman had marched right through the heart of the Confederacy, destroying everything in his path.

While 360,000 Union soldiers had died, 250,000 Confederate soldiers had been killed. Although smaller in number, a larger percentage of the Southern male population was lost. In all, one in 20 Southern whites had been either killed or wounded. Four million slaves who had been freed had nowhere to go and no way to make a living. Parts of the South had been devastated by Union troops in an effort to keep supplies from reaching the Confederate army. Homes, farms, shops, and factories had been set afire, and farm tools and machinery had been destroyed. Two-thirds of the railroad system in the South had been torn up, or the tracks had been bent so that they were useless. The economy was in no better shape than the landscape. Banks failed and creditors went without payment as the collapse of the government made Confederate money worthless.

Struggle for Control of the South

Before his death, Lincoln had drafted a policy toward the South that was lenient and very much in the spirit of his second inaugural: "with malice towards none." His policy had an eye towards "binding up the nation's wounds" rather than pouring salt in them. Among its provisions were that the states were to be readmitted to the Union after ten percent of the male citizens took an oath of loyalty to the United States. New state constitutions that banned slavery had to be written, and the states had to agree to establish schools to educate African Americans. Arkansas, Louisiana, Tennessee, and Virginia accepted Lincoln's provisions and established new governments.

A group in Congress known as "Radical Republicans" disagreed with Lincoln's plan. While the Radical Republicans did not control the Republican party, and the members of the group sometimes disagreed with one another, the group was able to influence Congress and succeeded in pushing through many of

Teaching Idea

Have students create a time line of Lincoln's life, from the beginning through to his assassination. Name other presidents that have been assassinated.

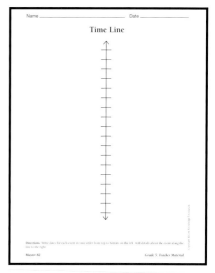

Use Instructional Master 82.

Cross-curricular Teaching Idea

Walt Whitman's poem "O Captain, My Captain," was written shortly after the assassination of Lincoln and pays tribute to Lincoln. You may wish to teach the poem after discussing the assassination.

II. The Civil War: Causes, Conflicts, Consequences

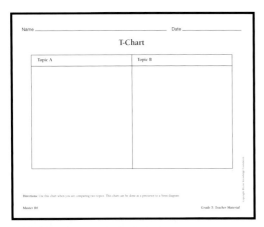

Name _____   Date _____
T-Chart

Topic A	Topic B

Directions: Use this chart when you are comparing two topics. This chart can be done as a precursor to a Venn diagram.

Master 84   Grade 5: Teacher Material

Use Instructional Master 84.

their policies. The Radical Republicans believed stronger measures were necessary to reconstruct the South and to protect the rights of the freed slaves. They wanted to make sure that former Confederates, almost all of whom were Democrats, would not, or could not, be elected to public office. When the four states noted above elected new members of Congress, the Radical Republicans blocked them from taking their seats.

After Lincoln's assassination, Vice President Andrew Johnson automatically became president. He had been a senator from Tennessee at the time of secession and had not followed his state out of the Union; he remained in the Senate. The Republicans had chosen him as Lincoln's running mate in 1864. Johnson, a self-made man, was a supporter of states' rights and the small farmer. For the most part, he agreed with Lincoln's plan for Reconstruction. To get around Congress's opposition, he took the opportunity of the Congressional recess later in 1865 to put it into effect. By the time Congress reconvened in December 1865, only Texas had not complied with the Presidential Reconstruction, as Johnson's plan was called.

The Radical Republicans refused the new members of Congress their seats. Congress formed a commission that found that Presidential Reconstruction was ineffective. The antagonism between the president and Congress worsened in 1866 over the Civil Rights Act and the 14th Amendment (see pp. 290–291). Johnson believed the first was unconstitutional because it violated the rights of states. He disapproved of the constitutional amendment for the same reason.

The election of 1866 hinged on whether the people supported Johnson's view or the Radical Republicans' view of the proposed 14th Amendment. The people supported the Radical Republicans, and they gained enough new members in Congress to override any veto from Johnson. The Radical Republicans were now in charge of Reconstruction. They threw out all the new state governments because many of the Southern constitutions had "black codes" that limited the rights of freed slaves. The exception was Tennessee, because it was the only state that had ratified the 14th Amendment.

The South was divided into five military districts and the army was dispatched to enforce the civil rights of former slaves and maintain order; in other words, the South was placed under martial law. The states had to write new constitutions guaranteeing African-American males the vote and had to ratify the 14th Amendment. Restrictions were placed on former Confederate officials.

Impeachment

The power struggle between President Johnson and the Radical Republicans continued. In 1867, Congress passed the Tenure of Office Act in an attempt to limit the president's power. According to this bill, a president would need the approval of the Senate before firing any federal official whom the Senate had confirmed. Included among these federal officeholders were the cabinet members. Johnson vetoed the bill, but Congress overrode his veto. In violation of the new law, Johnson fired a cabinet member who had sided with the Radical Republicans against him.

The House impeached Johnson; that is, it found enough evidence of wrongdoing to hand him over to the Senate for a trial. (The House's responsibility in this

situation is similar to that of a grand jury, which hands up an indictment and turns someone over for trial.) The Senate heard the evidence and voted three times, but each time Johnson's opponents could not muster enough votes. They were always one vote short. In the end the Senate acquitted Johnson, but his effectiveness in office was over.

Southern Governments

Radical Reconstruction banned former Confederate officers and officials from holding office again. Who then filled the new Southern legislatures and other government positions?

Who	Why
Northerners who moved South: federal government officials, teachers, missionaries Some, volunteers and employees of the Freedmen's Bureau	Supported Radical Republican policies Some, to profit economically from Reconstruction
Southerners who supported Radical Republican policies	Abolitionists, were against secession, and/or remained loyal to the Union during the war Some, to profit economically from Reconstruction
Free-born and freed African Americans	Participate in their own governance

cartoon of President Johnson during his impeachment

The new governments of the South were Republican, and most government positions were filled by members of three groups: Northerners, Southerners who worked with the Northerners, or freed African Americans. The Northerners, who had often served in the Union army or were working for the Freedmen's Bureau (see p. 290), moved south to help with Reconstruction. The Southern officials were whites who supported the efforts of Reconstruction. Ex-Confederates disparagingly called the Northerners "carpetbaggers" and the Southerners who collaborated with them "scalawags." The nickname "carpetbagger" supposedly came from the carpetbags (19th-century suitcases) that Northerners carried with them. Southerners said the Northerners were there to exploit the Southerners and take their money. The term *scalawag* means "rascal" or "scoundrel." In many Southern states, freed African Americans also held government positions, which was both symbolic and literal proof that efforts to reconstruct the South were, at least by some appearances, working. However, many white Southerners resented the new leaders and their policies, and some of the new government officials, particularly the carpetbaggers, were corrupt. The turmoil of Reconstruction led to years of political conflict for the South.

Freedmen's Bureau

Freed African Americans faced a bleak future. They had no place to live, no education, no money to buy food, and no experience in bargaining for a job or dealing with the law. The only last names they had were the names of their former owners. Many rectified that quickly by taking the names of Americans they admired. Among those were Lincoln, Washington, and Jefferson.

In 1865, the Freedmen's Bureau was established by the Department of War to look after the welfare of freed slaves. Agents of the bureau provided food for former slaves and helped them find housing and employment. The bureau provided

Freedmen's Bureau school

Teaching Idea

Have students imagine they are freed slaves. Talk about what it must have been like to have nothing but the clothes on their backs and no information about how to find a job, food, a place to live, how to read, how to use money, and so on.

Have students draw up a list of things that they would need, including kinds of information. If students do not mention education, talk about why knowing how to read and write was important to former slaves.

Teaching Idea

Before teaching the 13th–15th Amendments to the Constitution, review the Constitution and the first 12 Amendments.

legal aid and negotiated contracts for freed slaves to make sure their pay and working conditions were fair. To provide medical care, the bureau founded hospitals. **63**

The bureau established schools to teach African-American children and adults how to read and write. Within five years, some 300,000 African Americans were in school. The Freedmen's Bureau also established black colleges.

As the Civil War ended, many freed slaves came to expect that they would be given "40 acres and a mule." This promise stemmed from several sources but ultimately was not honored. Toward the end of the Civil War, General Sherman issued a proclamation that all freed slaves should be granted 40-acre parcels of land. This land was formerly owned by whites but would be given to freed slaves in an attempt to help them establish a homestead and to compensate them for their work as slaves. The Union army also had a surplus of mules it did not need, so Sherman ordered that the mules be distributed to the freed families as well. President Johnson rescinded Sherman's order once he became president on the grounds that it was unconstitutional, and President Johnson had all confiscated land returned to its former white owners. The Freedmen's Bureau also issued an act stating that freed slaves should be given up to 40 acres of land, but it was not passed by Congress. President Johnson vetoed any attempt to give land to African Americans, most of whom felt they were entitled to this opportunity based on the burden of their labor as slaves.

13th, 14th, 15th Amendments to the Constitution

The 13th, 14th, and 15th Amendments are known as "the Reconstruction Amendments." These three amendments were passed in response to slavery and extended the rights of African Americans.

13th Amendment

- outlawed slavery
- was passed and ratified in 1865 by the required 27 states, including Southern states
- stated that "Neither slavery nor involuntary servitude, except as punishment for crime whereof the party shall have been duly convicted, shall exist within the United States, or any place subject to their jurisdiction."

14th Amendment

- was the civil rights amendment
- extended certain rights to African Americans and denied certain rights to white Southerners
- was passed and ratified by Northern states and Tennessee in 1868
- was opposed by Johnson because he believed it violated the rights of the states
- stated that "All persons born or naturalized in the United States, and subject to the jurisdiction thereof, are citizens of the United States and of the state wherein they reside. No state shall make or enforce any law which shall abridge the privileges or immunities of citizens of the United States; nor shall any state deprive any person of life, liberty, or property, without due process of law; nor deny to any person within its jurisdiction the equal protection of the laws."

- provided that (a) the number of representatives for a state in the House of Representatives would be reduced in proportion to the number of citizens who were denied their voting rights by the state; (b) no former Confederate officer could hold office unless Congress pardoned him; (c) debts of the Confederate government would not be repaid; (d) former slave owners could not sue for the loss of their property, that is, slaves

15th Amendment

- was the African-American suffrage amendment
- was passed and ratified in 1870
- was considered necessary when Southern states continued to deny African-American men the right to vote
- stated that "The right of citizens of the United States to vote shall not be denied or abridged by the United States or by any state on account of race, color, or previous condition of servitude."

Black Codes

In response to Northern efforts to aid former enslaved African Americans—such as the establishment of the Freedmen's Bureau and ratification of the 13th Amendment—Southern legislatures passed a series of black codes in 1865 and 1866. These laws were similar to the old slave codes, which limited severely the activities of African Americans, that Southern towns, cities, and legislatures had passed in the 1700s and in the early 1800s.

In an attempt to reimpose some of the restrictions of slavery, the black codes typically required that former slaves be indoors by a curfew and have a permit to travel. In addition, a white person had to be present if former slaves wished to meet in a group. New regulations forbade former slaves from serving on juries, voting, owning land, and holding public office. Most troubling were those provisions that made it lawful to arrest and fine unemployed African Americans. An employer could pay the fine and then force the unemployed former slave to work in order to repay the fine. This amounted to a new form of servitude.

The Ku Klux Klan and "Vigilante Justice"

As early as 1866, groups of white Southerners began a campaign of terror against African Americans and their white supporters. Angry whites, many of whom were Confederate veterans returned from the war, organized into secret societies, such as the Knights of the White Camelia and the White League. Perhaps the most notorious, and certainly the largest, was the Ku Klux Klan.

Klan members dressed in white robes and masks and rode out under cover of night. Their aim was to keep former slaves and white Republicans from voting or holding public office. The Klan planted and burned crude wooden crosses in front of the homes and churches of people they wanted to frighten. When this failed to scare off African Americans, the Klan beat their victims. The violence escalated until "vigilante justice" took over in the late 1800s; several hundred victims of the Klan were abducted and hung in the South every year. (64)

Ida B. Wells-Barnett, an African-American female journalist, mounted a campaign in 1892 to bring lynching to the attention of the general public. By 1899, the number of lynchings in the South had dropped to 180 a year. This was down from 235 when Wells-Barnett had published her report in 1895. However, this form of vigilante justice continued in the South for several generations.

End of Reconstruction: Compromise of 1877

By the mid-1870s, Americans were tired of Reconstruction. The most prominent Radical Republicans had died or been replaced in Congress. Other problems and concerns, such as the economy, increasing immigration, and industrialization, replaced Reconstruction. In addition, business interests wanted relations with the South normalized. There was a desire among Northern businessmen to invest in and develop the resources of the South, which had been difficult while the states were under martial law.

By the election of 1876, only three states—Louisiana, Florida, and South Carolina—retained Reconstruction governments. In the election for president that year, the Democrats nominated Samuel J. Tilden of New York. The Republicans chose Rutherford B. Hayes, the governor of Ohio. It appeared that Tilden had won until Republican leaders in Louisiana, Florida, and South Carolina challenged and discarded large numbers of votes cast for Tilden.

To end the confusion, Congress established a commission of eight Republicans and seven Democrats that included Supreme Court Justices, senators, and members of the House of Representatives. The commission worked out a compromise that is known as the "Compromise of 1877." The Democrats supported Hayes in exchange for the following:

• the withdrawal of federal troops from the South and the end of Reconstruction

• funding for construction of the Texas and Pacific Railroad

• the appointment of a Southerner to the president's cabinet

With the Compromise of 1877, Reconstruction was over.

The Big Idea in Review

Slavery, the Civil War, and Reconstruction occupied much of the United States' attention and energy in the mid-19th century.

Review

Below are some ideas for ongoing assessment and review activities. These are not meant to constitute a comprehensive list. Teachers may also refer to the *Pearson Learning/Core Knowledge History & Geography* series for additional information and teaching ideas.

• Because of the number of people and places named in this section, have students play "Who/What Am I?" or create crossword puzzles to review the material. Have students create puzzles with at least 12 clues and then exchange them. Or have students work in teams of two to create five identifications. Then group two teams together and have them take turns asking the opposite team their identification questions.

• This section provides an opportunity for students to complete short research reports on Robert E. Lee, Ulysses S. Grant, Stonewall Jackson, Abraham Lincoln, and/or other important figures during the Civil War. Using the Language Arts section, provide the class with topics for short reports to write in formal style. Each day of a week, provide a mini-lesson on different aspects of report writing, such as correct paragraph form or bibliographies. Share these reports when completed.

• Have students explore primary sources for items mentioned in this section, such as the Constitution; the 13th, 14th, and 15th amendments; speeches; debates; and soldiers' letters. Ask the media specialist from your school to help find examples of these original sources and have the class read them. Have a class discussion on how to read and interpret primary sources. After studying the documents, have students write about reading these texts. How is it different from reading a textbook?

• At the end of the Civil War unit, give each student one piece of poster board. Tell the class that they may do anything that they want with their poster board, but it has to represent one aspect of the Civil War, and they have to include an element of writing with their project. Set a day to share the poster-board projects in class.

• Provide a list of important people from the Civil War for the class and have students choose one of the people from the list. Then, have students research that person's role during the Civil War. Students should write a brief description of the person on an index card from the first person point of view, as if they are that historical figure. Each student should read their description aloud and the class should guess who they are.

• Have students research the attitudes of people on both sides of the war. Use outside sources to discover how people felt about the war and why they felt that way. Have students present their findings in a paper where they write about either a person from the North or a person from the South. They must be able to present that person's argument and back it up with facts from the research.

• Write each date and event of the Civil War from the time line at the front of this section (pp. 264–265) on the top of an index card. Assign each student or pair of students a date and event. Students will be responsible for writing a short description of that event below the date and event name. Post these in order to form a time line of the Civil War on the wall outside the classroom.

• Choose one of the events of the 1850s that escalated the tensions between North and South over slavery. Have students write a paragraph describing the situation, the outcome, and its effect on anti- and proslavery feelings. Check that students use correct paragraph form for their writing. Share these aloud with the class.

• Invite students to write a letter to one of the figures they have learned about. In the letter they can comment on things they admire about the person, or ask questions about things they don't understand.

• Have students create a scrapbook from the perspective of someone during the Civil War. Students can choose to be a Union or Confederate soldier, a slave, a plantation owner, a politician, or anyone else they would like. The scrapbook pages should include illustrations to represent pictures of the person's life, along with captions describing each picture. Students can also create other items, such as letters, newspaper clippings, and other things that would be found in a typical scrapbook.

• You may also ask the following questions after completion of this unit of study.

1. Briefly identify: Harriet Beecher Stowe, John Brown, Ulysses S. Grant, Robert E. Lee, Stonewall Jackson, Jefferson Davis, John Wilkes Booth, Andrew Johnson.

   Harriet Beecher Stowe was the author of Uncle Tom's Cabin. *John Brown led a raid on Harpers Ferry to start a slave rebellion. Grant was the commander of Union forces. Lee was the commander of Confederate forces. Jackson was an able Confederate general. Davis was president of the Confederacy. Booth shot Lincoln. Johnson was the vice president who succeeded Lincoln and was impeached in the battle with Congress over Reconstruction.*

2. What did abolitionists want to abolish? Can you name any well-known abolitionists?

   Abolitionists wanted to abolish slavery. William Lloyd Garrison, Frederick Douglass, and Harriet Beecher Stowe were all abolitionists.

3. What event started the Civil War?

   The shelling of Fort Sumter marked the beginning of the war.

4. What happened during the first battle between the Union and the Confederacy?

   At the First Battle of Bull Run, the Confederates held firm and the Union soldiers retreated as best they could toward Washington.

5. While many battles went badly for the North, the Battle of Gettysburg was a Union victory. Why was this battle particularly important?

   General Robert E. Lee had hoped to take the war into Northern territory, win, and force the Union to ask for peace. The battle went on for three days. On the fourth, Lee, seeing no way to win, had to retreat South. He never took his army into the North again.

6. If the Emancipation Proclamation did not actually free any slaves, why was it considered important?

   The Emancipation Proclamation had a symbolic importance. It changed the focus of the war from merely preserving the Union to preserving the Union and ending slavery. It also helped prevent Great Britain from recognizing the South.

7. What role did William Tecumseh Sherman play in the Civil War?

   Sherman marched his Union army through Atlanta to the Atlantic Ocean, cutting the Confederacy in half and destroying its ability to contribute to the Confederate war effort.

8. Where and when did Lee surrender to Grant?

   Lee surrendered in 1865 in Appomattox Court House, Virginia.

9. What was the difference between President Andrew Johnson's policy for Reconstruction and the Radical Republicans' policy?

   President Johnson wanted to follow President Lincoln's plan for Reconstruction, which would allow states to reenter the Union after ten percent of males took a loyalty oath, new state constitutions banned slavery, and states agreed to establish schools to educate African Americans. Radical Republicans wanted to assure that former Confederate leaders could not be elected to public office, required states to write constitutions that ratified the 14th amendment and guaranteed African-American males the right to vote, and put restrictions on former Confederate officials.

More Resources

The titles listed below are offered as a representative sample of materials and not a complete list of everything that is available.

For students —

• *The Civil War,* edited by E. D. Hirsch, Jr. (Pearson Learning, 2002), a unit in the official *Pearson Learning/Core Knowledge History & Geography* series, is available as part of the bound book for Grade 5/Level 5 and also as a stand-alone module. A teacher's guide is also available. To order, call 1-800-321-3106.

• *Narrative of the Life of Frederick Douglass (Core Classics* abridged), by Frederick Douglass. (Core Knowledge Foundation, 1997).

• *American Voices from the Civil War,* by Susan Provost Beller (Benchmark Books, 2003). Uses primary source material. Hardcover, 104 pages, ISBN 0761412042. See also *Women & Families (Voices from the Civil War),* edited by Tom Head (Blackbirch Press, 2003). Library binding, 32 pages, ISBN 156711797X.

• *A Book of Americans,* by Rosemary and Stephen Vincent Benét (Henry Holt & Company, 1987). Contains poems on "Stonewall Jackson," "Abraham Lincoln," "Nancy Hanks," "Clara Barton," "Negro Spirituals" "Ulysses S. Grant," "Robert E. Lee," and "David Farragut." Paperback, 114 pages, ISBN 0805002979.

• *Bull Run,* by Paul Fleischman (HarperTropy, 1995). A historical novel for this age group. Paperback, 128 pages, ISBN 0064405885.

• *Children of the Emancipation: 1860s to 1890s,* by Wilma King (Carolrhoda Books, 2000). Note: Has a picture of one man's badly scarred back. Library binding, 48 pages, ISBN 1575053969.

• *A Confederate Girl: The Diary of Carrie Berry, 1864 (Diaries, Letters, and Memoirs),* edited by Suzanne Bunkers and Christy Steele (Blue Earth Books, 2000). A ten-year-old girl's diary during the Union attack on and occupation of Atlanta. Informative sidebars. Library binding, 32 pages, ISBN 0736803432.

• *Daily Life on a Southern Plantation,* by Paul Erickson (Puffin, 2000). Well illustrated with photos and drawings. Follows an imaginary family and their slaves through a typical day in 1853. Paperback, 48 pages, ISBN 140566686. See also *Life on a Plantation,* by Bobbie Kalman (Crabtree Publishing, 1997). Paperback, 32 pages, ISBN 0865054657.

• *50 American Heroes Every Kid Should Meet,* by Dennis Denenberg and Lorraine Roscoe (Lerrer Publications, 2005). Contains profiles of Frederick Douglass, Robert E. Lee, and Abraham Lincoln. Hardcover, 128 pages, ISBN 0761395482.

• *The Gettysburg Address,* by Abraham Lincoln and illustrated by Michael McCurdy (Houghton Mifflin, 1995). Striking woodcuts illustrate Lincoln's famous speech. Paperback, ISBN 0395883970.

• *Ironclads and Blockades in the Civil War,* by Douglas J. Savage (Chelsea House, 2000). Fascinating stories about the naval battles of the Civil War. Library binding, 64 pages, ISBN 0791054292.

• *John Brown's Raid on Harpers Ferry (Cornerstones of Freedom),* by Brendan January (Children's Press, 2000). Paperback, 32 pages, ISBN 0516270370. See also *Reconstruction,* by the same author.

• *Lincoln: A Photobiography,* by Russell Freedman (Clarion, 1989). Winner of the Newbery Award for excellence in children's literature. Paperback, 160 pages, ISBN 0395518482.

• *Nettie's Trip South,* by Ann Turner and illustrated by Ronald Himler (Aladdin Library, 1995). Young Nettie takes a trip from Albany to Richmond and sees many things she will never forget, including her first glimpse of slavery. Based on the diary of the author's great-grandmother. Paperback, 32 pages, ISBN 0689801173.

• *War, Terrible War: 1855–1865,* by Joy Hakim (Oxford University Press, 2002). Book 6 of the popular series *A History of Us.* Paperback, 160 pages, ISBN 0195153308. See also *Reconstruction and Reform,* in the same series.

More Resources continued

For teachers —

• *American Slavery As It Is: Testimony of a Thousand Witnesses,* edited by Theodore Dwight Weld (American Anti-Slavery Society, 1839). An incredible collection of contemporary reports on the practice of slavery in the United States prior to the Civil War. Available online through the "Documenting the American South" project of the University of North Carolina at Chapel Hill, http://docsouth.unc.edu/neh/weld/menu.html.

• *The Boys' War,* by Jim Murphy (Clarion, 1993). Honored by the Golden Kite Award committee for excellence in children's nonfiction. Contains some pictures of dead soldiers. Paperback, 128 pages, ISBN 0395664128.

• *The Civil War,* by Bruce Catton (Houghton Mifflin, 1988). A well-written overview by a respected historian and writer. Paperback, 382 pages, ISBN 0828103054.

• *Civil War (A Library of Congress Book),* by Martin W. Sandler (Harper Trophy, 2000). More than one hundred vintage posters, paintings, and photographs from the archives of the Library of Congress. Includes some gruesome battlefield scenes. Paperback, 96 pages, ISBN 0064462641.

• *The Civil War: A History in Documents,* by Rachel Seidman (Oxford University Press, 2001). Hardcover, 206 pages, ISBN 0195115589.

• *Escape from Slavery: The Boyhood of Frederick Douglass in His Own Words,* by Michael McCurdy (Knopf, 1994). Readable for some students, but the events are, not surprisingly, sometimes rough. Paperback, 80 pages, ISBN 0679846514.

• *The Illustrated Battle Cry of Freedom: The Civil War Era,* by James M. McPherson (Oxford, 2003). A very thorough and interesting reference. Hardcover, 804 pages, ISBN 0195159012.

• *Landmarks of the Civil War,* by Nina Silber (Oxford University Press, 2003). Hardcover, 144 pages, ISBN 0195129202. See also a companion website, Teaching with Historic Places at www.cr.nps.gov/nr/twhp, or phone 202-354-2213.

• *Slavery and the Coming of the Civil War, 1831–1861,* by Christopher and James Lincoln Collier (Marshall Cavendish, 2000). Library binding, 93 pages, ISBN 0761408177.

• *Uncle Tom's Cabin,* by Harriet Beecher Stowe (Bantam Classics, 1983). Paperback, 544 pages, ISBN 0553212184.

• Civil War Music can be found at www.civilwarmusic. net. The site includes lyrics, sheet music, digital song files, photographs, and more.

• Civil War Photographs from the Library of Congress, http://lcweb2.loc.gov/ammem/cwphtml/cwphome.html, contains more than a thousand photographs from the war, including many from the camera of Mathew Brady. Several show the brutality of war.

• The Valley of the Shadow: Two Communities in the American Civil War, www.iath.virginia.edu/vshadow2. Filled with primary source documentation comparing two counties—Augusta County in Virginia, and Franklin County, Pennsylvania—before, during, and after the Civil War. Winner of the first annual eLincoln Prize, and part of the Virginia Center for Digital History, University of Virginia. Also available as a book and/or CD-ROM from W.W. Norton.

III. Native Americans: Cultures and Conflicts

The Big Idea

Native American cultures were disrupted, displaced, and profoundly altered by the westward expansion and the government's policies in the 19th century.

Remember that each subject you study with students expands their vocabulary and introduces new terms, thus making them better listeners and readers. As you study historical people and events, use read alouds, independent reading, and discussions to build students' vocabularies.

The items below refer to content in Grade 5. Use time lines with students to help them sequence and relate events from different periods and groups.

1492	Estimated 5 million Native Americans in what is today the United States (minus Alaska)
1500s	Horses reintroduced into the Americas by the Spanish
1700s	Horses reach Plateau, Great Basin, and Plains native peoples
1824	Bureau of Indian Affairs established in War Department
1849	BIA moved to Department of Interior
1850s–1890	Plains Wars
1862	Homestead Act
1864	Sand Creek Massacre
1871	Indian Appropriation Act
1876	Battle of Little Big Horn

continued on next page

What Students Should Already Know

Students in Core Knowledge schools should be familiar with

Kindergarten

‣ Native American peoples, past and present

• representative peoples in all eight culture regions in what is today the United States (Pacific Northwest: Kwakiutl, Chinook; Plateau: Nez Perce; Great Basin: Shoshone, Ute; Southwest: Dine [Navajo], Hopi, Apache; Plains: Blackfoot, Comanche, Crow, Kiowa, Dakota, Cheyenne, Arapaho, Lakota [Sioux]; Northeast: Huron, Iroquois; Eastern Woodlands: Cherokee, Seminole, Delaware, Susquehanna, Mohican, Massachusett, Wampanoag, Powhatan)

Grade 1

‣ Earliest peoples

• hunters who historians believe either wandered over Beringia, a land bridge linking Asia and North America, or found a coastal route to North America

• the shift from hunting to farming in places

• the gradual development of towns and cities in places

Grade 2

‣ Sequoyah and the Cherokee alphabet

• forced removal to reservations and the Trail of Tears

• displacement of Native Americans by the railroad

• near extinction of buffalo and effect on Plains Native Americans

Grade 3

‣ Native Americans of the Southwest (Pueblos [Hopi, Zuni], Dine [Navajo], Apaches) and Eastern Woodlands, including woodland culture (wigwams, longhouses, farming, peace pipe, Shaman and Sachem) and major cultures (Cherokee Confederacy, Seminole, Powhatan, Delaware, Susquehanna, Mohican, Massachusett, Iroquois Confederacy)

Grade 4

‣ The French and Indian War, also known as the Seven Years' War and part of an ongoing struggle between Britain and France for control of colonies, including the French and British alliances with Native Americans

III. Native Americans: Cultures and Conflicts

continued from previous page

1880s	Near extermination of the Plains buffalo
1880s	Ghost Dance
1887	Dawes Act
1890	Wounded Knee Massacre; End of the Plains War

Text Resources

(65) *Battle of Little Big Horn*

Materials

Instructional Masters 37–39

Native American Culture Review, p. 302

Native American Culture Regions, p. 304

Native American Reservations, 1890, p. 307

sheet of brown construction paper, p. 303

crayons or colored markers, p. 303

stapler, p. 303

information from local universities about Native American speakers, p. 311

journals, p. 311

classroom library of Native American myth picture books, p. 311

materials to compile a class book, p. 311

What Students Need to Learn

Culture and Life

- ▸ Great Basin and Plateau (for example, Shoshone, Ute, Nez Perce)
- ▸ Northern and Southern Plains (for example, Arapaho, Cheyenne, Lakota [Sioux], Shoshone, Blackfoot, Crow)
- ▸ Extermination of buffalo
- ▸ Pacific Northwest (for example, Chinook, Kwakiutl, Yakima)

American Government Policies

- ▸ Bureau of Indian Affairs
- ▸ Forced removal to reservations
- ▸ Attempts to break down tribal life, assimilation policies, Carlisle School

Conflicts

- ▸ Sand Creek Massacre
- ▸ Battle of the Little Big Horn: Crazy Horse, Sitting Bull, Custer's Last Stand
- ▸ Wounded Knee
  - • Ghost Dance

Vocabulary

Student/Teacher Vocabulary

assimilate: to incorporate immigrants from other countries and people from other cultures into the American mainstream (S)

Bureau of Indian Affairs (BIA): organization established by the federal government to manage affairs with Native Americans (S)

Carlisle School: a school established by the federal government at Carlisle, Pennsylvania, to "assimilate" Native American children into mainstream American culture (S)

Crazy Horse: a chief of the Sioux; fought in the Battle of Little Big Horn (S)

Custer's Last Stand: another name for the Battle of Little Big Horn (S)

extermination: mass murder, elimination (S)

Ghost Dance: a Native American ceremony that the Native Americans believed would cause the settlers to disappear, the buffalo to reappear, dead Native Americans to be reborn, and land to be restored to the Native Americans (S)

Great Basin: one of the great Native American land areas; consists of intermountain lowlands (from Rocky Mountains to Sierra Nevada, across Utah and Nevada and parts of Idaho, Oregon, Arizona, California, and Wyoming); very dry and rocky with desert in places (S)

Little Big Horn: a battle in which Lieutenant Colonel George Custer and the 7th Cavalry were decimated by Sioux and Cheyenne warriors (S)

Pacific Northwest: a region of the United States, considered to include the states of Washington and Oregon (S)

plains: an extensive area of level, treeless land (S)

plateau: an extensive area of level land raised sharply above one side of an adjacent area of land (S)

Vocabulary continued

reservation: land allotted to the Native Americans by the U.S. government for their use (S)

Sand Creek Massacre: the slaughter of Cheyenne and Arapaho at a Native American gathering in Colorado in November 1864 by Colorado territorial volunteers under the command of "Colonel" John Chivington, a Methodist minister (S)

Sitting Bull (Tatanka Iyotake): the Dakota Indian chief who led the Sioux tribes in their efforts to resist American expansion (S)

Wounded Knee Massacre: the last armed encounter of the Plains Indian War; put an end to the Ghost Dance movement (S)

Domain Vocabulary

Native Americans and associated words:
culture region, geography, adapt, characteristic, woodlands, tent, buckskin, treatment, unfair, unjust, belief, nature, respect, sickness, trickster, Coyote, generation, teaching, way of life, myth, buffalo, hunter, horse, saddle, bridle, mane, Spanish, herds, raid, settlement, network, fishing, trading, hunting, mountains, desert, small game, semi-nomadic, wickiup, bark, grass mat, animal skin, sandal, plant fibers, horseback, farm, cattle, river, salmon, gathering, berries, round houses, earth, poles, reeds, mats, baskets, grass, guardian spirit, squash, sunflowers, tipi/teepee, buffalo hide, moccasins, fasting, spirit, death, disease, smallpox, starvation, white, farmers, ranchers, allied, scalp, massacre, surrender, coast, rainfall, halibut, shellfish, cod, whale, game, eagle, beaver, raven, bear, motif, carving, totem pole, hierarchical society, potlatch, social structure, ceremony, clothing, utensil, muscle, sinew, extinction, extinct, policies, European culture, religion, Christianity, property, sovereign, treaty, force, greed, corruption, government agent, head of household, parcel, federal funds, educate, civilize, mainstream, frontier, settlers, miners, fight, negotiate, peace, militia, attack, warpath, elderly, wipe out, invaded, sacred, cede, protest, encroach, order, comply, advance party, surround, kill, resistance, soldiers, disarm, encounter, ceremony, mystic, disappear, reappear, reborn, restored, believer, government, army, break up, arrest, buffalo soldiers

Cross-curricular Connections

Language Arts

Fiction and Drama

Myths and Legends

- Morning Star and Scarface: the Sun Dance (Plains legend, also known as "The Legend of Scarface")

- American Indian trickster stories (tales of Coyote, Raven, or Grandmother Spider)

Speeches

- "I will fight no more forever," Chief Joseph

> ## At a Glance
> The most important ideas for you are:
>
> ▶ Over time, the native people of the Great Basin, Plateau, and Plains culture regions had developed cultures that were adapted to the environment and shared similar cultural traits and characteristics.
>
> ▶ The coming of European Americans changed the way of life of the Native Americans.
>
> ▶ The federal government established the Bureau of Indian Affairs in 1824 to "safeguard" the well-being of Native Americans.
>
> ▶ From the 1860s to 1934, the Bureau of Indian Affairs forced Native Americans onto reservations, broke up tribal holdings, and attempted to impose a policy of assimilation.
>
> ▶ Between the 1850s and 1890, the army, settlers, miners, and ranchers fought a series of battles with the Native Americans that became known as the Plains Wars.

What Teachers Need to Know

Background

Anthropologists have categorized Native American peoples into culture regions in order to study and understand them. A culture region is a geographic area in which different groups have adapted to their physical surroundings in similar ways, and share similar cultural traits and characteristics, such as language, beliefs, customs, laws, dress, and housing. However, even within culture regions, groups still retain certain individual group characteristics. For the purpose of presenting information to your students, the diversity of the groups within areas is not discussed. For the most part, the emphasis in this lesson is on generalizations that apply to large numbers of peoples and nations within a culture region. In what is today the United States, there are eight Native American culture regions, namely, Eastern Woodlands, Southeast, Plains, Great Basin, Plateau, Southwest, Pacific Northwest, and California.

This section deals with some of the Native Americans west of the Mississippi—the Great Basin, Plateau, Northern and Southern Plains, and Pacific Northwest. These were the Native Americans whose lands stood in the way of European Americans on their mission to extend the United States from sea to sea.

At the points in history that are discussed here, native-born citizens and immigrants alike believed that Native Americans stood in the way of progress. They believed that these people, who lived in buffalo-hide tents instead of wooden or brick houses and who wore animal skins instead of cotton clothes, did not understand the value of the land or of hard work and were keeping enterprising Americans from actualizing that value. Today, many people feel that the United States' treatment of the native peoples was unfair and unjust.

It is important in teaching this unit to try to help students see how the pursuit of "manifest destiny" studied in earlier sections of the curriculum looked very different to the native peoples who were driven from their ancestral lands.

A. Culture and Life

There is no definitive way to know how many people were living in the Americas when Columbus first landed in the Caribbean. Various recent studies suggest that some 5,000,000 lived in what is today the contiguous United States and another 2,000,000 in Canada and Alaska. According to the 2000 United States Census, there were about 3,000,000 Native Americans living in the United States. Today, they live mostly in Oklahoma, California, Arizona, New Mexico, and Alaska.

Beliefs

According to Alvin M. Josephy,

"The life of almost all Indian societies was colored by a deep faith in supernatural forces that were believed to link human beings to all other living things. . . . [E]ach manifestation of nature had its own spirit with which the individual could establish supernatural contact."

Along with these beliefs was the sense that there was a balance, or harmony, in nature that people should respect. Disturbing this balance resulted in sickness, pain, and death.

Common to many Native American cultures are the hero and the trickster. These characters are the subjects of stories passed down orally from generation to generation, even to the present day. One character is the hero, who was responsible for teaching the people their way of life. The other is the trickster, often in the form of Coyote, who gets himself into all sorts of trouble.

Lifestyles

Students may have a stereotypical view of Native Americans as mounted buffalo hunters. However, only the Plains Native Americans and those from the Basin and Plateau areas, who acquired horses and moved onto the Plains to hunt buffalo, fit this description. Archaeologists have found evidence of prehistoric horses in North America, but the horses may have died out thousands of years ago for the same reason that mastodons died out. They were hunted to extinction, as they were a source of food, clothing, tools, etc., to early inhabitants of the continent.

Horses reappeared in the 1500s with the Spanish, who brought herds with them from Spain. As the Spanish moved across Mexico and north of the Rio Grande to found colonies, they went on horseback. By the 1600s, Native Americans were raiding Spanish settlements for horses, which they traded to other groups in a wide network. By the early 1700s, horses had reached Native Americans in the Plateau and Great Basin areas and greatly changed their ways of life. For example, the Shoshone (Sacagawea's people) moved into the Plains and became buffalo hunters rather than farmers. The Nez Perce turned from fishing and hunting to raising horses and trading them to hunting peoples. On the Plains, some groups that had been farmers, such as the Teton Sioux, turned to hunting

> **Cross-curricular Teaching Idea**
> You may wish to introduce students to Morning Star and Scarface: the Sun Dance (a Plains legend, also known as "The Legend of Scarface") as well as some Native American trickster stories as discussed in the Language Arts section, "Myths and Legends," on pp. 70–71. (27) (28) (29) (30)

III. Native Americans: Cultures and Conflicts

for their main source of food. The horse, which didn't become widespread on the Plains until the early- to mid-18th century, made it possible for a number of tribes living as agriculturalists along the rivers and fringes of the Plains to venture out onto the Plains following the bison herds.

Culture Areas

Great Basin

- Intermountain lowlands (from Rocky Mountains to Sierra Nevada, across Utah and Nevada and parts of Idaho, Oregon, Arizona, California, and Wyoming); very dry and rocky with desert in places

- Hunting small game

- Gathering seeds, nuts, plants, and roots

- Seminomadic groups that traveled on a regular cycle from lower lands to higher elevations in search of food

- Wickiups, cone-shaped houses made of poles covered with brush, bark, or grass mats

- Animal skins for clothes
  Sandals made of plant fibers
  Basketry hats for women

- Believed in what dreams told people

- Shoshone
  Acquired horses
  Moved into Plains to hunt buffalo from horseback
  Took on traits of Plains peoples, such as using buffalo skins for clothing
  Today, some 12,000 live on reservations

- Ute
  Acquired horses
  Moved into Plains to hunt buffalo from horseback
  Today, some 7,000 live on reservations and farm or raise cattle

Plateau

- Plateau of the Columbia and Fraser river basins in the area between the Rocky and Cascade Mountains (including Canada); changes of season with accompanying rain and snow; full rivers and lush forests

- Fishing, especially salmon, as major food source
  Gathering of plants and berries
  Hunting game

- In winter, round houses covered with earth
  In summer, poles tied together and covered with bark or reeds

- Clothing made of animal skins
  Wove mats and baskets from grass

- Believed that each person could acquire a guardian spirit for life, which could be the spirit of an animal, a force of nature, such as the wind, or a thing, such as rock

Use Instructional Master 37.

- Nez Perce
  Acquired horses in the 1700s and developed large herds; bred Appaloosas
  Turned from fishing for their main food source to hunting buffalo on the Plains on horseback
  Continued to live in the Plateau but traveled to the Plains to hunt
  Lost much of their land in the 1800s
  Today are farmers on an Idaho reservation

Plains

- From Canada to central Texas and from the Rocky Mountains to the Mississippi River; all changes of season with heavy to moderate precipitation

- Hunting buffalo and small game along with plant gathering on southern Plains
  Also seminomadic agriculture among some groups on northern Plains: farming corn, beans, squash, and sunflowers part of the year and hunting part of the year

- Tipi: cone-shaped structure made of poles and covered with buffalo hides

- Clothing made of animal skins, moccasins

- Vision quest in which a young man or woman fasted alone away from the village in the hope of dreaming of a spirit who would guard him or her for life

- Blackfeet
  Dyed their moccasins black, hence the name
  Relied on the buffalo for their way of life
  Many deaths from smallpox, lack of food when buffalo died out, actions of whites
  Today, some 10,000 live as farmers and ranchers on reservations

- Crow
  Allied with white soldiers in Plains Indian Wars of 1800s (frequently fought the Sioux)
  Scouts for General Custer at the Battle of Little Bighorn
  Today, around 5,000 on a reservation in Montana

- Sioux: three branches known as Dakota (Santee Sioux), Lakota (Teton Sioux), and Nakota (Yankton Sioux)
  Allies of the British in the American Revolution and War of 1812
  Fought as allies of Cheyenne at Little Bighorn
  Massacre of Sioux at Wounded Knee in 1890, end of Native American resistance
  Treaty giving Sioux the Black Hills ignored when gold found
  56-year court case (1923–1979) awards Sioux $105 million for Black Hills

- Cheyenne
  Once friendly toward whites
  Fought white encroachment on lands and massacre of Cheyenne at Sand Creek
  With Sioux, massacred General Custer and his soldiers at Little Bighorn
  Today, more than 7,000 on reservations

III. Native Americans: Cultures and Conflicts

Name _____ Date _____
Native American Culture Regions
Fill in the chart for each culture region. Then list the representative peoples of each region, giving specific facts about each.

Great Basin

Geographic	Climate	Housing	Clothing	Food	Beliefs

Representative Peoples:

_____
_____
_____
_____

Purpose: To identify major features of Native American culture regions

Master 38a   Grade 5: History & Geography

Use Instructional Masters 38a–38d.

- Arapaho
  Fought white encroachment and joined with Cheyenne to avenge Sand Creek
  Today, some 5,000 on reservations as farmers

Pacific Northwest

- Narrow strip of coast in what is today the United States and Canada from Prince William Sound to northern California; area with high annual rainfall and lush forests

  - Fishing: salmon, halibut, shellfish, cod
    Hunting whales
    Hunting game
    Gathering berries

  - Rectangular houses made of wooden planks

  - Clothing generally of shredded cedar bark
    In cold weather, animal skin robes
    Woven cone-shaped hats with wide brims to protect against rain

  - Spirit beings of the animal world: eagle, beaver, raven, bear, whale
    Use the spirit beings as design motifs in their carvings, especially in totem poles and masks
    Developed a hierarchical society in which social status was important; the potlatch confirmed one's rank in that social structure
    Practiced the potlatch ceremony, in which a wealthy member of the community gave away all his belongings to show how wealthy and important he was

- Kwakiutl
  Noted for their fine carving of animals in wood, slate, and shell
  About 15,000 when whites arrived
  Only a few thousand fishermen and farmers today

- Chinook
  Flattened children's foreheads to show social rank
  About 80 percent died during an outbreak of smallpox in 1829

- Yakima
  Originally lived on rivers in the Pacific Northwest and were primarily salmon fishers
  Today, about 7,500 live on the Yakima Reservation and earn a living through forestry

Plains Native Americans and Extermination of the Buffalo

The coming of the railroad and the influx of Easterners and European immigrants onto the Plains in the latter half of the 1800s changed the way of life of Plains Native Americans forever. Up until the 1860s, the northern and southern Plains had few European-American settlers. But the Homestead Act of 1862 encouraged settlement by giving 160 acres of land to any citizen or immigrant willing to live on and cultivate the land for five years and pay a modest processing fee. That land was home to Plains Native Americans, whose way of life depended on hunting buffalo.

Before the arrival of the white settlers, buffalo were plentiful on the Great Plains. Native Americans killed buffalo, but not in such numbers that the animals were endangered. The Native Americans generally used every part of the animal. They ate the meat for food and turned the skins into teepees, clothing, and storage vessels. Bones were used as utensils and tools. Muscle and sinew were used for sewing pieces of hide together. When the European-American settlers arrived, Native American hunters provided them with buffalo hides in exchange for manufactured goods. Later, European-American hunters killed buffalo themselves to feed the construction crews that built the transcontinental railroads across the plains and to supply hides to tanneries to be made into leather goods. Much of the killing was done between 1870 and 1883, and by 1890 less than a thousand buffalo remained. Some hunters also killed for sport, shooting buffalo from trains. Some scholars estimate that as many as 15 million buffalo were killed during the 1800s. By the turn of the twentieth century, the buffalo were gone in many places and the animal had become an endangered species. It is thought that there were only 34 buffalo left on the northern Plains. The combination of the land-taking and the extinction of the buffalo brought major changes to the lives of the Native Americans.

buffalo hide

B. American Government Policies

Bureau of Indian Affairs

The Bureau of Indian Affairs (BIA) was set up in 1824 by the United States Government within the War Department and transferred to the newly created Department of the Interior in 1849. The BIA's avowed purpose was to safeguard the welfare of Native Americans. However, in practice, the BIA implemented policies to remove Native Americans to reservations and to promote native accommodation and assimilation into European culture, which often meant destroying Native American culture and values. During the 1800s, there was a western European tradition of imposing Christianity and middle class morals and values on native peoples worldwide. This tradition was also practiced in the United States.

Forced Removal to Reservations

In 1871, the federal government passed the Indian Appropriation Act. Under the provisions of the law, the United States government withdrew recognition of separate Native American peoples as sovereign nations and stated that it would no longer enter into treaties with any Native American group. Treaties that were in force would be honored. That, however, proved to be a hollow promise whenever gold or silver was found on Native American lands or when American settlers wanted more land. (Native Americans were not granted U.S. citizenship until 1924.)

The Plains Native Americans were forced onto reservations. Although they were hunters, not farmers, the federal government tried to turn them into farmers. Not only did they not know how to farm, the reservations they were forced to live on were often not particularly suited to farming.

The BIA's purpose was to oversee the reservations and provide food, clothing, and other necessities to the Native Americans. However, greed and corruption

Teaching Idea

The decimation of the buffalo population during the 19th century is a sad chapter in American history. However, students may be pleased to know that the buffalo has recently made a comeback. You can find details on the web.

Teaching Idea

The BIA's title was changed to the Indian Service and still remains an agency of the Interior Department. Have students do research on the Internet and in newspapers and news magazines to find out what the Indian Service manages today.

Teaching Idea

The history of the treatment of Native Americans by the United States may be disturbing to students. Explore it in the context of earlier European attitudes toward Native Americans and Africans. Consider also the concept of manifest destiny if the class has studied Section I of American History and Geography for Grade 5. It is important that students be able to see how westward expansion must have looked to native peoples as well as white settlers.

often guided the actions of government agents in the BIA and the Native Americans saw little of the aid that was meant to sustain them in their new lives.

Attempts to Break Down Tribal Life

Corruption in the Bureau of Indian Affairs became so widespread that by the 1880s the protests of Native Americans and their supporters could no longer be ignored. In 1887, Congress passed the Dawes Act, which broke up the land holdings on the reservations. The land was divided into parcels of 160 acres, and each head of a household received a parcel. Any land that was not disposed of in this way could be sold to non-Native Americans. Native American families had to hold the land for 25 years, at which time they could sell it. Many did sell their land, and then had nothing to live on when the money was gone. By 1932, 96 million acres of the 138 million acres set aside for Native Americans in 1887 no longer belonged to them.

One of the reasons that advocates believed the reservations should be broken up was because they believed that the "communal life" of Native Americans—that is, living in and sharing with a large extended group—kept individuals from developing a sense of ambition and becoming more like white Americans. In breaking up the reservations, reformers believed they were trying to encourage personal initiative. As part of the Dawes Act, federal funds were to be used for educating and training Native Americans and encouraging them to adopt the habits of what western Europeans and white Americans considered "civilized life." These included owning land, settling in one place as opposed to moving around on a seasonal basis, farming or doing other kinds of modern labor, wearing European-style clothing, speaking English, learning to read and write, and accepting the Christian religion. The Dawes Act also made considerable quantities of land available in the West. The goal was to assimilate the Native Americans to the American way of life, in much the same way immigrants were assimilated.

Indian Schools

Well-meaning Americans set up schools to "civilize" and assimilate Native Americans. This experiment had been tried even in the colonial era. Benjamin Franklin recorded the results of one such attempt in which it was proposed to send several Native Americans to the College of William and Mary in Virginia in the 1740s. A chief wrote back to refuse the white man's offer:

> We know that you highly esteem the kind of learning taught in those Colleges, and that the Maintenance of our young Men, while with you, would be very expensive to you. We are convinced, that you mean to do us Good by your Proposal; and we thank you heartily. But you, who are wise must therefore not take it amiss, if our Ideas of this kind of Education happen not to be the same as yours. We have had some Experience of it. Several of our young People were formerly brought up at the Colleges of the Northern Provinces: they were instructed in all your Sciences; but, when they came back to us, they were bad Runners, ignorant of every means of living in the woods. . . neither fit for Hunters, Warriors, nor Counselors, they were totally good for nothing.

> We are, however, not the less oblig'd by your kind Offer, tho' we decline accepting it; and, to show our grateful sense of it, if the Gentlemen

of Virginia will send us a Dozen of their Sons, we will take Care of their Education, instruct them in all we know, and make Men of them.

After the Indian Wars in the West, similar efforts were made to educate young Native Americans for success in American society. The Carlisle Indian School in Carlisle, Pennsylvania, was one of 106 day and boarding schools for young Native Americans run by the federal government. Carlisle was founded by Captain Richard C. Pratt, who had fought in the Indian Wars and led a group of buffalo soldiers. Pratt's approach to educating Native Americans was summarized in a well-known phrase: "kill the Indian and save the man." That is, he wanted to kill off the "Indian" ways of thinking and living in order to create men and women who he believed could prosper in American society. Pratt explained his philosophy as follows:

> The Indians under our care remained savage, because forced back upon themselves and away from association with English-speaking and civilized people, and because of our savage example and treatment of them. . . .
>
> We have never made any attempt to civilize them with the idea of taking them into the nation, and all of our policies have been against citizenizing and absorbing them.
>
> . . .We invite the Germans to come into our country and communities, and share our customs, our civilization, to be of it; and the result is immediate success. Why not try it on the Indians? Why not invite them into experiences in our communities? . . . .
>
> It is a great mistake to think that the Indian is born an inevitable savage. He is born a blank, like all the rest of us. Left in the surroundings of savagery, he grows to possess a savage language, superstition, and life. We, left in the surroundings of civilization, grow to possess a civilized language, life, and purpose. Transfer the infant white to the savage surroundings, he will grow to possess a savage language, superstition, and habit. Transfer the savage-born infant to the surroundings of civilization, and he will grow to possess a civilized language and habit. . . .
>
> As we have taken into our national family seven millions of Negroes, and as we receive foreigners at the rate of more than five hundred thousand a year, and assimilate them, it would seem that the time may have arrived when we can very properly make at least the attempt to assimilate our two hundred and fifty thousand Indians . . .
>
> The school at Carlisle is an attempt on the part of the government to do this. . . . Carlisle fills young Indians with the spirit of loyalty to the stars and stripes, and then moves them out into our communities to show by their conduct and ability that the Indian is no different from the white or the colored, that he has the inalienable right to liberty and opportunity that the white and the negro have. Carlisle does not dictate to him what line of life he should fill, so it is an honest one. It says to him that, if he gets his living by the sweat of his brow, and demonstrates to the nation that he is a man, he does more good for his race than hundreds of his fellows who cling to their tribal communistic surroundings. . . .

Richard H. Pratt / "The Advantages of Mingling Indians with Whites", pp. 260–271. From an extract of the Official Report of the Nineteenth Annual Conference of Charities and Correction (1892), pp. 46–59.

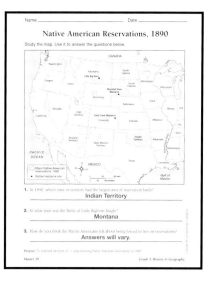

Use Instructional Master 39.

Teaching Idea

Indian schools like the Carlisle School raise important questions about national identity, assimilation, and diversity. How much assimilation must take place for a nation to remain a unified nation? To what extent is it important that the people in a country have the same culture, language, ideas, and ways of life? To what extent is it important that a nation not be totally homogenous, that there be diversity of thinking and various subcultures? How much do we have to have in common to prosper as a nation? These questions are still very much debated today, and students in Grade 5 can be introduced to the argument.

Teaching Idea

Pictures of students at the Carlisle School, as well as documents describing the school, are available on the web. Student may also be interested in learning about Jim Thorpe, a championship runner educated at the Carlisle School.

At the Carlisle School Native American children as young as seven years of age were sent to become Christians and English speakers. They were to forget their traditional ways and embrace the values of mainstream society. The school taught both academic subjects and preprofessional skills. Students learned reading, writing, and arithmetic. Boys studied carpentry, tinsmithing, and blacksmithing. Girls studied cooking, sewing, and baking. The boys wore uniforms and the girls wore Victorian-style dresses. Long hair was cut short. Shoes were required and no moccasins were allowed. Students were not allowed to speak their native languages. All of this was well intentioned, but in the attempt to assimilate children to a new culture, the educators at Carlisle were also systematically destroying the culture into which their students had been born.

C. Conflicts

The Plains Wars

The period from the 1850s to the 1880s on the narrowing frontier saw a number of conflicts between settlers and soldiers and the increasingly desperate and dwindling Native American population. These conflicts are sometimes called the Plains Wars. It was not surprising that some Indians resisted westward expansion. As United States General Philip Sheridan said:

> We took away their country and their means of support, broke up their mode of living, their habits of life, introduced disease and decay among them, and it was for this and against this that they made war. Could anyone expect less?

Sand Creek Massacre

In the 1850s, the Arapaho and Cheyenne in Colorado had been forced to accept a small area of land near Sand Creek for their reservation. Within ten years, gold had been found on the reservation and settlers and miners wanted Sand Creek. A conflict began and scattered fighting continued for three years until Chief Black Kettle and his band camped near Fort Lyon asking to negotiate for peace.

In November 1864, militia under the command of "Colonel" John Chivington, a Methodist minister, led an attack against Black Kettle's camp. Chivington and his men claimed to be seeking revenge on the Native Americans for an earlier attack on white miners. They attacked Black Kettle and his camp even though it was flying both a U. S. flag and the white flag of truce. Chivington and his force carried out their attack on a camp of sleeping men, women, children, and elderly. It is estimated that up to 500 Native Americans were killed (and in some cases mutilated) by Chivington's men.

Some Americans applauded Chivington's actions, but many others were disgusted. A Congressional committee investigated the attack and ultimately condemned Chivington's massacre.

Crazy Horse

Crazy Horse (Ta-sunko-witko), a chief of the Oglala Sioux, was one of the strongest leaders of the Native American resistance on the Great Plains. During the 1850s, he acquired a reputation as a great warrior, based on the bravery he displayed in conflicts with other groups of Native Americans. Later, Crazy Horse would turn these skills against the white men.

In the 1860s, Crazy Horse refused to remain on the reservation assigned to his people, insisting instead on venturing out to hunt buffalo. He also led attacks on the army and white settlers. In 1866 he led a party of roughly 1,000 warriors in an attack on soldiers near Fort Kearny in the Wyoming Territory. Crazy Horse led a decoy party that drew the commander and some soldiers out of the fort. The soldiers were then ambushed by a large Native American force and 80 soldiers were killed. The defeat, known as the Fetterman Massacre, was the worst defeat the army had suffered at the hands of the Native Americans up to that point.

In the 1870s, Crazy Horse led additional attacks on railroad workers and the army. He and his followers helped destroy the troops of George A. Custer at the famous battle of the Little Bighorn. After Little Bighorn, the army pursued Crazy Horse more intensively. He was forced to surrender in May 1877. Later that year, he was killed during a tussle with a guard. A memorial to Crazy Horse is currently under construction in South Dakota.

 ## Sitting Bull

Sitting Bull (Tatanka Iyotake) was the Dakota Native American chief who led the Sioux tribes in their efforts to resist American expansion. As a young man he gained a reputation for bravery and skill in battles against the Shoshone and other tribes, which gave the Dakota more land on which to hunt.

Sitting Bull began a long career of resistance to the U.S. Army and the white man in 1863. Along with Crazy Horse, he became a chief leader of Native American resistance.

In 1868 the Sioux made a peace treaty with the U.S. government that gave the Sioux a reservation in the Black Hills (current-day South Dakota). In 1876, the government ordered the Sioux onto reservations when gold was discovered in the area and white miners wanted to prospect for gold. Sitting Bull and others did not comply. The noncomplying Native American chiefs camped in the valley of the Little Bighorn River. Sitting Bull performed a ritual known as the Sun Dance and entered into a trancelike state. He reported that he saw the defeat of army soldiers, which foretold the defeat of General Custer and his men at the Battle of Little Bighorn.

After Little Bighorn, the Army applied additional pressure. By this point the buffalo population, on which the Sioux depended, was rapidly waning. Many of the Sioux suffered from hunger, and growing numbers began to surrender. Sitting Bull and other Sioux who continued to resist the government went to Canada and lived there from 1877 to 1881. He continued to lose followers to starvation and finally was forced to surrender.

For some time Sitting Bull was confined to a reservation. Then, in 1885 he was allowed to join Buffalo Bill's Wild West show. He was paid $50 a week for riding around the arena and he gained a popular following; however, Sitting Bull remained with the show for only four months.

Ghost Dance

The Ghost Dance was a ceremony associated with a movement that began among the Paiute [PIE-oot] in western Nevada in the 1880s. It was led by Wovoka [woh-VOH-ka], a Paiute mystic. He claimed that if the Ghost Dance was performed often enough, in time the settlers would disappear, the buffalo would reappear, dead Native Americans would be reborn, and land would be restored to the Native Americans.

III. Native Americans: Cultures and Conflicts

Cross-curricular Teaching Idea

You may wish to introduce students to "I will fight no more forever," by Chief Joseph as discussed in the Language Arts section, "Speeches," on pp. 83–90. Chief Joseph (1840–1904) was born in the Wallowa Valley in what is now northeastern Oregon. His tribal name was Hin-mah-too-yah-lat-kekt, or Thunder Rolling Down the Mountain. After succeeding his father as leader of the Wallowa band of Nez Perce in 1871, Chief Joseph refused to allow the U. S. government to force his people from their tribal lands. However, Chief Joseph was unable to resist the government and later died on the Colville Reservation in Washington. According to his doctor, he died of a broken heart. (32)

Teaching Idea

As you are discussing the various conflicts listed in this section, create a chart that will help students track them. Include the name, date, location, and key facts. Then, once all the conflicts have been studied, students can summarize what they learned in paragraph form.

The Ghost Dance conveyed a powerful message, inspiring hope in its believers. Word of the Ghost Dance was picked up by other bands and found its way onto the Plains. The government had the army break up the religion, fearing new outbreaks of violence just as the Plains Native Americans seemed to be subdued. Government officials gave orders to arrest Sitting Bull, one of the most important native leaders on the Plains and a supporter of the Ghost Dance. A scuffle broke out as officials were trying to arrest him, and Sitting Bull was accidentally killed.

Battle of the Little Bighorn

The Battle of the Little Bighorn is also known as "Custer's Last Stand." The Little Bighorn River flows through southeastern Montana. It was on its banks, on June 25, 1876, that Lieutenant Colonel George A. Custer and part of his Seventh Cavalry were completely destroyed. Sioux and Cheyenne, led by Chiefs Crazy Horse and Gall, carried out the attack.

The stage had been set for the battle when, in 1874, Custer invaded the Black Hills. This land was sacred to the Sioux and had been ceded to them in a treaty by the government. (See p. 309.) Custer already had a bad reputation among Native Americans. He had earlier led a raid on a peaceful Cheyenne village at Washita, killing many of the inhabitants.

On his expedition in 1874, Custer wanted to find out whether there was gold in the Black Hills. When the rumors of gold turned out to be true, word spread quickly and miners soon followed. The Native Americans protested the encroachment of people into the land, but the army seemed unable to remove the trespassers. In an effort to keep peace, the federal government offered to buy the Black Hills from the Sioux. The offer was refused because the Sioux felt they could not sell land that was sacred to them.

The government then ordered the Sioux onto reservations by February 1876. Sitting Bull and many others did not comply, and the federal government sent the army out looking for them. Custer was in charge of an advance party of 600 officers and enlisted men. There is debate about whether Custer misunderstood or ignored his orders, but when his scouts sighted a Native American village, he took part of his regiment and attacked. Unfortunately for him and his 236 men, they had located a small part of the major Sioux and Cheyenne encampment that housed 2,500 warriors. Custer and his men were surrounded and killed within minutes. His remaining troops narrowly escaped to the main army. (65)

The army gave chase and by winter 1876–77, most Sioux either had fled into Canada or, seeing no hope of outrunning and outlasting the army, had surrendered. Those who surrendered were sent to reservations. In 1881, Sitting Bull and his band returned from Canada to reservation life.

Wounded Knee

After the death of Sitting Bull, a group of Sioux joined Sitting Bull's half brother, Big Foot, and left the reservation. Like his half brother, Big Foot was a strong supporter of the Ghost Dance. About 500 U.S. Army troops set out after Big Foot's group, which included 100 warriors and 250 women and children. Big Foot was persuaded to lead his people to Wounded Knee, in what is today the Pine Ridge Indian Reservation in southwestern South Dakota, where they were to be disarmed and led to a reservation. When the army attempted to disarm the

Native Americans, many refused to surrender their weapons. A young warrior raised a rifle above his head and declared he would not give it up. A scuffle broke out and the warrior's rifle went off, probably accidentally. The frightened soldiers opened fire. By noon, 300 Native Americans, including Big Foot and many women and children, lay dead. The army suffered 25 dead and 39 wounded, though many of these were probably victims of friendly fire.

The Battle of Wounded Knee—some prefer to call it a massacre, not a battle—put an end to the Ghost Dance movement and, although scattered Native American resistance continued, Wounded Knee Massacre is widely seen as marking the end of the Indian Wars, one of the saddest chapters in American history.

Review

Below are some ideas for ongoing assessment and review activities. These are not meant to constitute a comprehensive list. Teachers may also refer to the *Pearson Learning/Core Knowledge History & Geography* series for additional information and teaching ideas.

• Consult with local universities or libraries to see if there is a Native American specialist (such as a professor, exchange student, or librarian) who can come to the class and give a presentation on an aspect of Native American culture and history. Before inviting the speaker, have students write personal letters to introduce themselves and ask a question that they would like answered. Deliver these letters to the specialist prior to the presentation.

• Have students choose a Native American group from this section and write a short research paper about that group. Have students focus on how the group's culture reflected where they lived. Students should consult three outside sources and then present their papers to the class. They may choose to also include a visual aid with their presentation. Check that students follow correct format for writing the short paper.

• While studying this section, focus on the concept of conflict and what causes conflict. Use other aspects of history to discuss this with the class, such as the Civil War and westward expansion. Have students reflect in journals about what we can learn about historical conflict and read those entries aloud. How will they apply what they have learned about history as they grow into adults?

• Work with your school media specialist and compile a classroom library of Native American myths written as picture books. Have each student choose a book, read it, and share a summary with the class. Then, meet with a kindergarten class while they are studying Native Americans and have book buddies share the Native American myths.

• Have students study an aspect of a Native American culture and write their own myth to describe the culture. After writing the myths, have students illustrate them and create a class book of Native American myths.

• You may also ask the following questions after completion of this unit of study.

The Big Idea in Review

Native American cultures were disrupted, displaced, and profoundly altered by the westward expansion of the United States and the government's policies in the 19th century.

1. How did the buffalo become almost extinct on the Plains?

Non-Native American hunters began to hunt buffalo for food, for their skins, and for sport.

2. Give an example of how the Bureau of Indian Affairs treated Native Americans.

Any one: forced Native Americans onto reservations; signed treaties with Native American nations recognizing their right to certain tracts of land and then taking the land back; tried to force Native Americans to assimilate into mainstream society; some BIA agents stole supplies meant for the Native Americans.

3. Why did the militia attack the Cheyenne at Sand Creek?

The militia, along with their colonel, John Chivington, wanted to rid the Sand Creek area of the Native Americans so they could have the land. Chivington and his men said they were also seeking revenge on the Native Americans for an earlier attack on white miners.

4. What happened at the Battle of the Little Bighorn?

Lieutenant Colonel George A. Custer took some of his Seventh Cavalry to a Sioux village ahead of the main army. When Custer saw the small village, he and his troops attacked. The village was part of a much larger encampment of Sioux and Cheyenne, and the soldiers were surrounded and killed within minutes.

5. Why did the Ghost Dance appeal to Native Americans on the Plains in the 1880s?

The Ghost Dance promised that European Americans would disappear, that all Native Americans who had died would reappear, that the buffalo would come back, and that the Native Americans would have their lands back. Considering that the Native Americans were forced onto reservations and depended on the federal government for their lives, it was not surprising that the Native Americans would find hope in the message of the Ghost Dance.

6. Which of the following was a result of the army's attempt to break up the Ghost Dance: massacre at Sand Creek, Battle of the Little Big Horn, or the Wounded Knee Massacre?

Wounded Knee Massacre was a result of the army's efforts to break up the Ghost Dance movement.

More Resources

The titles listed below are offered as a representative sample of materials and not a complete list of everything that is available.

For students —

• *Native Americans: Cultures and Conflicts*, edited by E. D. Hirsch, Jr. (Pearson Learning, 2002), a unit in the official *Pearson Learning/Core Knowledge History & Geography* series, is available as part of the bound book for Grade 5/Level 5 and as a stand-alone module. A teacher's guide is also available. To order, call 1-800-321-3106.

• *Calico Captive*, by Elizabeth George Speare (Houghton Mifflin, 2001). Excellent historical fiction generally based on *A Narrative of the Captivity of Mrs. [Susanna Willard] Johnson*, first published in 1796 (see below, teacher resources). Paperback, 288 pages, ISBN 0618150765. See also *The Sign of the Beaver*, a Newbery Honor book by the same author.

• *Exploration and Conquest: The Americas after Columbus (1500–1620)*, by Betsy and Giulio Maestro (Harper Trophy, 1997). Paperback, 48 pages, ISBN 0688154743.

More Resources continued

• *Indian Chiefs,* by Russell Freedman (Holiday House, 1992). Paperback, ISBN 0823409716. See also *Buffalo Hunt,* by the same author.

• *Wounded Knee: The Death of a Dream,* by Laurie A. O'Neill (Millbrook, 1994). Note: There is one mostly blurry photograph taken after the massacre showing several corpses. Paperback, 64 pages, ISBN 1562947486.

For teachers —

• *The Life and Death of Crazy Horse,* by Russell Freedman (Holiday House, 1996). Honored by the Orbis Pictus Awards program for excellence in children's nonfiction and written for young adults. Library binding, 166 pages, ISBN 0823412199.

• *The Life and Diary of David Brainerd,* by Philip E. Howard, Jonathan Edwards, and David Brainerd (Baker Book House, 1989). The edited journals of a young 18th-century Christian missionary to the Native Americans in New England. An unusual and insightful firsthand look at one encounter between Europeans and Native Americans during the colonial era. See especially Part VII. Paperback, 384 pages, ISBN 0801009766.

• *A Narrative of the Captivity of Mrs. [Susanna Willard] Johnson* was first published in 1796. A scanned facsimile of this book and later editions can be found at www. canadiana.org.

• *Native American Testimony: A Chronicle of Indian-White Relations from Prophecy to the Present, 1492–2000,* by Peter Nabokov (Penguin, 1999). Paperback, 506 pages, ISBN 0140281592.

• *With the Indians in the Rockies,* by James Willard Schultz (Confluence Press, 1996). Paperback, 144 pages, ISBN 0825303192.

IV. United States Geography

The Big Idea

The United States is made up of 50 states, which are often grouped into regions; each region has its own climate, landscape, and culture.

Remember that each subject you study with students expands their vocabulary and introduces new terms, thus making them better listeners and readers. As you study geography, use map work, read alouds, independent reading, and discussions to build students' vocabularies.

What Students Should Already Know

Students in Core Knowledge schools should be familiar with

Kindergarten

- naming town, city, or community, as well as state, where they live
- locating North America, the continental United States, Hawaii, Alaska, and own state

Grade 2

- the United States: 50 states; 48 contiguous states, plus Alaska and Hawaii; and territories
- Mississippi River, Appalachian and Rocky Mountains, Great Lakes, Atlantic and Pacific oceans, Gulf of Mexico

Grades 2–4

- Students should have begun learning the 50 states and their capitals.

What Students Need to Learn

- **Locate: Western Hemisphere, North America, Caribbean Sea, Gulf of Mexico**
- **The Gulf Stream and how it affects climate**
- **Regions and their characteristics: New England, Mid-Atlantic, South, Midwest, Great Plains, Southwest, West, Pacific Northwest**
- **50 states and capitals**

Vocabulary

Student/Teacher Vocabulary

capital: city in each of the 50 U.S. states that serves as the seat of government for that state (S)

climate: a summary of weather conditions; the general weather patterns, as opposed to the specific conditions on any particular day (S)

Gulf Stream: a warm ocean current originating off the coast of South America and flowing north into the Gulf of Mexico and along the coast of North America (S)

region: an area with shared characteristics (S)

Western Hemisphere: the western half of Earth, composed of North and South America and their surrounding waters (S)

Vocabulary continued

Domain Vocabulary

Geography and associated words:
North America, United States, land bridge, isthmus, South America, varied, rugged, mountainous, rocky, plains, flat, gently rolling, grasslands, agriculture, coastal plains, sandy beaches, scrub forest, erosion, Iroquois-Huron word, vast area, sparsely populated, few people, per square mile, Pacific Ocean, Arctic Ocean, Atlantic Ocean, borders, natural boundary, St, Lawrence River, St. Lawrence Seaway, New England, provinces, Commonwealth of Nations, Ottawa, Rio Grande, shallow river, Gulf of Mexico, Gulf of California, Belize, Guatemala, plateau, tableland, top of mountain, Sierra Madre Occidental, Sierra Madre Oriental, narrow, land bridge, connects, joins, independent, countries, Costa Rica, El Salvador, Honduras, Nicaragua, Panama, Caribbean Sea, steamy, dense

United States and associated words:
Alaska, similar, Great Plains, Pacific Ocean, Atlantic Ocean, noncontiguous, Guam, American Samoa, Virgin Islands, territories, Gulf of Mexico, New Orleans, south, below, tributaries, flow into, Ohio River, Missouri River, oldest, Newfoundland, Alabama, barrier, obstacle, movement, settlement, highest peak, mountaintop, Mount Mitchell, Maria Mitchell, astronomer, Hudson River, Delaware River, Susquehanna River, Potomac River, Tennessee River, New Mexico, Mount Elbert, formidable, harder, pass, route, South Pass, Wyoming, Oregon Trail, Continental Divide, separating line, Great Lakes, freshwater, chain, system, New York State, Minnesota, Ontario, Erie, Huron, Michigan, Superior, con-nected, joined, waterway, rivers, canals, locks, access through, St. Lawrence Seaway, *plus names of the 50 states*

Pacific Ocean and associated words:
largest, deepest, Arctic, Antarctica, North America, South America, Asia, Australia, islands, dot, chains, series, system, Bering Strait, South China Sea, Oceania, Guam, Marshall Islands, Japan, Philippines, New Zealand, Ring of Fire, volcanoes, active, inac-tive, lava, fire, molten rock

Atlantic Ocean and associated words:
second-largest, North America, South America, Europe, Africa, Arctic, Antarctica, ocean current, warm, Gulf of Mexico, flows, North Atlantic Drift, moderate, moderating influ-ence, warming, western Europe

New England and associated words:
Vermont, New Hampshire, Massachusetts, Connecticut, Rhode Island, Maine, cold winters, warm summers, milder winters, industry, trade, commercial fishing, commercial farming, Pilgrims, Puritans, first Thanksgiving, Boston, Lexington, Concord, American Revolution, lobsters, maple syrup, village squares, English colonists

Mid-Atlantic and associated words:
New York, New Jersey, Pennsylvania, Delaware, Maryland, mild winters, warm summers, high humidity, industry, trade, commercial farming, commercial fishing, New York City, the Statue of Liberty, Ellis Island, Philadelphia, the Liberty Bell, the Mummers Parade, first state to ratify the Constitution, crab cakes

South and associated words:
South, Maryland, Delaware, Virginia, North Carolina, South Carolina, Georgia, Florida, West Virginia, Kentucky, Tennessee, Alabama, Mississippi, Louisiana, Arkansas, Texas, Florida, humid subtropical, hot summers, mild winters, commercial farming, areas of industry, oil drilling, Delmarva Peninsula: Delaware, Maryland, Virginia, slavery, plantation economy, seceded, Confederate States of America, Nashville, country music, Disney World, birthplace of blues and jazz, Mardi Gras

Materials

Instructional Masters 40–43

Regions of the United States, p. 319

The Fifty States and Their Capitals, p. 321

Start the Match!, p. 322

Finish the Match!, p. 322

globe, p. 318

atlases, geography books, and similar books with maps of the United States, p. 319

access to computer lab for research, p. 323

index cards, p. 323

wooden puzzle of the United States, p. 323

information about each state's tourism office and addresses to use for writ-ing letters to that office, p. 323

access to local library or school media center, p. 323

Vocabulary continued

The Midwest and associated words:
Ohio, Michigan, Indiana, Illinois, Wisconsin, Minnesota, Nebraska, Iowa, Kansas, Missouri, cold winters, warm summers, major commercial farming, manufacturing, Chicago, meat-packing industry, Detroit, auto city, Upper Midwest, Germans, Scandinavians, Mississippi River, annual flooding, Minnesota, land of 10,000 lakes, Lake Superior, largest, Great Lakes, Lake Michigan, very cold, snowy winters, Paul Bunyan, Babe, the blue ox

Great Plains and associated words:
Montana, Wyoming, Colorado, North Dakota, South Dakota, Nebraska, Kansas, Oklahoma, Texas, cold winters, warm summers, major commercial farming, cattle ranching, tornadoes, dust storms, buffalo, Native Americans hunting on horseback, last Indian wars, cattle trails, railheads, Dust Bowl

The Southwest and associated words:
Arizona, New Mexico, Utah, Colorado, Texas, hot, dry, desert, mountain areas, cattle, light industry, cliff dwellings, Anasazi, Pueblo Native Americans, Navajo weavings, turquoise jewelry, cactus, Mexican food, Spanish heritage

The West and associated words:
Montana, Wyoming, Colorado, New Mexico, Idaho, Utah, Arizona, Nevada, Washington, Oregon, California, arid, semiarid, mountainous, hot summers, southern coast, mild winters, summers, mining, cattle ranching, light industry, lumbering, paper, wood products, dairy products, mining towns, California Gold Rush, cowhands and cattle ranching, Spanish influences in architecture, place names, Northwest Native Americans

Other regional names and associated words:
Gulf Coast, Gulf of Mexico, Florida, Alabama, Mississippi, Louisiana, Texas, Southeast, North and South Carolinas, Tennessee, Georgia, Arkansas, Rocky Mountains, New Mexico, Colorado, Wyoming, Montana, Utah, Washington, Idaho, Far West, California, Pacific Northwest, Oregon, temperature, mild winters, summers, lumbering, wood products, paper, dairy products, Northwest Native Americans, Columbia River, Lewis and Clark Expedition, Asian populations

50 states and their capitals and associated words:
city, town, seat, state government, capital building, executive branch, governor, legislative branch, judicial branch, making laws, citizens, laws on taxation, education, labor

---

At a Glance
The most important ideas for you are:

- Students should be able to locate the Western Hemisphere, North America, the Caribbean Sea, and the Gulf of Mexico.
- There are many ways to categorize the states of the United States.
- The regions of the United States are New England, Mid-Atlantic, South, Midwest, Great Plains, Southwest, West, Pacific, Northwest.
- Students should be able to identify all 50 states and their capitals.

What Teachers Need to Know

Location

 Western Hemisphere

Because Earth is round, it cannot be seen completely at any one time. Even an astronaut in space can see only half the world at once. One half of the world is called a hemisphere, meaning half of a sphere, or ball. The northern part of Earth is called the Northern Hemisphere and the southern part is called the Southern Hemisphere. But Earth can also be looked at as having a Western Hemisphere and an Eastern Hemisphere. Every continent is in at least two hemispheres at once. For example, North America is in the Northern Hemisphere and the Western Hemisphere.

Around the center of Earth is an imaginary line called the Equator. It is halfway between the North and South Poles. This is the place where the Northern and Southern Hemispheres divide. The dividing lines for the Eastern and Western Hemispheres are the Prime Meridian (also called the Greenwich meridian) and the 180th meridian. The Prime Meridian refers to 0° longitude, an imaginary line that runs from the North Pole to the South Pole going through the Royal Observatory in Greenwich, a suburb of London, England. The International Date Line also runs from the North Pole to the South Pole, generally following the 180th meridian (it deviates in a few places to avoid dividing Siberia and again to include the Aleutian Islands with Alaska). The Prime Meridian (0° longitude) and the 180th meridian are on opposite sides of Earth, and together divide the globe into Eastern (0° to 180° east of the Prime Meridian) and Western (0° to 180° west of the Prime Meridian) Hemispheres.

 North America

North America is the third-largest continent and is in both the Northern Hemisphere and the Western Hemisphere. The continent stretches from the Isthmus of Panama to the Arctic Ocean, and includes Greenland, Canada, the United States (including Hawaii), Mexico, the Caribbean Islands, and the Central American nations of Belize, Costa Rica, El Salvador, Guatemala, Honduras, Nicaragua, and Panama. North America is bordered by the Arctic Ocean in the north, the Atlantic Ocean in the east, the Pacific Ocean and Bering Sea in the west, and the continent of South America to the south.

 Caribbean Sea

The Caribbean Sea is an arm of the Atlantic Ocean and is bordered to the north and east by the West Indies, to the south by South America, and to the west by Central America. Since the early 1900s, the Caribbean has been linked to the Pacific Ocean through the Panama Canal.

The Caribbean Sea has four major island groups known collectively as the West Indies. The groups are the Bahamas, the Greater Antilles, the Lesser Antilles, and the Netherlands Antilles.

The islands have a generally warm and sunny climate. Most of the islands fall within the tropics and would be very hot if not for the breezes that move inland from the sea and keep the temperature around 80°F. Many of the islands are prime vacation spots because of their warm weather and sandy beaches.

Starting with the voyages of Christopher Columbus in 1492, Europeans began to colonize and then fight over possession of the islands. Some islands changed hands several times. Today, the Spanish heritage in Cuba, Puerto Rico, and the Dominican Republic is very evident, as are African influences, especially in music. Haiti's predominant cultural influences are French and African. The British stamp is apparent in many of the island nations, such as Trinidad and Tobago, the Bahamas, and Barbados. The Netherlands Antilles were colonized by the Dutch in the seventeenth century and remain a part of the Kingdom of the Netherlands.

Gulf of Mexico

The Gulf of Mexico, like the Caribbean, is known for its warm waters. The Gulf is bordered by the southeast coast of North America, from the tip of Florida to the Yucatán Peninsula. Its eastern boundary is the island of Cuba. The Strait of Yucatan links the Gulf to the Caribbean, and the Strait of Florida links it to the Atlantic.

The Gulf Stream and Climate

The Gulf Stream is a warm ocean current that originates off the coast of South America and flows to the Gulf of Mexico and up the coast of North America. The water temperature of the Gulf Stream is around 80°F. As it moves north, away from the Equator, the water cools.

The Gulf Stream passes from the Gulf of Mexico through the Strait of Florida and moves northeast until it meets the North Atlantic Drift off Newfoundland, Canada. The merged ocean current then flows toward Western Europe. As the North Atlantic Drift flows past the coasts of northwest Europe, the warm water of the ocean current moderates the climate. Considering the northern latitudes of countries like Ireland and England, one would expect much colder winters than the 40°F days they typically enjoy. The difference is the presence of the North Atlantic Drift. The southwestern coast of England is warm enough in a few places for palm trees to grow.

Regions and Their Characteristics

We sometimes talk about the United States in terms of regions, such as New England and the Southwest. These categories are determined by cultural characteristics as well as physical location. As a result, and depending on the context, one state may appear in more than one region.

New England

States: Maine, Vermont, New Hampshire, Massachusetts, Connecticut, Rhode Island

Climate: in the northernmost states, cold winters and warm summers; in the more southerly areas, milder winters and warmer summers

Economy: industry, trade, commercial fishing, commercial farming

Cultural literacy characteristics: The region is associated with

- Pilgrims and Puritans, the first Thanksgiving.
- Boston, Lexington, Concord, and the beginning of the American Revolution.
- Lobsters, maple syrup, and village squares.

Other: The term *New England* was used by the English colonists to refer to what they thought they were creating in their colonies—a "new" England.

 ## Mid-Atlantic

States: New York, New Jersey, Pennsylvania, Delaware, Maryland

Climate: relatively mild winters and warm summers, often with high humidity

Economy: industry, trade, commercial farming, some commercial fishing

Cultural literacy characteristics: The region is associated with

- New York City, the Statue of Liberty and Ellis Island.
- Philadelphia, the Liberty Bell and the Mummers Parade.
- the first state to ratify the Constitution (Delaware).
- crab cakes.

Other: With the exception of Pennsylvania, these states border the Atlantic Ocean, hence the name. Historically, Maryland and Delaware are also considered Southern states because they had slave economies.

 ## South

States: Maryland, Delaware, Virginia, North Carolina, South Carolina, Georgia, Florida, West Virginia, Kentucky, Tennessee, Alabama, Mississippi, Louisiana, Arkansas, Texas

Climate: humid subtropical; hot summers and mild winters; for much of the area precipitation is in the form of rain rather than snow, especially the more southerly parts of the region

Economy: commercial farming, areas of industry, oil drilling

Cultural literacy characteristics: The region is associated with

- Delmarva Peninsula: Delaware, Maryland, and Virginia.
- slavery and a plantation economy. Most states seceded and joined the Confederate States of America.
- Nashville and country music.
- Disney World.
- birthplace of the blues and jazz.
- Mardi Gras.

Other: During the Civil War, Maryland and Delaware were border states. They did not join the Confederacy, but remained slave states until the end of the war.

 ## The Midwest

States: Ohio, Michigan, Indiana, Illinois, Wisconsin, Minnesota, Nebraska, Iowa, Kansas, Missouri

Climate: cold winters and warm summers; precipitation may vary from year to year and from area to area; much of the winter precipitation is in the form of snow

Economy: major commercial farming with manufacturing

Teaching Idea

Duplicate Instructional Master 40, *Regions of the United States,* and distribute one to each student. Provide atlases, geography books, and similar references that include maps of the United States. Have students identify and label each state within the regions. As an alternative and as a check on student knowledge, make an overhead of the map. Have the class try to fill in the state names without looking at any references. Try not to rely on the same few students. When most students are unable to identify the remaining states, ask students to use the reference books to fill in the missing names on their maps.

When students have finished filling in state names, have them color each region a different color and create a key for the map.

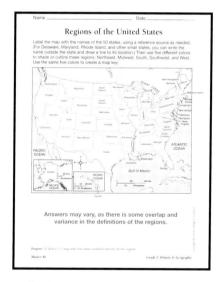

Use Instructional Master 40.

Cultural literacy characteristics: The region is associated with

- Chicago and the beginning of the meat-packing industry.
- Detroit, the auto city, "Motown."
- settlement of the upper Midwest by Germans and Scandinavians.
- the origin of the Mississippi River; annual flooding.
- Minnesota, the land of 10,000 lakes.
- Lake Superior, the largest of the Great Lakes; Lake Michigan.
- very cold, snowy winters.
- the home of Paul Bunyan and Babe, the blue ox.

Other: Part of the Midwest overlaps with the Great Plains region.

Great Plains

States: Montana, Wyoming, Colorado, North Dakota, South Dakota, Nebraska, Kansas, Oklahoma, Texas

Climate: cold winters and warm summers; precipitation may vary from year to year and from area to area. Much of the precipitation is in the form of snow

Economy: major commercial farming including cattle ranching

Cultural literacy characteristics: The region is associated with

- tornadoes and dust storms.
- buffalo, Native Americans hunting on horseback, and the last Indian wars.
- cattle trails and railheads to get cattle to Chicago.
- settlement in later phases of westward expansion, after the Homestead Act.
- Dust Bowl of the 1930s.

Other: Parts of these states are not within the Great Plains but are mountainous, and those areas have arid and semiarid climates. The Great Plains region overlaps with the Midwest, the West, and the South.

The Southwest

States: Arizona, New Mexico, Utah, Colorado, Texas

Climate: hot, dry, and in many places, desert; the mountain areas of these states receive snow in the winter

Economy: cattle, light industry

Cultural literacy characteristics: The region is associated with

- cliff dwellings of the Anasazi.
- Pueblo Native Americans.
- Navajo weavings, turquoise jewelry.
- desert, cactus.
- strong Spanish influence, dating back to the period when much of the Southwest was part of Mexico.
- Mexican food.

Other: The first Europeans to colonize these states were Spanish, and the Spanish heritage is very apparent in architectural styles and place names.

The West

States: Montana, Wyoming, Colorado, New Mexico, Idaho, Utah, Arizona, Nevada, Washington, Oregon, California

Climate: arid and semiarid in the mountainous areas; hot summers and cool winters along the southern coast; mild winters and summers but very rainy all year round in the northwest

Economy: mining, cattle ranching, light industry, lumbering, paper, wood products, dairy products

Cultural literacy characteristics: The region is associated with

- mining towns.
- California Gold Rush.
- cowhands and cattle ranching.
- Spanish influences in architecture and place names.
- Northwest Native Americans.

Other: The region overlaps with the Pacific Northwest and the Southwest.

 ### The Pacific Northwest

States: Washington, Oregon

Climate: temperate with mild winters and summers, but very rainy all year round

Economy: lumbering, wood products, paper, dairy products

Cultural literacy characteristics: The region is associated with

- Northwest Native Americans.
- Columbia River and Lewis and Clark Expedition.
- Asian populations.

Other: The region overlaps with the West.

Other Regional Names

Additional terms that appear in history texts and in contemporary news reports are

- Gulf Coast, referring to the states along the Gulf of Mexico: Florida, Alabama, Mississippi, Louisiana, and Texas.
- the Southeast, namely North and South Carolina, Tennessee, Georgia, Alabama, Florida, Mississippi, Arkansas, and Louisiana.
- Rocky Mountain states, namely New Mexico, Colorado, Wyoming, Montana, Utah, Washington, Idaho.
- Far West, namely California, Oregon, and Washington.

Some of these regions overlap. Which term is used depends on what the topic is. For example, someone interested in finding out which states border the Gulf Coast would not want to know what states were in the Southeast, only which states were Gulf States.

50 States and Their Capitols

Each of the 50 states has a city or town that is the capital. The capital city is the seat of state government. Most states have a capitol building in which much of the business of state government takes place. Each state has an executive branch of government (headed by the governor), a legislative branch, and a judicial branch.

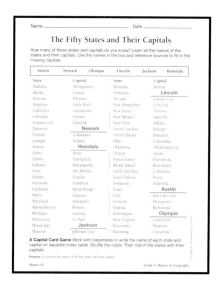

Use Instructional Master 41.

IV. United States Geography

Teaching Idea

To help students become more familiar with the 50 states and their capital cities, make a copy of Instructional Masters 42 and 43, *Start the Match!* and *Finish the Match!*, for each student.

The legislative branch varies from state to state. Some states have fulltime legislators, while others meet only periodically. Each state is responsible for making laws that apply to the citizens of that state, such as laws on taxation, education, labor, etc.

It is a *Sequence* goal in Grade 5 that students learn the names of the 50 states and their capitals. They should also know the name of the governor of their home state.

Use Instructional Masters 42 and 43.

State	Capital
Alabama	Montgomery
Alaska	Juneau
Arizona	Phoenix
Arkansas	Little Rock
California	Sacramento
Colorado	Denver
Connecticut	Hartford
Delaware	Dover
Florida	Tallahassee
Georgia	Atlanta
Hawaii	Honolulu
Idaho	Boise
Illinois	Springfield
Indiana	Indianapolis
Iowa	Des Moines
Kansas	Topeka
Kentucky	Frankfort
Louisiana	Baton Rouge
Maine	Augusta
Maryland	Annapolis
Massachusetts	Boston
Michigan	Lansing
Minnesota	St. Paul
Mississippi	Jackson
Missouri	Jefferson City
Montana	Helena
Nebraska	Lincoln
Nevada	Carson City
New Hampshire	Concord
New Jersey	Trenton
New Mexico	Santa Fe
New York	Albany
North Carolina	Raleigh
North Dakota	Bismarck
Ohio	Columbus
Oklahoma	Oklahoma City
Oregon	Salem
Pennsylvania	Harrisburg
Rhode Island	Providence
South Carolina	Columbia
South Dakota	Pierre
Tennessee	Nashville
Texas	Austin
Utah	Salt Lake City
Vermont	Montpelier
Virginia	Richmond
Washington	Olympia
West Virginia	Charleston
Wisconsin	Madison
Wyoming	Cheyenne

Teaching Idea

Have students create displays for states of choice. Ensure that all 50 states are represented. (This project can be a nice activity for the entire grade level to share.) Students can conduct research on their state, noting required information as well as other facts they find interesting. If students have learned to sing "Fifty Nifty," host a "Fifty Nifty State Fair" for parents and caregivers. Start by singing the song and then allow guests to tour each state's display. The state fair is also a meaningful end-of-the-year activity.

Review

The Big Idea in Review

The United States is made up of 50 states, which are often grouped into regions; each region has its own climate, landscape, and culture.

Below are some ideas for ongoing assessment and review activities. These are not meant to constitute a comprehensive list. Teachers may also refer to the *Pearson Learning/ Core Knowledge History & Geography* series for additional information and teaching ideas.

• Have students write about another region of the country and create a class presentation in which they share interesting facts about the other region. At the end of the presentations, have students write about the question, "If you could live in another part of the country, where would it be and why?"

• Have students pick another state to research. Create a list of facts to learn about that state, such as the capital, state bird, state flower, state motto, date admitted to the union, and number of congressmen and senators. Have students use computers in the computer lab to create a way to present this information to the class, such as handouts, puzzles, or Microsoft PowerPoint presentations.

• A fun way to assess student knowledge is to have students play "Concentration" or "Jeopardy" using the states and their capitals as the topic of the games. Students could make their own game cards using index cards. Alternatively, use a wooden puzzle of the United States to accomplish the same assessment. Have students take turns choosing a state and identifying the name of the state and its capital. Students who answer correctly may remove the puzzle piece; the student who collects the most pieces wins.

• Have students choose a state and write to that state's tourism office to learn more information. Make sure that students use the correct letter-writing format to ask for materials. Then, using that information, have students create a brochure for the state, including information and interesting areas to visit. Each brochure should have a short written summary about the state's history. Encourage students to decorate their state's brochures, as well.

• Use the resources at the local library or school media center for students to find books about United States geography. The books may focus on the entire country or on a more specific region. Have each student complete a written book report and a class presentation.

• You may also ask the following questions after completion of this unit of study.

1. Locate on a globe the Western Hemisphere, North America, the Caribbean Sea, and the Gulf of Mexico.

2. Identify three different regions in the United States and the states in each region.
   Any three: New England: Maine, Vermont, New Hampshire, Massachusetts, Connecticut, Rhode Island. Mid-Atlantic: New York, New Jersey, Pennsylvania, Delaware, Maryland. South: Maryland, Delaware, Virginia, North Carolina, South Carolina, Georgia, Florida, West Virginia, Kentucky, Tennessee, Alabama, Mississippi, Louisiana, Arkansas, Texas. Midwest: Ohio, Michigan, Indiana, Illinois, Wisconsin, Minnesota, Nebraska, Iowa, Kansas, Missouri. Great Plains: Montana, Wyoming, Colorado, North and South Dakota, Nebraska, Kansas, Oklahoma, Texas. Southwest: Arizona, New Mexico, Utah, Colorado, Texas. West: Montana, Wyoming, Colorado, New Mexico, Idaho, Utah, Arizona, Nevada, Washington, Oregon, California. Pacific Northwest: Washington, Oregon.

IV. United States Geography

More Resources

The titles listed below are offered as a representative sample of materials and not a complete list of everything that is available.

For students —

• *Geography of the United States*, edited by E. D. Hirsch, Jr. (Pearson Learning, 2002), a unit in the official *Pearson Learning/Core Knowledge History & Geography* series, is available as part of the bound book for Grade 5/Level 5 and as a stand-alone module. A teacher's guide is also available. To order, call 1-800-321-3106.

• *Alaska (Land of Liberty)*, by Xavier Niz (Capstone, 2003). One volume in a nicely presented library of the 50 states and Washington, D.C. Library binding, 64 pages, ISBN 0736815708.

• *My First Pocket Guide About North Carolina*, by Carole Marsh (Gallopade Publishing Group, 2002). Part of a series on all 50 states. Hardcover, 96 pages, ISBN 0635013231.

• *V is for Volunteer: A Tennessee Alphabet (Discover America State by State, Alphabet Series)*, by Michael Shoulders and illustrated by Bruce Langton (Sleeping Bear Press, 2001). Each book in this series tells interesting facts about each state in short verse while going through the alphabet. Hardcover, 40 pages, ISBN 1585360333. See other books in this series on Georgia, Ohio, South Carolina, Texas, and more, including the book *A is for America* with an accompanying CD of songs. Teacher's guides are also available. For more information, contact Sleeping Bear Press at www.sleepingbearpress.com or 1-800-487-2323.

• *Wyoming (From Sea to Shining Sea)*, by Alexandra Hanson-Harding (Children's Press, 2003). Highlighted by beautiful photography and an encyclopedialike text, this is one of several titles in a series. Though written at roughly a seventh-grade level, these books will make accessible reference works for many Grade 5 students. Library binding, 80 pages, ISBN 0516224905.

For teachers —

• *Across This Land: A Regional Geography of the United States and Canada*, by John C. Hudson (Johns Hopkins University Press, 2002). Clearly organized and well written. A good reference. Paperback, 504 pages, ISBN 0801865670.

• *Goode's World Atlas 20th Edition*, edited by John C. Hudson (Rand McNally & Company, 1999). Long a standard reference in classroom libraries. Hardcover, 384 pages, ISBN 0528843362.

• Nystrom, www.nystromnet.com or 1-800-621-8086, and Rand McNally, www.k12online.com or 1-800-678-7263, both offer a variety of maps and other geography teaching aids. One advantage of choosing a single company from which to purchase maps is that classroom wall maps and student maps will correspond, helping to eliminate confusion over scale, perspective, etc.

• The National Geographic Society, www.nationalgeographic.com/education. Multifeatured website includes a map machine, printable maps, and online adventures, to name a few.

• TerraServer, at http://terraserver-usa.com, may be one of the most useful online tools to help students see the relationship between their own home and a topographical map. Zoom in to see aerial or topographic maps of the continental United States up to a resolution of two meters. You can also purchase inexpensive topographical maps from the United States Geological Survey.

• The United States Geological Survey, www.usgs.gov. From the home page, click on the link for "Students and Teachers" to view a wide range of resources. There is also a comprehensive glossary of terms on this site. To reach it from the "Students and Teachers" page, scroll to the bottom of the column labeled "Explorers" and click on the picture labeled "Glossary," or type in the address http://interactive2.usgs.gov/learningweb/explorer/geoglossary.htm.

Visual Arts

Percentages beside major topics provide
a rough guide for allocating time for
Visual Arts during the year.

Visual Arts in Fifth Grade

Students who have been in Core Knowledge schools should arrive in Grade 5 with some understanding and appreciation of the visual arts from their experiences in earlier grades. They should be familiar with specific pieces of art by famous artists, and should have been introduced to architecture and to works of art from other countries, cultures, and times.

The visual arts of each culture and era are quite distinct. It is important for students to begin to appreciate the significance of art in all cultures, not just their own. They will learn that people have created artworks for thousands of years. They will also extend their knowledge about the different genres of art and the different purposes that art has played in different societies.

The European Renaissance remains perhaps the most influential period in Western art. The French term *Renaissance* comes from the Latin word meaning "rebirth." Initially, the Renaissance was a revival of ideas from classical Greek and Roman art and literature. Artists looked back to classical times, studying ancient architecture and sculpture. They did not blindly copy these earlier precedents, but culled particular aspects to create a unique style. For instance, domes, columns, and other architectural elements were used in new and visually impressive ways.

The status of artists also changed dramatically during the Renaissance. Previously, individual artists were deemed artisans practicing a trade. Now, the concept of "genius" emerged, and artists such as Michelangelo were celebrated for their talent. Patronage was no longer limited to the church; powerful Italian city-states and wealthy, ruling merchant families (such as the Medici) also now vied for artists' services. Patrons used impressive commissions to signal their power and prestige.

Ancient precedents did not affect the northern European Renaissance to nearly the same degree as they did in Italy. Instead, among the most powerful cultural forces were religious reform, the return to Christian values, and the revolt against the authority of the Roman Catholic Church. While Italian Renaissance artists created naturalistic yet idealized pieces, Northern artists in the 16th century strove for precisely accurate observations in their works. They tended toward genre scenes (scenes of everyday life) and portraiture instead of the biblical, mythological, or grand historical themes that were common in the south.

Even centuries later, Renaissance art continued to influence artists, including those in the United States. Most professional American artists trained in Europe or at least went to see the Renaissance masterpieces firsthand. However, while the techniques and themes were old, artists in the United States were intent on capturing the emerging nation. Artists traveled throughout the Northeast and also ventured to the West, capturing the majesty of the land.

In the Far East, Japan began its own artistic legacy in prehistoric times. Over the centuries, other cultures, particularly those of China and Korea, influenced Japanese styles and themes. Buddhism strongly affected Japanese art, architecture, and landscape gardens. A reverence for nature also figures into much traditional Japanese art; nature is the subject matter in paintings, ceramics, and prints.

I.  rt of the Renaissance

The Big Idea

The European Renaissance was one of the greatest periods for achievements in art, literature, science, and philosophy in the Western world.

What Students Should Already Know

Students in Core Knowledge schools should be familiar with

Kindergarten, Grades 1, 2, and 3

- ▸ Elements of Art: color, line, shape, texture, light, space, and design
- ▸ Sculpture
- ▸ Kinds of Pictures: portraits, still life, and landscapes
- ▸ Pieter Bruegel, *The Hunters in the Snow, Children's Games*

Grade 1

- ▸ Art from long ago
- ▸ Leonardo da Vinci, *Mona Lisa*

Grade 2

- ▸ Architecture (Parthenon)
- ▸ *The Discus Thrower*

Grade 3

- ▸ Art of ancient Rome (The Pantheon, Pont du Gard) and Byzantine civilization
- ▸ Pieter Bruegel, *Peasant Wedding*

Grade 4

- ▸ Art of the Middle Ages in Europe
- ▸ Islamic Art and Architecture

What Students Need to Learn

- ▸ The shift in world view from medieval to Renaissance art, a new emphasis on humanity and the natural world
- ▸ The influence of Greek and Roman art on Renaissance artists (classical subject matter, idealization of human form, balance and proportion)
- ▸ The development of linear perspective during the Italian Renaissance
  - • The vantage point or point of view of the viewer
  - • Convergence of orthogonal lines toward a vanishing point, the horizon line
- ▸ Observe and discuss works in different genres—such as portrait, fresco, Madonna—by Italian Renaissance artists, including
  - • Sandro Botticelli, *The Birth of Venus*

I. Art of the Renaissance

Materials

Art Resources 1–14

Sandro Botticelli, *The Birth of Venus*

Leonardo da Vinci, *The Vitruvian Man*

Leonardo da Vinci, *Mona Lisa*

Leonardo da Vinci, *The Last Supper*

Michelangelo, *The Creation of Adam*

Raphael, *Marriage of the Virgin*

Raphael, *The Virgin and Child with Saint John the Baptist*

Donatello, *Saint George*

Michelangelo, *David*

Filippo Brunelleschi, *Dome of Florence Cathedral*

Michelangelo, *Dome of St. Peter's Basilica*

Pieter Bruegel, the Elder, *The Peasant Wedding*

Albrecht Dürer, *Self-Portrait at 28*

Jan van Eyck, *The Arnolfini Portrait*

Instructional Masters 44–45, 83

Linear Perspective, p. 336

Take the Renaissance Art Challenge, p. 346

Venn Diagram, p. 347

journals, pp. 331, 338

outline sketch of *Mona Lisa*, 1 per student, p. 335

drawing paper, p. 337

masking tape, p. 340

materials for the class to practice painting, fresco, or sculpture, p. 347

information on local artists or art teachers to visit the class, p. 347

information on local museums or galleries, p. 347

a collection of pictures of local or state buildings that have Renaissance features, p. 347

What Students Need to Learn continued

- Leonardo da Vinci, *The Proportions of Man* (also called *The Vitruvian Man*), *Mona Lisa*, *The Last Supper*
- Michelangelo, Ceiling of the Sistine Chapel, especially the detail known as *The Creation of Adam*
- Raphael: *The Marriage of the Virgin*, examples of his Madonnas (such as *Madonna and Child with the Infant St. John*, *The Alba Madonna*, or *The Small Cowper Madonna*)

▸ Become familiar with Renaissance sculpture, including
- Donatello, *Saint George*
- Michelangelo, *David*

▸ Become familiar with Renaissance architecture, including
- The Florence Cathedral, dome designed by Filippo Brunelleschi
- St. Peter's in Rome

▸ Observe and discuss paintings of the Northern Renaissance, including
- Pieter Bruegel, *Peasant Wedding*
- Albrecht Dürer, *Self-Portrait* (such as from 1498 or 1500)
- Jan van Eyck, *Arnolfini Wedding* (*Giovanni Arnolfini and His Wife*)

What Students Will Learn in Future Grades

In Grade 6, students will learn about major periods in Western art, including classical and Renaissance art.

Vocabulary

Student/Teacher Vocabulary

balance: the harmony of different elements in a painting (S)

chiaroscuro: Italian for "light-dark"; the technique of using shading to create the impression of three-dimensionality (rather than using line to create the same effect) (T)

commissioned art: art that is requested by a patron, usually for a specific portrait, statue, or building (S)

cupola: a roof in the form of a dome (T)

fresco: a painting technique in which pigments are applied to wet plaster; also, a painting made in this way (S)

gable: a triangular wall space or decorative panel on the end of a building between two sides of a pitched roof (T)

genre: a kind of art or literature, e.g., a portrait, a still life, or a Madonna in art (T)

genre painting: painting that portrays scenes from everyday life (S)

horizon line: the division of Earth and sky as seen by the observer (S)

humanism: the intellectual and cultural interest during the early Italian Renaissance in the art and literature of antiquity; also concerned with the study of humanity and its writings and activities (T)

Vocabulary continued

linear perspective: a technique that creates the illusion of spatial depth on two-dimensional works by delineating a horizon line and many imaginary orthogonal lines which recede to meet at one or more vanishing points on the horizon (S)

Madonna: in art, a painting or depiction of the Virgin Mary (S)

orthogonal line: a line running back into represented space or a vanishing point in a picture; orthogonals are perpendicular to the imagined picture plane or surface of the picture (T)

pediment: a triangular gable on the end of a building, usually over doors, windows, or porticoes (e.g., the Pantheon) (T)

portrait: a drawing or painting of a person (S)

proportion: the relationship of size among the parts of a whole (S)

Renaissance: French term that comes from the Latin word meaning "rebirth"; period in Europe from around 1400 to 1600 CE (S)

sfumato: the technique of blurring the edges of objects, thus making them appear as if they are far away (T)

single point perspective: see "linear perspective" (S)

vanishing point: point at which receding orthogonal lines seem to meet when shown in linear perspective (S)

vantage point: position from which something is viewed; also called "point of view" (S)

Domain Vocabulary

Art of the Renaissance and associated words:
art, artist, basilica, cathedral, monastery, dome, nunnery, St. Peter's, Sistine Chapel, realism, illusion, depth, perspective, dimension, rebirth, Medici, Florence, Rome, Catholic Church, pope, painting, depict, subject, masterpiece, commission, canvas, brush, brushstroke, philosophy, symbolism, patron, subject matter, historical, mythological, biblical, religious, Old Testament, New Testament, Greek, Roman, workshops, guild, craftsman, genius, "old master," frieze, church, gothic, sacred, divine, altar, altarpiece, ceiling, portrait, mural, technique, Northern Renaissance, Renaissance Man, chisel, sculptor, sculpture, hammer, marble, carve, bronze, stone, canvas, pigment, brush, architect, architecture, column, arch, hoist, medieval, stained glass, gigantic, impressive, pedestal, niche, scaffold, *plus words describing colors, e.g.,* red, blue, light, dark, *etc., plus words that describe things in the artworks, e.g.,* Venus, God, Adam, Jesus, Judas, apostles, Last Supper, Virgin Mary, peasant, *etc.*

Cross-curricular Connections

Language Arts

Fiction and Drama

• Stories

Don Quixote (de Cervantes)

• Drama

Shakespeare

History and Geography

World: European Exploration, Trade, and the Clash of Cultures

World: The Renaissance and the Reformation

Music

Listening and Understanding

• Music from the Renaissance

I. Art of the Renaissance

Cross-curricular Connections continued

Mathematics	Science
Computation	**The Human Body**
Measurement	• The Vitruvian Man
Geometry	

At a Glance

The most important ideas for you are:

▸ The Italian Renaissance revived the ideals, learning, and styles of ancient Greece and Rome.

▸ Both the Christian Church and wealthy and powerful patrons from the independent city-states of Italy commissioned art in order to broadcast their power and wealth.

▸ Italian Renaissance art included religious, mythological, and historical themes as well as portraits of the elite.

▸ Renaissance painting and sculpture aimed to reproduce the world around them. This style became known as realism.

▸ Precise observation of the natural world pervaded the northern Renaissance style.

▸ The Renaissance produced some of the most famous artists the world has ever known.

What Teachers Need to Know

Background

What exactly was "reborn" during the European Renaissance? The Renaissance, which is generally said to have lasted from around 1400 to 1600, was a "rebirth" of learning, art, and awareness, based largely on classical Greek and Roman art and literature. The ancients saw beauty in the world and tried to capture it in their artwork. They made beautiful sculptures, buildings, and other works of art. However, the civilizations of ancient Greece and Rome both declined, and the latter was replaced by the dominance of the Church during the period we call the Middle Ages. During the Middle Ages, some classical texts and many classical works of art were lost or forgotten. New styles emerged in art and architecture, such as the Gothic style, which students in Core Knowledge schools should have studied in Grade 4.

The humanists and artists of the Renaissance defined themselves in opposition to the Gothic style. Instead of gargoyles and stained glass, they wished to return to classical elements and styles—to pillars, domes and friezes. Even when they built a cathedral, they wanted to build it with Greek and Roman

elements. The influence of classical styles eventually proved to be very fruitful, and the Renaissance developed into one of the greatest ages for art and artists in the history of the world. Spurred by trade, the growth of cities, and a renewed interest in the civilizations of ancient Greece and Rome, great advances were made in literature, scholarship, navigation, astronomy, engineering, philosophy, education, and art.

Note that the topics in this section are closely connected with the Renaissance topics in the World History and Geography section "The Renaissance and the Reformation," (pp. 164–188), as well as with certain topics in the Music and Language Arts sections. We suggest that you teach this unit on Renaissance art in tandem with your study of other aspects of the Renaissance. Your students' understanding of the works discussed below will be much increased if they are able to connect the artists and artworks described in this section to the humanists, patrons, and city-states described in the history section.

Note: The descriptions and activities in the main text below are intended to help you become familiar with the artworks before presenting them to students; however, some of the activities might be adapted for classroom use. Activities intended specifically for students can be found in the Teaching Idea sidebars. The Looking Questions given below are also printed on the reverse side of the *Art Resources*, and have been written with students in mind, so that they might be used as a rough plan for class discussion. You should feel free to use these questions or develop questions of your own. Be sure students have time to look at the reproductions carefully before asking the Looking Questions.

Developments in Art

 ### Patronage

The Roman Catholic Church remained a significant patron of the arts during the period of the Renaissance, as it had been in the Middle Ages. The popes commissioned artists like Raphael and Michelangelo to decorate cathedrals and other church buildings. However, wealthy merchant families (such as the Medici) and independent city-states (such as Florence, Pisa, Bologna, etc.) also commissioned works of art that announced their wealth and power. Wealthy persons or institutions who supported artists and commissioned works were (and still are) known as patrons. Patrons generally dictated subject matter, which might include religious, historical, or mythological scenes, as well as portraits of patrons and their families. You can read more about the Medici as patrons of art in the World History and Geography section "The Renaissance and the Reformation," pp. 164–188.

 ### The Increasing Status of Artists

During the Renaissance, the modern concept of artists as individuals with creative genius emerged. Previously, artists were generally considered mere artisans and manual laborers of a trade. From the earliest times, they had worked in workshops producing art that was often more functional than decorative. During the Renaissance, many continued to work collaboratively. An expert painter might be assisted by a handful of apprentices who were learning the trade. However, at the same time, a number of individual artists became well known. One sign of the new status of art and the artist was that many painters began to

Teaching Idea

Pair students, and have one "commission" the other for a particular type of art, just as patrons would have done during the Renaissance. The "patrons" should give specific instructions about the work's scene, story, and mood. Have pairs switch roles, so the "artists" become the "patrons" and vice versa. Afterward, have students write journal entries about what it was like to have to create art according to another person's dictates. What are the advantages and disadvantages as compared to drawing whatever you want?

I. Art of the Renaissance

sign their names on the works they created. Before the Renaissance this was much less common.

 ## Types of Art

Renaissance artists made important advances in many media. There were major frescos painted on walls and ceilings, as well as portraits and everyday scenes painted on canvas. Many great sculptures were also produced, including some that were free standing, rather than attached to a wall or building, as had been the custom in the Middle Ages.

Renaissance architecture adapted the geometry and symmetry of classical Greek and Roman buildings such as the Parthenon and Pantheon. Builders used columns, carved or painted scenes, friezes, and pediments. They abandoned the highly ornate Gothic style of the Middle Ages with its vaults, flying buttresses, stained-glass windows, and gargoyles.

 ## Growing Realism

One important characteristic of Renaissance art is an increased degree of realism. In the Middle Ages, a great deal of beautiful art was created, but much of this art did not put a high premium on realism. Saints and religious figures were often depicted in a way that looks somewhat flat and/or abstract. This was partly because some classical knowledge about how to make flat pictures appear three-dimensional had been lost. But it also reflected the priorities of medieval artists and their patrons. The painters and patrons of the medieval period were eager to inspire religious thoughts in the viewer, and this did not always require exact realism.

The artists of the Renaissance looked back to classical models. Greek and Roman sculptors had created some very realistic figures, especially in their sculptures, and these became the inspiration for a new emphasis on realism in sculpture and painting.

Renaissance artists and scholars also rediscovered specific techniques that allowed them to make more realistic depictions. The rediscovery and development of linear perspective in paintings promoted the illusion of depth as the human eye sees it in the natural world. In linear, or single-point perspective, lines seem to converge on a vanishing point along the horizon line. Artists used this technique not only to foster a sense of depth, but also to focus the viewer's eye. (For more on perspective, see the discussion of Leonardo da Vinci's *The Last Supper* on pp. 336–337.)

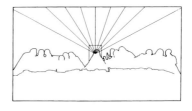

Artists who began this revolutionary change to Renaissance style included Giotto, who painted in the late 13th and early 14th centuries. He painted in a less Byzantine and more naturalistic way, imitating nature and using anatomy,

perspective, and expressive human detail in his works. Giotto's works influenced the style of Masaccio, a 15th-century Italian painter who employed perspective, three-dimensionality, and the use of light to create natural and realistic art. Through the works of these and other artists, the Renaissance brought about a slow evolution from medieval, Church-dominated culture to one more "modern" in which the artist could develop his or her individual expression.

The increased focus on realism can be seen as one aspect of the gradual growth of scientific observation. Indeed, some of the artists studied in this section—including Leonardo da Vinci—could be considered scientists as well as artists. Leonardo did engineering work as well as painting, and his sketches of the human body were based in part on his examination of cadavers.

The Renaissance in Northern Europe

The Renaissance began in Italy but eventually spread to other parts of Europe. Artists in 16th-century Netherlands and Germany learned much from Italian painters but also developed distinguishing characteristics of their own. In particular, they strove for precisely accurate depictions. Artists in the north paid enormous attention to detail in their portraits, religious scenes, and genre paintings.

Looking at the Included Reproductions

art resource 1

Sandro Botticelli, *The Birth of Venus* (c. 1485)

Renaissance artists sometimes painted mythological themes, looking back to classical literature for inspiration. One of the best-known mythological paintings of the Renaissance is *The Birth of Venus* by Sandro Botticelli (1444–1510). Lorenzo de' Medici, a member of the great Florentine family, commissioned this painting for his villa at Castello.

Botticelli himself was born in Florence. As a young man he was apprenticed first to a goldsmith, then to Fra Filippo Lippi (a well-known painter and subject of a poem by Robert Browning) where he worked with Andrea del Verrocchio, in whose shop Leonardo da Vinci later apprenticed. Botticelli did many works for the Medici family. After the 1490s, Botticelli appears to have been heavily influenced by a fiery preacher named Savonarola. Botticelli's style of painting changed to be less natural and idealized as he became more focused on politics and religion.

How does Botticelli indicate that the scene is clearly not of this world? His central figure, Venus, the goddess of love in Roman mythology, stands on an enormous seashell that somehow floats on water whose very waves create a beautiful pattern rather than portraying real ripples. On the left, the wind gods Zephyr and Aura blow Venus toward shore. On the right is one of the three Horae, or goddesses of the seasons, who were attendants of Venus; this hora personifies spring. She is clothed in a billowy gown, ready to drape the newly born (and therefore nude) goddess in a flowered cape.

Although the scene derives from classical mythology, in Renaissance times it reflected a Christian meaning as well. Venus's birth represented the mystery through which God gifts the world with beauty. Thus, in her purity, Venus represents sacred love in an exquisite, divine realm.

I. Art of the Renaissance

This painting was done with tempera on canvas. Botticelli may have been inspired to paint this subject after reading the work of the ancient Greek writer Lucian. Lucian describes a number of masterpieces from ancient Greece that had been lost by Botticelli's time.

The Birth of Venus is now in the Uffizi Gallery in Florence. It is sometimes jokingly referred to as "Venus on the Halfshell." Part of the painting is depicted on one side of the 10-cent euro coin.

Looking questions

- **What do you see?** *Answers will vary.*

- **What in this painting indicates that it does not represent real life?** *The woman is floating on a shell. There are also flying figures. The design of the landscape and the colors used in the work all indicate that it does not represent real life.*

- **What are the two floating figures doing on the left?** *They are blowing Venus to shore.*

- **Why is *The Birth of Venus* a good example of Renaissance interest in ancient Greece and Rome?** *The work is a good example of Renaissance interest in ancient Greece and Rome because it shows the renewed interest in classical subject matter, as well as the depiction of the nude, idealized human figure in a harmoniously balanced composition.*

- **It is said that Botticelli was a master of line. What evidence do you see to support that statement?** *The curving lines of the shell and surrounding figures focus attention on Venus. Also, the strong horizon line and vertical trees counterbalance the curves.*

art resource

(2) Leonardo da Vinci, *The Vitruvian Man (The Proportions of Man)* (c. 1492)

The mind of Leonardo da Vinci (1452–1519) has been a topic of endless fascination and discussion among scholars. How could one person have so many ideas about so many things? We are most fortunate that more than 5,000 pages of the artist's drawings and notes (in his curious mirror-image handwriting) survive. They tell us that he pondered all facets of the physical and natural worlds.

Leonardo was an especially great observer of human anatomy. This drawing of the proportions of the human body (sometimes called *The Vitruvian Man* or *The Proportions of Man*) is based on a mathematical analysis of the proportions between parts and the whole. The figure both stands in a square and, with extended limbs, stretches to touch a circle. The image reflects the belief that the perfect geometry of the human form relates it directly to the mathematical construction of the universe. To Renaissance thinkers the human form was as a microcosm of the macrocosm. **(66)**

You can read more about Leonardo da Vinci in the World History and Geography section "The Renaissance and the Reformation," pp. 164–188.

Looking questions

- **Where is the center of the circle?** *The center of the circle is located at the navel of the figure.*

- **What kind of triangle is formed, or implied, by the legs and feet of the extended figure?** *An equilateral triangle is formed by the legs and feet.*

- **What ideas and interests of the Renaissance does this figure represent?** *The figure represents an interest in the human figure and in the scientific and mathematical analysis of the physical world. It also expresses a belief in the importance of the role of humankind in the universe. The drawing also reminds the viewer that the laws ruling the human body are related to the laws ruling geometry, and both kinds of laws are part of the rational harmony of all heaven and earth.*

- **Why would you not expect an artist from medieval times to take the same kind of interest in understanding the physical world as a Renaissance artist?** *Medieval artists were focused on the spiritual aspects of the universe; they did not believe that humankind had the ability to shape its own destiny.*

- **Many of the ideas and projects that Leonardo was working on were original, or even in violation of the law. Why might he have used mirror-writing (backwards writing) for his notes?** *Answers will vary. Some people believe that he did it to deter others from studying his notebooks.*

- **Why might an artist's notebook be of more interest than a finished work of art?** *Answers will vary. Students might mention that an artist's notebook probably describes what the artist was thinking, his calculations, and his plans for completing the work.*

³ Leonardo da Vinci, *Mona Lisa* (1503–1506)

Leonardo da Vinci was the epitome of the "Renaissance Man"—a great artist of his time who also excelled in engineering, architecture (from churches to fortresses), military science, geology, aerodynamics, optics, hydraulics, botany, music, and literature.

His *Mona Lisa* is perhaps the most well-known portrait in the western world. Nearly 500 years after Leonardo laid down his brush, she still looks out with an enigmatic smile that has confounded scholars for generations. Why is the attractive woman smiling? At whom is she smiling? Did Leonardo want her gaze to meet ours or not?

Leonardo's fascination with the science of light and nature affected his art. He noticed that objects were not really made of lines, but of shadows and highlights. He used dark and light shades in a technique called chiaroscuro [kee-ahr-uh-SKYUR-oh], giving his images a softer, more realistic, three-dimensional look, as evident in *Mona Lisa*'s face. Leonardo also observed that objects in the far distance appear less distinct and so employed *sfumato*—blurring the edges of objects, thus making them appear as if they are far away. Sfumato is evident in the *Mona Lisa*'s landscape background, which recedes into deep space, defying the painting's actual flat surface.

Looking questions

- **How does Leonardo draw your eye through the painting?** *The use of light in the upper half of the painting and in the hands draws your eye in a circular motion through the painting. Leonardo also used a pyramid design, placing the woman in the center of the painting, forming the base with her hands, and the peak at the top of her head.*

Teaching Idea

Do an outline sketch of the Mona Lisa and draw an empty "thought bubble" above her head. Invite students to color the portrait and fill in the thought bubble with what Mona Lisa might have been thinking.

Teaching Idea

The Mona Lisa is often imitated and changed in advertisements. Some people say that imitation is the highest form of flattery. Have students find examples in magazines or on the Internet of changed images of the Mona Lisa. What is the company trying to sell with this image? How does this relate to the product in question? How does it make you feel to see the image changed?

- **Leonardo used a technique called *sfumato*, the blurring between light and dark and blending of different colors. How does this technique contribute to the realistic look of Mona Lisa?** *The depth of her face, especially around the eyes and corners of her mouth, was created using this technique. It creates a lively feeling and a sense of three-dimensionality.*

- **Is the background of the painting realistic? Why or why not?** *Answers will vary. Students should support their answers with specific references to the work.*

- **The young woman's expression is mysterious. What do you think she is feeling?** *Answers will vary. Explain that in drawing, expression rests mainly in two features: the corners of the mouth and the corners of the eyes. Leonardo deliberately left these parts hard to see by letting them merge into a soft shadow. That is probably why we are never quite certain what mood Mona Lisa's expression is conveying.*

art resource 4 Leonardo da Vinci, *The Last Supper* (1498)

Italian Renaissance painting was typically made for a specific purpose and location. What more logical subject to paint in the dining hall of the Dominican monastery in Milan than *The Last Supper*? While eating, the monks could contemplate the moment in which Christ tells his disciples, "One of you will betray me." How do the figures react? Leonardo captures each one's powerful response— questioning, denial, horror, shock, and disbelief. The story of *The Last Supper* is told in the book of Luke, chapter 22, verses 1–23 in the Bible. (See *More Resources*.)

Leonardo emphasizes Christ's centrality by placing him in the center, and also draws attention to his serene face through linear perspective. The lines made by the tops of the doorways, the meeting of wall and ceiling, and the roof beams all converge in a vanishing point just above his head. Judas, the disciple who will betray Christ, is on Christ's right. He is the only one drawing back and whose face is in shadow.

Leonardo tried something new with this work. He painted on dry plaster rather than using the traditional fresco technique of applying pigments to wet plaster, which absorbs the paint and makes for a strong, durable work. Unfortunately, the technique failed, and the paint began to flake off even in Leonardo's time. Restoration to preserve this masterpiece has continued to this day. **67**

Looking questions

- **What do you see?** *This is a depiction of Jesus' final meal with his disciples as imagined by the artist, Leonardo da Vinci. Christians believe that the Last Supper was on a Thursday, and Jesus was crucified on Friday and rose from the dead on Sunday, which is celebrated as Easter Sunday.*

- **How does Leonardo draw your eye to the main figure?** *The figure is centrally located and isolated within the door frame. Also, the vanishing point is at Jesus' head.*

- **One of Jesus' disciples will betray him to the Romans. Do you think the disciples have learned of this yet? Why?** *Answers will vary, but should include that the disciples appear surprised, shocked, or sad.*

Teaching Idea

Help students understand linear perspective with Instructional Master 44, *Linear Perspective*. Make sure they understand that Leonardo used linear perspective to underscore the meaning of the scene, Christ's centrality in the story of *The Last Supper*.

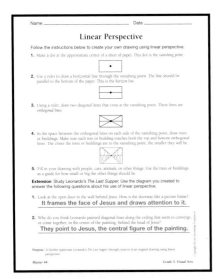

Use Instructional Master 44.

- **What do you feel looking at this work?** *Answers will vary.*
- **Did Leonardo use linear perspective in the same way in both** *The Last Supper* **and** *Mona Lisa*? *Answers will vary.*

5 Michelangelo, *The Creation of Adam* (Sistine Chapel ceiling, detail) (1508–1512)

Pope Julius II commissioned art to reflect the growing power of the Catholic Church in Rome. He hired Michelangelo (1475–1564) to paint the Sistine Chapel in the Vatican, even though the artist desperately did not want the enormous and painful task of painting the entire chapel ceiling; he was already working on Julius's tomb. The pope, papal advisors, and theologians dictated the subject matter: scenes from the Old Testament book of Genesis. In the center of the ceiling are nine rectangular panels, including *The Creation of Adam*. This story is told in the book of Genesis, chapter 2, verses 4b–25 of the Bible.

Michelangelo does not show God creating Adam's body, but rather the exact moment in which God will give Adam life: breath and soul. God gestures forcefully forward. Adam's arm is limp as he reclines weakly into the ground, not yet alive. Michelangelo makes clear God's power to give life to man.

Michelangelo spent over four years painting the ceiling of the Sistine Chapel. He built enormous scaffolding and then climbed up every day to paint. He had assistants to help him, but he did not like the way they painted, and so he did most of the painting himself. There are 145 pictures on the ceiling with over 300 figures in them. (68) (69)

The walls of the Sistine Chapel feature paintings by other Renaissance painters, including Botticelli. For more on Michelangelo, see the World History and Geography section "The Renaissance and the Reformation," pp. 164–188.

Looking questions

- **Explain to students that this scene is from the book of Genesis in the Old Testament. Here, God is said to have "breathed life" into Man. Ask: What is happening between the two figures?** *Their hands are outstretched between Heaven and Earth, and they are about to touch.*
- **Who might the older figure represent, considering his age and the heavenly figures around him in the sky?** *The figure might represent God.*
- **What is the contrast in energy in the forms of Man and God? Why is that?** *God is the life force; Man is barely alive in this instant before he is touched by God.*
- **How does Michelangelo draw our eyes to the two hands?** *He uses the silhouette of the nearly touching fingers against a light, empty background.*
- **In what type of building do you think this image of God creating the first man, Adam, would appear?** *It would probably appear in a religious building; in fact, it is in the Sistine Chapel.*

6 Raphael, *Marriage of the Virgin* (1504)

The master painter Raphael Sanzio (1483–1520) was born in Urbino but settled in Florence. His style was influenced by the works of Leonardo and Michelangelo. He is best known for his paintings of the Virgin Mary, also known as Madonna. He did a great deal of work in the Vatican for Pope Julius II and was the chief architect of Saint Peter's Basilica under Pope Leo X.

Teaching Idea

Show students additional pictures of details from the ceiling of the Sistine Chapel. If possible, also show a picture that shows the entire ceiling, so students can see the scope of the project. Pictures are widely available in books and online. If it's not against your school's policy, you can build on this assignment by reading the stories from Genesis on which the paintings are based and then asking students to discuss the paintings in light of the stories.

Teaching Idea

Explain that Michelangelo spent four years painting the ceiling of the Sistine Chapel. Contrary to popular myth, he most likely did not paint while lying on his back. However, he did stand on scaffolding and had to paint overhead, often bending back to reach the ceiling. Talk about what it must have been like to do this—how tired his arm must have gotten; how the paint must have run down his arm. Ask them to try it out. You might do this in class, but it would probably be a better homework assignment.

Give each student a piece of drawing paper and tell them to take it home and tape it as far over their heads as they can reach. They should ask an older sibling, parent, or a caregiver to time them for 10 minutes. Then the students should try drawing with a marker or crayon—not paint—for 10 minutes straight. When the other person calls time, students should untape their pictures and write a brief paragraph describing what it was like painting, how they felt, and what they think of Michelangelo.

Display their artwork on the ceiling of the class.

I. Art of the Renaissance

Teaching Idea

When you discuss perspective in Raphael's *Marriage of the Virgin*, you may wish to review from Grade 3 foreground, middle ground, and background. For contrast, examine paintings that do not create an illusion of depth, for example, *Madonna and Child on a Curved Throne*. (See Grade 4 Art Resources, "Art of the Middle Ages".)

Teaching Idea

You may wish to show students additional paintings by Raphael. One of special interest is his *School of Athens*, which shows great thinkers from antiquity like Plato and Aristotle along with Renaissance figures like Leonardo da Vinci. This is a classic expression of the Renaissance's artists' appreciation for the classical world.

Teaching Idea

Ask if students have been to a wedding, participated in a wedding, or seen a wedding on television. If they have, ask students to share their favorite memory of the wedding in a painting or drawing, and supplement it with a journal entry.

Teaching Idea

Review linear perspective with students. Then ask them to determine where the vanishing point is in Raphael's *Marriage of the Virgin*. (the open doorway) Why is its location important? (directly above Joseph putting a ring on Mary—the center of the action)

In his *Marriage of the Virgin*, Raphael sets the stage carefully. He conveys the importance of this marriage through his positioning of the main characters and background architecture. Everything, including the lines on the ground, draws our eye to Joseph and Mary, shown front and center, at the moment of their marriage. The joining of the couple is an important event leading to the eventual birth of Jesus. This story is told in the book of Matthew, chapter 1, verses 18–24 of the Bible.

Raphael inserts a bit of drama into the seemingly serene scene. Joseph's staff blossoms, signifying that God has chosen him to marry Mary. The staffs of the suitors behind him remain bare. And the frustrated suitor in the foreground even breaks his staff in half. Raphael heightens the sense of disappointment by playing it against the quiet perfection of the rest of the scene.

As noted above, prior to the Renaissance, artists typically did not sign their work. The concept of painters and sculptors as great geniuses who deserved fame from their work developed during this time. Raphael's painting is an example of the trend. He painted *Raphael Vrbinas (Raphael of Urbino)* and the date, 1504, in the building's fictive center arch—thus letting everyone know he created the work.

Looking questions

- **Explain that this scene represents the marriage of the Virgin Mary (the mother of Jesus) to Joseph in an Italian Renaissance setting. What moment in the marriage ceremony is being depicted?** *Joseph is about to place a ring on Mary's hand.*

- **Where is the vanishing point in this painting?** *The open doorway of the building is the vanishing point.*

- **Raphael establishes a foreground, middle ground, and background to give the painting depth. Which figures mark these areas of the painting?** *The wedding party is in the foreground; there are people in the middle of the plaza; and there are people in the distance atop the steps of the building.*

- **Raphael was praised for his ability to portray lifelike figures. How does he accomplish this in this painting?** *The figures have strength and energy. The man on the right is bending or breaking a stick over his knee. Joseph and Mary are caught in the middle of a movement.*

- **The Florentines (residents of Florence) were quite proud of their architecture. How does Raphael give a major role to architecture in this painting?** *The building occupies the upper half of the painting and seems to preside over the ceremony in the foreground.*

- **Does the building show evidence of Renaissance interest in ancient Greek and Roman architecture?** *Yes, the interest is apparent in the building elements (columns, arches, friezes) and the idealized figures.*

- **Raphael and other Renaissance artists placed biblical scenes in Italian Renaissance settings and peopled them with figures in Renaissance clothing. Why might they have depicted scenes this way?** *Answers will vary.*

(7) Raphael, *The Virgin and Child with Saint John the Baptist* (1507)

Raphael became famous for his Madonna and Child paintings. The theme was not new; the tradition of painting the Virgin and baby Jesus had existed for about 1,000 years. But Raphael's figures have more volume—a sense of fullness—which made them appear more lifelike than those from previous periods.

As in *Marriage of the Virgin,* Raphael positions his figures in a manner that communicates information. The Virgin Mary is in the center. She is the embodiment of love and nurturing, encompassing and protecting Jesus and his cousin John the Baptist. Mary is most likely holding a devotional prayer book. Jesus is holding a crucifix in his hand. John the Baptist is the figure on the right, and he is wearing the garment of a desert-dweller. Both John and Mary are focused on the figure of Jesus.

Notice too the strong diagonal Raphael builds from Mary's head down through that of Jesus, and then John the Baptist. The diagonal changes direction when forming the triangle. The only thing that breaks the line is the cross—an important symbol of the Christian religion. Raphael focuses both John and Mary's gaze on the cross so that we understand its importance.

Finally, Raphael forms the trio into a solid triangle that won't tumble out of the picture's round shape. **70**

Looking questions

Note: Cover up the title on the front of the print before showing to students.

- **This may look like a scene of two children and a woman, or their mother, but do you see indications that it is a religious scene as well?** *One child is holding a crucifix; the other (trace with your finger) has a halo above his head: the halo is a symbol of grace, divinity, and holiness.*

- **Explain that this is a portrait of the Virgin Mary with her son Jesus and John the Baptist, who is said to be Jesus' cousin. John the Baptist preached in the wilderness and baptized people there. Baptism welcomes people into the Christian community. Which child do you think is John the Baptist?** *He is the one on the right. He wears the garment of a desert-dweller.*

- **How can you tell that Jesus is the most important figure?** *Both John the Baptist and Mary are looking at him.*

- **What strong horizontal line balances the circular shape of the painting?** *The band of water and trees balances the circular shape of the painting.*

- **Despite the deep space of the background, how does Raphael keep your eyes focused on the figures?** *The figures are large, in the immediate foreground, and are placed so that they "block" your view.*

- **What geometric shape do the three figures create in the composition?** *The figures create a triangle.*

- **What do you think appealed to people about Raphael's works? Is there anything that appeals to you now?** *Answers will vary.*

art resource

8 ## Donatello, *Saint George* (c. 1415–1417)

The sculptor Donatello (1386–1466) was well known early in the Renaissance for his dramatic, life-sized figures. Born in Florence, Donatello was apprenticed to a goldsmith. Later he would benefit from the patronage of Cosimo de' Medici. He was a friend of the architect Brunelleschi.

Donatello posed Saint George in a rather simple manner. He stands facing us directly, feet apart, shoulders square, with his shield and hands at the ready. He is at rest but leans ever so slightly forward, ready to leap into action at any moment.

Teaching Idea

Find other, older depictions of Mary and Jesus along with additional paintings by Raphael and compare the figures. Ask students to try to describe the unique nature of Raphael's paintings.

Teaching Idea

Raphael's figures sit in a realistic landscape. He creates a sense of deep space in a similar way as Leonardo da Vinci did in his famous portrait *Mona Lisa*. Have students note how both artists blurred the details in the distance. The outlines of the landscape are indistinct in comparison to those of the nearby figures. This visually imitates the way humans actually see—objects grow fainter the farther away they are from us.

I. Art of the Renaissance

Saint George's expression is intense. His furrowed brow suggests passion and dedication. Donatello visually tells us that Saint George is the brave hero who saves the king's daughter from the menacing dragon.

The Armorers' Guild commissioned this work from Donatello for the Or San Michele Church. This was a guild church on the main road in Florence that had fourteen niches for sculpture. Saint George originally sat in one of the niches. A copy has since replaced it; the original is now in the National Museum of the Bargello in Florence. Different guilds commissioned different artists to represent their patron saints. Given the nature of its work, the Armorers' Guild demanded that Saint George be depicted fully armed. Despite the limitations this imposed, Donatello imbued his *Saint George* with a deep expressive quality.

Students who were in Core Knowledge schools in Grade 4 should be familiar with the story of Saint George and the dragon, though you may wish to review it. At a minimum, explain that Saint George is the patron saint of England. Around the time of the First Crusade, he is said to have slain a dragon that was holding a Libyan king's daughter captive. As his reward, he asked that the king and all his people convert to Christianity, and his request was granted.

Looking questions

- **What object is the figure holding and what is he wearing?** *He is holding a shield and wearing armor.*
- **What do these items suggest about the man's duty?** *The items suggest that the man is a knight or warrior.*
- **What does the figure's stance indicate about his attitude towards fighting?** *His stance indicates that he is courageous and determined.*
- **What do you think his facial expression suggests?** *Answers will vary. Students should support their answers with specific references to the image.*
- **Where do you see evidence that this warrior is a Christian knight?** *The sign of the crucifix is on his shield.*

art resource 9 — Michelangelo, *David* (c. 1501–1504)

Michelangelo (1475–1564) referred to himself as a stonecutter, believing it his foremost skill. (Notice the three-dimensional quality of his painted figures in the Sistine Chapel.)

At a mere 26 years of age, in Florence, Michelangelo carved a huge piece of marble—about 14 feet long—into a 13-foot tall statue of the biblical hero, David. Michelangelo's figure imitates the scale and idealization of ancient Greek sculpture, which celebrated beauty, youth, balance, and harmony. Michelangelo studied the human body to see how the muscles and skin moved; thus his statue has very obvious muscles and veins. The statue is leaning on one leg, as do many of the ancient Roman sculptures that copied the Greek style.

In the Old Testament story, David is a young boy who faces the giant warrior Goliath. This story can be found in the Bible, first book of Samuel, chapter 17, verses 1–58. Why did Michelangelo depict a heroic and strapping older youth? Although the sculpture has a religious theme, it was displayed in Florence's government center and served as a symbol of republican civic pride.

At that time, Florence was an independent city-state that had just ousted the

Medici rulers. *David* was originally located in the square in front of the city hall in Florence, Italy. It is now located in the Accademia delle Belle Arti in Florence, to protect it from the elements and pollution. (71)

Students will undoubtedly notice that David is nude. Remind students that the Greeks competed in the nude during the Olympics, and many Greek and Roman statues show figures in the nude. In general, the classical civilizations were less squeamish about nudity than we are today. While medieval artworks generally avoid nudity, Renaissance painters and sculptors followed the example of the classical artists before them by depicting many figures in the nude. Not everyone is comfortable with this nudity, and there are some Renaissance paintings in which the original figures were nude and a painter of a later era painted clothing on top of the naked bodies!

We urge schools to teach the selected works, which are great works of art and have also become part of cultural literacy. However, if you, your administrators, or parents of your students are extremely uncomfortable with nudity, you may wish to substitute other works by the same artists that feature clothed figures.

Looking questions

- **How did Michelangelo make the figure look real?** *Answers will vary, but students should note the muscles on the torso, veins on the hands, and the shifted-weight stance.*

- **How did Michelangelo create a sense of movement in the standing figure?** *The bent knee of the figure gives it a sense of movement.*

- **What details show the normal strain of the human body when it is twisting slightly?** *David's neck muscles are standing out; his ribs aren't level; most of his weight is on one foot.*

- **The Florentines were expecting the statue of a hero. Why do you think Michelangelo shows David in this pose, and not slinging a stone toward Goliath?** *Answers will vary. One of the reasons this statue is so striking is that this hero is perfectly composed and at ease. He is the image of confidence.*

- **The *David* is more than twice life-size and is placed on a high pedestal. How might it feel to stand at its base?** *It would feel overwhelming; the figure physically looms over the viewer, creating an intense mood.*

- **Given how David is standing and the sling over his shoulder, what do you think is on his mind?** *Answers will vary.*

- **How do the *David* and Donatello's *Saint George* reflect the Renaissance belief that humankind could shape its own destiny?** *Both heroes triumphed in the face of adversity, using their own will and strength.*

Filippo Brunelleschi, Dome of Florence Cathedral (1420–1436)

The Renaissance was a time of great accomplishments in art and architecture. The dome of the Florence Cathedral, built by Brunelleschi [broon-ell-ESS-key], is one of its greatest achievements. The cupola was the largest dome built since the Pantheon in Rome and the highest one ever created up to that time.

Brunelleschi was born and raised in Florence. He excelled in many fields. As

Teaching Idea

Read the story of David and Goliath to your students before they look at Michelangelo's sculpture *David*. Ask them to sketch or describe how they would portray David, and in which part of the story. Afterward, have students compare and contrast their versions to Michelangelo's as a way to begin the discussion about this sculpture. Students should note that Michelangelo left it to us to decide whether he depicts the moment before or after David killed Goliath.

Teaching Idea

Michelangelo wrote poetry. After defining any necessary vocabulary, have students discuss what the following example indicates about Michelangelo's concept of beauty and how this is evident in his own art. (Students should particularly understand the connection Michelangelo makes between beauty and the divine.)

> My eyes longing for beautiful things
> Together with my soul longing for salvation
> Have no other power
> To ascend to heaven than the contemplation of beautiful things

Have students write a poem that describes the statue of David, and have them focus on describing the beauty of the sculpture. They may also choose to write a poem to describe Michelangelo. Share these with the class.

I. Art of the Renaissance

Teaching Idea

Compare the architecture of the Florence Cathedral with other cathedrals. Discuss similarities and differences. This topic provides an opportunity for collaboration with students in Grade 4, who should be studying famous European cathedrals from the Middle Ages, including Notre Dame.

a youth, he was trained as a goldsmith. Later he became a painter and helped rediscover the lost art of perspective. Brunelleschi was also a well-known sculptor. In 1401, he entered a sculpture competition that was to decide who would be commissioned to make the elaborate bronze reliefs for the doors to an important religious building in Florence called the Baptistery. Brunelleschi completed a beautiful statue of the sacrifice of Isaac from the book of Genesis in the Old Testament, but his archrival Lorenzo Ghiberti was chosen to do the project.

Perhaps partly because of his frustration and disappointment at not winning the Baptistery competition, Brunelleschi began to focus more on architecture. His crowning achievement in his field was the building of the dome of the Florence Cathedral. Other architects had concluded that the dome could not be completed: they were sure it would collapse. But Brunelleschi thought otherwise. In 1418 he entered a competition meant to choose the best design for the dome. Once again he was competing against his rival Ghiberti. But this time Brunelleschi was selected as the winner. He developed an innovative plan for building the dome, based in part on building techniques of the ancient Romans. Rather than using a traditional wooden centering structure, Brunelleschi built his dome using stone beams and bricks. The bricks were placed in a special herringbone pattern between the beams. The design also used tension chains for additional support. Brunelleschi invented hoists and other equipment that made it easier to lift heavy supplies to the workmen high up on the construction site. He even arranged to have wine and food vendors placed within the construction so that the workers did not have to come down to the ground to eat. The work paid off. Brunelleschi succeeded in combining aesthetic beauty and sound engineering. His dome would serve as a model for Michelangelo's later work on the dome of St. Peter's in Rome.

Looking questions

- **Brunelleschi made several trips to Rome to study classic architecture. Which building would have been of particular interest to him?** *The Pantheon would have been particularly interesting to him. Encourage students to draw parallels between the Pantheon and this cathedral.*

- **How is this dome similar in structure to the one built later by Michelangelo on St. Peter's in Rome?** *Both have a drum, a ribbed dome, and a lantern. (Note: The drum was part of the Florence cathedral before Brunelleschi started his work.)*

- **What words would you use to describe the dome?** *Answers will vary, but students could use words such as massive, symmetrical, or harmonious.*

- **The streets of Florence are very narrow and winding. What feeling might you have walking down a street, looking up, and suddenly seeing the dome?** *Answers will vary, but should show a recognition of the size and awe-inspiring nature of the construction.*

- **Although it sits atop a religious building, the dome has always been a source of great civic pride for residents of Florence. Why do you think this is the case?** *Answers will vary.*

- **Why are the dome and its construction viewed as excellent examples of the Renaissance spirit?** *The influence of ancient Rome is evident in the construction. Brunelleschi's new scientific and engineering ideas reflect the Renaissance interest in exploring the physical world and the aesthetic preference for balance, harmony, and classic proportions.*

art resource

11 Michelangelo, Dome of St. Peter's Basilica (1546–1564)

At age 71 and in ill health, Michelangelo accepted the pope's commission to complete St. Peter's Basilica in Rome. A redesign of the church with an interior shaped like a cross had begun in 1506, but the project had outlasted several previous head architects. Michelangelo redesigned the exterior and the enormous dome.

Michelangelo referred back to ancient times in finishing the building. He infused the building with the same grandeur and geometrical symmetry as its ancient Roman and Greek antecedents, such as the Parthenon of ancient Greece and the Pantheon of ancient Rome. (Students in Core Knowledge schools should have learned about these buildings in Grade 2 and Grade 3.) Michelangelo also used ancient architectural styles that included pediments, columns, and the like. But he adapted the ancient features to create a "sculpted," upwardly thrusting exterior like no other building before it. The dome decreases in width and decoration as it gets taller: it starts with the colonnade-surrounded drum, then the visible ribs glide up toward the slim lantern, and a Christian cross decorates the top.

Explain that St. Peter's Basilica is a monument to Peter. According to the teachings of the Roman Catholic Church, Jesus chose him as the chief apostle, declaring that Peter was the rock on which he would build the Church. Because Rome was the capital of the Roman Empire, Peter, along with the apostle Paul, came to the city to spread the faith early in the first millennium. The popes claimed that Peter was the first head of the church and that they were his successors.

St. Peter's Basilica still dominates Rome's skyline today as it did as in the High Renaissance. The dome of St. Peter's was an important model for the U.S. Capitol in Washington, D.C.

Looking questions

- **Is the architecture symmetrical (exactly even on both sides) or asymmetrical?** *The architecture is symmetrical.*

- **What clue does the object at the very top of the dome give you about the building's function?** *The cross tells you that the building is used for Christian religious purposes.*

- **Explain that the height from the pavement of the church to the oculus of the lantern resting upon the dome is 404.8 feet, while the height to the summit of the cross surmounting the lantern is 434.7 feet. How is a dome of this size in keeping with the purpose of other grand designs of this type?** *Answers will vary. Like the dome of the Pantheon, the Hagia Sophia, or St. Paul's in London, the design is meant to overwhelm the viewer with sheer vastness, making him or her feel humble. This building communicates the power and prestige of this faith.*

12 Pieter Bruegel, the Elder, The *Peasant Wedding* (c. 1568)

Pieter Bruegel [BROI-gull] (1525–1569) is sometimes known as "Peasant" Bruegel because of his affinity for depicting village and farming life. Though he traveled to Italy and was influenced by Italian painters, including Raphael, Bruegel showed less interest in classical subject matter, idealized visions of the

St. Peter's square

Teaching Idea

Michelangelo studied ancient Roman architecture. Have students look at both the dome of the ancient Roman Pantheon (images can be found on the Internet) and Michelangelo's St. Peter's. Have them calculate how many years passed between the completion of the two buildings (c. 1564 CE [St. Peter's]–c. 125 CE [The Pantheon] = 1439). Then have students identify the classical elements in the Pantheon that Michelangelo adapted in his later dome (e.g., columns, tall drum, triangular pediments). Have students become architects, drawing proposals for a dome to top your school, using what they learned to make a grand, visual statement. You may wish to extend this comparative assignment by adding Brunelleschi's dome and the dome of the U.S. Capitol.

Teaching Idea

Show students additional pictures of St. Peter's. The interior is every bit as magnificent as the exterior and the dome. You may even be able to find pictures or a videotape of a pope performing a mass in St. Peter's.

I. Art of the Renaissance

Teaching Idea

Have students draw an event in their own genre setting that incorporates aspects of Bruegel's work, such as realistic figures and everyday activities.

Teaching Idea

Students in Core Knowledge Schools should already be familiar with some paintings by Bruegel. *Children's Games* (which shows children playing dozens of games, some of which are still played today) and *Hunters in the Snow* are in the curriculum for kindergarten, and *Peasant Wedding* is a featured artwork in Grade 3. You may wish to review some of these paintings by Bruegel and/or introduce new ones. A famous Bruegel painting that combines realistic depiction of life and landscape with a mythological theme is *Landscape with the Fall of Icarus.*

world, and nude figures. He chose instead to show believable figures in everyday settings (genre scenes). He was especially good at depicting people against the background of a landscape.

When looking at Bruegel's paintings, we are instantly engaged in the story we see unfolding. We say to ourselves, "What is going on?" The boisterous *Peasant Wedding* has been placed in a threshing room. Activity abounds. A careful observer will note the landlord and clergyman at the end of the table, and the lawyer (responsible for the contract of marriage) seated in a formal chair near the bride. The groom is not in evidence because, according to custom, he did not make an appearance until later in the celebration.

Bruegel is known as Pieter Bruegel the Elder because he had two sons who were also distinguished painters, Jan Bruegel and Pieter Bruegel the Younger. Jan was known as "Velvet Bruegel" and Pieter the Younger as "Hell Bruegel" because of his frequent depiction of fiery and Hellish scenes. The family name is sometimes spelled with an 'h': Brueghel. As noted above, the father was known as "Peasant Bruegel."

Looking questions

- **Explain that this is a wedding from more than 475 years ago. How does Bruegel draw your attention to the bride?** *A large dark area of color frames the bride, drawing the eye to her.*

- **How does the artist use red to lead your eye through the composition?** *The red begins at the child's hat, moves to the clothing at the right end of the table, to the bagpiper, to the doorway, and back.*

- **Why did Bruegel paint the foreground figure in the center with a bright blue shirt and a large white apron? What role does it play in the design of the painting?** *The cool, bright area jumps out at you and draws your eye right into the scene so that you immediately feel a part of it.*

- **What device did Bruegel use to both give you a sense of space beyond the room and prevent your eye from wandering away from the wedding activity?** *There is an open doorway, but it is almost entirely blocked by the crowd.*

- **In what ways would a wedding scene painted by an Italian Renaissance artist be different from this one?** *A Renaissance artist would have been more likely to have depicted wealthy people or nobility. The scene would likely have had a harmonious, tranquil air and depicted a "classic" environment.*

- **Have you ever been to a wedding? Was it anything like this?** *Notice what the guests are paying attention to. Is it the bride? No, it's the music, food, and drink.*

art resource
(13) Albrecht Dürer, *Self-Portrait at 28* (1500)

One of the important changes for artists that took place during the Renaissance was the transformation of their role in society. Medieval artists were viewed as artisans. During the Renaissance, individual artists became well known. Many of them were recognized as geniuses and held high places in society. The new attitude was a natural outcome of the Renaissance belief in the importance of the individual.

No one can doubt that Albrecht Dürer (1471–1528) viewed himself as a person of significance. His distinctive initials are found on all of his work, which includes paintings as well as a number of distinctive engravings and woodcuts. He was also the first artist to make a lifelong study of himself. His first self-portrait dates from when he was thirteen. The one in Münich, painted at twenty-eight, is a depiction of Dürer when he was already recognized as an eminent artist throughout Europe.

The inscription on the right side of the painting says, "I, Albrecht Dürer of Nuremberg, painted myself thus, with undying colors at twenty-eight years." One could say that the artist viewed the painting as a documentation of his talent and craftsmanship.

Looking questions

- **From which direction does the light in the portrait come?** *The light comes from the left.*

- **How would you describe the space in this painting?** *The space is very tight; there is no place for the eye to wander. The figure is placed immediately before you.*

- **What characteristics of this work would lead you to conclude that it was painted by a Northern Renaissance artist?** *The attention to detail and differentiation of textures could lead you to conclude that it was painted by a Northern Renaissance artist.*

- **How has Dürer posed his body? What impression does that give?** *His body is posed in a fully frontal position that commands respect and imparts a sense of power.*

- **How does Dürer use this self-portrait to make a statement about his skill and craftsmanship?** *Answers will vary.*

- **If you had to describe the artist based on this painting, what would you say? Consider physical and personality traits.** *Answers will vary.*

art resource (14) Jan van Eyck, *The Arnolfini Portrait (Portrait of Giovanni Arnolfini and His Wife)* (1434)

This painting by the Flemish painter Jan van Eyck [yahn van IKE] (c. 1390–1441) demonstrates the changing social makeup of Northern Renaissance society. Here, a wealthy merchant, Giovanni Arnolfini, is the artist's patron, instead of royalty or the church. Arnolfini was an Italian merchant who was working in the north at the time this was painted. Van Eyck, one of the early masters of oil painting, was commissioned to record Arnolfini's marriage.

This work is a portrait of Arnolfini and his wife, but it is probably not intended to be a record of the actual wedding (although the painting is sometimes referred to as *The Arnolfini Wedding*). Some scholars believe this scene is meant to be a vision for the couple's future—a fruitful and devoted marriage. Others interpret the painting as a sort of visual marriage certificate.

Arnolfini raises his right hand as he faces his guests, maybe as a greeting. His bride is not pregnant, though this is what viewers often think. She is holding up her full-skirted dress in what was then the stylish way.

The mirror on the rear wall reflects two figures in the doorway. Above the mirror, the artist wrote, "Jan van Eyck was here." Some people believe the painter

Teaching Idea

Students who have been in Core Knowledge schools for several years should have discussed Albrecht Dürer's *Young Hare* in Grades 1 and 2. Dürer was a Northern Renaissance artist. He was primarily a printmaker—and the greatest of his time. The multiple copies of his prints (which were less expensive than individual paintings) spread throughout northern and southern Europe, helping Dürer secure his reputation as the "Leonardo of the North." You may wish to review this painting or share additional pictures by Dürer. Some possibilities include additional self-portraits or engravings.

Teaching Idea

If students have studied the Reformation, they may be interested to know that Dürer was a friend and devoted follower of Martin Luther. Remind students that the Renaissance and Reformation were two movements that overlapped. While the Italian Renaissance artists they have been studying lived in Catholic areas and often received patronage from the pope, northern artists like Dürer lived in areas that inclined towards Protestantism. They sometimes received commissions from local princes and rulers, many of whom supported Luther.

Use Instructional Masters 45a–45b.

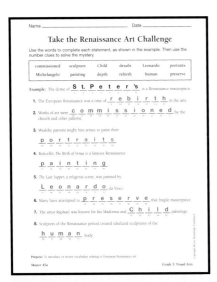

Use Instructional Masters 45a–45b.

is one of the two figures shown in the mirror. However, the figures in the mirror are very small and it is hard to be certain.

Measure out this painting on the board or a large piece of paper, then notice the extraordinary detail van Eyck included in the relatively small panel ($32\frac{1}{4}$ x $23\frac{1}{2}$ in. or 82 x 60 cm). Every item is distinct, so that you can tell the difference in texture between even the dog's fur coat and the fur trim on Giovanni's cloak. Like other Northern Renaissance artists, van Eyck paid meticulous attention to detail. Nothing in the composition is random; each object supports the painting's overall meaning.

This painting is highly realistic and yet it is also awash in symbolism. Some of this symbolism can be hard to understand; symbols that would have been clear to knowledgeable contemporaries do not convey the same meanings today. The dog symbolizes fidelity between husband and wife. The burning candle in the chandelier represents the presence of God. The figures have removed their shoes, an act of devotion. The ten miniature medallions in the mirror's frame depict scenes from the life of Christ—religious symbolism indicating that marriage is a sacred event ordained by God. The woman's stance, along with the fruit on the windowpane and table, symbolize hopes for children.

Looking questions

- **How many different textures can you find in the painting?** *Nearly everything in the room has a well-defined texture.*
- **Van Eyck was very interested in how light reflected on things to give them solidity and detail. Where do you see light reflected in this painting?** *Light is reflected on the mirror, of course, but also on the chandelier, which looks amazingly like real brass.*
- **What in van Eyck's painting indicates the relationship between the man and the woman?** *The couple is turned towards one another; they are holding hands; they have removed their shoes.*
- **What in this painting reveals that the couple is wealthy?** *Their sumptuous clothing and the decor indicate that the couple is wealthy.*
- **How do you think it would feel to step inside this room?** *Answers will vary.*

Review

Below are some ideas for ongoing assessment and review activities. These are not meant to constitute a comprehensive list.

• This section provides an opportunity for students to complete short research reports, either on any of the Renaissance artists included in the *Sequence*, or on a type of artistic style. Provide the class with topics for short reports to write in formal style (see the Language Arts section "Writing and Research," pp. 1–14, for guidance on report writing). Each day of a week, provide a mini-lesson on different aspects of report writing, such as correct paragraph form or bibliographies. Share these reports when completed.

• As a class, brainstorm two lists: one list of the elements of medieval art and one list of the elements of Renaissance art. Have students plot the lists on Instructional Master 83, *Venn Diagram*. Then, have students write a paragraph comparing and contrasting the two styles of art, using their diagrams as a guide. Ask students to use specific works of art to support any arguments they make in their paragraphs.

• Give the class an opportunity to practice some of the techniques from this section, such as painting a portrait, creating a fresco, or making a sculpture. Then, invite another class to an art show and have your students act as docents (guides), explaining their art and what influenced them. Provide examples of the art from this section to show the inspiration for each piece.

• Invite a local artist or art teacher to conduct a lesson on a specific type of artistic technique from the Renaissance. Allow students to make a piece of art using the technique that is demonstrated, and display the student art in the front hallway of the school.

• After studying this section, arrange a visit to a local museum or gallery. Have students write a letter to the owner of the gallery or to the director of the museum explaining what they have studied and asking what they might be able to view that is similar to what they have studied. Have students write papers after the field trip to describe what they examined on their trip.

• After studying the features of Renaissance architecture, have the class examine buildings in their local community or state to see if they can find some of these features, such as large domes, pediments, or gables. Assemble a collection of pictures of buildings to share with the class, and have students describe any Renaissance-inspired styles they notice. You can also encourage students to bring in pictures of any buildings they have noticed in town and then share these with the class.

• Use the Art Resources for this grade as flash cards to review the works that have been studied. Ask students to remember the names of the artists and the artworks, and see if they can remember additional facts as well.

• In general, the best time to ask questions about a specific work of art is while students are looking at it. However, by the end of the unit, students should be able to answer questions like the following:

1. What does the French term *Renaissance* mean?
   The term means "rebirth."

2. What was "reborn" during the European Renaissance?
   There was a rebirth (or rediscovery) of the values, ideas, and styles of classical Greece and Rome.

3. About when did the Renaissance take place?
   The Renaissance took place from roughly 1400 to 1600. (Students need not give exact dates.)

4. What does single-point (or linear) perspective do?
   Single-point, or linear, perspective creates the illusion of depth on a two-dimensional surface.

5. Who commissioned art during the European Renaissance?
   The church, city-states, and wealthy merchants all commissioned art during the Renaissance.

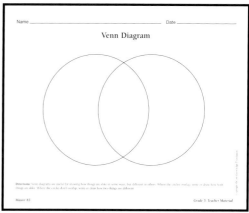

Use Instructional Master 83.

6. What do we call a person who supports the arts?

   We call a person who supports the arts a patron.

7. What kind of painting is a Madonna?

   A Madonna is a painting of the Virgin Mary.

8. How many Renaissance artists can you name?

   Students may mention Leonardo da Vinci, Michelangelo, Sandro Botticelli, Raphael, Donatello, Pieter Bruegel, Albrecht Dürer, or Jan van Eyck.

9. How is a fresco made?

   A fresco is made by adding color to wet plaster.

10. Who painted the *Mona Lisa*?

    Leonardo da Vinci painted the **Mona Lisa**.

11. Who sculpted the most famous Renaissance statue of *David* and also served as architect for the dome of St. Peter's Basilica?

    Michelangelo was the man behind both works.

12. What were some cities in Italy that were important centers of artistic life during the Renaissance?

    Students should mention Florence and Rome, and may also mention other Italian cities and city-states, e.g., Venice, Padua, Mantua, Urbino.

More Resources

The titles listed below are offered as a representative sample of materials and not a complete list of everything that is available.

For students —

• *Rats, Bulls, and Flying Machines: A History of the Renaissance and Reformation,* by Deborah Mazzotta Prum (Core Knowledge Foundation, 1999). An interdisciplinary history of the period, touching on history, literature, art, and music.

• *The Renaissance,* edited by E. D. Hirsch, Jr. (Pearson Learning, 2002), two units in the official *Pearson Learning/Core Knowledge History & Geography* series, available as part of the bound books for Grade 5/Level 5. A teacher's guide is also available for each unit. To order, call 1-800-321-3106.

• *The Genius of Leonardo,* by Guido Visconti (Barefoot Books, 2000). A great overview of Leonardo's life as told by his ten-year-old assistant. Library binding, 40 pages, ISBN 184148301X.

• *The Life and Work of Leonardo da Vinci,* by Sean Connolly (Heinemann, 2001). Paperback, 32 pages, ISBN 1588102831.

• *The Life and Work of Michelangelo Buonarroti,* by Richard Tames (Heinemann, 2001). Paperback, 32 pages, ISBN 1588102890.

• *Michelangelo,* by Mike Venezia (Children's Press, 1994). Part of the "Getting to Know the World's Great Artists" series. Paperback, 32 pages, ISBN 0516422936. Series also contains volumes on Leonardo da Vinci, Raphael, Bruegel, Giotto, Botticelli, and many others.

For teachers —

• *Rats, Bulls, and Flying Machines: A History of the Renaissance and Reformation,* by Deborah Mazzotta Prum (Core Knowledge Foundation, 1999) is a student book accompanied by a teacher's guide. An interdisciplinary history of the period, touching on history, literature, art, and music.

• Art Print Resources (209 Riverdale Avenue, Yonkers, NY 10705, www.artprintresources.com, or 1-800-501-4278) sells a set of posters of the art works in the *Sequence* for this grade.

• Art Sense (www.artsense.net) provides an art program using videos and trade books.

More Resources continued

• Art to the Core (Davis Publications, www.davis-art. com or 1-800-533-2847). A kit of materials that includes slides of artworks, lessons plans, assessment masters, and vocabulary masters, all keyed to the *Core Knowledge Sequence* for this grade.

• *Brunelleschi's Dome: How a Renaissance Genius Reinvented Architecture,* by Ross King (Penguin Books, 2000). Paperback, 167 pages, ISBN 0142000159.

• Crizmac (www.crizmac.com) sells a wide range of art education materials.

• *Drawing with Children,* by Mona Brookes (J.P. Tarcher, 1996). Teaches the basics of realistic drawing—the five "elements of shape"—to children as young as four or five. Useful for any age level. Paperback, 272 pages, ISBN 0874778271.

• *Holy Bible, New International Version Textbook Edition* (Zondervan, 1984). Hardcover, 1280 pages, ISBN 0310903262.

• *How to Teach Art to Children,* by Joy Evans and Tanya Skelton (Evan-Moor Corporation, 2001). An excellent companion to *Drawing with Children.* Covers color, patterns, designs, textures, and more. Paperback, 160 pages, ISBN 1557998116.

• *Leonardo Da Vinci,* by Kenneth Clark (Penguin, 1993). Originally published in 1939, perhaps the classic text on Leonardo. Paperback, 272 pages, ISBN 0140169822.

• *Leonardo Da Vinci,* by Diane Stanley (Morrow Junior Books, 1996). Hardcover, ISBN 0688104371.

• *Leonardo's Horse,* by Jean Fritz and illustrated by Hudson Talbott (Putnam, 2001). Hardcover, 48 pages, ISBN 0399235760.

• *Lives of the Artists (Oxford's World Classics),* by Giorgio Vasari (Oxford University Press, 1998). Paperback, 586 pages, ISBN 019283410X.

• *Michelangelo and the Pope's Ceiling,* by Ross King (Penguin Books, 2003). Paperback, 318 pages, ISBN 0142003697.

• *What Makes a Leonardo a Leonardo?,* by Richard Muhlberger (Viking Children's Books, 1994). Written for young adults, this provides a good overview of Leonardo's life and work. Paperback, 48 pages, ISBN 0670857440. See other books in this series, including *What Makes a Rembrandt a Rembrandt?*

• Exploring Leonardo, www.mos.org/sln/Leonardo, features a visit to his inventor's workshop, explores perspective, and considers the puzzle of his unusual style of mirror-writing. Includes additional links to other sites on the inventor.

• Michelangelo Buonarroti (1475–1564), www.michelangelo.com/buonarroti.html, takes a detailed look at the life of the artist.

• Usborne (www.edcpub.com) has a wide range of art books, coloring books, and workbooks for the early grades.

The Big Idea

As the young nation expanded in the 19th century, Romantic idealism permeated much of American art.

Text Resources
(72) *Mathew Brady*

What Students Should Already Know

Students in Core Knowledge schools should be familiar with

Kindergarten, Grades 1, 2, and 3

 ▶ Elements of Art: color, line, shape, texture, light, space, and design

Grade 2

 ▶ Kinds of Pictures: landscapes

Grade 4

 ▶ Art of a New Nation: the United States

What Students Need to Learn

 ▶ Become familiar with the Hudson River School of landscape painting, including
 • Thomas Cole, *The Oxbow (The Connecticut River Near Northampton)* (also known as *View from Mount Holyoke, Northampton, Massachusetts, after a Thunderstorm*)
 • Albert Bierstadt, *The Rocky Mountains, Lander's Peak*
 ▶ Become familiar with genre paintings, including
 • George Caleb Bingham, *Fur Traders Descending the Missouri*
 • William Sidney Mount, *Eel Spearing at Setauket*
 ▶ Become familiar with art related to the Civil War, including
 • Civil War photography of Mathew Brady and his colleagues
 • *The Shaw Memorial* sculpture of Augustus Saint-Gaudens
 ▶ Become familiar with popular prints by Currier and Ives

Vocabulary

Student/Teacher Vocabulary

genre painting: painting that portrays scenes from everyday life (S)

Hudson River School: a group of artists who painted landscapes of areas on the east coast of the United States (S)

landscape: a painting or other artwork that portrays the outdoors (S)

relief sculpture: a sculpture that is attached to a background plane (S)

Romanticism: an artistic movement that encouraged freedom of form in art and literature, placing an emphasis on imagination in artistic expression (T)

sculpture in the round: a freestanding, three-dimensional artwork (S)

Vocabulary continued

Domain Vocabulary

Art of the 19th century United States and associated words:
paint, painting, painter, artist, light, shade, dark, color, depict, nation, romantic, scale, natural world, wilderness, idyllic, pastoral, nature, glory, sublime, supernatural, bounty, civilization, pioneering, picturesque, New England region, expansion, industry, rural, rustic, explorers, society, genre, vista, art tradition, photographer/photographic, portray, composition, Civil War, soldiers, African American, charge, Fort Wagner, memorial, document, battlefield, military, honor, bravery, war, historical, image, promotion, print, magazine, advertisement, palette, *plus words that describe things in the artworks, e.g.,* landscape, mountain, peak, boat, river, spear, storm, soldier, *etc.*

Cross-curricular Connections

Language Arts

Poetry
• "Battle Hymn of the Republic" (Howe)
• "I Hear American Singing" (Whitman)

Speeches
• Lincoln: Gettysburg Address

History and Geography

American: Westward Expansion
• Bierstadt, *The Rocky Mountains, Lander's Peak*

American: The Civil War
• Photographs by Brady
• The Shaw Memorial

American: Native Americans: Culture and Conflicts
• Bingham, *Fur Traders Descending the Missouri*

American: U.S. Geography

Materials

Art Resources 15–21

Thomas Cole, *The Oxbow*

Albert Bierstadt, *The Rocky Mountains, Lander's Peak*

George Bingham, *Fur Traders Descending the Missouri*

William Sidney Mount, *Eel Spearing at Setauket*

Mathew Brady Studio, *Battery at Attention*

Augustus Saint-Gaudens, *The Shaw Memorial*

Currier and Ives, *Central Park in Winter*

Instructional Master 46
Designing a Memorial, p. 357

information on a trip to a museum or gallery that contains contemporary landscape art, p. 353

map of the U.S., p. 355

watercolors, p. 359

one disposable camera per two students, p. 359

collection of photography books for the classroom, p. 359

information on a local photographer, p. 359

At a Glance

The most important ideas for you are:

▸ A sense of romanticism pervaded much early 19th-century American art.

▸ Many artists in the United States during the first half of the 19th century drew inspiration from the natural world. They were also influenced by existing European art traditions.

▸ The Civil War was one of the first wars to have been recorded by photographers.

What Teachers Need to Know

Note: The descriptions and activities in the main text below are intended to help you become familiar with the artworks before presenting them to students; however, some of the activities might be adapted for classroom use. Activities intended specifically for students can be found in the Teaching Idea sidebars. The Looking Questions given below are also printed on the reverse side of the *Art Resources,* and have been written with students in mind, so that they might be used as a rough plan for class discussion. You should feel free to use these questions or develop questions of your own. Be sure students have time to look at the reproductions carefully before asking the Looking Questions.

Romantic Views of the American Scene

How old was the United States by the mid-19th century? With the new government just under 100 years of age, the country's artists retained strong links to western European art traditions. Many professional artists in America were born, trained, and/or studied in Europe.

Nonetheless, 19th-century artists in America did not slavishly reproduce European art or represent the same subjects. Instead, they adapted established ways of painting and sculpting to suit a new need—depicting the ever-expanding United States in the best light possible.

Although the United States didn't have a long-established history, it did have land—lots of it. The public hungered for images of the country's glory, splendor, and bounty. Artists largely ignored the often-unpleasant realities of life on the frontier; they deliberately painted as if looking though rose-colored glasses. Painters like George Caleb Bingham, in his *Fur Traders Descending the Missouri,* portrayed the humble lifestyle of those who made their living off the land. (See the discussion on pp. 354–355.) Bingham chose not to show any of the actual hardships involved in the pioneering life; the figures look out serenely, as if they had not a care in the world.

Landscape painters initially thrived along the East Coast. The Hudson River School artists, such as Thomas Cole (whose work students in Core Knowledge schools should have discussed in Grade 2), painted unsullied, pastoral views of the New York and New England regions. The typically vast vistas of the painters of the Hudson River School captured the light in mists, sunsets, and other memorable idyllic moments.

However, American landscape art was not just an East Coast phenomenon. It followed the country's explorers and pioneers as they moved across North America. Artists—like explorers, surveyors, and scientists—ventured into "new lands," bringing their amazing visual expressions back to eastern audiences.

Albert Bierstadt's paintings, including *The Rocky Mountains, Lander's Peak,* immortalized the West's natural scenery. (See discussion on p. 354.) Through size, scale, and a wide range of color, Bierstadt painted pictures that evoked a religious sense of awe and admiration for the land.

Most artists, like society itself, paid little attention to the Native Americans who had inhabited the country for some 10,000 years before Europeans arrived. Native peoples are absent from Bingham's fur trading genre paintings, though Native American hunting talents were crucial to the fur trade. Even when Native Americans are included, as they are in Bierdstadt's composition, they are generally not the focus.

Looking at the Included Reproductions

15 Thomas Cole, *View from Mount Holyoke, Northampton, Massachusetts, after a Thunderstorm—The Oxbow* (1836)

Ironically, British-born artist Thomas Cole (1801–1848) is best known for his romantic views of the American landscape. For him, the young country's rustic, rugged beauty, interspliced with areas of pastoral charm, epitomized the United States. Cole celebrated the divine "New World" with bright, almost supernatural, color and light. One of the popular ideas of Romanticism was that there was an intimate connection between God and nature, that nature was permeated and infused with holiness and divinity. Looking at Cole's landscape paintings, one sometimes feels that they are artistic representations of this romantic idea about the intimate connection between God and nature.

Cole came to Philadelphia from England at age 17. He studied in both the United States and Europe, but was ultimately drawn to America. Here, he painted vistas of the wilderness that would soon vanish as the population and industry encroached upon the virgin land.

Look at the included reproduction of *The Oxbow*. What is the weather like in this view? Cole detailed the sunlight on the lingering mist after a thunderstorm. Although realist artists like Cole appear to work in a nearly photographic style, they often change certain elements in their scenes. They might move, eliminate, enlarge, decrease, and/or add items in their compositions. It is important not to confuse realism and reality.

Cole divided the painting into two. The left half represents the powerful, uncontrollable, yet sublime aspect of nature, symbolized by the broken tree trunk and dark clouds. On the right, Cole painted a quiet, pastoral, sunny view, "civilized" by humans, who have cultivated nature into bucolic, prosperous farms. Cole's painting reflects the debate among Americans during his day: Would civilization wipe out the wilderness or could the two coexist?

Looking questions

Note: Cover up the title on the front of the print before showing to students.

- **What do you see?** *Answers will vary. Point out the lone figure.*
- **What is the lone figure doing?** *It is a self-portrait of the artist at work.*
- **Why did Cole make his self-portrait so small? (Hint: How does his size affect the way you see the rest of the scene?)** *The size of the self-portrait greatly enhances the grandeur and enormity of nature.*

Teaching Idea

If possible, take students to visit a museum or gallery that contains contemporary landscape art. What do recent depictions of the country reveal about the way artists wish to portray the United States now, as compared to over 125 years ago? Do any of the modern artists seem to have a viewpoint or "message" they wish to convey?

II. American Art: Nineteenth-Century United States

Cross-Curricular Teaching Idea

You may want to study *The Rocky Mountains, Lander's Peak* while studying "Westward Expansion" in American History and Geography (see pp. 232–263).

Teaching Idea

Have students compile a list of adjectives and adverbs inspired by Bierstadt's painting, supporting their examples with specific references to the scene. Afterwards, have students use these words as the basis for poems that convey the feelings they might have walking straight into the landscape.

Teaching Idea

George Caleb Bingham was a master of genre scenes—images of everyday life. Have students make quick genre scene sketches of people who have jobs outdoors today. Remind them to use color and placement to create the mood they want to convey about the job. Is it a hard, tiring job? Is it seemingly easy and enjoyable?

- **What two different aspects of nature did Cole present? Compare the left half to the right.** *On the left, Cole presented the rustic, wild side of nature. On the right side, he depicted the idyllic, pastoral side.*

- **What clues in the painting might lead you to believe that Cole saw the wilderness receding in the presence of civilization? What was Cole's message about civilization?** *Answers will vary, but he implies that civilization is good and orderly.*

- **This painting is called** *The Oxbow.* **Why do you think the artist chose this title?** *Students may identify the bow shape. Explain that the river makes the shape of an oxbow, a curved harness that is put over the necks of oxen.*

16 Albert Bierstadt, *The Rocky Mountains, Lander's Peak* (1863)

Albert Bierstadt (1830–1902) ventured to the Rocky Mountains with surveying expeditions, making sketches and photographs for his artwork. The dramatic grandeur of the mountains he depicts suggests the Alps, and indeed, Bierstadt was trained in Europe and born in Germany, but it was in America that he painted.

Bierstadt used his preparatory sketches and photographs to compose paintings back in his New York studio. He deliberately exaggerated reality, making mountains appear higher and scenes perfectly idyllic. He presented the great outdoors the way Americans in the second half of the 19th century wanted to see the West—through a romantic lens. His works were enormous; this one is over 6 feet long and 10 feet high. Bierstadt's art, in fact, did draw tourists from the East to the newly acquired western lands, much as Bingham's had done some twenty years earlier.

Looking questions

- **What first catches your eye in this enormous painting?** *Answers will vary, though the waterfall in the middle ground is a central focus.*

- **How does Bierstadt draw your gaze to certain parts of the painting?** *He makes frequent use of contrasting lights and darks.*

- **How did Bierstadt suggest the huge scale of this scene?** *The scale of the scene is suggested in the actual size of the canvas, the towering peaks in the distance, and the way the landscape dwarfs the Native American camp.*

- **How did Bierstadt use atmospheric perspective to give the viewer a sense of deep space?** *The mountains in the background are painted with much lighter colors and much less detail so that they seem far away.*

- **How did Bierstadt include reference to his own role as an artist?** *He included the camera in the lower left center of the work.*

- **Why do you think Bierstadt included his camera in the painting?** *Answers will vary.*

17 George Caleb Bingham, *Fur Traders Descending the Missouri* (1845)

George Caleb Bingham (1811–1879) moved from Virginia to Missouri with his family when he was a boy. He worked as a cabinetmaker and later became a painter of portraits, traveling from place to place. Other than a few months at an art school in Pennsylvania, Bingham was self-taught until he was in his forties,

when he studied in Europe. Bingham is best known for his paintings of scenes along the Missouri River.

In this picture, Bingham presents a single moment of the vanishing frontier way of life. All the figures look straight at the artist, making us aware of Bingham's role as visual recorder as well as pulling us directly into the scene. Bingham's painting is not, however, an exact replica of reality. His alluring, harmonious colors and blanketing tranquility offer a highly romantic vision that appealed to northeastern audiences.

How did Bingham enhance the stillness of his scene? He evenly balanced the composition. The boy displays the duck he has shot, which hangs over the edge of the covered box on which the young man leans. The background trees sit nearly dead center and frame the canoe like a halo. The water is so still you can see reflections in it, almost undisturbed. This type of painting was the "tourist brochure" of the age.

Looking questions

Note: Cover up the title on the front of the print before showing to students.

- **What is happening in this painting?** *Two traders with their goods and a fox are in a canoe.* Explain that the painting was first called **French Trapper/Half-Breed Son,** *which tells us more about these two figures. A "half-breed" was a crude term for someone who was half Native American.*

- **What mood does this painting suggest to you?** *Answers will vary.*

- **How did Bingham create the sense of a calm early morning?** *Answers will vary, but students should note the still water, the mist-covered background, the strong horizontal lines, and that there is little action in the work.*

- **Compare this work to** *The Rocky Mountains, Lander's Peak.* **What do the artists want us to think about the West?** *Answers will vary, but it should be noted that in both works, the solemn, still scenes immortalize the vanishing world of the American frontier.*

18 William Sidney Mount, *Eel Spearing in Setauket* (1845)

Born in Setauket on New York's Long Island, William Sidney Mount (1807–1868) is most well known for his images of everyday American life. He is particularly noteworthy for his (somewhat stereotypical) inclusion of African Americans in his work.

Mount drew inspiration from the local town and rural life on Long Island. *Eel Spearing in Setauket* draws its name from the activities surrounding the plentiful local sea life. It is an idyllic, romantic scene, but nonetheless it is a snapshot that captures the pastimes, garb, landscape, and social context of Long Island life in 1845. These scenes by Mount became wildly popular when they were made into engraved reproductions and thus became widely disbursed. They tapped into the same fascination with the simple life of American folk that Mark Twain would explore later in the century.

Looking questions

- **What characteristics of Mount's painting recall the work of Pieter Bruegel?** *The similarities include the attention to detail and the interest in the everyday life of common people.*

Teaching Idea

In order to give students a feel for the world of the Midwest in the 1840s and 1850s—the world in which Abraham Lincoln grew up and became a politician—show them a series of Bingham's paintings. Some paintings that are particularly relevant for understanding the life and career of Lincoln are *Family Life on the Frontier, Raftsmen Playing Cards, Stump Speaking, The County Election,* and *Canvassing for a Vote.*

Cross-curricular Teaching Idea

Have students locate the Missouri River and surrounding areas on a map. (The traders in the painting were probably headed to the market in St. Louis.) Help students research which Native American peoples lived in these areas and would likely have been the ones with whom the fur traders interacted. Use this activity as a jumping-off point to study the fur trade and/or Native American/United States relations during this era.

- What effect do the broad horizontal bands made by the sky, land, water, and canoe have on the mood of the painting? *The bands establish a calm, tranquil mood.*

- How did Mount break the horizontal lines and keep the painting from seeming visually boring? *Mount placed some vertical trees on the left and right, the woman creates a vertical line that breaks into the sky areas, and the pole and paddle are very strong diagonals.*

- How did Mount use line and color to tie the two figures together despite the wide space between them? *If the line of the paddle were extended up it would intersect the pole. Also, bright red is used only on the woman's kerchief, and the boy's hat and cushion.*

- It has been said that a good writer could create a whole story based on one of Mount's paintings. Do you agree? Why or why not? *Answers will vary.*

- How might your thoughts about this painting be different from those of a fifth-grader seeing it in 1845? *Answers will vary.*

Art Related to the Civil War

The American Civil War tore the young nation apart. During the Civil War, many artists witnessed the war firsthand, and depicted in their artwork both the horrors and courage they observed. The American Civil War was the first American combat that was documented with photography.

Mathew Brady Studio, *Battery at Attention*

Mathew Brady was a famous portrait photographer who turned his interests to the Civil War. Although many pictures are attributed to him, Brady actually spent most of his time managing traveling photographers whom he had hired to work directly in the battlefield. These photographers captured every aspect of the war—soldiers in camps and preparing for battles, devastated ruins, officers, corpses on battlefields, ships, and railroads. These men chronicled the harsh images of war's reality in stark black and white for the public back home. Brady exhibited some of the gruesome images in 1862. The *New York Times* wrote that the photographs of battlefield corpses from Antietam brought "home to us the terrible reality and earnestness of war." Brady's team had made more than 7,000 images by the end of the war. However, Brady didn't credit any of his cameramen nor allow them to retain the negatives they took on their own time.

Although Brady had many photographers working with him, he too risked his life on the battlefield. Brady said, "I had to go. A spirit in my feet said 'Go,' and I went." Brady, along with many Union soldiers, had to flee after the Union defeat at the First Battle of Bull Run. After three days, he showed up in Washington, hungry and exhausted, where he bought more equipment, rounded up additional cameramen, and returned to the front. Later in the war he was present at Antietam and Gettysburg. He also made photographs of the rival generals, Grant and Lee. Interestingly enough, the war brought financial ruin for Brady. He had invested approximately $100,000, thinking that the government would want to buy his photographs when the war was over. However, the government showed no interest (until many years later) and Brady lost his investment, went bankrupt, and died in poverty and neglect. (72)

Cross-Curricular Teaching Idea

The most logical time to introduce Brady's Civil War photographs is during the American history unit on "The Civil War." (See pp. 264–296.)

Teaching Idea

The Library of Congress has a collection of Civil War photographs (more than 1,000, including many Mathew Brady shots). These can be viewed online, free of charge. (See *More Resources.*) There are also other websites devoted to Civil War photography. Print several photos to share with students during your unit on the Civil War.

Teaching Idea

Artists in the past often romanticized war. Have students carefully study the photograph by Mathew Brady and identify in writing some of the harsh realities of combat revealed in his photographs. Remind students to examine clothing, facial expressions, body poses, surroundings, and general atmosphere—what the people were feeling. Have students use the information to write a letter to someone back home in the voice of one of the subjects.

Looking questions

- **Who are these men and when would you date this scene?** *These are Civil War soldiers standing at attention. The date is between 1861 and 1865.*

- **Is this a painting?** *No, it's a photograph (made with film in a camera). The photographer is Mathew Brady.*

- **Was it Brady's aim to create art? Explain your opinion.** *Answers will vary. Brady's intention was to capture images of war for the first time on film, which he succeeded in doing. He recognized the importance of composition and lighting, but his aims were not strictly artistic.*

- **How has Brady positioned his camera not only to cover the scene visually, but also for the sake of line and composition?** *Our eye follows the line of the earthworks toward the furthest point of the battery. We look along the line of men, as if we were inspecting them.*

art resource 20 Augustus Saint-Gaudens, The Shaw Memorial (1900)

The sculptor Augustus Saint-Gaudens (1848–1907) created The Shaw Memorial some 35 years after the conflict to which it pays tribute. The memorial honors the Massachusetts 54th regiment—1,000 soldiers who formed the fifth African-American troop organized for the Civil War. Robert Gould Shaw, a white officer, was the leader of the regiment. (See p. 285.) His regiment attacked Fort Wagner in the harbor at Charleston, South Carolina. Shaw and one-third of the regiment died in the battle, and the regiment failed to capture the fort. Despite the defeat, President Lincoln believed it was a turning point in the war. The regiment also helped legitimize the participation of African Americans in the military. The bravery of the African-American soldiers was widely recognized and helped overturn stereotypes.

Like many war sculptures, Saint-Gaudens's first proposal was for a work of Colonel Shaw seated on his horse. Shaw's mother felt it was too grandiose. It took Saint-Gaudens some 14 years to be fully satisfied with his final version of a military parade. Saint-Gaudens's sculpture is stirring both because of its size and because of the individuality of each man portrayed. He spent approximately 14 years perfecting the work, which combines relief sculpture with a nearly freestanding equestrian figure. He created many clay sketches, seeking to represent a range of ages and physical characteristics. In each successive sketch, he would shift the tilt of a head or wrist to get the exact expression he desired. The sculpture portrays Shaw as he leads his men in a military procession. Saint-Gaudens finally produced an enlarged plaster model that was cast in bronze and unveiled in the Boston Common on Memorial Day, 1897.

Looking questions

- **Who are the people in this sculpture?** *The people are soldiers. Explain that this sculpture honors Colonel Robert Gould Shaw and his troops, the 54th Massachusetts Volunteer Regiment, the first all-black regiment in the Civil War, who launched a heroic offensive on Fort Wagner.*

- **How does Saint-Gaudens show us who the leader is?** *The leader is the only figure on horseback.*

- **Do you see a figure over the heads of the soldiers? (You may have to trace it.)** *There is an angel over the heads of the men.*

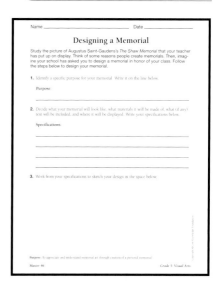

- Soldiers usually march in rows. Why did the sculptor choose to show the legs of the men and the horse in this way? *It creates a strong sense of movement.*

 Nathaniel Currier and James M. Ives, *Central Park in Winter*

Nineteenth-century America was the perfect place for Nathaniel Currier (1813–1888) and James M. Ives (1824–1895) to build a flourishing business printing and selling mass-produced lithographs. The public, accustomed to obtaining the latest news from a rapidly growing newspaper industry, was eager to have images illustrating the news and other items of interest.

In 1857 Currier and Ives formed a partnership that resulted in the creation of more than 7,000 works that were reproduced in mass quantities. They hired a variety of artists to depict the scenes that were then printed and hand-painted at a factory in New York City. Some of the more popular subject categories included disaster scenes, firefighting, politics, trains, ships, portraits, and city and rural scenes. The larger prints sold for a couple of dollars and the smaller ones were only a few cents. This was well within the price range of the lower and middle classes at a time of national prosperity and, thus, Currier and Ives were insured of a large and continuous customer base.

Looking questions

- What is going on in this scene? *Answers will vary.*

- How does this print give you a clear sense of depth? *The distinct foreground, middle ground, and background with objects and figures getting smaller as they recede into the distance all give a sense of space.*

- Why might the small section of stone outcropping, or wall, have been placed in the lower right corner? *The artist might have placed the wall there to give the viewer a sense of where they are "standing" in relation to the scene—perhaps a small hill or terrace overlooking it.*

- How are light and dark used to help build the design of the scene? *The large expanses of light created by the snow, ice, and sun are balanced by the dark of the trees, sleighs, and shadows and provide an alternating pattern of light and dark.*

- The colorists who hand-painted Currier and Ives prints were each assigned one color and used a master print placed before them as a guide. If you were a nineteenth-century colorist, would you have enjoyed this job? Why or why not? *Answers will vary.*

- What is the mood of this scene? What helps create that mood? *Answers will vary.*

- Why could the more than 7,500 subjects produced by Currier and Ives in the second half of the nineteenth century be considered historical documents? *The works provide a detailed visual record of many aspects of American life at that time.*

Teaching Idea

In order to give your students a sense of the range of subjects depicted in Currier and Ives prints, you will need to go beyond the single print provided in the Art Resources. You can find many Currier and Ives prints online by using a search engine to search for "Currier and Ives." You may wish to show a number of these prints in conjunction with the American History units for this grade as a way of deepening students' understanding of nineteenth-century America. Alternatively, you might use a set of Currier and Ives prints of well-known places in conjunction with the geography unit on U.S. regions.

Review

Below are some ideas for ongoing assessment and review activities. These are not meant to constitute a comprehensive list.

• This section provides an opportunity for students to complete short research reports on any of the artists included in this section or on a type of artistic style, such as the Hudson school. Provide the class with topics for short reports to write in formal style (see the Language Arts section "Writing and Research," pp. 1–14, for guidance on report writing). Each day of a week, provide a mini-lesson on different aspects of report writing, such as correct paragraph form or bibliographies. Share these reports when completed.

• When studying the landscape paintings from this section, ask students to observe the elements artists included in their works. Have students sketch a local landscape with pencil and then paint their pictures using watercolors. To practice helping students observe details in the landscape, take the class outside to look at the landscape (or cityscape) around the school. You may also have the class brainstorm adjectives to describe their local area. In the paintings, ask students to experiment with using colors that depict the mood and the environment. When the landscapes are finished, have students write descriptions to post next to their paintings.

• See if you can have a set of disposable cameras donated to the class or buy a camera for pairs of students in your class. After studying the Civil War photographs and how the photographer catches the mood of a moment, have pairs of students circulate outside and around school to take pictures that depict life at school. Be sure that you clear this project with the administration and inform other classes of the project, and that you have permission from parents to photograph students. When you have the pictures developed, have students arrange their photographs in a collage depicting the school. You can then photocopy the collages so they are in black and white, closer to the way photographs were in the Civil War. Have students write about their experiences and the different mood represented by the color and black and white photos.

• Work with your local librarian or school media specialist to assemble a collection of photography books so that students can further explore the techniques of photography. Ask students to search newspapers or magazines at home and bring in one example of a photograph that catches their interest. They should share this photograph with the class and then write a paragraph describing the picture and why it is interesting to them.

• Invite a photographer to class to talk about black and white, color, and digital photography. Also talk to the students about portraits, artistic arrangement, and other techniques for photography.

• Ask students to write a description of one landscape that they have seen. Ask them to use vivid adjectives and clear descriptions. Pair students and then ask them to trade writings. See if they can draw a picture to illustrate the landscape the other student described. Discuss how using vivid descriptions makes this activity easier for the artist.

The Big Idea in Review

As the young nation expanded in the 19th century, Romantic idealism permeated much of American art.

- In general, the best time to ask questions about a specific work of art is while students are looking at it. However, by the end of the unit, students should be able to answer questions like the following:

1. What was a popular subject matter in American painting during the first half of the 19th century?

   Images of nature were a popular subject matter.

2. Who are some of the American artists we have studied?

   Student may name Thomas Cole, Albert Bierstadt, George Caleb Bingham, or William Sidney Mount.

3. What area of North America that was as yet unseen by the majority of citizens did landscape painting describe?

   The West was an area that the majority of citizens had never seen that was described by landscape painting.

4. What war did Mathew Brady and his team of photographers document?

   They documented the Civil War.

5. What does St. Gaudens's Shaw Memorial commemorate?

   The Shaw Memorial commemorates the assault on Fort Wagner by African-American Union troops.

More Resources

The titles listed below are offered as a representative sample of materials and not a complete list of everything that is available.

For students —

- *I Wanna Take Me a Picture: Teaching Photography and Writing to Children,* by Wendy Ewald and Alexandra Lightfoot (Beacon Press, 2002). Paperback, 176 pages, ISBN 0792263707.

- *Photography Guide For Kids,* by Neil L. Johnson (National Geographic, 2001). Paperback, 80 pages, ISBN 0792263707.

For teachers —

- *Albert Bierstadt (Famous Artist),* by Matthew Baigell (Watson-Guptill Publications, 1988). Paperback, 88 pages, ISBN 0823004937. Part of the *Famous Artists* series, which also includes volumes on other artists described in this section.

- Art Print Resources (209 Riverdale Avenue, Yonkers, NY 10705, www.artprintresources.com, or 1-800-501-4278) sells a set of posters of the artworks in the *Sequence* for this grade.

- Art Sense (www.artsense.net) provides an art program using videos and trade books.

- Art to the Core (Davis Publications, www.davis-art.com or 1-800-533-2847). A kit of materials that includes slides of artworks, lessons plans, assessment masters, and vocabulary masters, all keyed to the *Core Knowledge Sequence* for this grade.

- *Brady's Civil War: A Collection of Civil War Images Photographed by Mathew Brady and his Assistants,* by Webb Garrison (The Lyons Press, 2002). Paperback, 256 pages, ISBN 1585746932.

- Crizmac (www.crizmac.com) sells a wide range of art education materials.

- *Nineteenth-Century American Art (Oxford History of Art),* by Barbara Groseclose (Oxford University Press, 2000). Paperback, 234 pages, ISBN 0192842250.

- Selected Civil War Photographs from the Library of Congress, http://memory.loc.gov/ammem/cwphtml/cwphome.html, contains more than 1,000 photographs from the war, including many from the camera of Mathew Brady. Several show the brutality of war.

III. Art of Japan

The Big Idea

Simplicity of form and design, attentiveness to the beauty of nature, and overall subtlety are characteristics of traditional Japanese art.

What Students Should Already Know

Students in Core Knowledge schools should be familiar with

Kindergarten, Grades 1, 2, and 3

- Elements of Art: color, line, shape, texture, light, space, and design
- Sculpture
- Looking at and Talking About Works of Art

Kindergarten

- Katsushika Hokusai, *Tuning the Samisen*

Grade 2

- Katsushika Hokusai, *The Great Wave at Kanagawa Nami-Ura* from *Thirty-six Views of Mt. Fuji*

Grade 3

- Native American art
- Art of Ancient Rome and Byzantine Civilization

Grade 4

- Art of the Middle Ages in Europe
- Islamic Art and Architecture
- The Art of Africa
- The Art of China
- The Art of a New Nation: The United States

What Students Need to Learn

- **Become familiar with the art of Japan including**
  - **The Great Buddha (also known as the Kamakura Buddha)**
  - **Landscape gardens**

III. Art of Japan

Materials

Art Resources 22–24

The Great Buddha of Kamakura

Ryōan-ji Temple Garden

Suzuki Harunobu, *Woman Admiring Plum Blossoms at Night*

Instructional Masters 47–48

Traditional Japanese Art, p. 363

A Japanese Garden, p. 366

instructions to create a simple origami animal, p. 365

gravel, p. 366

small rocks and pebbles, p. 366

cardboard box lids, p. 366

Styrofoam meat trays, p. 367

different sizes of wood blocks and oil paint, p. 367

large pieces of heavy white paper, p. 367

Vocabulary

Student/Teacher Vocabulary

Buddha: meaning "Enlightened One," the founder of Buddhism (S)

Buddhism: one of the main religions in Japan; the goal of Buddhism is to achieve enlightenment by self-purification (S)

haiku: an unrhymed Japanese poem of three lines of 5, 7, and 5 syllables respectively (T)

landscape garden: a garden that is decorated or developed in an artistic manner (S)

kabuki: a traditional Japanese dramatic form that includes highly stylized singing and dancing (T)

origami: the art of folding paper into decorative objects (T)

Shinto: "way of the gods;" the oldest and largest religion in Japan; emphasizes reverence for family, nature, and the ruling family as direct descendant of the gods (T)

ukiyo-e: "the art of the floating world;" Japanese art (typically woodcuts) that described life around the district of Edo (now Tokyo) (T)

Domain Vocabulary

Art of Japan and associated words:
nirvana, gigantic, enlightenment, personal desires, spiritual, stone, carved, simplicity, elegance, cohesive, culture, subtlety, harmony, serene, perfection, ruling class, calligraphy, paper-art, Korea, China, Edo period, woodcut, prints, rock garden, temple, rocks, sand, trees, water, bronze, mold, quiet, peaceful, tranquil, tree, soothing, relaxing, rake, natural, brushstrokes, landscape, Edo, Tokyo, city, bridge, water, meditate, kimono, robe, samurai, wood, tea, ceremony, drink, sip, cup, pour, plus words that describe things in the *artworks*, e.g., waterfall, pebbles, bridges, Zen, *etc.*

Cross-curricular Connections

History and Geography

World: Feudal Japan

> ### At a Glance
> The most important ideas for you are:
> - Simplicity of form and design, attentiveness to the beauty of nature, and overall cohesiveness are key elements of much traditional Japanese art.
> - The arrival of Buddhism to Japan in the mid-sixth century significantly shaped early Japanese art and culture.
> - Japanese gardens reflect a sensitivity to the beauty of nature.

What Teachers Need to Know

Background

Many cultures have influenced Japan's history, culture, and art throughout the ages. Chinese and Korean influence dominated from the seventh to the ninth centuries. Europe began to have an influence in the sixteenth century as did the United States after 1868. Despite the variety of outside influences, Japanese art has distinct characteristics. One is simple elegance in form and design. Notice the careful inclusion of details in Suzuki Harunobu's Girl Viewing Plum Blossoms at Night. (See discussion on p. 366.) Japanese art also demonstrates a keen sensitivity to the sublime aspect of nature. Japanese gardens honor nature's splendor while subtly shaping the outdoors into three-dimensional artistic experiences. (See discussion on pp. 365–366.) Subtlety, too, pervades sculpture, even in such a monumental piece as The Great Buddha of Kamakura. *Draped over Buddha's quiet body, the pleats in his robe create only the slightest hint of repeated pattern. (See discussion on pp. 364–365.)*

Note: The descriptions and activities in the main text below are intended to help you become familiar with the artworks before presenting them to students; however, some of the activities might be adapted for classroom use. Activities intended specifically for students can be found in the Teaching Idea sidebars. The Looking Questions given below are also printed on the reverse side of the *Art Resources*, and have been written with students in mind, so that they might be used as a rough plan for class discussion. You should feel free to use these questions or develop questions of your own. Be sure students have time to look at the reproductions carefully before asking the Looking Questions.

Cross-curricular Teaching Idea

You may wish to teach the section "Feudal Japan" from World History and Geography (see pp. 220–230) in conjunction with this unit.

Teaching Idea

After introducing the basic concepts and ideas in this section, use Instructional Master 47, *Traditional Japanese Art,* to reinforce the important ideas relating to Japanese art.

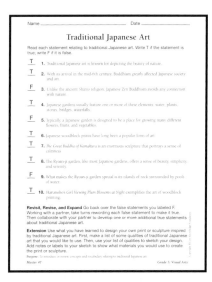

Use Instructional Master 47.

History of Japanese Art

 ### The Early Years

Some of the earliest surviving Japanese art dates from as early as 10,000 BCE, and consists of expressive clay vessels and figurative sculpture. By about the 3rd century CE, sculptors modeled clay figures of humans and animals to serve as funeral items for the ruling class, and metalworkers cast bronze ritual bells and decorated mirrors.

 ### Buddhism Arrives

The introduction of Buddhism from Korea and China in the mid-6th century greatly affected Japanese society and art. Until the 10th century, Japanese artists mainly reworked the existing Chinese and Korean art styles. Sculpture was largely tied to Buddhism. Painters depicted both Buddhist and non-Buddhist themes. Like the Chinese, Japanese painters historically worked with ink and water-soluble colors on paper or silk. They likewise worked with established Chinese subjects—narratives, landscapes, and portraits. In both Japan and China, calligraphy was considered an art form, critiqued for the visual qualities of the ink strokes.

III. Art of Japan

Teaching Idea

Have students conduct research to find out more about Japanese gardens and tea ceremonies. Students can even re-create a tea ceremony as a culminating activity for the unit.

Teaching Idea

You can find more pictures of Japanese gardens by searching the web for "Japanese Garden."

Teaching Idea

You can find dozens of additional images of Japanese art prints online to share with students by searching for keywords such as "ukiyo-e." You can also search using the names of ukiyo-e artists, such as Hokusai, Hiroshige, Utamaro, and Harunobu.

Teaching Idea

Find additional images of the Buddha online using a search engine. Share these pictures with students. Discuss some of the common elements of Buddha images, e.g., the fact that he is usually shown seated. Why is this? (One reason is because meditation is generally done in a seated position.)

Three-Dimensional Landscape Art

Japanese Zen Buddhism and the ancient Shinto religion were both key to the development of Japanese gardens. Both religions connect deeply to nature. According to Shinto belief, spirits or gods manifest themselves in all aspects of nature, including trees, rocks, and waterfalls. (See the World History and Geography section "Feudal Japan," pp. 220–230, for more information on Shinto.) Nature, therefore, reflects the beauty of the gods. Zen Buddhists from the 1200s through the 1400s taught that the best way to gain the wisdom of Buddha was through contemplation and by living in simple harmony with nature. Japanese gardens offer sanctuaries where humans can become closer to the divine.

Japanese gardens take many forms, but the most essential ingredients are water, plants, stones, waterfalls, and bridges. However, whether a dry rock garden such as Ryōan-ji (see discussion on pp. 365–366), or one lush with trees and ponds, all Japanese gardens utilize nature to produce a beautiful, serene place for people to reflect and meditate.

Among the aristocracy, Zen Buddhism gave rise to the tea ceremony, a pre-scribed ritual for drinking tea that involved all the senses. Potters made exquisite, minimally designed bowls, water jars, and tea-powder holders. Hanging scrolls depicting natural scenes were hung on walls and in niches. The ritual gestures for pouring, passing, drinking, and sharing the tea enhanced the slow pace in which participants relished the rarified peace and beauty of the entire experience.

Prints

Although learning about Japanese prints is not in the *Sequence* as a learning goal for Grade 5, we have included it in this discussion if you wish to expand your discussion on Japanese art. The first Japanese woodblock prints were made at temples and distributed free to the faithful. The later prints of the Edo period (1603–1867), called *ukiyo-e* [ooh-key-oh-yay], were also popular, but highly secular in nature. Ukiyo-e artists depicted scenes in Edo (now Tokyo). The scenes celebrated beauty, wealth, fame, and love. The wealthy merchant class hungered for these images of famous courtesans and handsome kabuki actors. (See the discussion of *Woman Admiring Plum Blossoms at Night* on p. 366.) Today, ukiyo-e prints are collected both in Japan and abroad, but originally they were considered only minor enterprises within Japanese society. In fact, it was the French Impressionists and post-Impressionists in Paris during the late 19th century who first recognized their artistic importance.

Japanese woodblock prints became available in Paris during the 1860s. Their radical compositions (daring perspectives and cropping of figures) as well their depictions of daily life greatly influenced many French Impressionists and post-Impressionists.

Looking at the Included Reproduced Artworks

The Great Buddha of Kamakura (1252)

Buddhists try to escape the constant cycle of birth, suffering, and death by breaking free of the world of illusion to achieve personal enlightenment (a state called nirvana). *The Great Buddha of Kamakura* visually demonstrates a part of this process. The Buddha is depicted deep in meditation, a practice through

which believers try to extinguish their personal desires and passions. Everything about the enormous sculpture depicts a deep sense of spiritual calm. The Buddha's downcast eyes indicate inner focus, as do his relaxed hands and posture.

The figure is fairly idealized, rather than a specific portrait of a historical figure. Buddha's perfect outward body posture is meant to indicate his inner, spiritual perfection.

Looking questions

- **What type of person do you think this figure represents? What in the art specifically supports your idea?** *Answers will vary.*

- **What do you think the figure is doing? What clues can you find?** *Answers will vary, but the posture and the expression of the figure should lead students to the conclusion that Buddha is meditating.*

- **Why do you think the sculpture is so large?** *The size of the sculpture increases the emotional impact of the work. It emphasizes the importance of Buddhism in the culture.*

- **How did the designer of this sculpture use line to make the figure seem approachable and not frightening?** *There are no harsh, strong vertical or horizontal lines. Most lines are soft and curving.*

art resource 23 Ryōan-ji Temple Garden (1499)

Japanese garden design existed at least as early as the eighth century. In fact, the Japanese word for "garden" initially indicated a purified place for worship of native Shinto spirits. Zen dry rock gardens were developed later and were designed as fixed spaces with large rocks on gravel. Japanese gardens are intended to create a sense of peace and simplicity.

Ryōan-ji rock garden in Kyoto is one of the most famous rock gardens in Japan. Ryōan-ji means "Temple of the Peaceful Dragon." It measures 30 meters by 10 meters and contains 15 large rocks. However, the rocks are arranged in such a way that only 14 can be viewed from any one vantage point. It is said that only those who have achieved genuine spiritual enlightenment can see all 15 rocks at once. At Ryōan-ji, onlookers view the austere beauty from the temple terrace. Where is the "water" that is so typical of Japanese gardens? One possible interpretation is that the rock formations are intended to represent islands floating in the sea, represented by the pebbles or gravel.

Looking questions

- **What makes this a garden?** *It's outside, it's made from natural materials, and it's clearly designed.*

- **This garden is meant for meditation. What qualities does it have that might encourage thoughtful reflection?** *Answers will vary. The simplicity and gentle lines are restful, without demanding a great deal of attention the way that a lush flower garden would.*

- **This garden has 15 stones. As you walk in the garden, you can see only 14 stones at any one time. How might this feature encourage meditation?** *The scene changes slowly, but never surprisingly. You make progress, but simultaneously do not progress. This is in the Buddhist tradition of learning to be in the moment within your thoughts, i.e., in the present.*

III. Art of Japan

Use Instructional Master 48.

- **What materials form this garden?** *Materials include gravel, dirt, boulders, and rocks.*
- **What elements of art are used?** *Answers will vary, but should include line (raked pattern), texture (gravel and rocks), shape, and light.*
- **How would you feel if you were sitting in this garden?** *Answers will vary, but students could mention concepts such as calm, contemplative, and in harmony with nature.*

art resource 24 Suzuki Harunobu, *Woman Admiring Plum Blossoms at Night* (c. 1764–1770)

Ukiyo-e ("the art of the floating world") became wildly popular with the merchant class in the 18th century. The woodblock prints could be reproduced in large numbers and, therefore, sold inexpensively. Middle-class people bought prints of actors and fashionable "social" women, much as modern Americans buy entertainment magazines with pictures of celebrities today.

The Chinese invented woodcuts during the Tang dynasty (618–906 CE), and this art form came to Japan during the 8th century. Japanese artists perfected the medium, using separate blocks to print every color. An individual wooden block was carved for every area that had a particular color. For example, one block would be carved for all the lines and areas that would appear in black. Another block was carved for shapes that would be yellow, and so forth. Printers printed one block on top of another. They had to line each new block up carefully to exactly match the existing, emerging image so that the final picture looked like a single piece.

Suzuki Harunobu's beautiful young woman on the veranda lights up the night with her lantern. Harunobu (1725–1770) picks up the same bright color in the blossoms, which will quickly lose their beauty with the change of seasons.

Note: This work, although not in the *Sequence,* has been added to give students another example of Japanese art.

Looking questions

- **How did Suzuki Harunobu indicate the time of day?** *There is a lantern lighting up the scene, and the background is black, indicating night.*
- **Where are the two strong diagonals in this print?** *There is a diagonal in the veranda, in the implied line from the tree branch to the lantern, and through the woman's body.*
- **What visual clues did Harunobu provide about the woman's life—if it was a hard existence or one of luxury?** *Answers will vary, but students should note the woman's adorned hair, elegant kimono, and leisure activity.*
- **This figure could be described as "flat." Can you see why?** *The emphasis is on line and the pattern of clothes rather than on defining the three-dimensional form of the figure.*

Review

Below are some ideas for ongoing assessment and review activities. These are not meant to constitute a comprehensive list.

• This section provides an opportunity for students to complete short research reports on any of the genres of Japanese art. Provide the class with topics for short reports to write in formal style. (See the Language Arts section "Writing and Research," pp. 1–14, for guidance on report writing.) Each day of a week, provide a mini-lesson on different aspects of report writing, such as correct paragraph form or bibliographies. Share these reports when completed.

• Have students write comparisons of the art of the Renaissance and the art of Japan. As a class, brainstorm a list of features of each kind of art. Have students create a Venn diagram using the items on their lists. Then have the class write paragraphs comparing and contrasting both kinds of art. Have them use specific examples when they are writing about each kind of art.

• Pose the question to students, "How does art reflect the culture of a people?" Ask students to write a response to the question, and then read these responses aloud to the class.

• Experiment with using wood blocks and oil paint to create pictures. Although the intricate carving of lines and shapes may not be possible, see if students can use wood blocks of different sizes and oil paint to create nature pictures on white paper. When finished, ask students to write a description of their work. Discuss how this process was different from the Japanese artists. How was it the same?

• In general, the best time to ask questions about a specific work of art is while students are looking at it. However, by the end of the unit, students should be able to answer questions like the following:

1. What are some kinds of Japanese art we have looked at?
   Some kinds of Japanese art we've looked at are prints, sculpture, and landscape gardens.

2. Which religions had a great impact on Japanese society?
   Buddhism and Shinto both had a great impact on Japanese society.

3. Why is the Buddha often shown sitting?
   He is shown sitting because this is the typical posture of meditation.

4. How would you describe a Japanese Zen rock garden to someone who had never seen one?
   Answers will vary, but students should mention the presence of rocks and the intention to allow for thinking or contemplation.

Teaching Idea

Have students try to create their own block print to reinforce the challenge and patience required. Have students draw a simple pattern on paper. Students should select a color for each part of their picture, and then draw each separate part on a different piece of Styrofoam (like the meat trays from grocery stores). Then, they should apply the correct paint color to each of their "templates" and press them on a piece of paper to build the final print pattern. Students will have to try to match up the position of the template and the print with each template application. After a few attempts, students should be able to produce their own block print.

The Big Idea in Review

Simplicity of form and design, attentiveness to the beauty of nature, and overall subtlety are characteristics of traditional Japanese art.

More Resources

The titles listed below are offered as a representative sample of materials and not a complete list of everything that is available.

For students —

• *Hokusai: The Man Who Painted a Mountain*, by Deborah Kogan Ray (Frances Foster Books, 2001). Hardcover, 40 pages, ISBN 0374332630.

For teachers —

• *Art of Japan: Wood-Block Color Prints (Art Around the World)*, by Carol Finley (Lerner, 1998). Hardcover, 64 pages, ISBN 082252077X.

• Art Print Resources (209 Riverdale Avenue, Yonkers, NY 10705, www.artprintresources.com, or 1-800-501-4278) sells a set of posters of the artworks in the *Sequence* for this grade.

• Art Sense (www.artsense.net) provides an art program using videos and trade books.

• Art to the Core (Davis Publications, www.davis-art.com or 1-800-533-2847). A kit of materials that includes slides of artworks, lessons plans, assessment masters, and vocabulary masters, all keyed to the *Core Knowledge Sequence* for this grade.

• Crizmac (www.crizmac.com) sells a wide range of art education materials.

• *Hokusai: One Hundred Views of Mt. Fuji*, edited by Henry D. Smith (George Braziller, 1999). Paperback, 224 pages, ISBN 080761453X.

• *Japanese Prints: The Art Institute of Chicago*, by James T. Ulak (Abbeville Press, 1995). Hardcover, 320 pages, ISBN 0789206137.

• The Freer Gallery of Art and the Arthur M. Sackler Gallery comprise the National Museum of Asian Art at the Smithsonian Institution in Washington, D.C. Their website, www.asia.si.edu, is a source of images and other information on Japanese art.

Music

Music in Fifth Grade

There are many ways for students to enjoy music: they may listen to it, sing it, perform it, move to it, and more. In Grade 5, students will explore all these forms of musical participation and, in the process, expand their knowledge of theory, notation, and music history.

Music is made up of several basic elements, including rhythm, melody, harmony, form, and timbre. Students will explore these elements through active participation, developing a sense of how each element is musically significant. This year, students will learn several new terms, including *accelerando, ritardando, crescendo,* and *decrescendo*. Students will begin to work with more elaborate uses of rhythm. They will also continue to expand their knowledge of music notation as they learn several new symbols, including the eighth rest, sixteenth notes, and a new time signature. Students will build their performance skills through two- and three-part singing, and begin to perform from scores. In addition, they will review and strengthen the concepts and skills learned in previous years.

This year introduces students to two new composers: Ludwig van Beethoven and Modest Mussorgsky. Students will learn a few facts about each composer's life and then listen to at least one representative work, thereby learning a little about music history and gaining exposure to several famous and accessible works of music. In connection with their study of the Renaissance in the World History section, students will also be introduced to some of the music of that era. Furthermore, their study of *A Midsummer Night's Dream* in Language Arts will be supplemented with music, composed by Felix Mendelssohn, that was inspired by the play.

Students will learn to sing a repertoire of traditional songs. These songs provide an accessible and fun way for students to master short musical works. Through the process of learning these songs, students will develop a valuable intuitive sense of the elements of music at work. These songs also provide a way to connect the study of music to other disciplines through contextual information. For example, students will explore the tradition of spirituals and learn about their origins in African-American history. Other selections from this year are folk songs that have historical roots in other world cultures, and songs from the Civil War and the era of westward expansion.

Music can be a source of great pleasure and satisfaction; at the same time, the observational and analytical skills used to understand music are valuable in making sense of any form of art and many other aspects of the world around us. Ideally, in Grade 5, students will enjoy the pleasures of music and, in the process, gain a more sophisticated understanding of it.

I. Elements of Music

The Big Idea

Music has its own language and is described with terms such as rhythm, melody, harmony, form, dynamics, and timbre.

What Students Should Already Know

Students in Core Knowledge schools should be familiar with

Kindergarten through Grade 4

- recognizing a steady beat, accents, and the downbeat; playing a steady beat
- moving responsively to music
- recognizing short and long sounds
- discriminating between fast and slow; gradually changing tempo
- discriminating between differences in pitch (high and low)
- discriminating between loud and soft; gradually changing dynamics
- understanding that melody can move up and down
- humming the melody while listening to music
- echoing short rhythms and melodic patterns
- playing simple rhythms and melodies
- singing in unison, both unaccompanied and accompanied
- recognizing harmony; singing rounds
- recognizing verse and refrain
- recognizing timbre (tone color) and phrasing
- names of musical notes, scales, and singing the C-major scale using "do-re-mi"
- understanding notation: treble clef (including names of lines and spaces); staff; bar line; measure; repeat sign; whole, half, quarter, and eighth notes; whole, half, and quarter rests; tied and dotted notes; sharps and flats; *Da capo [D.C.] al fine*; meter signatures ($\frac{4}{4}$, $\frac{2}{4}$, $\frac{3}{4}$); dynamic markings (quiet: *pp*, *p*, and *mp*, and loud: *mf*, *f*, and *ff*)
- understanding *legato* (smoothly flowing progression of notes) and *staccato* (crisp, distinct notes)
- singing canons
- recognizing introduction and coda
- recognizing theme and variations, and listen to Mozart, *Variations on "Ah! vous dirai-je Maman"* (familiarly known as "Twinkle, Twinkle, Little Star")

I. Elements of Music

Materials

Instructional Masters 49–59

Reading Rhythms, p. 377

Simultaneous Rhythms, p. 378

Melody Listening Guide, p. 378

Tied Notes, p. 387

Dotted Notes, p. 387

The Sound of Silence, p. 388

Name That Notation!, p. 389

Name the Notes, p. 391

Time Signatures, p. 392

Meter and Dynamics, p. 393

Words and Music, p. 395

CD, audiotape, or videotape

Symphony no. 5, Beethoven, pp. 378, 382

"God Bless America" or "Greensleeves," p. 378

A Midsummer Night's Dream, Mendelssohn, p. 383

note-value cards, pp. 376, 388

variety of percussion music, p. 376

recording of two versions of "Jingle Bells," p. 377

cards that say *staccato* and *legato*, p. 379

professional recording of a traditional song that students have learned (two different arrangements, if possible), p. 381

recording of a theme and its variations, p. 382

recording of *Variations on "Ah! vous dirai-je Maman*," p. 382

compact disc player, pp. 383, 395

dynamic cards, pp. 383, 396

chart board, pp. 383, 395

What Students Need to Learn

› **Increase ability to recognize elements of music learned in previous grades**

› **Play a steady beat, a simple rhythm pattern, simultaneous rhythm patterns, and syncopation patterns**

› **Understand *accelerando* and *ritardando***

› **Understand *crescendo* and *decrescendo***

› **Sing in two and three parts**

› **Recognize interlude in musical selections**

› **Understand the following notation:**

  • **eighth rest**

  • **grouped sixteenth notes**

  • **meter signature: $\frac{6}{8}$, common time is $\frac{4}{4}$**

What Students Will Learn in Future Grades

In Grade 6, students will extend their knowledge of musical terms and notation, including

  • recognize frequently used Italian terms, including *grave* (very, very slow), *largo* (very slow), *adagio* (slow), *andante* (moderate; "walking"), *moderato* (medium), *allegro* (fast), *presto* (very fast), *prestissimo* (as fast as you can go)

  • identify chords [such as I (tonic), IV (subdominant), V (dominant), V7]; major and minor chords; chord changes; intervals (third, fourth, fifth)

  • understand what an octave is

  • understand notation: bass clef; naturals

Vocabulary

Student/Teacher Vocabulary

accelerando: "getting faster"; this notation indicates that the music should gradually speed up (S)

accent: (noun) a regularly recurring stress or special emphasis of a tone in a measure; (verb) emphasize a note (S)

accidental: a general term for a sharp, flat, or natural sign; a symbol used to raise or lower a note, or to return a note to its normal pitch (S)

arrangement: a specific rendition of a piece, specifying the instruments used, the exact notes of the accompaniment, the harmony parts, etc. (T)

bar: one measure of music (S)

bar line: a vertical line that divides the staff into measures (S)

beam: in music notation, the horizontal line, in place of flags, that connects groups of short notes, i.e., eighth notes, sixteenth notes, and thirty-second notes (T)

beat: the steady pulse that can be felt during a piece of music (S)

Vocabulary continued

canon: a melody that is imitated by a different voice that begins a short interval of time after the original voice (S)

chorus: the section of a song that is usually repeated, also called the refrain (S)

clef: a symbol in written music placed at the beginning of each staff to indicate the pitches of the notes (S)

C-major scale: an important scale found on the white keys of the piano, from one C to the next C (S)

coda: a section of a musical piece that occurs only once, at the end, and brings the music to a conclusion (S)

common time: the notation **C** is a type of time signature that stands for $\frac{4}{4}$ (S)

consonant: adjective describing sounds that are pleasing to the ear (T)

crescendo: "increasing"; this notation indicates that the music should gradually get louder (S)

Da capo [D.C.] al fine: [DAH KAH-po AHL FEEN-eh] Italian for "from the head, to the end"; an indication meaning that the performer is to continue playing by returning to the beginning of the piece and playing until he or she reaches the word *fine* in the score (S)

decrescendo: "decreasing"; this notation indicates that the music should gradually get softer (S)

dissonant: adjective describing sounds that are unpleasant to the ear (T)

dotted note: a dot written beside a note; indicates that the length of the note is increased by half of its original value (S)

dynamics: the element of music that has to do with volume—loudness and softness (S)

flag: a line or lines extending from the right side of a stem of a note, indicating whether the note is an eighth note, sixteenth note, or smaller (T)

flat: a symbol (♭) placed next to a notehead to lower the pitch of that note by one half-step (S)

form: the element of music that deals with musical structures and patterns (S)

half rest: two beats of rest or silence (in $\frac{4}{4}$ meter) (S)

half-step: the interval between any two adjacent notes of a piano (including black keys); the smallest interval used in most music (T)

harmony: a combination of sounds that is pleasing to the ear (S)

interlude: a short piece of music that is used to bridge together sections of a longer piece of music (S)

interval: the distance in pitch between two notes (T)

introduction: a section of a musical piece that occurs only once, at the beginning, and leads into the main part of the piece (S)

legato: Italian for "bound together"; a marking that indicates a technique of playing consecutive notes as a smooth, continuous line, without breaks between notes (S)

measure: the space between two bar lines (S)

melody: an organized sequence of single pitches making up the tune (S)

meter: the specific way the beat is organized in a piece of music; number of beats per measure (T)

mezzo forte, forte, fortissimo (mf, f, ff): dynamic markings meaning "moderately loud," "loud," and "very loud" (S)

Materials continued

flash cards that say *accelerando, ritardando, crescendo,* **and** *decrescendo,* **p. 384**

two pieces of music— one that reviews notes students have learned and another with sixteenth notes, p. 386

recorder or guitar, p. 387

resonator tone bars or Orff® tone bar instruments, p. 388

variety of sheet music, pp. 389, 396, 397

transparency of the treble clef staff, p. 389

overhead projector, p. 389

xylophone, resonator bells, or a piano to demonstrate music, pp. 382, 387, 390

poster board, pp. 393, 396, 397

ball, p. 394

materials for students to use when interpreting music, such as tissue paper, scarves, or paper plates, p. 394

index cards, p. 395

pieces of paper with bars and time signatures on the side, p. 395

variety of simple instruments, p. 395

large piece of paper for each student to create a notation collage, p. 396

piece of yarn, 1 per pair of students, p. 396

information to visit a choir in the local community or at the local high school, p. 397

Vocabulary continued

middle C: the C that falls just below the bottom of the treble clef; found near the middle of the piano keyboard (S)

notation: a way of representing sounds on paper (S)

note: a written symbol used in music to represent a sound of a particular duration (S)

phrase: a musical sentence (S)

pianissimo, piano, mezzo piano (pp, p, mp): dynamic markings meaning "very soft," "soft," and "moderately soft" (S)

pitch: the highness or lowness of a note (S)

quarter rest: one beat of rest or silence (in $\frac{4}{4}$ meter) (S)

refrain: the section of a song that is usually repeated, also called the chorus (S)

repeat sign: a kind of bar line (distinguished by two dots alongside it) indicating that a whole section of the score is to be repeated before continuing to the next bar (S)

rhythm: the pattern of long and short note values in music (S)

ritardando: "getting slower"; this notation indicates that the music should gradually slow down (S)

round: a vocal canon for two or more voices; each voice begins shortly after the other, singing the same melody and lyrics; when a voice reaches the end, it can then start over, continuing indefinitely (S)

scale: a series of eight notes in order (S)

scale degree: one of the seven differently named pitches that make up a scale, in terms of its position in the scale. For example, E is the third scale degree of the C-major scale (C D E F G A B C). The eighth degree has the same tone as the first, so it is considered a duplication. (T)

score: a piece of notated music (T)

sharp: a symbol (♯) placed next to a notehead to raise the pitch of that note by one half-step (S)

solfège: [SOLE-fezh] the syllables "do re mi fa so la ti" that are traditionally sung to the pitches of the scale in rising order (T)

staccato: Italian for "detached"; a marking that indicates a technique of playing consecutive notes as very short and disconnected from one another (S)

staff: the five horizontal lines upon which music is written (S)

syncopation: the placement of rhythmic accents on weak beats or weak portions of beats; the effect created when music falls into a rhythm that does not align with the underlying beat in a simple way (S)

tempo: the speed of a musical performance (S)

theme: the musical subject of a piece, usually the melody (S)

theme and variations: a musical form that presents the theme of the piece and then restates it in different ways (S)

tie: a curved line connecting two notes of the same pitch, indicating they are to be played as one (S)

timbre: tone color and quality of a musical instrument or voice (S)

time (or meter) signature: the numbers at the beginning of a piece of music. The top number indicates the number of beats in a measure. The bottom number indicates the type of note that receives one beat. (S)

Vocabulary continued

treble clef: a symbol (𝄞) that, when placed on the staff, indicates that the lines of the staff, from bottom to top, will represent E, G, B, D, and F (S)

variation: a musical theme that has been melodically, harmonically, or rhythmically changed from its original form (S)

verse: a set of lyrics that tells the story of a song; unlike the chorus (or refrain), the verses generally differ from stanza to stanza (S)

whole rest: four beats of rest or silence (in $\frac{4}{4}$ meter) (S)

Domain Vocabulary

Elements of music and associated words:
speed, fast, slow, tune, line, up, down, row, air, vibration, work, perform, dance, march, skip, jump, clap, play, stress, color, high, low, rising, falling, dynamics *and associated words* (loud, louder, soft/quiet, softer/quieter), form *and associated words* (bridge, phrase, section, movement, piece, composer, song, writer), instruments *and associated words* (guitar; piano; percussion, wind, string, and brass families), songs *and associated words* (performance, tune, melodic, lyric, sing, singer, voice, two-part and three-part harmony, harmonic, harmonize, choral, bass, soprano, tenor, alto, soloist, singing, listening, accompaniment, musicians, choir, glee club, concert, performance), theory *and associated words* (scale, "do re mi fa so la ti," solfège, major, minor, tone, chord, cadence, octave), notation *and associated words* (symbol, whole note, half note, quarter note, eighth note, sixteenth note, notehead, stem, rest, $\frac{4}{4}$, $\frac{3}{4}$, $\frac{6}{8}$), *plus words in song lyrics*

Cross-curricular Connections

Language Arts

Writing, Grammar, and Usage
- Notation as the written language of music

Mathematics

Numbers and Number Sense
Fractions and Decimals
Computation
- Rhythm, meter, and note durations interact mathematically and often as fractions.

At a Glance

The most important ideas for you are:

- *Accelerando* and *ritardando* indicate gradual changes in tempo: *accelerando* means "grow faster"; *ritardando* means "grow slower."
- *Crescendo* and *decrescendo* indicate gradual changes in dynamics: *crescendo* means "grow louder"; *decrescendo* means "grow softer."
- An interlude is a section in a piece of music that appears somewhere in the middle and provides a contrast with what comes before and after it.
- Common time is another name for the $\frac{4}{4}$ time signature.
- Students should review all concepts from previous grades.

What Teachers Need to Know

Background

Though we tend to enjoy music as a whole, it is made up of several different basic elements. Rhythm, melody, harmony, form, dynamics, and timbre are some of the most fundamental of these elements, each contributing something unique to the music. Being able to make observations about each of these individual elements is useful for listeners and performers alike. Awareness of these elements can be a tool to help us better understand how music works, but it can also be a way to deepen our enjoyment. The better we are at identifying what it is that we are hearing, the more we are able to become involved with it and respond. In Kindergarten through Grade 4, students in Core Knowledge schools should have learned about these basic elements of music. It would be helpful to review them with students and fill in gaps as you introduce new elements and songs. You may also use some of the classical pieces in Section II, "Listening and Understanding," on pp. 399–409 and some of the songs in Sections III and IV, "American Musical Traditions" and "Songs," on pp. 410–418 to demonstrate the concepts to be reviewed or introduced.

Many musical concepts are best learned through active participation. Emphasize classroom activity involving interaction with music: singing, clapping rhythms, moving responsively, playing instruments, etc. When introducing concepts from this section, try to use this year's songs and listening selections as examples to help students understand how these concepts are relevant. For example, students can listen to "Dona Nobis Pacem" sung as a round to recognize harmony. "Havah Nagilah" lends itself naturally to responsive rhythmic movement.

Rhythm

In order to understand rhythm, it is important to first understand beat. The steady beat is the most basic way music is organized. This is a steady, constant pulse that can be felt underneath a whole piece of music. When we clap or tap in time to music, we are intuitively marking the steady beat. Being aware of the steady beat is central to the experience of understanding music; it is the foundation upon which all music is built.

Individual steady beats always occur at regular intervals. For example, in the line "Twinkle, twinkle, little star," there are steady beats on "TWIN," "KLE," "TWIN," "KLE," "LIT," and "TLE." These marked steady beats reflect the meter, the specific way the beat is organized in a piece of music. This song has the most basic meter of $\frac{4}{4}$, meaning there are four beats per measure and each beat in the measure is a quarter note.

When teaching students about notes and rests, it is best to use examples in this basic $\frac{4}{4}$ meter. "Battle Hymn of the Republic" (p. 413) and "Red River Valley" (p. 415) are two examples of songs in this grade with $\frac{4}{4}$ meter. Students were introduced to $\frac{2}{4}$ and $\frac{3}{4}$ meter in previous grades. You may wish to review these meter signatures with them. Songs in Grade 5 to use as examples include "Shenandoah" and "Dona Nobis Pacem."

Teaching Idea

To review rhythms, prepare a set of note-value cards, with each card having a single eighth note, quarter note, half note, or whole note drawn on it. The set will need multiple copies of cards with each type of note value. Students can use these cards to create $\frac{4}{4}$ measures. This gives students the chance to create simple rhythms for the class to count and clap out. To help them better understand the relationships between the various note values, students could compare and contrast the different measures created. Once sixteenth notes have been taught, create sixteenth-note cards to allow students to practice creating rhythms with them, too.

Teaching Idea

Play a variety of percussion music for the class, focusing on the rhythms heard and what can be done with rhythm without melody.

The rhythm of the song itself is found in the actual pitches of the music. Unlike the pulses of the steady beat, musical pitches do not all last the same amount of time; some are longer, and some are shorter. The exact arrangement of long and short pitches, arranged against the steady beat, makes up the rhythm of the music. In the line "Twinkle, twinkle, little star," notice that the seventh pitch (on the word *star*) is a longer sound than the first six pitches (the syllables "TWIN," "KLE," "TWIN," "KLE," "LIT," "TLE"). In fact, it is exactly twice as long. This particular relationship of long and short pitches or sounds is part of what defines this song, and even when we change the speed of the steady beat (known as the tempo), these proportions will not change. Fast and slow performances of the same song all have the same rhythms.

Rhythms can be performed by themselves (by playing them on a drum, clapping, or speaking in time), and they can also be performed as part of melodies in songs, instrumental works, etc. Have the class pay attention to the rhythms in the listening selections and try to echo them.

Downbeat

The downbeat is the first and strongest beat of every measure of music. Students should have already learned that individual steady beats always occur at regular intervals, but not all beats are equal in emphasis: some are accented, and we call these the downbeats. In "Battle Hymn of the Republic," the downbeat falls on the first note of every measure. Try playing this song for students and see if they can feel the downbeat. It will feel like the most natural place to take a step in time with the music.

Simultaneous and Syncopated Rhythms

Simultaneous rhythms are when two or more rhythm patterns are being played or sung at the same time. It is important for students to have exposure with simultaneous rhythms because when playing in bands or orchestras or singing in choirs, it is common for many rhythms to occur at once. Therefore, students need to learn how to maintain a given rhythm even when other patterns are occurring around them.

Syncopation is the placement of rhythmic accents on weak beats or weak portions of beats. There are many ways to slightly alter rhythms to create syncopation. One of the most common ways is to tie the last part of a count to the next count. For example, when tying an eighth note to a quarter note, the eighth note would be emphasized but because of the tie, the quarter note would not. The placement of the accent on a weaker beat creates syncopation. Jazz music often features syncopation. Two strategies that jazz musicians often use to create syncopation are anticipation and delay. Anticipation is when a note is played right before the regular beat. Delay is when a note is played right after the regular beat.

Changes of Tempo: *Accelerando* and *Ritardando*

In previous grades, students should have learned that music has a speed, or tempo. Sometimes, a composer will change the tempo in the middle of the piece for a musical effect. The tempo may change suddenly, or it may change gradually, speeding up or slowing down. *Accelerando*, abbreviated as *accel.*, means "getting faster" and is used to indicate that the performer should gradually speed up.

Teaching Idea

Help the class to understand that just as 4 quarters make up a dollar, 4 quarter notes last as long as a whole note. Have them clap or speak rhythms from notation using Instructional Master 49, *Reading Rhythms*. After they have had some practice with reading notation, you may wish to try presenting them with a simple rhythm and having them draw the notation.

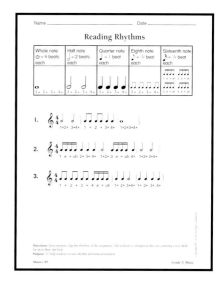

Use Instructional Master 49.

Teaching Idea

To help students better understand syncopation, play two versions of "Jingle Bells" for the class. The first version could be a traditional version students are used to hearing and singing, where the rhythms are regular. The second version could be a jazz rendition that contains syncopation. Have the class compare and contrast the rhythms. Students could then share which version they like more and why.

Music   **377**

I. Elements of Music

Use Instructional Master 50.

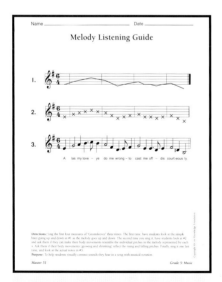

Use Instructional Master 51.

Accelerando can be used to build excitement or tension; listen for one near the end of the final movement of Beethoven's *Symphony no. 5* (see pp. 401–403). Play the movement for students, and see if they can identify the accelerando. Have students close their eyes and raise their hands when they think they hear the gradual increase in speed (tempo). *Ritardando*, abbreviated as *rit.*, means "getting slower" and is used to indicate that the performer should gradually slow down. Ritardando can create the reverse effect of relaxing or losing energy.

Melody

Melody is the "tune" of a piece of music. We recognize a melody based on its rhythm and on the arrangement of its pitches. We recognize a melody by the particular way it travels up and down, and where it starts and where it ends. When we say a sound is "high" or "low," we are describing its pitch. Melody is the arrangement of several pitches in a row. Play "Danny Boy" for the class. Have students listen for features of a melody: does it start by moving up or down? When does it change direction? Does it stay on some pitches for longer than others?

Listen to "Greensleeves" and encourage students to "grow" and "shrink" as they hear the music get higher and lower. You may wish to let students then look at the melody and study whether the notes are traveling up or down on the staff. Have students grow and shrink again, not only when they hear the music getting higher and lower but also when they see it happening on the music as well. Once they have done this, invite students to look at **Instructional Master 51**, *Melody Listening Guide*, to help them visually connect with what they are hearing when they listen to "Greensleeves." Help them discriminate between differences in high and low pitches.

Some students may forget to attend to the rhythm when they are singing or playing melodies. Call students' attention to the fact that all melodies have rhythm by isolating the rhythms of some familiar songs, such as "God Bless America" or "Greensleeves." Have students speak the words in rhythm before they attempt to play or sing the melody. You can even play a guessing game where students try to identify a tune when only its rhythm is performed.

▶ Two Phrasing Techniques: *Legato* and *Staccato*

Legato (Italian for "bound together") is a marking that indicates a technique of playing consecutive notes as a smoothly connected, continuous line, without any breaks between notes. This requires that each note be held for its full length. Legato playing generally sounds very smooth and easy, and as a result, relaxed. On the other hand, the technique can also be used to give a phrase the expressive quality of the human voice, which might be used for an emotionally intense effect. On a stringed instrument, this might mean changing the pitch while playing a continuous stroke with the bow, or on a woodwind instrument, changing the pitch during a continuous breath. A piano, which has different strings for each note, can be played legato only by carefully letting each note last fully until the next one begins—maybe even allowing them to overlap slightly, to increase the sense that they are connected. This technique is notated on music by a curved line over or under a series of notes. This curved line is called a slur. When a slur is written on the music, the musician needs to play or sing using a legato style.

Staccato (Italian for "detached") is just the opposite: a marking that indicates a technique of playing consecutive notes as very disconnected, held for significantly

less than their full length. Staccato notes can sound nervous or violent in their suddenness; they can also seem tentative or humorous due to their short length. A composer can simply write *staccato* in a score, but there are other ways to indicate this technique: the most common is to place a dot directly above the head of the note (or below, if the stem extends upward).

When listening to the musical selections from Section II, "Listening and Understanding," on pp. 399–409, have students listen to the phrasing techniques used by the instruments. Have cards with the words *staccato* and *legato* written on them, with a simple illustration completed by the students to help them remember the difference between the two words. Students should hold up the "staccato" card when they hear staccato phrasing, and the "legato" card when they hear legato phrasing. Keep practicing this all year long with a variety of musical pieces.

Harmony

When two or more pitches occur at the same time, combined with one another, we hear harmony. Harmony is the element of music that deals with the relationships between simultaneous tones. Harmony can be one of the most subtle and complex elements of music to understand. This is because the kinds of effects created by combinations of notes vary subtly, depending on the relationship between the tones.

An interval is the distance between two pitches. Different intervals suggest different amounts of tension: an interval that feels satisfying and settled is called consonant, while one that feels unsettled is called dissonant.

Have students listen to pairs of harmonic intervals played on the piano. Harmonic intervals are notes played at the same time. Ask students to listen for the difference between "pretty" harmony (consonance) and "weird or ugly" harmony (dissonance). Students could even be encouraged to explore different expressions based on the harmony that they hear. If they hear the "pretty" harmony, then they are to strike a pose or expression that represents that consonant sound. If students hear more dissonance, then they should choose a different expression or pose to represent that type of sound.

Finding the best pitches to produce a satisfying harmony can sometimes be difficult. One good way to start exploring harmony is by singing rounds. A round is a song for two or more voices. Each voice begins shortly after the other, singing the same melody and lyrics. When a voice reaches the end, it can then start over, continuing indefinitely. A round has only one tune, but it can create harmony with itself. "Dona Nobis Pacem" is a familiar example of a round. See Section IV, "Songs," on pp. 410–418, for more about rounds.

Rounds are essentially a vocal form of canons. Canons are musical compositions in which the initial melody is played, and then after an interval, that melody is echoed back, either at the same or a different pitch. One or more imitations of the initial melody can be heard in a canon.

Performance: Score-Reading and Part-Singing

In previous years, students have acquired a substantial understanding of music notation. Students have also become more and more comfortable with unison singing and singing in rounds. This year they will begin performing from

Teaching Idea

Have students explore how melodies can represent emotions or moods. For example, play 3 or 4 contrasting instrumental melodies for the class. Ask students to pick one melody that they think best represents how they are feeling that day. Students can then write a couple of sentences explaining why they picked that melody.

Teaching Idea

Ask students to pick 2 activities that they do daily that if "underscored with music" would need a legato style of music, and choose two activities that would be more staccato. For example, reading in the library and getting ready for bed could be legato activities. Jumping rope at recess and cleaning up their room might be more staccato.

Teaching Idea

When you are introducing a round, such as "Row, Row, Row Your Boat," have students listen to a vocal arrangement of the song in a round and then discuss what they are hearing. Why are there people starting at different times? Why are there people singing different words at different times? This type of discussion is a good way to segue into the study and exploration of rounds. Note that "Row, Row, Row Your Boat" is an easier song to begin with because most students are familiar with this piece, and the words are simple to understand and follow.

Teaching Idea

While singing rounds, let students take turns "conducting" by indicating when each group should begin. The second voice should start singing after the first voice sings the first line and the third voice after the second. You may also wish to set aside a group of students as an audience. Have them try to listen to all the parts at once, or try to follow the voices of just one part as it travels through the round. You may wish to start with an easier song like "Row, Row, Row Your Boat" and then move to a more challenging round like "Dona Nobis Pacem."

Teaching Idea

To help students understand the concept of form and phrasing in music, teach students the chorus of "Down by the Riverside," found in the Text Resources. Tell them you are going to sing each verse and they are going to sing the refrain, or chorus, together when you lift up your arms. You can repeat this activity with other songs listed in Sections III and IV on pp. 410–418.

scores and singing in two- and three-part harmony. Help students become comfortable working from scores by first singing or playing each phrase to them while they follow in their scores. Then you may ask them to sing the phrase back. Finding notes and intervals from a score can be quite difficult. It is more important for students to have the sensation that they are reading the music from the score than it is for them to be able to actually find their part from the score alone.

A good transition piece into the experience of singing in parts is "Dona Nobis Pacem," from this year's song list. Even though it is constructed as a round, the phrases are so long that the experience of singing it is not too different from the experience of singing a nonrepeating piece in three-part harmony. Have all students learn each part of the song separately prior to singing it in harmony. As students begin singing in harmony, make sure to focus on the intervals formed between the parts long enough for the students to feel and hear what it is like for two or more different sung notes to be in harmony with one another. A large part of singing in harmony is being able to listen while you sing; encourage students to do just that.

A large body of music has been written specifically for students' voices in two- and three-part harmony. Any competent arrangement will serve the purpose of providing students with the opportunity to build their reading and singing skills. Don't feel limited to the songs on the list. Choose several songs or song arrangements from any genre that you think your class would particularly enjoy performing, and then practice singing from the score regularly. Have the class exchange parts periodically so that everyone gets a chance to read and sing every part. This kind of work is invaluable in giving students active involvement with the musical concepts they have been learning.

Form

Melody, harmony, and rhythm are all ways in which the individual notes of a piece of music are organized and structured, but if we stand back and look at the big picture, we might see many other kinds of structure. Just as letters make up words and words make up sentences, so individual notes combine into phrases, and, in turn, phrases can be arranged and combined into even larger units. The word *form* refers to all these other levels of structure and organization.

Form is the shape and order of music; it describes how the melody or melodies are organized over the course of the whole piece. Students are not expected to explore form in great detail this year, though you may wish to have them try to describe the order of musical events in a piece of music: how many different melodies were there? Did the melodies repeat? Change? Go away and then come back?

One of the simplest ways a piece can have form is by repeating sections. In many traditional songs, such as "Shenandoah," there is only one phrase, which repeats over and over for each new verse of the lyrics. Another simple and very common form for songs is to have two distinct sections that alternate, often called the verse and refrain (or chorus); "Down by the Riverside" is an example. The song has several different verses sung to the same tune; each verse is followed by a singing of the chorus (see p. 412).

Verse and Refrain

Verse and *refrain* are terms for contrasted sections of a song. The refrain (or chorus) always has the same or virtually the same lyrics when it appears, while the verse varies from one appearance to another, often telling a story as the lyrics progress.

Not all songs have a verse-and-refrain structure; "Shenandoah," for example, has only one section, of which the lyrics change with each repetition. "Old MacDonald Had a Farm" is an example of a simple song that also has only one section, with the different animal names and sounds substituted in each time the song is sung.

Issues of form can be among the most elusive aspects of music. Even with something as straightforward as verse and refrain, it can sometimes be difficult to pin down exact definitions. There are too many exceptions and variations. It is best, then, not to spend time trying to offer precise definitions of verse and refrain for students. Simply note what constitutes the verse and the refrain in the various songs you sing as they come up. Once the song sections have been identified this way, you may call on the class to sing "just the refrain" of a particular song, etc. As the year progresses and students become familiar with hearing these terms applied to many examples, they will develop a suitable intuitive understanding of the definition. By the end of the year, you might prompt them to identify the verse and refrain in newly learned songs; they should be able to do so without difficulty.

Introduction and Coda

In the early grades, students' knowledge of musical form was limited to the concepts of verse and refrain, concepts that have been sufficient to describe the form of nearly every song learned in previous years. However, some songs, and most works of classical music, cannot be described solely in terms of verse and refrain. Consider the song "Do-Re-Mi" that students learned in Grade 2. What would we call the section that opens the song, with the lyrics "Let's start at the very beginning / a very good place to start. . . ."? It certainly isn't the refrain, nor is it a verse: it never comes back, and in many ways it's very different from the rest of the song. It doesn't have a particularly memorable melody, and if you listen to the accompaniment, you'll hear how the music stays in one place, almost as if it's waiting for the song to really begin. This section of the song simply starts things off and leads into the main body of the song, and so it's called an introduction. An introduction is a section of a musical piece that occurs only once, at the very beginning, and allows the main part of the piece to start in a satisfying way. Introductions occur in many classical works (for examples from this year's listening selections, see the Overture from *A Midsummer Night's Dream*), partly as a way of signaling that the piece that's going to follow is big and important. The introduction to "Do-Re-Mi" serves a slightly different purpose: not only does it help explain what the song is about, but it helps make the transition into the song a little smoother.

A coda is the reverse of an introduction: it is a section of a piece of music that happens only once, at the very end of the piece, and is there to wrap things up satisfactorily. For a clear example of a coda, consider reviewing the end of the second movement of Haydn's "Surprise" Symphony from Grade 4 or the final

Teaching Idea

Listen to a professional recording of one of the traditional songs that students have learned, and discuss what the performers have done to create a more finished piece. Have they added an introduction and coda? What kind of accompaniment do they provide? Have they added new harmony parts for voices or instruments? These details are called the arrangement of the song. If possible, find 2 different arrangements of the same song and compare them as a class.

movement of Beethoven's *Symphony no. 5* from this grade (discussed on pp. 401–403). The last few bars have different harmonies and a different orchestral texture than anything that has come before in the movement. The real body of the movement ends with the loud statement of the theme at the end of the final variation, but if the movement ended there, it would feel somehow unexpected and unsatisfying. The coda eases us out of the movement so that by the time it ends, the listener is prepared to leave it and move on. Another brief coda can be found at the end of Britten's *The Young Person's Guide to the Orchestra*, after the main theme has finally made its reappearance.

If students have listened to professional recordings of any of the classroom songs from this year or previous years, they have probably heard brief introductions and codas added to songs that don't otherwise have any. Song performances lacking introductions and codas would seem to start and stop with unsatisfying abruptness. A typical technique when performing such a song is to create a miniature introduction out of music found elsewhere in the song, and to create a miniature coda by repeating the final phrases.

Theme and Variations

Introduction and coda are concepts that can be added to verse and refrain, but many pieces have forms that include neither verse nor refrain and are built on entirely different principles. One such principle is that of theme and variations. In a piece constructed in this form, the listener is first presented with a theme, something fairly memorable and usually also simple, to best serve in the variations that follow. Each variation is a version of the theme that has been decorated, elaborated, or altered. The listener is invited to hear both the ways in which each variation is tied to the original theme and the ways in which it is distinctive in its own right.

Play a recording for students of Mozart's *Variations on "Ah! vous dirai-je Maman"* (Ah! Let me tell you, Mother) from the Grade 4 curriculum. Here, Mozart applies the form of theme and variation to a children's song we know as "Twinkle, Twinkle, Little Star." Having intentionally chosen a very simple theme, Mozart shows what sorts of alterations and elaborations can be added to any material, and the piece is a sort of tour through various piano textures that Mozart liked to write. Several of the variations play the melody in one hand, while the other hand plays an elaborate decorative line. Mozart does other variations, such as changes in key, inverting the melody (playing it "upside down"), and changing the rhythm and tempo—all variations that alter the texture and sound of the piece. As with many variation sets, Mozart orders these variations so that they progress from variations that closely resemble the theme to variations with more markedly distinct characters. This "patterning" and predictability is what makes Mozart the consummate classical composer. As students listen to each variation, discuss the similarities and differences that they hear. Which was their favorite? What did they like about it?

Two other works are built around a theme and variations: Britten's *The Young Person's Guide to the Orchestra*, and the second movement of Haydn's "Surprise" Symphony. Again, students in Core Knowledge schools should be familiar with these pieces from their Grade 4 curriculum. Haydn's original theme remains intact and present through most of the movement. Britten's variations, on the

---

Teaching Idea

After taking time to study and listen to various introductions and codas, students could study a new piece of music that doesn't have an introduction or coda. Students should listen and look carefully at a simple traditional song and then explore as a class what sections of the melody they could use for an introduction and coda. If possible, play the different ideas they create on the piano and then let the class pick the ones they like best for the introduction and coda.

Teaching Idea

Play a recording of a theme and its variations, either a sample from last year or a new one. Have students first listen to the main theme and share what it reminds them of. What do they picture in their heads as they listen? Then play one of the variations and, after listening, have students share how their thoughts have changed. Did the original idea or picture change when the melody was altered? Play another variation to further demonstrate how the melody can be altered in many ways.

other hand, reflect the great stylistic leaps made in the 150 years separating him from Haydn and Mozart, and by comparison are extremely free in their reinterpretations of the original theme. In fact, Britten's piece begins with several restatements of the theme that he did not even consider variations. They differ from the original theme more than many of Haydn's variations do from their theme. The actual variations in Britten's set are progressively less and less tied down to the melodic, rhythmic, and harmonic world of the original theme, and by the time the percussion variation begins, hardly anything recognizable of the original theme can be discerned. This progression away from the theme makes it all the more satisfying when Britten brings back the original theme after the fugue at the end of the piece. He has added to the basic form of theme and variations in a way that makes good dramatic and musical sense.

▶ Interlude

An interlude is a short piece of music that is used to bridge together sections of a longer piece of music. The function of a true interlude is to provide a musical connection from one major dramatic or musical unit to the next. One example of an interlude is the Scherzo from Mendelssohn's *A Midsummer Night's Dream* (see p. 407); this section begins just after the curtain falls on Act One and ends as the curtain rises on Act Two. Play the Scherzo section of *A Midsummer Night's Dream* for students when you discuss interludes.

Dynamics

Since Kindergarten, students have been observing that music can be loud or soft. This important aspect of musical performance is known as dynamics. A composer may use dynamic markings to indicate dynamics to almost any degree of precision. The dynamics may change in any way at any point the composer chooses. Although dynamics can be indicated simply by writing words like *loud* and *soft* on the score, it is standard for composers to use a certain set of notations. Students should have learned that *p* means *piano*, or "soft," and *f* means *forte*, or "loud." They also were introduced to four variants of these basic dynamic indications: *pp*, *pianissimo*, for "very soft"; *mp*, meaning *mezzo piano*, or "moderately soft"; *mf*, meaning *mezzo forte*, or "moderately loud"; and *ff*, *fortissimo*, for "very loud." These six indications from softest to loudest are: *pp*, *p*, *mp*, *mf*, *f*, *ff*. The general use of Italian terms for musical indications like these dates back several centuries in the European classical tradition. When a performer sees *p* in a score, he or she knows to play that section of the score softly, whereas *f* appears in sections of the score that are meant to be played loudly.

When students hear that *piano* means "soft," they will probably want to know why the instrument of the piano is called that. The reason is that the full Italian name for the instrument of the piano is actually the *pianoforte*—which might seem even stranger, since it means "soft-loud." But before the piano was invented, there were only harpsichords and instruments like them, which can only play at one dynamic level. The pianoforte, therefore, was named for the thing that made it unique: its ability to play both soft and loud, depending on how the keys are struck. Of course, in our time, very few people still play harpsichords and the other keyboard instruments that can't play both soft and loud, and the pianoforte is rarely called by its full name.

Teaching Idea

Once students have studied interludes and have listened to many examples in class, ask them to listen to a CD they have at home and try to identify a song that contains an interlude. Have students bring their CDs to class and play the example for the class. This kind of activity helps students recognize that interludes are used in all types of music, even today's popular music. You may wish to have students consult with you on song choices to be sure all material being played is appropriate.

Teaching Idea

For a fun and interactive way to make sure students understand the meaning of dynamic markings, make a set of dynamic cards, with several *pp*, *mp*, *p*, *mf*, *f*, and *ff* cards. On a large chart board, write up a song that the class will sing. Invite students, one at a time, to post the dynamic cards wherever they choose on the music. Then have the class sing the song following those dynamics.

I. Elements of Music

Teaching Idea

To demonstrate change in dynamics, sing "God Bless America," found in the Text Resources, with your class. Tell students that you want them to sing the first verse of the song soft, or piano (*p*). Have them sing the first 4 lines of the second verse at a moderately loud volume, or mezzo forte (*mf*). Finally, ask them to sing the last 4 lines starting at a loud volume, or forte (*f*), and gradually increasing their volume (crescendo) to a very loud volume, or fortissimo (*ff*) at the end. Discuss with students how change in dynamics is effective in connection with the lyrics.

Teaching Idea

Practice the terms *accelerando, ritardando, crescendo,* and *decrescendo* by applying them to the performance of class songs. When the class is singing (see "Songs," pp. 410–418), hold up flash cards with these musical terms and ask students to respond appropriately. When it becomes challenging to stay together during the accelerandos and ritardandos, suggest that a conductor may be needed to keep the group together and that gestures may be a better way to convey the ideas rather than signs. Simple conducting gestures can be created by moving gradually faster and slower and by using gestures that are gradually larger or smaller to indicate dynamics. Students will also enjoy serving as the conductor of the class.

► Change of Dynamics: *Crescendo* and *Decrescendo*

Students should already be aware of dynamics, or how loud or soft a piece of music is. They should also be familiar with several markings, such as *forte* and *piano*, which can be used to specify specific dynamics. (They have already learned the abbreviations *pp*, *p*, *mp*, *mf*, *f*, *ff*.) Composers may change the dynamic level during the course of a piece by placing a new dynamic marking at the place in the score where they want the change to occur. However, often a composer will want to create a gradual, rather than sudden, change in dynamics. These changes are indicated and described by two terms: *crescendo* and *decrescendo*. *Crescendo* is from the Italian meaning "increasing" and indicates that the music gets gradually louder; *decrescendo* means "decreasing" and indicates that the music gets gradually softer.

Crescendos tend to create the sense that the energy level of a piece is rising; decrescendos may cause a piece to seem to relax or retreat. Crescendo is often indicated by the abbreviation *cresc.*, and decrescendo by the abbreviation *decresc.* Crescendo and decrescendo are also indicated by the notational symbols < and >, respectively. The width of the wedge shapes suggests the volume of the music: as the wedge narrows, the music gradually becomes softer, and as it widens, the music gradually becomes louder. When one of these symbols occurs, it applies only to the part of the score in which it appears, and so they may be many different sizes, depending on how long the crescendo or decrescendo is meant to last.

Timbre

Timbre, or tone color, concerns the qualities of the musical sound itself. In particular, instruments have different timbres—the sound of a piano and the sound of a flute are clear and recognizable, though we may not always have the words to describe what it is about the timbre that we recognize. The timbre of an instrument has a lot to do with how the instrument produces sound. In string instruments, a taut string vibrates to produce the sound. In woodwind and brass instruments, air blown into the instrument produces the sound. Percussion instruments vibrate to produce sound when they are struck. (See Section II, "Listening and Understanding," on pp. 399–409, for more about the different families of instruments.)

In Grade 1, students studied *Peter and the Wolf.* You may wish to review this as you discuss the elements of music. Help students become familiar with the timbres of different instruments. (You will need to teach students about the instruments and their timbres prior to making a connection to this listening exercise.) Point out, while listening, that different combinations of instruments produce unique timbres, just as colors can be combined to form new colors.

Notation

There are many musical traditions in the world that have been passed from musician to musician without ever being written down. However, in our present-day musical culture, written music serves a very large role; a great deal of the music we encounter has been transmitted from composers to performers through written scores. Musicians use a special system of symbols, or notation, to write down music. A piece of notated music, known as a score, contains many different kinds of information about the music it describes. In addition to specifying what pitches are used in a piece and in what order they appear, a score also records exactly how long each pitch lasts, how each pitch relates to the underlying beat, how loud or soft each pitch is, how fast the piece is meant to be performed, and many other details. Some of this information is conveyed with words or instructions written right into the score, but most of it is written in its own special way.

The system of notation that we use is several hundred years old and has its origins in the European classical music tradition. Today it is used all over the world. Comprehending notated music is a valuable way to improve our musical understanding, just as reading is beneficial to our understanding of language. Music can sometimes be a difficult thing to explain in words; notation is a tool for describing music clearly and precisely.

Whole Note, Half Note, Quarter Note, and Eighth Note

As you might guess from looking at a score, each little circle represents a note of music. The notes are read, like a book, in order from left to right. The duration of each note is indicated not by the spacing, as you might expect, but by the way the circle, or notehead, is written. It is important to notice whether a notehead is solid black or just an outline, and whether or not it has a line extending from it, known as a stem. The pitch is indicated by a note's vertical location on the staff. Notes of high pitch are placed higher on the staff; notes of low pitch are placed lower on the staff.

Three common durations are the whole note ο, half note ♩, and quarter note ♩. Notice that the whole note, which lasts the longest, has an open notehead and no stem. When a stem is added, it becomes a half note, which lasts exactly half as long as a whole note. When the half note is darkened, it becomes a quarter note, lasting half as long as a half note, or one quarter as long as a whole note.

Another very common note value is the eighth note ♪, which lasts half as long as a quarter note (one eighth of a whole note) and is indicated with a darkened notehead and a stem that bears an attachment known as a flag. When several eighth notes appear consecutively in a score, their flags often are connected to form a continuous horizontal bar, or beam. When eighth notes appear individually, the flag hangs down on the right side of the stem. An effective way to teach eighth notes is to teach them as pairs, with two eighth notes connected with a horizontal bar. This way students can truly see that it takes a pair of eighth notes to make a quarter note.

Teaching Idea

Listen to the musical selections from Section II, "Listening and Understanding," (pp. 399–409). Have students close their eyes and listen to the timbre of the instruments. Can they identify a certain instrument? If so, they are hearing the different timbres. Students should try to name the instruments they hear. Keep practicing this all year long with a variety of musical pieces. With practice, students will become better at identifying instruments, and naming instrument families as well (e.g., woodwind, brass, percussion, and string).

Teaching Idea

If one is available, show students a score to one of the listening selections, and remind them that everything they hear in the music is notated in the score. Explain that the score is what the composer created when he or she first wrote the piece. Reinforce the idea that music is a universal written language; everyone follows the same "rules" so people can play the same music around the world.

Teaching Idea

Review the whole, half, quarter, and eighth notes by drawing each on the board. Ask students to indicate each note's relationship to the other notes and then its name. Encourage them to notice the pattern of halved values and to apply what they know about fractions from the Mathematics section.

I. Elements of Music

Teaching Idea

Have students look at musical notations of songs and identify the notes. Guide the class in counting and clapping the rhythms. Writing the counts under the rhythms is a very visual and helpful strategy and often makes the counting easier. You may wish to have students circle the rhythms that last longer than 1 beat. For example, if a $\frac{4}{4}$ measure reads quarter note (1+), quarter note (2+), half note (3+4+), the student should draw a circle around the half note and the counts to visually reinforce that the half note owns both the 3+4+ beats.

Teaching Idea

Once students are able to visually locate sixteenth notes within music, begin to explain the duration of these rhythms and how they relate to the other notations. Start by breaking the class into 2 groups. One group should begin clapping steady quarter notes, while saying "quarter, quarter." The second group should then begin to clap twice as fast, creating eighth notes, while speaking "eighth notes, eighth notes." The class should stop and review how the eighth note is half the value of the quarter note. Next explain that the sixteenth note works the same way but it is half the value of the eighth note; it will take 2 sixteenth notes to make 1 eighth note. To demonstrate this, have the first group begin to clap and speak "eighth notes." The second group should then come in clapping and speaking "sixteen, sixteen." As an extra challenge, divide the class into 3 groups, with quarter, eighth, and sixteenth notes being clapped all at once.

Sixteenth Notes

Until now, students have been aware of whole notes, half notes, quarter notes, and eighth notes. It should not come as too great a surprise to them, therefore, to find that the next duration they will encounter is the sixteenth note ♪. Sixteenth notes last half as long as eighth notes, or exactly one-sixteenth as long as whole notes. They look like eighth notes in every respect except that their flag (the line extending from the end of the stem) contains two parallel lines instead of only one.

Because sixteenth notes are so short, it is possible to fit many of them into a single bar—so many that it can sometimes be challenging to make sense of them rhythmically. For this reason, it is very important to become comfortable with the appearance of grouped sixteenth notes. Notes with flags are grouped together when two or more of the same kind of note appear in a row. The separate flags turn into a horizontal beam that connects the adjacent notes into groups, usually of two, three, or four. Sixteenth notes are grouped with a double-lined bar or beam. These beamed groups are occasionally used to indicate phrasings, but much more often, they simply help the performer to see how the various shorter notes fit into the meter. They provide this help because the groups are always made to correspond to the larger divisions of the beat. For example, a bar in $\frac{4}{4}$ time that contained all 16 possible sixteenth notes would be notated as four groups of four sixteenth notes each , corresponding to the quarter-note divisions of the beat, and each connected by double horizontal beams. Use the beamed groups to help you make sense of elaborate rhythms. Remember, the first note in a group is most likely to fall on one of the quarter beats in the bar.

To introduce what sixteenth notes look like, display two pieces of music. The first piece should contain all the rhythms students have learned about (half notes, quarter notes, eighth notes, whole notes, etc.). Ask students to name all of the different rhythm notations they recognize in the music. List these, along with their durations, on the board. Next display a second piece of music that contains sixteenth notes, and ask students if this piece has any rhythms in it that the other piece does not. Students should identify the sixteenth notes and then discuss how they look different than eighth notes (two beams or flags). Have students practice drawing sixteenth notes with flags and sixteenth notes that are grouped and connected with beams.

Note Names

Musical tones are named after the first seven letters of the alphabet, ABCDEFG. These tones can be found in order on the white keys of the piano. You can identify them by their relationship to the groups of black keys, as seen below.

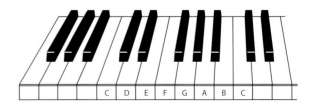

On the piano, the musical alphabet keeps repeating itself all the way up the keyboard. After every G comes an A again. Therefore, there are many repeated tones on the piano. A tone is a musical sound. What makes repeated tones different from each other is the pitch. Pitch is the highness and lowness of a sound. The greater the number of sound waves produced per second, the higher the sound or pitch we hear. The fewer the sound waves, the lower the sound or pitch we hear. For example, there are a total of eight A's on the piano; some have higher pitches and some have lower pitches but they all have the same A tone; therefore, they are all A's.

Tied Notes

When two consecutive notes on the same line or space are connected to one another by a small curved line between the noteheads, these notes are tied, and the curved line is called a tie. When two notes are tied, the second note is not played—it represents an extension of the first note's duration. When a note must extend beyond the end of a bar and into the next bar, a tie is the only proper way to represent this.

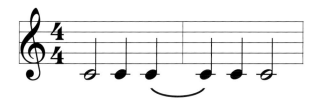

Dotted Notes

Another way to extend the duration of a note is to make it into a "dotted note." When a dot is placed to the side of a notehead, the duration of that note is increased by 50%. This means that a dotted quarter note actually lasts as long as a quarter note plus an eighth note, and a dotted half note lasts as long as a half note plus a quarter note.

Have students look through various pieces of music in search of dotted rhythms. Ask them to circle their examples and then guide the class in charting them on the board. First the class could write what the value of the rhythm is without the dot and then determine what the value is with the dot.

Sharps and Flats

An accidental is a general term for a sharp, flat, or natural sign. In Grade 4, students were introduced to only sharps and flats, which you should review in Grade 5. Sharps and flats are used in music to slightly alter the pitch of notes. When a sharp ♯ is placed in front of a notehead, it raises the pitch of that note by one half-step; when a flat ♭ is placed in front of a notehead, it lowers the pitch of that note by one half-step. Half-steps can be identified easily on a piano. A half-step is the distance between any two consecutive keys on the piano keyboard, regardless of whether the keys are black or white. When a C, for example, is given a sharp, this raises the note to C-sharp, the black key that falls immediately above every C. An F-flat, however, lowers an F down a half-step, which is the white key

Use Instructional Master 52.

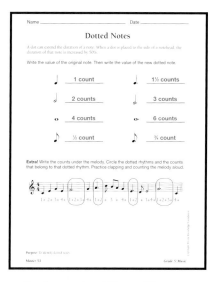

Use Instructional Master 53.

I. Elements of Music

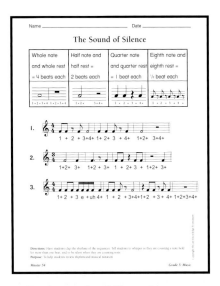

Use Instructional Master 54.

just before the F. The resulting pitches are always named by saying the letter name of the unaltered note followed by the name of the symbol that altered it. Therefore, a D with a flat in front of it is called D-flat.

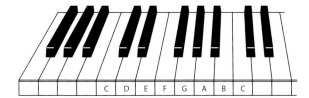

Note that sharps and flats can be applied even when they don't lead to a black key note. An F with a flat next to it is called F-flat, regardless of the fact that this is the same pitch as E.

To help students understand sharps and flats, allow them to manipulate resonator tone bars or Orff® tone bar instruments.

Rests

A rest is a musical pause of a determined length. Rests are just as important as the notes themselves in creating music, but since they are, by definition, silent, they can sometimes go overlooked. The notational symbols for three basic rests are shown below.

whole   whole   half   half   quarter   quarter
note   rest   note   rest   note   rest

Sometimes silence is part of the music. A whole rest lasts as long as a whole note. A half rest lasts as long as a half note. A quarter rest lasts as long as a quarter note.

The whole rest and half rest symbols can be confusingly similar. When they appear off the staff (as they occasionally do), they are almost indistinguishable. The crucial difference is, of course, that the half rest extends upward from a line, while the whole rest extends downward. When the rests are placed on the staff, they appear in the third space, either extending down from the fourth line or up from the third line. With practice, you and the students will grow accustomed to distinguishing one from the other.

To remember which symbol takes which value, it may be helpful to keep this tip in mind: think of the rest symbol as a bucket. When the bucket is only half-full, it rests on top of the line, but when it is completely full, it is so heavy that it drops below the line.

Another way for students to remember the difference between whole and half rests is to imagine the rest is a top hat and they are back in the "olden days." When a man walked into a room where ladies were present, he was considered a true, or "whole," gentleman if he completely took his hat off and tipped it over to greet the ladies. If the man only slightly lifted his hat straight up, he was only considered a "half" gentleman. Students may enjoy acting out the motions of a whole and half gentleman with each other. Once they act the motions out, have them practice looking at music and identifying the two different kinds of "hats" on the staff.

It is common for students to omit or distort rests while singing or playing melodies. Draw their attention to the importance of observing rests by singing or performing a familiar song but omitting the rests (thus distorting the rhythm . . . this can actually be difficult to do intentionally!) and asking them what was missing. If they have difficulty recognizing the problem, suggest that they try clapping in rhythm. Getting students to observe the fact that silence can be a necessary element of music will encourage them to handle rests more carefully in their own performances.

Eighth Rest

Students in Grade 5 should be introduced to the eighth rest. The eighth rest ɣ indicates a pause lasting exactly as long as one eighth note. Notice that the eighth rest does not resemble the eighth note, nor does it resemble the quarter, half, or whole rests! Counting rests and maintaining a sense of the meter becomes even more difficult at the eighth-note level. In each bar, pay careful attention to how many eighth notes have passed and how many are left, in order to be sure of performing the rests in the proper place.

The Staff and the Treble Clef

The staff is the set of five parallel lines on which music notation is placed. Notes placed higher on the staff will sound higher, notes placed lower on the staff will sound lower, and any two notes placed on the same line or space of the staff will have the same pitch. The presence of a clef lets the musician know the names of the notes on the staff. When the treble clef appears on the staff, the lines and spaces, from bottom to top, represent the pitches shown below.

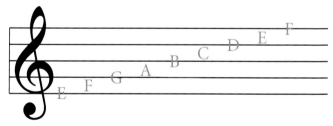

Without a clef, the staff isn't complete; a note on a staff without a clef could be any number of different notes, depending on which clef was intended. For now, we will be dealing only with the treble clef, but be sure that students understand that the identities they have learned for the spaces and lines of the staff are only true because the treble clef is present.

Music is read from left to right along the staff, just like English. Notice that the treble clef is not the only possible clef that the staff can take. Consider that there are only nine positions (lines or spaces) on a staff, but 52 white keys on a piano. To be able to present all the possible notes, the staff has to be able to "move" up or down the keyboard. Different clefs place the staff in different ranges. The treble clef designates a range known as the treble. This is the range in which students are generally most comfortable singing, and is traditionally the range (and clef) in which most melodies are notated.

Well-known mnemonic devices, such as "Every Good Boy Does Fine," are meant to help students memorize the names for the lines of the treble clef staff in ascending order. The names of the notes in the spaces spell "FACE." It is more important that students understand that they can derive all the rest of the letters

Teaching Idea

Give students copies of various songs and instrumental pieces. Have them search through the music and circle any rests they see. Challenge them to pick 3 or 4 rests that they circled and label them with the correct name and length of silence. You may wish to use the sheet music that is included as part of the Text Resources.

Teaching Idea

Once students have started learning about the musical staff, guide them in seeing how the musical alphabet is repeated on the staff. Show students a transparency of the treble clef staff on an overhead projector and have the class help write in the names of the lines and spaces to see how the alphabet repeats.

Use Instructional Master 55.

as long as they know any one of them. A student who knows that the bottommost line is an E can fill in the letters simply by working upward through the scale and filling in each line and space. It is also important for students to learn that when they encounter notes on a staff, they should first always locate the clef before trying to name the notes. Even though students in Grade 5 will only be learning treble clef at this point, it is still a good habit to always locate the clef. That way, when they begin reading bass and other clefs as they get older, they will already be used to this important step in identifying note names.

Middle C

Middle C is the C that falls just below the bottom of the treble clef. This note can be represented by a note placed exactly at the height where a C would be if the staff lines continued. Musicians draw a horizontal line through it to suggest the imaginary extra staff line on which it would fall; this horizontal line is called a ledger line. Middle C is so-called because it is found very near the middle of a piano keyboard. It is the fourth C up from the bottom of the keyboard, and the fifth C down from the top. Middle C is often used as a reference point because many instruments, high or low, can reach this note, or at least near to it, as can most singing voices.

Middle C

Teaching Idea

Students need to be actively involved in the sounds before they are presented with the notation. To introduce scales to students, begin by playing a C scale on a xylophone, on resonator bells, or even on a piano before showing students the notation. Another idea is to use a "stairstep ladder" on which tone bar resonator bells can be placed to create a C-major scale.

Scales

A scale is a series of notes in order. Students will be working with the C-major scale, which consists of the notes C, D, E, F, G, A, B, and C. To play the C-major scale on the piano, first locate a C. (The black keys are grouped in sets of two and three; a C is always the first key immediately below a set of two black keys.) Then, beginning on that C, play only the white keys, moving upward along the keyboard (to the right) until you reach the next C, for a total of eight notes. Students should become familiar with the name and sound of this scale and be able to recognize it, sing along with it, and if possible, play it on their instruments.

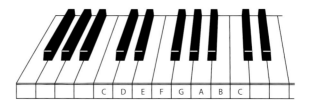

"Do re mi" Syllables

The syllables "do re mi fa so la ti" are traditionally sung to the pitches of the scale in rising order. These syllables (sometimes called solfège [SOLE-fezh] syllables) are a standard way to sing any major scale. Students should use these syllables when singing the scale as a tool to help them articulate and remember the individual notes that constitute it. For this purpose, the solfège syllables are preferable to the letter-names of the notes for several reasons. First, they are simply better sounds for singing. (F, for example, doesn't lend itself very well!) Second, unlike the letter-names, these syllables have another meaning besides their musical significance and thus form a stronger association with the pitches on which they are sung.

The most important reason for using these syllables is that while major scales can be sung beginning on any pitch, singing the letter names C D E F G A B C is only correct when the first pitch is a C, which for most students (and adults) will require referring to an instrument. It is much more important that students become comfortable with the sound of the major scale in general than that they are able to sing a C; the "do re mi" syllables are correct no matter where a student begins singing a scale. Thus scale-singing (and the "Do-Re-Mi" song) may be practiced independently of any instrument or accompaniment.

The form of solfège described here is called the "movable 'do'" system, rather than the "fixed 'do'" system. "Movable 'do'" is thought to be most effective with young students. "Mi," for example, is always the third note of a major scale, no matter what letter-name that note happens to have. This third note is known as the third scale degree. "Do re mi," etc., then, are names for the degrees of the major scale.

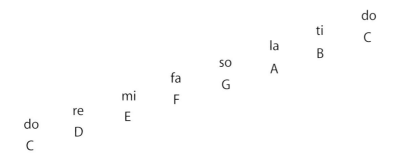

Teach students the "Do-Re-Mi" song and connect the solfège to the names of the notes on the staff. They can also act out the music by adding movements to help them remember the words. "Do-Re-Mi" is a particularly fun song, because it has a fun play-on-words ("Doe—a deer, a female deer; Ray—a drop of golden sun; Me—a name I call myself," etc.).

Once students are familiar with the song "Do-Re-Mi," have eight students hold out the initial syllable of each line as it is sung so that the class can more clearly hear the scale underlying the song. If you like, try learning the second part of the song ("do mi mi/mi so so . . ."), which is good practice for singing the notes of the scale out of order.

Teaching Idea

Once students are comfortable singing the scale in "do re mi," have them practice singing the scale in descending order: "do ti la so fa mi re do." Singing the scale in both directions helps students to be more aware of the identities of the individual notes, rather than just memorizing the ascending scale as a single "chunk." You may even wish to challenge students to sing the notes in other orders, or sing melodies with these syllables. Students could sing "Taps" using solfège. They would sing "so so do/so do mi/so do mi so do mi so do mi/do mi so/mi do so/so so do."

Active awareness of these scale degrees is an important step toward music theory that students will be learning in years to come. For now, it is most important that students be comfortable with singing them in order.

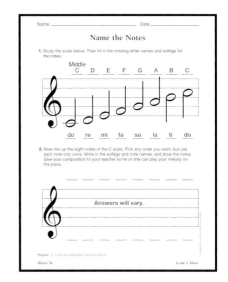

Use Instructional Master 56.

I. Elements of Music

Teaching Idea

The feeling of a waltz often doesn't come alive until students actually move to a waltz. Tchaikovsky's "Waltz of the Flowers" from *Nutcracker Suite* is a good piece to feel this $\frac{3}{4}$ meter and move to it. Students may enjoy learning to dance the waltz without partners while listening to this piece.

Teaching Idea

Students often learn best by hearing contrasting examples. Play 2 pieces side by side, one with a strong sense of 2 or 4 and the other with a strong sense of 3 to give students a stronger sense of contrasting meters. The sheet music in the Text Resources can provide good examples of songs with these meters. Use "The Battle Hymn of the Republic" as an example of a strong 2 or 4 meter and use "Shenandoah" to demonstrate $\frac{3}{4}$ time.

Use Instructional Master 57.

Meter and Bar Lines

The meter of a piece of music is the way that the steady beat is divided into equal groups (or measures). Students have intuitively understood this concept when they learned to find the downbeat, which is the first beat of every measure. Measures are generally of two, three, or four beats each. To capture this way of structuring rhythm in notation, we use meter signatures (or time signatures) such as $\frac{2}{4}$, $\frac{3}{4}$, and $\frac{4}{4}$. Though these time signatures resemble fractions, their meaning is quite different, and they are read "two-four," "three-four," and "four-four." The upper number indicates the number of beats per measure. The lower number usually indicates what note value is being used to represent the beat. $\frac{4}{4}$ means that each measure will have four beats in it, and each beat will have the value of one quarter note. Common time is another name for the meter signature $\frac{4}{4}$, so-called because it is indeed the most common time signature. One way to indicate common time is by placing a **C** on the staff in the place of a meter signature. Common time and $\frac{4}{4}$ time are identical in every respect; they are simply two names and two notations for the same meter. $\frac{3}{4}$, on the other hand, means that each measure will have the value of three quarter notes. The lower number in a time signature is usually a 1, 2, 4, 8, or 16—indicating a beat counted in whole notes, half notes, quarter notes, eighth notes, or sixteenth notes (which last half as long as eighth notes and which students have encountered in this grade). Other numbers are meaningless; the time signature $\frac{4}{3}$ is impossible because there is no such thing as a "third note." By far, the most common time signatures are those measured in half notes, quarter notes, and eighth notes.

Although time signatures can be used in various ways, some tend to have their own rhythmic character. A piece in $\frac{2}{4}$ time might feel fast or high-energy. The meter of two beats can also feel a bit like the alternation of feet in a march. $\frac{4}{4}$ time has a regular, steady feel to it. Pieces in $\frac{3}{4}$ time have their own rather distinctive character. The rhythm of three beats tends to give a feeling of graceful motion. Waltzes are a common example of music in $\frac{3}{4}$.

The time signature appears at the left edge of the staff, just to the right of the clef at the very beginning of a piece of music. Usually only one time signature appears in a whole piece. However, throughout the music from beginning to end, the meter is represented in a different way: the beginning and end of each measure is marked by a vertical line across the staff. These lines, known as bar lines, break the music into boxes, or bars, that each contain one measure of music. Most bar lines are just a single line; however, some are two close parallel lines. These are known as double bar lines, and indicate the end of a major section of the music (such as the verse or chorus), or of the whole piece.

(Clef) (time signature)   (bar line)   (bar line)   (bar line)   (double bar line)

6/8 Meter Signature

This year, students will be learning about a new time signature, $\frac{6}{8}$. In this meter, there are six beats in every measure and the eighth note gets the beat. Up to this point, in all the time signatures students have studied ($\frac{2}{4}$, $\frac{3}{4}$, and $\frac{4}{4}$) the quarter note always got the beat. However, $\frac{6}{8}$ is quite different and it will take time for students to become comfortable understanding this meter when reading music. Students should listen to music in $\frac{6}{8}$ so they can begin to recognize how this meter sounds and feels within music. "Git Along, Little Dogies" is an excellent song to demonstrate $\frac{6}{8}$, and the "Il Vecchio Castello" movement from *Pictures at an Exhibition* by Mussorgsky (discussed in Section II, "Listening and Understanding," on pp. 403–406) is a clear example of the distinctive feel of the $\frac{6}{8}$ meter.

Repeat Sign

Another kind of bar line is the repeat sign, which is a double bar with two dots arranged alongside it. This symbol indicates that a whole section of the score (the section on the side of the double bar line with the dots) is to be repeated as part of the piece. Often, the repeat sign will require the performer to go all the way to the beginning of the score again. Other times, a previous repeat sign with the dots on the right will indicate the start of the section to be repeated, and the performer will not have to return all the way to the beginning.

Repeat signs are useful for songs with several verses that use the same music, or for songs that are meant to begin again as soon as they end. Sometimes, repeat signs are useful simply as a way of saving space in a score! Almost every style of music uses repetition, and so there is almost always a way to use a repeat sign as a shortcut in creating the score for an entire piece.

Da capo [D.C.] al fine

The phrase *Da capo* (often abbreviated "D.C.") is Italian for "from the head," and when it appears in music notation (almost always at the bottom of the last page of the score) it means that the performer is instructed to continue playing by returning to the beginning of the piece. In many ways, *Da capo* is similar to a repeat sign, though *Da capo* is often necessary because repeat signs have been used elsewhere in the piece and thus a simple repeat sign at the end would not send the performer all the way back to the beginning. *Al fine* means "to the end," and so *Da capo al fine* means "return to the beginning and play until the end." When *Da capo al fine* appears, the word *fine* has been placed somewhere in the score to indicate where the piece will ultimately end, and the performer plays until reaching this indication.

The following is a common example of the use of *Da capo al fine*: a piece has a first section, A, which ends with a repeat sign. It is followed by a section, B, which has the word *fine* at the end. The score continues with a third section, C, that ends with the indication *Da capo al fine*. The performer begins the piece by playing A twice and then B. He or she then continues on to C, ignoring the *fine* for the time being. At the end of C, the performer returns to the beginning of the piece (*Da capo*) and plays A again, this time only once—it is customary to skip repeat signs when one is playing a section for the second time, *Da capo*. Finally, B is played for a second time, and when the performer reaches the word *fine* at the end of this section, the piece ends. In other words, the score "A (repeat sign) B (*fine*) C (*Da capo al fine*)" is to be played as AABCAB.

Use Instructional Master 58.

I. Elements of Music

Teaching Idea

Teach *Da capo al fine* by asking the class to line up so that students are facing the front of the room. Give the last student in line a sign that says *"Da capo al fine"* and another student in line a sign that says *"fine."* Have students pass a ball through the line to represent movement through a piece of music. You may wish to play music as the ball moves through the line. When the "music" starts, the students should pass the ball from one person to the next and continue back to the beginning once the last student holding the *"Da capo al fine"* sign receives the ball. Then repeat the process of passing the ball until the ball reaches the student with the *"fine"* sign or the end of the song.

The Big Idea in Review

Music has its own language and is described with terms such as rhythm, melody, harmony, form, dynamics, and timbre.

Learning by Participating

Students in Grade 5 are expected to gain familiarity with all the terms for the elements of music and to increase their ability to recognize elements of music learned in previous grades. By singing, marching, and performing, they can learn to recognize such elements as short and long sounds, phrases, and beat; as well as discriminate between high and low sounds, fast and slow pieces, loud and soft, etc. The songs in Section IV, "Songs," on pp. 410–418, lend themselves to this type of learning.

In order to teach students to recognize like and unlike phrases, for example, start with "Twinkle, Twinkle, Little Star." Have students sing the song once with the words, and a second time just singing "la la" in place of the words. Next, have students sing "Baa, Baa, Black Sheep"—the first time with the words and the second time just singing "la la" in place of the words. Finally, divide the class into two groups—have one sing the tune of "Twinkle, Twinkle, Little Star," while the other group sings "Baa, Baa, Black Sheep" at the same time. What do students notice about the melody? (The melodies are the same, or "like" each other.) What do students notice about the words? (The words are different, or "unlike" each other.) The "Alphabet Song" could also be used with this activity. Using three songs would demonstrate even further how melodies of different songs could be very similar.

Refer back to this exercise in the next section, "Listening and Understanding," when listening to pieces of music. Encourage students to find phrases (or short melodies) that sound the same (like), and ones that sound different (unlike).

When teaching notation concepts, show students a score from one of this year's listening selections or songs, and indicate the different elements of the score that can be heard in the music: dotted and tied notes, dynamic markings, etc. It can be very valuable in building understanding of notation for students to sing or listen to a recording while looking at the corresponding score.

Review

The best time to ask questions about a musical piece is usually immediately after the students have listened to it, or even in the middle of the piece. Below are some ideas for ongoing assessment and review activities. These are not meant to constitute a comprehensive list.

• Play pieces of music and have students move interpretively. This activity could be a good way to incorporate physical education class activities. Before starting, divide students into small groups, and have them talk about how the music makes them feel. Also review how music can illustrate different kinds of movement. Then, play the music and have small groups show the class how they interpret the music's mood through movement. You may also want to provide simple props like scarves, tissue paper, or paper plates.

• Have students create decks of flash cards using index cards. On one side of the card, draw a picture of a musical notation. Then have students define the notation on the back of the card in complete sentences. If the card has a note, also give the mathematical equivalent of counting that note. You may wish to have a set of these cards for classroom use and allow students to take home the cards they make for additional practice and review. You may include terms and notations from previous grades, but be sure to add new terms from Grade 5, such as *crescendo, ritardando, interlude, sixteenth notes,* $\frac{6}{8}$ *time signature,* and *eighth rests.*

• Hum or play the melodies of familiar songs for the class. The class should try to guess the name of the song based on the arrangement of pitches and their rhythms.

• Echo-clapping is a game in which students repeat, or echo, the teacher's clapped rhythms. To begin, teachers should clap a rhythm with a strong sense of meter. Teachers could start by clapping an easy pattern of 4 to establish the meter. If students are having trouble feeling the meter, the teacher can quietly chant "1, 2, 3, 4" while the students echo-clap. When they are very successful at this, the students can then begin leading the echo-clapping in 4. For a challenge, echo-clapping rhythms can be made more difficult by the inclusion of long or unexpected rests. The teacher can begin more difficult rhythms and then have students take turns leading. In trying to stump each other with unusual rhythms, students will hone their counting skills and awareness of rests.

• Give students pieces of paper with bars and time signatures on the side. Using what they know about notation, have students write music that illustrates the appropriate time for each measure.

• Give students opportunities to compose songs. They may use their knowledge of simple notation and then write songs to illustrate concepts they have learned in other subjects. Have them write the notes and words to accompany them.

• Provide a variety of simple instruments in the room for students to practice rhythm, melody, and form. Students can practice reading and playing pieces of music and then have a performance for other classes.

• As a way to review musical terms, ask students to choose a song and bring that song in to play for the class. Before the assigned day to share, have students sign up with the songs they have chosen so you can approve the choices. On the day to share, each student will play a song on a CD player and identify any terms that apply to that song, e.g., introduction, coda, verse, refrain, theme, or variation. You may also wish to chart each song and mark the elements identified by the class. Finally, you may wish to use **Instructional Master 59**, *Words and Music,* to review the terms and concepts introduced in this section.

• Choose a song from Section IV, "Songs," pp. 410–418, with which students are familiar, and have students sing the song once using staccato, and once using legato. Students could also switch back and forth between these two styles. One phrase might be marked staccato and then the next two legato. Discuss the difference between the two versions. Did the staccato version sound short and choppy? Did the legato version seem easier to sing because the notes are connected? Is it easier to maintain the rhythm when singing staccato or legato? Then have students review other songs, and discuss when they hear staccato and when they hear legato. How does the use of staccato or legato affect the feeling of the piece?

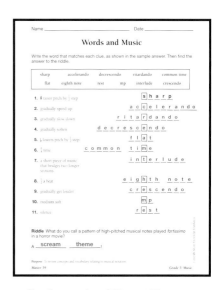

Use Instructional Master 59.

- To review rhythms, play "Follow My Rhythms," which is similar to the game "Follow the Leader." Clap out a variety of short simple rhythms, and have students copy (or echo) your rhythms. This activity is an excellent "transition" activity to get students back on task. For a more involved activity, you may wish to sometimes have the rhythms written out so students can visually study what they are hearing and copying back. As students get better at copying your rhythms, make the rhythms more and more complex. Students can also take turns being the rhythm leader. Another variation on this activity is to break the students into small groups and challenge the groups to try and write out the rhythmic notation that they heard and copied. The notations created by the groups could then be discussed, clapped, and counted out by the entire class.

- To review dynamics, create a "dynamic" board to hang in the classroom, with a card for *pp*, *mp*, *p*, *mf*, *f*, and *ff*. Explain to students that at any time during class, you may post a certain dynamic marking on the board and they will have to reflect that dynamic. For example, if the class is working in small groups on an activity, you could post a *pp* on the board. The students would then know that they had to do their work and discussions following that dynamic. You could change the board many times throughout a class period, not only as a way to keep students on their toes, but to help reiterate what these musical notations mean.

- To review various instruments, play a piece of music and ask students to focus on one specific instrument's sound. Invite students to draw a picture of what they are hearing or seeing in their minds as they listen to this instrument. Students could then listen to the same piece of music again but focus on a new instrument when they are listening and drawing. How are the pictures they created similar? How are they different? What do these pictures tell us about the timbre or tone of these instruments? The class could share and discuss.

- Have students create a "Notation Collage" where they post musical notation they have already learned in previous grades or elsewhere. Students may also post notation they have seen somewhere, but whose name or meaning is unfamiliar. Once the collage is complete, the class can then talk about each symbol and review its meaning if it is something they are familiar with, or you can briefly introduce new notation and explain that the class will be exploring such symbols later.

- Give students sheet music to songs with familiar melodies. Have students add two flats and two sharps to the music anywhere they want to put them. Remind students that the symbols need to be drawn to the left of the notehead and on the same line or space as the notehead. Once students have added their accidentals, play the melodies with the new alterations put in. Students can listen and discuss how the sharps and flats change the melodies.

- Assign each student a note value (using sixteenth, eighth, quarter, half, and whole notes). Each student's note value could be drawn on poster board. Pair students up by giving two students a piece of yarn and asking each of them to hold an end so they are "tied together." The class should study each of the pairs and identify the total count value for each tied pair. To challenge students, ask them to find a partner to tie themselves with that would give them "a total value of ___."

Students would have to explore the other note values in the room to find a correct "tied" match.

- On poster board, write rhythm patterns consisting of a variety of whole, half, quarter, eighth, and sixteenth notes, with some rests as well. Post the time signature at the beginning of each pattern. Before clapping out the rhythm, point out that the pattern has no bar lines and then invite students to add bar lines where they are supposed to go. Students would then have to read what the time signature says and place bar lines in the appropriate spots. Continue practicing this concept by also displaying rhythm patterns that contain bar lines but no time signature. Students should count the beats in each measure to determine what the time signature should say.

- Divide students into groups of eight. Assign each student a solfège syllable, which can be written on a small piece of poster board. Students can work within their groups to create a melody using all eight tones of their solfège scale. Once they have their melodies complete, groups can try and sing each other's scale melodies.

- Arrange for an informal concert after the class has learned how to sing in two- and three-part harmony. You may want to invite another class and then discuss the dynamics of the music. Ask students to be able to explain the concept of singing in two- and three-part harmony and present a short explanation to the audience.

- Arrange for a trip to hear a choir either in the local community or at the high school. Before you go, ask the choir director to choose some pieces that include two- and three-part harmony or that demonstrate Grade 5 concepts, such as *crescendo* and *decrescendo,* and then share those with the class.

- Provide a variety of sheet music for the class to read as you are studying music throughout the year. You may also ask students to bring in examples from home. Be sure to include pieces that have the new notations from Grade 5: eighth rests, meter signatures, and grouped sixteenth notes.

- You may also ask the following questions after completion of this unit of study:

1. What should a performer do when faced with the indications "accel." and "decresc."?

   When the performer sees "accel.," he or she should speed up the tempo. When the performer sees "decresc.," he or she should get quieter.

2. How is a sixteenth note different from an eighth note?

   A sixteenth note lasts half as long as an eighth note. A sixteenth note has a double flag instead of a single one, and when it is beamed, it has a double beam instead of a single one.

3. What is an interlude?

   An interlude is a short piece of music that is heard between longer sections of a work.

4. If a composer creates a variation on a musical theme, what's something that might happen?

   Possible answers: the melody might be altered slightly, the rhythms might be different, or the meter might change.

5. Where would you find an introduction?

   An introduction is found at the beginning of a piece.

6. Where would you find a coda?

   A coda is found at the end of a piece.

7. Why is it sometimes important to have a coda at the end of a piece?

   A coda helps a piece to slowly come to an end instead of ending abruptly.

8. If you see a little dot above or below a notehead, what does that mean?

   The dot is a staccato marking, and the note would need to be played short and quickly.

More Resources

The titles listed below are offered as a representative sample of materials and not a complete list of everything that is available.

For students —

• *Core Knowledge Music Collection: Grades 3–5* (Core Knowledge Foundation). A multi-CD set that includes works listed in the *Sequence* for Grade 5, such as Mendelssohn's *A Midsummer Night's Dream.*

• Finale Notepad is free, downloadable software from the makers of the acclaimed music software, Finale. With this intuitive software, students will be able to create their own compositions with one or more instruments. Go to www.finalemusic.com to download a version for Windows or Mac.

• *The Story of the Orchestra,* by Robert Levine and illustrations by Meredith Hamilton (Black Dog & Leventhal, 2000). Accompanying CD includes 41 selections written by composers from Vivaldi to Bernstein. Covers the instruments, the music, and the composers who wrote the music. Hardcover, 96 pages, with accompanying CD, ISBN 1579121489.

For teachers —

• Essentials of Music Theory 2.0 (Alfred, 2002), is interactive software that starts at the beginning and can take interested students through the equivalent of a one-year high school course. For more information, go to www.alfred.com/sub_software/emtcdrom_v2.html. You may also wish to get the accompanying book by the same title (Alfred Publishing, 1999). Spiral-bound book and CD, ISBN 0882848976. Both can be ordered through The Mustard Seed, 711 Washington Avenue, Suite 11, Chestertown, MD, 21620 or phone 410-778-6707.

• *Thirty Days to Music Theory: Ready-to-Use Lessons and Reproducible Activities for the Music Classroom,* by Ellen Wilmeth (Hal Leonard, 2001). Paperback, 64 pages, ISBN 0634033506.

• *Usborne Music Theory for Beginners,* by Emma Danes and Gerald Wood (Usborne, 2003). A brief, but full introduction built around short (4–5 measure) excerpts from classic scores. Paperback, 48 pages, ISBN 0794503896.

II. Listening and Understanding

The Big Idea

Listening to and exploring pieces of music by great composers enhances students' appreciation of the music of different eras, such as the Renaissance.

Text Resources

(73) *Ludwig van Beethoven*

What Students Should Already Know

Students in Core Knowledge schools will be familiar with

- the music of Grieg, Hubert, Rogus, Saint-Saëns
- composers: Mozart, Prokofiev, Humperdinck, Dukas, and Tchaikovsky
- Vivaldi and *The Four Seasons*
- Bach and *Minuet in G major; Jesu, Joy of Man's Desiring; Toccata and Fugue in D minor*
- Beethoven and *Symphony no. 6 ("Pastoral")*: first movement and from "Thunderstorm" to end of symphony
- Tchaikovsky and *Suite from Swan Lake*
- Sousa and *Stars and Stripes Forever*
- Copland and *Fanfare for the Common Man*; "Hoedown" from *Rodeo*, "Simple Gifts" from *Appalachian Spring*
- Rimsky-Korsakov: *Scheherazade*, part one: "The Sea and Sinbad's Ship"
- Handel and "Hallelujah Chorus" from *Messiah*
- Haydn and *Symphony no. 94 ("Surprise")*
- Mozart and selections from *The Magic Flute*, including: Overture; Introduction, "Zu Hilfe! Zu Hilfe!" (Tamino, Three Ladies); Aria, "Der Vogelfänger bin ich ja" (Papageno); Recitative and Aria, "O zittre nicht, mein lieber Sohn!" (Queen of the Night); Aria, "Ein Mädchen oder Weibchen" (Papageno); Duet, "Pa-pa-gena! Pa-pa-geno!" (Papageno and Papagena); Finale, Recitative and Chorus, "Die Strahlen der Sonne" (Sarastro and Chorus)
- Gregorian chant

What Students Need to Learn

- **Ludwig van Beethoven: *Symphony no. 5***
- **Modest Mussorgsky: *Pictures at an Exhibition* (as orchestrated by Ravel)**
- **Renaissance music (such as choral works by Josquin Desprez, and lute songs by John Dowland)**
- **Felix Mendelssohn: Overture, Scherzo, and Wedding March from *A Midsummer Night's Dream***

What Students Will Learn in Future Grades

In Grade 6, students will extend their learning about classical music by studying the baroque, classical, and romantic periods.

II. Listening and Understanding

Materials

Instructional Masters 60–62

Music Appreciation Ideas for Young Students, p. 402

Questions to Ask Students About Music, p. 402

A Classical Crossword, p. 405

CD, audiotape, or videotape

Symphony no. 5, Beethoven, pp. 402–403

Pictures at an Exhibition (as orchestrated by Ravel), Mussorgsky, pp. 404–406

Renaissance music of Desprez and Dowland, pp. 406–407

Overture, Scherzo, and *Wedding March* from *A Midsummer Night's Dream,* Mendelssohn, p. 407

recordings of Renaissance music, p. 406

information on a local lute player, p. 408

photographs of lutes and recordings of lute music, p. 408

chart paper, p. 408

Vocabulary

Student/Teacher Vocabulary

chamber music: music intended for performance in a small room (or chamber) by only a few musicians (T)

choral: relating to a chorus or a choir (S)

incidental music: music used in a play (or movie) to create a mood or enhance the dramatic action (S)

lute: a stringed instrument related to the guitar but with its own distinctive timbre; the most popular solo instrument during the Renaissance (S)

motet: in the Renaissance, a choral composition, generally based on a sacred text (T)

overture: an instrumental piece played before the start of a dramatic work such as a play or opera, sometimes introducing musical ideas to be heard later in the work (S)

promenade: a stately walk, or music that accompanies such a walk (T)

scherzo: "joke"; an energetic, rhythmically driven piece (or movement), often lighthearted and often in a meter of three (S)

symphony: a musical piece for a large orchestra; usually consists of four movements or sections (S)

Domain Vocabulary

Ludwig van Beethoven and associated words:
Haydn, classical, Romantic era, Bonn, Vienna, deafness, early middle and late periods, "Ode to Joy," motif, unified, Fate

Modest Mussorgsky and associated words:
The Mighty Handful, folk music, Night on Bald Mountain, orchestration, exhibition, "Gnomus," "Il Vecchio Castello," "Tuileries," "Bydlo," "Limoges," "Baba Yaga," "Kiev," ballet, catacombs

Renaissance and associated words:
art, architecture, Josquin Desprez, John Dowland, masses, church, liturgy, lute songs

Felix Mendelssohn and associated words:
Shakespeare, Puck, Wedding March

Instruments and associated words:
orchestra, strings (violin, viola, cello, bass), woodwinds (flute, piccolo, clarinet, oboe, bassoon, saxophone), brass (trumpet, trombone, french horn, tuba), percussion (timpani, snare drum, xylophone, glockenspiel, tambourine, bass drum), guitar, keyboard, piano, organ, harpsichord

Musical forms and associated words:
concerto, opera, song, string quartet, march, dance, sonata, movement, suite

Cross-curricular Connections

Language Arts	History and Geography	Visual Arts
Fiction and Drama	**World: The Renaissance and the Reformation**	**Art of the Renaissance**
Drama	The Renaissance	
• *A Midsummer Night's Dream*		

At a Glance

The most important ideas for you are:

▸ Ludwig van Beethoven was a German composer whose works had unparalleled importance in changing musical styles at the start of the 19th century.

▸ Beethoven's nine symphonies are some of the most important and influential works in all of classical music. His *Symphony no. 5,* beginning with the famous four-note figure, shows his masterful style.

▸ Modest Mussorgsky was one of the most original and accomplished Russian composers of the 19th century. He belonged to a group that wanted to create a new and distinctly Russian style.

▸ Mussorgsky's *Pictures at an Exhibition* is a musical depiction of an exhibition of paintings and drawings by a friend of the composer.

▸ The period of the Renaissance was, in music as in the other arts, a time of major stylistic advances that broke away from the limitations of the Middle Ages.

▸ Josquin Desprez was one of the foremost composers of the Renaissance, known for his expressive vocal works. John Dowland was a prolific Renaissance composer, noted particularly for his writing for the lute.

▸ Felix Mendelssohn's *A Midsummer Night's Dream* is incidental music meant to accompany Shakespeare's play, but it became popular on its own as well.

What Teachers Need to Know

A. Composers and Their Music

Ludwig van Beethoven: *Symphony no. 5*

Ludwig van Beethoven (1770–1827) is one of the central figures in the history of European classical music and in many ways the most influential. His life spanned a period of major stylistic advancement in music, and many of the innovations of his personal style guided the next several generations of composers. His earliest works are in a classical style very similar to that of his teacher, Haydn. But early on, he began developing the distinctive voice that was to be so fundamental to the composers of the Romantic era. He wrote more adventurous music that used startling extremes to obtain expressive effects never before heard.

Beethoven was born in the German town of Bonn, the son of a local musician. After a childhood spent cultivating his musical talent, he moved to Vienna to study with Haydn and pursue a career as a composer and pianist. He would stay there for the rest of his life.

His reputation as one of the greatest composers of the era grew steadily. During the first decade of the 19th century, his name and works became known throughout Europe. He was known for having remarkably bad manners and a hot temper, but we now know part of the reason why his behavior often seemed antisocial—he was gradually going deaf. The knowledge that his hearing was slowly failing embarrassed and depressed him deeply. For a while he kept it a secret, knowing that it would be a great humiliation for a composer to admit he was unable to hear. He was essentially completely deaf by 1819. For the last 10 years of his life he composed without being able to hear a note of what he had written, guided only by his inner ear and the skills he had learned from a lifetime of composition. **(73)**

Musicians often refer to Beethoven's works as being divided into three periods, each with its own distinctive style. His early period, 1794–1800, contains works written within the tradition he inherited from Haydn. The middle period, 1801–1814, contains most of Beethoven's most beloved works. These pieces show him in full command of a more expansive and freely expressive style than what preceded. The late period, 1814–1827, found Beethoven's style becoming more and more personal and challenging. The most famous of the late works is his great *Symphony no. 9*, the choral finale of which contains one of the world's most celebrated melodies, the "Ode to Joy."

Beethoven composed in many genres, including an opera, *Fidelio* (1805–1814), a *Violin Concerto* (1808), songs, and many chamber works (works for small instrumental groups). However, his greatest achievements are generally held to be his sets of five piano concertos, 32 piano sonatas, 16 string quartets, and the nine symphonies.

Beethoven's nine symphonies are central to the orchestral repertoire and, in the 200 years since their composition, have always been considered some of the greatest achievements in classical music. *Symphony no. 5* (1807–1808) is one of the most familiar of the symphonies, with its opening phrase among the most widely known musical motifs in the world. The symphony is a good example of two aspects of composition that particularly interested Beethoven. First, he liked to compose music by assembling small, simple building blocks to make larger structures. Second, he didn't want the separate movements of his symphonies to feel like several unrelated pieces, so he created different kinds of connections between the movements to make the symphony feel more unified, like one long piece.

The first movement is the most famous example of Beethoven's ability to construct elaborate works using a single, simple idea as a building block. Almost everyone can hum the first four notes of this movement, but it is what happens afterward that shows Beethoven's genius. The entire movement is built around the

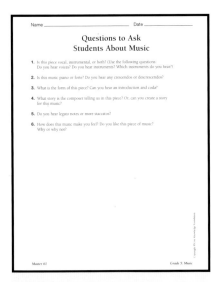

Use Instructional Master 60.

Use Instructional Master 61.

four-note motif. Listen as Beethoven uses that simple idea in all sorts of different ways: stringing several versions of it in a row or stacking it up on top of itself, extending or abbreviating it, bringing it into the foreground or pushing it into the background, using one statement of it to punctuate another, etc. Every section of the movement seems to develop as a natural outgrowth of that little four-note phrase.

As in most symphonies of Beethoven's time, the second movement is slow. Many slow movements of that era are songlike in melody and construction, and this one is no exception. Two gentle, singable tunes alternate through the movement: the first has a lilting quality and finishes with the winds making a beautiful "sigh"; the second has a more steady and noble tone. These themes are varied each time they appear with more and more elaborate decoration by the strings.

The third movement is called Scherzo, which means "joke." (In some versions it might be called "Allegro.") It was traditional for third movements of symphonies to be rather fast and light, and they almost always took the form of either a minuet (a light dance in a meter of $\frac{3}{4}$) or scherzo (an energetic, rhythmically driven piece, also often in $\frac{3}{4}$). This particular scherzo, however, is uncharacteristically dark and heavy. In many ways, its main theme is more of a march than a scherzo. However, the middle section, with its scurrying strings, captures something of the traditional spirit of a scherzo. Notice that the marchlike music is based on a rhythm that is essentially the same as the four-note phrase from the first movement. This rhythm appears in all four movements and helps tie the piece together as a whole. The prominent way it is used in this third movement makes sure that the audience can hear the relationship.

Instead of the traditional break between movements, Beethoven writes the third movement so that it leads directly into the fourth movement without any pause. This is another way in which he indicates that he is thinking of the symphony as one large unified piece, and not as four disconnected movements. The fourth movement is triumphant in spirit. By connecting the movements in this way, Beethoven creates the effect that the triumph of the final movement is a resolution to the dark, ominous quality of the preceding movements. To make this effect even stronger, Beethoven puts a little reminder of the third movement into the fourth, just before the ending. This emphasizes the way that the triumphant finale "answers" the earlier movement.

The symphony is often discussed as being representative of man's struggle with (and ultimate triumph over) Fate. This is accomplished through repetition of the insistent motif from the first movement. Interpretations of this sort were extremely popular in the 19th century.

Modest Mussorgsky: *Pictures at an Exhibition*

Until the second half of the 19th century, Russia had no real classical music tradition of its own, and Russian composers generally wrote in styles modeled after the great German composers. In the 1860s, five major Russian composers formed a group (nicknamed the "Mighty Handful," after the five fingers of the hand) that was dedicated to creating a truly Russian style of classical music that would not be as derivative of the music of western Europe. The most original and noteworthy of these five was Modest Mussorgsky (1839–1881). While other

Teaching Idea

The coda to the final movement of Beethoven's *Symphony no. 5* prominently features the piccolo; this is one of the earliest pieces to make use of the piccolo. What does it bring to the texture? How does Beethoven use the instruments of the orchestra to enhance the effect of his symphony? While listening to the piece, discuss its orchestration as a class. Pay attention to the contrast between phrases played by solo instruments, phrases played by whole sections of the orchestra, and phrases played by the entire orchestra.

Teaching Idea

Beethoven's *Symphony no. 5* is more than half an hour long and is one of the most structurally elaborate works that students will have studied to this point. Allow sufficient time for the class to become familiar with the piece. This will require many repeated listenings and perhaps even more active involvement with the themes of the different movements. You may wish to have the class break into 4 groups, and assign each to study 1 of the 4 movements and present their findings to the class. Make copies of the score available to these groups and encourage them to identify the major themes and structures of each movement.

II. Listening and Understanding

Teaching Idea

Pictures of Mussorgsky show that he was a large man, weighing nearly 300 pounds. The theme in *Pictures at an Exhibition*, stated over and over again, suggests a very large man walking along. Without specifically mentioning this to students, have them walk to the music. Then ask how a person who walks to such a "ponderous" movement might look (or what his or her size might be).

Teaching Idea

Once students understand the premise of the piece and have had the titles of the individual movements explained to them, have them draw what they imagine the pictures to look like. Some editions of the score include pictures similar to those that inspired the music. (The original pictures have been lost.) Some of these are also available online. You can show them to students, but only after they have created their own versions. Ask students how the composer depicts these images with musical sounds.

members of the "Mighty Handful" attempted to create the Russian sound by using melodies from Russian folk songs, Mussorgsky did not borrow any actual melodies, but adapted his compositional style to have audible similarities of harmony and rhythm to the style of Russian folk music. His compositions do indeed sound somehow "Russian," even though they are completely original.

Mussorgsky did not receive much training as a composer, and as a result, his music is not always particularly polished. On the other hand, many people feel that the raw and sometimes surprising sounds that he composed only enhance the appeal of his works and contribute to the sense that they are somehow as native to Russia as its folk music.

Mussorgsky's greatest achievement is his opera *Boris Godunov* (1874) but far better known are two other works—*Night on Bald Mountain* (1867) (which many people know from the memorable sequence in the film *Fantasia*), and *Pictures at an Exhibition*. In 1874, an exhibition of paintings and drawings by the Russian artist Victor Hartmann was held in Moscow. Hartmann was a close friend of Mussorgsky's and had been attempting to do for the visual arts what Mussorgsky and the "Mighty Handful" wanted to do for music—create a Russian style that did not depend on foreign influences. Mussorgsky attended the exhibition and was inspired to depict several of the artworks in musical form. The work he composed not only represents these works but also the person who is viewing them. This helps tie the unrelated images into a more cohesive whole structured around the idea of the exhibition.

Mussorgsky originally wrote *Pictures at an Exhibition* for piano, but in 1924, the French composer Maurice Ravel arranged the music for orchestra. It is in the orchestrated form that the work is most often heard.

As you play the piece for your students, stop and discuss the items below.

- Promenade

The piece opens with a stately theme, which is meant to represent the composer (or any viewer at the exhibition) as he or she strolls from one picture to the next. This theme will return occasionally throughout the piece, and is the one idea that ties the whole set together.

1. "Gnomus" (The Gnome)
   The image is of a threatening and grotesque dwarf.
- Promenade

   The viewer quietly walks onward to a reprise of the Promenade theme.

2. "Il Vecchio Castello" (The Old Castle)
   This picture depicts a night scene of an Italian castle, with a singer standing in the foreground. The music, in imitation of Italian folk music, is mysterious and shifting, appropriate to a night setting. Eventually the song drifts away into the distance. Listen for Ravel's rare orchestral use of the saxophone.
- Promenade

   Another brief reprise of the Promenade, this one is more forceful than before.

3. "Tuileries" (Famous Garden in Paris)
   The scene portrays children at play in the park having an argument. The sounds of the children are depicted quite literally: the opening figure mimics the universal taunting melody of "nyah-nyah!" which is interspersed with quick, light, bubbling figures that sound very much like children's giggling laughter. Wind instruments (flutes, clarinets, piccolos) are used to depict the children.

4. "Bydlo"

This movement portrays an image of a huge, heavy Polish ox-wagon, making its lumbering way down the road. Listen to the way Mussorgsky uses a steady, rocking figure in the bass to give a sense of the wagon's weight.

• Promenade

This version of the Promenade begins quite tentatively—perhaps something has troubled the viewer. However, the next picture will probably lighten his spirits; we hear a brief preview of it before the final notes of this movement.

5. "Ballet of the Chicks in Their Shells"

The original drawing that inspired this movement was of whimsical "unhatched egg" costumes for a ballet. The music imagines a comical dance of chickens and eggs, using chirping sounds that imitate the actual sounds of chicks. Clarinets are used to depict the chickens' chirping sounds.

6. "Samuel Goldenberg and Schmuyle"

Sometimes called "The Rich Jew and the Poor Jew," this movement is a response to two contrasting portraits—one of a rich businessman, and the other of a shivering beggar in the street. The imposing and severe theme of the rich man, and the chattering desperation of the beggar, are heard first separately and then combined.

7. "Limoges: The Marketplace"

In this scene, women argue in a bustling French marketplace. The frantic and constant movement of the music captures the sense of the endless activity of the marketplace. The piece seems to capture the cries of the different sellers and combines them in a progressively more chaotic and surprising way, each interrupting the previous.

8. "Catacombae: Sepulchrum Romanum"

In this drawing, the artist himself is seen in the Roman catacombs in Paris, an underground system of tunnels and burial chambers with skulls stacked on the ground nearby. Ominous chords capture the gloom and power of the scene.

• "Cum Mortuis in Lingua Mortua" (Speaking to the Dead in a Dead Language)

Mussorgsky explained this movement as representing his reaction to the drawing of the catacombs. In the drawing, the artist can be seen examining ancient skulls. Mussorgsky envisioned this as a sort of conversation between the living and the dead, and he is prompted to his own thoughts on death. The Promenade theme returns, but altered, as though seen through the murk of the catacombs. The whole piece is colored by shifting chords reflecting thoughts of mortality.

9. "The Hut on Fowls' Legs"

This movement is also known as "Baba Yaga." Baba Yaga was a witch from Russian folklore who lived in a hut that could walk on the legs of a bird. Her hut not only had a bird's legs but also could fly, aided by the blood of victims who were crushed when the house landed. Students should be able to identify what is going on in this piece, based on a description of the hut and what it represents. The pounding, rhythmic opening notes suggest a giant bird, bouncing on its legs. A quieter chase theme follows, in which the hut obviously gains speed and leaps into the air. The quiet, steady theme on the violins represents the house circling, looking for a victim. There is an almost cartoonlike quality to the rhythm. It is followed by a lower and lower tone, as the house circles, until a single chord shows that the hut has thudded to the ground, presumably on top of a victim. Soon enough, the pounding rhythm returns, and the hut begins to bound into the air, building to a frenzy that leads immediately into . . .

Use Instructional Master 62.

10. "The Great Gate of Kiev"

This movement, the final piece in the set, is a response to an architectural drawing of an enormous gate, imagined in a traditional Russian style. The great, noble theme that Mussorgsky uses to depict the gate also expresses a patriotic sentiment. This same sentiment can be felt in the quiet hymnlike passages that interrupt the main theme. Toward the end of the piece, the set as a whole is wrapped up by the introduction of the Promenade. A grand final statement of the "Gate" theme, suggesting a grand and royal procession through the gate, follows.

B. Musical Connections

The Renaissance

Note that Renaissance music is closely connected with the Renaissance topics in the History section (pp. 164–168), as well as with certain topics in the Visual Arts and Language Arts sections. We suggest that you teach about Renaissance music in tandem with your study of other aspects of the Renaissance. Your students' understanding of the works discussed below will be much increased if they are able to connect the composers and music described in this section to the humanists, patrons, and city-states described in the History section.

As in the other arts, the Renaissance was a time of great advances in the sophistication and variety of music. Before the Renaissance and during the Middle Ages, music was written under considerable limitations—some resulting from the limited theoretical understanding of music, and some resulting from the specific religious and ceremonial purpose of most musical composition. As the Renaissance began in the mid-15th century, a rising interest in the rich artistic cultures of ancient Greece and Rome inspired composers to try to write more expressive works. Attention began to be devoted to music theory, and as a result, a much broader, more sophisticated musical language became available to Renaissance composers. This change, of course, took place very gradually over a long period of time.

One of the greatest Renaissance composers was Josquin Desprez [zyos-CAN duh-PRAY] (c. 1445–1521). His works are some of the finest of the entire Renaissance, despite the fact that he lived at the very beginning of this period. His music is entirely for voice, which was the norm for his time; before the late 15th century, instrumental music was almost never notated or published. Desprez's major works are masses (large works based on the church liturgy for use in services) and motets (shorter vocal works, usually in four parts, based on Latin texts). His reputation rests in great part on the expressive qualities of his writing for voice; he was a master of capturing the emotion of a text in his music and making sure the text could be understood. His music communicated with its audience in a way no music had before. If you wish to play Desprez's music for students, try the CD *Josquin Desprez: Motets & Chansons*.

John Dowland (1562–1626) was an English Renaissance composer, famed for his lute songs. A lute is a stringed instrument played somewhat like a guitar, but with a different and distinctive timbre. The lute was the most popular solo instrument of the Renaissance. For this reason, many composers, such as Dowland, wrote songs for a solo singer to be accompanied on the lute. Dowland's songs are noted for their subtle and expressive attention to the texts. Such songs also mark the first time that the melody of a work and its accompaniment were written out

Cross-curricular Teaching Idea

The sounds of Renaissance music may seem new and different to students. The most important thing for them is to become accustomed to the musical world of that era. Play recordings of Renaissance music while studying Renaissance art and history. This will help set the scene; this will also help students to build associations and a sense of the cultural context for those less familiar musical sounds. Ask students if they see connections among the music, the paintings, and the architecture of the Renaissance.

Teaching Idea

If recordings of Dowland's songs are available, listen to the words and discuss with the class the ways in which the music attempts to capture their emotions. Since the words are really Elizabethan poems, some of which can be hard to understand, you may want to discuss the lyrics before playing a song. If you can't find a recording in your community, check for recordings online.

in full. In the past, the instrumental accompaniment had either been improvised or simply passed from performer to performer. It was typical of the Renaissance spirit, however, to begin devoting artistic attention to the composition of the instrumental accompaniment. You may wish to acquire the boxed set of John Dowland's complete lute collection for classroom use.

You may wish to introduce "Greensleeves," which is also a lute song, when discussing John Dowland's lute songs.

Mendelssohn: *A Midsummer Night's Dream*

Felix Mendelssohn (1809–1847) was one of the leading German composers of the early 19th century. He avoided the Romantic leanings of his time and held to his own style—more classical in spirit and less weighty in tone. He was particularly skilled at writing music that was vibrant and picturesque, a skill that he put to good use in his incidental music to Shakespeare's *A Midsummer Night's Dream* (1842). Mendelssohn had always been fond of this play and had written the Overture much earlier, in 1826, at the age of 17. Mendelssohn captured the spirit of the play so well that his incidental music is still used quite often for productions of *A Midsummer Night's Dream*.

The Overture brings us into the world in which the play takes place, conveying a sense of mystery, magic, and humor. Though it is built on traditional classical principles, it is the mood and color that are most important here. The Scherzo, to be played between Acts One and Two, portrays the fairies, and in particular Puck, flitting through the forest like fireflies. This helps set the scene for what is to come. Mendelssohn creates a sense of mischievous motion that never slows or rests until the piece is done and the scene begins. The famous Wedding March, now heard at weddings all over the world, originally fell between Acts Four and Five, preceding the wedding scene. While this delightful march is a genuinely grand and celebratory piece for a wedding, it also manages to fit right in with the whimsical world of the other movements.

Mendelssohn's music for *A Midsummer Night's Dream* and Mussorgsky's *Pictures at an Exhibition* were both composed in response to other kinds of art: a play, and a collection of drawings and paintings, respectively. Sometimes one kind of art will become the inspiration for another. Can the class think of any other examples of this? Encourage students to try writing music or to find examples of music that reflect their responses to works of literature and visual art encountered this year.

Review

The best time to ask questions about a musical piece is usually immediately after the students have listened to it, or even in the middle of the piece. Below are some ideas for ongoing assessment and review activities. These are not meant to constitute a comprehensive list.

• Provide a time for students to listen to the pieces of music from this section several times. After they are familiar with a number of pieces, have them write a paragraph describing which is their favorite piece of music and why. They should include reasons for their opinions, and they should be encouraged to use vocabulary about specific elements of music.

Cross-curricular Teaching Idea

Incidental music is music that is used in a play (or a movie) to help create a mood or enhance the action. Mendelssohn wrote his music for *A Midsummer Night's Dream* to enhance certain moods and feelings he experienced while watching the play. Can you think of any music that might be suitable incidental music for a dramatic version of any of the literature read this year? Challenge students to bring in recordings of songs or pieces of music that set the mood for specific stories. See if the class can guess the movie or play for which the music was written. (This will be possible for popular movie music, such as *Star Wars*.)

Cross-curricular Teaching Idea

You may wish to teach Mendelssohn's *A Midsummer Night's Dream* at the end of the Language Arts unit when Shakespeare's play is taught. Students may enjoy making a connection between the play and the music.

The Big Idea in Review

Listening to and exploring pieces of music by great composers enhances students' appreciation of the music of different eras, such as the Renaissance.

• Play selections of Beethoven, Mussorgsky, Desprez, Dowland, and Mendelssohn from this section. Have students write about the music, reflecting on the similarities and differences of the pieces.

• If possible, have a local musician who plays the lute come in and play for the class. If you cannot find a musician, show students several photographs of lutes and play various lute pieces on CD by Dowland and other artists.

• Many pieces of music are based on a story. Select some of the musical pieces studied in Grade 5 that are based on a story, and break the class into groups with each group assigned one of these pieces of music. Students should listen to the piece many times, create a story that they feel goes with the music, practice acting it out, and present it to the class. Once all groups have presented, have students research the piece to find out what the composer's story was. They can present this research to the class as well.

• This section provides an opportunity for students to complete short research reports on any of the composers included in this section or on a type of music they enjoy. Provide the class with topics for short reports to write in formal style. Each day of a week, provide a mini-lesson on different aspects of report writing, such as correct paragraph form or bibliographies. Have students share their reports with the class.

• Arrange students in small groups, and have each group create a biography web about one composer from this section. It is fine to have more than one group research the same composer. Have students put the composer's name in the middle of a piece of chart paper, and then ask each student to find one fact about the composer. Students should write their facts extending from the composer's name. Post these webs around the room for use when writing about each composer. The class will have access to many facts about that person upon which to base paragraphs or other writing about each composer.

• When studying music from the Renaissance, have students think about how music reflects the culture of a people. Have them write paragraphs or reflect in a journal about other civilizations they have studied and how the music from those places sounded. For example, compare and contrast the music of the Renaissance to other world civilizations and their music.

• You may also ask the following questions after completion of this unit of study:

1. Which of the composers we have studied went deaf late in life?
   Beethoven went deaf late in life.

2. What is something you learned about Beethoven's *Symphony no. 5*?
   Possible answers include: it has four movements; there is a theme that recurs and varies each time; the third movement is in $\frac{3}{4}$ time; etc.

3. Who wrote *Pictures at an Exhibition*?
   Mussorgsky wrote **Pictures at an Exhibition.**

4. What nationality was Mussorgsky? How did it affect his music?
   Mussorgsky was Russian. He wanted to create a new, Russian style of classical music, and so he wrote in a style sometimes inspired by Russian folk music.

5. Which of the composers we have studied wrote music based on Shakespeare's play?
   Mendelssohn wrote **A Midsummer Night's Dream** *based on Shakespeare's play.*

6. What is incidental music?

Incidental music is music used in a play or movie to help support the mood or the action.

7. What was the most commonly played solo instrument during the Renaissance?

The lute was the most commonly played solo instrument during the Renaissance.

8. Who were two famous Renaissance composers?

Desprez and Dowland were two famous Renaissance composers.

More Resources

The titles listed below are offered as a representative sample of materials and not a complete list of everything that is available.

For students —

• *Core Knowledge Music Collection: Grades 3–5* (Core Knowledge Foundation). A multi-CD set that includes works listed in the *Sequence* for Grade 5, such as Mendelssohn's *A Midsummer Night's Dream.*

• *Rats, Bulls, and Flying Machines: A History of the Renaissance and Reformation,* by Deborah Mazzotta Prum (Core Knowledge Foundation, 1999). An interdisciplinary history of the period, touching on history, literature, art, and music.

• *Ludwig van Beethoven* (*Getting to Know the World's Great Composers*), by Mike Venezia (Children's Press, 1996). Paperback, 32 pages, ISBN 0516200690.

• *Mussorgsky: Pictures at an Exhibition,* performed by Evgeny Kissin (RCA, 2002). Though we often are more familiar with listening to *Pictures* as arranged for a full orchestra, this recording is a performance of Mussorgsky's piano score. CD, ASIN B00005UED7.

• *Pictures at an Exhibition,* by Anna Harwell Celenza (Charlesbridge Publishing, 2003). The accompanying CD includes both piano and orchestral renditions. Hardcover, 32 pages, book & CD, ISBN 1570914923. See also *The Heroic Symphony,* by the same author and publisher.

• *The Story of the Orchestra,* by Robert Levine and illustrations by Meredith Hamilton (Black Dog & Leventhal, 2000). Accompanying CD includes 41 selections written by composers from Vivaldi to Bernstein. Covers the instruments, the music, and the composers who wrote the music. Hardcover, 96 pages, with accompanying CD, ISBN 1579121489.

For teachers —

• *Rats, Bulls, and Flying Machines: A History of the Renaissance and Reformation,* by Deborah Mazzotta Prum (Core Knowledge Foundation, 1999). An interdisciplinary history of the period, touching on history, literature, art, and music. Comes with a teacher's guide.

• *Beethoven and His World,* edited by Scott Burnham and Michael P. Steinberg (Princeton University Press, 2000). Paperback, 350 pages, ISBN 0691070733.

• *Beethoven as I Knew Him,* by Anton Felix Schindler, edited by Donald W. MacArdle (Dover, 1996). A translation of *Biographie von Ludwig van Beethoven,* originally published in 1860. Paperback, 560 pages, ISBN 0486292320.

• *Composer Posters* (available through Music in Motion, www.musicmotion.com or 1-800-445-0649). Two sets of 20 posters each—16" x 20" portraits by Flemish artist Jean Keuterick. Short biographies printed on back and in a separate booklet. Includes Beethoven and Mendelssohn. See the website or catalog for biographies of composers, games, software, and much more.

III. American Musical Traditions and IV. Songs

The Big Idea

Spirituals are religious songs from the African-American tradition. Singing these and other traditional songs enhances appreciation for different types of songs.

What Students Should Already Know

Students in Core Knowledge schools in Kindergarten through Grade 4 should have become familiar with and sung many songs. (See *Sequence* for a list of titles.)

What Students Need to Learn

> • **Spirituals: Originally by African Americans, many spirituals go back to the days of slavery.**
> • **The lyrics and melodies of the spirituals and songs in this section**

Vocabulary

Student/Teacher Vocabulary

klezmer: a tradition of Jewish dance music, originating in eastern Europe (T)

spiritual: religious song from the African-American tradition, many dating back to the era of slavery (S)

Domain Vocabulary

Spirituals and associated words:
slavery, Christianity, church, services, African and African-American cultures, civil rights movement, hymns, psalms, oppression, work songs, plantation, religion, baptism, God, Jesus, cope, hardship, afterlife, freedom, *plus words in song lyrics, e.g.,* wayfaring, toil, danger, roam, Jordan, pathway, riverside, sword, shield, *etc.*

American songs and associated words:
melody, tune, lyrics, lyricist, composer, round, folk songs, verse, refrain, chorus, protest song, carol, lute, Renaissance, tradition, immigrants, Irish, English, German, anthem, abolition, patriotism, amateur, cowboy, yodel, gold rush, *plus words in song lyrics, e.g.,* dogies, cowpuncher, spur, chuck wagon, yoke, cattle, hog, allegiance, guide, prairie, foam, glory, Lord, trample, vintage, wrath, loose, fateful, sword, Hallelujah, dew, damp, righteous, gospel, burnished, pipes, glen, meadow, shadow, kneel, Ave, tread, *etc.*

Cross-curricular Connections

History and Geography

World: European Explorations
Trade and Slavery
• Spirituals

World: England from the Golden Age to the Glorious Revolution
England in the Golden Age
• "Greensleeves"

World: Feudal Japan
• "Sakura"

American: The Civil War
• "Battle Hymn of the Republic"

American: Western Hemisphere
• "Git Along, Little Dogies"
• "Red River Valley"
• "Shenandoah"
• "Sweet Betsy from Pike"

At a Glance

The most important ideas for you are:

▸ Spirituals are religious songs from the African-American tradition, many of which date back to the era of slavery.

▸ Songs can capture or reflect other cultures or historical eras.

What Teachers Need to Know
III. American Musical Traditions

Spirituals

Spirituals are religious songs from the African-American tradition, many of which date back to the era of slavery. Religion was very important to many slaves in coping with the incredible hardships of their lives, and many Christian churches held services for slaves. However, unlike the Christian church of the late 1700s, many African cultures placed a great emphasis on singing and dancing as part of worship. Slaves often gathered after services, or held secret meetings, in order to share their feelings of pain, hope, and religious belief with one another through song. These songs, known as spirituals, were based partly on the African music that many of the slaves had learned before being brought to the United States, and partly on the Christian hymns and psalms sung during church services. The songs were passed down orally from generation to generation. After the revivalist movement of the 1850s, song became an important part of Christian worship even outside of the slave community, and after the Civil War, slave spirituals began to be heard and enjoyed by a wider audience. During the civil rights movement of the 1950s and '60s, spirituals were sung in support of rights for African Americans. Many spirituals from the slave era were adapted to the fight for civil rights, while other spirituals were newly created in a style similar to the originals.

The lyrics of the early spirituals combine expressions of Christian faith with themes of slave life—the pain of oppression and dreams of freedom. Some of these songs also functioned as work songs, sung by slaves to relieve the tedium and pain of repetitive physical labor.

Materials

Instructional Masters 63–64
Two African-American Spirituals, p. 412
Git Along, Little Dogies, p. 414
videotape of Martin Luther King, Jr. giving his "I Have a Dream" speech, p. 412
index cards, p. 416
bingo cards for students with titles of songs from this section, p. 416
materials to make song posters, p. 416
chart paper, p. 416
song lyrics and titles from this section cut apart and put in envelopes, p. 416
information on local spiritual choirs from churches or other organizations, p. 416

Teaching Idea

You may wish to review spirituals introduced in earlier grades, which include "Swing Low Sweet Chariot," "He's Got the Whole World in His Hands," and "This Little Light of Mine."

Cross-Curricular Teaching Idea

Give students lyrics of spirituals to read and analyze. Students could first read the text and then draw or write about what it means to them or how the words affect them. How could singing songs help provide comfort to slaves? Have students discuss or write their responses. Once the class has studied the text, they then could listen to the text sung as a spiritual. Did hearing the music change the thoughts they had? Did the music help intensify the meaning of the words?

Use Instructional Masters 63a–63b.

Teaching Idea

You may wish to introduce spirituals by asking students if they have sung or heard any in church, at home, or at camp: for example, "Jacob's Ladder." You could invite students to share any spirituals they know. (Note that students with a non-Christian background may not have heard of spirituals, much less sung them.)

Teaching Idea

Invite students to share if and when they have heard "We Shall Overcome." Play a videotape of Martin Luther King, Jr.'s "I Have a Dream" speech, which references this spiritual.

"Down by the Riverside"

This song describes the many ways in which the singer will enter a religious and peaceful life "down by the riverside." The implication is that the singer is going to be baptized. Baptism was considered a spiritual cleansing and an entry into the Christian life. In some churches, baptism is performed in an actual river rather than in the church. "The Prince of Peace" mentioned in later verses is Jesus. (74)

"Sometimes I Feel Like a Motherless Child"

"Sometimes I Feel Like a Motherless Child" is a moving example of a spiritual composed as an expression of the grief and pain in the life of a slave. The song is based on a simile in which the slave's experience is compared to the experience of a lost child. The lyrics describe feeling as lost and helpless as an infant while yearning to fly to freedom. The mournful melody seems to capture the slave's deep sadness. In fact, many slaves were motherless children because slaves were frequently separated from their families. (75)

"The Wayfaring Stranger"

"The Wayfaring Stranger" combines the themes of suffering and religious redemption. Again, the song is based on a simple simile, or comparison, in which life is compared to a journey and heaven is compared to a "fair land" where one arrives at the end of the journey. The message of the song is that although life may be a painful struggle, heaven will be the reward; we only pass through life as a "wayfaring stranger" on our way back to heaven. It is heaven that is being described in the verse "But there's no sickness, / Toil, nor danger / In that bright world to which I go." The expression "a-goin' over Jordan" is another expression that refers to the afterlife. This comes from the Old Testament, in which Moses and the Hebrew people escaped from bondage in Egypt and had to wander for many years before finally reaching the promised land of Canaan. They entered Canaan by crossing the Jordan River. Many spirituals draw on the story of Moses and the Hebrew people. The slaves drew a comparison between themselves and the enslaved Hebrews. (76)

"We Shall Overcome"

The most important spiritual of the civil rights movement, "We Shall Overcome" was assembled in the 1950s from two earlier sources. The lyrics were adapted from the 1900 gospel song "I Will Overcome," while the music was drawn from an early slave spiritual, "No More Auction Block for Me." "We Shall Overcome" became an anthem for the civil rights struggle and has gone on to be used by many other groups fighting for social causes. (77)

IV. Songs

Songs come from many cultures and have many different purposes. Many songs tell stories about people, places, or historical events. Songs often were passed from one generation to another orally before being written down.

Students should have a chance to listen to songs, to study and discuss the lyrics, to sing along, and (as opportunities permit) to perform for parents and caregivers or other classes.

 ## "Battle Hymn of the Republic"

Julia Ward Howe, wife of the prominent Boston philanthropist Dr. S. G. Howe, wrote the lyrics to this inspirational anthem. In 1861, she visited a military camp in Virginia. There, she heard the soldiers singing the song "John Brown's Body," about the abolitionist and leader of the raid at Harpers Ferry. A friend encouraged Howe to write a new set of lyrics to the song, which she did soon after. The lyrics were published in *The Atlantic Monthly* in February 1862 and immediately became popular. Howe's lyrics use religious language and imagery derived from the Bible to express patriotic, strongly pro-Union, pro-war, and abolitionist sentiments. In the lyrics, the Civil War is envisioned as the coming of an angry, belligerent God to Earth, with a sword in his hand, in order to defeat the South, crush the "serpent of rebellion," and end slavery ("make man free"). Though the origins of the tune are less clear, the most likely composer is an amateur musician and insurance salesman from Philadelphia named William Steffe. Steffe claimed to have written the song in 1855 or '56 for Philadelphia's firefighters with entirely different lyrics, under the title "Say, Brothers, Will You Meet Us." (84)

 ## "Danny Boy"

This sentimental tune has become one of the world's most beloved melodies and is commonly thought of as quintessentially Irish. However, the lyrics are actually by an Englishman, Frederick Weatherly, who was already an extremely successful songwriter when he wrote "Danny Boy" in 1910. The lyrics are spoken by a woman to her beloved. She says that they must part, but she also looks forward to Danny's return the next summer, and she imagines what might happen if she is dead when he returns. The tune Weatherly originally composed is not the one we know today. In 1912 his sister sent him the music to a traditional Irish melody known as "Londonderry Air." Weatherly was pleased to find that the "Danny Boy" lyrics fit it perfectly. This version was published in 1913. "Londonderry Air" was first collected in 1855 but even at the time was known to be a much older part of the Irish musical tradition. (78)

 ## "Dona Nobis Pacem" (round)

"Dona Nobis Pacem" (Latin for "Bring us peace") is a three-part round in the classical style that uses a traditional 16th-century Christian text. "Dona Nobis Pacem" was the European equivalent of a mantra, a repetitive phrase sung or said over and over again to instill calmness and peace. The phrase is actually taken from the Latin mass, and one can imagine it being sung by monks in a monastery. To this point, students have sung rounds (for example, "Row, Row, Row Your Boat") in which the parts enter at the end of each phrase. In "Dona Nobis Pacem," each part in the round is quite a bit longer, which allows for more involved

Give students the lyrics for "Say, Brothers, Will You Meet Us" and "Battle Hymn of the Republic," and have them compare and contrast the text from a literary view. Students should study the words, phrasing, meaning, etc. Students could share their analyses with the rest of the class.

Cross-Curricular Teaching Idea

Introduce "Battle Hymn of the Republic" during the American History section on the Civil War. You may first wish to teach the lyrics to "John Brown's Body," which is sung to the same tune. Also, you may wish to recall relevant songs from Grade 2, including "Dixie," "Follow the Drinking Gourd," and "When Johnny Comes Marching Home."

Teaching Idea

If appropriate, you might want to teach a cluster of songs about love by grouping "Danny Boy," "Red River Valley," and "Greensleeves" together. Students could look for similarities between these songs.

Use Instructional Master 64.

harmonies to occur. "Dona Nobis Pacem" is a good transition between singing simple rounds like "Row, Row, Row Your Boat" and the large body of music written in four independent parts. Particular emphasis should be placed on singing this song over the course of the year. Once students have grown comfortable singing it as a round, begin to practice starting the song with all three separate parts simultaneously. (85)

"Git Along, Little Dogies"

"Git Along, Little Dogies" is one of the great cowboy songs collected at the beginning of the 20th century, but sung since the mid-1800s. These songs reflect the lonely, rugged life of the cowman. In this particular song, the singer suggests his affection for the herd of cattle, or "dogies." But he also declares he intends to drive them to their destination. A "cowpuncher" is another name for a cowboy. Many cowboy songs are known to have been derived from pre-existing songs when singers improvised new lyrics to describe life on the plains. "Git Along, Little Dogies" is believed to be based on an Irish melody from the 1700s. (86)

"God Bless America"

This popular patriotic song is by one of America's great songwriters, Irving Berlin (1888–1989). In 1918, he composed the song for a stage show, but decided that the song was too serious for the rest of the show, and set it aside. In 1938, with the threat of war looming in Europe, Berlin decided it would be appropriate to write a patriotic song in a spirit of peace. Berlin revised "God Bless America" from what he'd drafted 20 years earlier and included a brief introduction that alludes to the storm brewing in Europe: "While the storm clouds gather far across the sea." The song was first sung by Kate Smith on a radio broadcast on Armistice Day, 1938. It was an immediate hit and has remained one of the best-known and best-loved "American" songs. (79)

"Greensleeves"

The original lyrics to this old English folksong tell of the singer's dismay at being cast aside by his lover, Lady Greensleeves. Starting in 1580, many versions of these lyrics began appearing in England, and judging from the style of the music, it is unlikely that the melody dates from any earlier. The song was popular in Shakespeare's time, during the reign of Queen Elizabeth I. Today, the melody is best known as the Christmas carol "What Child Is This?" with lyrics written in America at the end of the 19th century by William Chatterton Dix. (80)

"The Happy Wanderer"

Although it's meant to sound like a German folk song, "The Happy Wanderer" was actually written in 1954, with music by Friedrich W. Moller and words by Antonia Ridge. The song was a popular hit and was recorded in many styles (polka, jazz, etc.) and in many languages. The lyrics, with their yodel-like chorus of "Val-de-ri, val-de-ra," have made the song particularly popular with hikers and scouting organizations. (81)

"Havah Nagilah"

This celebratory song is probably the most widely known Israeli folk song. The Hebrew lyrics mean "Let us rejoice and be glad / Let us sing / Awaken, brothers, with a cheerful heart." The most recognizable version of the song is an example of klezmer music, a tradition of Jewish dance music that originated in eastern Europe. This particular tune actually comes from the Ukrainian Jewish tradition, and was only incorporated into the klezmer style in the 1960s. (82)

"If I Had a Hammer"

The American folksinger and songwriter Pete Seeger composed this straightforward and catchy melody in 1949, to words by the poet Lee Hays. The lyrics are an impassioned plea for brotherhood, repeated in verses about a hammer, a bell, and a song, all of which the singer pledges to use in calling attention to his or her cause. The song has been used to rally support for various social causes such as the civil rights movement and the anti-war protests of the 1960s. (87)

"Red River Valley"

This song is often thought to be from Texas because of the Red River there, but it actually comes from Canada and is about the Red River in Manitoba. The song is believed to have originated during a military occupation there in 1870. The song's lyrics are about the love of a local woman for a soldier who will now be leaving. However, because of the confusion about Texas, the song is most often heard sung as a cowboy's song about his departing sweetheart. (88)

"Sakura"

This traditional Japanese song describes the cherry blossoms ("sakura") blooming at the beginning of spring. The simple and delicate melody is a popular selection for children. (83)

"Shenandoah"

Named for a Native American chief living on the Missouri River, this beautiful song was actually a chantey sung on riverboats and later at sea, dating from around the 1820s. Later it became associated with the American West. The melody is a blend of elements from several folksong traditions, including Irish and African American. The songs of many cultures were sung on American ships and in that environment, songs like "Shenandoah" were created. (89)

"Sweet Betsy from Pike"

Most likely dating from the gold rush of 1849, "Sweet Betsy from Pike" is a humorous ballad of a couple's attempt to make the difficult journey over the mountains to California. The text is certainly meant to be humorous, but it also captures the danger and exhaustion of life on the trail. Earlier versions of this song include quite a lot of verses recounting the adventures of Betsy and Ike during their travels, usually ending with them reaching California and getting married (and then immediately divorced). (90)

Teaching Idea

If students are familiar with major and minor chords, point out that although we often associate minor chords with sadness, "Havah Nagilah" uses minor chords for a joyous effect. To demonstrate this effect to students, play the melodies of songs or pieces that are in minor keys, for example, "Greensleeves" or the first movement of Beethoven's *Symphony no. 5,* and then talk about how these depict a sad mood. Next play a recording of "Havah Nagilah" to demonstrate how minor keys can be joyous, too.

Teaching Idea

Discuss the lyrics of "If I Had a Hammer" as a class. What do students think the lyrics "I'd hammer out a warning; I'd hammer out love between my brothers and my sisters" mean? What do they think the warning would be about? The lyrics talk about trying to promote justice with a hammer, a bell, and a song. Ask, "How does this song try to promote justice? How can a song be used as a tool?"

Cross-curricular Teaching Idea

Introduce "Sweet Betsy from Pike" and "Git Along, Little Dogies" when students are learning about westward expansion and cattle drives after the Civil War. You may wish to review other songs related to westward expansion as well.

Teaching Idea

"Sweet Betsy from Pike" has a lot of rich visual content. Invite students to draw pictures of one of the scenes depicted in the lyrics.

The Big Idea in Review

Spirituals are religious songs from the African-American tradition. Singing these and other traditional songs enhances appreciation for different types of songs.

Review

The best time to ask questions about a musical piece is usually immediately after the students have listened to it, or even in the middle of the piece. Below are some ideas for ongoing assessment and review activities. These are not meant to constitute a comprehensive list.

• These songs provide an opportunity for both research and student performance. Have small groups of students research and write a short paragraph about the origin of a song on index cards. Schedule an opportunity for students to perform the songs for another class, and have students introduce each song by reading the prepared index cards.

• Play musical bingo with the class. Provide cards with the names of songs in each square, and play short excerpts of each song. If students can identify the song and they have the song listed on their bingo card, they should cover it with a counter. The first student to cover a row wins.

• Encourage students to share their thoughts and feelings about the songs in this unit by creating song posters. Using pieces of chart paper, put the title of a song on each piece of paper. Let students circulate around the room and write a fact they learned about the song, share their reaction to the song, or draw a picture illustrating the song. Post the song posters in the hallway, and invite other students to read them.

• Provide song lyrics and titles in envelopes, and allow students to sequence the song lyrics on sentence strips. When the song is sequenced, sing the song aloud.

• Research to see if there are local church choirs or other organizations that can perform spirituals for the class. Seeing these choirs sing is a way to experience the uplifting energy of the music. After the concert, have students write a letter to the choir members describing how they felt during the concert.

• Have students write an acrostic poem to describe how they feel while listening to the spirituals from this section. They should use one of the titles from a spiritual song from this section or perhaps some lyrics from the song. Students should use the first letter of each word of the title or phrase for each line of the poem. The poem should express something the students have learned about spirituals or how the song made them feel. Post these poems in the classroom.

• Have the class study the lyrics of a song from this unit in detail. When studying the songs, have the words written on chart paper for the students to read. Structure a lesson around the song lyrics, reviewing parts of speech, identifying rhyming words, and defining vocabulary words. After studying the song, ask students to try to write another verse to add to the song, and have the class sing the new verse.

• When studying "Havah Nagilah," you may wish to teach the students to dance the hora. This folk dance is often performed at weddings and other joyous festivals. The original version of this dance requires the dancers to cross one foot over another, which is difficult for some fifth graders. An easier version is to move sideways (rather than crossing over) four steps and then take two kick steps:

1   2   3   4
Step, close, step, close,

1   2   3   4
kick, step, kick, step.

Once the basic, simplified steps are learned, students can join hands in a line or circle when doing the dance.

- You may also ask the following questions after completion of this unit of study:

1. Which song was used as an anthem of the civil rights movement?

   "We Shall Overcome" is the song used as an anthem of the civil rights movement.

2. What country does "Greensleeves" come from?

   "Greensleeves" comes from England.

3. What kind of song is "Dona Nobis Pacem"?

   "Dona Nobis Pacem" is a three-part round.

4. What kinds of subjects are the lyrics of spirituals about?

   Spirituals are about the life of the slave: religion, faith, suffering, and yearning for freedom. Some later spirituals are about the fight for civil rights.

5. What are some songs we studied that are about westward expansion?

   Students may mention "Git Along, Little Dogies," "Sweet Betsy from Pike," "Shenandoah," and "Red River Valley."

6. Why do you think it is important to study spirituals today?

   Spirituals are an important way to remember what African Americans went through before gaining their freedom. Spirituals are also significant because they are often sung and used today for civil rights and other social causes.

More Resources

The titles listed below are offered as a representative sample of materials and not a complete list of everything that is available.

For students —

- *A Band of Angels: A Story Inspired by the Jubilee Singers,* by Deborah Hopkinson (Atheneum/Anne Schwartz Books, 1999). Hardcover, 40 pages, ISBN 0689810628.

- *Slave Spirituals and the Jubilee Singers,* by Michael L. Cooper (Clarion Books, 2001). "In 1862, Colonel Thomas Wentworth Higginson, commander of the first regiment of newly freed slaves to join the Union Army, became fascinated by the songs his men sang. He wrote down the words to these spirituals as well as the former slaves' explanations of the origins" (*School Library Journal*). Hardcover, 96 pages, ISBN 0395978297.

For teachers —

- *The Books of American Negro Spirituals,* by James Weldon Johnson and John Rosamond Johnson (Da Capo Press, 2002). Paperback, 384 pages, ISBN 0306812029.

- *From Sea to Shining Sea: A Treasury of American Folklore and Folk Songs,* edited by Amy L. Cohn and illustrated by Molly Bang (Scholastic, 1993). Diverse and delightful collection of stories, poems, and songs. Includes a very useful subject index and suggestions for further reading. Illustrated by 11 Caldecott-winning artists. Textbook binding, ISBN 0590428683.

- *Go in and Out the Window: An Illustrated Songbook for Young People,* by Dan Fox (Metropolitan Museum of Art New York, 1987). Includes "Greensleeves," "Red River Valley," "Shenandoah," "Sweet Betsy from Pike." Hardcover, 144 pages, ISBN 0805006281.

More Resources continued

• *Slave Songs of the United States*, compiled by William Francis Allen, Charles Pickard Ware, and Lucy McKim Garrison (Applewood Books, 1996). "This 1867 landmark book represents the first systematic effort to collect and preserve the songs sung by the plantation slaves of the Old South. Most of the 130 songs, arranged by geographic area, were recorded directly from the singers themselves. Includes the melody line and all known verses to each song, directions for singing, and a commentary on each" (from the publisher). Paperback, 168 pages, ISBN 1557094349.

• "Battle Hymn of the Republic," on the Library of Congress's I Hear America Singing website (http://lcweb2.loc.gov/cocoon/ihas/loc.natlib.ihas.200000 003/default.html), includes a simple history of the song, sheet music, song sheets, sound recordings, and links to other sites.

• The Teacher's Guide, www.theteachersguide.com/ childrensSongs, is a wonderful website that has a great comprehensive list of popular children's songs. Very helpful for the classroom.

• Sheet Music Direct, www.sheetmusicdirect.com, is a wonderful website for sheet music and songbooks. Search under "African-American Spiritual" for a comprehensive list of popular spirituals.

Mathematics

Follow your math program for time allotments, adding additional time for Sequence topics not covered.

Mathematics in Fifth Grade

The purpose of this chapter is to provide background information in mathematics for Grade 5 teachers. It is not intended to be a complete curriculum. For that purpose, an already existing, sound, commercial mathematics program that coordinates topics for all of the elementary school grades is the best bet. Some suggestions for instruction are given in this chapter, but its main purpose is to provide mathematical insights at the adult level and to illuminate the meaning of the Grade 5 mathematics content guidelines in the *Core Knowledge Sequence*. Frequent reference is made to the *Sequence*.

In Grade 5, students will be introduced to several new topics in the *Core Knowledge Sequence*. **Ratio and Percent**, **Probability and Statistics**, and **Pre-Algebra** are all areas of mathematics that are found for the first time in this grade. Students in Grade 5 are learning the prerequisites and building the foundation that will enable them to feel comfortable with the specific subjects found in high school mathematics. Success is dependent upon students' mastery of multiplication tables and other basic operations in previous grades. There can be no substitute for students' understanding of the concepts behind these basic operations and positive, repeated practice that gives students the knowledge, mastery, and confidence to proceed with what they will learn in Grade 5.

In **Numbers and Number Sense**, students will deal with exponents by reviewing perfect squares and square roots to 144. They will use the terms *squared, cubed,* and *to the nth power,* and read and evaluate numerical expressions with exponents.

In **Ratio and Percent**, students will express simple ratios and use ratios to create simple scale drawings. They will also solve problems on speed using rate. In the section "Percent," students will learn to express equivalences between fractions, decimals, and percents, and memorize common equivalences.

A new topic in **Fractions and Decimals** is determining the least common denominator (LCD) of fractions with unlike denominators. Another topic introduced in Grade 5 is identifying the reciprocal of a given fraction and understanding that the product of a given number and its reciprocal is equal to 1. Students will add, subtract, multiply, and divide both fractions and decimals.

Students will review multiplication and division in **Computation**, and in **Measurement**, they will review linear measurement, weight (mass), and capacity (volume).

New topics in **Geometry** include using a compass to draw circles with a given diameter or radius, and finding the area of a circle using a formula. Students will find areas of triangles, parallelograms, and irregular figures by dividing them into regular figures. They will also find the surface area of rectangular prisms.

In **Probability and Statistics**, students will understand probability as a measure of the likelihood that an event will happen and, with simple models, express probability of a given event as a fraction, as a percent, and as a decimal between 0 and 1. Students will collect and organize data in graphic form and graph simple functions.

Pre-Algebra topics include recognizing variables and solving basic equations using variables. Students will also find the value of expressions, given replacement values for the variables.

I. Numbers and Number Sense

The Big Idea

Writing, identifying, and comparing numbers and data are fundamental parts of developing number sense.

The mathematics concepts outlined in the *Core Knowledge Sequence* do not constitute a complete Grade 5 mathematics program. The Grade 5 mathematics section of the *Core Knowledge Sequence* provides a comprehensive set of guidelines as to the mathematical concepts and skills that ought to be taught in Grade 5. The Core Knowledge Foundation recommends that you choose a structured, well-sequenced mathematics program (one that allows for distributed practice of fundamental math operations) and then compare the scope and sequence of this program with the *Core Knowledge Sequence* Grade 5 topics. In this way, you can identify any content gaps in the program that you have chosen and be certain to make any needed additions to the instructional program. Contact the Foundation for a list of mathematics programs that have been used with success in Core Knowledge schools.

What Students Should Already Know

Students in Core Knowledge schools should be familiar with

Kindergarten

- establishing concepts of likeness and difference by classifying and sorting objects according to various attributes: size, shape, color, amount, function, etc.
- defining a set by the common property of its elements
- in a given set, indicating which item does not belong
- recognizing patterns and predicting the extension of a pattern using concrete objects and pictorial representations
- extending a sequence of ordered concrete objects
- using concrete objects and pictorial representations, comparing sets: same as (equal to), more than, less than, most, least
- counting: forward from 1 to 31; backward from 10; from 1 to 10 by twos; by fives and tens to 50
- recognizing and writing numbers 1–31
- identifying ordinal position, first (1st) through sixth (6th)
- identifying pairs
- interpreting simple pictorial graphs
- identifying $\frac{1}{2}$ as one of two equal parts of a region or object, and finding $\frac{1}{2}$ of a set of concrete objects

Grade 1

- recognizing and writing numbers 0–100 and counting: from 0 to 100 by ones, twos, fives, and tens; by tens from a given single-digit number; forward and backwards; using tallies
- identifying ordinal position, first (1st) through tenth (10th)
- identifying dozen; half-dozen; pair
- recognizing place value: ones, tens, hundreds
- given a number, identifying one more and one less; ten more and ten less
- comparing quantities using the signs <, >, and =
- recognizing fractions as part of a whole: $\frac{1}{2}, \frac{1}{3}, \frac{1}{4}$
- creating and interpreting simple pictorial graphs and bar graphs

What Students Should Already Know continued

Grade 2

- recognizing and writing numbers to 1,000; reading and writing words for numbers from one to one-hundred
- ordering and comparing numbers to 1,000 using the signs $<$, $>$, and $=$
- counting: by threes; by hundreds to 1,000; by fifties to 1,000; forward and backward
- using a number line
- identifying ordinal position, 1st through 20th, and writing words for ordinal numbers, first to twentieth
- identifying even and odd numbers
- recognizing place value up to thousands
- writing numbers up to hundreds in expanded form (for example, 64 = 60 + 4; 367 = 300 + 60 + 7)
- rounding to the nearest ten
- identifying and extending numerical and symbolic patterns
- recording numeric data systematically (for example, tossing a die) and finding the lowest and highest values in a data set

Grade 3

- reading and writing numbers (in digits and words) up to six digits
- recognizing place value up to hundred-thousands
- ordering and comparing numbers to 999,999 using the signs $<$, $>$, and $=$
- identifying ordinal position, 1st through 100th
- rounding to the nearest hundred
- identifying perfect squares (and square roots) to 100, and recognizing the square root sign: $\sqrt{}$
- identifying Roman numerals from 1 to 20 (I–XX)
- understanding what negative numbers are in relation to familiar uses (such as temperatures below zero)
- locating positive and negative whole numbers on a number line
- creating and interpreting line graphs
- recording outcomes for a simple event (for example, tossing a die) and displaying the results graphically

Grade 4

- reading and writing numbers (in digits and words) up to nine digits
- recognizing place value up to hundred-millions
- ordering and comparing numbers to 999,999,999 using the signs $<$, $>$, and $=$
- locating positive and negative whole numbers on a number line

I. Numbers and Number Sense

Materials

What Students Should Already Know continued

- identifying perfect squares (and square roots) to 144
- rounding to the nearest thousand
- identifying Roman numerals from 1 to 1,000 (I–M), and identifying years written in Roman numerals
- plotting points on a coordinate plane (grid) using ordered pairs of positive whole numbers
- knowing the meanings of *multiple, factor, prime number,* and *composite number*

What Students Need to Learn

- **Read and write numbers (in digits and words) up to the billions**
- **Recognize place value up to billions**
- **Locate positive and negative integers on a number line**
- **Compare integers using the signs <, >, and =**
- **Know that the sum of an integer and its opposite is 0**
- **Add and subtract positive and negative integers**
- **Round to the nearest hundred-thousand**
- **Using the terms *squared* and *cubed* and *to the nth power*, read and evaluate numerical expressions with exponents**
- **Identify the powers of ten up to 10^6**
- **Identify a set and the members of a set, as indicated by { }**
- **Identify numbers under 100 as prime or composite**
- **Identify prime factors of numbers to 100, and write using exponential notation for multiple primes**
- **Determine the greatest common factor (GCF) of given numbers**
- **Determine the least common multiple (LCM) of given numbers**

What Students Will Learn in Future Grades

The *Core Knowledge Sequence* for mathematics emphasizes the importance of reviewing and building on prior knowledge. Related topics from the Grade 6 *Sequence* are listed below, and subsequent grades will continue to focus on strengthening and expanding these skills.

Grade 6

- read and write numbers (in digits and words) up to the trillions
- recognize place value up to hundred-billions
- determine whether a number is a prime number or composite number
- round to the nearest million
- compare and order whole numbers, mixed numbers, fractions, and decimals, using the symbols $<$, $>$, $=$
- write numbers in expanded notation using exponents

Vocabulary

Student/Teacher Vocabulary

base ten system: a number system that groups numbers in sets of ten (T)

binary operation: an operation that combines two numbers to make a new number, e.g., addition, subtraction, multiplication, and division (T)

composite number: a counting number, other than 1, that is not a prime number (S)

expanded form: a way of writing numbers that shows the place value of each digit, e.g., 743 = 700 + 40 + 3 (T)

exponent: the number that tells how many factors there are of a number, e.g., $5 \times 5 \times 5 \times 5 = 5^4$, where 5 is the base and 4 is the exponent (S)

factor: one of two or more numbers that divides evenly into another number without a remainder, e.g., 1 and 12, 2 and 6, and 3 and 4 are factors of 12 (S)

greatest common divisor: another name for the greatest common factor (T)

greatest common factor: the largest of the factors common to two numbers, e.g., the greatest common factor for 12 and 18 is 6 (S)

inequality: a mathematical statement that compares two unequal values (T)

integer: any number in the set { . . . , –3, –2, –1, 0, 1, 2, 3, . . . } (S)

least common multiple: the smallest of all of the common multiples of two numbers, e.g., the least common multiple of 6 and 9 is 18 (S)

multiple: the product of a number and any other number; a number that can be divided evenly by another number without a remainder, e.g., 12 is a multiple of 4 because it can be divided by 4 with no remainder (S)

number line: a line that uses equally spaced marks to represent numbers (T)

perfect square: any number that is a product of a whole number and itself (S)

place value: the value of the position of a digit in a number, e.g., the digit 5 in 549 is in the hundreds place, and its value is 500 (T)

power of ten: the product of multiplying tens together, e.g., the numbers 10, 100, 1,000, and 10,000 are all powers of ten (S)

prime number: a number that has two and only two different factors, itself and 1 (S)

set: a collection of objects; the members or elements of the set are listed in brackets. For example, the set consisting of the numbers 2, 6, and 9 is {2, 6, 9}. (S)

square root: the square root of a number N is the number which, multiplied by itself, equals N; if $a \times a = b$, then a is the square root of b, e.g., 4 is the square root of 16 because $4 \times 4 = 16$ (S)

whole number: any number in the infinite set { 0, 1, 2, 3, 4, . . . } (T)

Domain Vocabulary

Numbers and number sense and associated words:
add, subtract, multiply, divide, compare, greater, less, larger, smaller, positive, negative, symbol, sum, round, rounding, rounded, nearest, powers, square, squared, cubed, digit, order, count, computation, estimate, divisible by, divisor, dividend, multiplication, division, ones, tens, hundreds, thousands, millions, billions, number, numeral, equal, equivalent, total, opposite, prime, composite

Cross-curricular Connections

Visual Arts	Music
Art of the Renaissance	**Elements of Music**
• perspective	• rhythms and patterns

At a Glance

The most important ideas for you are:

- Numbers can be expressed using numerals or written words.
- Number lines can be used to count, compare values, round numbers, examine integers, and strengthen students' understanding of place value.
- Place value is a system that assigns a value to the position of a digit in a number.
- Quantities can be compared using the signs $<$, $>$, and $=$.
- Students should explore the relationships between multiplication, perfect squares, square roots, exponents, and powers of ten.
- Learning how to round numbers helps students when measuring or performing mental calculations.
- Exploring the concepts of factors, multiples, prime numbers, and composite numbers will allow students to later build on these skills in other areas of math.
- It is important that students develop a deep, practiced understanding of numbers so they will be able to not just learn but to understand the algorithms and math in this grade and beyond.

What Teachers Need to Know

Background

Since the dawn of civilization, people have struggled to find efficient and reliable ways to count and to calculate. A landmark in that struggle was the introduction of the base ten system of numbers, used throughout the world today. The system of Arabic numerals, or Hindu-Arabic numerals, most likely originated in India and was introduced to Europe through contact with Islamic culture. This base ten system of numbers spread through Europe during the Renaissance, and subsequently to other parts of the globe. Before the proliferation of the modern base ten system, Roman numerals were widely used in Europe and in other parts of the former Roman Empire.

Whole Numbers

As students in Core Knowledge schools should have learned in previous grades, the set of whole numbers is the set of all counting numbers together with the number 0. In other words, a whole number is any number in the collection {0, 1, 2, 3, . . . }. The way we write whole numbers uses the idea of place value. Place value in the base ten system of numbers is the fundamental ingredient for understanding arithmetic. Only ten different digits are needed to write any whole number. They are:

0, 1, 2, 3, 4, 5, 6, 7, 8, 9

Being able to express numbers as written words is a language arts skill that students will need later in daily life. For example, writing a check in dollar amounts in order to pay a bill or make a deposit requires this skill.

There are slightly different conventions for writing number words, so it is a good idea not to be too insistent about them. However, there are a few helpful guidelines that you may wish to review with students. A commonly accepted convention is the use of the dash (-) for number words that follow the words *twenty, thirty, forty, fifty, sixty, seventy, eighty,* and *ninety.* For example, the dash is used in these expressions:

twenty-one   fifty-six   ninety-nine

A standard convention is to avoid using the word *and* in expressions for whole numbers. Following this convention, do not write or say "eight hundred *and* twenty-six." Instead, the correct way to write or say this number is:

eight hundred twenty-six

As another example, the number 103 should be written as "one hundred three" rather than "one hundred *and* three."

The reasoning behind this rule is so that the word *and* can be reserved for writing words for decimals or mixed numbers. For example, the mixed number $32\frac{1}{10}$ is written (and verbalized) as "thirty-two *and* one tenth." The decimal 32.1 (which is the same number as $32\frac{1}{10}$) is written the same way, "thirty-two *and* one tenth," or as "thirty-two point one."

Commas are generally used in number words in the same locations as in figures. For example, for the number 835,426, write:

eight hundred thirty-five thousand, four hundred twenty-six

Notice the location of the comma after the word *thousand* just as in the figure. For a review of comma placement in figures, see the subsection below, "The Base Ten System and Place Value."

The Base Ten System and Place Value

It is impossible to understand how and why the standard operations of arithmetic work without a thorough understanding of the base ten system of numbers. Students in Core Knowledge schools in Grade 4 should have learned place value of whole numbers to nine digits. The Grade 5 *Sequence* reviews and extends this topic.

You may wish to use concrete manipulatives, such as base ten blocks, to allow students to review and explore these concepts as they learn how to read and write numbers up to the billions. Charts can also help students to understand the

> **Teaching Idea**
>
> Emphasize to students that the number 10 plays a critical role in the base ten number system. Each place value is 10 times greater than the next lower place value to its right. This is true not only for whole numbers, but also for decimal numbers such as 3,456.78. For example, there are 10 hundredths in one-tenth, 10 tenths in one, 10 ones in ten, 10 tens in one hundred, 10 hundreds in one thousand, and so on.

base ten system, and students may have seen charts like these in previous grades. As an example, the number 156,837,261,549 can be displayed using a chart like this one to label the place value of each digit.

100,000,000,000s	10,000,000,000s	1,000,000,000s	100,000,000s	10,000,000s	1,000,000s	100,000s	10,000s	1,000s	100s	10s	1s
1	5	6	8	3	7	2	6	1	5	4	9

Commas are a valuable aid in reading large numbers. The general rule is to group the digits in a numeral by threes from the right to the left. For example, the commas help us see that 156,837,261,549 can be understood as 156 billion, 837 million, 261 thousand, 549. The commas may be understood as separating the ones, thousands, millions, and billions in this example. The next group of three digits designates trillions. Just as a billion is a thousand millions, one trillion is a thousand billions, that is, $1,000 \times 1,000,000,000$.

The numeral 234,837,261,549 is read aloud as "two hundred thirty-four billion, eight hundred thirty-seven million, two hundred sixty-one thousand, five hundred forty-nine."

Writing numbers in expanded form helps students to recognize the meaning of place value. Writing 234,837,261,549 in expanded form looks like this:

200,000,000,000 + 30,000,000,000 + 4,000,000,000
+ 800,000,000 + 30,000,000 + 7,000,000 + 200,000
+ 60,000 + 1,000 + 500 + 40 + 9

Comparing Whole Numbers

Place value makes it easy to compare whole numbers. Entering fifth graders should already have had practice comparing large numbers, so you should be able to build on earlier skills.

The symbol $<$ is read aloud as "is less than" and the symbol $>$ is read aloud as "is greater than." Mathematical statements using these symbols to compare two unequal values are called inequalities. For example, the statement "5 is less than 8" may be expressed as the inequality

5 < 8

Likewise, the statement "25 is greater than 0" may be written more concisely as

25 > 0

How can large whole numbers be compared systematically? The base ten structure provides the answer. Read each number from left to right. The first placeholder in which the digits are different determines which number is larger. The reason is that any single (non-zero) digit in a placeholder to the left is worth more than the value of all the digits to its right put together. The 1 in 1,999 represents 1,000 and that is greater than the value of 999 from all of the digits to the right of the 1.

As an example, compare 823,549 to 823,651. The 8 in the hundred-thousands place is the same for both numbers, as is the 2 in the ten-thousands place and the 3 in the thousands place. Continuing to read from left to right, the digits in the next placeholder, the hundreds column, are different; in one case there is a 5 and in the other a 6. Because 5 < 6,

823,549 < 823,651

Notice that the digits in the tens column and in the ones column played no role in deciding which of these two numbers is greater than the other.

This same rule works even when the number of digits differ in the two numbers being compared, provided that 0 is used as a placeholder in the smaller number. As another example, compare 12,345 to 9,876. A possible mistake students might make is to compare the first digits that appear in the two numerals and conclude incorrectly that 9,876 is greater than 12,345 because 9 > 1. Why is this wrong, and what is the correct way to compare digits? The number 9,876 may be thought of as having a 0 in the ten-thousands' place, so that for purposes of this comparison, 9,876 may be thought of as 09,876. Now looking at the ten-thousands' place in 12,345 and 09,876, we see that 1 > 0 and therefore,

12,345 > 9,876

If students are having trouble comparing numbers, have them line them up horizontally, starting with the ones place and copying the number to the left.

823,549

823,651

Then, starting from the left, students can draw lines between the numbers that are the same, and stop when they are different. The number with the larger digit is the larger number.

This same strategy is especially useful with numbers that do not have the same number of digits.

12,345

9,876

In this case, the students can tell at a glance which number is larger.

Number Lines and Integers

The number line is a powerful teaching tool. It is important at many levels of mathematics, even the university level. Number lines can help students reach several Core Knowledge benchmarks. In addition to using number lines to locate positive and negative numbers, they can be used as a teaching tool for instruction on rounding numbers. The topics of rounding whole numbers and rounding decimal numbers are discussed in the subsections "Rounding Whole Numbers," on pp. 432–433, and "Rounding Decimals," on pp. 470–471.

The set of integers is the collection of numbers { . . . , –3, –2, –1, 0, 1, 2, 3, . . . }. An integer is any number in this set. Therefore, an integer is either a counting number (1, 2, 3, etc.), 0, or the opposite (the negative) of a counting number (–1, –2, –3, etc.). The number line below is a standard way to exhibit the integers.

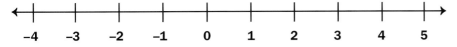

Teaching Idea

Students sometimes confuse the two inequality signs, > and <, and forget which one means "is greater than" and which means "is less than." It might help students to think of these symbols as arrow heads that always point to the smaller number. Another way to remember is that both symbols ">" and "<" open up toward the larger number. A story to go with this could involve a hungry fish that knows that it gets more to eat when it opens its mouth toward the larger number.

Teaching Idea

Make a number line for the front of your classroom that begins with 0. The space between tick marks and the size of the numbers should be large enough so that students can read the number line from any seat in the classroom. Some teachers place the number line on the wall just above the board and let it wrap around the room so that it includes large numbers. Some teachers also have students help create the number line by writing the numbers on register tape and wrapping that around the room. Make sure that you can point to any number using a yardstick or a pointer. Don't forget to leave room to add numbers to the left of 0 for when you begin your discussion of negative numbers.

The positive integers lie to the right of 0 on a number line, and the negative integers lie to the left of 0. Like whole numbers, integers on the number line are ordered from left to right with the smaller numbers to the left and larger numbers to the right. Integers can be compared using the symbols for "less than" or "greater than":

$$-4 < -3 < -2 < -1 < 0 < 1 < 2 < 3 \text{ etc.}$$

These inequalities tell you that -4 is less than -3, which is less than -2, and so forth. The number 0 is greater than any negative number and less than any positive number. Any positive number is greater than any negative number. An intuitive way to understand the ordering of integers is to think of temperature. For example, $-2°$ is colder than $0°$ and $-2 < 0$ (or $0 > -2$).

Students in Core Knowledge schools may have been introduced to negative numbers through temperature, and you may wish to use this topic to review negative numbers in Grade 5. A thermometer can be thought of as a number line that includes negative numbers. Usually, the number line on a thermometer is vertical instead of horizontal.

Addition of integers may be explained with a number line. We begin with the addition of two positive integers. This builds on earlier grade experience. The addition expression $2 + 3 = 5$ can be represented this way:

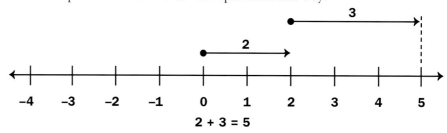

$$2 + 3 = 5$$

The first arrow has length 2 and the second has length 3. Both arrows point to the right because both 2 and 3 are positive. The same idea applies when one or both of the addends (the numbers being added) are negative. Arrows for negative addends point to the left, as the arrow for -3 in this example: $-3 + 2 = -1$.

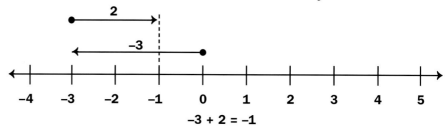

$$-3 + 2 = -1$$

When both addends are negative, both arrows point to the left, as for $-3 + (-2) = -5$.

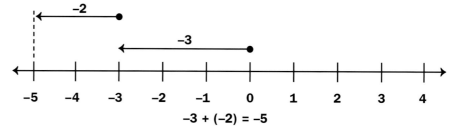

$$-3 + (-2) = -5$$

The addition problem 3 + (−2) = 1 gives the same result as the subtraction problem 3 − 2 = 1. Both can be illustrated this way:

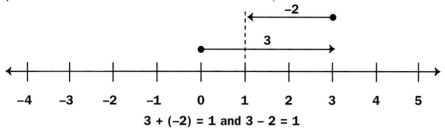

3 + (−2) = 1 and 3 − 2 = 1

In order to understand how to subtract integers, we need a new concept: the opposite of an integer. Every integer has an opposite. The opposite of any positive integer is a negative integer, and the opposite of any negative integer is a positive integer. For example, the opposite of 1 is −1, and the opposite of 2 is −2. The opposite of −3 is 3, and the opposite of −17 is 17. The opposite of the number 0 is 0; 0 is its own opposite.

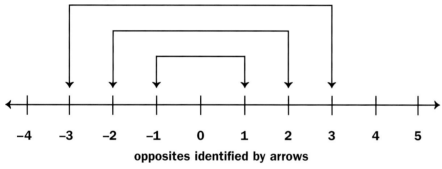

opposites identified by arrows

When an integer is added to its opposite the result is 0. For example, 4 +(−4) = 0 and −7 + 7 = 0.

Now we are ready to subtract integers. Here is the definition of subtraction.

For any integers A and B, A − B means A + (−B)

The minus sign (−) is used in three different ways: to indicate a negative number, to indicate the opposite of a number, and to indicate the operation of subtraction. This can be confusing to students. In some texts, an elevated minus sign, as in ⁻4, is used to indicate "the opposite of," in this case the opposite of 4. The usual minus sign refers to subtraction, as in 5 − 4. With that convention, one would write "3 minus the opposite of 4" as "3 −(⁻4)." However, most people do not use different symbols, and we follow the usual convention here.

Let's look at some examples. First, let's compare familiar subtraction statements involving only positive integers to this definition. An example discussed above is 3 − 2 = 1. According to the definition of subtraction of integers,

3 − 2 means 3 + (−2)

We saw earlier that 3 + (⁻2) = 1, so this new definition of subtraction is consistent with students' earlier understanding of subtraction. The value of this new definition of subtraction is that we get the same answers to subtraction problems as before when all numbers were positive, and we can now extend the operations of addition and subtraction to negative integers. The definition allows us to change any subtraction problem to an addition problem. To illustrate, let's calculate ⁻3 − 4:

Teaching Idea

If students are struggling, reinforce the abstract number line addition and subtraction with wooden blocks. Use 3 blocks, and then take away 2 to demonstrate that 3 + (−2) = 1 is the same as 3 − 2 = 1.

$$-3 - 4 \text{ means } -3 + (-4)$$

$$A - B \text{ means } A + (-B)$$

$$(A = -3 \text{ and } B = 4)$$

We can use a number line to find that $-3 + (-4) = -7$. Therefore $-3 - 4 = -7$.

As another example, consider the subtraction problem $-3 - (-4)$, that is -3 minus -4.

$$-3 - (-4) \text{ means } -3 + (-(-4))$$

$$A - B \text{ means } A + (-B)$$

$$(A = -3 \text{ and } B = -4)$$

To evaluate $-3 + -(-4))$, we use the fact that $-(-4) = 4$ (the opposite of -4 is 4). Then,

$$-3 - (-4) = -3 + (-(-4)) = -3 + 4 = 1$$

The key to addition of integers is the number line, and the key to subtraction of integers is to write the subtraction problem as an addition problem.

Rounding Whole Numbers

Rounding is an important number sense skill. It is useful in measurements and for mental estimations of arithmetic calculations. Rounding is particularly useful in cases where you need only an approximate number, not an exact number. Grade 4 Core Knowledge students should have learned to round whole numbers to the nearest thousand. In Grade 5, these topics should be reviewed and expanded. There are two issues to focus on with regard to rounding: explaining a rule to round numbers, and explaining the concept behind this rule. Begin with the concept.

The basic idea behind rounding a number to the nearest ten illustrates the idea for rounding a number to any place value. For this reason, it is a good idea to begin a review of rounding numbers to the nearest ten. Rounding can be explained through the use of a number line. Rounding a number to the nearest ten, except in one special case, means finding the closest multiple of 10 to that number. As an example, consider rounding 56 to the nearest ten. To round 56 to the nearest ten we must find the multiple of 10 closest to 56. Which of these numbers is 56 the closest to: 0, 10, 20, 30, 40, 50, 60, 70, etc.?

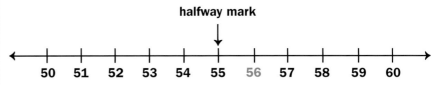

Since 56 lies between 50 and 60, these are the two candidates for the answer. The number 56 lies to the right of the halfway mark, 55, and is closer to 60. Therefore 56 rounded to the nearest ten is 60.

How do we round a number to the nearest ten when it falls exactly halfway between two multiples of ten? These are the exceptions, or special cases, to this approach to rounding. For example, instead of 56, suppose we want to round 55 to the nearest 10. To which multiple of 10 is 55 closest? It is equally close to 50 and 60; 55 is exactly halfway between them. The usual convention is to round "halfway numbers" like 55 up to the larger of the two closest multiples of 10. Following this convention, 55 rounded to the nearest 10 is 60.

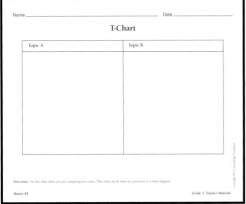

Use Instructional Master 84.

Notice that any integer with a "5" in the ones column is halfway between two multiples of 10.

Rounding to the nearest hundred or to the nearest thousand is similar. Rounding a number to the nearest hundred means finding the multiple of 100 that is closest to that number. The multiples of 100 are: 0, 100, 200, 300, etc. Rounding a number to the nearest thousand means finding the multiple of 1,000 that is closest to the number. The multiples of 1,000 are: 0, 1,000, 2,000, 3,000, etc. Similarly, rounding a number to the nearest ten-thousand or hundred-thousand means finding the appropriate multiple that is closest to the number. In all cases, numbers that fall halfway between the appropriate multiples are rounded up.

As an example, round 34,192 to the nearest thousand. Between which two multiples of 1,000 does 34,192 lie on the number line? The answer is 34,000 and 35,000. Therefore 34,192 rounded to the nearest thousand must be 34,000 or 35,000. Students can see from a number line that the correct answer is 34,000 because 34,192 is closer to 34,000 than to 35,000 (or any other multiple of 1,000).

halfway mark

34,000   **34,192**   **34,500**   **35,000**

To round 34,500 to the nearest thousand, round up, because 34,500 falls exactly halfway between 34,000 or 35,000.

Once students understand the idea of rounding to the nearest ten, hundred, or higher place value using the number line, they can apply a general rule for rounding. This rule will also work for decimal numbers. (See the subsection "Rounding Decimals," on pp. 470–471.)

◗ Rule for Rounding (whole numbers)

Step 1. Circle the digit in the place you want to round to.

8, ⑦ 6 3

↑

hundreds place

Step 2. Underline the digit just to the right of the circled digit.

8, ⑦ 6 3

↑

digit to the right

Step 3. If the underlined digit is 5 or greater than 5, increase the circled digit by one. If the underlined digit is 4 or less than 4, do not change the circled digit. Change all digits to the right of the circled digit to zeros.

8,763 rounded to the nearest hundred is 8,800

Teaching Idea

For students who need a more concrete exercise to understand and practice how to round numbers, make sets of index cards with a digit (0–9) written on each one. Give each student or group of students 2 or more sets of cards. Then read a number aloud. Have students arrange the index cards to match the number you read aloud. Check their work. Then have students place a colored marker (a round bingo marker, for example) on the place that will be rounded to. Students should inspect the digit to the right of the marker to see if it's larger or smaller than 5, and then round. Then they should rearrange their cards to represent the rounded number, adding new cards and removing others as necessary. You could also use a similar strategy to have students practice rounding with ones, tens, hundreds, and thousands manipulatives.

Perfect Squares, Square Roots, and Exponents

Fourth graders in Core Knowledge schools should have learned about perfect squares up to 144 and the corresponding square roots. The Grade 5 *Sequence* includes a review of these topics.

You may wish to review with students that any number that is a product of a whole number with itself is called a perfect square. The list of perfect squares to 144 is: 0, 1, 4, 9, 16, 25, 36, 49, 64, 81, 100, 121, 144. Each of these numbers is equal to some whole number times itself. For example,

0 = 0 x 0
1 = 1 x 1
4 = 2 x 2
9 = 3 x 3
16 = 4 x 4

Look at the models below to see how these multiplication sentences can be visually represented as squares. The same technique can be used for any perfect square:

4 = 2 x 2   **9 = 3 x 3**   **16 = 4 x 4**

There is some notation with which teachers should be familiar. For any number *a*,

a^2 means a x a

For example, 5^2 means 5×5, so $5^2 = 25$. This is read aloud as "five squared equals twenty-five." The equation $5^2 = 25$ can also be read aloud as "five to the second power equals twenty-five." You may wish to point out the geometrical roots of the terms "squared" and "cubed" (see the subsections "Area of Rectangles," pp. 516–518, "Area of Parallelograms and Triangles," pp. 519–521, and "Volume and Surface Area of Rectangular Prisms," pp. 521–523).

The square root of a number N is the number which, multiplied by itself, equals N. For example, the square root of 9 is 3 because $3 \times 3 = 9$. The square root of 25 is 5 because $5 \times 5 = 25$.

In the middle school grades, students will learn that positive numbers have two different square roots, a positive square root and a negative square root. For example, students will learn that one square root of 9 is 3 and the other square root of 9 is –3. This is because a negative number times a negative number is a positive number. In particular, $-3 \times -3 = 9$. So the two square roots of 9 are 3 and –3. This is not an appropriate topic for class instruction in most Grade 5 classrooms. However, it is a good idea for teachers to be aware of negative square roots. It is always possible that a motivated student who has received enrichment in mathematics outside of class could raise this topic.

There is a mathematical symbol for square roots. It is called the square root symbol (or sometimes the radical symbol). The square root of the number N is written this way: $\sqrt{N}$. For example,

$$\sqrt{4} = 2 \text{ because } 2^2 = 4$$
$$\sqrt{64} = 8 \text{ because } 8^2 = 64$$
$$\sqrt{81} = 9 \text{ because } 9^2 = 81$$
$$\sqrt{1} = 1 \text{ because } 1^2 = 1$$
$$\sqrt{0} = 0 \text{ because } 0^2 = 0$$

Teaching Idea

Discuss the relationship between multiplication equations and square roots. Then, have students review common square roots. For example:

$2 \times 2 = 4$, therefore $\sqrt{4} = 2$

$3 \times 3 = 9$, therefore $\sqrt{9} = 3$

$4 \times 4 = 16$, therefore $\sqrt{16} = 4$

$5 \times 5 = 25$, therefore $\sqrt{25} = 5$

To find $\sqrt{36}$, students should ask themselves what number multiplied by itself equals 36? The answer is $6 \times 6 = 36$. Therefore $\sqrt{36} = 6$.

Exponents provide a shorthand way to write the product of a number with itself, or how many factors the number has.

If A is a number, and n is a counting number (n = 1 or 2 or 3, etc.), then

$$A^n = \underbrace{A \text{x} \ldots \text{x} A}_{n \text{ factors of } A}$$

Also, for any number A that is not zero, $A^0 = 1$.

The number n is called the exponent, and A is called the base in the expression A^n. Here are some examples:

$$7^0 = 1$$
$$7^1 = 7$$
$$7^2 = 7 \text{ x } 7 = 49$$
$$2^3 = 2 \text{ x } 2 \text{ x } 2 = 8$$
$$2^4 = 2 \text{ x } 2 \text{ x } 2 \text{ x } 2 = 16$$

Students sometimes make mistakes like interpreting 2^4 to mean 2×4. Remind them that the exponent is the number of times that the base is a factor. That is, 2^4 means that 2 is a factor 4 times.

The first equation above, $7^0 = 1$, is read aloud as "seven to the zero power equals one." The second equation is read aloud as "seven to the first power equals seven." Any number raised to the first power is equal to itself. The third equation may be verbalized as "seven to the second power equals 49," or "seven squared equals 49." The next line tells us that two to the third power, or two cubed, equals eight. The last line is read as two to the fourth power equals 16.

Any number, except 0, raised to the zero power, is by definition equal to 1. For example, $32^0 = 1$. The expression 0^0 is undefined. It has no meaning. The definition of the zero exponent makes it possible to simplify algebraic expressions that students will encounter in later courses.

The reason that A^2, or A to the second power, is often verbalized as "A squared" is that a square whose sides each have length A has area A^2. Similarly A^3 is often read aloud as "A cubed" because a cube whose sides each have length A has volume A^3. Students will benefit from seeing a visual representation of these concepts, and you may want to provide many examples of squares and cubes. (See the subsections "Area of Rectangles," pp. 516–518, "Area of Parallelograms and Triangles," pp. 519–521, and "Volume and Surface Area of Rectangular Prisms," pp. 521–523.)

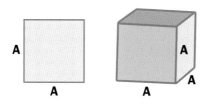

A power of ten is the product of multiplying tens together. For example, the numbers 10, 100, 1,000, and 10,000 are all powers of ten. Powers of ten are important in scientific notation, a topic taken up in the Grade 7 Core Knowledge curriculum. In Grade 5, students should learn the following powers of ten:

$$10^0 = 1$$
$$10^1 = 10$$
$$10^2 = 100 = 10 \times 10$$
$$10^3 = 1,000 = 10 \times 10 \times 10$$
$$10^4 = 10,000 = 10 \times 10 \times 10 \times 10$$
$$10^5 = 100,000 = 10 \times 10 \times 10 \times 10 \times 10$$
$$10^6 = 1,000,000 = 10 \times 10 \times 10 \ \times 10 \times 10 \times 10$$

Notice that a power of ten equals "1" followed by zeros, and the number of zeros is the exponent. For example, 10^6 (one million) is "1" followed by 6 zeros. This is because each time we multiply a counting number by 10, we place an extra digit of 0 in the numeral for the product.

Parentheses and Order of Operations

When evaluating numerical expressions that contain exponents, we must be familiar with and follow the order of operations rule. Addition, subtraction, multiplication, and division are binary operations. That means that each of these operations combines two numbers to make a new number. For example, consider this expression:

$$1 + 2 \times 3$$

Let's perform the calculations in two different orders and compare answers. Going from left to right, if we add first, we get $1 + 2 = 3$. Then $3 \times 3 = 9$. On the other hand, if we multiply first, we get $2 \times 3 = 6$. Then adding, $1 + 6 = 7$. We are left with two choices for this expression

$$1 + 2 \times 3 = \begin{cases} 9? \\ \text{or} \\ 7? \end{cases}$$

We will resolve this ambiguity below to see that the correct answer is actually 7. However, before doing that, we will review the use of parentheses in mathematical expressions.

Operations inside a pair of parentheses are to be carried out before the operations outside the parentheses. For example,

$$(1 + 2) \times 3 = 3 \times 3 = 9$$
$$1 + (2 \times 3) = 1 + 6 = 7$$

More than one pair of parentheses can appear in an expression, as in $(27 - 19) \times (36 \div 4)$. Working inside the parentheses first, the expression may be systematically evaluated:

$$(27 - 19) \times (36 \div 4) = 8 \times 9 = 72$$

There is universal agreement, worldwide, to use the order of operations rule. According to this rule, if there are no parentheses,

> **Teaching Idea**
>
> Encourage students to write equations that show the steps of their calculations, as in $(5 + 3) \times 4 = 8 \times 4 = 32$. This is a valuable habit to develop in students and one that will help them as they move into algebra.

First: Calculate exponents.

Second: Perform multiplications and divisions from left to right.

Third: Perform additions and subtractions from left to right.

If there are parentheses in an expression, perform the operations in this same order within parentheses first.

The order of operations rule tells us how to evaluate the expression $1 + 2 \times 3$. There are no parentheses or exponents; so according to the order of operations rule, we must first multiply and, only after that, add. Therefore, $1 + 2 \times 3$ means the same thing as $1 + (2 \times 3) = 7$.

As another example, consider this expression:

$$4 + 2 \times 3^2$$

The order of operations rule tells us to first calculate the exponent, then multiply, and only then add:

$$4 + 2 \times 3^2 = 4 + 2 \times 9 = 4 + 18 = 22$$

Notice that

$$4 + 2 \times 3^2 \neq 4 + (2 \times 3)^2$$

Instead,

$$4 + 2 \times 3^2 \text{ means } 4 + (2 \times 3^2)$$

In some cases, the placement of parentheses does not affect the answer. For example,

$$2 \times (3 \times 4) = (2 \times 3) \times 4$$

This is because

$$2 \times 12 = 6 \times 4$$

The "left to right rule" (which is part of the order of operations rule), tells us that $2 \times 3 \times 4$ means $(2 \times 3) \times 4$, even though it doesn't matter where the parentheses go in this example. This is due to the fact that multiplication (and addition) are associative operations. Subtraction and division are not associative, however, so the left to right rule is important in expressions such as $2 - 3 - 4$. By the convention, this means $2 - 3 - 4 = (2 - 3) - 4 = (-1) - 4 = -5$, not $2 - (3 - 4) = 2 - (-1) = 3$.

Sets

A set is a collection of objects called members or elements of the set. "Curly" brackets like these { } are customarily used to indicate a set. For example, the set consisting of the numbers 2, 6, and 9 is written this way:

$$\{2, 6, 9\}$$

The same set may also be written as {9, 2, 6}. This is because the elements of a set may be written in any order. Sets can be finite like the one above, or infinite. The set of counting numbers may be written this way: {1, 2, 3, . . . } and the set of whole numbers may be written as {0, 1, 2, 3, . . . }. Both sets are infinite, that is, they have infinitely many members. The set of whole numbers includes all of the counting numbers together with 0. While most of the sets considered at this level are sets of numbers, the elements of sets do not have to be numbers. For example, {a, b, c} is a set whose elements are a, b, and c. The alphabet, all of the

I. Numbers and Number Sense

students in a class, or all of the books in a library can be considered objects in a set as well. Sets can be used to model fractions, where the whole is the entire set of objects, such as counters, and fractional parts can be represented with some of the elements in the set. Students will continue to learn more about sets in later grades, and they should develop a good understanding of the basic concept this year.

Factors, Multiples, Prime and Composite Numbers

Students in Grade 5 will continue to develop their number sense by learning more about factors, multiples, prime numbers, and composite numbers. This section deals with the set of counting numbers {1, 2, 3, . . . }, and in this context the word *number* means "counting number." In the statements below, the letters A and B represent counting numbers.

Students should have been introduced to the term *factor* in Grade 4. A factor is one of two or more numbers that divides evenly into another number without a remainder. The statement "A is a factor of B" means that B is equal to some whole number times A. For example, 4 is a factor of 12 because $12 = 4 \times 3$ and 7 is a factor of 35 because $35 = 5 \times 7$. People sometimes communicate the same information by saying that B is divisible by A, or by saying that B is a multiple of A. A multiple is the product of a number with any other number. It can also be thought of as a number that can be divided evenly by another number without a remainder. The following statements all have exactly the same meanings:

4, when paired with 3, is a factor of 12

12 is divisible by 4

12 is a multiple of 4

All of these statements mean that some number times 4 equals 12. As an alternative, students can think of the statement "B is divisible by A" to mean $B \div A$ has 0 remainder. Notice that this just means that B equals A times some counting number.

Every counting number except the number 1 has at least two different factors, the number itself and 1. For example, $12 = 12 \times 1$, so 12 and 1 are both factors of 12. But the number 12 also has other factors. The complete list of factors of 12 is 1, 2, 3, 4, 6, and 12.

A prime number, or prime, is a number that has two and only two different factors. The two factors of any prime number are the prime number itself and the number 1. For example, 5 is a prime number because the only factors of 5 are 1 and 5 ($5 = 5 \times 1$). The list of all prime numbers begins this way:

2, 3, 5, 7, 11, 13, 17, 19, 23, 29, 31, . . .

There is no largest prime number; there are infinitely many prime numbers. For the same reason, it is impossible to count up all of the prime numbers. This fact was first proven by the ancient Greeks. Notice that the number 1 is not a prime number because it has only one factor: 1.

A composite number, or composite, is a counting number other than 1 that is not a prime number. The number 1 is called a unit; it is neither prime nor composite. Each composite number has three or more factors. The smallest composite number is 4. The factors of 4 are: 1, 2, 4. There are infinitely many composite

Have students work with partners or in small groups to make rectangles by arranging square tiles or by shading in squares on grid paper. Instruct the groups to find as many different ways to make a rectangle using the numbers 2, 5, 10, and 12 as they can. Students will find that there is only one way to make a rectangle for 2 and 5 (using 1 × 2 and 1 × 5 squares, respectively), but there are more ways to make rectangles for 10 and 12 (for example, you can make 1 × 10 and 2 × 5 rectangles for 10). Explain to students that the dimensions of the rectangles are the factors of each number. For example, 2 is a prime number with only the factors 1 and 2, while 10 is a composite number with the factors 1, 2, 5, and 10. Students can continue to practice making rectangles to identify factors for other prime and composite numbers.

numbers. Every even number, except for 2, is a composite number. This is because every even number is divisible by 2; that is, 2 is a factor of every even number. The list of composite numbers begins as follows:

4, 6, 8, 9, 10, 12, 14, 15, 16, 18, 20, 21, 22, . . .

Notice that while every even number except 2 is composite, not every composite number is even. For example, 21 is an odd number, but it is also a composite: $3 \times 7 = 21$.

Any composite number can be written as a product of prime numbers, and except for the order in which the prime numbers are written, this can be done in only one way.

For example, 12 can be written as a product of prime factors this way and in no other way (except for changing the order of 2, 2, and 3):

12 = 2 x 2 x 3

Using exponents, we can write

12 = 2^2 x 3

When a composite number is written as a product of prime numbers, we say that it has been factored into a product of prime numbers. This unique factorization of any positive integer greater than 1 into a product of prime numbers is known as the fundamental theorem of arithmetic. While the order of the prime numbers listed can vary, the set of prime numbers is unique for each number. To appreciate how far-reaching the fundamental theorem of arithmetic is, consider a much less transparent example.

57,967 = 7^3 x 13^2

The composite number 57,967 may be factored as a product of prime numbers as above (with a little time, you can check this by calculating $7 \times 7 \times 7 \times 13 \times 13$). Because of the fundamental theorem of arithmetic, we are guaranteed that there is no other way to factor 57,967 as a product of prime numbers (except to write the primes in different orders). Students in Grade 5 are not expected to factor such large numbers or to identify the fundamental theorem of arithmetic by name. This example serves only to demonstrate what the theorem is really saying.

The fundamental theorem of arithmetic has important consequences in more advanced courses in mathematics. One modern application of multiplying large prime numbers is the creation of secret codes that are almost impossible to break. These codes are used by government agencies throughout the world.

Finding factors that two numbers have in common is useful for simplifying (renaming) fractions, a topic explained in the section "Fractions and Decimals," on pp. 450–476. When the numerator and the denominator of a fraction have a common factor greater than 1, the fraction may be simplified. Students can get practice for this important skill by solving problems like this one:

Find all common factors of 12 and 18.

Solution:

By testing all numbers up to 12, we find the factors of 12 are 1, 2, 3, 4, 6, 12.

By testing all numbers up to 18, we find the factors of 18 are 1, 2, 3, 6, 9, 18.

Teaching Idea

Students may find it interesting to study patterns made by multiples on a hundreds chart. Give each student several copies of a hundreds chart. (You may wish to create a handout that has several small versions of a hundreds chart on one page.) Ask students to choose a number less than 10 and to circle that number and all of its multiples with a colored pencil. Each number and its multiples will form a pattern, either in diagonal lines or in columns. Have students experiment with several different numbers and then share and discuss their discoveries with the class.

1	2	3	4	5	6	7	8	9	10
11	12	13	14	15	16	17	18	19	20
21	22	23	24	25	26	27	28	29	30
31	32	33	34	35	36	37	38	39	40
41	42	43	44	45	46	47	48	49	50
51	52	53	54	55	56	57	58	59	60
61	62	63	64	65	66	67	68	69	70
71	72	73	74	75	76	77	78	79	80
81	82	83	84	85	86	87	88	89	90
91	92	93	94	95	96	97	98	99	100

Teaching Idea

Have students identify all prime numbers under 100 using a hundreds chart. Students should first circle 2 and then cross out all multiples of 2. Next, they should circle 3 and cross out all multiples of 3. Students should do the same thing for 5 and 7. After completing these steps, all numbers (except the number 1) that are not crossed out are prime numbers. This activity of eliminating numbers that are not prime is called the sieve of Eratosthenes, named after a Greek astronomer.

The factors common to both lists are 1, 2, 3, and 6.

The largest of these common factors for 12 and 18 is 6. The largest of the factors common to two numbers is called the greatest common factor or the greatest common divisor. The greatest common factor is often abbreviated as GCF. It is also possible to find the greatest common factor of three or more numbers by listing the factors that the numbers have in common and choosing the largest one.

The multiples of a number may be found by counting by that number, or by multiplying that number by the counting numbers 1, 2, 3, 4, and so forth. For example, the multiples of 2 are 2, 4, 6, 8, etc., and the multiples of 3 are 3, 6, 9, 12, etc. Finding the multiples that two numbers have in common is a useful skill in the study of fractions. This skill will help students to find common denominators for different fractions. Students can get practice by solving problems like this one:

Find two common multiples of 6 and 9.

The multiples of 6 are 6, 12, 18, 24, 30, 36, and so forth.
The multiples of 9 are 9, 18, 27, 36, 45, and so forth.
Two multiples common to both lists are 18 and 36.

The list of multiples for 6 and 9 (and any other number) never ends. However, the most important common multiple of two numbers is called their least common multiple. The least common multiple or LCM of two numbers is the smallest of all of the common multiples of the two numbers. In the example above, the least common multiple of 6 and 9 is 18. All other common multiples are greater than 18. Students will learn that the least common denominator for two fractions is the least common multiple of their denominators.

It is also possible to find the least common multiple of three or more numbers by listing the multiples that the numbers have in common and choosing the smallest one.

The Big Idea in Review

Writing, identifying, and comparing numbers and data are fundamental parts of developing number sense.

Review

Below are some ideas for ongoing assessment and review activities. These are not meant to constitute a comprehensive list.

• Organize a math center in the room with activities, puzzles, and challenging math problems. You may want to use your math center to reinforce some of the new topics from this chapter, such as practicing with positive and negative integers. Create time in your daily schedule for students to explore a variety of math activities that might interest them and encourage them to bring in other activities from home. Arrange for math programs to be installed on the class computer. You may also want to create some time at the end of the week during math class for students to share what they have been working on that week.

• Create a daily problem of the day to practice the skills found in this section. Write problems on index cards and have a student draw the problem for the day from a box. Then, give the class an opportunity to solve the problem. Check together. After solving the problem of the day, have students create another problem to solve using the first as a model. Trade problems and solve for correct answers.

- Create flash cards with a number written on one side and its name spelled out on the other. For example, write "1,234,222" on one side of the card and write "one million, two hundred thirty-four thousand, two hundred twenty-two" on the other side. Students can use either side of the card to quiz classmates, depending on which answer they would like to review. Make sure students are using numbers up to the billions.

- Start a class math dictionary where students record math vocabulary and definitions. Post this dictionary of math terms in your classroom on chart paper. Use it daily in your instruction and make sure that students know the vocabulary associated with mathematical terms and functions. Include time throughout the year for students to write about their math solving process using the correct vocabulary.

More Resources

A good mathematics program follows sound cognitive principles and allows many opportunities for thoughtful and varied practice to build mastery of important skills. For advice on suitable mathematics programs, contact the Foundation.

The titles listed below are offered as a representative sample of materials and not a complete list of everything that is available.

For students —

- *Everything You Need to Know About Math Homework,* by Anne Zeman and Kate Kelly (Scholastic, 1994). A clear guide for students in Grades 4–6 that covers numbers and the number system, basic math functions, measurement, geometry, money, graphs, statistics, and computers. Paperback, ISBN 0590493590.

- *G is for Google: A Math Alphabet Book,* by David M. Schwartz and illustrated by Marissa Moss (Tricycle Press, 1998). A creative and educational challenge. Hardcover, 57 pages, ISBN 1883672589.

- *How Math Works,* by Carol Vonderman (Reader's Digest, 1996). Hardcover, 192 pages, ISBN 0895778505.

- *On Beyond a Million: An Amazing Math Journey,* by David M. Schwartz (Dragonfly, 2001). Introduces the names of larger numbers and powers of ten. Paperback, 32 pages, ISBN 0440411777.

For teachers —

- *Usborne Illustrated Dictionary of Math,* by Tori Large and others (Usborne, 2004). Paperback, 128 pages, ISBN 0794506623.

- Figure This!, www.figurethis.org, provides math challenges designed for middle school students.

II. **R**atio and Percent

The Big Idea

Ratios and percents are closely related to fractions and decimals and can be used to compare quantities.

What Students Should Already Know

Students in Core Knowledge schools should be familiar with

Grade 2

- ▸ recognizing these fractions as part of a whole set or region and writing the corresponding numerical symbols: $\frac{1}{2}, \frac{1}{3}, \frac{1}{4}, \frac{1}{5}, \frac{1}{6}, \frac{1}{8}, \frac{1}{10}$

Grade 3

- ▸ recognizing fractions to $\frac{1}{10}$
- ▸ knowing and writing decimal equivalents to $\frac{1}{4}, \frac{1}{2}, \frac{3}{4}$
- ▸ reading and writing decimals to the hundredths

Grade 4

- ▸ recognizing fractions to $\frac{1}{12}$
- ▸ reading and writing decimals as fractions (for example, $0.39 = \frac{39}{100}$)
- ▸ writing decimal equivalents for halves, quarters, eighths, and tenths

What Students Need to Learn

Ratios

- ▸ **Determine and express simple ratios**
- ▸ **Use ratio to create a simple scale drawing**
- ▸ **Ratio and rate: solve problems on speed as a ratio, using the formula $S = \frac{D}{T}$ (or $D = R \times T$)**

Percents

- ▸ **Recognize the percent sign (%) and understand percent as "per hundred"**
- ▸ **Express equivalences between fractions, decimals, and percents, and know common equivalences:**

  $\frac{1}{10} = 10\%$

  $\frac{1}{4} = 25\%$

  $\frac{1}{2} = 50\%$

  $\frac{3}{4} = 75\%$

- ▸ **Find the given percent of a number**

What Students Will Learn in Future Grades

The *Core Knowledge Sequence* for mathematics emphasizes the importance of reviewing and building on prior knowledge. Related topics from the Grade 6 *Sequence* are listed below, and subsequent grades will continue to focus on strengthening and expanding these skills.

What Students Will Learn in Future Grades continued
Grade 6

- ▶ solve proportions, including word problems involving proportions with one unknown
- ▶ use ratios and proportions to interpret map scales and scale drawings
- ▶ set up and solve proportions from similar triangles
- ▶ understand the justification for solving proportions by cross-multiplication
- ▶ convert between fractions, decimals, and percents
- ▶ find the given percent of a number, and find what percent a given number is of another number
- ▶ solve problems involving percent increase and decrease
- ▶ find an unknown number when a percent of the number is known
- ▶ use expressions with percents greater than 100% and less than 1%

Materials

fraction strips, p. 445

geoboard, p. 445

grid paper, p. 445

maps, pp. 446, 448

scale drawings, p. 446

fraction models, p. 447

hundreds chart, p. 447

two wide mouth jars, large enough for students to take an object from the jar, p. 447

11 red counters, p. 447

99 blue counters, p. 447

chart paper, p. 447

math journals, p. 448

access to computer lab, p. 448

rulers, p. 448

variety of menus from local restaurants, p. 448

Vocabulary

Student/Teacher Vocabulary

equivalent: having the same value (S)

percent: a ratio that compares a number to 100 using the symbol %, which stands for "per hundred" or hundredths (S)

rate: a ratio of two quantities with different units of measurement, for example, miles per hour, or gallons per minute (S)

ratio: a comparison of two numbers or measurements, e.g., 2 to 3, $\frac{2}{3}$, or 2:3 (S)

scale drawing: a drawing with the same shape but a different size as the object being drawn (S)

Domain Vocabulary

Ratio and percent and associated words:
show, stand for, smaller, larger, map, key, proportion, formula, percent sign, percentage, hundred, compare, fraction, decimal, half, quarter, tenth, part, whole, *plus words from story problems involving ratio and percent*

> ## At a Glance
> The most important ideas for you are:
> - A ratio is a comparison of two numbers or measurements.
> - Ratios can be used to find rate and speed using the formula $S = \frac{D}{T}$ or $D = R \times T$.
> - Maps and scale drawings are created using ratios.
> - Fractions, decimals, and percents are closely connected; each value can be written in the other forms.
> - Equivalent fractions, decimals, and percents can be identified with the aid of fraction models.
> - Students should practice until they learn common equivalences between fractions, decimals, and percents to the point of automaticity.

What Teachers Need to Know

Background

Ratios and percents are a new topic for Grade 5, but students will be building on skills learned in previous grades. Students cannot understand ratios and percents if they do not have a thorough knowledge of fractions and decimals. Ratios compare two numbers or measurements, and they are very closely tied to fractions. Likewise, percents can simply be seen as another way to express fractions and decimals.

In Grade 5, it is important for students to gain an understanding of these new topics, which will appear in future grades and math courses. Effective instruction and practice in Grade 5 with ratios and percents is essential for students to succeed in Grade 6 and beyond.

A. Ratio

Simple Ratios

A ratio is a comparison of two numbers or measurements. The ratio "A to B" is the division of A by B, that is, $\frac{A}{B}$. A ratio can also be considered a quotient of two numbers, A and B. When looking at special ratios like rate, the division becomes more apparent.

Look at an example of a simple ratio. Suppose that in a Grade 5 classroom there are 15 boys and 20 girls. The ratio of boys to girls in that classroom is 15 to 20, or $\frac{15}{20}$. The fraction $\frac{15}{20}$ may be simplified as $\frac{3}{4}$, so we may also describe the ratio of boys to girls as 3 boys to 4 girls. This ratio is sometimes written as 3:4 (read aloud as "three to four"). More generally, the ratio of A to B, or $\frac{A}{B}$, may be written as A:B.

Fractions and ratios are very closely related; in fact, all fractions are ratios. Fractions compare parts (the numerator) to the whole (the denominator). Ratios can also be used to compare parts or wholes. Let's look at some examples of ratios

to see how they compare parts and wholes. The ratio comparing the part of the class that is boys to the whole class is 15 to 35, or $\frac{15}{35}$. This ratio is most like a fraction, because the numerator describes part of the class (the boys) and the denominator describes the total number of students, or the whole class. Likewise, the ratio comparing the part of the class that is girls to the whole class is 20 to 35, or $\frac{20}{35}$.

The example above can be turned around. Suppose we know that the ratio of boys to girls in a particular classroom is 3:4 and there are 20 girls. Can we deduce the number of boys? Yes. The calculation may be posed this way:

$$\frac{3}{4} = \frac{?}{20}$$

To find the numerator designated by the question mark, we can calculate (see the subsection "Equivalent Fractions," on pp. 454–456):

$$\frac{3}{4} = \frac{3 \times 5}{4 \times 5} = \frac{15}{20}$$

It follows that there are 15 boys in the class.

When working with ratios, students can use manipulatives that are used in the study of fractions, decimals, geometry, and other areas of math to compare numbers and lengths and to concretely demonstrate ratios. For example, fraction strips can be used to create two lengths that are a certain ratio, such as 2:3. Students can also use geoboards or grid paper to create shapes that are similar to (or like) a given example, but larger.

Ratio and Rate

A rate is a ratio of two quantities with different units of measurement. An important example of rate is speed. The speed 60 miles per hour is the ratio $\frac{60 \text{ mi.}}{1 \text{ h.}}$, where "mi." is an abbreviation for "miles" and "h." is an abbreviation for hours. This ratio is a rate because the unit for the numerator is miles and the unit for the denominator is hours, and these are different units. This ratio, $\frac{60 \text{ mi.}}{1 \text{ h.}}$, is more commonly written as 60 mph (miles per hour).

Any ratio of the form $\frac{\text{Distance}}{\text{Time}}$ is a rate or speed, and the average rate or speed of a moving object over an interval of time T is the distance D the object travels during that interval of time divided by T. In abbreviated form the average rate R or speed S is given by these formulas:

$$R = \frac{D}{T} \text{ or } S = \frac{D}{T}$$

Both of these formulas show the same thing, but many math educators and textbooks prefer to use the version where rate equals R.

Suppose that a fifth grader jogged a distance of 720 feet in 1 minute. Then his average speed was $\frac{720 \text{ feet}}{1 \text{ minute}}$, which may be written as 720 feet per minute. In abbreviated form this is 720 ft./min. This same average speed may also be expressed as a number of feet per second. Since 1 minute is the same as 60 seconds, the student's average speed S was $\frac{720 \text{ feet}}{60 \text{ seconds}}$, and this may be simplified.

$$S = \frac{720 \text{ feet}}{60 \text{ seconds}} = \frac{36 \text{ feet}}{3 \text{ seconds}} = 12 \text{ ft./sec.}$$

The student's average speed was 12 feet per second.

Teaching Idea

Give each student a geoboard or a piece of dot grid or grid paper. Have students create a small shape, and then ask them to create other shapes that are like the first shape only larger. Students will have to create a ratio by multiplying the length of each side by the same number.

Teaching Idea

Students may also be interested in rates for racecars, airplanes, fast and slow animals, etc. Money problems offer an excellent opportunity for finding rate too; a price is a ratio of a money amount to a certain quantity. You can even use the *Guinness Book of World Records* to calculate silly rates. For instance, if the world's fastest hot dog eater can eat 26 hot dogs in two minutes, his rate is 13 hot dogs per minute.

Students should have multiple opportunities to work with and discuss different kinds of rates, not just miles per hour. Introduce students to some rates they might find interesting. For example, in connection with thunder and lightning, the following two rates may be of interest. The speed of sound in air is 1089 feet per second, which is about 743 miles per hour. The speed of light in empty space is a little more than 186,000 miles per second. That is fast enough to travel around Earth at the equator more than seven times in one second! The large difference between these two rates explains why we see lightning before we hear thunder.

Suppose that we know the average rate R of an object and we want to know the distance D it travels during a specific length of time T. A formula that answers this type of question is

$$D = R \times T$$

For example, suppose that our average rate in a car on the freeway is 60 miles per hour, and we drive for 3 hours. How far do we travel? Using this formula, we can calculate $D = 60 \times 3 = 180$, or if we include the units:

$$D = 60 \text{ miles per hour} \times 3 \text{ hours} = 180 \text{ miles}$$

Simple Scale Drawings

A scale drawing is a drawing with the same shape as the object being drawn, but a different size. Both maps and scale drawings depend on ratios of distances. A map might be drawn to this scale: 1 inch on the map corresponds to 2 miles of actual distance. This scale might be written on a map as: 1 inch = 2 miles. It is important to understand that this information determines all ratios of inches on the map to actual miles. If two points on the map are M inches apart, then they correspond to towns or places that are an actual distance of A miles apart, where

$$\frac{A}{M} = \frac{2}{1} = 2$$

Suppose that two towns are placed 4 inches apart on this map. What is the actual distance between them? Since $\frac{A}{4} = 2$ it follows that $A = 4 \times 2$ miles = 8 miles. Although the terminology is not important for this type of problem, the ratio $\frac{2 \text{ miles}}{1 \text{ inch}}$ may be identified as a rate because the numerator and denominator have different units (miles and inches). This ratio of 2 miles of actual distance per inch on the map allows us to convert easily from map distances to actual distances. Just multiply the number of inches of distance on the map by 2 to find the actual distance in miles.

B. Percent

You may wish to introduce percents in connection with fractions and decimals because the three topics are so closely related. Percents are just another way to express the same values that can be expressed as fractions or decimals. Percent is a ratio that compares a number to 100 using the symbol %. The symbol % is read as "percent" and means "per hundred" or hundredths.

$$N\% \text{ means } \frac{N}{100} \text{ and } \frac{N}{100} = N\%.$$

For example, 10% means 10 hundredths. That can be written as 0.10 or $\frac{10}{100}$, which may be simplified to $\frac{1}{10}$. Therefore $\frac{1}{10} = 10\%$. Similarly, $25\% = 0.25 = \frac{25}{100} = \frac{1}{4}$; $50\% = 0.50 = \frac{50}{100} = \frac{1}{2}$; and $75\% = 0.75 = \frac{75}{100} = \frac{3}{4}$.

Help students see the relationship between hundredths and percent by studying an example such as $\frac{50}{100}$, 0.50, and 50%. Both the fraction and decimal are read aloud as "fifty hundredths." Percent is simply another way of expressing hundredths, and the word *percent* can be thought of as a substitute for hundredths.

Give students time to explore the relationship between fractions, decimals, and percents using manipulatives such as fraction models or a hundreds chart. For example, ask students to shade in half of the boxes on a hundreds chart. How many boxes are shaded in? What are other ways this number can be expressed? (0.50 and 50%)

Once students have a conceptual understanding of the relationship between decimals and percents, you can teach them a simple rule for converting from percent to decimals and vice versa. To write a percent as a decimal, move the decimal point two places to the left. To write a decimal number as a percent, move the decimal point two places to the right. For example, 37% = 0.37. This is because

$$37\% = \frac{37}{100} = 0.37$$

The decimal 0.37 results from 37% by moving the decimal point in 37 two places to the left: .37 This decimal point movement should be clear if students understand that percents are simply another way of expressing hundredths.

In the subsection "Adding, Subtracting, Multiplying, and Dividing Fractions and Mixed Numbers" (see pp. 454–467), the word *of* is identified with multiplication. (*Of* means "times.") That identification is essential for solving problems involving percents. As an example, let's see how to compute 43% of 121. This sequence of steps shows how to understand this problem as a multiplication problem.

$$43\% \text{ of } 121 =$$

$$\frac{43}{100} \text{ of } 121 =$$

$$\frac{43}{100} \times 121 =$$

This calculation can be completed by multiplying fractions, $\frac{43}{100} \times \frac{121}{1}$, or by writing $\frac{43}{100}$ as 0.43, in which case the calculation is 0.43 × 121. Performing this multiplication tells us that 43% of 121 = 0.43 × 121 = 52.03.

Review

Below are some ideas for ongoing assessment and review activities. These are not meant to constitute a comprehensive list.

• Create journal activities for students to think about ratio and percent and how they understand the concepts. As an introduction, prepare two jars with counters. In one jar, place 1 red counter and 9 blue ones. In the other jar, place 10 red counters and 90 blue ones. Tell the students that they will have a chance to choose a counter from the jar, without looking, and if they choose a red one, they can receive a prize. Make a chart to record the jar that each student chooses

The Big Idea in Review

Ratios and percents are closely related to fractions and decimals and can be used to compare quantities.

to select a counter and then ask why they chose from that jar. When finished, explain that each jar had the same chance for success. Most often, students believe 1 chance out of 10 is better than 10 chances out of 100, but the ratio of counters is the same. Have students write about this activity in math journals.

• As a class, practice the ways to write a ratio using words (eight to twelve), symbols (8:12), and fractions ($\frac{8}{12}$). Have students create word problems to share with the class, and then have the class present the ratio from the word problem three different ways. Model a word problem for students before they write their own. Share answers.

• Math computer programs give students an opportunity to work with ratio and percent. Schedule a time to go to the computer lab and have students work with programs to convert ratio to percent and create graphs based on their computations. Share these with the class.

• Bring a variety of maps to class and have students explore the map scales to find the distance between cities and states. Students will need rulers to use the map scale and represent how many miles are equal to the distance on the map. Have students practice showing this distance as a ratio and then calculating the actual mileage.

• Provide a variety of menus from local restaurants and have students choose one to use for this activity. Ask students to choose what they would want for a meal and then add up the price of the meal. When they have calculated their final price, have them calculate the local tax (from your area) and then ask them to figure out the tip for their meal, using the figure of 20% for excellent service. What is the final price of their meal? Check for accuracy in multiplying and calculating the percentages.

More Resources

A good mathematics program follows sound cognitive principles and allows many opportunities for thoughtful and varied practice to build mastery of important skills. For advice on suitable mathematics programs, contact the Foundation.

The titles listed below are offered as a representative sample of materials and not a complete list of everything that is available.

For students —

• *Everything You Need to Know About Math Homework,* by Anne Zeman and Kate Kelly (Scholastic, 1994). A clear guide for students in Grades 4–6 that covers numbers and the number system, basic math functions, measurement, geometry, money, graphs, statistics, and computers. Paperback, ISBN 0590493590.

• *How Math Works,* by Carol Vonderman (Readers Digest, 1996). Hardcover, 192 pages, ISBN 0895778505.

• *If You Hopped Like a Frog,* by David M. Schwartz and illustrated by James Warhola (Scholastic, 1999). "If you hopped like a frog, you could jump from home plate to first base in one mighty leap" (from the book). Several examples like this encourage students to multiply their own height, weight, etc., to see what they could do if they had proportionally the same abilities as animals. Library binding, 32 pages, ISBN 0590098578.

• *Percents and Ratios (Math Success),* by Lucille Caron and Philip M. St. Jacques (Enslow, 2000). Library binding, 64 pages, ISBN 0766014355.

More Resources continued

For teachers —

• *Key to Percents (Keys to Math)*, by Steve and David Rasmussen (Key Curriculum Press, 1972). Self-paced, self-guided workbooks described by one reviewer as "very motivational for kids burned out on textbooks" (Love to Learn, www.lovetolearn.net). Set of four paperbacks, available individually or as a set from Key Curriculum Press, www.keypress.com, or 1-800-995-MATH. Answer keys and notes, as well as reproducible tests, are also available.

• *Usborne Illustrated Dictionary of Math,* by Tori Large and others (Usborne, 2004). Paperback, 128 pages, ISBN 0794506623.

• Figure This!, www.figurethis.org, provides math challenges designed for middle school students.

III. Fractions and Decimals

The Big Idea

Fractions and decimals can be written, compared, added, subtracted, multiplied, and divided.

What Students Should Already Know

Students using the Core Knowledge curriculum should be familiar with

Kindergarten

- identifying $\frac{1}{2}$ as one of two equal parts of a region or object
- finding $\frac{1}{2}$ of a set of concrete objects

Grade 1

- recognizing fractions as part of a whole: $\frac{1}{2}, \frac{1}{3}, \frac{1}{4}$

Grade 2

- recognizing these fractions as part of a whole set or region, and writing the corresponding numerical symbols: $\frac{1}{2}, \frac{1}{3}, \frac{1}{4}, \frac{1}{5}, \frac{1}{6}, \frac{1}{8}, \frac{1}{10}$
- recognizing fractions that are equal to 1

Grade 3

- recognizing fractions to $\frac{1}{10}$
- identifying numerator and denominator
- writing mixed numbers
- recognizing equivalent fractions (for example, $\frac{1}{2} = \frac{3}{6}$)
- comparing fractions with like denominators using the signs $<$, $>$, and $=$
- knowing and writing decimal equivalents to $\frac{1}{4}, \frac{1}{2}, \frac{3}{4}$
- reading and writing decimals to the hundredths

Grade 4

- recognizing fractions to one-twelfth
- changing improper fractions to mixed numbers and vice versa
- putting fractions in lowest terms
- renaming fractions with unlike denominators to fractions with common denominators
- comparing fractions with unlike denominators, using the signs $<$, $>$, and $=$
- solving problems in the form of $\frac{2}{3} = \frac{?}{12}$
- adding and subtracting fractions with like denominators
- expressing simple outcomes as fractions (for example, 3 out of 4 as $\frac{3}{4}$)
- reading and writing decimals to the nearest thousandth
- reading and writing decimals as fractions (for example, $0.39 = \frac{39}{100}$)
- writing decimal equivalents for halves, quarters, eighths, and tenths

What Students Should Already Know continued

- comparing fractions to decimals using the signs $<$, $>$, and $=$
- writing decimals in expanded form
- rounding decimals to the nearest tenth; to the nearest hundredth
- comparing decimals using the signs $<$, $>$, and $=$
- reading and writing decimals on a number line
- adding and subtracting with decimal numbers to two places

What Students Need to Learn

Fractions

- **Determine the least common denominator (LCD) of fractions with unlike denominators**
- **Identify the reciprocal of a given fraction; know that the product of a given number and its reciprocal is equal to 1**
- **Add and subtract mixed numbers and fractions with like and unlike denominators**
- **Multiply and divide fractions**
- **Multiply mixed numbers and fractions**
- **Round fractions to the nearest whole number**
- **Write fractions as decimals (e.g., $\frac{1}{4} = 0.25$; $\frac{17}{25} = 0.68$; $\frac{1}{3} = 0.3333\ldots$ or 0.33, rounded to the nearest hundredth)**

Decimals

- **Read, write, and order decimals to the nearest ten-thousandth**
- **Round decimals (and decimal quotients) to the nearest thousandth**
- **Estimate decimal sums, differences, and products by rounding**
- **Add and subtract decimals through ten-thousandths**
- **Multiply decimals: by 10, 100, and 1,000; by another decimal**
- **Divide decimals by whole numbers and decimals**

What Students Will Learn in Future Grades

The *Core Knowledge Sequence* for mathematics emphasizes the importance of reviewing and building on prior knowledge. Subsequent grades will continue to focus on strengthening and expanding these skills.

Materials

paper plates, p. 453

cardboard, foam board, plastic, or plastic coffee can lids, p. 453

fraction strips, geoboards, grid paper, tiles, blocks, and other fraction manipulatives, p. 455

money manipulatives, pp. 465

blank 10 x 10 grid, p. 465

materials for a decimal or fraction center, p. 476

index cards for flash cards and to make a concentration game, p. 476

construction paper, enough for 1 page per student p. 476

dice, 1 pair for each pair of students in class, p. 476

pocket chart, p. 476

daily fraction or decimal problem, p. 476

Vocabulary

Student/Teacher Vocabulary

algorithm: standard mathematical procedure that shows each step in a process (T)

common denominator: any common multiple of the denominators of two or more fractions; also called *like denominator* (S)

decimal number: a number written using a decimal point and based on place value (S)

denominator: the number on the bottom of a fraction, or the number of pieces into which a whole, region, or set has been divided (S)

fraction: a number that represents parts of a whole, region, or set (S)

least common denominator: the smallest possible common denominator of two or more fractions (S)

mixed number: a counting numeral followed by a fraction with a value between 0 and 1 (S)

numerator: the number on the top of a fraction, or the number of pieces being considered (S)

reciprocal: the fraction that can be multiplied by another fraction to make a product of 1, e.g., the reciprocal of the fraction $\frac{3}{4}$ is the fraction $\frac{4}{3}$ (S)

Domain Vocabulary

Fractions and decimals and associated words:
whole, part, region, group, set, equivalent, improper fraction, lowest terms, like denominator, regroup, rename, outcome, terms, like, unlike, product, reduce, simplify, multiply, add, subtract, divide, calculate, plus, minus, sum, point, ones, tenths, hundredths, thousandths, ten-thousandths, expanded form, number line, differences, estimate, round

At a Glance

The most important ideas for you are:

- Fractions consist of a numerator and a denominator.
- Mixed numbers include a counting numeral and a fractional part.
- Equivalent fractions can be identified with the aid of fraction manipulatives.
- Fractions with like denominators can be compared, added, subtracted, multiplied, and divided by examining the numerators. Fractions with unlike denominators can be compared, added, subtracted, multiplied, and divided by finding a common denominator.
- Fractions and decimals are closely connected; fractions can be written as decimal numbers and vice versa.
- Decimal numbers use decimal points to separate the ones place from the tenths, hundredths, thousandths, and ten-thousandths places.
- Decimal numbers can be rounded, compared, and placed on a number line.
- Decimal numbers can be added, subtracted, multiplied, and divided using the addition and subtraction algorithms.
- Students should practice until they learn fractions and decimals to the point of automaticity.

What Teachers Need to Know

Background

A. Fractions

The study of fractions is arguably the most important component of the Grade 5 Core Knowledge mathematics curriculum. Without mastery of fraction concepts, students cannot understand decimal numbers and percents, topics of great practical importance. The arithmetic of fractions also introduces principles and methods that are needed for algebra courses in middle and high school.

Students in Core Knowledge schools during Grade 4 should have learned to recognize equivalent fractions; put fractions in lowest terms; rename fractions with unlike denominators to fractions with the same denominators; represent mixed numbers as improper fractions and vice versa; add and subtract fractions with the same denominators; and compare fractions with the same and different denominators. Teachers in Grade 5 will need to build upon these skills to teach the four operations of arithmetic for fractions and mixed numbers.

Reviewing Basic Fraction Concepts

Whenever graphics or pictures are used to illustrate fractions, it is important to refer to an agreed-upon unit, or whole. For the fractions illustrated below, the unit is the first completely shaded circle. A "whole" means one filled-in circle (or disk).

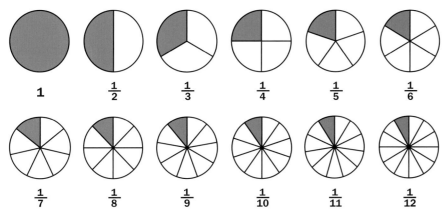

Point out to students that whenever figures are used to illustrate fractions, the figures should be divided into parts with equal areas. For example, if a circle is used to illustrate the fraction $\frac{1}{12}$, it should be divided into 12 identical sectors. Each of these pieces represents $\frac{1}{12}$ of the whole.

The numerator of a fraction is the number above the fraction bar (i.e., the number on top), and it describes the number of pieces being considered. The denominator of a fraction is the number below the fraction bar (i.e., the number on the bottom), and it tells the number of parts into which a whole, region, or set

Teaching Idea

Use a drawing of a pizza to review fractions. Draw circles on the board and divide each into the fractions you are teaching, for example $\frac{1}{2}$ and $\frac{1}{3}$. Then shade in one "piece" of each pizza. For distinguishing which is larger, $\frac{1}{2}$ or $\frac{1}{3}$, ask students to create models of $\frac{1}{2}$ and $\frac{1}{3}$ using paper plates, compare them, and demonstrate which is larger, $\frac{1}{2}$ or $\frac{1}{3}$. You can repeat this procedure with a variety of fractions.

Teaching Idea

Any sturdy material, such as cardboard, foam board, or plastic, can be used to create fraction manipulatives. One inexpensive idea is to collect plastic coffee can lids in different colors. Use one coffee lid as a base, and then remove the rims of different color lids and cut them into halves, fourths, etc. Students can manipulate the fraction pieces inside the inverted lid to explore fractional relationships.

Teaching Idea

In illustrating fractions, it seems natural to most of us to use circles divided into slices, in the same way pizzas and pies are divided. However, this is only one way to show a fraction. You can also use other shapes, e.g., $\frac{1}{4}$ can be shown as a square divided into fourths. The danger of always using round shapes to illustrate fractions is that students may come to think that fractions are somehow directly connected with circles, whereas in fact fractions are ways of showing a portion of a whole, which might be represented by many shapes.

Teaching Idea

When studying fractions, it is helpful to make connections to liquids, such as $\frac{1}{2}$ a glass of water, or $\frac{3}{4}$ of a container of milk. Fractions may also be directly connected to standard volume measurements. There are 2 cups in a pint, so a cup is $\frac{1}{2}$ of a pint. Since there are 4 quarts in a gallon, a quart is $\frac{1}{4}$ of a gallon. A gallon container is also made up of 8 pints, so a pint is $\frac{1}{8}$ of a gallon.

Teaching Idea

To teach fractions, use whole squares and squares divided into equal segments. For example, if a square is divided into 8 equal segments, one segment equals $\frac{1}{8}$. An uncut square is not divided into any segments. It is equal to $\frac{1}{1}$. And the whole square with 8 equal segments can be expressed as $\frac{8}{8}$.

Teaching Idea

Point out to students that two fractions may be equivalent even though neither numerator is a factor of the other and neither denominator is a factor of the other. For example, $\frac{2}{4}$ and $\frac{3}{6}$ are equivalent fractions. They are equal, and they both may be simplified to $\frac{1}{2}$. See the discussion of equivalent fractions on pp. 454–456.

has been divided, "the denominations." When reading fractions aloud, the numerator is read as a counting number, while the denominator is read as an ordinal number. Thus, $\frac{1}{6}$ is read as "one-sixth." One exception is $\frac{1}{2}$, which is read as "one-half."

For Grade 5, the denominator of a fraction can be any positive counting number (this excludes 0 as a denominator), and the numerator can be any whole number (even 0). When the numerator of a fraction is 0, the fraction itself equals 0. For example, $\frac{0}{4} = 0$. In later grades, the numerators and the denominators of fractions may be integers. (Remember, integers include negative numbers.)

In Grade 4, students who were in Core Knowledge schools should have become familiar with fractions to $\frac{1}{12}$. Use a variety of manipulatives, illustrations, and other resources to help students review these fractions.

Equivalent Fractions

An important idea concerning fractions is that two different fractions can represent the same number. For example, $\frac{1}{2}$ is the same number as $\frac{2}{4}$ and $\frac{3}{6}$. The Grades 3 and 4 guidelines from the *Sequence* address this important topic, but it should be carefully reviewed in Grade 5 before other fraction skills are introduced.

Pictures and diagrams can help students to review equivalent fractions. For example, to see why $\frac{1}{2}$ and $\frac{2}{4}$ represent the same part of a whole, consider this illustration.

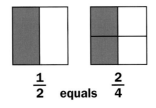

$$\frac{1}{2} \text{ equals } \frac{2}{4}$$

Start with the picture on the left for the fraction $\frac{1}{2}$. There are two pieces; one that is shaded and one that is unshaded. Imagine dividing each of these two pieces exactly in half. The resulting picture is the one on the right showing the fraction $\frac{2}{4}$. The important point here is that cutting both of the halves in half did not change how much of the square is shaded. The conclusion is that $\frac{1}{2} = \frac{2}{4}$. Notice that because you cut each half in half, both the numerator and the denominator of the fraction $\frac{1}{2}$ are doubled, the result is the fraction $\frac{2}{4}$, and this represents the same amount, that is, the same number as $\frac{1}{2}$. Try this same idea with another example. Start with $\frac{1}{2}$ again, but divide each half into three equal pieces. The picture looks like this:

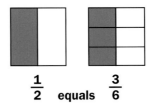

$$\frac{1}{2} \text{ equals } \frac{3}{6}$$

Dividing each half into three equal pieces triples the total number of pieces, and it triples the number of pieces that are shaded. The fractions $\frac{1}{2}$ and $\frac{3}{6}$ are equal, and $\frac{3}{6}$ results from $\frac{1}{2}$ by multiplying both the numerator and the denominator of $\frac{1}{2}$ by 3.

Manipulatives such as fraction strips, geoboards, grid paper, folded paper, tiles, blocks, or pie pieces allow students to review this concept in a concrete way. Encourage students to find alternative ways to express fractions in daily lessons. For example, students can use fraction strips to model $\frac{1}{2}$. Ask students to find as many other ways as they can to make strips of the same length using fraction strips with different denominators. Students will find that $\frac{2}{4}$, $\frac{3}{6}$, $\frac{5}{10}$, etc., are the same length as their $\frac{1}{2}$ strip. During class discussion, see if students notice relationships between equivalent fractions: multiplying the numerator and denominator by the same counting number results in an equivalent fraction.

All of the examples above illustrate the following important general principle:

Multiplying both the numerator and the denominator of a fraction by the same counting number produces a fraction equal to the first one.

For example, if you multiply both the numerator and the denominator of $\frac{3}{4}$ by 25, the resulting fraction is $\frac{75}{100}$ and this fraction equals $\frac{3}{4}$.

Consider the problem $\frac{2}{3} = \frac{?}{12}$. Students can solve this problem by recognizing that $\frac{2}{3} = \frac{2 \times 4}{3 \times 4} = \frac{8}{12}$. Exercises similar to this one will give students valuable practice in finding equivalent fractions and prepare them to learn how to put fractions in lowest terms.

Putting a fraction in lowest terms is often referred to as simplifying, reducing, or renaming a fraction. Reducing a fraction may be thought of as the reverse of the process of multiplying the numerator and denominator by the same counting number. If both the numerator and the denominator of a fraction are divisible by the same whole number, then an equivalent fraction is obtained by dividing both the numerator and the denominator by that whole number. As an example, consider the fraction $\frac{8}{12}$.

Because both 8 and 12 are divisible by 4,

$$\frac{8}{12} = \frac{8 \div 4}{12 \div 4} = \frac{2}{3}$$

The fraction $\frac{8}{12}$ expressed in lowest terms is $\frac{2}{3}$. The fraction $\frac{2}{3}$ cannot be simplified further. This is because 2 and 3 have no common factors greater than 1. Dividing both numerator and denominator of a fraction such as $\frac{8}{12}$ by their greatest common factor, or GCF, always results in a fraction simplified to lowest terms. (See the subsection, "Factors, Multiples, Prime and Composite Numbers," on pp. 438–440.) For the fraction $\frac{8}{12}$, the GCF of 8 and 12 is 4. Therefore we are guaranteed that dividing both the numerator and the denominator of $\frac{8}{12}$ by 4 results in a fully simplified fraction.

Students might not always find the largest possible number that is a factor of both the numerator and the denominator of a particular fraction (that is, the GCF of the numerator and denominator). For example, students might first simplify $\frac{75}{90}$ by dividing both the numerator and the denominator by 3 instead of by 15:

$$\frac{75}{90} = \frac{75 \div 3}{90 \div 3} = \frac{25}{30}$$

Teaching Idea

The term *reduce* in relation to renaming a fraction can be misleading to some students as they may think that the actual size of the fraction is reduced. Point out to students that the size of the fraction does not change when both the numerator and the denominator are divided by a whole number. Instead, when we reduce a fraction, we rename it with smaller numbers. To help avoid misconceptions, some teachers choose to talk about "simplifying" or "renaming" a fraction rather than "reducing" it.

Teaching Idea

Students can concretely model problems such as $\frac{2}{3} = \frac{?}{12}$ by using fraction strips, pie pieces, counters, grid paper, or other objects as models to find the missing number. The fractional representation will remain the same size, but the numbers will change.

There is nothing wrong with this as a first step. But students should also observe that $\frac{25}{30}$ may be expressed in lower terms by dividing both the numerator and denominator by 5. The entire calculation can be presented this way:

$$\frac{75}{90} = \frac{75 \div 3}{90 \div 3} = \frac{25}{30} = \frac{25 \div 5}{30 \div 5} = \frac{5}{6}$$

When two fractions have the same denominator, we say that they have common denominators. When two fractions have different denominators, it is always possible to find two new fractions with the same denominator, each equivalent to one of the original pair of fractions.

One choice for a new common denominator for any two fractions is the product of their denominators. However, there are other common denominators that are often more convenient. The smallest possible common denominator, or least common denominator, for two fractions is the least common multiple, or LCM, of the denominators of two fractions. (See the subsection "Factors, Multiples, Prime and Composite Numbers," on pp. 438–440.)

For example, a common denominator for the fractions $\frac{5}{6}$ and $\frac{7}{9}$ is the product of the two given denominators: $6 \times 9 = 54$. Then,

$$\frac{5}{6} = \frac{5 \times 9}{6 \times 9} = \frac{45}{54}$$

$$\frac{7}{9} = \frac{7 \times 6}{9 \times 6} = \frac{42}{54}$$

However, students might observe that 6 and 9 are each divisors of 18 and, therefore, 18 may be used as a common denominator for the fractions $\frac{5}{6}$ and $\frac{7}{9}$. The calculation would then continue this way:

$$\frac{5}{6} = \frac{5 \times 3}{6 \times 3} = \frac{15}{18}$$

$$\frac{7}{9} = \frac{7 \times 2}{9 \times 2} = \frac{14}{18}$$

Notice that 18 is the least common multiple of 6 and 9. In both cases, the fractions $\frac{5}{6}$ and $\frac{7}{9}$ have been changed to equivalent fractions with common denominators. One advantage of using the product $6 \times 9 = 54$ as the common denominator for $\frac{5}{6}$ and $\frac{7}{9}$ is that the fraction calculations are not complicated by the necessity for students to understand the concept of least common multiple. It is a good teaching strategy to introduce ideas and skills in their simplest contexts first.

Finding a common denominator for two fractions enables us to add, subtract, and compare fractions. Addition and subtraction are explained later in this section.

When comparing two fractions, first look at their denominators. If the fractions have the same denominator, the smaller fraction is the one with the smaller numerator. For example, $\frac{2}{6} < \frac{5}{6}$ because $2 < 5$.

When comparing two fractions with unlike denominators, first rewrite the fractions so that both fractions have common denominators, and then compare the numerators. For example, to compare $\frac{1}{2}$ and $\frac{1}{3}$, first rewrite the fractions with common denominators. Since $\frac{1}{2} = \frac{3}{6}$ and $\frac{1}{3} = \frac{2}{6}$, and $3 > 2$, it follows that $\frac{1}{2} > \frac{1}{3}$.

Add and Subtract Fractions and Mixed Numbers

In Grade 4, students in Core Knowledge schools should have learned how to add and subtract fractions with the same denominator. In Grade 5, students will significantly expand their skills in this area. You may wish to begin with a review of the Grade 4 content.

The sum of two fractions with the same denominator is a fraction with that denominator, whose numerator is the sum of the numerators of the two addends (the two fractions being added). For example,

$$\frac{3}{8} + \frac{2}{8} = \frac{3+2}{8} = \frac{5}{8}$$

Subtracting one fraction from another, when the denominators are the same, is carried out in a similar fashion. For example,

$$\frac{9}{11} - \frac{3}{11} = \frac{9-3}{11} = \frac{6}{11}$$

You may wish to allow students to review adding and subtracting fractional amounts by using concrete objects and manipulatives, such as fraction strips. Students can gain an intuitive understanding of the process by counting the total pieces when adding or the remaining pieces when subtracting.

In order to calculate explicitly a sum or difference of fractions that do not have a common denominator, it is necessary first to find equivalent fractions with a common denominator. As an example, consider the problem of adding the fractions $\frac{1}{12}$ and $\frac{3}{8}$. The first step is to find a common denominator for these fractions. Until students gain proficiency with fraction addition, it is a good idea for them to choose the common denominator that is the product of the denominators of the original fractions. Choosing the denominator $12 \times 8 = 96$, we can calculate

$$\frac{1}{12} = \frac{1 \times 8}{12 \times 8} = \frac{8}{96}$$

$$\frac{3}{8} = \frac{3 \times 12}{8 \times 12} = \frac{36}{96}$$

Therefore,

$$\frac{1}{12} + \frac{3}{8} = \frac{8}{96} + \frac{36}{96} = \frac{44}{96}$$

The sum, $\frac{44}{96}$, can be simplified by dividing both numerator and denominator by 4. The result is $\frac{1}{12} + \frac{3}{8} = \frac{11}{24}$.

An advantage of using the least common denominator for two fractions is that this last step, simplifying the sum, can sometimes be avoided entirely. The least common denominator of two fractions is the least common multiple of their denominators. In the case at hand, the denominators are 12 and 8, and the least common multiple is 24. Using this we get:

$$\frac{1}{12} = \frac{1 \times 2}{12 \times 2} = \frac{2}{24}$$

$$\frac{3}{8} = \frac{3 \times 3}{8 \times 3} = \frac{9}{24}$$

Therefore, $\frac{1}{12} + \frac{3}{8} = \frac{2}{24} + \frac{9}{24} = \frac{11}{24}$, and the sum is already expressed in lowest terms. The procedure for subtraction is similar. For example, to calculate $\frac{2}{9} - \frac{1}{6}$, we may proceed as follows

$$\frac{2}{9} - \frac{1}{6} = \frac{4}{18} - \frac{3}{18} = \frac{1}{18}$$

When the numerator of a fraction is less than the denominator, it is called a proper fraction (such as $\frac{3}{4}$). A fraction whose numerator is greater than or equal to its denominator is called an improper fraction. For example, $\frac{17}{3}$ and $\frac{5}{5}$ are improper fractions. Proper fractions are less than 1 and improper fractions are greater than or equal to 1. A mixed number is a counting numeral followed by a fraction between 0 and 1. For example, $4\frac{3}{8}$ and $2\frac{3}{4}$ are mixed numbers. A mixed number is just shorthand notation for a sum. The mixed number $4\frac{3}{8}$ means $4 + \frac{3}{8}$, and $2\frac{3}{4}$ means $2 + \frac{3}{4}$. Remind students that when reading mixed numbers aloud, they should use the word *and* between the whole number and the fraction. For example, $2\frac{3}{4}$ is read aloud as "two *and* three-fourths."

Any mixed number can be written as an improper fraction, and any improper fraction can be written either as a whole number or a mixed number. You may wish to allow students to use concrete objects, manipulatives, and pictures to review the relationship between mixed numbers and improper fractions. For example, give each student 11 one-fourth fraction pieces. How could they express this many pieces as a fraction? Counting the pieces will lead students to determine that there are 11 one-fourth pieces, or $\frac{11}{4}$. What are some other ways students can think to name this amount? Eight of the pieces will create 2 wholes, with 3 one-fourth pieces left over, which can be expressed as 2 wholes and $\frac{3}{4}$, 2 and $\frac{3}{4}$, or $2 + \frac{3}{4}$. Students can then easily make the transition to see that the mixed number $2\frac{3}{4}$ is just another way of expressing this amount.

When formally reviewing how to rename mixed numbers as improper fractions, the first step is to write whole numbers as fractions. Any whole number can be written as a fraction whose denominator is 1. For example,

$$5 = \frac{5}{1} \qquad 17 = \frac{17}{1} \qquad 1 = \frac{1}{1} \qquad 0 = \frac{0}{1}$$

Once a whole number is expressed as a fraction whose denominator is 1, we can use the methods of the subsection "Equivalent Fractions" (pp. 454–456) to write whole numbers as fractions with any denominator. For example,

$$4 = \frac{4}{1} = \frac{4 \times 7}{1 \times 7} = \frac{28}{7}$$

This shows that 4 is equal to the improper fraction $\frac{28}{7}$.

We also know that we may reverse the process by dividing the numerator and denominator by the same whole number. Suppose we started with the improper fraction $\frac{28}{7}$. Divide both numerator and denominator by the common factor of 7:

$$\frac{28}{7} = \frac{28 \div 7}{7 \div 7} = \frac{4}{1} = 4$$

A shortcut is simply to divide the numerator by the denominator.

$$\frac{28}{7} = 28 \div 7 = 4$$

This natural identification of the fraction bar with division was introduced in the Grade 4 *Sequence,* and it is important for algebra courses in later grades.

Division of whole numbers plays an important role in expressing improper fractions, not only as whole numbers, as in the above example, but also as mixed numbers. To review how to convert an improper fraction to a mixed or whole number, use long division to divide the numerator by the denominator. The quotient is the whole number part of the mixed number. The remainder is the numerator for the fraction part of the mixed number. The denominator stays the same. If the remainder is zero, then the improper fraction is a whole number.

Here is a sample problem to review this procedure: Express $\frac{17}{3}$ as a mixed number.

Solution:
$$\begin{array}{r} 5 \\ 3\overline{)17} \\ \underline{15} \\ 2 \end{array}$$

The quotient for $17 \div 3$ is 5 and the remainder is 2. Therefore $\frac{17}{3} = 5\frac{2}{3}$.

How can a mixed number be written as an improper fraction? Using the same ideas as before, students can understand how to write mixed numbers as improper fractions and exactly why the method works. As an example, let's start with the mixed number $5\frac{2}{3}$ and use mathematical principles to write it as an improper fraction. Now, $5\frac{2}{3}$ means $5 + \frac{2}{3}$, so

$$5\frac{2}{3} = 5 + \frac{2}{3} = \frac{5}{1} + \frac{2}{3} = \frac{15}{3} + \frac{2}{3} + \frac{15+2}{3} = \frac{17}{3}$$

Before introducing a formal method of adding mixed numbers, you may wish to allow students to use concrete objects, manipulatives, and pictures to explore on their own. For example, give each student a set of $\frac{1}{5}$ fraction pieces and ask them to add $1\frac{2}{5} + 3\frac{1}{5}$. Students can use a variety of methods to find the sum, such as creating and then adding the whole numbers first and then adding the fractional parts, or by counting the individual pieces to find an improper fraction that they then turn into a mixed number.

Although it is often awkward to do so, you can calculate sums of mixed numbers by first writing them as improper fractions, and then adding. For example, to compute the sum $4\frac{3}{7} + 5\frac{2}{3}$, we can first write each of the addends as a fraction (these calculations are carried out explicitly in the previous subsection) and then add.

$$4\frac{3}{7} + 5\frac{2}{3} = \frac{31}{7} + \frac{17}{3}$$

A common denominator for the two fractions on the right is 3×7, or 21.

$$4\frac{3}{7} + 5\frac{2}{3}$$
$$= \frac{31}{7} + \frac{17}{3}$$
$$= \frac{93}{21} + \frac{119}{21}$$
$$= \frac{212}{21}$$

The sum $\frac{212}{21}$ may be expressed as a mixed number by dividing the numerator by the denominator: dividing 212 by 21 gives 10 with a remainder of 2, that is, $212 = 21 \times 10 + 2$. Therefore,

$$4\frac{3}{7} + 5\frac{2}{3} = \frac{212}{21} = 10\frac{2}{21}$$

Subtracting one mixed number from another can be carried out using the same basic strategies used for addition. Again, you may wish to use concrete manipulatives before demonstrating how to subtract mixed numbers on paper, especially when regrouping is necessary. Performing mixed number addition or subtraction vertically may require regrouping. To focus on regrouping, consider an example that does not require finding a common denominator:

$$7\frac{2}{5} - 4\frac{3}{5} = ?$$

The result is that $7\frac{2}{5} - 4\frac{3}{5} = 2\frac{4}{5}$. Here is a detailed justification of the important regrouping step, $7\frac{2}{5} = 6\frac{7}{5}$.

$$7\frac{2}{5}$$
$$= 7 + \frac{2}{5}$$
$$= (6 + 1) + \frac{2}{5}$$
$$= 6 + (1 + \frac{2}{5})$$
$$= 6 + (\frac{5}{5} + \frac{2}{5})$$
$$= 6 + \frac{7}{5}$$
$$= 6\frac{7}{5}$$

The third equality follows from the associative property of addition. It is valuable for students to see this kind of explanation of regrouping because it illustrates how computation depends on fundamental mathematical principles.

Students can check the subtraction calculation $7\frac{2}{5} - 4\frac{3}{5} = 2\frac{4}{5}$ by adding to verify that $4\frac{3}{5} + 2\frac{4}{5} = 7\frac{2}{5}$.

The method of computing sums of mixed numbers described at the beginning of this subsection may also be used to calculate differences without the need for regrouping.

$$7\frac{2}{5} - 4\frac{3}{5} = \frac{37}{5} - \frac{23}{5} = \frac{14}{5} = 2\frac{4}{5}$$

Students will benefit by calculating sums and differences of mixed numbers by all of the methods described here, not just by following one approach. Understanding the principles behind fraction and mixed number calculations will give students an advantage in algebra courses.

Multiply and Divide Fractions and Mixed Numbers

Multiplying and dividing fractions and mixed numbers are new topics for students. It is important to help students develop a conceptual understanding of these operations before teaching them the algorithms.

You may wish to begin by having students use fraction manipulatives to explore a problem such as $2 \times \frac{3}{4}$. Ask students to estimate what the product may be and to use their fraction models to find two sets of three-fourths. You can then ask students to use fraction models to gain an understanding of multiplying two fractions. Students are often confused because the product of fractions is smaller than the factors, and it is beneficial to explore these topics when using concrete models.

When multiplying fractions, it is important for students in Grade 5 to know how to perform the multiplication as well as how to use fraction multiplication to solve problems.

Applying fraction multiplication to problem solving is an important skill for fifth graders. A key step to that end is understanding the meaning of the statement: *of* means "times." For example, "$\frac{1}{2}$ of 12" means the same thing as "$\frac{1}{2} \times 12$." Both expressions equal 6.

As another example, $\frac{1}{3}$ of $\frac{1}{2} = \frac{1}{3} \times \frac{1}{2} = \frac{1}{6}$. This may be visualized by splitting halves into three equal parts, as in this diagram:

$$\frac{1}{3} \text{ of } \frac{1}{2} = \frac{1}{6}$$

A number line may also be used to visualize the meaning of fraction multiplication. As an example, compute $\frac{2}{3} \times \frac{3}{4} = \frac{6}{12} = \frac{1}{2}$. To illustrate the multiplication $\frac{2}{3} \times \frac{3}{4} = \frac{1}{2}$, the length of each arrow below is one-third of the distance from 0 to $\frac{3}{4}$. Two of these arrows laid end-to-end as below have a combined length of $\frac{2}{3}$ of $\frac{3}{4}$, that is, $\frac{1}{2}$.

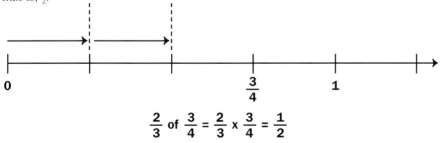

$$\frac{2}{3} \text{ of } \frac{3}{4} = \frac{2}{3} \times \frac{3}{4} = \frac{1}{2}$$

Another good way to model multiplication of fractions pictorially is with a unit rectangle, i.e., a rectangle that is assigned an area of 1. Then $\frac{3}{4}$ can be pictured by dividing the rectangle vertically into fourths and shading three of the four vertical bars. Now divide the rectangle into thirds horizontally, shading two of the horizontal bars differently than the others to represent $\frac{2}{3}$. The intersection automatically gives $\frac{2}{3}$ of $\frac{3}{4}$ and it is clearly seen to be $\frac{6}{12}$ or $\frac{1}{2}$ of the unit rectangle.

Here is a sample word problem connected with this calculation: Mrs. Pistolesi gave her thirsty son a pitcher of lemonade that was $\frac{3}{4}$ full. Her son drank $\frac{2}{3}$ of the lemonade in the pitcher. When the pitcher is full it holds 1 liter of fluid. How much lemonade did Mrs. Pistolesi's son drink?

Solution: Mrs. Pistolesi's son drank $\frac{2}{3}$ of $\frac{3}{4}$ of a liter of lemonade. Therefore he drank $\frac{2}{3} \times \frac{3}{4}$ liters. Mrs. Pistolesi's son drank $\frac{1}{2}$ liter of lemonade.

After giving students an opportunity to explore with models and examples like these, you can introduce the definition and algorithm.

Suppose that *a*, *b*, *c*, and *d* are whole numbers and that *b* and *d* are not 0. The rule for multiplying the fractions $\frac{a}{b}$ and $\frac{c}{d}$ is:

$$\frac{a}{b} \times \frac{c}{d} = \frac{a \times c}{b \times d}$$

For example, $\frac{2}{3} \times \frac{4}{5} = \frac{2 \times 4}{3 \times 5} = \frac{8}{15}$. Here $a = 2$, $b = 3$, $c = 4$, and $d = 5$. This rule for multiplication holds for all choices of *a*, *b*, *c*, and *d*, as long as neither denominator equals 0.

A shortcut for fraction multiplication is to cancel common factors from the numerator of one fraction with the denominator of another.

For example, using cancellation, we can compute

$$\frac{2}{3} \times \frac{1}{2} = \frac{\cancel{2}}{3} \times \frac{1}{\cancel{2}} = \frac{1}{3}$$

Cancellation should be explained and justified. One explanation proceeds this way:

$$\frac{2}{3} \times \frac{1}{2} = \frac{2 \times 1}{3 \times 2} = \frac{2}{6} = \frac{2 \div 2}{6 \div 2} = \frac{1}{3}$$

The point of cancellation in this example is to avoid multiplying and dividing the numerator and denominator by the same factor, 2. Cancellation is a shortcut. A more direct explanation that relies on the concept of fraction multiplication and the commutative property of multiplication proceeds as:

$$\frac{2}{3} \times \frac{1}{2} = \frac{2 \times 1}{3 \times 2} = \frac{1 \times 2}{3 \times 2} = \frac{1}{3} \times \frac{2}{2} = \frac{1}{3} \times 1 = \frac{1}{3}$$

In this calculation, the 2s cancel because $\frac{2}{2}$ is equivalent to 1. Explanations like these connect computational methods to mathematical reasoning. Students should not be taught cancellation until after they thoroughly understand fraction multiplication without the use of canceling.

In order to introduce division with fractions, you may wish to begin by reviewing the concept of division itself and then allowing students to explore division with fractions using fraction models.

What does it mean to divide one fraction by another fraction, and what is the rule for finding the quotient? The answer depends on the concept of the reciprocal of a fraction.

The reciprocal of the (nonzero) fraction $\frac{c}{d}$ is the fraction $\frac{d}{c}$.

For example, the reciprocal of the fraction $\frac{3}{4}$ is the fraction $\frac{4}{3}$. To find the reciprocal of a fraction, just "turn it upside down." The reciprocal of $\frac{4}{3}$ is $\frac{3}{4}$. The reciprocal of 5 is $\frac{1}{5}$ (because $5 = \frac{5}{1}$) and the reciprocal of $\frac{1}{5}$ is $\frac{5}{1}$ or 5. The number 0 $\left(\frac{0}{1}\right)$ has no reciprocal because the denominator of a fraction can never be zero.

What is important about reciprocals? The key fact is that any fraction multiplied by its reciprocal equals 1.

$$\frac{3}{4} \times \frac{4}{3} = \frac{12}{12} = 1$$

$$\frac{1}{5} \times \frac{5}{1} = \frac{5}{5} = 1$$

The procedure for fraction division can be explained in terms of reciprocals. Dividing one fraction by a second fraction is the same as multiplying the first fraction by the reciprocal of the second. More explicitly,

$$\frac{a}{b} \div \frac{c}{d} = \frac{a}{b} \times \frac{d}{c}$$

Rule for fraction division

For example, $\frac{2}{3} \div \frac{3}{4} = \frac{2}{3} \times \frac{4}{3} = \frac{8}{9}$. To divide $\frac{2}{3}$ by $\frac{3}{4}$, multiply $\frac{2}{3}$ by the reciprocal of $\frac{3}{4}$, that is multiply $\frac{2}{3}$ by $\frac{4}{3}$.

To gain some intuition and check that this rule does what it should when the fractions equal whole numbers, suppose we write $6 = \frac{6}{1}$ and $2 = \frac{2}{1}$. Does the procedure for dividing fractions tell us that $6 \div 2 = 3$, as it should? Let's find out. According to the rule:

$$6 \div 2 = \frac{6}{1} \div \frac{2}{1} = \frac{6}{1} \times \frac{1}{2} = \frac{6}{2} = 3$$

So, fraction division gives the correct answer for this example, and in a similar way, it will also give the correct answer for any whole number division problem. This particular example illustrates the fact that a number divided by 2 equals one-half of that number (i.e., that number multiplied by $\frac{1}{2}$).

Now, instead of dividing 6 by 2, let's divide 6 by $\frac{1}{2}$.

$$6 \div \frac{1}{2} = \frac{6}{1} \div \frac{1}{2} = \frac{6}{1} \times \frac{2}{1} = \frac{12}{1} = 12$$

What is the intuition for $6 \div \frac{1}{2} = 12$? What does it mean? The quotient 12 is the answer to the question: what number times $\frac{1}{2}$ equals 6? Since 12 halves equals 6, the quotient is 12. A word problem to go with $6 \div \frac{1}{2} = 12$ is, How many half cups of water are required to fill a container that holds 6 cups? This particular division problem can be explained in terms of repeated subtraction. How many times can $\frac{1}{2}$ be subtracted from 6? The answer is 12 times. However, it is important to realize that repeated subtraction cannot be used to explain most examples of fraction division, and cannot explain the rule for fraction division.

This "invert and multiply rule" may be explained to students using a numerical example, such as

$$5 \div \frac{2}{3} = ?$$

The goal is to find the number designated by the question mark. Because division is the inverse operation for multiplication, the answer must satisfy

$$? \times \frac{2}{3} = 5$$

Students in Core Knowledge schools should have learned in Grade 4 that, "equals multiplied by equals are equal." So we can multiply both sides by the reciprocal of $\frac{2}{3}$, that is, by $\frac{3}{2}$.

$$? \times \frac{2}{3} \times \frac{3}{2} = 5 \times \frac{3}{2}$$

Since $\frac{2}{3} \times \frac{3}{2} = 1$, this gives

$$? = 5 \times \frac{3}{2}$$

In other words, $5 \div \frac{2}{3} = 5 \times \frac{3}{2}$. This method works for all examples, and it justifies the "invert and multiply" rule.

The rule for fraction division allows us to understand fractions as quotients. To illustrate, consider the division problem $2 \div 3 = ?$

$$2 \div 3 = \frac{2}{1} \div \frac{3}{1} = \frac{2}{1} \times \frac{1}{3} = \frac{2}{3}$$

This shows that $\frac{2}{3} = 2 \div 3$. In the same way, any fraction is equal to its numerator divided by its denominator ($\frac{a}{b} = a \div b$). The fraction bar separating the numerator from the denominator may be understood as a symbol for division.

Multiplying Mixed Numbers

Products of mixed numbers can be calculated by first expressing them as fractions. The first step for multiplying mixed numbers is to write them as fractions. Then the fractions are multiplied. For example,

$$5\frac{2}{3} \times 2\frac{4}{5} = \frac{17}{3} \times \frac{14}{5} = \frac{17 \times 14}{3 \times 5} = \frac{238}{15}$$

The improper fraction $\frac{238}{15}$ may be written as a mixed number. Carrying out the division, $238 \div 15$ is 15 with a remainder of 13, that is, $238 = 15 \times 15 + 13$. So,

$$\frac{238}{15} = 15\frac{13}{15}$$

Students in Core Knowledge schools should have had extensive practice rounding both whole and decimal numbers in Grade 4, and these topics are further developed in Grade 5. (See the subsections "Rounding Whole Numbers," on pp. 432–433, and "Rounding Decimals," on pp. 470–471.) Students benefit from learning rounding in stages, so you may wish to review rounding whole numbers before teaching students how to round fractions.

Rounding fractions follows the same principles as rounding whole and decimal numbers. As an example, the fraction $\frac{17}{3}$ rounded to the nearest whole number is 6. This is because $\frac{17}{3} = 5\frac{2}{3}$, and $5\frac{2}{3}$ is closer to 6 than to 5. When the fraction part of a mixed number is greater than or equal to $\frac{1}{2}$, the mixed number is rounded up to the next largest whole number, as in this case. When the fraction part of a mixed number is less than $\frac{1}{2}$, the mixed number is rounded down to the whole number part of the mixed number. For example, $4\frac{3}{7}$ rounded to the nearest whole number is 4 because $\frac{3}{7} < \frac{1}{2}$. To give students concrete practice rounding fractions and mixed numbers, consider using fraction models or a number line.

Writing Fractions as Decimals

In Grade 4, students in Core Knowledge schools should have learned how to read and write decimals as fractions; how to write decimal equivalents for halves, quarters, eighths, and tenths; and how to compare fractions and decimals. Students will continue to develop these skills in Grade 5 by learning how to express additional fractions as decimals.

You may wish to begin this topic by reviewing the concept that fractions and decimals are just two different ways to express the same number. This same idea will be addressed when students study ratios and percents. (See "Ratio and Percent," pp. 442–449.)

For example, you know that $0.5 = \frac{5}{10}$ and that $\frac{5}{10} = \frac{1}{2}$. Hence,

$$\frac{1}{2} = \frac{5}{10} = 0.5$$

If the denominator of a fraction divides 10, 100, 1,000, or some other power of 10 (see the subsection "Perfect Squares, Square Roots, and Exponents," on pp. 434–436), then the fraction can be written as a finite decimal. To illustrate, consider the fraction $\frac{17}{25}$. Because 25 is a factor of 100, we can find an equivalent fraction whose denominator is 100.

$$\frac{17}{25} = \frac{17 \times 4}{25 \times 4} = \frac{68}{100}$$

Since $\frac{68}{100} = 0.68$, it follows that $\frac{17}{25} = 0.68$. In a similar way, multiplying the numerators and the denominators of $\frac{1}{4}$ and $\frac{3}{4}$ by 25 gives the important results

$$\frac{1}{4} = \frac{25}{100} = 0.25$$

$$\frac{3}{4} = \frac{75}{100} = 0.75$$

Students following the *Core Knowledge Sequence* in Grade 4 should have learned to express fractions as decimals using this method. Students often gain a better understanding of decimal numbers and fractions when they are connected to money amounts, and you may wish to use this approach as well. For example, $0.01 means one cent. Since there are 100 cents in a dollar, one cent is $\frac{1}{100}$ of one dollar. This may help students to recognize 0.01 as $\frac{1}{100}$.

Students may interpret decimals with two place holders to the right of the decimal point directly in terms of hundredths, so that they recognize, for example, that $0.67 = \frac{67}{100}$.

The relationships that $0.25 = \frac{25}{100} = \frac{1}{4}$ and that $0.75 = \frac{75}{100} = \frac{3}{4}$ can be explained in terms of money. A quarter, the coin for 25¢, is $\frac{1}{4}$ of 1 dollar because 4 quarters make a dollar. A quarter is also worth 25 pennies or $\frac{25}{100}$ of 1 dollar (since there are 100 pennies to a dollar). This might help students to see that $\frac{25}{100} = \frac{1}{4}$. Similarly, 3 quarters make 75¢ and so $\frac{3}{4}$ of 1 dollar is the same as $\frac{75}{100}$ of 1 dollar. Therefore $\frac{75}{100} = \frac{3}{4}$. Now write decimals for $\frac{1}{4}$ and $\frac{3}{4}$.

$$\frac{1}{4} = \frac{25}{100} = 0.25$$

$$\frac{3}{4} = \frac{75}{100} = 0.75$$

You may wish to provide money manipulatives for students to use while demonstrating the relationship among fractions, decimals, and money. This connection can also be made using other simple manipulatives, such as a blank 10 × 10 grid. Students can shade in 25 of the squares to represent the fraction $\frac{25}{100}$ and the decimal number 0.25, as in the example above. Using a marker or colored pencil, next have them draw lines to divide the grid into four equal parts, as in the picture on p. 466. This visual representation makes it easier to see that $\frac{25}{100}$ and 0.25 are the same as $\frac{1}{4}$.

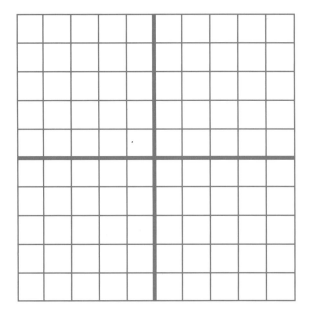

An important alternative method to express fractions as decimals is also appropriate for students in Grade 5:

To find a decimal expression for a fraction, divide the numerator by the denominator.

For example, to express the fraction $\frac{3}{4}$ as a decimal, perform this long division calculation:

$$
\begin{array}{r}
.75 \\
4\overline{)3.00} \\
\underline{28} \\
20 \\
\underline{20} \\
0
\end{array}
$$

The conclusion is: $\frac{3}{4} = 0.75$.

Before dividing the numerator of a fraction by its denominator, simplify the fraction to lowest terms. That will make it easier to perform the division calculation for the decimal representation of the fraction.

What about fractions whose denominators have prime factors other than 2 or 5? An example of such a fraction is $\frac{1}{3}$. Dividing the numerator by the denominator results in a never-ending string of 3s following the decimal point. The calculation below may be continued without end.

$$
\begin{array}{r}
.33 \\
3\overline{)1.000} \\
\underline{9} \\
10 \\
\underline{9} \\
1 \text{ etc.}
\end{array}
$$

The correct decimal representation for $\frac{1}{3}$ is 0.333333 . . . . The ellipsis (. . .) indicates that the decimal continues forever.

B. Decimals

Decimal notation is part of the base ten system, and it has great practical importance in measurement and calculation. Decimal notation provides a convenient way to write and calculate with mixed numbers whose fractional parts have denominators that are powers of 10: 10, 100, 1,000, etc. You will see that this system for writing mixed numbers has great flexibility, as well as some limitations that you need to understand.

It may be helpful to review with students that decimals are simply another way of writing fractions, and vice versa. Exploring the connections between fractions and decimals is key to helping students gain an understanding of both concepts. For example, students must learn that 0.50 is simply another way of expressing $\frac{1}{2}$; these are just two different ways to write the same number. When teaching decimals to students, use many of the same fraction models and manipulatives you use when teaching fractions. These manipulatives will help students have concrete experiences with decimal numbers, and the manipulatives will also help reinforce the connection between fractions and decimals.

The Sequence asks teachers in Grade 5 to review and build upon the skills and understandings students should have gained in Grade 4. Students in Grade 5 learn the standard procedures (or standard algorithms) for addition, subtraction, multiplication, and division of decimal numbers.

Decimal Notation and Place Value

You may wish to review with students that decimal numbers are written using a decimal point and are based on place value. Examples of decimal numbers include 4.75, 1.687, 0.5, and 2.25. In a decimal number, any number to the left of the decimal point (except for the 0 used as a visual cue that a decimal point is present) is 1 or greater, and each number to the right of the decimal point is less than 1. For instance, in the number 4.75, 4 is a whole number greater than 1, and .75 is less than 1. The decimal point is used to separate the ones place from the places less than one.

Students should remember from their studies of the base ten system (see pp. 427–428) that each place to the left of the decimal point increases its value ten times as you move to the left. For example, 10 is 10 times 1, and 100 is 10 times 10. This pattern continues to the right of the decimal point, with the value of each place to the right of the decimal point becoming ten times smaller. Another way to think of this is that the value of each place to the right of the decimal point is divided by ten.

The first placeholder to the right of the decimal point is the tenths place. The digit in the tenths place indicates the number of tenths. For example, 0.1 means $\frac{1}{10}$ and 0.3 means $\frac{3}{10}$.

The next placeholder to the right of the tenths place is the hundredths place. The digit in the hundredths place indicates the number of hundredths. For example, 0.01 means $\frac{1}{100}$ and 0.04 means $\frac{4}{100}$.

The next placeholder to the right is the thousandths place. The digit in the thousandths place indicates the number of thousandths. For example, 0.001 means $\frac{1}{1,000}$ and 0.009 means $\frac{9}{1,000}$. The placeholder to the right of the thousandths place is the ten-thousandths place. The digit in the ten-thousandths place indicates the number of ten-thousandths. For example, 0.0001 means $\frac{1}{10,000}$ and 0.0007 means $\frac{7}{10,000}$.

What about numerals that have nonzero digits in more than one place to the right of the decimal? For example, what is the meaning of 0.67?

$$0.67 \text{ means } \frac{6}{10} + \frac{7}{100}$$

This is because the 6 is in the tenths column and therefore represents 6 units of $\frac{1}{10}$ (that is $\frac{6}{10}$), and the 7 is in the hundredths column and therefore represents 7 units of $\frac{1}{100}$ (that is, $\frac{7}{100}$). The two fractions above may be added by using the common denominator of 100. Then,

$$0.67 = \frac{6}{10} + \frac{7}{100} = \frac{60}{100} + \frac{7}{100} = \frac{67}{100}$$

$$0.67 = \frac{67}{100}$$

The decimal 0.67 is read aloud as "sixty-seven hundredths" or as "zero point six seven," and not as "zero point sixty-seven." It is also correct to write .67 instead of 0.67 and this is read aloud as "point six seven." However, including the 0 in the ones place helps the reader to see the decimal point.

Any decimal numeral with placeholders only in the tenths and hundredths positions may be recognized directly as a fraction in the same way. The two digits together form the numerator of a fraction whose denominator is 100. For example, $0.36 = \frac{36}{100}$. Notice that this fraction can be simplified:

$$\frac{36}{100} = \frac{36 \div 4}{100 \div 4} = \frac{9}{25}$$

It is good practice for students to write decimal numbers as fractions and then simplify those fractions when possible.

It is particularly important that students understand that zeros to the right of all nonzero digits, following the decimal point, do not change the value. For example, 0.3 = 0.30 = 0.300.

With this understanding of the connections between decimals and fractions, numerals like 3.5 and 6.25 may be directly interpreted by students as mixed numbers:

$$3.5 = 3\frac{5}{10} = 3\frac{1}{2}$$

$$6.25 = 6\frac{25}{100} = 6\frac{1}{4}$$

Decimal numbers greater than 1 are read aloud much as mixed numbers are. When reading these decimal numbers aloud, read the decimal point as *and*. For example, the decimal number 1.25 is read aloud as "one *and* twenty-five hundredths." This number can also be read aloud as "one point two five." In order to help students see the connection between fractions and decimals, encourage them to use the form that names the decimal place values of tenths, hundredths, thousandths, or ten-thousandths.

Teaching Idea

Show students that the relationship of 0.3 = 0.30 = 0.300 may be seen by simplifying the fractions $\frac{300}{1,000}$ and $\frac{30}{100}$ to $\frac{3}{10}$. However, a natural and easy way to understand this is in terms of place value: 0.300 means $\frac{3}{10} + \frac{0}{100} + \frac{0}{1,000}$. Adding the three fractions gives $\frac{3}{10} + 0 + 0 = \frac{3}{10}$; so 0.300 = 0.3, and similarly 0.30 = 0.3.

Charts such as this one may be used to explain place value to fifth graders.

hundreds	tens	ones		tenths	hundredths	thousandths
100s	10s	1s		$\frac{1}{10}$s	$\frac{1}{100}$s	$\frac{1}{1,000}$s
1	2	3	.	4	5	6

This chart displays the meaning of the number 123.456 as

$$123.456 = 100 + 20 + 3 + \frac{4}{10} + \frac{5}{100} + \frac{6}{1,000}$$

Many students can recognize directly that $0.456 = \frac{456}{1,000}$, and therefore $123.456 = 123\frac{456}{1,000}$. This immediate recognition should be encouraged. However, it is also important that teachers emphasize the actual meaning of decimal numbers in terms of place value. Exactly why does 0.456 equal $\frac{456}{1,000}$? By definition, $0.456 = \frac{4}{10} + \frac{5}{100} + \frac{6}{1,000}$. The sum may be computed using the common denominator 1,000.

$$\frac{4}{10} + \frac{5}{100} + \frac{6}{1,000} = \frac{400}{1,000} + \frac{50}{1,000} + \frac{6}{1,000} = \frac{456}{1,000}$$

Decimals and Number Lines

The base ten structure of the decimal system makes it easy to compare decimal numbers. The method is the same as for comparing whole numbers. (See the subsection, "The Base Ten System and Place Value," on pp. 427–428.)

As in the case of whole numbers, to compare two decimal numerals, read the digits in each from left to right. The first placeholder where the digits are different determines which number is larger. As an example, consider the decimal numbers 456.769 and 456.796. Which one is larger? The 4 in the hundreds place is the same for both numbers, as is the 5 in the tens place and the 6 in the ones place. Continuing to read from left to right, the digit 7 in the tenths column is the same, but in the hundredths place there is a 6 for the first number and a 9 for the second number. Since 6 < 9, 456.769 < 456.796. Observe that the digits in the thousandths place play no role whatsoever in determining which of these two numbers is larger. The same technique described here is used to compare and order all decimal numbers.

Representing decimals on a number line strengthens students' commonsense understanding of numbers, sometimes referred to as "number sense." One approach to teaching number lines with decimal numerals is to ask students to imagine magnifying portions of number lines. To illustrate, let's start with a portion of a number line for whole numbers:

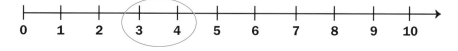

III. Fractions and Decimals

Teaching Idea

To reinforce the connection between the whole numbers on a number line and the decimal numbers between them, divide the section between 2 whole numbers with 10 small tick marks. Compare this section to a centimeter ruler, where there are also 10 units between measurements. This demonstration may help students gain a better understanding of decimal numbers on a number line.

In order to represent decimal numbers between 3 and 4, imagine magnifying, or "zooming in" on the encircled portion of the number line above, and marking off intervals of length 0.1 with tick marks.

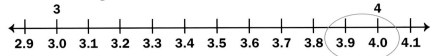

We can zoom in again. For example, a magnification of the interval between 3.9 and 4 looks like this:

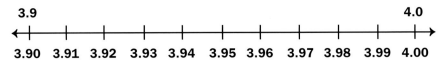

In these displays we have used the relationships 3 = 3.0, 4 = 4.0 = 4.00, and 3.9 = 3.90. Displaying numbers with three or more placeholders to the right of the decimal point may be done in a similar way.

Rounding Decimals

Lessons on rounding whole numbers should be given well in advance of explanations of rounding decimal numbers to place values to the right of the decimal point. Students benefit from learning rounding in stages.

Rounding decimal numbers to the nearest 10, 100, 1,000, etc. is done the same way as rounding whole numbers to the nearest 10, 100, 1,000, etc. (See "Rounding Whole Numbers," on pp. 432–433.) The decimal portion of the numeral plays no role in the process or in the final answer. Here are some examples:

34.899 rounded to the nearest ten is 30

5,658.456 rounded to the nearest hundred is 5,700

Rounding a decimal number to the nearest tenth means finding the whole number multiple of 0.1 that is closest to the number. The whole number multiples of 0.1 are: 0, 0.1, 0.2, 0.3, 0.4, 0.5, 0.6, 0.7, 0.8, 0.9, 1.0, 1.1, 1.2, 1.3, and so on. The list of the whole number multiples of 0.1 may be found by "counting by 0.1s," that is, by counting by tenths. Any number with at most one placeholder to the right of the decimal point is a whole number multiple of 0.1.

As an example, let's round 3.671 to the nearest tenth. The first step is to find the whole number multiples of 0.1 that are closest to 3.671. The number 3.671 lies between 3.6 and 3.7. Students can see from the number line that the correct answer to the problem is 3.7 because 3.671 is closer to 3.7 than to 3.6 (or any other whole number multiple of 0.1).

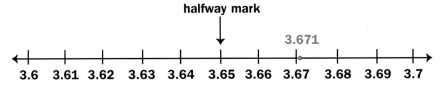

As with the previous cases, a number falling exactly halfway between two whole number multiples of 0.1 is rounded up. For example, 3.65 rounded to the nearest tenth is 3.7. The ideas for rounding to the nearest one (that is, the nearest whole number) and for rounding to the nearest hundredth or thousandth are the same. The rule for rounding whole numbers applies to decimals.

Rule for Rounding (decimals)

Step 1. Circle the digit in the place you want to round to.

9 ⑦ . 5 3
↑
ones place

Step 2. Underline the digit just to the right of the circled digit.

9 ⑦ . 5̲ 3
↑
digit to the right

Step 3. If the underlined digit is 5 or greater than 5, increase the circled digit by one. If the underlined digit is 4 or less than 4, do not change the circled digit. Change all digits to the right of the circled digit to zeros. If the digits to the right of the circled number are also to the right of the decimal point, they are deleted.

97.53 rounded to the nearest whole number is 98

Here are some other examples:

0.547 rounded to the nearest tenth is 0.5

3.5 rounded to the nearest one is 4

0.004 rounded to the nearest hundredth is 0.00

39.699 rounded to the nearest hundredth is 39.70

Adding and Subtracting Decimals

In Grade 4, students in Core Knowledge schools should have learned to add and subtract decimal numbers with two placeholders to the right of the decimal point. Hence, most fifth graders will have little or no difficulty with the procedures for adding or subtracting decimal numbers but may benefit from a review.

To add or subtract decimal numbers, align the decimal points vertically, add or subtract the numbers as if they were whole numbers, and bring down the decimal point. For example, to calculate the sum 4.5693 + 2.7961, apply the addition algorithm in the same way as to 45,693 + 27,961, except bring the decimal down vertically in the sum.

$$
\begin{array}{r}
{\scriptstyle 1\ 1\ 1} \\
4.5693 \\
+\ 2.7961 \\
\hline
7.3654
\end{array}
$$

To help students understand what the addition algorithm is really doing, point out that you could start by writing the addends in expanded form. Here is one way to do this:

4.56 = 4 ones + 5 tenths + 6 hundredths

2.78 = 2 ones + 7 tenths + 8 hundredths

To find the sum, add hundredths, then tenths, and finally ones.

$$
\begin{array}{r}
4 \text{ ones} + 5 \text{ tenths} + 6 \text{ hundredths} \\
+\ 2 \text{ ones} + 7 \text{ tenths} + 8 \text{ hundredths} \\
\hline
6 \text{ ones} + 12 \text{ tenths} + 14 \text{ hundredths}
\end{array}
$$

III. Fractions and Decimals

Teaching Idea

The use of money amounts to review the addition and subtraction algorithms for decimals gives students a concrete understanding of tenths and hundredths placeholders. However, identifying decimals with money amounts does not work well for numbers with three or more placeholders to the right of the decimal. Teachers should encourage students to understand the addition and subtraction algorithms not only in terms of money amounts, but also directly in terms of the base 10 system.

The next step is the regrouping step. At this point, identifying the placeholders with money amounts can illuminate regrouping for students who need extra help. Identify ones with dollars, so that 1 refers to one dollar. Then one-tenth means $\frac{1}{10}$ of a dollar, or one dime. Students can regroup 12 tenths as 1 dollar and 2 tenths, or dimes. Similarly, one-hundredth means $\frac{1}{100}$ of a dollar, or one penny, which can be regrouped as one dime and four pennies. Subtraction problems can be explained in the same way.

It is often helpful to use estimation to check the reasonableness of an answer. If we estimate before we perform calculations, we can tell if our calculations are reasonable. Rounding numbers helps to make the estimation easier, and in some cases, the estimation may be done mentally. For example, in the example above, we could round both numbers to the nearest whole number. The numbers 4.5693 and 2.7961 round to 5 and 3, respectively. We can add these numbers mentally and get 8. We know that the sum should be about 8. The exact sum (7.3654) is close to 8, so we know our exact answer is reasonable.

Using the addition and subtraction algorithms for decimal numbers requires greater understanding of the base ten system than was required for whole numbers. For example, consider the subtraction problem $7.6 - 4.39 = ?$ Students may try to calculate the difference by writing this:

$$\begin{array}{r} 7.6 \\ -\ 4.39 \\ \hline \end{array}$$

At this point, they may be stumped, or worse; some students might simply bring down the 9 in the hundredths column and then proceed to subtract the remaining underlined digits from those on top. To use the subtraction algorithm correctly for this example, students must first recognize that $7.6 = 7.60$. The problem can then be completed, using regrouping, in this way:

$$\begin{array}{r} ^{5\ 1} \\ 7.\!\!\not{6}0 \\ -\ 4.39 \\ \hline 3.21 \end{array}$$

Multiplying Decimals

Multiplication of decimals is a new topic for fifth graders. Students need a thorough understanding of multiplication of whole numbers before they can successfully learn to multiply decimal numbers.

In Grade 4, students should have learned how to mentally multiply numbers by 10 by adding a 0. The same idea can be used to demonstrate multiplying a decimal number by 10.

$$10 \times 3.169 = 31.69$$

move the decimal point

one place to the right

This rule applies even to multiplication of whole numbers by 10. Beginning fifth graders should already know that multiplication of a whole number by 10 is accomplished by writing a 0 to the right of the digits in the other whole number

factor. This is a consequence of the rule for multiplying decimal numbers. For example, we may think of 10 × 31 as 10 × 31.00 because 31 = 31.00. To multiply 31 by 10, move the decimal in 31.00 one digit to the right to get 310.0, that is, 310.

The rules for multiplying by 100 and by 1,000 follow from the rule for 10. Since 100 = 10 × 10, to multiply a number by 100, multiply it by 10 two times. The result is that the decimal point in the number is moved two places to the right. Similarly, since 1,000 = 10 × 10 × 10, to multiply a number by 1,000, move the decimal point three placeholders to the right.

The multiplication algorithm for decimals is almost the same as the multiplication algorithm for whole numbers. Our purpose here is to explain the procedure for multiplying decimal numbers in terms of the procedure for whole numbers. We start with a description of the procedure by way of an example, 4.06 × 27.3 = 110.838:

$$
\begin{array}{r}
\overset{1}{} \\
\overset{4}{} \\
\overset{1}{4}.0\,6 \\
\times \quad 2\,7.3 \\
\hline
1\,2\,1\,8 \\
2\,8\,4\,2\,0 \\
+\ 8\,1\,2\,0\,0 \\
\hline
1\,1\,0.8\,3\,8 \\
\end{array}
$$

↑

place the decimal point

3 digits from the right

The calculation displayed here is identical to the calculation for 406 × 273 = 110,838, except for the presence of the decimal points. The final step in the calculation for 4.06 × 27.3 is the placement of the decimal point among the digits of the product. The rule is to first count the number of digits to the right of the decimal point in the two factors, 27.3 and 4.06 (one for 27.3 and two for 4.06), add those numbers (1 + 2 = 3), and then count that many places (3 places) to the left from the last digit on the right, and place the decimal there. The product is 110.838.

To see that the rule for the decimal point of the product is correct, calculate the product 4.06 × 27.3 this way:

$$(4.06) \times (27.3) = \left(406 \times \left(\frac{1}{100}\right)\right) \times \left(273 \times \left(\frac{1}{10}\right)\right) = 406 \times 273 \times \frac{1}{1,000}$$

This example illustrates a general rule. To multiply decimal numbers, first apply the standard multiplication algorithm for whole numbers, as if the factors were whole numbers. Then count the number of digits to the right of the decimal point in each of the factors and find the total number of digits to the right for all factors. Finally, count from the far right digit of the product that many places to the left. Place the decimal point there.

As with any calculation, it is a good idea to estimate an answer before performing the calculation. In the previous example, we could round 4.06 to 4 and 27.3 to 30 and then multiply mentally to find that our answer should be about 120. This is extremely valuable when checking to see if the decimal point in the calculation is located correctly, and it can also help students gain a conceptual understanding of the algorithm.

Dividing Decimals

The division algorithm for whole numbers is discussed in detail in the subsection "Dividing Whole Numbers." (See pp. 491–493.) In this subsection, we focus on how the division procedure for decimal numbers is related to the standard division algorithm for whole numbers.

The long division algorithm for decimals is almost the same as the division algorithm for whole numbers. When the divisor is a whole number, the division procedure is carried out exactly as in the case of whole numbers, but with the decimal point for the quotient placed directly above the decimal point of the dividend, as shown below in the calculation for 9.36 ÷ 4.

For a whole number divisor, place the decimal point for the quotient directly above the decimal point for the divisor.

$$4 \overline{)\ 9.36} \quad \rightarrow \quad 2.34$$

Why is this rule for the decimal point of the quotient correct? Calculate the quotient 9.36 ÷ 4 this way:

$$9.36 \div 4 = (936 \div 100) \div 4 = \frac{936}{100} \div 4 = \frac{936}{100} \times \frac{1}{4} = \frac{936}{4 \times 100} = \frac{936}{4} \times \frac{1}{100}$$

This calculation shows us that

$$9.36 \div 4 = \frac{936}{4} \div 100 = (936 \div 4) \div 100$$

In words, we may first perform the whole number calculation 936 ÷ 4. Then to divide by 100, we can move the decimal point for the quotient two places to the left. This is what the rule for the decimal point accomplishes for us in the long division algorithm for decimals when the divisor is a whole number.

How does the long division algorithm work when both the dividend and the divisor are decimal numbers? To illustrate the procedure, consider the problem 52.93 ÷ 6.7. The procedure is to move the decimal point in the dividend, in this case 52.93, and in the divisor, in this case 6.7, the same number of places, so that the new divisor is a whole number.

$$6.7\, \overline{)52.93}$$

For this problem, we move the decimal point one place to the right so that the resulting division problem is 529.3 ÷ 67. The decimal is moved one place to the right in order to change the divisor, 6.7, to a whole number, 67. The answer, i.e., the quotient, to both division problems is the same. The calculation is to find

$$67 \overline{)529.3}$$

You can see that the decimal point movement is correct by demonstrating this step with fractions:

$$\frac{52.93}{6.7} = \frac{52.93}{6.7} \times \left(\frac{10}{10}\right) = \frac{529.3}{67}$$

The procedure for dividing a decimal number by a whole number and the reasons for the procedure are described above.

The calculation for 529.3 ÷ 67 (which equals 52.93 ÷ 6.7) proceeds this way:

```
         7.9
67 )5 2 9.3
    4 6 9
      6 0 3
      6 0 3
            0
```

This calculation tells us that 529.3 ÷ 67 = 52.93 ÷ 6.7 = 7.9.

Once again, it is a good idea to estimate the answer before performing the calculations. In this problem, we could round the divisor 6.7 to 7 and round 52.93 to 53. We know that 53 divided by 7 is more than 7 but less than 8, so our answer of 7.9 seems reasonable.

This problem is unusual because the actual quotient is a finite decimal. A typical decimal division problem can continue indefinitely. For example, the calculation for 579.3 ÷ 67 proceeds this way:

```
        8.646
67 )579.300
    536
     433
     402
       310
       268
         420
         402
          18
```

If this calculation were continued we would get 8.6462686567164179 . . . , and eventually we would see that a large block of digits in the decimal repeats over and over again without end, since there are only as many possible remainders as the size of the divisor. That is, continuing the computation above, the shortest repeating block must be no longer than 66 digits since 0 to 66 are the only possible remainders. If, after we start "bringing down zeros," we ever hit a remainder of 0, the quotient terminates. If not, there are only 66 different remainders possible, so in 67 steps (and maybe long before) there must be a repetition. That repetition completely determines the repeating block of the corresponding digits in the quotient forever after. It is a fact that the quotient of two decimal numbers (including whole numbers) is a decimal number that has a repeating block of digits in its decimal.

To indicate what part of a remainder repeats, draw a bar above the digit(s) that repeat. For example,

$$\frac{1}{3} = .\overline{3}$$

The Big Idea in Review

Fractions and decimals can be written, compared, added, subtracted, multiplied, and divided.

Review

Below are some ideas for ongoing assessment and review activities. These are not meant to constitute a comprehensive list.

• Provide students with opportunities to practice recognizing fractions and decimals in a classroom math center for use throughout the year. Make sure you include fractions to one-twelfth and decimals including tenths, hundredths, thousandths, and ten-thousandths. You may want to have students create flash cards with a fraction on one side and the decimal on the other. Also, students could put the fraction on one side and draw a picture representing it on the other side. Have students quiz each other.

• Have students fold paper to construct fractional parts. Review how to fold pieces of construction paper to show equal halves, thirds, fourths, and sixths. Then pair students. Have each student fold a piece of paper to practice fractional equivalency. Give students sheets of paper of the same size. Have one student fold a sheet into $\frac{1}{2}$ or $\frac{2}{4}$ and the other student fold a sheet into $\frac{3}{6}$ to explore equivalent fractions. Have them try to fold other equivalent fractions as well.

• Make a concentration game for the class using equivalent fractions and decimal equivalents for halves, quarters, eighths, and tenths. Make a set of cards that has fraction and decimal equivalents in the deck. Place all cards on a pocket chart and have students request that two cards be turned over at a time. If the cards are equivalent, the student identifies them and keeps the two cards. The student with the most cards at the end wins.

• Have students practice writing fractions by rolling dice. Divide students into groups of two and give each group a pair of dice. Then instruct them to roll the dice and write a fraction representing what they rolled. Students will need to practice writing proper fractions by putting the smaller number as the numerator and the larger number as the denominator, and practice writing improper fractions by doing the opposite. Students should practice reading the fractions to their partner. You may also wish to invite students to illustrate at least some of the fractions, to simplify the fractions, or to compare the fractions generated by two rolls of the dice.

• Since Grade 5 is a critical grade for students to become comfortable with fractions, provide a fraction or decimal problem daily. At the beginning of class, have a problem posted on the board or in a box. Give the class a chance to solve the problem and then review it as a class. Start this at the beginning of the year and continue as you cover new fraction and decimal concepts.

More Resources

A good mathematics program follows sound cognitive principles and allows many opportunities for thoughtful and varied practice to build mastery of important skills. For advice on suitable mathematics programs, contact the Foundation.

The titles listed below are offered as a representative sample of materials and not a complete list of everything that is available.

For students —

• *Everything You Need to Know About Math Homework,* by Anne Zeman and Kate Kelly (Scholastic, 1994). A clear guide for students in Grades 4–6 that covers numbers and the number system, basic math functions, measurement, geometry, money, graphs, statistics, and computers. Paperback, ISBN 0590493590.

• *Fractions and Decimals (Math Success),* by Lucille Caron and Philip M. St. Jacques (Enslow, 2000). Library binding, 64 pages, ISBN 0766014304.

• *How Math Works,* by Carol Vonderman (Reader's Digest, 1996). Hardcover, 192 pages, ISBN 0895778505.

• *Janice VanCleave's Math for Every Kid,* by Janice VanCleave (John Wiley & Sons, 1991). Paperback, 224 pages, ISBN 0471542652.

For teachers —

• *Key to Fractions (Keys to Math),* by Steve Rasmussen (Key Curriculum Press, 1980). Self-paced, self-guided workbooks described by one reviewer as "very motivational for kids burned out on textbooks" (Love to Learn, www.lovetolearn.net). Set of four paperbacks, available individually or as a set from Key Curriculum Press, www.keypress.com, or 1-800-995-MATH. Answer keys and notes, as well as reproducible tests, are also available. See also *Key to Decimals,* by the same publisher.

• *Math The Easy Way (Fourth Edition),* by Anthony and Katie Prindle (Barron's, 2003). A simply written book that can be used as a refresher course or as extra practice for students. Paperback, 234 pages, ISBN 0764120115.

• *Usborne Illustrated Dictionary of Math,* by Tori Large and others (Usborne, 2004). Paperback, 128 pages, ISBN 0794506623.

• Figure This!, www.figurethis.org, provides math challenges designed for middle school students.

The Big Idea

Learning multiplication and division algorithms and properties is essential for computation and problem solving.

What Students Should Already Know

Students in Core Knowledge schools should be familiar with

Kindergarten

- adding and subtracting to ten, using concrete objects
- recognizing the meaning of the plus sign (+)
- subtraction: the concept of "taking away"; recognizing the meaning of the minus sign (−)

Grade 1

- knowing what a "sum" and a "difference" are
- knowing addition facts to 10 + 10 and corresponding subtraction facts (untimed mastery)
- adding in any order and knowing that when you add three numbers, you get the same sum regardless of grouping of addends
- knowing what happens when you add zero
- writing addition and subtraction problems horizontally and vertically
- solving two-digit addition and subtraction problems with and without regrouping, and mentally subtracting 10 from a two-digit number
- writing an addition or subtraction equation to solve basic one-step story and picture problems in the form of ___ − 2 = 7; 5 + ___ = 7.

Grade 2

- achieving timed mastery of addition facts (2 seconds) and mastering subtraction facts
- knowing how to check a sum by changing the order of addends
- knowing addition and subtraction "fact families"
- estimating the sum and the difference
- solving two-digit and three-digit addition and subtraction problems with and without regrouping; adding three two-digit numbers
- practicing doubling (adding a number to itself)
- understanding addition and subtraction as inverse operations; using addition to check subtraction
- recognizing the "times" sign (×) and knowing what "factor" and "product" mean
- understanding that you can multiply numbers in any order
- multiplication facts: knowing the product of any single-digit number × 1, 2, 3, 4, and 5; and knowing what happens when you multiply by 1, by 0, and by 10

What Students Should Already Know continued

- solving simple word problems and equations with addition, subtraction, or multiplication

Grade 3

- mentally estimating sums and differences, and estimating products
- using mental computation strategies
- addition and subtraction with and without regrouping: finding the sum (up to 10,000) of any two whole numbers and finding the difference given two whole numbers of 10,000 or less
- mastering basic multiplication facts to 10×10 and mentally multiplying by 10, 100, and 1,000
- multiplying two whole numbers, with and without regrouping, in which one factor is 9 or less and the other is a multi-digit number up to three digits
- writing numbers in expanded form using multiplication, for example: $9{,}278 = (9 \times 1{,}000) + (2 \times 100) + (7 \times 10) + 8$
- solving two-step word problems and solving word problems involving multiplication
- knowing basic division facts to $100 \div 10$ and the meaning of *dividend, divisor,* and *quotient*
- knowing that you cannot divide by 0 and that any number divided by 1 is equal to that number
- dividing two- and three-digit dividends by one-digit divisors; solving division problems with remainders
- understanding multiplication and division as inverse operations; checking division by multiplying (and adding remainder)
- solving equations in the form of ___ $\times$ 9 = 63; 81 $\div$ ___ = 9
- solving problems with more than one operation, as in $(43 - 32) \times (5 + 3) =$ ___
- reading and writing expressions that use parentheses to indicate order of multiple operations

Grade 4

- identifying multiples of a given number; common multiples of two given numbers
- multiplying two-digit and three-digit numbers
- using mental computation strategies for multiplication, such as breaking a problem into partial products, for example: $3 \times 27 = (3 \times 20) + (3 \times 7) = 60 + 21 = 81$
- checking multiplication by changing the order of the factors
- multiplying three factors in any given order
- identifying different ways of writing division problems: $28 \div 7$, $7\overline{)28}$, $\frac{28}{7}$

What Students Should Already Know continued

- estimating a quotient
- identifying factors of a given number; common factors of two given numbers
- dividing dividends up to four digits by one-digit and two-digit divisors
- solving problems with more than one operation, as in $(72 \div 9) \times (36 \div 4) =$ ___
- equality properties: knowing that equals added to equals are equal; equals multiplied by equals are equal
- using letters to stand for any number, as in working with a formula (for example, area of rectangle: $A = l \times w$)

What Students Need to Learn

- **Commutative, associative, and distributive properties of addition and multiplication: know the names and understand the properties**
- **Multiply two factors of up to four digits each**
- **Write numbers in expanded form using multiplication**
- **Know what it means for one number to be "divisible" by another number**
- **Estimate the quotient**
- **Know how to move the decimal point when dividing by 10, 100, or 1,000**
- **Divide dividends up to four digits by three-digit divisors**
- **Solve division problems with remainders; round a repeating decimal quotient**
- **Check division by multiplying (and adding remainder)**
- **Solve word problems with multiple steps**

What Students Will Learn in Future Grades

The *Core Knowledge Sequence* for mathematics emphasizes the importance of reviewing and building on prior knowledge. Related topics from the Grade 6 *Sequence* are listed below, and subsequent grades will continue to focus on strengthening and expanding these skills.

Grade 6

- understand addition and subtraction, and multiplication and division, as inverse operations
- add, subtract, multiply, and divide with integers, fractions, and decimals, both positive and negative
- multiply multi-digit factors, with and without a calculator
- estimate a product
- distributive property for multiplication over addition or subtraction, that is, $A \times (B + C)$ or $A \times (B - C)$: understand its use in procedures such as multi-digit multiplication

What Students Will Learn in Future Grades continued

‣ divide multi-digit dividends by up to three-digit divisors, with and without a calculator

‣ solve problems with more than one operation, according to order of operations (with and without a calculator)

Vocabulary

Student/Teacher Vocabulary

algorithm: standard mathematical procedure that shows each step in a process (T)

associative property: property that says that the grouping of addends or factors can be changed without changing the sum or product, e.g., (A + B) + C = A + (B + C) and A × (B × C) = (A × B) × C (S)

commutative property: property that says that the order of addends or factors can be changed without changing the sum or product, e.g., A + B = B + A and A × B = B × A (S)

distributive property: property that says that one of the factors of a product can be written as a sum and each addend multiplied before adding without changing the product, e.g., A × (B + C) = (A × B) + (A × C) (S)

divide: to separate into equal parts or measures (S)

dividend: the number being divided (S)

divisible: can be divided by another number without leaving a remainder, e.g., 10 is divisible by 2 (S)

divisor: the number by which another number is to be divided (S)

equation: a statement that two mathematical expressions are equal (T)

estimate: (verb) to find a number close to an exact amount (S)
        (noun) a number close to an exact amount (S)

factor: one of two or more numbers multiplied in a multiplication problem (S)

multiply: to find the product of two or more numbers (S)

polynomial: an expression with two or more terms (T)

product: the answer to a multiplication problem (S)

quotient: the answer to a division problem (S)

remainder: the number left after a division problem is complete; the remainder is always less than the divisor (S)

Domain Vocabulary

Computation and associated words:
number, strategies, partial, operations, regrouping, inverse, add, subtract, times sign, sum, difference, zero, digit, property, more, less, fewer, base ten, single-digit, multi-digit, any order property, place value, column, round, greater than, less than, placeholder, superscript, array, multiple, partition, equal shares, calculate, compute, figure, greatest common factor, greatest common divisor, operation, mental computation

IV. Computation

Materials

blocks, pp. 486, 491

grid paper, pp. 487, 492

base ten squares and strips, p. 487

counters, p. 491

flash cards with multiplication and division facts, p. 495

math journals, p. 495

estimation jar, p. 495

index cards, p. 495

daily time/materials to share multiplication and division problems, p. 495

overhead projector, markers, and overhead film, p. 495

At a Glance

The most important ideas for you are:

- Addition, subtraction, multiplication, and division facts must be mastered in order for students to successfully solve more complicated computations.
- The commutative, associative, and distributive properties make it easier to find a sum or product by allowing the order and grouping of a problem to be changed.
- Multiplication and division are inverse operations.
- Estimation can be used to find answers that are close to an exact amount and to check the outcome of problem.
- Algorithms offer students a procedure for solving more difficult problems.
- Mental computation strategies can be used to break a problem down into simpler parts.
- Multiplication and division of multi-digit numbers can be broken down into simple single-digit facts.
- Developing problem-solving skills is a critical part of students' mathematical development.
- Students should practice until they learn computation skills to the point of automaticity.

What Teachers Need to Know

Background

The Grade 5 guidelines for computation with whole numbers are focused on multiplication and division. However, some students may benefit from a review of addition and subtraction procedures for multi-digit whole numbers. These procedures are prerequisites for learning the standard procedures for multiplying and dividing numbers.

An algorithm is a step-by-step procedure for performing a calculation. The standard multiplication and division algorithms should have been introduced in Grade 3 and further developed in Grade 4. The term regrouping is used in connection with the addition, subtraction, and multiplication algorithms. In the context of addition and multiplication, regrouping is sometimes called "carrying," and in the context of subtraction, it is sometimes called "borrowing."

The standard algorithms of arithmetic are important for practical purposes and that alone is significant. Students should continue to develop speed and facility with these algorithms. Beyond knowing how to calculate, it is also important for students to understand why the arithmetic algorithms work.

This understanding will help students to avoid mistakes and increase their number sense. Understanding the "whys" behind the standard algorithms of arithmetic also lays the groundwork for mastering parts of algebra, especially addition, subtraction, multiplication, and division of polynomials and rational expressions involving polynomials.

A. Addition

Students in Core Knowledge schools should have been introduced to the concept of the commutative property of addition in previous grades, but this is the first year they are required to recognize and name the property. The commutative property says that for any two numbers A and B, it is always true that

A + B = B + A

As an example, if A is 21 and B is 53, the commutative property of addition tells you, even without calculating, that:

21 + 53 = 53 + 21

The associative property of addition says for any three numbers A, B, and C,

(A + B) + C = A + (B + C)

For example, if A = 3, B = 4, and C = 5, the associative property of addition says that:

(3 + 4) + 5 = 3 + (4 + 5)

Performing the additions in parentheses first, the associative property of addition just tells us that:

7 + 5 = 3 + 9

The associative property of addition can be used for some mental calculations. As an example, consider the addition problem:

79 + 98 = ?

A good strategy here is to take 2 away from 79 and "give the 2" to the 98. Here are the mathematical steps:

$$79 + 98 = (77 + 2) + 98$$
$$= 77 + (2 + 98)$$
$$= 77 + 100$$
$$= 177$$

The associative property of addition was used to go from the first line to the second; because of the associative property, (77 + 2) + 98 = 77 + (2 + 98).

Used together, the commutative and associative properties allow us to change the order of addends and regroup them to make an addition calculation easier or to check the correctness of a calculation. These properties are also important for understanding the principles behind arithmetic and for algebra.

Teaching Idea

Teach students to rearrange numbers in order to simplify addition. This strategy helps students perform mental calculations. Consider the following:
9 + 8 + 1 + 5 + 2 = ?
In this example, teach students to look for groups of 10. For example, 9 + 1 = 10 and 8 + 2 = 10. Students can add these sums together, finding that 10 + 10 = 20. The remaining number is 5, so the 20 and 5 are added, which equals 25. Have students practice many ways to find and make groups of 10—sometimes even with 3 numbers (for example 2, 3, and 5). Teach students to cross out the numbers as they are adding so they do not add the same numbers again. They should also practice mental computation whenever possible.

B. Multiplication

Properties of Multiplication

The commutative property of multiplication says that for any two numbers A and B, it is always true that

A x B = B x A

For example, if A = 5 and B = 7, the commutative property says that $5 \times 7 = 7 \times 5$. The commutative property of multiplication tells us that two numbers may be multiplied in either order, and the answer (the product) will be the same. This remarkable fact should be explained and not merely stated. For students to appreciate the significance of the commutative property of multiplication, it is essential that they have a clear understanding of what multiplication of whole numbers really means. For example,

7 x 5 means 5 + 5 + 5 + 5 + 5 + 5 + 5

5 x 7 means 7 + 7 + 7 + 7 + 7

In other words, 5×7 means 5 groups of 7, whereas 7×5 means 7 groups of 5. How is it possible to understand, without even adding, that the two sums above must be the same? Even without adding, the commutative property of multiplication guarantees that:

5 + 5 + 5 + 5 + 5 + 5 + 5 = 7 + 7 + 7 + 7 + 7

A concrete way to demonstrate this concept to students is to have them make or draw rows of objects to represent these numbers and verify that the product is the same. They will see that 5 rows of 7 is the same as 7 rows of 5. See the example below:

```
★ ★ ★ ★ ★ ★ ★          ★  ★  ★  ★
★ ★ ★ ★ ★ ★ ★          ★  ★  ★  ★
★ ★ ★ ★ ★ ★ ★          ★  ★  ★  ★
★ ★ ★ ★ ★ ★ ★          ★  ★  ★  ★
★ ★ ★ ★ ★ ★ ★          ★  ★  ★  ★
                       ★  ★  ★  ★
                       ★  ★  ★  ★
```

5 rows of 7 = 35   7 rows of 5 = 35

Students should use this strategy with many different numbers to prove to themselves that changing the order of factors does not change the product.

The associative property of multiplication says that for any three numbers A, B, and C,

A x (B x C) = (A x B) x C

For example if A = 2, B = 3, and C = 4, the associative property of multiplication tells us that

2 x (3 x 4) = (2 x 3) x 4

Performing the multiplications inside the parentheses first, this equation says that

2 x 12 = 6 x 4

Both sides of the equation above equal 24, demonstrating the truth of the associative property of multiplication for this example.

The commutative and associative properties for multiplication guarantee that three or more numbers may be multiplied in any order with the same result. For example, calculating $2 \times 173 \times 5$ is easy when it is done this way:

2 x 173 x 5 = 173 x (5 x 2) = 173 x 10 = 1,730

It is difficult to overstate the importance of the distributive property. In algebra, it is the principle behind adding "like terms," factoring, and multiplying polynomials. At the elementary school level, the distributive property is the standard procedure for multiplying multi-digit numbers. This property is sometimes called the distributive property of multiplication over addition. The distributive property says that for any three numbers A, B, and C,

A x (B + C) = (A x B) + (A x C)

For example, if A = 3, B = 2, and C = 5, the distributive property of multiplication says

3 x (2 + 5) = (3 x 2) + (3 x 5)

Remember, the order of operations rule tells you that on the right side of the equation, the multiplications must be performed before the addition. (The order of operation rule is discussed in the subsection "Parentheses and Order of Operations," on pp. 436–437.) Performing these multiplications along with the addition inside the parentheses on the left side gives

3 x 7 = 6 + 15

21 = 21

Pictures such as the ones below can help to illustrate why the distributive property is true for the case of whole numbers:

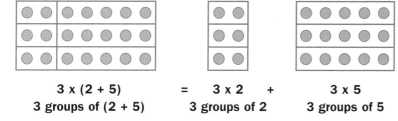

3 x (2 + 5)	**= 3 x 2 +**	**3 x 5**
3 groups of (2 + 5)	**3 groups of 2**	**3 groups of 5**

Reviewing Basic Skills for Multiplication

It is essential that students memorize the single-digit multiplication tables before they tackle more advanced topics in multiplication. Drilling students who need the practice with the multiplication tables is time well spent.

You may also wish to review the meaning of multiplication. Multiplication by whole numbers other than 1 is just shorthand notation for repeated addition. For example,

3 x 4 means 4 + 4 + 4

Think of 3 groups of 4 objects. Notice that the meaning of 4×3 is $3 + 3 + 3 + 3$, and this is different from the meaning of 3×4, even though the result is the same.

A concrete way to represent multiplication to students is to create an array, or rectangle, that shows numbers being multiplied. Using the example above, create a rectangle that has 3 rows of 4 squares each. The array would look like this:

3 x 4

Students can draw or make their own arrays using blocks or other objects. If you turn the rectangular array 90°, you can also show students that the rectangle now has 4 rows of 3 squares each. This can be linked to the discussions of the commutative property of multiplication. (See pp. 484–485.)

Multiplication can be thought of as repeated addition even for larger numbers. However, larger numbers demonstrate how much easier it is to multiply instead of add. Think of 5 groups of 72 objects.

5 x 72 means 72 + 72 + 72 + 72 + 72

A good way to review multiplication with students is to pose a problem, such as this one:

Five students each brought two books to return to the library. How many books will be returned to the library?

Ask students to think of a way to solve the problem, and give them manipulatives to use. Many students will probably use repeated addition to find a solution, by adding

2 + 2 + 2 + 2 + 2 = 10

Encourage students to record their strategy on paper. Then show them how you can change the addition problem to a multiplication problem:

5 x 2 = 10

Multiplication by 10 deserves special attention and can be explained in terms of place value and the base ten structure of numbers. Multiplication by 10 is accomplished by writing a 0 to the right of the other whole number factor. For example, the product of 3×10 is 3 followed by a 0, i.e., 30. Another way of saying this is that $3 \times 10 = 10 + 10 + 10$.

What about multiplying a two-digit number, or an even larger number by 10? The same rule applies: a whole number of tens (except 0) is always the digits of that whole number followed by a 0.

The rules for multiplying by 100 or 1,000 follow from the rule for multiplying by 10. This is because

100 = 10 x 10

1,000 = 10 x 10 x 10

Multiplying a number by 100 is the same as multiplying the number by two factors of 10. Therefore, multiplying a whole number by 100 is accomplished by writing the number followed by two zeros. Multiplying a number by 1,000 is the same as multiplying the number by three factors of 10. Therefore, multiplying a whole number by 1,000 is accomplished by writing the number followed by three zeros.

Teaching Idea

Be sure to go beyond "knowing the rule," and ensure that students understand why multiplication by 10s and 100s is unique (and easy).

Multiplying Whole Numbers

There are two important topics for the multiplication algorithm: teaching correct procedures, and explaining why those procedures work. To help students review and gain a conceptual understanding of multiplication with a multi-digit number, try this activity that builds on the multiplication array used earlier to demonstrate single-digit multiplication. Using base ten grid paper, first review single-digit multiplication by drawing a rectangle on the grid paper that is 3 ones (single squares) by 4 ones. Ask students how many "ones" are inside the rectangle (12). Now draw a larger rectangle that is 3 ones by 4 tens (ten squares). Ask students how many tens are in the rectangle. Students can shade in units of ten squares to find that there are 12 tens in the rectangle. By using their knowledge of place value, students can change 12 tens to 1 hundred and 2 tens, or 120. This number can be confirmed by counting the single squares in the rectangle.

Allow students to repeat this exercise several times with rectangles of different sizes. Instead of using grid paper, you could provide rectangles made on poster board or other large paper and have students fill them with physical base ten squares and strips. These approaches will allow students to gain a conceptual understanding of multiplication before you review the algorithm.

Writing numbers in expanded form also helps to explain why the multiplication algorithm works. For example, we know that 530,927 in expanded form looks like this:

530,927 = 500,000 + 30,000 + 900 + 20 + 7

A more explicit version of expanded form makes use of multiplication:

530,927 = (5 x 100,000) + (3 x 10,000) + (0 x 1,000)
+ (9 x 100) + (2 x 10) + 7

This expression uses multiplication to emphasize that 530,927 means 5 groups of 100,000; 3 groups of 10,000; 0 groups of 1,000; 9 groups of 100; 2 groups of 10; and 7 ones.

Prior to multiplying two-digit numbers, review the multiplication algorithm when one factor is 9 or less. When reviewing the multiplication algorithm, it makes sense to begin with an example that does not involve regrouping.

$$\begin{array}{r} 23 \\ \times\ 3 \\ \hline 69 \end{array}$$

This calculation, using the multiplication algorithm, is carried out in two steps: $3 \times 3 = 9$ for the ones column, and $3 \times 2 = 6$ for the tens column. The multiplication algorithm reduces a problem involving large numbers to a series of single-digit multiplications using place value. When explaining the algorithm to students, you may wish to emphasize that multiplication with multi-digit numbers is simply a series of single-digit multiplication facts.

That example did not require regrouping, but most multi-digit multiplication problems do. Consider the problem 3×27. It is important that students see how the distributive property is used in this example, and how it can often help us find products mentally. For example, to find the product of 3 and 27, we know that $3 \times 27 = 3 \times (20 + 7)$. We can apply the distributive property directly to the right side of this equation.

$$3 \times (20 + 7) = 3 \times 20 + 3 \times 7$$
$$= 60 + 21$$
$$= 81$$

It is valuable for fifth graders to realize that the standard multiplication algorithm (this means the standard procedure for multiplying numbers) uses the same ideas. The standard procedure for multiplying whole numbers is fundamentally based on the distributive property and base ten structure of numbers.

Fourth graders in Core Knowledge schools should have learned the multiplication algorithm for the product of two-digit and three-digit numbers. Fifth graders extend the algorithm for two factors of up to four digits.

You may wish to review the steps of calculating products of two-digit numbers. As an example, consider 63×27, which, due to the commutative property of multiplication, is the same as 27×63. Using the distributive property, start the calculation this way:

$$27 \times 63 = 27 \times (60 + 3) = (27 \times 60) + (27 \times 3)$$

In other words, 27 groups of 63 items is the same amount as 27 groups of 60 items plus 27 groups of 3 items. That is essentially what the distributive property tells you here. The calculation on the right side of the equation above may be carried out this way:

```
  ²27          ⁴27            ¹81
  x  3         x 60        + 1,620
  ────         ─────        ───────
    81         1,620          1,701
```

The standard form of the multiplication algorithm combines all of the calculations above, but in a more compact form:

```
      ⁴
     ²27
   x  63
   ──────
      81
 + 1,620
 ───────
   1,701
```

The multiplication algorithm is really just an efficient way to apply the distributive property to calculate products of multi-digit numbers. Students have a straightforward way to check multiplication calculations, like this one, by using the commutative property of multiplication.

Since $63 \times 27 = 27 \times 63$, we can compute the product as above or this way:

```
     ²63
   x  27
   ──────
     441
 + 1,260
 ───────
   1,701
```

Teaching Idea

If students experience difficulty aligning the numbers when using the multiplication algorithm, have them multiply on grid paper, writing 1 digit in each small square.

The answers are the same for the two calculations (as they must be by the commutative property of multiplication), but the intermediary steps are different. For this reason, multiplying numbers in the opposite order can help students catch mistakes. Checking multiplication by changing the order of the factors is an important strategy to teach students.

Here is a sample calculation for the product of two three-digit numbers.

```
        1
        4
        1
      406
    x 273
      1218        (3 x 406) ⟵
  + 28420        (70 x 406) ⟵
    81200      (200 x 406) ⟵
   110838
```

The product may be read off from the bottom row: 110,838.

This calculation may be understood in terms of the distributive property in this way:

**273 x 406 = (200 + 70 + 3) x 406 =
(200 x 406) + (70 x 406) + (3 x 406)**

Calculations for products of four-digit numbers using the multiplication algorithm are similar, and follow as above from the distributive property and the base ten structure of the number system.

Estimating Products

To check the reasonableness of a product, it is helpful to estimate the product before calculating the exact product. We can estimate the product by rounding one or more of the factors before multiplying. For example, to estimate the product for 6×384, students can round 384 to the nearest hundred and then multiply by 6. The estimation is then 6×400. Students should calculate products like this mentally. They can calculate the product this way:

6 x 400 = 6 x 4 x 100 = 24 x 100 = 2,400

Notice that the estimate of 2,400 must be larger than the exact product because 384 was rounded up before the calculation.

An alternative version of this problem is to ask students to estimate the cost of 6 items if each one costs $3.84. After rounding to the nearest dollar, the estimated cost is given by $6 \times \$4.00$. To help students calculate this mentally, describe this problem verbally as 6×4 dollars, which is easily seen to be 24 dollars and is written as $24.00.

When both factors are multi-digit numbers, it is often appropriate to round each of them. For example, to estimate 23×361, you can round 23 to the nearest ten, and 361 to the nearest hundred. The estimation is then 20×400, which can be computed as $2 \times 4 \times 10 \times 100 = 8,000$.

For another example, to estimate 273×406, we could round 273 to 300 and 406 to 400 and then multiply mentally to find that our answer should be about 120,000. Although 406 is rounded down to 400, it is so much closer than the rounding of 273 up to 300 that the result is assured to be an estimate that is greater than the actual product.

Teaching Idea

If your mathematics program doesn't teach multiplication in this manner, you may want to supplement your program with the models and activities provided here. Multiple strategies and lots of practice are the key to deepening student understanding of multiplication.

Teaching Idea

As you teach students to estimate the product, be sure to break this into small steps. First have them break down the problems as a class, one step at a time, discussing the steps along the way. Once students become familiar with these steps, they can try them on their own. The goal is to structure learning so that they understand *why* they are following certain steps, not simply following the steps without understanding what they are doing. Ask students to tell you how and why they reached the results.

Word Problems with Multiplication

There is a huge variety of word problems that involve multiplication in one or more steps for the problem. Fifth graders need practice with word problems. Consider this example:

There are 39 bags of cement on a truck. If each one weighs 124 pounds, how much do they all weigh?

To solve this problem, multiply 39 bags times 124 pounds per bag to find a total weight of 4836 pounds.

Further discussion of word problems is given below in the subsection "Solving Problems and Equations," on p. 494.

C. Division

Long division is the most challenging of the four arithmetic algorithms. The division algorithm incorporates the multiplication and subtraction algorithms as part of its own computational process. Division also relies heavily on number sense and estimation skills.

The division algorithm is not just a computational method; it is also an important tool for understanding concepts. It reappears in middle school and plays a critical role in explanations of rational and irrational numbers at that level. Essentially the same algorithm is used in algebra to divide polynomials, and later in calculus to divide "power series."

Relating Multiplication and Division

What does division mean? Division can mean dividing something into equal measures or partitioning something into equal shares. Division should be understood directly in terms of multiplication; division is the inverse operation for multiplication in the following sense:

A ÷ B = C means A = B x C

For example,

12 ÷ 4 = 3 means 12 = 4 x 3

Just as addition and subtraction are inverse, or opposite, operations, so too are multiplication and division inverse operations. To solve the problem $72 \div 8 = ?$, students should identify it with $? \times 8 = 72$, or 8 times what number equals 72? The answer to the multiplication problem is the answer to the division problem.

As part of the review of division topics, remind students of the special status of the number 0. The number 0 cannot be a factor of any number because it is impossible to divide by 0. Students might ask why division by 0 is never allowed. This is a good question, and it is valuable for you to understand the answer. As an example, think about what $5 \div 0$ means. Remember, from the meaning of division given at the beginning of this subsection:

5 ÷ 0 = C means 5 = 0 x C

A ÷ B = C means A = B x C

$0 \times C = 0$ no matter what number C is. Therefore, $0 \times C$ cannot be 5. This means that there is no possible answer for $5 \div 0$. This same argument shows that no nonzero number can be divided by 0. Another way to think of this is that in

its most elemental form, multiplication is repeated addition. How many zeros does it take to make some nonzero number? Since repeated addition of zeros is always just 0, there is no answer. Therefore, dividing a nonzero number by 0 has no answer that could be checked by multiplication. You can even demonstrate this concept to students by using manipulatives such as blocks. Ask students to divide 3 blocks into 0 groups. They will quickly realize that you cannot divide 3 blocks into 0 groups.

It is also true that not even 0 itself can be divided by 0, but the explanation is a little more subtle. The reason that $0 \div 0$ makes no sense is because you could say the answer is any number, and the definition would be satisfied. For example, we could say that $0 \div 0 = 17$ because $0 = 0 \times 17$. We could just as well say that $0 \div 0 = 582$ because $0 = 0 \times 582$. Any number C satisfies the definition for $0 \div 0$:

$$0 \div 0 = C \text{ means } 0 = 0 \times C$$
$$A \div B = C \text{ means } A = B \times C$$

Since there is no single possible correct answer for $0 \div 0$, this operation is excluded from arithmetic and from all of mathematics. Division by 0 is never possible.

Dividing by 0 is never allowed, but dividing 0 by different numbers is allowed and the answer is always 0. For example, $0 \div 5 = 0$, because $0 = 0 \times 5$. The number 0 cannot be the divisor, but it can be the dividend and the quotient.

Dividing Whole Numbers

Fifth graders in Core Knowledge schools should be able to calculate quotients for four-digit dividends and two-digit divisors. However, students will benefit from a review and clear explanation of those procedures.

Calculators cannot substitute for mastery of long division. Before attempting to learn the long division algorithm, it is imperative that students memorize the multiplication tables and the corresponding division facts.

Just as multiplication of whole numbers is really repeated addition, division may be understood as repeated subtraction. For example, $12 \div 4 = 3$ means $12 = 4 \times 3$, but we can also interpret $12 \div 4$ as the number of times that 4 can be subtracted from 12. How many times can this be done until we reach 0? Subtracting once gives 8, subtracting 4 again gives 4, and then subtracting 4 once more gives 0. If you successively subtract 4 three times, starting with 12, you finally arrive at 0. So, $12 \div 4 = 3$. You can take 4 objects away from 12 objects three times before you run out of objects. To demonstrate this concretely to students, give each student 12 counters and have them divide the counters into groups of 4. They can take away a group of 4 three times before running out of objects.

Students in Core Knowledge schools should already have experience performing division calculations for quotients and remainders by using this box symbol: $\overline{)}$ instead of $\div$. To calculate 13 divided by 4, they learn to write

$$
\begin{array}{r}
3 \\
4\overline{)13} \\
\underline{12} \\
1
\end{array}
$$

> **Teaching Idea**
>
> A good way for students to review the concept of division is to explore the relationships between multiplication, subtraction, and division. Have students demonstrate a simple division problem with manipulatives, explaining how they multiplied and subtracted to solve the problem.

This tells us that $13 \div 4 = 3$ remainder 1; that is $13 = 4 \times 3 + 1$. To concretely explain this to students, use the subtraction method described above. Subtract 4 from 13 three times, and there will be 1 left over. Think of 13 objects divided equally among 4 children, and use this example to demonstrate the concept concretely. When each of 4 children receives 1 object, the total number of objects is reduced by 4. If each child receives 3 objects, the number 13 is reduced by $3 \times 4 = 12$. There is 1 object left over. The process ends when the number of objects left is less than the number of children. Notice that the answer of 3 remainder 1 can be checked by calculating $4 \times 3 + 1$ and verifying that the answer is 13. This same way of checking works for any long division problem.

Fifth graders are expected to be able to solve division problems with two- or three-digit divisors, such as $5{,}738 \div 17$. You may wish to first review division problems with one- and two-digit divisors before introducing three-digit divisors. In the previous example, ask students to imagine 17 students dividing 5,738 apples equally among themselves. Here, focus mainly on procedures. Estimation is an important part of the process.

$$17\overline{)5738}$$

To find the quotient and remainder, you must first decide where the first digit (the highest place value digit) of the quotient will be placed. Above which digit in 5,738 should you begin writing the quotient? This can be decided systematically. Working from left to right with the digits of the dividend, ask, "Does 17 go into 5?" or more precisely, "Is 17 less than or equal to 5?" The answer is no. Moving one digit to the right, ask, "Does 17 go into 57?" (or, "Is 17 less than or equal to 57?"). The answer is yes. This tells you that the highest place value digit of the quotient will be placed above the 7 in 5,738.

Proceed to the next question: "How many times does 17 go into 57?" (Because of the place value locations of 5 and 7 in 5,738, you are really trying to find the answer to this question: "How many 1,700s may be subtracted from 5,700?") Through trial and error students must recognize that

3 x 17 < 57 and 4 x 17 > 57

This leads to

$$
\begin{array}{r}
3 \\
17\overline{)5738} \\
51 \\
\hline
6
\end{array}
$$

Now pause to check that the remainder, 6, is less than the divisor, 17. If the remainder at this stage were greater than or equal to 17, it would mean that you made a mistake in the previous step. Because the digit 3 is in the hundreds column of the quotient, this first step corresponds to "allocating 300 apples to each student." Next bring down the 3 in 5,738:

$$
\begin{array}{r}
3 \\
17\overline{)5738} \\
51 \\
\hline
63
\end{array}
$$

At this stage you need to find the number of times that 17 may be subtracted from 63. The answer is 3 because

3 x 17 < 63 and 4 x 17 > 63

Therefore, you can place a 3 in the tens column of the quotient, then multiply 3 by 17 and subtract the product from 63 as below:

$$
\begin{array}{r}
33 \\
17\overline{)5738} \\
51 \\
\hline
63 \\
51 \\
\hline
12 \\
\end{array}
$$

Because this 3 is written in the tens column, it corresponds to "allocating an additional 30 apples to each student." Notice that the remainder, 12, is less than the divisor, 17, as it should be. The final step is written this way:

$$
\begin{array}{r}
337 \\
17\overline{)5738} \\
51 \\
\hline
63 \\
51 \\
\hline
128 \\
119 \\
\hline
9 \\
\end{array}
$$

Choosing 7 in the ones column of the quotient is based on the estimate

7 x 17 < 128 and 8 x 17 > 128

This calculation tells you that each student can receive 337 apples and there will be 9 apples left over. The calculation can be checked by verifying that

5,738 = 17 x 337 + 9

Long division problems involving three-digit divisors are similar and should be practiced by students.

To check the reasonableness of a quotient, it is helpful to estimate the quotient before calculating the exact answer. We can estimate the answer to the previous example by rounding 17 to 20 and 5,738 to 6,000. We can then divide 6,000 by 20 mentally and get a quotient of 300. This tells us that our answer should be about 300.

In addition to learning the long division procedure, it is important to learn how to divide by 10, 100, and 1,000. From the rules for multiplying by 10, 100, and 1,000, we can deduce corresponding rules for dividing by 10, 100, or 1,000. Since multiplying a number by 10 moves the decimal point one place to the right, dividing a number by 10 must move the decimal point to the left one place. This is because multiplying a number by 10 and then dividing that product by 10 results in the original number.

41.57 ÷ 10 = 4.157

move the decimal point

one place to the left

Similarly, dividing a number by 100 is accomplished by moving the decimal in the number two places to the left, and dividing a number by 1,000 is achieved by moving the decimal point three places to the left.

Decimal quotients may be rounded by following the rules for rounding decimals. (See the subsection "Rounding Decimals," on pp. 470–471.)

D. Solving Problems and Equations

Problem solving and practice of skills are crucially important in the mathematical education of students. No mathematics curriculum is complete without these components, and the Grade 5 Core Knowledge curriculum is no exception.

Fifth graders need lots of practice with straightforward fraction, decimal, and whole number computation. If students do not master the basic arithmetic algorithms, they will have difficulty solving problems that require multiple steps and more than one operation. Frequent practice of skills is a good idea. Word problems consolidate these skills and illustrate practical applications of mathematics. For example, consider the following problem:

**A cubic foot of water weighs about 62 pounds.
What is the approximate weight of water in a full aquarium
that is 4 feet long, 3 feet wide, and 2 feet high?**

To solve this problem students must calculate the volume of the aquarium and multiply the volume by the density of water: $2 \times 3 \times 4 \times 62$. The approximate weight is 1,488 pounds. This is the number of cubic feet in the aquarium times the approximate weight of 1 cubic foot of water.

Fifth graders should solve many word problems involving fractions. After some practice with word problems that you assign, ask your students to invent their own word problems that have a specific solution. For example, ask them to write a word problem whose solution is $\frac{2}{3} \times \frac{3}{4}$. Here are some possible answers:

**A recipe for fudge used $\frac{3}{4}$ of a stick of butter. If John
ate $\frac{2}{3}$ of all the fudge, how much butter did he eat?
Answer: $\frac{2}{3} \times \frac{3}{4} = \frac{1}{2}$, $\frac{1}{2}$ of a stick of butter**

**A rectangular plot of land is $\frac{2}{3}$ of a mile wide
and $\frac{3}{4}$ of a mile long. What is its area?
Answer: $\frac{2}{3}$ mile x $\frac{3}{4}$ mile = $\frac{1}{2}$ square mile**

**The average speed of a frog is $\frac{2}{3}$ mile per hour.
How far will the frog go in 45 minutes?
Answer: Since 45 minutes is $\frac{3}{4}$ of an hour,
the distance traveled is $\frac{2}{3}$ mile/hr. x $\frac{3}{4}$ hr. = $\frac{1}{2}$ mile.**

Multiple step problems may combine topics from geometry, measurement, fractions, decimals, or other topics. For example, consider the following problems:

**A music class lasts $\frac{5}{6}$ of an hour and recess lasts $\frac{1}{3}$ of an hour.
How many minutes long are 2 music classes and 2 recesses?**

**The length of a rectangle is twice its width. If the perimeter of the
rectangle is 48 inches, what is its length? What is its area?
Now suppose that the perimeter of the rectangle is 4.8 inches
instead of 48 inches. What is its length? What is its area?**

These are only a few of the many kinds of problems that can support a Grade 5 math curriculum based on the *Core Knowledge Sequence.*

Teaching Idea

Encourage students to write equations that show the steps of their calculations, as in (5 + 3) x 4 = 8 x 4 = 32. This is a good habit to develop in students as early as possible. Although fifth graders can probably perform many calculations in less organized ways, writing the equations in a step-by-step fashion will help them to avoid mistakes, and it is essential for algebra classes in later grades. In addition, students should be able to articulate and verbally explain steps in a process.

Review

Below are some ideas for ongoing assessment and review activities. These are not meant to constitute a comprehensive list.

• If any students are not proficient with their math facts, have several sets of flash cards for multiplication and division facts in the classroom. Make them available in a center, or use them during math or when there is extra time. Students can also make their own flash cards on index cards to use at home.

• Have students keep a math journal where they can solve and create problems. At the beginning of each day or each math period, post a problem of the day for students to solve in their journals. Students should also write out the process they used to solve the problem. This will help students practice thinking about how to solve problems. You may have students read their process aloud to the class and discuss different problem-solving strategies. Or, you may wish to talk through a problem with the class as a whole. These discussions allow students to see the thinking that leads to the solution.

• Have an estimation jar in the room filled with objects such as marbles, erasers, or paper clips. Have students guess how many objects are in the jar. On the day when you reveal the number, first empty the jar and put 10 of the items back to show the class what that number looks like. Ask if any of them want to change their original estimates based on that new information. Share the number of items with the class and consider giving a prize to the student who guesses the number or closest to it. Have that student explain the process behind the winning estimate.

• Practice word problems and the connection between addition and multiplication. Have students choose objects that have an equal number of parts in common—for example, a truck with eight wheels or a flower with five petals. Then model creating a word problem with this object. For example, students would say, "I have three trucks with eight wheels. How many wheels do I have altogether?" Model the addition equation first, $8 + 8 + 8 = 24$. Then ask students to make the multiplication problem $3 \times 8 = 24$. Have students write their problems on index cards, modeling the form above. Then, have them read their problem aloud to the class and ask the class to solve the problem using addition and multiplication.

• Each day, give students a multiplication or division problem to solve, and then ask for a volunteer to show on the board or on an overhead projector how they solved the problem. Have other students propose different ways to solve the problem. Keep a bank of these problems so students can use them to review for tests and quizzes.

• Each day, practice how many computation problems students can do in a minute. Start with problems with the same operation, and then change to mixed operations. By the end of the year, students should have very automatic computation skills. You can even have students graph their progress. *The Mad Minute* (see *More Resources*) provides pre-created worksheets for you to use.

More Resources

A good mathematics program follows sound cognitive principles and allows many opportunities for thoughtful and varied practice to build mastery of important skills. For advice on suitable mathematics programs, contact the Foundation.

The titles listed below are offered as a representative sample of materials and not a complete list of everything that is available.

For students —

• *Anno's Mysterious Multiplying Jar,* by Masaichiro and Mitsumasa Anno (Puffin, 1999). Paperback, 48 pages, ISBN 0698117530.

• *Dazzling Division: Games and Activities that Make Math Easy and Fun,* by Lynette Long (John Wiley & Sons, 2000). Starts with very simple concepts. Paperback, 128 pages, ISBN 0471369837.

• *Everything You Need to Know About Math Homework,* by Anne Zeman and Kate Kelly (Scholastic, 1994). A clear guide for students in Grades 4–6 that covers numbers and the number system, basic math functions, measurement, geometry, money, graphs, statistics, and computers. Paperback, ISBN 0590493590.

• *Far-Out Science Projects with Height and Depth,* by Robert Gardner (Enslow, 2003). Interesting experiments for the classroom or at home. Require good understanding of multiplication and division. Library binding, 48 pages, ISBN 0766020169. Also by the same author: *Heavy-Duty Science Projects with Weight* (ISBN 0766020134); *It's About Time! Science Projects* (ISBN 0766020126); *Really Hot Science Projects with Temperature* (ISBN 0766020150); *Split-Second Science Projects with Speed* (ISBN 0766020177); and *Super-Sized Science Projects with Volume* (ISBN 0766020142).

• *How Math Works,* by Carol Vonderman (Reader's Digest, 1996). Hardcover, 192 pages, ISBN 0895778505.

• *Multiplication and Division (Math Success),* by Lucille Caron and Philip M. St. Jacques (Enslow, 2001). Library binding, 64 pages, ISBN 0766014312. See also *Addition and Subtraction* in the same series.

• *On Beyond a Million: An Amazing Math Journey,* by David M. Schwartz (Dragonfly, 2001). Introduces the names of larger numbers and powers of ten. Paperback, 32 pages, ISBN 0440411777.

• *Whodunit Math Puzzles,* by Bill Wise and illustrated by Lucy Corvino (Sterling, 2001). Hardcover, 96 pages, ISBN 080695896.

For teachers —

• *The Mad Minute: A Race to Master the Number Facts,* by Paul Joseph Shoecraft and Terry James Clukey (Dale Seymour Publications, 1981). Paperback, ISBN 0201071401.

• *Usborne Illustrated Dictionary of Math,* by Tori Large and others (Usborne, 2004). Paperback, 128 pages, ISBN 0794506623.

• Figure This!, www.figurethis.org, provides math challenges designed for middle school students.

V. easurement

The Big Idea

Learning how to convert to common units and how to regroup units of measurement are important problem-solving skills.

What Students Should Already Know

Students in Core Knowledge schools should be familiar with

Kindergarten

- identifying familiar instruments of measurement, such as ruler, scale, thermometer
- comparing objects according to linear measure, weight (mass), capacity (volume), and temperature
- sequencing and comparing duration of events and orienting them in time
- reading a clock face and telling time to the hour
- naming the days of the week and the months of the year

Grade 1

- linear measure: measuring length using nonstandard units, inches, feet, and centimeters
- weight (mass): comparing weights of objects using a balance scale and measuring weight in nonstandard units and in pounds
- capacity (volume): estimating and measuring capacity in cups; identifying quart, gallon
- temperature: associating temperature in degrees Fahrenheit with weather
- reading a clock face and telling time to the half-hour
- knowing the days of the week and the months of the year, both in order and out of sequence

Grade 2

- linear measure: knowing that one foot = 12 inches and the abbreviations: ft., in.
- measuring and drawing line segments in inches to $\frac{1}{2}$ inch
- estimating linear measurements, then measuring to check estimates
- estimating and measuring weight in pounds, and knowing abbreviation: lb.
- measuring liquid volumes in pints, quarts, gallons
- comparing U.S. and metric liquid volumes: quart and liter (one liter is a little more than one quart)

V. Measurement

- measuring and recording temperature in degrees Fahrenheit to the nearest 2 degrees and knowing the degree sign: °
- reading a clock face, telling time to five-minute intervals, and knowing how to distinguish time as AM or PM; understanding noon and midnight
- solving problems on elapsed time (how much time has passed?)
- using a calendar, identifying the date, day of the week, month, and year
- writing the date using words (for name of month) and numbers

Grade 3

- making linear measurements in yards, feet, inches, centimeters, and meters
- knowing that one yard = 36 inches; 3 feet = 1 yard; 1 meter = 100 centimeters; 1 meter is a little more than one yard
- measuring and drawing line segments in inches (to $\frac{1}{4}$ inch), and in centimeters
- estimating and measuring weight in pounds and ounces; grams and kilograms
- knowing abbreviations: oz., g, kg
- estimating and measuring capacity in liters
- knowing that 1 quart = 2 pints; 1 gallon = 4 quarts
- measuring and recording temperature in degrees Celsius
- identifying freezing point of water as 32°F = 0°C
- reading a clock face and telling time to the minute as either AM or PM; telling time in terms of both "minutes before" and "minutes after" the hour
- writing the date using only numbers

Grade 4

- making linear measurements in yards, feet, inches (to $\frac{1}{8}$ in.), and in millimeters
- estimating and measuring liquid capacity in teaspoons, tablespoons, cups, pints, quarts, gallons, and milliliters
- knowing the following equivalents among U.S. customary units of measurement, and solving problems involving changing units of measurement, including the relationships among inches, feet, yards, and miles (linear measure); ounces, pounds, and tons (weight); and fluid ounces, cups, pints, quarts, and gallons (capacity/volume)
- knowing the following equivalents among metric units of measurement, and solving problems involving changing units of measurement, including millimeters, centimeters, meters, and kilometers (linear measure); milligrams, centigrams, grams, and kilograms (mass); and millimeters, centiliters, and liters (capacity/volume)
- time: solving problems on elapsed time

Materials

small conversion chart for each student, p. 503

math journals, p. 503

newspapers, 1 per student or pair of students, p. 503

examples of recipes, p. 503

What Students Need to Learn

> **Convert to common units in problems involving addition and subtraction**

> **Regroup when multiplying and dividing amounts of time**

What Students Will Learn in Future Grades

The *Core Knowledge Sequence* for mathematics emphasizes the importance of reviewing and building on prior knowledge. Related topics from the Grade 6 *Sequence* are listed below, and subsequent grades will continue to focus on strengthening and expanding these skills.

Grade 6

> solve problems requiring conversion of units within the U.S. customary system, and within the metric system

> associate prefixes used in metric system with quantities:

    kilo = thousand

    hecto = hundred

    deka = ten

    deci = tenth

    centi = hundredth

    milli = thousandth

> time: solve problems on elapsed time; express parts of an hour in fraction or decimal form

Vocabulary

Student/Teacher Vocabulary

capacity: the volume of a solid shape expressed in units of liquid measurement (T)

mass: a measure of the quantity of matter (T)

measure: (noun) the length, capacity, dimensions, or quantity of something (T)
        (verb) to find the length, dimensions, capacity, or quantity of something (S)

temperature: the degree of hotness or coldness of an object or space (S)

volume: the amount of space inside a solid shape (T)

weight: the force of gravity on an object, or a measure of the heaviness of an object (S)

Domain Vocabulary

Measurement and associated words:
feet, inches, centimeters, line segment, scale, pound, ounce, ton, cup, pint, quart, gallon, gram, kilogram, liter, Fahrenheit, Celsius, noon, midnight, elapsed time, calendar, week, month, year, ruler, scale, thermometer, short, long, longer, shorter, tall, heavy, light, glass, can, bottle, clock, hour, minute, second, common, time, regroup

V. Measurement

At a Glance

The most important ideas for you are:

- Students should become fluent with the standard units for each type of measurement and understand when it is appropriate to use each one.
- Students should learn standard equivalents in U.S. and metric units of measurements and be able to solve problems that require a change in a unit of measurement.
- Problems with different units of measurement may need to be converted to common units in order to find a solution.
- Regrouping units of measurement may be necessary to solve problems.
- Students should practice by measuring real-world objects until they learn these skills to the point of automaticity.

What Teachers Need to Know

Familiarity with units of measurement of length, weight, volume, and time gives students a foundation for applications of mathematics, science, and everyday life. Core Knowledge students learn both the U.S. customary units of measurement and the metric system. Students will encounter feet, inches, pounds, tons, quarts, and gallons from the U.S. customary system in their everyday lives. Units from the metric system, such as meters, centimeters, grams, kilograms, and liters, are more common outside of the United States, and these metric units are used worldwide for scientific purposes.

Reviewing Equivalents

Students in Core Knowledge schools should have learned the following equivalents among U.S. customary units of measurement, and should be able to solve problems involving changing units of measurement:

Linear Measure	Weight	Capacity (volume)
1 ft. = 12 in. 1 yd. = 3 ft. = 36 in. 1 mi. = 5,280 ft. 1 mi. = 1,760 yd.	1 lb. = 16 oz. 1 ton = 2,000 lb.	1 cup = 8 fl. oz. (fluid ounces) 1 pt. = 2 c. 1 qt. = 2 pt. 1 gal. = 4 qt.

Students should also know the following equivalents among metric units of measurement and should be able to solve problems involving changing units of measurement:

Linear Measure	Mass	Capacity (volume)
1 cm = 10 mm (millimeters) 1 m = 1,000 mm 1 m = 100 cm 1 km = 1,000 m	1 cg (centigram) = 10 mg (milligrams) 1 g = 1,000 mg 1 g = 100 cg 1 kg = 1,000 g	1 cl (centiliter) = 10 ml (milliliters) 1 liter = 1,000 ml 1 liter = 100 cl

Students in Core Knowledge schools should have learned the equivalents stated above and how to solve problems involving changing units of measurement. You may wish to review how to convert from one unit of measurement to another using the information in these tables. For example, since 1 yard is 3 feet, and 1 foot is 12 inches, it follows that 1 yard is 3 × 12 inches, or 36 inches. Using long division, students can deduce the number of yards in one mile from the number of feet in one mile. Since 1 yard is 3 feet, the number of yards in a mile is 5,280 ÷ 3 = 1,760. Students can solve problems such as finding the number of inches in 25 yards (25 × 36 in. = 900 in.), or the number of feet in 10 miles (10 × 5,280 ft. = 52,800 ft.).

The relationships among metric units are simpler. For example, since there are 100 centimeters in a meter, 17 meters is the same length as 17 × 100 cm, or 1,700 cm. To appreciate how large the number 1,000,000 is, students can calculate the number of millimeters in one kilometer. Since one kilometer is 1,000 meters and one meter is 1,000 millimeters, it follows that

1 km = 1,000 x 1,000 mm = 1,000,000 mm

Students can solve problems that require comparing different units within the metric system, or within the U.S. customary system of measurements. As an example, students might be asked to decide which weighs more, a 1 lb. 7 oz. book, or a container full of feathers whose total weight is 25 oz. Since 1 lb. 7 oz. = 16 oz. + 7 oz. = 23 oz., the container full of feathers weighs more. Calculations using metric units are more straightforward. For example, to find the number of grams in 3 kg, calculate 3 × 1,000 g = 3,000 g.

Students can also use equivalents for volume and capacity to solve problems such as calculating the number of milliliters in 4 liters (4 × 1,000 ml = 4,000 ml). In the U.S. customary system, students can compare volumes in different units. For example, ask which is the larger volume, 1 gallon or the combination of 1 cup, 1 pint, 1 quart, and 1 half-gallon. This comparison is most easily carried out by converting all measurements to cups.

**1 gallon = 16 cups, whereas 1 cup, 1 pint, 1 quart, and
1 half-gallon is the same as 15 cups.**

Converting to Common Units

To add or subtract measurements given in U.S. customary units, various kinds of regrouping are necessary. For example, to add 5 ft. and 7 in. to 2 ft. and 8 in., we can calculate this way: add the inches first. Then regroup 15 in. as 1 ft. and 3 in.

$$\begin{array}{r} \text{5 ft. 7 in.} \\ + \text{2 ft. 8 in.} \\ \hline \end{array} \qquad \text{15 in. = 1 ft. 3 in.}$$

Finally, complete the problem by carrying the 1 ft. and adding.

$$\begin{array}{r} \text{1 ft.} \\ \text{5 ft. 7 in.} \\ + \text{2 ft. 8 in.} \\ \hline \text{8 ft. 3 in.} \end{array}$$

V. Measurement

This addition problem could also be completed by first converting all measurements to inches, and then writing the sum in terms of feet and inches.

Subtraction problems can be calculated in a similar way as above. Consider the problem of subtracting 2 lb. and 11 oz. from 15 lb. and 3 oz.:

$$\begin{array}{r} \textbf{15 lb.\ \ 3 oz.} \\ \underline{-\ \textbf{2 lb. 11 oz.}} \end{array}$$

It is not possible to take 11 oz. from 3 oz., so the calculation begins by regrouping 15 lb., 3 oz. as 14 lb., 19 oz. (because there are 16 ounces in one pound), and proceeds by subtracting by columns.

$$\begin{array}{r} \textbf{14 lb. 19 oz.} \\ \underline{-\ \textbf{2 lb. 11 oz.}} \\ \textbf{12 lb.\ \ 8 oz.} \end{array}$$

Adding and subtracting metric measurements is generally best done by converting all measurements to the same unit. For example,

3 kg + 50 g = 3,000 g + 50 g = 3,050 g or 3.05 kg

Allow students significant time to practice converting units and adding and subtracting to solve problems.

Solving Problems on Elapsed Time

Addition and subtraction of time as measured in years, days, hours, minutes, and seconds can be solved in a similar way. The regrouping must take into account how these measurements of time are related to each other.

The following is an example of an elapsed time problem appropriate for students in Grade 5:

A flight leaves Charlottesville, Virginia, for New York City at 11:55 AM. If the flight lasts 3 hours and 35 minutes, what time does it arrive in New York City?

The solution, 3:30 PM, may be found using a number of strategies. Students may first wish to add the whole number amounts to find that 3 hours past 11:00 AM is 2:00 PM. You may need to remind students of the switch from AM to PM at noon. Next, students would add 35 minutes to 55 minutes to find a total of 90 minutes, which would be regrouped as $1\frac{1}{2}$ hours. If they add $1\frac{1}{2}$ hours to 2:00, they will reach the solution of 3:30 PM.

Students should be offered many opportunities to practice solving problems with elapsed time, particularly ones that involve regrouping and careful consideration of AM and PM in the answers.

Fifth graders also learn to multiply and divide with time. For example, consider the following problem:

A teacher gives her students 4 hours and 20 minutes of instruction each day, Monday through Friday. How many hours of instruction does she give per week?

Solution: 5 × (4 hours + 20 minutes) may be calculated this way. Start by multiplying the minutes.

$$
\begin{array}{r}
\text{4 h. \quad 20 min.} \\
\times\ 5 \\
\hline
\text{100 min.}
\end{array}
$$

Before multiplying the hours by 5, regroup the 100 min. as 1 h. and 40 min.

$$
\begin{array}{r}
\text{1 h.} \\
\text{4 h. \quad 20 min.} \\
\times\ 5 \quad \text{100 min.} = \text{1 h. 40 min.} \\
\hline
\text{21 h. \quad 40 min.}
\end{array}
$$

The total instruction time per week is 21 hours and 40 minutes.

A regrouping procedure is also possible for division, but it is simpler to carry out a division by first converting a time measurement to a single unit. For example, consider the following problem:

A bicycle racer goes around a track four times in 10 minutes and 32 seconds. If he travels at constant speed the whole time, how long does it take him to go around the track once?

Solution: 10 min. and 32 sec. is 632 sec.

$$
\begin{array}{r}
158 \\
4\overline{)632} \\
\underline{4} \\
23 \\
\underline{20} \\
32 \\
\underline{32} \\
0
\end{array}
$$

Then, 632 sec. divided by 4 is 158 sec. This is the same as 2 min. and 38 sec. The bicyclist travels around the track once every 2 min. and 38 sec.

Again, allow students significant time to explore how to regroup when multiplying and dividing problems with elapsed time.

Review

Below are some ideas for ongoing assessment and review activities. These are not meant to constitute a comprehensive list.

• Provide students with a small conversion chart to use as a reference in their math journals. Provide a daily conversion problem that covers the different measurement conversions. By the middle of the year, have students solve problems without their charts.

• Use the daily newspaper to practice converting units of measurement. You may find articles in the sports section where students are able to convert linear measure, such as feet to inches or miles to feet. You may also bring in recipes and ask students to change units of capacity from cups to ounces. How would the recipe or the article read differently with the conversion? Check for mathematical accuracy.

The Big Idea in Review

Learning how to convert to common units and how to regroup units of measurement are important problem-solving skills.

• Students might find it interesting to calculate how many units of time they use when they perform a certain activity in their lives. For example, ask students to choose something that they do every day and then calculate how many hours, minutes, or seconds in a week, a month, or a year they perform that activity, like brushing their teeth, playing soccer, or playing video games. How do they view this activity differently when they think about how much time it consumes each week, month, or year? Have students record their thoughts in their math journals and share with the class.

More Resources

A good mathematics program follows sound cognitive principles and allows many opportunities for thoughtful and varied practice to build mastery of important skills. For advice on suitable mathematics programs, contact the Foundation.

The titles listed below are offered as a representative sample of materials and not a complete list of everything that is available.

For students —

• *Everything You Need to Know About Math Homework,* by Anne Zeman and Kate Kelly (Scholastic, 1994). A clear guide for students in Grades 4–6 that covers numbers and the number system, basic math functions, measurement, geometry, money, graphs, statistics, and computers. Paperback, ISBN 0590493590.

• *Far-Out Science Projects with Height and Depth,* by Robert Gardner (Enslow, 2003). Interesting experiments for the classroom or at home. Require good understanding of multiplication and division. Library binding, 48 pages, ISBN 0766020169. Also by the same author: *Heavy-Duty Science Projects with Weight; It's About Time! Science Projects; Really Hot Science Projects with Temperature; Split-Second Science Projects with Speed;* and *Super-Sized Science Projects with Volume.*

• *How Math Works,* by Carol Vonderman (Reader's Digest, 1996). Hardcover, 192 pages, ISBN 0895778505.

• *Janice VanCleave's Math for Every Kid,* by Janice VanCleave (John Wiley & Sons, 1991). Paperback, 224 pages, ISBN 0471542652.

For teachers —

• *Key to Metric Measurement (Key Math Series),* by Betsy Franco (Key Curriculum Press, 1972). Self-paced, self-guided workbooks described by one reviewer as "very motivational for kids burned out on textbooks" (Love to Learn, www.lovetolearn.net). Set of four paperbacks, available individually or as a set from Key Curriculum Press, www.keypress.com, or 1-800-995-MATH. Answer keys and notes, as well as reproducible tests, are also available. See also *Key to Measurement,* by the same publisher.

• *Usborne Illustrated Dictionary of Math,* by Tori Large and others (Usborne, 2004). Paperback, 128 pages, ISBN 0794506623.

• Figure This!, www.figurethis.org, provides math challenges designed for middle school students.

VI. Geometry

The Big Idea

Plane and solid figures can be identified, compared, and measured. Lines, angles, and triangles can be classified and named.

What Students Should Already Know

Students in Core Knowledge schools should be familiar with

Kindergarten

- identifying left and right hand; top, bottom, middle
- knowing and using terms of orientation and relative position, such as closed, open; on, under, over; in front, in back (behind); between, in the middle of; next to, beside; inside, outside; around; far from, near; above, below; to the right of, to the left of; here, there
- identifying and sorting basic plane figures: square, rectangle, triangle, circle
- identifying basic shapes in a variety of common objects and artifacts (windows, pictures, books, buildings, cars, etc.)
- recognizing shapes as the same or different
- making congruent shapes and designs
- comparing size of basic plane figures (larger, smaller)

Grade 1

- drawing basic plane figures: square, rectangle, triangle, circle
- describing square, rectangle, and triangle according to number of sides
- identifying basic solid figures: sphere, cube, cone

Grade 2

- measuring perimeter in inches of squares and rectangles
- identifying solid figures—sphere, cube, pyramid, cone, cylinder—and associating solid figures with planar shapes: sphere (circle), cube (square), pyramid (triangle)
- identifying lines as horizontal, vertical, perpendicular, parallel
- naming lines and line segments (for example, line AB; line segment CD)
- identifying a line of symmetry, and creating simple symmetric figures

Grade 3

- polygons: recognizing vertex (plural: vertices); identifying pentagon, hexagon, and octagon (regular)
- identifying angles by letter names (for example, $\angle ABC$); identifying a right angle; knowing that there are four right angles in a square or rectangle

VI. Geometry

What Students Should Already Know continued

- computing area in square inches (in.²) and square centimeters (cm²)
- recognizing and drawing congruent figures; creating symmetric figures
- identifying solid figure: rectangular solid

Grade 4

- identifying and drawing points, segments, rays, and lines
- identifying and drawing lines: horizontal, vertical, perpendicular, parallel, intersecting
- identifying acute and obtuse angles
- identifying polygons: quadrilateral (regular), parallelogram, trapezoid
- identifying and drawing diagonals of quadrilaterals
- circles: identifying radius (plural: radii) and diameter; radius = $\frac{1}{2}$ diameter
- recognizing similar figures
- knowing the formula for area of a rectangle (area = length × width) and solving problems involving finding area in a variety of square units (such as mi.²; yd.²; ft.²; in.²; km²; m²; cm²; mm²)
- computing volume of rectangular prisms in cubic units (cm³, in.³)

What Students Need to Learn

- **Measure the degrees in angles, and know that right angle = 90°; acute angle: less than 90°; obtuse angle: greater than 90°; straight angle = 180°**
- **Identify and construct different kinds of triangles: equilateral, right, and isosceles**
- **Know what it means for triangles to be congruent**
- **Identify polygons: rhombus**
- **Know that regular polygons have sides of equal length and angles of equal measure**
- **Identify and draw diagonals of polygons**
- **Circles: identify arc and chord**
- **Using a compass, draw circles with a given diameter or radius**
- **Find the circumference of a circle using the formulas $C = \pi d$, $C = 2\pi r$, using 3.14 as the value of pi**
  - **Find the area of triangles, using the formula $A = \frac{1}{2}(b \times h)$**
  - **Find the area of parallelograms, using the formula $A = b \times h$**
  - **Find the area of an irregular figure (such as a trapezoid) by dividing into regular figures for which you know how to find the area**
- **Find the surface area of a rectangular prism**
- **Compute volume of rectangular prisms in cubic units (cm³, in.³), using the formula $V = l \times w \times h$**

What Students Will Learn in Future Grades

The *Core Knowledge Sequence* for mathematics emphasizes the importance of reviewing and building on prior knowledge. Related topics from the Grade 6 *Sequence* are listed below, and subsequent grades will continue to focus on strengthening and expanding these skills.

Grade 6

- ▸ identify and use signs that mean
  - congruent $\cong$
  - similar $\sim$
  - parallel $\parallel$
  - perpendicular $\perp$
- ▸ construct parallel lines and a parallelogram
- ▸ construct a perpendicular bisector
- ▸ know that if two lines are parallel, any line perpendicular to one is also perpendicular to the other; and, that two lines perpendicular to the same line are parallel
- ▸ angles:
  - bisect an angle
  - construct an angle congruent to a given angle
  - construct a figure congruent to a given figure, using reflection over a line of symmetry, and identify corresponding parts
  - show how congruent plane figures can be made to correspond through reflection, rotation, and translation
- ▸ triangles:
  - know that the sum of the measures of the angles of a triangle is 180°
  - construct different kinds of triangles
  - known terms by which we classify kinds of triangles:
    - by length of sides: equilateral, isosceles, scalene
    - by angles: right, acute, obtuse
- ▸ identify congruent angles and sides, and axes of symmetry, in parallelograms, rhombuses, rectangles, and squares
- ▸ find the area (*A*) and perimeter (*P*) of plane figures, or given the area or perimeter, find the missing dimension, using the following formulas:
  - rectangle

    $A = lw$

    $P = 2(l + w)$
  - square

    $A = s^2$

    $P = 4s$

VI. Geometry

- triangle

  $A = \frac{1}{2}bh$

  $P = s1 + s2 + s3$

- parallelogram

  $A = bh$

  $P = 2(b + s)$

▸ circles:

- using a compass, draw circles with a given diameter or radius
- solve problems involving application of the formulas for finding the circumference of a circle using the formulas $C = \pi d$, and $C = 2\pi r$, using 3.14 as the value of pi
- find the area of a circle using the formula $A = \pi r^2$

▸ find volume of rectangular solids, or, given the volume, find a missing dimension, using the formulas $V = lwh$, or $V = bh$ (in which b = area of base)

Vocabulary

Student/Teacher Vocabulary

angle: the union of two rays that have the same endpoint; can be classified as acute, obtuse, or right (S)

arc: one of two curves on a circle created when a chord is drawn on a circle (S)

area: a measure of the space inside a plane figure (S)

chord: a line segment whose endpoints lie on a circle (S)

circle: the set of all points in a plane that are the same fixed distance from a single point (S)

circumference: the distance around a circle; also can be described as a circle's perimeter (S)

compass: a tool for drawing a circle (S)

congruent: adjective describing figures with the same shape and size (S)

cube: a solid figure with six square faces at right angles with each other (S)

diagonal: a line segment that connects opposite vertices of a polygon (S)

diameter: the distance across a circle along a line segment through the center of the circle; twice the length of the radius (S)

equilateral triangle: a triangle with three sides of equal length (S)

hexagon: a polygon with six sides and six vertices (S)

horizontal line: a line that is parallel to the ground (S)

intersect: to cross or meet at a point (S)

Vocabulary continued

isosceles triangle: a triangle with at least two sides of equal length (S)

line: a straight path that passes through two different specific points and extends forever in both directions (S)

line segment: the part of a line that lies between two endpoints (S)

octagon: a polygon with eight sides and eight vertices (S)

parallel lines: two lines in the same plane that have no point in common (S)

pentagon: a polygon with five sides and five vertices (S)

perimeter: the distance around a plane figure (S)

perpendicular lines: two lines that meet to form four right angles (i.e., four 90-degree angles) (S)

plane: a flat surface that extends forever in all directions (S)

polygon: a closed figure made of line segments (S)

quadrilateral: a polygon with four sides and four vertices (S)

radius: the distance from any point on the circle to the center of the circle; one-half of the diameter of a circle (S)

ray: a half line that continues forever in one direction but has an endpoint in the other direction (T)

rectangle: a four-sided figure with four right angles (S)

rectangular solid: a three-dimensional figure that has six rectangular faces at right angles to one another (S)

rhombus: a parallelogram with four sides of equal length (S)

right triangle: a triangle that has a right angle (S)

square: a rectangle with all sides the same length (S)

trapezoid: a quadrilateral with exactly one pair of opposite sides parallel (S)

triangle: a three-sided figure (S)

vertex: the common endpoint where two lines, line segments, or rays meet to form an angle or a corner of a polygon (plural = vertices) (S)

vertical line: a line that is perpendicular to the ground or perpendicular to any line parallel to the ground (S)

volume: the number of unit cubes that fit inside a solid figure, such as a rectangular prism (S)

Domain Vocabulary

Geometry and associated words:
rectangular, sphere, cubic, pyramid, cone, cylinder, regular polygon, perimeter arc, horizontal, vertical, line of symmetry, intersecting, intersection, symmetric, point, right angle, obtuse angle, acute angle, regular polygon, square unit, square centimeter, square inch, similar, perpendicular, parallel, length, width, algebra, equation, measure, measurement, ruler, side, construct, isosceles, center, equilateral, dimension, geometry, distance, centimeter, degree, linear, straight, midpoint, draw, height, inch, edge, center, protractor, straightedge

Materials

geoboards, pp. 514, 516

paper cutouts of several sizes of squares, rectangles, and circles, pp. 516, 519–520, 523

square inch or centimeter tiles, pp. 516–523

base 10 grid paper, pp. 517, 519–520

common rectangular objects, such as index cards, business cards, notebook paper, playing cards, same-sized books, etc., p. 517

photocopy of a flattened prism, p. 521

tape, p. 521

1-cm cubes, p. 522

boxes, blocks, sugar cubes, and other cubes of different sizes, p. 522

examples of visual art pieces from this grade level, p. 523

self-sticking notes, p. 523

rulers, p. 524

chart paper, p. 524

compasses, 1 per student, p. 524

At a Glance

The most important ideas for you are:

- Lines, segments, and rays can be identified as horizontal, vertical, perpendicular, parallel, or intersecting.

- Lines, line segments, and rays can be named using the names of their points.

- Angles can be identified as right, acute, obtuse, or straight.

- Triangles can be identified as equilateral, right, or isosceles.

- Polygons are closed figures made of line segments and can be identified by the number of sides they have.

- Plane figures, such as squares, rectangles, triangles, and circles, are two-dimensional and can be identified by their shape.

- The distance from any point on the circle to the center of the circle is called the radius of that circle. The diameter of a circle is two times the radius.

- A compass can be used to draw a circle with a specific radius or diameter.

- Two geometric figures are congruent if they have the same size and shape.

- Area is a measure of the space inside a plane figure such as a square or rectangle. Formulas can be used to find the area of many shapes.

- Volume can be explained as the number of cubic units that fit inside a solid figure such as a rectangular prism. A formula can be used to find the volume of rectangular prisms.

What Teachers Need to Know

Background

Geometry is an ancient subject known to many civilizations, most especially to the ancient Greeks. It is a subject that is both fascinating for its own sake, and rich in modern applications. Geometry topics, such as volume, area, and perimeter, can be combined with arithmetic and developed through word problems. Student understanding and intuition will increase by solving problems of a visual and geometric nature.

Reviewing Points, Lines, Segments, and Rays

Students in Core Knowledge schools should have learned about points, lines, segments, and rays in previous grades. However, a review of these basic geometric topics would be wise.

One of the fundamental ideas of geometry is that two points determine a line. That means that there is one and only one line that passes through two different specific points. Think of a point as an exact location in space. Points are sometimes labeled with capital letters of the alphabet, such as A, B, C, D, etc., as below.

There are two points indicated above. One is called A, and the other is called B. There is only one (straight) line that contains both A and B.

line *AB*, or $\overleftrightarrow{AB}$

The arrows in the picture above serve as a reminder that a line must go on forever in both directions. We can identify, or name, a line by any two points that it contains. Since the line in this picture contains the two points A and B, we can call the line, line *AB*. Line *AB* is sometimes written this way: $\overleftrightarrow{AB}$. This same line could just as well be described as line *BA* or $\overleftrightarrow{BA}$. The part of a line that lies between two points is called a line segment. A line segment can be labeled or named by its two endpoints. The line segment below is called line segment *AB* and is sometimes written this way: $\overline{AB}$. This line segment can also be called line segment *BA* or $\overline{BA}$.

line segment *AB*, or $\overline{AB}$

A ray is a half line with an endpoint like the one pictured here.

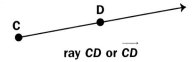

ray *CD* or $\overrightarrow{CD}$

The arrow is a reminder that the ray continues in one direction forever (but not the other direction). A ray can be named by its endpoint and any other point on the ray. The ray pictured above may be described as ray *CD* or as $\overrightarrow{CD}$. The first letter, C, names the endpoint of the ray.

Two lines that have a point in common are said to intersect. For example, the two lines drawn below intersect at point A.

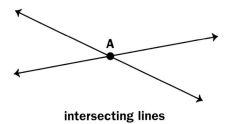

intersecting lines

A plane is a flat surface that extends forever—think of an infinite tabletop that extends forever in all horizontal directions. Two lines in the same plane are parallel if they have no point in common, that is, if they don't intersect, no matter how far they are extended in either direction.

two parallel lines

Two lines are perpendicular if they intersect to form four right angles, i.e., 90-degree angles. (See the next subsection.) A horizontal line and a vertical line are perpendicular to each other.

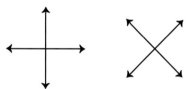

two pairs of perpendicular lines

A line or line segment that is parallel to the ground is called horizontal. If a line or line segment is perpendicular to the ground (or perpendicular to a horizontal line), it is said to be vertical. These are practical terms used to describe the orientation of objects. For example, a telephone pole is vertical and telephone wires may be described as horizontal.

Angles

An angle can be formed by two rays that have the same endpoint.

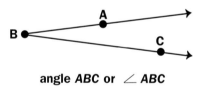

angle *ABC* or ∠ *ABC*

This angle is the union of the two rays, $\vec{BA}$ and $\vec{BC}$, that both have the same endpoint B. A name for this angle is ∠ABC. This is read aloud as "angle ABC." Another name for this same angle is ∠CBA. The letter B must be the middle letter because it is the endpoint of the two rays, but the other two letters can be interchanged. The common endpoint B of the two rays is called the vertex of the angle.

To every angle there corresponds a number between 0 and 180 called the measure of the angle. A protractor may be used to measure angles. For example, if ∠ABC is a right angle, it is 90°. A right angle may be thought of as a quarter turn (90°). A rotation of less than a quarter turn is called an acute angle (less than 90°). A rotation that is more than a quarter turn but less than a half turn is called an obtuse angle (greater than 90° but less than 180°). The measure of a straight angle is equal to 180°.

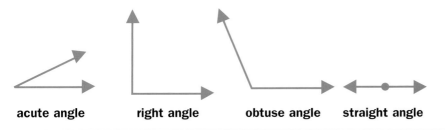

acute angle   **right angle**   **obtuse angle**   **straight angle**

Polygons

Polygon means "many-sided figure." More specifically, a polygon is a closed figure made of (straight) line segments.

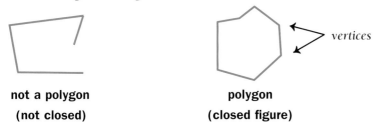

not a polygon   **polygon**
(not closed)   **(closed figure)**

A "corner" of a polygon, where two sides meet, is called a vertex. The plural of vertex is vertices [ver-ti-sees]. A polygon with three sides is called a triangle. A triangle has three vertices. If the triangle has a right angle, it is called a right triangle. If all three sides of a triangle are equal in length, it is called an equilateral triangle. If at least two of its sides are equal in length, it is called an isosceles triangle.

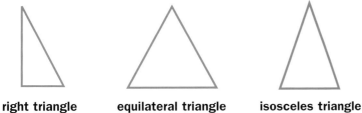

right triangle   **equilateral triangle**   **isosceles triangle**

A polygon with four sides is called a quadrilateral.

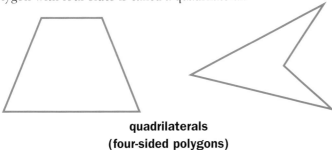

quadrilaterals
(four-sided polygons)

A rectangle is an example of a polygon with four sides and four vertices. A rectangle is a quadrilateral with four right angles. If all four sides of a rectangle are equal in length, it is called a square.

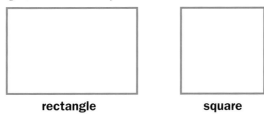

rectangle   **square**

A quadrilateral whose two pairs of opposite sides are parallel is called a parallelogram. A parallelogram is a rhombus if all four sides have the same length.

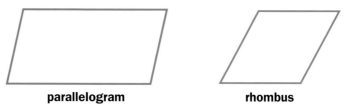

parallelogram　　　　**rhombus**

A quadrilateral that has exactly one pair of opposite sides parallel is called a trapezoid.

trapezoid

A polygon that has five sides and five vertices is called a pentagon. A hexagon has six sides and six vertices, and an octagon has eight sides and eight vertices. Any polygon whose sides all have the same length, and whose angles are all congruent to each other, or equal in measure (see "Congruence," on p. 516), is called a regular polygon. The pentagon, hexagon, and octagon shown below are regular polygons.

pentagon　　　　**hexagon**　　　　**octagon**

Teaching Idea

Have students demonstrate what each polygon looks like on a geoboard.

A polygon can be named by assigning letters to its vertices (which are points). For example the triangle below may be named triangle *ABC* and the rectangle may be named rectangle *DEFG*.

A

B　　　C

E　　　D

F　　　G

The vertices for the triangle can be listed in any order, but those for the rectangle cannot be written next to each other unless they are connected by a side. For example, rectangle *DEFG* can be described as *FGDE* or *EFGD*, but not as *EGDF* or *FDEG*. With the vertices properly labeled, it is easy to refer to a specific side of a polygon. For example, the side on the bottom of rectangle *DEFG* is segment *FG* or $\overline{FG}$.

A diagonal of a polygon is a line segment that connects opposite vertices. Any diagonal of a quadrilateral divides it into two triangles.

E　　　D

F　　　G

The line segment $\overline{EG}$ is a diagonal for the rectangle *DEFG*. The other diagonal for *DEFG* is the line segment connecting F to D (not drawn in the above diagram).

Circles

A circle is the set of all points in a plane that are a fixed distance from a particular point in the plane called the center of the circle. The distance from any point on the circle to the center of the circle is called the radius of that circle (plural = radii). The diameter of a circle is the distance across the circle along a line segment through the center of the circle. The diameter of a circle is two times the radius (and the radius is one-half of the diameter). A chord is a line segment whose endpoints lie on a circle. A chord divides a circle into two arcs (the smaller of the two arcs for a chord is identified below).

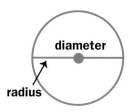
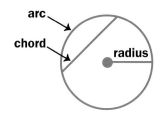

A diameter and a radius can be numbers or line segments, depending on the context in which the words are used. For example, in the circles below, the diameters can be referred to as line segment *XY* or as 2 in.

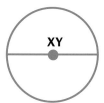
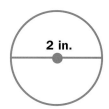

A compass is a tool for drawing a circle. To use a compass, select a radius for a circle and a point for its center. Place the point of the compass at the center of the circle and then rotate the compass about the center to draw the circle. If you wish to draw a circle with a particular diameter, use the measure of the circle's radius to draw the correct size.

The distance around a circle is called its circumference. The circumference of a circle is its perimeter. The ratio $\frac{C}{d}$ of the circumference to diameter is the same for any circle. That ratio is called *pi* [pie] and is represented by the Greek letter π. The number π is defined by this equation:

$$\frac{C}{d} = \pi$$

Multiplying both sides by the diameter *d* results in an equation for the circumference of a circle:

$$C = \pi d$$

Now since $d = 2r$, where *r* is the radius, it is also true that $C = 2\pi r$.

The number π is an irrational number. That means that the exact value of π is an infinite decimal that has no block of digits that repeats over and over again.

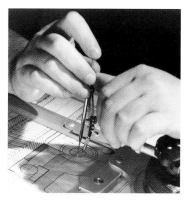

compass

A standard decimal approximation for π is 3.14. Another widely used approximate value for π is the fraction $\frac{22}{7}$. Neither of these numbers exactly equals π, nor do they equal each other, but they are both reasonably close to π.

To find the circumference of a circle with a diameter of 3 ft., use the following steps:

$$C = \pi d$$
$$C = 3.14 \times 3$$
$$C = 9.42$$

The circumference is approximately 9.42 ft.

To find the circumference of a circle with a radius of 5 cm, use the following steps:

$$C = \pi d$$
$$C = 2 \times 3.14 \times 5$$
$$C = 3.14$$

The circumference is approximately 31.4 cm.

The value of π to the first 50 decimal places is 3.14159265358979323846264338327950288419716939937511, but the exact value is an infinite decimal. As of December 6, 2002, the world record for the calculation of π was 1.24 trillion digits, using a supercomputer. However, there are no practical applications for such high precision.

Congruence

Two geometric figures are congruent if they have the same size and shape. This means that two figures are congruent if one of them could be placed on top of the other with an exact fit. The triangles below are congruent.

Teaching Idea

Have students experiment with congruent shapes by giving them paper cutouts of various shapes. Encourage students to place 1 shape on top of another to see if they can find a perfect match (2 congruent shapes). You can also do this same activity using tracing paper.

Area of Rectangles

Students in Core Knowledge schools should have been introduced to the concept of area in Grade 3 and should have learned how to find the area of a rectangle using a formula in Grade 4. You may wish to review both of these before teaching students how to find the area of triangles, parallelograms, and irregular figures.

Area, or the space inside a figure, is based on the idea of the number of unit squares that "fit inside" a shape, such as a square or rectangle. A good way to have students review the concept of area is to use a variety of square manipulatives to measure the area of different-sized rectangles or squares. For example, use square inch or square centimeter tiles and pre-drawn rectangles and have students determine how many tiles it takes to fill up each rectangle. Explain to students that the tiles must touch but not overlap each other. How many tiles can fit inside? That

number is the area of the rectangle. You can also have students use geoboards or count the square units in rectangles drawn on base ten grid paper to find area. Allow students significant opportunities to experiment with manipulatives and models and to review the concept of area.

Using standard units of measurement to find area is important, just as it is when performing other types of measurements. When communicating about area, it is necessary first to choose a unit of length, for example, inches or centimeters. Once a unit of length is selected, the square unit becomes the basis for defining what area means, and for calculating it. For example, if the unit for measuring length is the centimeter, then the area of a figure is some number of square centimeters. A square centimeter (cm²) is a square whose sides are each 1 centimeter long.

Teaching Idea

Use creative manipulatives to allow students to find the area of squares and rectangles. Index cards, business cards, notebook paper, playing cards, same-sized books, and other everyday objects in the shape of a square or rectangle can be used to find the space inside a figure. You can also use graph paper to find the square units inside a figure.

1 cm

1 cm

square centimeter

Similarly, a square inch (in.²) is a square, each of whose sides is one inch long. An abbreviation for one square centimeter is 1 cm² and the abbreviation for one square inch is 1 in.². This kind of notation works for other units as well. For example, 1 yd.² means one square yard and 1 mi.² stands for one square mile.

To help explain the meaning of area for rectangles whose sides have whole number lengths marked, consider a rectangle whose sides are 3 cm and 5 cm.

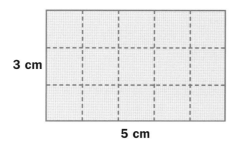

3 cm

5 cm

The area of this rectangle is the number of square centimeters it takes to fill up the inside of the rectangle. The square centimeters must lie entirely inside the rectangle, and they must not overlap. Notice that there are 3 rows of unit squares (each one is a square centimeter), and there are 5 unit squares in each row. Instead of counting the squares you can multiply the length of the sides to find the area:

Area = 5 cm x 3 cm = 15 cm²

The area is 15 cm² or 15 square centimeters. For rectangles, there is a formula for finding area:

Area = length x width, or Area = base x height

In the second formula, the base is the length and the height is the width. Writing the formula this way will help students understand the formulas for areas of triangles and parallelograms (see below).

It is important to emphasize that area does not mean length times width. Multiplying the length and the width of a rectangle gives the correct area in square units, but the area of rectangles whose sides have whole number lengths means the number of unit squares that fit inside the rectangle, as described in this subsection. Teaching the concept of area only through the formula Area = length × width can cause serious misconceptions. Other figures, such as triangles and circles, have different formulas for their areas, but the meaning of area for these other figures is based on the idea of the number of unit squares that "fit inside." Students who don't understand the meaning of area for rectangles sometimes try incorrectly to apply the formula Area = length × width to any geometric figure. The use of manipulatives and models along with instruction on the formula for area should allow students to gain a strong understanding of the concept and build on this foundation in later grades.

Perimeter is not mentioned in any of the guidelines in the *Sequence* for Grade 5. In Grade 2, students should have learned how to find the perimeter of squares and rectangles, and you may wish to review this in Grade 5.

Many Grade 5 math textbooks include lessons on both area and perimeter, and students sometimes confuse the two. The perimeter of a plane figure is the distance around it. The perimeter of a polygon is the sum of the lengths of its sides. The perimeter of a rectangle is the sum of the lengths of its four sides. You can find the perimeter of the rectangle below by adding the lengths of its sides:

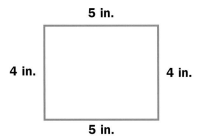

perimeter = 5 in. + 4 in. + 5 in. + 4 in. = 18 in.

Because of the commutative and associative properties of addition (see "Addition," on p. 483), the four lengths can be added in any order with the same answer for the perimeter. Some students might also observe that the perimeter can also be found this way:

perimeter = (2 x 5) + (2 x 4) inches = 10 + 8 inches = 18 inches

It is important that students have a clear understanding that these two concepts, area and perimeter, are different. An illustration like this one might help.

area = no. of unit squares inside **perimeter = distance around**

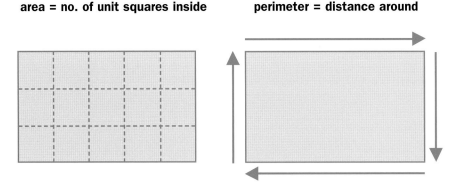

Area of Parallelograms and Triangles

After reviewing the concept of area and the formula for finding the area of rectangles, students should be ready to learn how to find the area of parallelograms and triangles. Remember, rectangles are just a special kind of parallelogram. If you cut up a parallelogram, you can move the pieces to make a rectangle. Fifth graders can gain insight into this strategy and the formula for the area of a parallelogram with the help of diagrams like this one.

To find the area of the parallelogram at the left, imagine cutting the triangle off the left end of the parallelogram and pasting it to the right end as indicated above. The result is a rectangle with the same base and height as the parallelogram. Because the area of a rectangle is $b \times h$, the formula for the area of the parallelogram is also $A = b \times h$, where h is the distance between the base and the side opposite the base on the parallelogram (which has the same length).

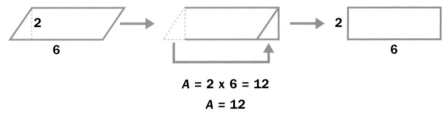

$$A = 2 \times 6 = 12$$
$$A = 12$$

Diagrams can also aid students in understanding the formula for the area of a triangle. In the case of right triangles, start with the triangle and use a congruent copy to form a rectangle:

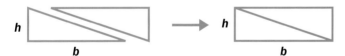

Because two identical triangles together form a rectangle whose area is base times height, the area of each triangle must be half that amount. Therefore the area of the triangle is $A = \frac{1}{2}(b \times h)$, where h and b are identified in the diagram.

To concretely demonstrate the concept of forming two triangles from a rectangle, give students paper cutouts of rectangles and allow them to cut them in half to form two triangles. Students can find the area of an individual triangle and of the entire rectangle to prove the formula to themselves. Likewise, students could draw rectangles on grid paper, draw a diagonal to create two triangles, and use the same technique to explore the concept.

The formula $A = \frac{1}{2}(b \times h)$ is valid not only for right triangles, but for any triangle, and this may be deduced using arguments similar to the one for right triangles. But what is meant by the base and the height of a triangle when it does not have a right angle? Any side of the triangle may be chosen to be the base. Once the base is chosen, the height of the triangle is the length of a line segment called an altitude of the triangle. The altitude is perpendicular to the line containing the base; it has one endpoint on that line and the other endpoint at the opposite vertex of the triangle. Each of the blue line segments shown below is an altitude.

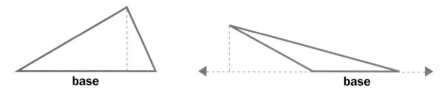

base   base

In the formula for the area of a triangle, h represents the length of the altitude (one of the blue line segments), and b represents the length of the base.

$$A = \frac{1}{2}(b \times h)$$

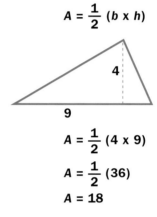

4

9

$$A = \frac{1}{2}(4 \times 9)$$

$$A = \frac{1}{2}(36)$$

$$A = 18$$

The area of a trapezoid may be found by cutting the trapezoid into two triangles as shown below, calculating the area of each triangle, and adding those areas.

A general formula for the area of a trapezoid may even be deduced using this idea. Areas of more complicated polygons may be calculated by partitioning their interiors into triangles and rectangles.

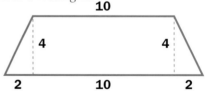

10

4   4

2   10   2

Begin by finding the area of the rectangle.

$$A = 10 \times 4 = 40$$

Then calculate the area of the first triangle.

$$A = \frac{1}{2}(2 \times 4) = \frac{1}{2}(8) = 4$$

Teaching Idea

When teaching students how to find the area of parallelograms and irregular figures, it is a good idea to let them use manipulatives such as paper cutouts and grid paper to explore the idea of rearranging or partitioning the shapes to form ones they know. A thorough understanding of the concept of finding area in this way will help make formulas more meaningful and provide a strong foundation for continued studies in later grades.

Next, calculate the area of the second triangle.

$$A = \frac{1}{2}(3 \times 4) = \frac{1}{2}(12) = 6$$

Finally, add the areas of each shape within the trapezoid.

A (trapezoid) = 40 + 4 + 6 = 50

Volume and Surface Area of Rectangular Prisms

Students should have learned how to find volumes of rectangular boxes, or rectangular prisms, in Grade 4. A rectangular prism, or rectangular box, looks like a cardboard box or a cereal box. It has six faces that are rectangles. Adjacent faces form right angles with each other, and opposite faces are parallel.

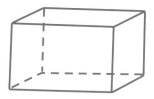 

rectangular prisms

The surface area of a rectangular prism is the sum of the areas of all of its faces. Imagine a rectangular prism like the one on the right, but made out of cardboard. What would it look like if you cut it along some of its edges and laid it flat? Here is a diagram of one way to lay the box out flat.

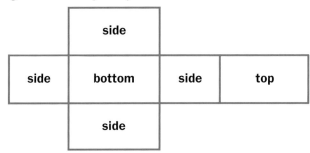

The surface area of the rectangular prism is the sum of the areas of all the rectangles shown here. Students can calculate surface areas of a rectangular prism if they are given the length, width, and height of the prism.

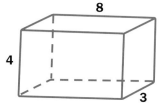

Surface area of rectangular prism =
area of six rectangles that make up prism
Area of ends = 2 (4 x 3) = 24
Area of top and bottom = 2 (8 x 3) = 48
Area of sides = 2 (8 x 4) = 64
Sum of areas = 24 + 48 + 64 = 136

> **Teaching Idea**
>
> Allow students the opportunity to construct a rectangular prism so that they can see the connection between the formulas and the solutions (as shown above). This connection can easily be made when students are given tape and a photocopy of a flattened prism. You can find many examples on the Internet using a search engine.

Point out to students that a cube is a special kind of rectangular prism. The edges of a cube all have the same length and the faces are all congruent squares.

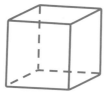 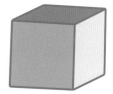

cubes

A rectangular prism may be thought of as a three-dimensional version of a rectangle, and a cube may be thought of as a three-dimensional version of a square. Just as the area of a rectangle is the number of unit squares that fit inside the rectangle, the volume of a rectangular prism is the number of unit cubes that fit inside the rectangular prism.

As with area, in order to understand volume, it is necessary first to choose a unit of length, such as inches or centimeters. Once a unit of length is selected, the cubic unit becomes the basis for defining what volume means and for calculating it. For example, if the unit for measuring length is the centimeter, then the volume of a figure is some number of cubic centimeters. A cubic centimeter is a cube whose sides are each 1 centimeter long.

1 cm 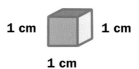 **1 cm**

1 cm

The volume of a rectangular prism whose sides have whole number lengths is just the number of unit cubes that fill it. The unit cubes must lie entirely inside the prism and they may not overlap. As an example, if each of the small cubes filling the rectangular prism below is a cubic centimeter, then the volume of the prism is 24 cm³.

4 cm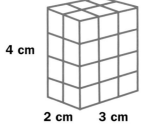

2 cm   **3 cm**

Students should explore the concept of volume using manipulatives such as boxes, blocks, sugar cubes, and other cubes that can be used to fill a rectangular box.

As with areas of rectangles, volumes of rectangular prisms may be calculated using multiplication. The formula for the volume of a rectangular prism is

Volume = length x width x height

To see why this formula is correct, imagine cutting the rectangular prism above into the four sections shown below. You can find the number of unit cubes

in each section, for example the top section, by multiplying the length times the width.

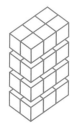

4 sections:

3 x 2 unit cubes in each section

The length times the width of the top section is 3×2. The total number of unit cubes is then $3 \times 2 \times 4$ because there are 4 sections just like the top section. Therefore, the volume = length $\times$ width $\times$ height. In Grade 4, students should have learned how to find the volume of rectangular prisms in the cubic units of cm^3 and $in.^3$. You may wish to review the connection of cm^3 and $in.^3$ with students.

Review

Below are some ideas for ongoing assessment and review activities. These are not meant to constitute a comprehensive list.

• The study of geometry can be nicely integrated with the study of visual arts. Post one of the pieces from the visual arts section in front of the class. Provide each student with a self-sticking note labeled with a topic studied in this section, such as line, polygon, angle, or solid figure. Then have each student come forward and place their self-sticking note on the art print to identify a place where they see that geometric concept. Students can also create their own pictures with the shapes and lines from this section.

• Play a congruency game with the class. Make two sets of congruent shapes by stacking two sheets of different color construction paper on top of each of each other and cutting out multisided polygons. Make one shape for each student in the class. To play, pass out one shape to each student, and ask the students to examine the shapes. Then, each student has to find the classmate with the congruent shape (matching shape and size). After the students have found each other, have them discuss what strategies they used to find a congruent pair.

• Go on a geometry scavenger hunt throughout the school. Give students a list of items that they are trying to find, using topics studied in this section. Have students record where in the school they find examples of each geometric concept. For example, the opposite sides of a bookcase have parallel lines. After the scavenger hunt, have students share their findings with the class.

• Provide groups of students with several different sizes of square and rectangle cutouts to have them practice finding area. Provide square tiles for the group to manipulate. Before computing area, have the groups estimate the area of each square and rectangle and write it on a recording sheet. Then find the area and record that measurement. How accurate were their estimates?

The Big Idea
in Review

Plane and solid figures can be identified, compared, and measured. Lines, angles, and triangles can be classified and named.

• Provide several different size cutouts of circles and have students measure the radius and diameter of each. Alternatively, list several different diameters and radii on the board and have students practice using a compass to draw circles of that size. You may also wish to have students find the circumference of each circle.

• Provide groups of students with several different sizes of cubes, and have them measure each side with a ruler in order to find the length, width, and height of each cube. Then have them practice finding the volume of each cube in cubic units. Have students write out their formulas and show their work.

• Give students an opportunity to create a picture using the shapes and forms they have studied from this section. Before starting, brainstorm with the class the geometric terms they have learned, define them, and write them on chart paper for reference. Tell the class that they must use at least 10 shapes, forms, or lines in their pictures. After creating their pictures, have students write a paragraph describing their pictures using correct terms and definitions from this section.

• Enlist the help of parents and caregivers to create a "geometry quilt." Allow each student to create a quilt square that illustrates one element of geometry studied or create a square that is geometric in nature. Be sure each student has a different element to illustrate. Then, parents can sew the quilt together. If a less complex culminating activity is preferred, you can simulate a quilt using construction and butcher paper. Students should create and write an explanation of their square. See the website listed in *More Resources* for examples.

More Resources

A good mathematics program follows sound cognitive principles and allows many opportunities for thoughtful and varied practice to build mastery of important skills. For advice on suitable mathematics programs, contact the Foundation.

The titles listed below are offered as a representative sample of materials and not a complete list of everything that is available.

For students —

• *Everything You Need to Know About Math Homework,* by Anne Zeman and Kate Kelly (Scholastic, 1994). A clear guide for students in Grades 4–6 that covers numbers and the number system, basic math functions, measurement, geometry, money, graphs, statistics, and computers. Paperback, ISBN 0590493590.

• *Geometry (Math Success),* by Lucille Caron and Philip M. St. Jacques (Enslow, 2001). Library binding, 64 pages, ISBN 0766014339.

• *How Math Works,* by Carol Vonderman (Reader's Digest, 1996). Hardcover, 192 pages, ISBN 0895778505.

• *Janice VanCleave's Geometry for Every Kid,* by Janice VanCleave (John Wiley & Sons, 1994). Paperback, 221 pages, ISBN 0471311413.

• *Math Trek 2: Adventures in the MathZone,* by Ivars Peterson and Nancy Henderson (John Wiley & Sons, 2000). Focuses on principles of geometry. Paperback, 128 pages, ISBN 0471315710.

• *Mental Math Challenges,* by Michael L. Lobosco (Sterling Publications, 1999). "… offers detailed instructions on the construction of mathematical models of two and three dimensions and related activities" (*School Library Journal*). Many of these problems will be tough for fifth graders. Hardcover, 80 pages, ISBN 1895569508.

• *Shape Up! Fun With Triangles and Other Polygons,* by David A. Adler (Holiday House, 1998). Activity-based, fun, and educational. Library binding, 32 pages, ISBN 0823413462.

More Resources continued

• *Sir Cumference and the Great Knight of Angleland: A Math Adventure,* by Cindy Neuschwander (Charlesbridge, 2001). Creative introduction to angles in a whimsical, medieval setting. Library binding, 32 pages, ISBN 1570911703. See also *Sir Cumference and the First Round Table* and *Sir Cumference and the Sword in the Cone* (geometric solids).

For teachers —

• *Key to Geometry (Keys to Math),* by Newton Hawley, Patrick Suppes, George Gearhart, and Peter Rasmussen (Key Curriculum Press, 1972). Great for individual or classroom instruction. The complete set of eight workbooks (also available individually) covers lines and segments, circles, constructions, perpendiculars, squares and rectangles, angles, and more. To view sample pages or to order, visit Key Curriculum Press, www.keypress.com, or phone 1-800-995-MATH. Answers and notes, as well as reproducible tests, are also available.

• *Math The Easy Way (Fourth Edition),* by Anthony and Katie Prindle (Barron's, 2003). A simply written book that can be used as a refresher course or as extra practice for students. Paperback, 234 pages, ISBN 0764120115.

• *Usborne Illustrated Dictionary of Math,* by Tori Large and others (Usborne, 2004). Paperback, 128 pages, ISBN 0794506623.

• Figure This!, www.figurethis.org, provides math challenges designed for middle school students.

• Mathematical Quilts products can be found at www.keypress.com/catalog/products/supplementals/Prod_MathQuilts.html.

VII. Probability and Statistics

The Big Idea

Data can be organized, displayed, and interpreted in many ways.

What Students Should Already Know

Students in Core Knowledge schools should be familiar with

Kindergarten

- interpreting simple pictorial graphs

Grade 1

- using tallies
- creating and interpreting simple pictorial graphs and bar graphs

Grade 2

- recording numeric data systematically (for example, tossing a die) and finding the lowest and highest values in a data set

Grade 3

- creating and interpreting line graphs
- recording outcomes for a simple event (for example, tossing a die) and displaying the results graphically

Grade 4

- plotting points on a coordinate plane (grid) using ordered pairs of positive whole numbers

What Students Need to Learn

- **Understand probability as a measure of the likelihood that an event will happen; using simple models, express probability of a given event as a fraction, as a percent, and as a decimal between 0 and 1**
- **Collect and organize data in graphic form (bar, line, and circle graphs)**
- **Solve problems requiring interpretation and application of graphically displayed data**
- **Find the average (mean) of a given set of numbers**
- **Plot points on a coordinate plane, using ordered pairs of positive and negative whole numbers**
- **Graph simple functions**

What Students Will Learn in Future Grades

The *Core Knowledge Sequence* for mathematics emphasizes the importance of reviewing and building on prior knowledge. Related topics from the Grade 6 *Sequence* are listed below, and subsequent grades will continue to focus on strengthening and expanding these skills.

Materials

coins, p. 529

dice, pp. 529, 530

counters, p. 532

maps, p. 533

copies of local newspaper, p. 535

access to school computer lab, p. 535

a collection of books for a class library on probability and statistics, p. 536

games, p. 536

What Students Will Learn in Future Grades continued
Grade 6

- find the range and measures of central tendency (mean, median, and mode) of a given set of numbers
- understand the differences among the measures of central tendency and when each might be used
- understand the use of a sample to estimate a population parameter (such as the mean), and that larger samples provide more stable estimates
- represent all possible outcomes of independent compound events in an organized way, and determine the theoretical probability of each outcome
- compute the probability of any one of a set of disjoint events as the sum of their individual probabilities
- given a set of data, find the mean, median, range, and mode
- construct a histogram and a tree diagram
- coordinate plane:
  - use the terms *origin* (0,0), *x-axis*, and *y-axis*
  - graph simple functions, and solve problems involving use of a coordinate plane

Vocabulary

Student/Teacher Vocabulary

bar graph: a graph that uses bars or wide lines to represent data (T)

circle graph: a graph that uses a circle divided into sections to display how parts make up a whole (S)

coordinate plane: a flat grid that can be used to show the exact location of points (S)

function: a relationship between numbers that can be expressed as an equation (e.g., y = x − 2), or graphed on a coordinate plane (S)

line graph: a graph that uses lines to represent data (T)

mean: the sum of a set of numbers divided by the number of numbers in the set; also called the average (S)

median: the number exactly in the middle of a set of numbers listed from least to greatest, e.g., in the set of numbers {1, 3, 5, 6, 10}, the number 5 is the median; if the set has two middle numbers, the median is the mean of the two middle numbers, e.g., in the set of numbers {3, 6, 7, 9, 12, 20}, 8 is the median (T)

mode: the number that appears most often in a set of numbers, e.g., in the set {1, 3, 4, 5, 4, 7}, the mode is 4. It is possible for a set of numbers to have no mode or to have more than one mode. (T)

ordered pair: a pair of numbers that indicates the exact location of a point on a coordinate plane (S)

probability: a measure of how likely it is for something to happen (S)

Mathematics   **527**

Vocabulary

Domain Vocabulary

Probability and statistics and associated words:
models, collect, organize, data, graphs, bar line, interpretation, application, coordinate, pairs, chance, odds, likelihood, probable, improbable, likely, unlikely, outcome, event, result, toss, roll, die/dice, spin, spinner, gamble, Las Vegas, casino, cards, game, up, down, more, less, show, depict, illustrate, axis, *x*-axis, *y*-axis, plot, average, tally, count, illustrate, show, record, frequency, part, whole, percentage, percentile, sum, divide

At A Glance

The most important ideas for you are:

- Probability can be expressed as a fraction, percent, or decimal.
- Data can be organized and displayed in bar graphs, line graphs, circle graphs, and coordinate planes.
- Information from graphs can be used to solve problems.
- Finding the mean, or average, of a set of numbers has many practical applications.
- Points and functions can be plotted on a coordinate plane.

What Teachers Need to Know

Background

The Core Knowledge probability and statistics guidelines constitute a relatively minor part of the Grade 5 mathematics curriculum, but it is still important to introduce students to these topics. Probability and statistics are present in our everyday lives in a multitude of forms, from studying population trends to determining the possibility that a person will contract a disease. Graphs are used in textbooks, reports, advertisements, and opinion polls, and in many other common places. Learning how to find, display, and interpret information is an important life skill for students.

Probability

Probability is a measure of how likely it is for something to happen. The probability of an event (something that happens) can be expressed as a number between 0 and 1. The larger the probability, the more likely the event. Events that are certain to occur have probability 1, and events that are certain not to occur have probability 0.

A simple example of a probability experiment is a coin toss. If the coin is fair, the event of getting "heads" has probability $\frac{1}{2}$ and the event of getting "tails" also has probability $\frac{1}{2}$. These probabilities may also be written as decimals or percents.

The probability of getting heads on a coin toss is 0.5 or 50%, and this is also the probability of tails.

There is a simple way to find probabilities of outcomes when all of the outcomes are equally likely:

If there are _n_ equally likely outcomes to an experiment, then the probability of each outcome is $\frac{1}{n}$.

For example, our experiment might be to toss a die. A die looks like a cube and has six faces. ("Dice" is the plural of "die.") The faces are numbered 1, 2, 3, 4, 5, and 6. If the die is fair (not "loaded," or weighted on one face) then the faces are all equally likely to result after a single toss of the die. In this case, $n = 6$, and the probability of rolling any one of the numbers is $\frac{1}{6}$. The significance of this probability ($\frac{1}{6}$) to practical experience is that after many tosses of a fair die, each number on the die will appear about one-sixth of the total number of tosses.

Often, people are interested in the probability of an event that includes more than one individual outcome. For example, we could ask for the probability of rolling an even number with one toss of a fair die. That is, we could ask for the probability of rolling 2, 4, or 6 in one toss.

Here is the rule for finding probabilities of events that correspond to one or more individual outcomes, when all the outcomes are equally likely:

The probability of an event is the fraction whose numerator is the number of ways the event can occur, and whose denominator is the number of ways that anything can happen in the experiment.

For example, we can use this rule to find the probability of rolling an even number—a 2, 4, or 6—with a single toss of a fair die. The numerator of our fraction is 3 because there are three ways to roll an even number: 2, 4, and 6. The denominator of the fraction is 6 because altogether there are six possible outcomes for this experiment: 1, 2, 3, 4, 5, and 6. The probability of rolling an even number is therefore $\frac{3}{6}$, which may be simplified to $\frac{1}{2}$.

The probability of an event when all outcomes are equally likely may be understood as this fraction:

$$\frac{\text{number of ways an event can occur}}{\text{total number of possible outcomes}}$$

If E is an event, the probability that E does not happen (let's write this as "not E") is given by this formula:

P(not E) = 1 − P(E)

Suppose that a weatherman predicts a 25% chance of rain on a particular day. What is the probability that it does not rain on that day? If _E_ is the event that it rains, then _not E_ is the event that it does not rain. Then,

P(not E) = 1 − P(E) = 1 − 25% = 1 − 0.25 = 0.75 = 75%

So, the probability that it does not rain is 75% (which is the same as 0.75 or $\frac{3}{4}$).

Organizing Data in Graphs

Before data can be displayed on a graph, it must be collected and organized in a systematic way. Tally marks are often useful for this purpose. Core Knowledge students should have had practice using tallies starting in Grade 1. To review, remind students that tallies are useful for keeping track of categories. To

Teaching Idea

Point out the probability of events to reinforce the daily use of probability. For example, track the weather forecast and actual weather for 2 weeks at a time.

Teaching Idea

Play a variety of probability games with your class. First, have students predict results, and then explain outcomes through fractions and percentages. For example:

• _Heads or Tails?_ How many times will the coin land on its head? On its tail?

• _Roll the Dice._ How many times will the die land on each number? For a more complicated version, use 2 dice and predict the total of both dice. Be sure to roll the dice or flip the coin enough that the averages begin to come out.

• _Game Day._ Have students play games of chance and guess the probability of winning. How does the probability change when more or fewer players are added to the game? Are there certain strategies students use to win?

identify the numbers of girls and boys in the class, you might use tallies. As you name the students, a volunteer can place a tally mark in the row for boys or the row for girls, as follows. After four tally marks in either row, have the volunteer use the fifth tally mark in that row to cross the bundle of four; this indicates a bundle of five altogether. The result of such a process might look like this:

Boys ⅢⅡ ⅢⅡ ⅢⅠ

Girls ⅢⅡ ⅢⅡ ⅠⅠ

Students can count the crossed bundles by fives then count the remaining tallies by ones. The tally count shown indicates 26 students altogether, with 14 boys and 12 girls.

Here is another example of using tallies to keep track of data. Toss a die (one of two dice) 30 times. Collect the results in a table.

Face of Die	Frequency (number of times out of 30)	
1	ⅢⅡ	5
2	ⅢⅡ ⅠⅠ	7
3	ⅠⅠⅠⅠ	4
4	ⅠⅠⅠ	3
5	ⅢⅡ	5
6	ⅢⅡ Ⅰ	6

Students should make one tally mark in the middle column after each toss of the die. The third column is filled out only after the 30th, and final, toss of the die. In this way, students can keep track of the data systematically. Of course, the results for this experiment will vary, so students are likely to get numbers different from those above. After many more tosses of a fair die, the numbers in the right column should be nearly the same. Each number in the right column would be equal to about one-sixth of the total number of tosses of the die.

The type of data from the experiment above can be displayed well as a bar graph such as the following:

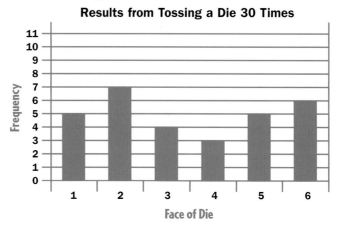

Students should have been introduced to bar graphs in Grade 1, but it may be helpful to review their features again. A bar graph uses bars, or wide lines, to represent a number. The vertical axis has an incremental scale used to indicate

amounts of data. The horizontal axis lists items or categories of data, with a bar drawn above each item or category. The height of the bar indicates the quantity of data, using the scale on the vertical axis.

In contrast to bar graphs, line graphs use lines to show data, and are better used to show how data changes over time. Points are plotted to represent data, and the points are connected to create a line. The horizontal axis often has an incremental scale to show a measure such as an amount of time. The vertical axis has numbers for what is being measured. Line graphs are used to show how data changes over time, such as increases or decreases in temperature or population size.

As an example, suppose that daily high temperatures were tracked for a week. The results may be collected in a table like this one:

Date	Temperature
Monday, Sept. 20	70°
Tuesday, Sept. 21	76°
Wednesday, Sept. 22	78°
Thursday, Sept. 23	71°
Friday, Sept. 24	84°
Saturday, Sept. 25	78°
Sunday, Sept. 26	76°

The type of data from the experiment above can be displayed well as a line graph such as the following:

> **Cross-curricular Teaching Idea**
>
> Have students conduct research on other topic areas from the *Core Knowledge Sequence* and find data about that topic that can be shown in graph form. For example, students might research casualties during Civil War battles. Teach students to choose which graph will best display their data—bar, line, or circle. Additionally, encourage students to include graphs in research reports they present to the class.

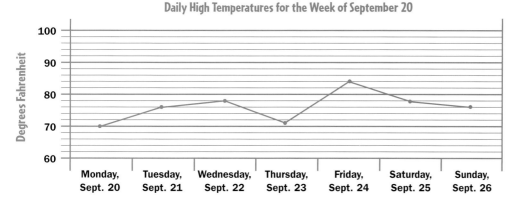

Daily High Temperatures for the Week of September 20

Each point shows the temperature on that day. The line segments connect the points to show how the high temperatures changed each day. It is important for students to be able to interpret information given to them in graphical form. Here are some sample questions to ask students related to this line graph:

Which day had the highest high temperature? (Friday)

Which day had the lowest high temperature? (Monday)

What was the change in high temperature from Thursday to Friday? (13°F)

How much warmer was the high temperature on Saturday than on Monday? (8°F)

A circle graph, or pie chart, can be used to display how parts make up a whole. Each section of the circle represents part of the whole. For example, the circle graph below might be used to display the percentage of annual rainfall for each season in a given city. Each season, or part of the whole year of rainfall, is represented by a section of the circle.

Percentage of Annual Rainfall by Season in Rainbow City

Annual Rainfall: 24 inches

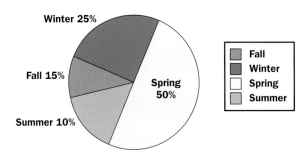

You may want to ask questions like the following:

In which season (or part of the whole year) does the most rain fall? (spring)

How many inches of rain fall in the winter? (6 in.)

How much more rain falls in the spring than in the summer? (9.6 in.)

Finding the Average (Mean)

Statisticians sometimes refer to the mean, median, mode(s), and the range of a list of numbers.

In Grade 5, students will learn how to find the mean, and they will learn how to find the median, mode, and range in Grade 6.

The mean, or average of a list of numbers, is the sum of the numbers divided by the number of numbers. For example, the mean of the list of numbers 1, 3, 8 is

(1 + 3 + 8) ÷ 3 = 4

The mean, or average, of three numbers is the sum of the numbers divided by 3.

For a concrete way to demonstrate mean, have students stack counters in columns to represent the numbers being averaged. For the example above, students would make a column of 1 counter, a column of 3 counters, and a column of 8 counters. Next, ask students to move counters around between columns until each column has the same number of counters. The number of counters now in each stack is the mean, or average.

There are many practical applications for finding the mean. For example, mean can tell the average number of students who buy milk each day, or it can be used to find the average of a student's math test scores.

The Coordinate Plane

Students should have been introduced to the idea of a coordinate plane in Grade 4, but they were only required to learn how to plot points associated with ordered pairs of positive whole numbers. Students' graphing skills are extended in Grade 5.

Coordinate planes, or grids, offer another way to organize and display data by plotting points. Planes and points are discussed in "Geometry," on pp. 508–525. Think of a plane as a flat surface, like a tabletop or a flat paper map. A point may be understood as an exact location in the plane. Students in Grade 5 should have learned that a point in a plane may be identified using just two numbers.

The diagram below shows two number lines. One number line is horizontal. This is called the *x*-axis, and the vertical axis is called the *y*-axis. These names are standard in many middle and high school algebra textbooks, so it is a good idea for students to begin to use those terms.

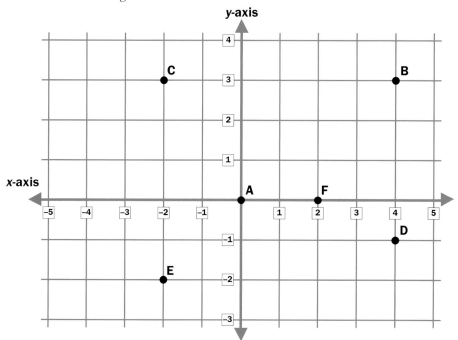

Two numbers together name a point. These numbers are called an ordered pair, or the coordinates of the point. The first number tells how many steps to move along the *x*-axis, and the second number tells how many steps to move up or down (or vertically) parallel to the *y*-axis. The point labeled *A* above has coordinates (0,0). This is because *A* is located at the zero point on both the *x*-axis and the *y*-axis.

The coordinates (4, 3) name the location of point *B* pictured above. The coordinates tell us to first move 4 units (or steps) to the right, and then 3 units up to find point *B*. The first number 4, is the *x*-coordinate and the second number, 3, is the *y*-coordinate. The *x*-coordinate is always listed first, as in (4, 3).

If the *x*-coordinate of a point is negative, then starting at the origin (0, 0) first move to the left. For example, the coordinates of point *C* are (–2, 3). To locate *C*, move two units to the left (because –2 is negative), and then 3 units up. If the *y*-coordinate is negative, we must go down instead of up for the second step. For

Teaching Idea

Set up a "coordinate plane" on the floor of your classroom. Have students describe the locations of their desks based on the coordinate plane. You can also have students move on the coordinate plane and then draw their corresponding movements on a piece of graph paper. This activity will reinforce the connection between the physical coordinate plane and the ones on their paper.

Teaching Idea

Students can practice finding points on a coordinate plane by using a map index to find a specific location. Maps often use grids labeled with letters and numbers. You may wish to create a map scavenger hunt for students. Give them the *x*- and *y*-coordinates of certain points and have them identify the points on the map. Afterwards, students can create their own list of coordinate points and swap them with a partner to continue practicing.

example, the coordinates of point *D* are (4, –1). The coordinates tell us to move 4 steps to the right, and then 1 step down (because the *y*-coordinate, –1, is negative).

Both coordinates can be negative as for point *E*. The coordinates of *E* are (–2, –2); take 2 steps to the left, then 2 steps down. The coordinates of point *F* are (2, 0). To find *F*, move 2 units to the right, but no unit up or down (because the *y*-coordinate is 0).

Graphing Simple Functions

Students in Grade 5 learn to graph simple functions, such as $y = x - 2$. The first step is to find pairs of numbers, one for *x* and one for *y*, that satisfy the equation. The next step is to treat these pairs of numbers as coordinates and plot them.

To find pairs of numbers satisfying $y = x - 2$, you can first choose *x* to be any number you wish, and then calculate *y*. For example, if $x = 3$, then $y = 3 - 2 = 1$; if $x = 0$, then $y = 0 - 2 = -2$. A table like this one can be helpful for organizing *x* and *y* values that satisfy the equation.

Table for

$y = x - 2$

x	y
0	–2
1	–1
2	0
3	1
4	2
–1	–3
–2	–4

The numbers for *x* may be freely chosen; they can even be fractions or decimals. For simplicity, only integers appear in this table. For each value of *x* in the first column, the value for *y* in the second column is determined by the equation, $y = x - 2$.

The next step is to plot the points from the table: (0, –2), (1, –1), (2, 0), etc.

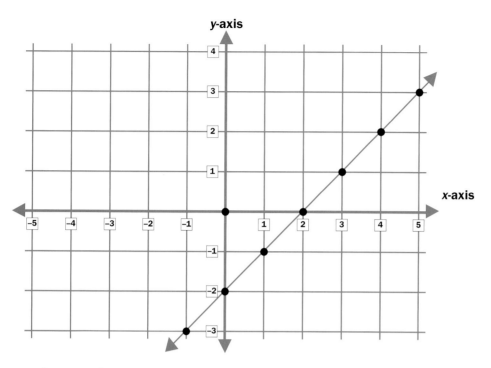

y-axis

x-axis

The points from the table lie on a straight line. If more points satisfying the equation $y = x - 2$ are plotted, they will also lie on the line shown on the graph. Students learn in algebra classes in later grades that the graph of any equation of the form $y = mx + b$, where m and b are numbers, is a straight line. In our case, $m = 1$ and $b = -2$. However, teachers should be aware that the graphs of many functions are not straight lines. For example, the graph of the equation $y = x^2$ is a parabola, which is not a straight line. Graphing exercises like the one above for $y = x - 2$ give students practice for future algebra and science classes.

─────────────────────────────

Review

Below are some ideas for ongoing assessment and review activities. These are not meant to constitute a comprehensive list.

• During the week, have copies of the local newspaper delivered to the class. In the paper, have students search for data that has been presented in graphs or in any type of chart. Ask students to write a paragraph describing the information provided in the graph or chart. Share these with the class.

• Computer programs provide an opportunity for students to input information and then to display their information in a variety of charts and graphs. Use your school computer lab to have students use these programs to construct graphs. Have students share their work with the class.

• Remember to incorporate graphs into other areas of Core Knowledge study. For example, students may vote on the most influential person of the Civil War and then post the results on a bar graph. You may have the class refer to the graph when you ask comprehension questions during the Civil War unit. For example, if 12 students choose Abraham Lincoln as the most influential person of the Civil War, ask students to give three reasons they chose him.

The Big Idea in Review

Data can be organized, displayed, and interpreted in many ways.

VII. Probability and Statistics

• Have the media specialists or librarian assemble a collection of books on probability and statistics. Students might find it interesting to see what the probability of certain events is for weather or science, such as the probability of an object being struck by lightning. Ask students to write a paragraph explaining how they use probability and statistics in their daily lives. Share these with the class.

• Once a week, present the class with some data in a word problem, and ask them to present it in some type of graph. Students must draw their graphs and explain why they chose to represent the data in that way. Discuss whether there is a better way to display some types of data.

• Encourage students to bring in games from home and provide a variety of games in the room to practice skills from this section. For example, simple card games provide opportunities to count numbers or predict the probability of events. Once a month, organize a game day to practice math skills.

More Resources

A good mathematics program follows sound cognitive principles and allows many opportunities for thoughtful and varied practice to build mastery of important skills. For advice on suitable mathematics programs, contact the Foundation.

The titles listed below are offered as a representative sample of materials and not a complete list of everything that is available.

For students —

• *Everything You Need to Know About Math Homework,* by Anne Zeman and Kate Kelly (Scholastic, 1994). A clear guide for students in Grades 4–6 that covers numbers and the number system, basic math functions, measurement, geometry, money, graphs, statistics, and computers. Paperback, ISBN 0590493590.

• *How Math Works,* by Carol Vonderman (Reader's Digest, 1996). Hardcover, 192 pages, ISBN 0895778505.

• *Plotting Points and Position (Math for Fun),* by Andrew King (Copper Beech, 1998). Library binding, 32 pages, ISBN 0761308520.

• *Tiger Math: Learning to Graph From a Baby Tiger,* by Ann Whitehead Nagda and Cindy Bickel (Henry Holt, 2002). Paperback, 32 pages, ISBN 080507161X.

For teachers —

• *The Complete Idiot's Guide to Statistics,* by Robert A. Donnelly (Alpha, 2004). Paperback, 400 pages, ISBN 1592571999.

• *Usborne Illustrated Dictionary of Math,* by Tori Large and others (Usborne, 2004). Paperback, 128 pages, ISBN 0794506623.

• Figure This!, www.figurethis.org, provides math challenges designed for middle school students.

VIII. Pre-Algebra

The Big Idea

In algebra, variables are used to stand for unknown numbers, and equations are used to solve problems.

What Students Should Already Know

Grade 1

▶ writing an addition or subtraction equation to solve basic one-step story and picture problems in the form of ___ − 2 = 7; 5 + ___ = 7.

Grade 2

▶ solving simple word problems and equations with addition, subtraction or multiplication

Grade 3

▶ solving two-step word problems and solving word problems involving multiplication

▶ solving equations in the form of ___ × 9 = 63; 81 ÷ ___ = 9

▶ reading and writing expressions that use parentheses to indicate order of multiple operations

Grade 4

▶ equality properties: knowing that equals added to equals are equal; equals multiplied by equals are equal

▶ using letters to stand for any number, as in working with a formula (for example, area of rectangle: $A = l \times w$)

What Students Need to Learn

▶ **Recognize variables and solve basic equations using variables**

▶ **Write and solve equations for word problems**

▶ **Find the value of an expression given the replacement values for the variables; for example: what is 7 − *c* if *c* is 3.5?**

What Students Will Learn in Future Grades

The *Core Knowledge Sequence* for mathematics emphasizes the importance of reviewing and building on prior knowledge. Related topics from the Grade 6 *Sequence* are listed below, and subsequent grades will continue to focus on strengthening and expanding these skills.

Grade 6

▶ recognize uses of variables, and solve linear equations in one variable

▶ solve word problems by assigning variables to unknown quantities, writing appropriate equations, and solving them

VIII. Pre-Algebra

Materials

index cards, p. 540

math journals, p. 540

information on meeting with middle school or high school algebra class, p. 541

What Students Will Learn in Future Grades continued

- find the value for an expression, given replacement values for the variables; for example: what is $\frac{7}{x} - y$ when x is 2 and y is 10?
- simplify expressions with variables by combining like terms
- understand the use of the distributive property in variable expressions such as $2x(2y+3)$

Vocabulary

Student/Teacher Vocabulary

algebra: a type of mathematics in which letters are used to represent unknown quantities (S)

equation: a mathematical statement that two expressions are equal (S)

expression: a variable or a combination of variables, numbers, and operations that show a mathematical relationship (S)

variable: a symbol that stands for a number (S)

Domain Vocabulary

Pre-Algebra and associated words:
values, solve, find, side, substitute, equal, multiply, divide, add, subtract, times, plus, minus, equals

At A Glance

The most important ideas for you are:

- Variables are symbols that stand for unknown numbers in expressions and equations.
- Algebraic equations with variables can be used to solve problems.
- The value of expressions can be solved by substituting values for the variables.

What Teachers Need to Know

Background

The Core Knowledge curriculum gradually introduces concepts from algebra in the elementary school grades. Part of the reason for doing this is that it eases the transition into algebra classes for students in middle school. In Grade 4, students in Core Knowledge schools should have learned to substitute numbers for variables in mathematical expressions. They should have also learned the algebraic principles "equals added to equals are equal" and "equals multiplied by equals are equal." Topics in Grade 5 will help students continue to develop their problem-solving skills and prepare them for further studies in algebra in the later grades.

Using Variables in Expressions and Equations

A variable is a symbol that stands for an unknown number. An expression is a variable or a combination of variables, numbers, and operations that show a mathematical relationship. For example, $4 + x$, a^2, and $2b - 7$ are all algebraic expressions. The most basic Grade 5 guideline, which asks students to be able to find the value of an expression given the replacement values for the variables, reinforces Grade 4 skills. For example, what is $7 - c$ if c is 3.5?

If $c = 3.5$, then $7 - c = 7 - 3.5 = 3.5$. As fourth graders, Core Knowledge students should have learned to substitute numbers for variables in a variety of contexts, including the calculation of areas of rectangles via the formula $A = l \times w$ (area equals length times width). Fifth graders can review and expand upon this skill by substituting integers, fractions, and decimals for variables as appropriate in mathematical expressions.

An equation is a mathematical statement that two expressions are equal. For example, in the equation $x - 29 = 53$, $x - 29$ has the same value as 53. When introducing the solving of equations to Grade 5 students, you might begin by asking students to suppose that x is a "mystery number." The goal is to find the number x if we know that

$$x - 29 = 53$$

Now, many students will quickly realize that the value of x may be found by adding 29 and 53. It is likely that they encountered problems similar to this one in earlier grades. However, a fruitful way to approach this problem is to add 29 to both sides of this equation. The resulting equation is:

$$x - 29 + 29 = 53 + 29$$

The next step is to recognize that $x - 29 + 29 = x$. Students may understand it this way: start with a number x, subtract 29, and now add 29 back again. The result is the original number x. So, continuing with the problem above,

$$x = 53 + 29$$
$$x = 82$$

Students can write equations to go with word problems such as this one: After eating 29 blueberries, Peter had 53 left. How many blueberries did he start with?

Encourage students to clearly identify an unknown variable. In this case, let x be equal to the number of blueberries that Peter started with. Then follow as above:

$$x - 29 = 53$$

$$x = 82 \text{ blueberries}$$

Here's another example of an equation that can be written to solve a word problem.

Barbara bought 2 mystery books and 1 magazine. The magazine cost $5 and she spent a total of $25. Assuming the 2 mystery books cost the same amount, what was the cost of each mystery book?

In this case, students again need to identify an unknown variable, which is the price of each mystery book. Students can let B be equal to the price of 1 mystery book and create the following equation to solve the problem:

$$B + B + 5 = 25$$

In this equation, B is equal to the price of a mystery book, 5 is the price of a magazine, and 25 is the total amount Barbara spent. Students will use the following steps to solve the equation:

$$B + B + 5 = 25$$

$$2B + 5 = 25$$

$$2B + 5 - 5 = 25 - 5$$

$$2B = 20$$

$$\frac{2B}{2} = \frac{20}{2}$$

$$B = 10$$

Each mystery book cost $10.

The Big Idea in Review

In algebra, variables are used to stand for unknown numbers, and equations are used to solve problems.

Review

Below are some ideas for ongoing assessment and review activities. These are not meant to constitute a comprehensive list.

• Make a set of numbered index cards with a word problem written on each one. Give each student a card and have him or her solve the problem. After a few minutes, have students switch cards with their neighbor and solve the next problem, being sure to mark the number of the word problem on their paper. Continue swapping cards so that each student has a chance to solve all of the word problems. When the class has finished, have each student share the answer to the last problem he or she solved and check with the class to see if everyone got the same solution.

• Present an algebra equation each day for students to solve in their math journals. Students should share their answers and approaches aloud with the class.

• Plan a day when the class pairs up with students from an upper grade to work on algebra problems together. In pairs, have an older and younger student share and solve problems. You may also want to have an algebra teacher from the middle or high school prepare a short talk about the study of algebra in the world around us.

More Resources

A good mathematics program follows sound cognitive principles and allows many opportunities for thoughtful and varied practice to build mastery of important skills. For advice on suitable mathematics programs, contact the Foundation.

The titles listed below are offered as a representative sample of materials and not a complete list of everything that is available.

For students —

• *How Math Works*, by Carol Vonderman (Reader's Digest, 1996). Hardcover, 192 pages, ISBN 0895778505.

• *Pre-Algebra and Algebra (Math Success)*, by Lucille Caron and Philip M. St. Jacques (Enslow, 2000). Library binding, 64 pages, ISBN 0766014347.

For teachers —

• *Key to Algebra (Keys to Math)*, by Julie King and Peter Rasmussen (Key Curriculum Press, 1991). The first three workbooks in this series cover the basics: operations on integers; variables, terms and expressions; and equations. To view sample pages or to order, visit Key Curriculum Press, www.keypress.com, or phone 1-800-995-MATH. Answers and notes, as well as reproducible tests, are also available.

• *Math The Easy Way (Fourth Edition)*, by Anthony and Katie Prindle (Barron's, 2003). A simply written book that can be used as a refresher course or as extra practice for students. Paperback, 234 pages, ISBN 0764120115.

• *Usborne Illustrated Dictionary of Math,* by Tori Large and others (Usborne, 2004). Paperback, 128 pages, ISBN 0794506623.

• Figure This!, www.figurethis.org, provides math challenges designed for middle school students.

Supplemental Essay #1

Math and the Magical Number Seven

by E. D. Hirsch, Jr.

One of the most famous articles in modern psychology is "The Magical Number Seven—Plus or Minus Two" by George A. Miller. It's famous because it brought to people's attention a crucial absolute limit in the human mind that constrains both math geniuses and ordinary mortals. Seven is the approximate number of separate things that we can hold in mind before they start to evaporate into oblivion. We have to put those things together quickly in some meaningful way before they disappear, or else we will lose the opportunity to make sense of them. This small, momentary storage place of the mind is called working memory or short-term memory. It's where all of our conscious mental operations first take place. One of the reasons that novices in math have a hard time with some of the simplest problems is not that they lack understanding, but that they lack the ability to put together one step of a multistep problem quickly before they forget what it is they were trying to do.

Take for instance the simple problem of adding 4 and 8 and 9. Very young beginners know the principle of how to add things. If you ask them to add one and one, they can do it without a mistake. But if you ask them to add 4 and 8 and 9 they may get the answer wrong not because they don't understand, but because they have run up against the limits of short-term memory. Think of a five-year-old who still adds by finger counting. "One two, three, four, that's four and then five, six, seven, eight, nine, ten, eleven, twelve, thirteen, that's four plus nine. And then what was I supposed to add to that? Oh, dear, I have to start over again!" So the student may give up, or give a wrong answer, not because she doesn't understand, but because the underlying processes are too slow, making one part of the problem evaporate from memory before the problem is complete.

How is this limit overcome? Not by gaining a deeper understanding of addition, which children (and some animals) are born with, but rather by using a faster processing method. Processing speed is what makes the big difference between novices and experts in any subject, and processing speed is increased not by making the mind work faster, which none of us can do, but by using two other devices: making some of the procedures unconscious and automatic, and by already knowing in advance certain facts such as 4 plus 8 is 12. Experts do the underlying math processes very fast (and partly unconsciously). This allows them to overcome the limits of short-term memory by using shortcuts like just knowing that 4 and 8 is 12, and 12 plus 9 is 21. By having these already-familiar elements quickly available, the expert can keep all the elements in mind with ease.

In this respect doing math is like reading. To understand the phrase "When in the course of human events it becomes necessary for one people to dissolve the political bands which have connected them with another," you have to be able to turn those letters into sounds and words very fast and automatically so you can hold in mind all the words of the phrase. Otherwise, some of them will drift out of memory. That's why gaining "automaticity," that is, being able to do the underlying processes fast and unconsciously, is the key to reading and the key to under-

standing math at all levels, and going on to gain still deeper understanding and achievement. That's why the education war between proponents of drill and proponents of deep understanding is a very big mistake. These two sides should get together. You can't have deep understanding in math without enough drill to make the basic math processes fast and automatic.

Math Fluency and Familiarity Versus Math Phobia

by E. D. Hirsch, Jr.

A lot of people think that math is a subject that you are innately good at or you hate.

Some math experts have said that one of the great barriers to American achievement in math is a vicious cycle whereby elementary teachers themselves have math phobia, and math aversion, and this rubs off on students, and also causes teachers to spend less time on math, which in turn causes students to dislike math even more and fail to fulfill their potential. These same experts say that these students have much greater math potential than we may believe, and that this is proved by the fact that all young students perform rather well in math in those countries that have a tradition of math emphasis in the early grades.

In "Math and the Magical Number Seven," we explained why familiarity and speed are important in understanding math problems and getting them right. Fluency is equally important in avoiding math phobia and bringing out the math potential in our students.

Think of how important familiarity is in reading. Suppose I wrote a sentence using Cyrillic letters. You would have trouble reading it:

СУППОЗ АЙ

РОТ а СЭНТЭНС

ЮЗИН СЫРИЛИК

ЛЭТРС.

I wrote: "Suppose I wrote a sentence using Cyrillic letters." Yet what I wrote was easy to understand when it was presented in familiar letters.

The same is true in math. We have to make our students *familiar* with the symbols and with the operations of math, and as they become truly familiar, their pleasure in the subject will increase. And so will their understanding. Believe it or not, drill is the friend of taking pleasure in math, because drill is the road to fluency and familiarity.

We teachers who were not given the math education we deserve need to break the cycle of math aversion for our students. In doing so, we may very well find that we have an ever greater liking for the subject ourselves.

Supplemental Essay #3

How to Help Children Understand Why They Make Math Errors

Think back to when you were a student in elementary school. Your answers to a worksheet of math problems have just been returned—or maybe a classmate has graded them in class—and you're dismayed to see that certain types of problems have stumped you again. Maybe it's addition problems that require regrouping. Or maybe it's subtraction when you must borrow from the tens column—that operation always gives you trouble. Or maybe the difficulty centers on (as it did for this writer) the mysterious "zero." When is it only a placeholder? And why can't you subtract 5 from zero? Won't the answer be 5?

As a teacher, you probably see errors like these committed by your students again and again. Some students seem to have a mental block about a particular operation. And because they tend to miss the same type of problem, they begin to give up—"I just don't get it!" You sympathize with their angry face-rubbing and frustration, but when a math answer is wrong, it's just wrong—isn't it?

Actually, an effective way of helping students "get it" springs from understanding how they think. The old proverb "Practice makes perfect" is true in some circumstances; but if students don't recognize the math errors they make again and again, the saying might as well be "Practicing mistakes can make them permanent."

▶ Overlapping Waves Theory

How our thinking becomes more sophisticated as we grow—or the process of cognitive development—has been the subject of intense research for nearly a century. The Swiss psychologist and historian Jean Piaget (1896–1980) devoted his long and influential career, for example, to answering the question: How does knowledge grow? His answer was that gaining knowledge is a series of progressive steps. Lower, less powerful logical thoughts are folded into, and gradually overtaken by, higher and more powerful ones up to adulthood. Therefore, students' logic and modes of thinking start out entirely different from those of adults.

More recently, Robbie Case's book *The Mind's Staircase* (1992) uses a simple image to expand on Piaget's explanation about knowledge-building. According to Case, children think a particular way for awhile (a tread on a staircase); then their thinking undergoes a breakthrough—"Oh, I get!" (the riser on a staircase); then they think on a different and higher plane for another extended period (the next tread), and so on. Often, specific stages of cognitive development are said to be typical of a child's age level, too. Five-year-olds tend to solve simple addition problems by counting from 1; seven-year-olds by counting from the larger addend; and nine-year-olds by coming up with the answer from memory.

But studies by Robert S. Siegler at Carnegie Mellon University, and his colleagues, have pointed out a simple fact that most veteran teachers already know: students will use different strategies to figure out what they want to know. On a trial-by-trial basis, people will approach a problem in different ways—whether the task is reasoning, language, memory, attention, or motor activity—and whether they are infants, toddlers, preschoolers, elementary children, teenagers, or adults. Although called "variable strategies," these attempts are not random. Students *adapt* and *refine* their strategies as they go, sometimes falling back and rehearsing the old approaches—not discarding them quite yet—before trying a new strategy. This means that the staircase image of students going "up and up" in knowledge and learning does not describe what students really do (but if you think about it, many math textbooks take the "up and up" approach in the way they present material). A better image would be that knowledge and learning in a student's mind are like a tide coming in: the waves fall back (old strategies), then curl forward and fall on the shore (new strategies), and the waterline surges higher and higher up the beach. In fact, this explanation of cognitive change is called "overlapping waves theory."

Studies conducted to explore overlapping waves theory indicate that students gradually select strategies that ultimately result in rapid and accurate solutions. As they discover more successful strategies, they learn more about the problem at hand. Correct solutions become more strongly linked with problems, and students opt for the most efficient strategy. Often, they first must rely on a more time-consuming technique before they discover a faster way. But many factors—including practice, reasoning, tasks with new challenges and adult help—contribute to improved problem solving.

So for you, the classroom teacher, the question is: How can I get students to experiment with different strategies for finding the right answer to a division problem, for instance?

Go Fly a Kite

First, to show that trying different strategies is a necessary step in learning, let's create an activity outside the classroom. Imagine this: you take your students outside, and give a kite to teams of three students. All the kites are exactly the same. Then you state the problem and give instruction about solving it: "Get the kite to fly. Kites fly by going against the wind." (You demonstrate.) "You can check the direction of the wind by tossing a few blades of grass in the air." (You demonstrate.) "The goal is to get the kite to fly higher until your string runs out." This is basically similar to putting a math problem on the board and giving instruction about getting the answer (the goal) by steps you recommend.

As you would expect, in both kite-flying and math problem situations, students will take different approaches and use different strategies. As Siegler writes, "Children who are presented the same instructional procedure often construct quite different strategies." To solve the kite-flying problem, some students will pull their kite behind a bike; some will go around the building in search of more wind; others will shorten the kite's tail. They may go back and adapt a strategy that seemed promising and combine it with a new one; say, shortening the kite's tail, but using a bike to pull it this time.

And this is important: you'll hear them *talk through what they're doing*—suggesting reasons, offering new ideas, recommending new approaches. Siegler and his colleagues call this "self-explanations." Self-explanations are inferences about the connections between objects and events—the "hows" and "whys" events happen. The kite keeps nose-diving? Maybe the tail's too heavy. Or the string could be too slack, too. Try keeping the string stretched tight this time. Let's try it. Moreover, when the kite does fly, the team can explain what did or didn't work and why.

Making Connections

The ability to make causal connections—to explain the causes of events—seems to be a fundamental trait of human beings. Even very young children can do it. Consequently, math teachers—and science teachers, too—can become exasperated when students' ability to make connections suddenly seems to have vanished. As if they were blindly following a recipe, students can perform a procedure in math and have no idea why it works—or doesn't. Siegler calls such situations "failures of self-explanation." Siegler explains, "For example children often borrow [regroup] across a zero without decrementing the number from which the borrowing was done. On $704 - 377 =$ ___, this would produce the answer 477. Such procedures may reflect children knowing the superficial form of the long subtraction algorithm but not understanding why it generates the answers that it does." Self-explanation has the power to reveal to the student where he or she went wrong—or right. It's the key to *error analysis*.

In a number of studies, the difference between better and worse learners has been shown to come down to the degree to which they try to explain what they are learning. Studies of textbook reading, for example, indicate that how often students explain to themselves the logic of statements in a textbook is positively related to learning the material. In Japan, classroom discussions about logic often revolve around why some math procedures that are only slightly different yield the same answer, while procedures that make sense on the surface result in incorrect answers. Drawing on the research of some of his colleagues, Siegler writes, "Encouraging children to explain why the procedures work appears to promote deeper understanding of them than having the [teacher] describe the procedures, provide examples of how they work, and tell children to practice them—the typical approach to mathematics instruction in U.S. classrooms."

Specifically, self-explanation helps students learn in these ways:

• Encouragement to explain increases the likelihood that the learner will seek an explanation at all. When students are told an answer is wrong, they simply accept the fact without thinking about why it's wrong.

• Encouragement to explain increases the depth of students' search for an explanation. Students in experiments who were asked to explain both correct and incorrect answers worked harder at finding reasons why.

• Students asked to explain correct and incorrect answers drop their old strategies more rapidly. Realizing why a certain path of reasoning is faulty, they tend to abandon it faster.

• The more time a student spends thinking about why one answer is correct and another isn't, the more likely the student is to be learning.

• Learning is more enjoyable when the act of making connections becomes a motivator.

How You Can Help

Bringing the benefits of research-based teaching strategies into your classroom may require some changes in your teaching. You may even find yourself going against your instincts.

For example, when students respond incorrectly to a math problem, many teachers instinctively encourage students to "try again" to figure out the correct answer on their own. A study by Siegler involving 45 children, however, suggests that there may be other, more constructive responses that a teacher might make.

Children were divided into three groups and individually shown two parallel rows of blocks. Then the experimenter changed a row by lengthening it spatially, shortening it, or removing a block. The experimenter asked whether the child thought the transformed row had more objects, fewer objects, or the same number.

The first group of children was given feedback only: "That's right," or "No, look again." The second group was given feedback, and then the experimenter asked the child to explain his or her answer. The third group gave their answers and received feedback concerning the correct answer; then the experimenter asked, "How do you think I knew that?"

The results of the experiment indicated that the third approach was most successful. Providing the correct answer and then encouraging the children to explain the reasoning behind the answer led to greater learning—more than receiving the feedback "to look again" or feedback and a request to explain their own answer. Gains were largest, in fact, with more difficult problems. What this indicates is that students must be led on a path of discovering reasons, finding out why something happened without being told how to do so. As students grow older, they will be able to use self-explanation to lead themselves toward discovery.

So here is one way to bring the benefits of research-tested teaching strategies to your classroom: If a student provides an incorrect response to a math problem or question, provide the correct response AND then immediately ask the student to show or explain why your answer is correct. For example, if a student states that $3 + 2 = 4$, you could say, "The correct answer is that $3 + 2 = 5$. Can you use these counting blocks to show me how I knew that the correct answer was 5, instead of 4?" You can also have the students explain other students' correct and incorrect answers.

Another finding from the experiment involving three groups of students has to do with the concept of "variability of reasoning." Careful observation revealed that children showed a variety of ways of thinking about the block problem, both before and during the test. In other words, "thinking through"—adapting and refining explanations, discarding old strategies in favor of better ones, as overlapping waves theory predicts would happen—was part of the process of learning.

So another way to bring the benefits of research to your classroom is this: Recognize and encourage various ways of thinking through a problem. Model how to "talk through" your thought process out loud as you figure out a problem and encourage students to do the same. For example, "The question is what is $3 + 4$? Hmmm, well, I know that $4 + 4 = 8$, and 3 is one less than 4, so $3 + 4$ must be one less than 8. That means $3 + 4 = 7$." Recognize that other students may solve the same addition problem correctly using different strategies and encourage them to share these strategies as well.

When students have provided incorrect answers, listen carefully to students' explanations to see if there is a fundamental misunderstanding that contributed to their error. For example, if a student has answered that $7 - 5$ is 3 and then explains that it's 3 by stating "You have to count backwards from 7. See—7 (shows 1 finger)—6 (shows 2 fingers)—5 (shows 3 fingers)—4 (shows 4 fingers)—3 (shows 5 fingers)," you know that the student understands the process of subtraction as counting backwards on a mental number line, but needs to be

taught to *start counting* backwards only *after* saying the first number—in this case, starting counting backwards with 6 . . . 5–4–3–2.

Finally, as a practical way of measuring whether your students' learning is surging further and further "up the beach," so to speak, you need to become familiar with typical math errors students make. One way to accomplish this is to administer a pretest and note the types of mistakes students make. It may also be helpful to familiarize yourself with what research says about the various strategies that students typically use to solve math problems.

For Teachers —

Alibali, M. W. 1999. How children change their minds: Strategy change can be gradual or abrupt. *Developmental Psychology* 35 (January):127.

Chen, Z., and R. S. Siegler. 2000. Across the Great Divide: Bridging the gap between understanding of toddlers' and older children's thinking. *Monographs of the Society for Research in Child Development* 65.

Griffin, S., and R. Case. 1997. Re-thinking the primary school math curriculum: An approach based on cognitive science. *Issues in Education 3*.

Siegler, R. S. In press. Microgenetic studies of self-explanation. In *Microdevelopment: Transition Processes in Development and Learning*, N. Granott and J. Parziale, eds. Cambridge, England: Cambridge University Press.

_____. 2000. The rebirth of children's learning. *Child Development* 71 (January/February): 26.

Further Readings —

Bower, B. 1999. Minds on the move. *Science News* 155 No. 12 (March 20): 184.

_____. 1999. Math discoveries catch kids unawares. *Science News* 155 No. 1 (Jan. 2): 5.

_____. 1995. Kids take mental aim at others' goals. *Science News* 148 (Sept. 16): 181.

Kuhn, D. 1995. Microgenetic study of change: What has it told us? *Psychological Science* 6 (May): 133.

_____. 2000. Metacognitive development. *Current Directions in Psychological Science* 8 (October): 178.

Miller, P. H., and T. R. Coyle. 1999. Developmental change: Lessons from microgenesis. In *Conceptual Development:* Piaget's Legacy, E. K. Scholnick, K. Nelson, S. A. Gelma, and P. H. Miller, eds. Mahway, N. J.: Erlbaum.

Science

Percentages beside major topics provide a rough guide for allocating time for Science during the year.

Science in Fifth Grade

Whether wondering about the weather, observing a rainbow, smelling a flower, or gazing at the stars, you are engaging in science. Science is a pursuit of knowledge about the world in which we live. Through the process of observation, we take in information about our world. Through continuous and systematic observation, we begin to hypothesize about and classify observed phenomena so that we may better understand our universe. Science is not only the process of gaining knowledge, it is also the knowledge obtained from that process. The information we have gained over the centuries about such broad-ranging phenomena of our world as mountains, earthquakes, weather, plants, animals, gravity, and electricity are included within the realm of science.

In Grade 5, students will continue their explorations in science by broadening and building on courses of study undertaken in previous grades. Expanding on their study of animal classification from Grade 3, students in Grade 5 will learn about a system scientists use to classify all living things, and they will be introduced to five major kingdoms in which all organisms can be grouped. As a natural extension of studying the classification system, students will have opportunities to hone their classification skills; the ability to classify information is an essential skill for organizing, analyzing, and understanding data.

Continuing with their study of life science, students in Grade 5 will begin an in-depth study of cells, the basic building blocks of life. Students will be introduced to the structures and processes of cells and will have opportunities to compare and contrast the cells of different organisms. Through their study of cells, students will also review and extend their understanding of tissues, organs, and body systems.

Students will re-examine plants and plant structures and will begin to learn about important plant processes including reproduction as well as photosynthesis, the process by which plants make their own food. Students will study the life cycle of plants from seed production to plant growth and will have opportunities to observe the life cycle of a plant throughout the year as they plant seeds and monitor the seeds' growth and development during class.

Building on the concept of life cycles developed during their study of plants, students will expand their understanding of life cycles as they learn that all living organisms, including themselves, go through a cycle of growth and development from birth to death. Students will also be introduced to the concept that all living things reproduce in order to continue the life of their species and that different organisms reproduce in different ways. Students will study sexual reproduction in animals.

Students will continue their study of the human body as they learn about the endocrine system, the body system involved in regulating a variety of body processes such as metabolism, growth, and development. They will also begin to explore the human reproductive system, the system that enables us to reproduce. Students will learn about changes that occur during adolescence as the result of hormones produced by the endocrine system and the maturation of the reproductive system.

Students will continue their study of matter as they examine the elements of which all matter is made. They will learn about the atom, the smallest unit of an element, and will learn that the atom can combine to form molecules and compounds that have properties and characteristics that are unique to the elements from which they are made. Students will learn about chemical and physical changes and will have opportunities to observe and distinguish between the two.

In learning about the scientific endeavors and contributions of Galileo Galilei, Percy Lavon Julian, Ernest Just, and Carl Linnaeus, students will begin to see science as a human endeavor and will be able to connect their studies of science, which often include abstract concepts, to human faces. They will also be able to see that scientific knowledge and views change and evolve over the years due to the continued work of scientists around the world. Students will learn that scientific knowledge can be applied for practical use to benefit society and will see that individual actions can have an impact on society. The science section will help students in Grade 5 learn why the world around them is the way it is.

I. Classifying Living Things

The Big Idea

Organisms are classified in order to easily identify and distinguish one species from another, and to study their relationships and how they fit in the natural world.

Remember that each subject you study with students expands their vocabulary and introduces new terms, thus making them better listeners and readers. As you study about classifying living things, use read alouds, independent reading, and discussions to build students' vocabularies.

What Students Should Already Know

Students in Core Knowledge schools should be familiar with

Kindergarten

▸ animals and their needs

  • Animals, like plants, need food, water, and space to live and grow.

  • Plants make their own food, but animals get food from eating plants or other living things.

  • Offspring are very much (but not exactly) like their parents.

  • Most animal babies need to be fed and cared for by their parents.

  • Pets have special needs and must be cared for by their owners.

Grade 1

▸ animal habitats and special classifications

  • Animals live in environments to which they are particularly suited.

  • specific habitats and what lives there

  • food chains

  • special classifications of animals, including herbivores (plant-eaters), carnivores (flesh-eaters), omnivores (plant and animal-eaters), and extinct animals

Grade 2

▸ life cycles

  • the life cycle: birth, growth, reproduction, death

    • from egg to egg with a chicken

    • from frog to frog

    • from butterfly to butterfly: metamorphosis

  • insects

Grade 3

▸ introduction to classification of animals

  • Scientists classify animals according to the characteristics they share, for example: cold-blooded or warm-blooded; vertebrates (have backbones and internal skeletons) or invertebrates (do not have backbones or internal skeletons).

  • different classes of vertebrates

  • fish: aquatic animals, breathe through gills

  • cold-blooded, most have scales, most develop from eggs that the female lays outside her body

What Students Should Already Know continued

- amphibians: live part of their lives in water and part on land, have gills when young, later develop lungs, cold-blooded, usually have moist skin
- reptiles: hatch from eggs, cold-blooded, have dry, thick, scaly skin
- birds: warm-blooded, most can fly, have feathers and wings, most build nests, hatch from eggs, most baby birds must be fed by parents and cared for until they can survive on their own (though some, like baby chickens and quail, can search for food a few hours after hatching)
- mammals: warm-blooded, have hair on their bodies, parents care for the young, females produce milk for their babies, breathe through lungs, most are terrestrial (live on land) though some are aquatic

What Students Need to Learn

- **Scientists have divided living things into five large groups called kingdoms, as follows:**
  - **Plant**
  - **Animal**
  - **Fungus (mushrooms, yeast, mold, mildew)**
  - **Protist (algae, protozoans, amoeba, euglena)**
  - **Moneran (bacteria, blue-green algae) (also known as Prokaryote)**
- **Each kingdom is divided into smaller groupings as follows:**

  Kingdom

        Phylum

              Class

                    Order

                          Family

                                Genus

                                      Species

                                        (Variety)

- **When classifying living things, scientists use special names made up of Latin words (or words made to sound like Latin words), which help scientists around the world understand each other and ensure that they are using the same names for the same living things.**
- *Homo sapiens*: **the scientific name for the species to which human beings belong (genus** *Homo*, **species** *sapiens***)**
- **Taxonomists are biologists who specialize in classification.**

I. Classifying Living Things

As a general rule of thumb, when choosing projects to do with your students, they should be well-thought-out and relate directly to the unit objectives and time allotments outlined in the beginning of each section. Projects have an important place, especially in the early grades when they help reinforce vocabulary and content and don't serve purely as time fillers. Throughout this subject, we have added teaching ideas with fun and purposeful extensions to further students' understanding.

What Students Need to Learn continued

▶ **Different classes of vertebrates and major characteristics: fish, amphibians, reptiles, birds, mammals**

Example: Classification of a collie dog

Kingdom: Animalia

Phylum: Chordata (Subphylum: Vertebrata)

Class: Mammalia (mammal)

Order: Carnivora (eats meat)

Family: Canidae (a group with doglike characteristics)

Genus: Canis (a coyote, wolf, or dog)

Species: familiaris (a domestic dog)

Variety: collie

What Students Will Learn in Future Grades

In future grades, students will review and extend their learning about animals.

Grade 6

▶ Oceans: Marine Life

Grade 7

▶ History of Earth and Life Forms

Vocabulary

Student/Teacher Vocabulary

algae: a group of living things that can make their own food; algae does not have true roots, stems, or leaves, but does have chlorophyll (S)

amoeba: a one-celled organism that moves by continually changing shape; can only be seen with a microscope (S)

class: a category in taxonomy ranking above the order and below the phylum categories (S)

classify: to group and study the relationships between organisms (S)

diaphragm: an important muscle located between the chest and abdomen in mammals; the diaphragm is used in respiration (S)

euglena: a tiny, single-celled organism; often classified as algae (S)

eukaryote: an organism made up of one or more cells, each of which has a defined nucleus and other organelles (membrane-bound compartments); unlike prokaryotes, many eukaryotes are multicellular organisms; human beings are eukaryotes (T)

extract: to draw out or remove (S)

family: a category in taxonomy ranking above the genus and below the order categories (S)

fertile: capable of reproducing (S)

fungus: a parasitic plant lacking chlorophyll, leaves, true stems, and roots; reproduces by spores (S)

Vocabulary continued

genus: a category in taxonomy ranking above the species and below the family categories (S)

gills: organs in fish and amphibians for breathing oxygen dissolved in water; made of thin, pliable layers of tissue lining the neck (S)

Homo sapiens: the Latin, or scientific, name for the human genus and species (S)

kingdom: the largest category of taxonomic classification, based on common characteristics and evolutionary history (S)

mammary gland: the gland responsible for the production of milk in female mammals (S)

moneran: an organism without a membrane-bound nucleus; also known as a prokaryote. Prokaryotes differ from eukaryotes, organisms whose cells have membrane-bound nuclei. The vast majority of prokaryotes consist of only a single cell. (S)

order: a category in taxonomy ranking above the family and below the class categories (S)

phylum: a category in taxonomy ranking above the class and below the kingdom categories (S)

prokaryote: see *moneran*, above (T)

protist: a unicellular or simple multicellular organism (S)

protozoan: a single-celled organism; classified as protists; most live in water (S)

species: a category in taxonomy ranking below the genus category (S)

taxonomist: a biologist who specializes in classification (S)

vertebrata: animals with a backbone made of bony segments (T)

Domain Vocabulary

Classifying living things and associated words:
identification, hierarchy, organize, inherit, inherited, evolution, Linnaeus, Darwin, specimen, specialist, specific, specificity, descendant, ancestor, adaptation, diversity, carnivore, herbivore, omnivore, terrestrial, aquatic, habitat, inhabit, denizen, extinct, endangered, system, characteristic, feature, compare, contrast, similar, alike, different, plant, animal, yeast, mold, mildew, bacteria, breeding, crossbreeding, reproduction, hybrids, unique, female, male, methods, variable, variation, variety, mutation, change, category, group, grouping, breed, interbreed, reproduce, offspring, leg, body, arm, spine, vertebrate, invertebrate, taxonomy, taxonomic, subphylum, subgroup, organism, naturalist, specimen, primate, Latin, binomial, fish, reptile, amphibian, mammal, bird, body plan, hair, fur, limb, mammary, organ, *plus the names of specific animals discussed (e.g., dog, cat, etc.) and words related to those animals* (paw, puppy, collie, beagle, fur, whiskers, kitten, litter, *etc.*)

Cross-curricular Connections

Language Arts

Poetry
• "A Bird Came Down the Walk"
• "The Eagle"
• "Jabberwocky"
• "The Tiger"
• "A Wise Old Owl"

Materials

Instructional Masters 65–67, 84

Introduction to Hierarchical Classification, p. 559

The Five Kingdoms, p. 562

Researching an Organism, pp. 564, 568, 569

T-Chart, p. 565

samples or pictures to represent plant, animal, and fungus kingdoms (e.g., geranium or other plant, hamster or goldfish, dry yeast or mushroom), p. 562

chart paper, p. 562

bone models or pictures of skeletons of animals from vertebrate class, p. 564

materials for working aquarium, pp. 565, 566

bird feeder to place near classroom window, p. 568

pictures of animals from vertebrate class, p. 570

paper bag, p. 570

pictures of various animals, p. 570

class set of library books about animals, p. 570

information on local zoo, p. 570

information about obtaining a small animal for the classroom (fish, gerbil, etc.), p. 570

At a Glance

The most important ideas for you are:

- Scientists divide living things into categories and subcategories.
- The system of classification introduced here divides organisms into five kingdoms and then into smaller subcategories. However, taxonomy is an evolving science, and this classification system is subject to revision based on future discoveries, particularly DNA research.
- Kingdoms are further divided into smaller groupings: phylum, class, order, family, genus, and species; subdivisions may branch out at any level.
- Latin nomenclature is used for worldwide classification schemes.
- Vertebrate classes within the animal kingdom are examples of how major characteristics and genetic information are used in the classification of an organism.

What Teachers Need to Know

Background

Billions of different organisms have lived on Earth over the last 3.5 billion years. In order to study organisms in an organized fashion, it was necessary for scientists to divide organisms into groups. Scientists developed several levels of ranked divisions for classifying organisms, moving from the generic to the particular. Biologists who specialize in the work of classification are called taxonomists, and their field of study is called taxonomy.

Introduction to Classification

Taxonomy is a field that has been changing constantly for many decades and continues to change today. The great pioneer in this field was the Swedish scientist Carl Linnaeus. (See "Science Biographies," pp. 634–646.) Linnaeus (1707–1778) collected a wide variety of organisms and developed a classification scheme to sort and categorize these organisms. His scheme began with very large general categories called kingdoms. These kingdoms were then subdivided into smaller categories, all the way down to the smallest categories, *genus* and *species*.

Linnaeus believed all organisms could be classified into one of two kingdoms, *plants* and *animals*. In the Linnean system, organisms that produce their own food and do not move are classified as plants, while animals that move and obtain their food by eating other organisms are classified as animals.

Little by little, scientific knowledge advanced, and eventually scientists came to believe that the two-kingdom system was not adequate. There were some organisms that did not seem to fall into either kingdom, or that combined features of the two kingdoms. Linnaeus had classified fungi (like mushrooms) as plants because they do not move. But scientists discovered that fungi do not make their own food. Rather, they take in nutrients from dead animals and plants, and so differ from plants in this regard. Scientists looking through microscopes also

discovered tiny single-celled organisms like bacteria. Some of these tiny organisms are able to move around, like animals, but many of them also make their own food, like plants. In other words, some bacteria exhibit features of both the plant and animal kingdoms. In response to these discoveries, scientists began to modify their classification systems. Eventually most scientists came to believe a third kingdom was necessary, then a fourth, and then a fifth.

The five-kingdom classification scheme was the most widely accepted scheme during the last decades of the 20th century and was included in the *Core Knowledge Sequence* for that reason. The five-kingdom scheme is also described in this book, which is intended to help you teach the topics in the *Sequence*. However, scientific knowledge continues to accumulate, and the latest discoveries suggest that the five-kingdom classification system itself needs some modification and refinement.

Until recently, taxonomists relied heavily on what is called morphological evidence. That is, they looked at the shape or body parts of an organism and classified it with other organisms with similar shapes or body parts. Animals with backbones or wings or mammary glands would be grouped together on the basis of these common features. Morphological evidence is still used in classification today. However, taxonomists are relying more and more heavily on DNA and genetic evidence. DNA evidence has confirmed many of the distinctions and classifications that were made based on morphological evidence, but it has also revealed some imperfections in the preexisting classification system. By comparing the DNA sequences of various species and noting the number of differences in these sequences, scientists are able to determine which organisms are most closely related. This has led to some surprising discoveries. Some organisms that scientists previously believed to be close cousins are now seen as being more distant relatives, while others now seem to be more closely related than was previously thought.

DNA evidence has also led many scientists to question whether the five-kingdom system is the most accurate way of classifying organisms. One widely held view, based on extensive DNA research, holds that organisms should in fact be divided into three large groups, which scientists have begun to call "domains": 1. bacteria, 2. prokaryotic single-celled organisms called "archaea," and 3. eukaryotes. The eukaryotes domain includes animals, plants, fungi, and other organisms.

DNA evidence also shows how much all organisms have in common. A simple bacteria has a surprising amount of DNA in common with a flower or a tiger. Scientists increasingly think of organisms as forming a "tree of life" in which all living things are descended from common ancestors. The illustration below shows one version of the tree of life (showing the branches specific for Domain Eukarya only).

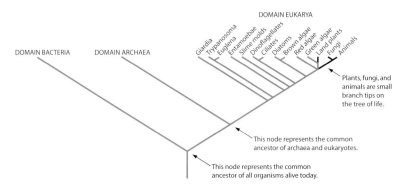

Teaching Idea

When introducing the concept of classification, you may want to draw upon students' prior knowledge of habitats and why certain animals live in certain habitats. Scientists classifying an organism may look at where the animal lives, how it gets its food, what body parts it has, and what its DNA tells us about its evolutionary history.

Teaching Idea

Introduce students to the concept of a taxonomic hierarchical structure using Instructional Master 65, *Introduction to Hierarchical Classification.*

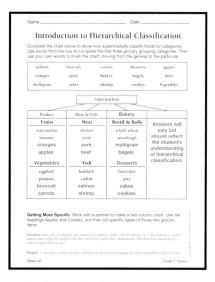

Use Instructional Master 65.

In short, it seems likely that the five-kingdom system presented here will be replaced or at least modified in some important ways in the near future. The new model will almost certainly be based on the findings of DNA research, and will probably resemble the tree of life shown on p. 559. However, the exact details of the new system are still coming together. That system will be included in future editions of the *Core Knowledge Sequence* once a degree of scientific consensus is reached and the details are sufficiently clear.

For the classroom teacher, this transitional situation may seem to be an inconvenience. It is difficult to teach a subject that will not "sit still." However, the situation can also be viewed as an opportunity to help students understand that scientific knowledge is constantly evolving. Students in Grade 5 are old enough to understand this. We therefore recommend that teachers teach the five-kingdom system but also try to help students understand that a new system is taking shape, and that the replacement of good approaches with even better ones is an integral part of the scientific process. As our knowledge grows, this new system may also be replaced one day.

The Five-Kingdom Taxonomic System

The taxonomic system described here classifies all living organisms into five large categories called kingdoms. Animals are assigned to one of these kingdoms based on common features and/or common evolutionary history. Each kingdom in our taxonomic system is divided further into smaller groupings as follows: phylum (plural: phyla), class, order, family, genus, and species. One kingdom might contain several phyla, and each of those phyla might contain several classes, and so on. A good way to remember the order of the various categories is to use a mnemonic device, or a memory aid, that substitutes other words that start with the same letters as the categories to make a memorable or silly sentence, such as "King Philip came over for good spaghetti" or "King Philip came over from Germany Saturday." Each word in the phrase stands for a category from largest (kingdoms) to smallest (species).

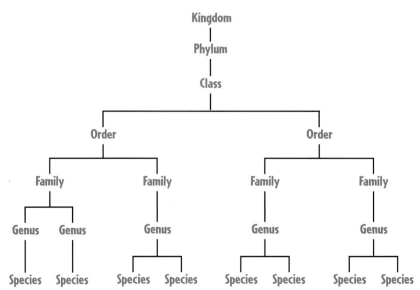

Classification of Organisms

In the five-kingdom classification system, the five kingdoms are plants, animals, fungi, protists, and prokaryotes (formerly known as monerans). Complex, multicellular organisms are divided into three kingdoms: the plant kingdom (Latin: Plantae), which includes all plants except algae; the animal kingdom (Latin: Animalia), which includes all multicellular animals; and the fungus kingdom (plural: Fungi), which includes all mushrooms, yeasts, mildew, and some molds. The other two kingdoms are composed of unicellular or simple multicellular organisms. The protist kingdom (Latin: Protista), includes protozoa, multicellular algae, slime molds, diatoms, and other lower eukaryotes, all of which have a nucleus. The moneran kingdom, also called Prokaryotae (Latin), or Prokaryotes (English), consists of unicellular organisms without a nucleus, which include bacteria and blue-green algae.

Organisms are classified into kingdoms based on what is known about them at the time. Sometimes organisms have to be reclassified when new information is uncovered that calls the old classification into question. For example, DNA testing may reveal that two organisms that appear to be very similar and have traditionally been classified together are in fact less closely related than they appear to be.

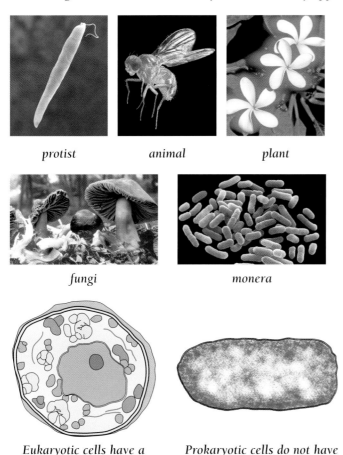

protist   *animal*   *plant*

fungi   *monera*

*Eukaryotic cells have a
membrane-bound nucleus.*   *Prokaryotic cells do not have
a membrane-bound nucleus.*

I. Classifying Living Things

Use Instructional Master 66.

Teaching Idea

On chart paper, create a large branching chart showing the 5 kingdoms, along with some of the most significant (or interesting) phyla, subphyla, and classes. Show students pictures of a number of living things, including at least 1 example from each of the kingdoms. You may wish to focus particularly on animals.

Ask students if they can name the animals shown in the pictures. Then show them where in the classification scheme each animal falls. After doing several animals in this way, you can ask students to predict where an animal will be classified. Then they can compare their predictions to the actual, current classifications. Some examples of animals that fall into different phyla and subphyla are rattlesnake, sea urchin, elephant, scorpion, blue jay, salmon, jellyfish, frog, sponge, and worm.

How Kingdoms Are Divided

The five-kingdom classification system is divided further into the categories of phylum, class, order, family, genus, and species; each grouping is more specific than any previous one. These categories can also be changed by adding the prefix *sub-* or *super-*. For example, scientists can recognize a superkingdom or a subphylum.

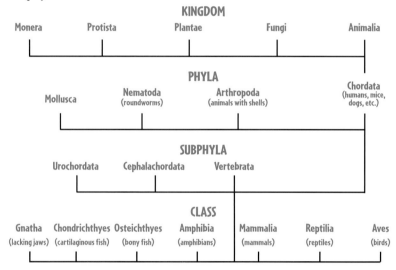

A kingdom is composed of phyla. There are over 30 different phyla in the animal kingdom. These include *Mollusca* (soft-bodied invertebrates including mussels and snails), *Nematoda* (roundworms), *Arthropoda* (animals with exoskeletons, including insects, crabs, and spiders) and *Chordata* (animals like humans, mice, dogs, fish, reptiles, etc.). Each of these phyla branches out into subphyla. The phylum *Chordata* consists of three subphyla; the largest one is called *Vertebrata*, or vertebrates, to which belong all animals with backbones and internal skeletons, including mammals, birds, reptiles, amphibians, and fish. When students think of animals, they generally think of vertebrates like cats, elephants, tigers, and dogs. However, most animal species are not vertebrates; over 90% of all animals are invertebrates, or animals lacking an internal skeleton. Invertebrates include worms, spiders, bees, and butterflies.

A subphylum can be further broken down into classes. For example, the subphylum *Vertebrata* is divided into classes for fish (three classes), mammals, birds, reptiles, and amphibians. A class consists of related orders. A subgroup within an order is a family. Under the family is the subgroup called genus, followed by the species.

A species is defined as a group of organisms that resemble each other and are capable of interbreeding to produce fertile offspring. If two organisms cannot reproduce, or if their offspring are infertile (incapable of reproducing), then the organisms are considered to belong to separate species. Each species of organism has inherited different characteristics by which that species is identified.

We classify organisms to show their relationships and as a means to study them. The genus and species names are given together to name a species. This two-part naming system is called "binomial nomenclature." (A nomenclature is a system of names; *binomial* means "two names.") Thus, humans are *Homo sapiens*;

Homo is the genus, meaning "man," and *sapiens* is the species, meaning "wise" or "knowing." Note that both names are italicized and the genus name is capitalized and the species name is not. Other examples include *Felis domesticus*, meaning "domestic house cat," and *Canis familiaris*, meaning "domestic dog." Below are the classifications for a human being, a dog, and a cat:

	Human	Dog	House cat
Kingdom:	Animalia	Animalia	Animalia
Phylum:	Chordata	Chordata	Chordata
Class:	Mammalia	Mammalia	Mammalia
Order:	Primata	Carnivora	Carnivora
Family:	Hominidae	Canidae	Felidae
Genus:	*Homo*	*Canis*	*Felis*
Species:	*sapiens*	*familiaris*	*domesticus*

varieties of dogs

The number of animal species presently identified totals about 1.5 million, of which 1 million are insects, and about 40,000 are vertebrates. Scientists believe there may be as many as 9.6 million other species of animals that have not yet been identified.

Within any species that interbreeds—that is, reproduces sexually—offspring always have slight variations in characteristics from those of the parents. If individuals with particular variations persist in breeding through many generations, variations in characteristics may become more pronounced. Examples of such characteristics in animals may be limb length, density of fur or hair, or eye shape; in plants, such characteristics might be height, hardiness, or flower color or size.

Humans have purposely created new subspecies, or varieties, of organisms for specific purposes. For example, humans have created some plant hybrids specifically for their appearance and others for their ability to produce fruits or vegetables that are larger, tastier, or more disease-resistant. They have raised corn with larger kernels and tomatoes with distinctive tastes. Humans have also bred animals for a particular service or purpose. The domestic dog is a good example of a species with a wide range of varieties. For example, dachshunds were originally bred to chase badgers into their burrows. Dalmatians were originally bred to serve as "coach dogs" that accompanied coaches, carriages, and other horse-drawn vehicles. Today, dalmations are often known as fire department mascots.

Why Latin Names?

Latin is the official language for naming organisms. The Swedish scientist Carl Linnaeus used Latin when he created the first classification system in the 18th century. Linnaeus chose Latin because, at that time, it was a common language that enabled scientists and scholars to communicate with one another across national borders. Modern scientists have continued using Latin because it is a static language; that is, it doesn't change and is the same worldwide. Animals have different names in various modern languages. For example, a dog is called "dog" in England and the United States, *chien* in France, and *sobaka* in Russia. French scientists might get confused if they tried to communicate with Russian scientists, but some of this confusion can be avoided when Latin is used as a common

Teaching Idea

You may want to teach about Carl Linnaeus while teaching this section. (See his biography in Section VII, "Science Biographies," on pp. 634–646.) Carl Linnaeus is the Latinized name of Carl von Linné. Invite students to figure out how their own names could be Latinized. (Hint: Most feminine singular names and words end in *-a*, and most masculine names end in *-us*.) Then have students choose an organism they know or put common names of organisms in a hat from which to pick, 1 name for each student in the class. Have students conduct research on their organisms to find out more about its classification, including the Latin names. As an extension, students could research the name of the animals in other languages to see how different they sound. This will reinforce the historical importance of Latin names as a universal language for classifying organisms.

I. Classifying Living Things

Cross-curricular Teaching Idea

You may wish to review the poem "Jabberwocky" from the Language Arts section while students are learning the connection between Latin names and animal classification. Have students invent a Latin scientific name for the Jabberwock.

Teaching Idea

Give students Instructional Masters 67a–67b, *Researching an Organism,* to reinforce what they have learned about classification and taxonomy. As you introduce each class of vertebrates including fish, amphibians, reptiles, birds, and mammals, have them research an organism in each class and record their observations. As an extension, they may research and record the classification of a particular organism as well.

Use Instructional Masters 67a–67b.

Teaching Idea

Bone models can be useful in illustrating vertebrate animals. Show students pictures of skeletons of human beings, dinosaurs, dogs, etc., and help them find the backbones, or vertebrae, in each one.

language for scientific names. In addition, many organisms do not have common names. The Latin system of names includes names not only for everyday animals we all know, like dogs and cats, but also for obscure, microscopic, and little-known organisms.

Whenever a new species is identified, the discoverer has traditionally been allowed the privilege of naming that organism, assigning a unique, two-part name. Generally the names selected are Latin names or words that are given Latin suffixes in order to retain consistency in naming.

The genus and species names are usually descriptive. The discoverer may name the species after him- or herself, or after a scientific colleague. An example is an ostrichlike bird in South America that was named *Rhea darwinii,* after Charles Darwin. The species name may reflect a characteristic or activity of the organism, such as the mosquito species names *punctor* (it punctures your skin) and *excrucians* (it causes excruciating pain). Other names are given whimsically, such as the new species of wasp in the genus *Lalapa* that was assigned *lusa* as its species name, making it sound like "lollapalooza," an English slang term meaning something unusual or outstanding.

wildebeest (Connochaetus gnu)   *woodchuck (Marmota monax)*

Invertebrate Animals

Animals can be divided into two main groups: invertebrates and vertebrates. Invertebrates, or animals without backbones, are by far more abundant. They make up more than 90% of animal species, most of which are insects. Invertebrate classifications are arranged by increasing complexity, characterized by their body plans. Body plans include the presence or absence of particular aspects, such as symmetry, a gut, a segmented body, organs, and organ systems. Simpler invertebrates lack some of these aspects, and more complex ones have many or all of the aspects.

Vertebrate Animals

Within the animal phylum *Chordata* (animals with some form of backbone) is the subphylum *Vertebrata,* which consists of five classes with particular structural characteristics: fish, amphibians, reptiles, birds, and mammals.

Three classes in the phylum *Chordata*—fish, amphibians, and reptiles—are all characterized, in common parlance, as "cold-blooded." The term is a category given to animals whose internal body temperature varies with the temperature of the surroundings. When it is cold outside, the internal temperature of a cold-blooded animal is also cold; if it is hot, the animal's internal temperature is also hot. Alligators are cold-blooded, and their behavior varies with temperature. When the temperature is low, alligators are sluggish, but when it heats up, they become more active.

Birds and mammals are characterized as "warm-blooded," which means they maintain a nearly constant body temperature regardless of the surrounding temperature, with only slight variations. The internal temperature of a human being may rise slightly as a result of fever, or dip if a person is exposed to severe cold over a prolonged period, but in order for life to continue, the internal temperature cannot rise too far above or fall too far below the average temperature of 98.6 degrees Fahrenheit.

Fish

Fish are cold-blooded and usually need to maintain a fairly constant internal temperature. Fish that live where the water temperature remains constant, such as deep in the ocean, keep a constant internal temperature. Tuna and swordfish are two examples of such fish. However, fish that live in shallow waters, such as minnows or trout, are likely to encounter varied water temperatures and have to swim around to find regions of water that have their optimal temperature; sharp changes in temperature can prove fatal. They must actively seek out the most optimal water temperature.

Fish obtain oxygen by taking in water through the mouth and then passing it across the gills, thin layers of skin that extract oxygen from the water and pump it into the blood vessels. The majority of fish are predators, feeding on invertebrates and other fish. For improved survival from predation, fish evolved thicker skins and, on top of that, most also developed flattened, rigid plates called scales. Most fish lay eggs externally, which are then fertilized by the male as he deposits his sperm while swimming over the eggs. Some fish eggs are internally fertilized and remain inside the body until they hatch into live young. Sharks are an example of this type of fish.

gills

As part of this section, be sure to introduce students to a few different kinds of fish. Some interesting fish include trout, salmon, tuna, sharks, barracuda, piranha, and swordfish. Note that although dolphins may seem a lot like fish, they are actually mammals.

Three fish that students may be interested in learning more about are salmon, barracuda, and piranha. Salmon are found in both the Atlantic and Pacific regions. These fish spend some of their time living in the ocean, and then head to streams and rivers to spawn, or produce offspring. The male Pacific salmon undergoes a series of changes during spawning season, including changing color and sometimes developing a hooked jaw. The salmon then swim upstream as many as 2,000 miles up the Yukon River, swimming against the rapids and jumping over waterfalls until they reach the spot where they traditionally spawn.

Teaching Idea

Divide students into groups to conduct research on the following fish: trout, salmon, tuna, sharks, barracuda, piranha, and swordfish. Generate a list of questions to which students should find the answers to share with the class; for example: What do they look like? Where do they live? What is unique about this fish? Do we eat this fish? What is the classification of this organism? Use Instructional Masters 67a–67b, *Researching an Organism*, for students to record their answers.

Teaching Idea

If possible, collect tadpoles from a local body of water, or order them from a science catalog, to allow students to examine and observe the tadpoles' metamorphosis into adult frogs. Prepare an aquarium with some water. Add rocks or branches that protrude above the surface of the water so the tadpoles can climb out of the water as they develop. Make sure to have a tight-fitting, but permeable, cover to prevent maturing frogs from jumping out of the tank. (If you collected tadpoles locally, return the adult frogs to the same area. Check a field guide on amphibians for frogs native to your region before ordering from a science supplier. If you cannot use native species, don't try this activity, since you will not have a place to let the frogs go once they have matured.)

Barracuda are fish usually found in warm or tropical oceans. They can range in size from small to large, with the largest about six feet long. Barracuda are very fast and powerful fish, and they prey on other fish and eat them with their many sharp teeth. Barracuda have even been known to attack humans swimming in the water.

In the fresh waters of South America live as many as 20 species of piranha. These small fish have sharp teeth and very strong jaws. The red-bellied piranha sometimes hunts for other fish in groups as large as 100, and when they hunt independently they send a signal to one another once prey has been found. The piranhas then have a feeding frenzy, with each one taking a bite and then swimming away to let other piranha in for a bite. Attacks on humans and other large animals are rare but do happen occasionally.

Amphibians

Amphibians are animals with characteristics somewhere between those of fish and reptiles. The word *amphibian* means "living two lives" or "living in two worlds." Most amphibians spend part of their lives in water and part on land. Amphibian females lay eggs externally, in water or in moist soil. The eggs are then fertilized by the male. The hatching young, or larvae, are aquatic and have gills to breathe in water. In most amphibians, as the larvae grow and develop, a metamorphosis occurs, which is a drastic change in body structure and corresponding change in lifestyle from aquatic to terrestrial as they reach adulthood.

Frogs provide a good example of an amphibian life cycle. Baby frogs are called tadpoles. Tadpoles swim in water and use gills. They begin their metamorphosis when they lose their gills and develop lungs for breathing air. Then legs develop, and mouth parts change from those adapted to feeding on plants to those for feeding on animals. Also, the tail is absorbed. The result is an adult frog, drastically altered from the larval tadpole.

life cycle of a frog

Amphibians have thin skin, usually without scales, that dries out easily. Amphibians use both skin and lungs to breathe, and some species use skin entirely and have no lungs. Some species of frogs and toads also produce toxins in their skin glands. Frogs and salamanders living in cold climates become dormant when the temperature decreases so much that they cannot find ways to maintain an efficient body temperature. Burrowing underground, or into mud beneath a body of

water that won't freeze to the bottom, they hibernate until conditions once more become favorable.

Students may be interested in learning some of the following fun facts about amphibians:

• Here is the difference between frogs and toads: Toads have glands behind their eyes and dry, bumpy skin. They are often a greenish brown color with a yellow stripe down their backs. Frogs have longer legs and moist skin, and they tend to be brown, green, yellow, and/or gray. Some frogs have the ability to camouflage their appearance to blend in with their surroundings.

• The West African Goliath frog is the world's biggest frog species; it is the size of a house cat!

• Poison arrow frogs of the Central and South American rainforests produce some of the most toxic biological substances known. One species of these frogs is especially poisonous: just 0.00001 gram of this frog's skin secretion can kill a human.

• Salamanders are unique amphibians because they have long tails as adults. Most salamanders can shed their tails if pursued by a predator; the tail continues to move after falling off, which often distracts the predator while the salamander escapes. The salamander has the ability to regenerate a tail.

• Caecilians are legless amphibians that usually live underground. They have sharp teeth and eat other animals, such as beetles, earthworms, and sometimes even small frogs and lizards.

Reptiles

Reptiles are cold-blooded, air-breathing vertebrates. Most reptiles have scaly or plated skin, and most of them lay eggs. Like fish and amphibians, reptiles are cold-blooded; that is, their internal body temperature can be adjusted largely by behavior, such as basking in the sun on warm rocks or hiding behind rocks or underground during the hot midday. Reptiles have lungs for breathing and were the first vertebrates to become truly terrestrial, freed from a dependency on water for survival. Two adaptations made this possible. Internal fertilization allowed the male to deposit sperm directly into the female's body. The second adaptation was the development of a new kind of egg, the amniote egg, which retains its own water supply, in the albumen, so that developing embryos can survive on dry land. Reptiles' eggs also have a large yolk as a food supply for embryos to develop to an advanced stage before birth. The eggs are surrounded by a membrane for protection and water retention, and, in most species, a leathery or hard, calcified shell. Some snakes and lizards are viviparous, which means they give birth to fully formed live young. Other reptiles are oviparous and lay eggs. When reptiles are born, the young have dry skin covered by protective scales.

Students will form a better composite idea of reptiles if they have an opportunity to study several specific reptiles. Snakes, alligators, and iguanas are all reptiles likely to be of interest to fifth graders.

Students may also enjoy learning some of the following fun facts about reptiles:

• Scientists used to believe that dinosaurs were reptiles; however, recent evidence suggests that dinosaurs were warm-blooded and that they may be more closely related to birds.

• Some species of turtles and tortoises can live for more than a century.

Teaching Idea

Divide students into groups to conduct research on the following amphibians: frogs, toads, salamanders, and newts. Generate a list of questions to which students should find the answers to share with the class; for example: What do they look like? Where do they live? What is unique about this amphibian? Is it poisonous? What is the classification of this organism? Use Instructional Masters 67a–67b, *Researching an Organism,* for students to record their answers.

I. Classifying Living Things

Teaching Idea

Divide students into groups to conduct research on the following reptiles: snakes, alligators, turtles, and iguanas. Generate a list of questions to which students should find the answers to share with the class; for example: What do they look like? Where do they live? What is unique about this reptile? Is it safe or dangerous to humans? What is the classification of this organism? Use Instructional Masters 67a–67b, *Researching an Organism,* for students to record their answers.

Teaching Idea

Divide students into groups to conduct research on some of the following birds: bald eagles, vultures, blue jays, cardinals, robins, penguins, albatrosses, geese, cisticolas, terns, whooping cranes, turkey vultures, and roadrunners, as well as any local birds. Generate a list of questions to which students should find the answers to share with the class; for example: What do they look like? Where do they live? What is their size? What is unique about this bird? How far do they travel? Do they migrate? What is the classification of this organism? Use Instructional Masters 67a–67b, *Researching an Organism,* for students to record their answers.

Teaching Idea

You may wish to study some common local birds so that students can recognize birds in their area. You could place a bird feeder near a classroom window to attract the local birds for firsthand observation.

• The emerald tree boa has special infrared heat receptors that allow it to sense the location of nearby animals. The emerald tree boa spends all of its time in trees, where it blends in with the leaves due to its bright green coloring.

• Although it's hard to tell the difference between a poisonous snake and a harmless snake just by looking at them, most snakes in the United States are harmless. Each year, more Americans die from bee and wasp stings than die from snake bites.

Students might be interested in learning about specific reptiles, such as the crocodile and the anaconda:

• Crocodiles are amphibious and live in tropical climates. They look like very large lizards and can range in length from 6 to 33 feet; the largest species can weigh up to a ton. Crocodiles do most of their hunting at night, and usually eat fish and small mammals. However, crocodiles occasionally attack humans and other large mammals. They use their strong tails to disable prey in the water and then hold the prey in their sharp jaw and shake it rapidly back and forth until it is dead.

• Anacondas are large snakes found in tropical regions of South America. They are usually olive green with black spots and can grow to over 30 feet long. Anacondas spend much of their time in the water, and they hunt nocturnally. They prey on animals like caiman and deer by wrapping themselves around their victims and constricting them. They also kill smaller animals, like birds and turtles, by biting them.

Birds

Birds are the only animals with feathers, which assist in flight, insulation, or both. Most birds have the ability to fly, but some, such as ostriches, emus, and penguins, are flightless. Birds are bipedal, or two-legged, with scales on their legs and feet. Their forelimbs are wings, which have feathers, strong muscles, and bones filled with air cavities, making them very lightweight. Bird feathers are believed to be a type of modified scale, having evolved from reptilian ancestors. This hypothesis is based on scientific studies of Archaeopteryx fossils. (The Archaeopteryx theory is based on fossils that are approximately 150 million years old and have some characteristics similar to modern birds, such as feathers and wings.) Wing muscles and bones attach to an enlarged, fused breastbone called a keel. These powerful but light structures, along with a high metabolic rate, are required to make flight possible. To achieve a high metabolic rate, birds must be warm-blooded.

Birds are the only class of animal that have no means of giving birth other than laying eggs. Bird eggs are yolk-filled like reptiles', and all have hard, calcified shells. Some birds, like chickens, are able to see, walk, and feed themselves almost immediately after hatching, but many birds are born in a very immature stage, and all require a lengthy period of parental care. During this period, the young need shelter from predators. The parents prepare shelters either by building a nest made of such materials as twigs and straw or mud, usually in a tree or thicket, or by cleaning out a hollow in a tree or a burrow in the ground.

Students will form a better composite idea of birds if they have an opportunity to study several specific birds. Bald eagles (our national symbol), vultures, blue jays, cardinals, penguins, flamingos, and roadrunners are all birds likely to be of interest to fifth graders.

Students may also enjoy learning some of the following fun facts about birds:

• Albatrosses can spend up to 10 years at sea without returning to land.

• Bar-headed geese may be the highest fliers of the bird world. Breeding in Tibet and wintering in India, they fly at over 27,000 feet to get through the Himalayan passes.

• The golden-headed cisticola [siss-ti-CO-la], a type of Australian warbler, uses thread from spiderwebs to stitch living leaves together to make an almost perfectly camouflaged nest.

• The Arctic tern roves over more of the planet than any other creature. Breeding north of the Arctic Circle, it migrates south to the Antarctic pack ice—about 10,000 miles away.

Mammals

Mammals are the only animals that have hair or fur and mammary glands in the females to nourish their young. (The word *mammal* is derived from the same root as *mammary.*) Like birds, mammals are warm-blooded; they have a high metabolic rate to maintain a high and constant internal body temperature. All mammals have lungs and a diaphragm that assists in pumping air to and from the lungs. Most mammals are placental; that is, the young are nourished inside the female's body until they are well developed. Some are fully developed at birth. Marsupials, such as opossums and kangaroos, are born at an extremely immature stage, but then move to a protective pouch and are there nourished by the mother's milk. Only a few mammals, the monotremes, which include the platypus and spiny anteater, lay eggs, but after hatching, their young are also fed with milk from the females. The young of all mammals are dependent on adults for an extended period while they learn to feed themselves and survive on their own. Mammals live in virtually every environment, as they are adaptable and can survive drastic changes in the environment. Most mammals are terrestrial, or land dwellers, but some, including walruses, seals, dolphins, and whales live in water or aquatic environments.

Students should have the opportunity to study several specific mammals, including humans, dogs, cats, tigers, lions, horses, giraffes, etc.

Students may also enjoy learning some of the following fun facts about mammals:

• The world's largest known land mammal lived more than 30 million years ago. This giant hornless ancestor to the rhinoceros lived in Asia, weighed an estimated 33 tons, and was so tall that a modern giraffe would just reach its shoulder.

• Humans are, biologically speaking, most closely related to chimpanzees—sharing more than 98% of the same genetic sequence.

• Even though they can fly, bats are mammals, not birds.

• Marine mammals, like dolphins, whales, and seals, evolved from mammals that lived on land. Even though they have become specialized to live in an aquatic environment, marine mammals share characteristics with all other mammals. For example, whales and dolphins have hair, and all marine mammals have lungs, not gills, and must breathe air to live.

I. Classifying Living Things

The Big Idea in Review

Organisms are classified in order to easily identify and distinguish one species from another, and to study their relationships and how they fit in the natural world.

Review

Below are some ideas for ongoing assessment and review activities. These are not meant to constitute a comprehensive list.

• Create a writing activity by collecting pictures of animals from the vertebrate classes studied in this section that students have already researched. Put all the pictures into a paper bag and have each student select a picture. Have students write about their animals, using correct paragraph form. Then have students share their paragraphs without naming the animal to see if the class can guess the identity of the animal from the written description.

• Have your students be amateur taxonomists. Split them into small groups and present each group with a set of animal pictures. Their first task is to determine whether the animal is a vertebrate or invertebrate. The next task is to match each vertebrate with the appropriate class: fish, amphibian, reptile, bird, or mammal. After each group has finished, reconvene and discuss the students' results. Be sure to have students explain why they matched an animal with a particular class. You may wish to include some of the following: hermit crab (invertebrate), bear (mammal), salamander (amphibian), bat (mammal), penguin (bird), komodo dragon (reptile), domestic dog (mammal), goldfish (fish), preying mantis (invertebrate), parakeet (bird), cobra (reptile), poison arrow frog (amphibian), whale (mammal), salmon (fish), and snail (invertebrate).

• Assemble a class library of books about a variety of animals from this unit. Have the media specialist assist you in collecting books that cover all the classes of vertebrates from this unit. Then assign a book report for the class. Each student should select a book from the library and write a book report. Have students include new facts that they learned about animals.

• Visit a zoo if there is one in the area. Before the visit, see if you can arrange to have one of the zoologists from the facility talk with the class. While touring the facility, you may wish to have students make a list of the animals and their scientific names, which are usually listed on the description outside the animal's cage. Have students write a thank-you letter to the zoologist, if they met one.

• Have students observe the wildlife around their neighborhoods or the school. For one week, have students draw pictures of any animals that they see and record their observations on a chart. Which animals did they see? To which classes do the animals belong? How many times did the students see the animals? Share the observations and findings, and collect them on a class chart to show the results of animal sightings.

• Have students observe any fish or other animals in the classroom, or arrange for them to visit another classroom that has an animal. What habits do the students notice during their observations of the animal? Assign groups of students to observe the animal for one week and record observations. Then research that animal and find out if the behaviors are normal for that classification of animal. Report findings to the class. Did each group notice similar behaviors or did groups notice different behaviors?

- You may also ask the following questions after completing this section:

1. Name the set of categories for classification in the five-kingdom classification scheme.

   The categories are, in order of most general to most specific, kingdom, phylum, class, order, family, genus, and species.

2. Why are organisms classified with a two-part name?

   The two parts identify the particular genus and species and distinguish them from other organisms.

3. What is the reasoning for giving Latin names to organisms?

   Latin is the same all over the world and it does not change, so scientists are able to be sure of the correct and unique name of any organism.

4. What is the name for a biologist who works with the classification of organisms?

   A taxonomist works with the classification of organisms.

5. Name the five classes of vertebrate animals. To which class do humans belong?

   The five classes of vertebrates are fish, amphibians, reptiles, birds, and mammals. Humans belong to the class of mammals.

6. What is the Latin, or scientific, name for the human genus and species?

   The Latin, or scientific, name for humans is Homo sapiens.

More Resources

The titles listed below are offered as a representative sample of materials and not a complete list of everything that is available.

For students —

- *Amphibian (DK Eyewitness Books)*, by Barry Clarke (DK Children, 2000). Hardcover, 64 pages, ISBN 0789457547.

- *The Kingdoms of Life: Classification (Come Learn with Me)*, by Bridget Anderson (Lickle Publishing, 2003). A clear introduction with lots of new vocabulary. Hardcover, 48 pages, ISBN 1890674176. See also *Animals Without Backbones: Invertebrates*, in the same series. Available directly from Lickle Publishing, www.licklepublishing.com or 1-866-454-2553.

- *Oxford First Book of Animals*, by Barbara Taylor (Oxford University Press, 2003). A fairly comprehensive and succinct overview of animal habitats, activity, and classification. Paperback, 48 pages, ISBN 0199109850.

- *Scales, Slime, and Salamanders: The Science of Reptiles and Amphibians (Science @ Work)*, by Patricia Miller-Schroeder (Raintree, 2000). Library binding, 48 pages, ISBN 0739801414.

- *Slime Molds and Fungi*, by Elaine Pascoe (Blackbirch Press, 1998). Includes many experiments. Library binding, 48 pages, ISBN 1567111823.

- *Sorting Out Worms and Other Invertebrates*, by Samuel Woods (Blackbirch Press, 1999). ISBN 1567113710.

- *The Usborne Living World Encyclopedia*, by Anna Craig and Cliff Rosney (EDC Publications, 2003). Why do leopards have spots? How do plants breathe? Includes a classification section, glossary, and index. Hardcover, 128 pages, ISBN 0794500056.

For teachers —

- *Animal Encyclopedia*, by Jayne Parsons, Ed., and Barbara Taylor (DK Children, 2000). Extensive information on habitats, homes, protection, etc., followed by an A–Z introduction of more than 2,000 species. Lavishly illustrated. Hardcover, 376 pages, ISBN 0789464993.

- *Biological Science*, by Scott Freeman (Pearson Education, Inc., 2004). Chapter 1 is easy to read and covers the latest developments in taxonomy. Hardcover, 1,283 pages, ISBN 0131409417.

More Resources continued

• *The Concise Animal Encyclopedia,* by David Burnie (Kingfisher Larousse Chambers, 2003). Hardcover, 320 pages, ISBN 0753455900.

• *The Firefly Encyclopedia of Insects and Spiders,* edited by Christopher O'Toole (Firefly Books, 2002). "With lush color photographs and lavishly detailed illustrations, this encyclopedia presents a striking abundance of information at a glance. Also noteworthy is the scholarly text, a comprehensive overview of these frequently studied phyla" (*Booklist*). Hardcover, 240 pages, ISBN 1552976122. Also in this series are *The Firefly Encyclopedia of Reptiles and Amphibians* and *The Firefly Encyclopedia of Birds.*

• *Handbook of Nature Study*, by Anna Botsford Comstock (Cornell University Press, 1986). Originally penned for elementary school teachers, this book has been a helpful guide to many for the 90-plus years it has been in print. Paperback, 887 pages, ISBN 0801493846.

• *Insects (Peterson Field Guides),* by Donald J. Borror and Richard E. White (Houghton Mifflin, 1998). Field guides are an excellent way to develop observation and thought about different characteristics of the living world. Organized by order. Paperback, 448 pages, ISBN 0395911702.

The Big Idea

All living things are composed of cells; in complex organisms, groups of cells form complex structures that work together for the survival of the organism.

Remember that each subject you study with students expands their vocabulary and introduces new terms, thus making them better listeners and readers. As you study cell structures and processes, use read alouds, independent reading, and discussions to build students' vocabularies.

What Students Should Already Know

Students in Core Knowledge schools should be familiar with

Kindergarten

‣ the five senses and associated body parts: sight (eyes), hearing (ears), smell (nose), taste (tongue), touch (skin)

‣ taking care of the body: exercise, cleanliness, healthy foods, rest

Grade 1

‣ body systems: skeletal, muscular, digestive, circulatory, nervous

‣ germs, disease, and preventing illness: taking care of your body; vaccinations

Grade 2

‣ cells: all living things are made up of cells, too small to be seen without a microscope

‣ Cells make up tissues; tissues make up organs; organs work in systems.

‣ the digestive and excretory systems
  • salivary glands, taste buds
  • teeth: incisors, bicuspids, molars
  • esophagus, stomach, liver, small intestine, large intestine
  • kidneys, urine, bladder, urethra, anus, appendix

‣ taking care of your body: the food pyramid, vitamins and minerals

Grade 3

‣ the muscular system
  • involuntary and voluntary muscles

‣ the skeletal system
  • skeleton, bones, marrow
  • musculo-skeletal connections, including ligaments, tendons (Achilles tendon), cartilage
  • skull (or cranium), spinal column (vertebrae), rib cage, sternum, scapula (shoulder blades), pelvis, tibia, fibula
  • joints, broken bones, and x-rays

‣ the nervous system
  • brain: medulla, cerebellum, cerebrum, cerebral cortex
  • spinal cord, nerves, and reflexes

II. Cells: Structures and Processes

Materials

Instructional Masters 68, 83

Venn Diagram, p. 579

Put Your Brain Cells to Work, p. 580

chart paper, p. 577

pictures of various kinds of cells, p. 578

pipe cleaners or yarn, assorted colors, p. 578

plastic bag, p. 578

bean seeds, p. 578

different-sized balls, p. 578

gelatin, p. 578

pictures of single-celled organisms, p. 580

onion, p. 581

simple microscope, p. 581

toothpick, p. 581

thin slices of cork, celery, or other plant or animal materials, p. 581

information about visiting a local clinic or hospital, p. 582

materials to make coloring books, e.g., paper, black markers, p. 582

information about having a health care professional visit the class, p. 582

$8\frac{1}{2}$" by 11" piece of paper for each student, p. 582

1 piece of construction paper for each student, p. 582

What Students Should Already Know continued

- vision: how the eye works
  - parts of the eye: cornea, iris and pupil, lens, retina
  - optic nerve
  - farsighted and nearsighted
- hearing: how the ear works
  - sound as vibration
  - outer ear, ear canal
  - eardrum
  - Three tiny bones (hammer, anvil, and stirrup) pass vibrations to the cochlea.
  - auditory nerve

Grade 4

- the circulatory system
  - pioneering work of William Harvey
  - heart: four chambers (auricles and ventricles), aorta
  - blood: red blood cells (corpuscles), white blood cells (corpuscles), platelets, hemoglobin, plasma, antibodies
  - blood vessels: arteries, veins, capillaries
  - blood pressure, pulse
  - coagulation (clotting)
  - filtering function of liver and spleen
  - Fatty deposits can clog blood vessels and cause a heart attack.
  - blood types (four basic types: A, B, AB, O) and transfusions
- the respiratory system
  - process of taking in oxygen and getting rid of carbon dioxide
  - nose, throat, voice box, trachea (windpipe)
  - lungs, bronchi, bronchial tubes, diaphragm, ribs, alveoli (air sacs)
  - smoking: damage to lung tissue, lung cancer

What Students Need to Learn

- **All living things are made up of cells.**
- **Structure of cells (both plant and animal)**
  - **Cell membrane: selectively allows substances in and out**
  - **Nucleus: surrounded by nuclear membrane, contains genetic materials, divides for reproduction**
  - **Cytoplasm contains organelles, small structures that carry out the chemical activities of the cell, including mitochondria (which produce the cell's energy) and vacuoles (which store food, water, or wastes).**
- **Plant cells, unlike animal cells, have cell walls and chloroplasts.**

What Students Need to Learn continued

- ▸ Cells without nuclei: monerans (bacteria)
- ▸ Some organisms consist of only a single cell: for example, amoeba, protozoans, some algae.
- ▸ Cells are shaped differently in order to perform different functions.
- ▸ Organization of cells into tissues, organs, and systems
  - • In complex organisms, groups of cells form tissues (for example, in animals, skin tissue or muscle tissue; in plants, the skin of an onion or the bark of a tree).
  - • Tissues with similar functions form organs (for example, in some animals, the heart, stomach, or brain; in some plants, the root or flower).
  - • In complex organisms, organs work together in a system. (Recall, for example, from earlier studies of the human body, the digestive, circulatory, and respiratory systems.)

What Students Will Learn in Future Grades
In Grade 7, students will study cell division and genetics.

Vocabulary

Student/Teacher Vocabulary

bacterium: a simple single-celled organism that does not have a membrane-bound nucleus and is a prokaryotic cell (plural: bacteria) (S)

cell: the basic structural unit of all living things (S)

cell membrane: the thin layer of membrane that surrounds the cytoplasm in a cell (S)

chlorophyll: a green molecule in plant cells that traps sunlight, uses the light energy to break down carbon dioxide and water and recombine them to form glucose and oxygen; gives plants their green color (S)

chloroplast: in plant cells, a chlorophyll-containing organelle in which photosynthesis takes place (S)

chromosome: a single long molecule of DNA and any associated proteins; carries the genetic information for a cell (S)

cytoplasm: a jellylike mass of material in a cell that contains DNA, the information for the cell's life processes (including reproduction) (S)

DNA: deoxyribonucleic acid; the genetic material organized in protein structures called chromosomes, passed on to each generation of cells (S)

enzyme: a protein produced by cells that catalyzes, or changes the rate of, biochemical reactions in the metabolism of living things (T)

epithelial tissue: tissue with tightly packed cells that lines, covers, and protects animal organs and other body parts from injury and infection; also connects parts of plants (S)

Vocabulary continued

eukaryote: an organism with complex cells with distinctive traits, including a nucleus; may be either unicellular or multicellular (T)

glucose: a simple sugar that green plants produce during photosynthesis (S)

mitochondria: organelles that break down organic molecules from nutrient substances (food) to produce energy for the cell to use (S)

moneran: a cell that has no defined nucleus; also known as a prokaryote (S)

nuclear membrane: the double membrane that surrounds the nucleus of a cell; also called the nuclear envelope (S)

nucleus: in eukaryotic cells, the part of the cell that contains the DNA (S)

organ: a combination of tissues functioning as a whole by working together (S)

organelle: a discrete, membrane-bound structure within a cell where cell activities are carried out (S)

prokaryote: a unicellular organism that has no defined nucleus, e.g., bacteria (T)

symbiosis: a cooperative relationship between individuals of two different species (adjective: symbiotic) (T)

system: a set of interacting elements, e.g., a set of organs that work together to perform a function (S)

tissue: a group of cells with similar functions that work together (S)

vacuole: a small space or cavity in the cytoplasm of a cell; usually used for storage of a fluid, e.g., water, food, or waste (S)

Domain Vocabulary

Cells: structures and processes and associated words:
algae, amoeba, protozoa, predator, disease, sickness, kingdom, species, organism, prey, scavenger, decomposer, producer, genes, photosynthesis, sun, energy, light energy, chemical energy, metabolism, synthesize, nutrient, nutrition, protein, carbohydrate, lipid, fat, organize, feature, characteristic, pore, stoma (singular), stomata (plural), reproduction, fertilization, digestion, similar, different, specialize, strengthen, support, survive, fluid, liquid, gas, absorb, molecule, pigment, coloration, albino, melanin, hereditary, genetic, inherited, generation, environment, convert, transfer, store, exchange, receive, transmit, conduct, assist, egg, sperm, present, absent, lack, fibrous, fiber, group, colony, function, structure, network, plants *(and specific names)*, animals *(and specific names)*, fungi *(and specific names)*, protist, activities, direct, control, evolve, evolution, simple, complex, primitive, numerous, multiple, multiply, benefit, advantage, disadvantage

At a Glance

The most important ideas for you are:

- Cells are basic structural units of life. All living things are made up of one or more cells.
- The structure of most cells, including plant and animal cells, includes a cell membrane, a nucleus, and cytoplasm.
- Plant cells differ from animal cells by the additional features of cell walls and chloroplasts.
- Some cells have no defined nucleus.
- Cells that perform different functions have different shapes.
- Cells in complex organisms are organized into groups; they form tissues, organs, and organ systems that carry out the many functions required for survival of the organism.

What Teachers Need to Know

Background

All living things are composed of one or more cells. A cell is an organized structure that is capable of independent survival and exact reproduction.

Biologists divide all cells into two types, prokaryotic and eukaryotic. While you may wish to avoid these terms with fifth graders, it will be useful for you to know the terms and understand the differences between the two kinds of cells. The most basic difference between the two types is that a prokaryotic cell does not have a nucleus, whereas a eukaryotic cell does. Organisms made up of eukaryotic cells are called eukaryotes. Organisms made up of prokaryotic cells are called prokaryotes.

The vast majority of prokaryotes are unicellular; that is, they consist of only one cell. Many (but not all) eukaryotes are complex, multicellular organisms. Human beings, cats, and mushrooms are all multicellular eukaryotes made up of large numbers of eukaryotic cells. Four of the five kingdoms described in the previous section of this handbook are made up of eukaryotic cells: animals, plants, fungi, and protists. Members of the fifth kingdom—monerans or prokaryotes—are made up of prokaryotic cells.

The sections that follow describe eukaryotic cells (noting differences between animals and plants) and then prokaryotic cells.

Eukaryotic Cells

Animal Cells

Cells in human beings and other multicellular animals are eukaryotic cells. Although the cells in various animals differ in certain ways, they have certain common features. Some common features of an animal cell are shown in the diagram on p. 578.

II. Cells: Structures and Processes

Teaching Idea

Although cells have certain features in common, they also differ in some ways. A good way to help students develop a composite idea of what a cell looks like is to show them pictures of various kinds of cells, e.g., white blood cells, red blood cells, plant cells, etc. You may also purchase slides of various kinds of cells. (See *More Resources*.)

Teaching Idea

As students are learning about cells, reinforce the fact that cells represent minisystems and are constantly in motion. Although they may appear to be static in pictures, they are actually very active and bustling entities.

Teaching Idea

Invite students to create their own cell model to gain a better understanding of parts of cells. Have them choose either an animal cell or a plant cell to model. Students can make a 2-dimensional model with colored pipe cleaners or yarn, cut and formed to represent membranes and other cell parts; or they may make a 3-dimensional model with materials such as a plastic bag, bean seeds, different-sized balls, and even gelatin. Encourage students to make a drawing of their finished model and label the parts they included. Make sure students include at least a cell membrane, nucleus, and/or DNA, and 2 or more types of organelles. Remind them that plant cells also have chloroplasts and cell walls.

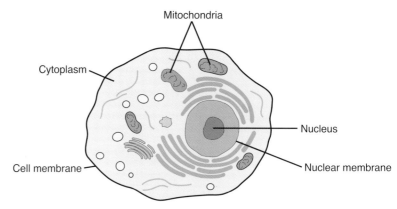

typical animal cell

The cell membrane, also called the plasma membrane, is a layer of molecules that surrounds the cell, keeping it separate from the external environment and controlling the passage of substances into and out of the cell. The cell membrane is composed mainly of phospholipids, or fatty compounds, carbohydrates, and proteins.

Inside the cell membrane is a jellylike substance called cytoplasm. Tiny filaments and tubules form a matrix in the cytoplasm to define a cell's shape. These filaments and tubes also help to hold various organelles in place. Organelles are small structures that carry out the chemical, or metabolic, activities of the cell. Each organelle is a discrete structure within the cytoplasm of a cell, and each is bounded by its own membrane.

One of the most prominent and important organelles in an animal cell is the nucleus. The nucleus is surrounded by a double membrane called the nuclear envelope, or the nuclear membrane. Each membrane consists of a lipid bilayer with proteins. Some of the proteins fuse and form pores, or passages, to and from the nucleus, thus allowing interactions between the nucleus and the cytoplasm of the cell. The nucleus carries the cell's DNA, which contains the hereditary instructions that are passed on to new cells each time the cell divides. The nucleus also influences the activities of the cell in various ways.

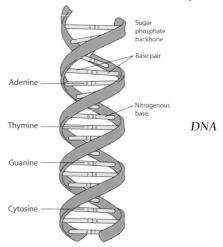

DNA

Mitochondria are larger organelles that break down organic molecules from nutrient substances (food) to produce energy for the cell to use. Mitochondria are often called the powerhouses of the cell. Mitochondria also contain a special kind of DNA called mitochondrial DNA.

Plant Cells

Plant cells are also eukaryotic cells. They contain all of the features of animal cells just noted, plus some additional features.

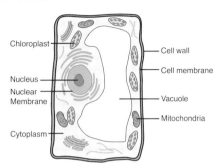

typical plant cell

Plant cells also contain organelles called chloroplasts. Chloroplasts are surrounded by a double membrane and contain molecules of enzymes and pigments. The greenish pigment in chloroplasts is chlorophyll. Chlorophyll gives chloroplasts (and green plants overall) their green color. Chlorophyll molecules absorb sunlight and convert the light energy to chemical energy to synthesize glucose, a sugar that serves as food for the plant cell. The process by which this is accomplished is called photosynthesis. (See Section III B, "Photosynthesis," on pp. 589–590.)

A second feature that is present in plant cells but absent in animal cells is a cell wall, found outside the cell membrane. Cell walls are composed of a type of carbohydrate called cellulose—fibrous glucose molecules bundled together.

Plant cells often contain large structures called vacuoles. These vacuoles are fluid-filled organelles that store food or wastes and improve nutrient absorption.

Single-Celled Organisms: Protists

In the section on classification, you learned about protists. These tiny organisms make up one of the kingdoms in the five-kingdom classification scheme. Protists are unicellular, which means that each one consists of a single cell. Protists are eukaryotes, which means that they have a nucleus.

Some of the simplest protists are amoebas, which are a type of protozoan or animal-like organism. (The root *proto-* means "first" or "early," and the root *zoan*, from which we get the word *zoo*, means "animal"; so a protozoan is an early animal-like organism.) Many amoebas are predators and hunt by stretching out part of their cytoplasm to surround and envelop prey. Once the victim is surrounded, specialized molecules begin to break down the amoeba's prey, turning it into nutrients for the amoeba.

Many amoebas and other protozoa are parasites that cause disease in humans and other animals. For example, African sleeping sickness, Chagas' disease, leishmaniasis, and malaria are all caused by protozoa. The protozoan *Plasmodium* causes malaria, which is spread to humans by mosquitos. If a person does not have natural immunity to malaria, the person can take drugs before and during a visit to an area where malaria is prevalent to prevent infection. The study of parasitic illnesses continues to be important for the medical community. With the development of better electron microscopes and increased genetic knowledge, scientists are collecting more information on these organisms.

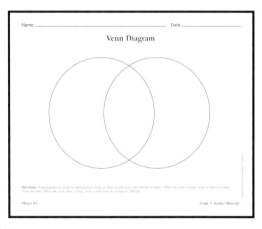

Science **579**

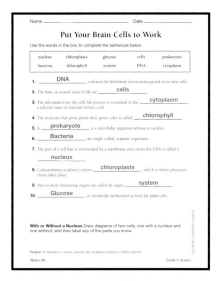

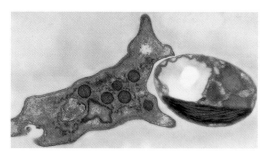

amoeba engulfing an organism

Prokaryotic Cells

Single-Celled Organisms: Prokaryotes

Another kind of single-celled organism is the prokaryote, also known as the moneran. Prokaryotes are tiny organisms that make up one kingdom in the five-kingdom classification scheme described in the previous section of this handbook. Prokaryotes are like protists in that they consist of only one cell; however, prokaryotic cells have a simpler structure and are lacking some of the features of eukaryotic cells.

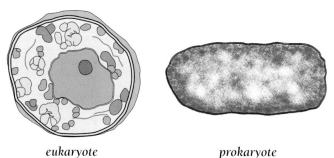

eukaryote   *prokaryote*

Like eukaryotic cells, prokaryotic cells have an outer cell membrane, genetic information coded in DNA, and cytoplasm. However, prokaryotic cells have neither a defined nucleus nor the types of organelles that eukaryotic cells have. In a prokaryote, the outer plasma membrane encloses a single compartment, and this compartment contains few or no separate organelles. In prokaryotic cells, the DNA cannot be held in the nucleus (since there is no nucleus), so it floats about in the cytoplasm. Also, whereas many eukaryotes are complex multicellular organisms (e.g., flowers, dogs, mushrooms), prokaryotes are almost always unicellular. In other words, each prokaryote cell is typically a complete, individual organism.

Some prokaryotes have whiplike projections called flagella that they can flap to move around. In general, prokaryotic cells are much smaller than eukaryotic cells. Most scientists believe the prokaryotes were the first organisms on our planet and that eukaryotes evolved from simple, primitive prokaryotic ancestors.

Prokaryotes include bacteria and cyanobacteria (from the Greek *kyanos,* meaning "having a bluish color"). Cyanobacteria are also sometimes called blue-green algae. Bacteria are able to live in virtually every environment on Earth. Some bacteria have chloroplasts and photosynthesize, while others break down inorganic molecules as an energy source, but most bacteria derive nutrients from the remains of other organisms.

Like other prokaryotes, bacteria are unicellular, or single-celled. Therefore, each cell is a separate organism capable of independent existence. When the cells divide, the resulting daughter cells do sometimes remain together, forming different types of groupings and even becoming colonies. Colonies are groups of cells that work toward a mutual benefit.

Although not all bacteria are harmful, some do cause diseases in human beings. Here are just a few diseases that are caused by bacteria: Lyme disease, anthrax, tetanus, food poisoning, acne, pneumonia, strep throat, and scarlet fever. Scientists fight bacterial diseases with medicines called antibiotics.

Organization of Cells

Prokaryotes are single-celled organisms. But many eukaryotes are complex multicelled organisms in which different sorts of cells are designed to perform specific functions. The cell structures of different organisms vary, depending on their functions. In complex organisms, such as animals and plants, cells that have similar functions have similar shapes. Groups of cells working together to perform a specialized activity are known as tissues. Several kinds of tissue can be distinguished, as each tissue consists of a particular kind of cell held together by a surrounding matrix. Epithelial tissue covers the surfaces and linings of organs. Your skin is composed largely of epithelial tissue. If you have ever had a sunburn, you may have experienced the peeling of the outermost layer. The cells in this layer of tissue have died and are continually being replaced by new cell tissue beneath.

Muscle tissues come in three different types: cardiac muscle is found in your heart; smooth muscle is found in other organs, such as in intestinal walls and blood vessels; and skeletal muscle is attached to the bones and allows your bones to move. Most meats used for food are skeletal muscle tissue.

The function of many plant tissues is to strengthen and support the plant. Bark is formed from tissues made of thick-walled, toughened cells. When these cells mature, they die and leave behind the tough cell walls. An onion bulb is a bud with a short stem and modified compacted leaves for food storage, with epithelial tissue between each leaf.

Organs are structures of combined tissues that perform a common task. In complex animals, the heart is an organ composed of cardiac muscle tissues. The stomach is made of smooth muscle tissues with types of digestive enzymes. The brain is composed of tissue masses of nerve cells that function to receive and transmit information to other parts of the body. Fluids circulate through the inner layers. Plants have organs, too. One plant organ is the root, which has tissues that are able to conduct water and nutrients from the soil to other parts of the plant. Flowers are the reproductive organs of some plants, consisting of tissues that function to assist in the fertilization of egg and sperm cells into a seed.

Organ systems are formed when two or more organs interact to assist in the entire organism's survival. For example, your digestive system consists of several organs (stomach, large and small intestines, etc.) that work to break down food into simple molecules that can then be used by individual cells of your body. Your circulatory system consists primarily of the heart, a network of blood vessels, and

Teaching Idea

Invite students to peel an onion and pull away a layer of epithelial tissue, which is the thin, transparent layer between each thick leaf layer of the bulb. If you have a microscope, you can also observe the individual cells and identify the rectangular cell walls and dark nucleus in the individual cells. You can also invite students to use a clean toothpick to scrape the inside of their cheek and place the scrapings onto a microscope slide for viewing some animal (human) epithelial tissue. (Note: You may prepare additional slides using thinly cut slices of cork, celery, or other plant or animal materials. Assortments of prepared slides also can be purchased from science suppliers.)

Teaching Idea

Ask students to explain the relationship between tissues, organs, and organ systems.

Teaching Idea

You may want to teach about Ernest Just in conjunction with this section. (See Section VII, "Science Biographies," on pp. 634–646.)

II. Cells: Structures and Processes

Teaching Idea

You can use discussion of tissues and organs to review the various body systems students should have studied in earlier grades, including the skeletal, muscular, digestive, circulatory, nervous, and respiratory systems.

The Big Idea in Review

All living things are composed of cells; in complex organisms, groups of cells form complex structures that work together for the survival of the organism.

blood, which transports materials to and from cells all over your body, and helps regulate body temperature. Your respiratory system provides oxygen to your body and eliminates carbon dioxide waste; your lungs exchange these gases through your blood.

Review

Below are some ideas for ongoing assessment and review activities. These are not meant to constitute a comprehensive list.

• Have students write a paper about the functions of the parts of a cell, using a metaphor to compare how the parts of a cell work together to another system with parts that work together. For example, students could compare the parts of a cell to a computer, where the outside of the computer would be like the cell wall and the computer chips inside like the nucleus. See how creative students can be in explaining the similarities of the parts of the cell and the other system in their writing, and also ask them to note where the comparison is not accurate.

• Schedule a trip to a hospital or clinic where the students would have an opportunity to look at a variety of different cells under microscopes. You may want to talk with a doctor or nurse in advance to have them prepare a variety of slides for students to view. Have students sketch the different cells and then write a description of what they saw under the microscope. You may also wish to purchase sets of slides of various types of cells for students to examine.

• Since second graders in Core Knowledge schools also study cells, have fifth graders create coloring books with pictures and sentences that give information about cells. Pair a fifth grader with a second grader to read the books and color the pictures. Ask the pairs to share with the class what they learned about cells.

• You may also have a health care professional visit the class to talk with students about what kinds of professionals work with cells, tissues, organs, and systems of the body. Students may be interested to hear about various health care opportunities and how much schooling is required for each profession. After the visit, have students write about what they learned from the presentation.

• Have students make a flap book to show how they understand the smallest to largest parts of the body: cells, tissues, organs, and organ systems. Take an $8\frac{1}{2}$" by 11" piece of paper and fold it lengthwise. Then have students cut out four "flaps" from the top fold of the paper. On the flaps, have students draw four pictures, one on each flap, of cells, tissues, an organ, and an organ system, and then under the flap on the bottom of the paper, have them write sentences to define each term and explain how cells build to eventually become parts of systems. Mount these on construction paper.

• You may also ask the following questions after completing this section:
1. What is a cell?
A cell is the basic structural unit of every living thing.

2. Are there any animals that are not made up of cells? What about plants?
   No. All animals and plants are composed of cells.

3. What are some basic structures that all cells have?
   All cells have a cell membrane, DNA, and cytoplasm.

4. What is a nucleus?
   A nucleus is a structure within a eukaryotic cell in which DNA is stored.

5. Do all cells have a nucleus?
   No. Prokaryotes/monerans (including bacteria) do not have a nucleus.

6. What are some ways in which plant cells differ from animal cells?
   Plant cells have additional features not found in animal cells, including a cell wall and chloroplasts.

7. What are the different levels of organized cell groupings that perform a common task?
   Cells organize into tissues, organs, and organ systems.

More Resources

The titles listed below are offered as a representative sample of materials and not a complete list of everything that is available.

For students —

• *Cell Division & Genetics (Cells & Life)*, by Robert Snedden (Heinemann, 2002). Paperback, 48 pages, ISBN 1588109348. See also *DNA and Genetic Engineering*, by the same author.

• *Cells (Science Concepts)*, by Alvin and Virginia Silverstein, and Laura Silverstein Nunn (Twenty-First Century Books, 2002). Library binding, 64 pages, ISBN 076132254X. See also *DNA*, by the same authors.

• *Cells and Systems (Life Processes)*, by Holly Wallace (Heinemann, 2001). Library binding, 32 pages, ISBN 1575723360.

• *Inside an Egg*, by Sylvia Johnson (Lerner, 1987). Paperback, 48 pages, ISBN 0822595222.

• *Janice VanCleave's Biology for Every Kid: 101 Easy Experiments that Really Work*, by Janice VanCleave (John Wiley & Sons, 1990). Paperback, 240 pages, ISBN 0471503819.

• *Understanding DNA: A Breakthrough in Medicine*, by Tony Allan (Heinemann, 2002). An interesting biographical look at this important discovery. Paperback, 32 pages, ISBN 1403400741.

For teachers —

• *The Double Helix: A Personal Account of the Discovery of the Structure of DNA*, by James D. Watson (Touchstone, 2001). Paperback, 256 pages, ISBN 074321630X.

• *The Language of Life: How Cells Communicate in Health & Disease*, by Debra Niehoff (Joseph Henry Press, 2005). Hardcover, 260 pages, ISBN 0309089891.

• *Outline of Molecular and Cell Biology*, by William Stansfield (McGraw-Hill, 1996). Paperback, 384 pages, ISBN 0070608989.

• *Rosalind Franklin: The Dark Lady of DNA*, by Brenda Maddox (Harper Perennial, 2003). Helps to correct the caricature of this important scientist given in *The Double Helix* (above). Paperback, 416 pages, ISBN 0060985089.

• Cell models can be purchased from Science Kit & Boreal Laboratories, www.sciencekit.com or 1-800-828-7777. They also offer Microslides™, which can be observed through an inexpensive viewer. Microslide™ sets include "Plant Mitosis," "Cell Structure," and "Animal Mitosis." Also see their wide assortment of microscopes and individual prepared slides of cells (plant, animal, cork section, and paramecium).

III. lant Structures and Processes

The Big Idea

Plants have structures to take in water and make their own food, and they have several different ways to reproduce.

Remember that each subject you study with students expands their vocabulary and introduces new terms, thus making them better listeners and readers. As you study plant structures and processes, use read alouds, independent reading, and discussions to build students' vocabularies.

What Students Should Already Know

Students in Core Knowledge schools should be familiar with

Kindergarten

 ▸ plants and plant growth
  • what plants need to grow: sufficient warmth, light, and water
  • basic parts of plants: seed, root, stem, branch, leaf
  • Plants make their own food.
  • flowers and seeds: seeds as food for plants and animals (for example, rice, nuts, wheat, corn)
  • two kinds of plants: deciduous and evergreen
  • farming: how some food comes from farms as crops; how farmers must take special care to protect their crops from weeds and pests; how crops are harvested, kept fresh, packaged, and transported for people to buy and consume

Grade 1

 ▸ living things and their environments
  • habitats
  • the food chain for plants: nutrients, water, soil, air, sunlight
  • environmental change and habitat destruction

Grade 2

 ▸ cycles in nature
  • seasonal cycles: four seasons and life processes
   • spring: sprouting, sap flow in plants
   • summer: growth
   • fall: ripening, migration
   • winter: plant dormancy
  • life cycles: from seed to seed with a plant

What Students Need to Learn

 ▸ **Structure: nonvascular and vascular**
  • **nonvascular plants (for example, algae)**
  • **Vascular plants have tubelike structures that allow water and dissolved nutrients to move through the plant.**
   •**parts and functions of vascular plants: roots, stems and buds, leaves**

Materials

Instructional Masters 69–71

K-W-L Chart, p. 588

Vascular and Nonvascular Plants, p. 589

Photosynthesis, p. 590

Reproductive Structure of Flowering Plants, p. 595

variety of books about plants, p. 588

plants or pictures of plants (e.g., common house-plants, ferns, and mosses), pp. 588, 589

tree cross-section, slice, p. 589

freshly cut celery stalk, p. 589

container with water, p. 589

food coloring, p. 589

magnifying glass or microscope, p. 589

aluminum foil, p. 589

materials to plant a school garden, seeds, seedlings, tools, pp. 589, 597

stem cuttings and leaf cuttings, p. 591

soil, p. 591

water, p. 591

plastic bag, p. 591

pictures or live samples of ferns and mosses, p. 592

seeds from a variety of plants, p. 592

natural cones (such as pine, fir, or spruce), p. 595

flower(s), preferably large (such as tulip, daylily, or iris), p. 595

knife, plastic with serrated edge, p. 595

What Students Need to Learn continued

▶ **Photosynthesis**

- Photosynthesis is an important life process that occurs in plant cells but not animal cells (photo = light; synthesis = putting together). Unlike animals, plants make their own food through the process of photosynthesis.
- role in photosynthesis of energy from sunlight, chlorophyll, carbon dioxide and water, xylem and phloem, stomata, oxygen, sugar (glucose)

▶ **Reproduction**

- asexual reproduction
  - example of algae
  - vegetative reproduction: runners (for example, strawberries) and bulbs (for example, onions); growing plants from eyes, buds, leaves, roots, and stems
- sexual reproduction by spore-bearing plants (for example, mosses and ferns)
- sexual reproduction of nonflowering seed plants: conifers (for example, pines), male and female cones, wind pollination
- sexual reproduction of flowering plants (for example, peas)
  - functions of sepals and petals, stamen (male), anther, pistil (female), ovary (or ovule)
  - process of seed and fruit production: pollen, wind, insect and bird pollination, fertilization, growth of ovary, mature fruit
  - seed germination and plant growth: seed coat, embryo and endosperm, germination (sprouting of new plant), monocots (for example, corn) and dicots (for example, beans)

Vocabulary

Student/Teacher Vocabulary

algae: a plant or plantlike organism, usually aquatic and containing chlorophyll (S)

angiosperm: a vascular plant whose seeds are covered or enclosed by an ovary (T)

anther: the tip of the stamen, the male reproductive structure in flowering plants; responsible for producing pollen grains (S)

asexual reproduction: any means of reproducing without the joining of male and female gametes (S)

bryophyte: a nonflowering, nonvascular plant such as a moss (T)

bulbs: buds with short stems, modified compacted leaves for food storage, and epithelial tissue between each leaf; form of vegetative reproduction (S)

carpel: the female reproductive structure; also known as the pistil (S)

III. Plant Structures and Processes

Materials continued

information on a local gardener or plant store owner, p. 597

different examples of flowers to dissect in class, p. 597

hand lens for each student, p. 597

variety of local field guidebooks for the area, pp. 596, 597

large index cards, p. 597

large wall map of the world, p. 598

variety of plants and flowers to plant in the classroom for observation throughout the year, p. 598

Vocabulary continued

chlorophyll: the molecule in plant cells that traps sunlight; uses the light energy to break down carbon dioxide and water and recombine them to form glucose and oxygen; gives plants their green color (S)

conifer: a tree or bush that has cones; usually an evergreen (S)

dicot: one of the two groupings of flowering plants; has two seed leaves, both of which photosynthesize for the seedling until the foliage leaves can take over to supply nutrients for the plant (S)

embryo: a mature zygote in the female ovule of a plant; eventually becomes a seed (S)

endosperm: tissue surrounding an embryo of seeds in a flowering plant; supplies nutrients to the embryo (S)

fertilization: the result of a sperm uniting with an egg (S)

flowering plant: plant in which the flower is the reproductive organ of the plant (S)

gamete: a mature sex cell, either male (sperm) or female (egg) (S)

germination: the process of the growth of the embryo in a plant (S)

gymnosperm: a plant, such as a conifer, that produces naked or uncovered seeds (T)

monocot: one of the two groupings of flowering plants; has one seed leaf, usually enclosed in a sheath that surrounds and protects the shoot (S)

node: a joint on a plant stem from which roots, leaves, or other structures can develop (T)

nonflowering plant: a plant that produces no flowers (S)

nonvascular plant: a plant that is relatively simple in form and lacks specialized tissues for support and fluid transport (S)

ovary: in seed-bearing plants, the place where fertilization takes place and seeds mature; when mature, the ovary is called a fruit (S)

petal: the brightly colored part of the plant designed to attract animal pollinators (S)

phloem: the set of tubelike structures in vascular plants that transport sugars, which are made primarily in the leaves, to other parts of the plant or store it for later use (S)

photosynthesis: a plant life process that traps sunlight and uses carbon dioxide and water to form carbohydrates (S)

pistil: the female reproductive structure in a plant; also known as the carpel (S)

pollen: male gametes of plants (T)

pollination: the act of transferring pollen from an anther to a stigma (S)

runners: stems that grow above ground in vegetative (asexual) reproduction (S)

seed coat: the structure that protects the plant embryo until favorable conditions allow the embryo to begin to grow (S)

sepal: one of the outermost structures of a flower, sepals protect the young flower while it begins to develop (S)

sexual reproduction: means of reproduction in which male and female gametes join (S)

spores: reproductive plant bodies, usually one-celled, each able to develop into a new organism (S)

stamen: the male reproductive structure in flowering plants (S)

stigma: the top of the pistil or carpel (S)

stoma: a minute opening in the outer layer of a plant through which gaseous interchange takes place (plural: stomata) (S)

Vocabulary continued

tissue: a group of cells working together to perform a similar task (S)

vascular plant: a plant that has specialized tissues to carry water and nutrients to all parts of the plant (S)

vegetative reproduction: asexual reproduction in which some plants grow stems that branch out along the ground; nodes on these stems are where new roots can grow, starting a whole new plant (S)

xylem: one type of vascular tissue; transports water and nutrients from the roots to the leaves (S)

Domain Vocabulary

Plant structures and processes and associated words:
specialize, egg, sperm, immature, mature, phase, light energy, chemical energy, combine, recombine, manufacture, synthesize, simple, complex, lack, transport, carbohydrate, glucose, starch, sugar, oxygen, carbon dioxide, hydrogen, zygote, development, sprout, shoot, stem, stalk, seedling, foliage, flower, fruit, ripen, regrowth, division, vegetative, tuber, leaf cutting, stem cutting, farming, agriculture, agriculturalist, bulb, structure, function, support, organ, plants, species, specimen, absorb, water, moisture, humidity, fluid, distribute, nutrient, internal, external, feature, characteristic, derive, descend, descendant, ancestor, inherit, life cycle, identical, variation, parent, clone, offspring, evolve, extract, reaction, drought, flood, freeze, favorable, extreme, conditions, environment, weather, climate, precipitation, dependent, independent, maintain, sustain, linked, whorl, opposite, pollinate, nectar, dormant, dormancy, emerge, photosynthesize, sunlight, moss, hornwort, liverwort, *plus the names of other plants*

Cross-curricular Connections

Language Arts
Fiction and Drama
• *The Secret Garden*

Visual Arts
Art of Japan
• Landscape gardens

At a Glance
The most important ideas for you are:

‣ Photosynthesis occurs in plant cells, allowing plants to make their own food.

‣ Chlorophyll, the molecule in plant cells that traps sunlight, uses the light energy to break down carbon dioxide and water and recombine them to form glucose and oxygen.

‣ Nonvascular plants are relatively simple in form and lack specialized tissues for support and fluid transport.

‣ Vascular plants have specialized tissues to carry water and nutrients to all parts of the plant.

‣ Specialized organs in vascular plants include roots, stems, and leaves.

‣ Plants may reproduce either asexually or sexually.

What Teachers Need to Know

Background

Most plants produce their own food from water and dissolved minerals, using sunlight as their source of energy. The plant kingdom is comprised mainly of vascular plants, with structures that transport and distribute water and nutrients throughout the plant. The rest of the plant kingdom consists of nonvascular plants, which lack internal tissue structures, true roots, stems, and leaves. Plants reproduce by both asexual and sexual methods.

A. Structure: Nonvascular and Vascular Plants

Many scientists believe that all plants derive from a common ancestor, which is thought to be originally a group of green algae. In the five-kingdom classification system, plants represent one kingdom. The plant kingdom is grouped into 10 divisions, or phyla. Plants are divided according to characteristics such as life cycle, tissue structure, and seed structure. They vary tremendously in terms of size: from a moss that rises only $\frac{1}{8}$ inch above the ground to a redwood tree that towers 300 feet in the air. The majority of plants (including most plants with which you would be familiar, such as all flowering plants, trees, grasses, shrubs, and many others) are vascular plants. Veinlike strands of tissues support vascular plants; these tissues also transport water and minerals through the plants' main organ structures—the roots, stems, and leaves.

Some plants are simpler in structure and lack the specialized tissues and organs of vascular plants. These comparatively simple plants are known as nonvascular plants, or bryophytes. There are three classes of bryophytes: mosses, hornworts, and liverworts. Most nonvascular plants are relatively small and low growing, seldom reaching more than 6 inches (15 centimeters) in height. Many species have developed structures that are rootlike, stemlike, and leaflike. These simpler structures allow the nonvascular plants to conduct processes such as taking in water or performing photosynthesis. For example, most species of nonvascular plants have structures called rhyzoids, which are elongated cells that attach to the soil and absorb water and nutrients. Rhyzoids are therefore rootlike, but they do not have the specialized cells and tissues of true roots. Most bryophytes are found in damp environments and are able to absorb moisture directly from the air.

Vascular plants have developed several specialized structures that have made them more adaptable to a wider range of environments. These structures include roots, which absorb water and nutrients and anchor the plant in surrounding soil; stems, which transport water and sugar to the other plant parts and support the plant; and leaves, where most photosynthesis occurs. Vascular tissues are groups of cells working together as a system. (If you have already taught Section II, "Cells: Structures and Processes," on pp. 573–583, students will be familiar with cells and tissues.) They conduct and distribute water and nutrients to all parts of the plant. Xylem [ZYE-lem], one type of vascular tissue, transports water and nutrients from the roots to the leaves. Xylem is composed of elongated, narrow cells that are open at each end and connect to each other into tubelike structures. These tubes are grouped into either bundles (like a bunch of straws) or rings (as in a tree trunk).

The other part of this transport system is made of phloem [FLOW-em], another set of tubelike structures. Phloem transports sugars, which are made primarily in the leaves, to other parts of the plant or stores them for later use.

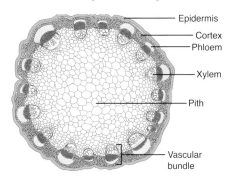

cross-section of a non-woody plant

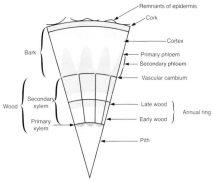

cross-section of a woody plant

Have students look at a cross-section of a tree and identify the location of the tree's xylem and phloem. The phloem is located in a ring just under the bark. Deer and other animals often scrape off the bark to eat the phloem because it contains nutrients (sugars). They usually do this during winter months when other food sources are scarce. Xylem is located inside the ring of phloem. Xylem forms the wood of a tree; a new ring of tissue is added during each year of the tree's life.

B. Photosynthesis

All living cells are capable of taking energy from their surroundings and using this energy to sustain themselves and to reproduce. The cells of green plants (and some types of bacteria and algae) use the energy of the sun's light to synthesize, or manufacture, their own food. This process is called photosynthesis. Photosynthetic cells contain the green pigment chlorophyll. Chlorophyll is found in a compartment within the cell called a chloroplast; this is where photosynthesis takes place. Plants use photosynthesis to make food products such as sugars, starches, and other carbohydrates. Through the process of photosynthesis, plants also produce and give off oxygen, an element used by nearly all organisms.

Plants need water, carbon dioxide, and light from the sun in order to carry out the process of photosynthesis. There are several steps to the process:

• First, plants trap the sun's light energy and use that energy to break down water (H_2O) into its components—hydrogen and oxygen. While the plants use some of the oxygen, much of it is released into the environment.

• Next, the carbon dioxide taken in by the plants, mainly in the leaves, is recombined with the remaining oxygen and the hydrogen to form glucose, a simple sugar.

• Additional reactions combine the glucose molecules into chains and form more complex carbohydrates, such as starch.

Other types of cells, such as animal cells, are unable to make their own food. These types of cells must extract the energy from other organisms for food. For example, humans get energy from food in the form of carbohydrates, proteins, and fats. They do this by eating parts of plants or by eating the meat of animals that ate plants.

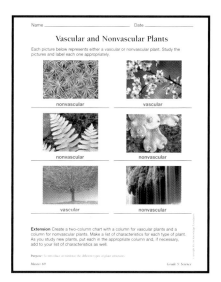

Use Instructional Master 69.

III. Plant Structures and Processes

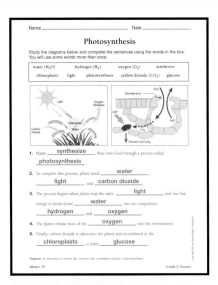

Use Instructional Master 70.

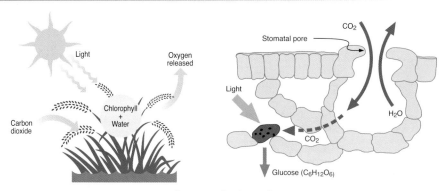

photosynthesis cycle

C. Reproduction

Plants have many different methods of reproduction, both asexual and sexual. (See section IV, "Life Cycles and Reproduction," on pp. 600–606.) Asexual reproduction is any means of reproducing without the joining of male and female gametes. Gametes are a plant's sex cells. When male and female gametes do join, sexual reproduction occurs. While there is only one method of sexual reproduction, there are many methods of asexual reproduction. In each asexual method, the new plant offspring is almost always a clone of the parent plant. That is, the new plant is genetically identical to the old plant. Occasionally, however, there will be slight variations or mutations, and these can lead to distinct species of plants. Sometimes, plants reproduce asexually by growing a whole new plant on one or more parts of the original plant, such as a root or a leaf. Other reproductive methods involve growth and development from a spore (asexual) or a seed (sexual) from the plant's mature reproductive organs.

Some plants reproduce asexually by growing stems that branch out along the ground. The nodes on these stems are places where new roots can grow, starting a whole new plant. If these stems grow aboveground, they are called runners. Strawberries and spider plants are examples of runner plants. A runner stem grows from the parent plant. At each node on the stem, roots may develop and continue to grow and develop into a whole organism.

Stems that grow below the ground are called rhizomes. Plants in which rhizomes occur include some grasses, irises, and bamboo. Aspen trees, found in parts of Colorado, also send up shoots from rhizomes. Each shoot becomes a mature tree. Separate trees above ground are all connected underground. The group of trees, or stand, can cover thousands of acres, and all of the trees are genetically identical, derived from a single parent tree. Some plants are able to extend their lives for many years via asexual reproduction. The oldest known plant is a clump of creosote bushes in the Mojave Desert; scientists believe this group is a clone of a plant that germinated 12,000 years ago!

corms

plantlets

rhizomes

Asexual reproduction has its disadvantages as well as its advantages. One major disadvantage is that organisms produced by asexual reproduction are generally genetically identical to the parent organism. That is, they have exactly the same DNA. This means that if a disease comes along and infects one organism, it is likely to also infect others that are clones of the first organisms. Sexual reproduction leads to new combinations of DNA: DNA from the male gamete combines with DNA from the female gamete, and the resulting organism is not identical to either parent, though it has aspects of both. This leads to genetic diversity and to stronger resistance to many diseases.

Cutting up parts of plants and growing entire new plants from the parts is another means of propagating, or reproducing, identical offspring. Farmers and other plant growers have long used plant part regrowth to assure uniform copies of many types of plants. New plants can be grown from almost any plant organ or tissue, including its buds, roots, stems, and leaves.

Phases of the Life Cycle

All plants have a life cycle. Many plants reproduce in two phases: the sporophyte phase and the gametophyte phase. (You don't have to use these terms with students, but it is useful for you to understand them.) A sporophyte is a plant that produces asexual spores. A gametophyte is a plant that produces sex-specific gametes, i.e., sperm or eggs, which can then fuse to make a zygote. The essential characteristic of the sporophyte is that its reproductive spores are asexual; by contrast, the gametophyte produces sexual gametes (sperm and eggs) that combine during sexual reproduction.

The diagram below shows a general version of what takes place in many different kinds of plants. The sporophyte produces spores. The spores develop into gametophytes. The gametophytes produce gametes, male and female. The male gametes are called sperm. The female gametes are called eggs. When a sperm fertilizes an egg, a zygote is created and this zygote develops into a sporophyte. And then the cycle begins again.

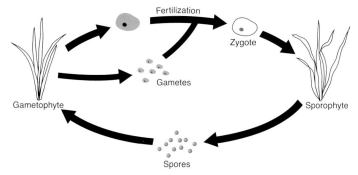

This process of alternating phases (also called alternation of generations) occurs in all plants, but not always in the same form. The exact details of reproduction differ from one kind of plant to another. It is helpful to look at several specific versions of this general process, each of which differs in small ways.

Let's begin with the example of mosses. In mosses, the gametophyte is large and long lived. The sporophyte depends on the gametophyte for its nutrition. The mature gametophyte is shown on the left in the illustration on p. 592. The gametophyte produces gametes. The female gametes (eggs) are formed in one part of the gametophyte, and the male gametes (sperm) are formed in another. If a

---

Teaching Idea

Demonstrate how plants propagate. Potato "eyes," or buds, will grow into a whole new plant when a piece of the potato and bud are planted. A sweet potato, which is a tuber, or enlarged root structure, can be suspended so that its base just touches water. The tuber will begin to develop into a long, vinelike plant. Geraniums and gardenias can grow new plants from stem cuttings. Simply cut off a growing shoot and plant the stem in soil or other growing medium. Each stem node that is in contact with the soil will grow new roots, thereby starting a new plant. New leaves will develop from nodes above the soil level. African violets propagate well from leaf cuttings. Cut off a leaf and place the leaf node so it is in contact with soil. Add water and cover with a plastic bag to make a mini-greenhouse. In a few weeks, tiny leaves will begin to grow. These and other methods are ways in which plant growers can grow plants that are identical to one another. Have students keep observation journals and write about what they learned from this at the end of the demonstrations.

sperm is able to swim to an egg, fertilization will occur. A layer of water, usually from rain or dew, must be present for the sperm to be able to swim to the eggs. The result of a sperm uniting with an egg is fertilization, and the fertilized egg, called a zygote, begins to grow into the sporophyte phase of the plant, which will develop to produce spores. In the sporophyte stage, spores are produced in spore cases or capsules called sporangia. When the spores are mature (ripe), the spore capsules burst open and the spores are released. Each individual spore is then able to germinate, or sprout, to grow and develop into a small plant with leaflike structures. These small plants are gametophytes. The gametophyte matures, and the cycle begins again.

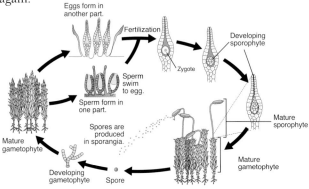

moss life cycle

Next, consider how the same general stages occur in ferns. In ferns, the sporophyte is long-lived, but when it is young, it depends on the gametophyte for nutrition. The mature sporophyte is shown on the left in the illustration below. The sporangia or spore capsules produce and release spores, which are dispersed by wind. Each spore has the potential to develop into a gametophyte. A mature gametophyte will produce gametes. Sperm are produced in one area and eggs in another. If a sperm can swim to an egg, fertilization will occur. (As is the case with moss, water is required.) After fertilization, a zygote develops. The young sporophyte develops on the gametophyte and depends on it for nutrition. Eventually, the sporophyte is fully mature and the process begins again.

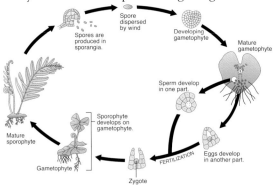

fern life cycle

With conifers (like pine trees), the general stages are the same, but there are some differences in the details. In these plants the sporophyte is dominant and the gametophyte depends on the sporophyte for nutrition. The illustration on p. 593 shows a mature sporophyte (a pine tree). The tree produces two kinds of cones. The pollen-bearing cones produce pollen grains, which are male gametophytes. The ovulate cones produce mother cells that develop into female

gametophytes. When pollen from a pollen-bearing cone lands on a scale from the ovulate cone, the pollen produces sperm, which can fertilize one of the eggs in the female gametophyte. An embryo then develops inside of a seed. The seed is dispersed by wind or by animals. If it germinates, it can grow into a mature sporophyte, at which point the process begins again.

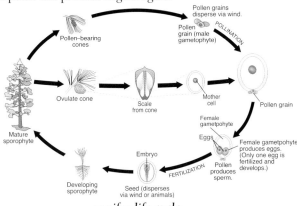

conifer life cycle

Finally, consider the life cycle of an angiosperm, or flowering plant with a covered seed. The mature sporophyte plant has flowers that contain both male and female reproductive structures. The male structures are called stamens. At the tip of each stamen is an anther, which produces pollen grains containing male gametophytes. The female structure is called the pistil or the carpel. At the base of the carpel is an ovary in which the female gametophytes develop. When a pollen grain containing a male gametophyte is blown by the wind (or carried by an insect) from an anther to the tip of a carpel, pollination occurs. The male gametophyte extends down the carpel to fertilize the female gametophyte, the egg. The fertilized egg develops into a zygote, and the zygote into an embryo with nutritive tissue. This tissue is the fruit that surrounds the seed. Eventually the fruit and seed fall to the ground. If conditions are suitable, the seed germinates. (If conditions are not favorable, the seed may remain dormant until water swells and splits the coat, triggering germination.) The seed then develops into a sporophyte, and the process begins again.

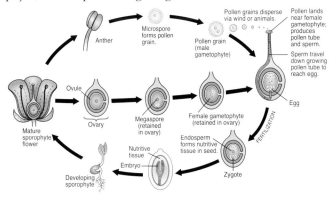

angiosperm life cycle

Notice that all of the life cycles described involve a sporophyte and a gametophyte phase. However, in the case of angiosperms, the male and female gametes develop inside the sporophyte, so the gametophyte phase is much less prominently visible than it is in the moss. In the case of the moss, the gametophyte is very prominent. It is a separate, long-lived plant. With the angiosperms, by contrast, the gametophyte has been greatly reduced in size, to the point where it generally consists of only a few cells. The gametophyte is no longer a separate plant as with the moss. Instead, it is embedded within the sporophyte and is therefore both less visible and less exposed to hazards of the environment than the moss gametophyte.

Seed-producing plants gained an advantage over spore-producing plants as Earth's climate (long-term temperature and moisture variations) became less humid over the course of millions of years. Spore-producing plants (like the moss described above) pass through a gametophyte stage in which they need a film of water for the sperm cells to travel to the egg cells, so conditions of drought and cold were unfavorable for these kinds of plants. Seed-producing plants evolved into structures that conserved water and protected the embryonic sporophyte plants. This protection is in the form of seeds, the mature ovules of the plants. Because of this protection, seed-producing plants were better able to survive in a less humid environment.

Cone-Bearing Plants

Seed-bearing plants consist of two major groupings: angiosperms, which have covered seeds (enclosed in an ovary) and gymnosperms, which have naked seeds (not enclosed in an ovary). Most flowering plants you are familiar with are angiosperms. The conifer described below is an example of a gymnosperm. Today angiosperms comprise about 90% of the plants on Earth. But this was not always the case. DNA and fossil records indicate that gymnosperms were once much more prevalent.

Gymnosperms consist of four groups: cycads, ginkgoes, gnetophytes, and conifers.

angiosperm   *cycad*   *conifer*

ginkgo   *gnetophyte*

All gymnosperms produce two types of spores. Conifers (cone-bearers) are the most numerous of the gymnosperms and include pines, firs, and spruces. Each of the two types of spores produced develops into a separate kind of cone. The male, or pollen, cones produce spores that develop into pollen grains—immature sex cells (male gametes)—that get blown by wind. The female, or seed cones, produce spores that develop into female gametophytes (egg cells) in the ovule. The ripening ovule in the female cone secretes a sticky liquid that traps pollen. When pollen grains carried by the wind get stuck in the liquid, pollination—the transfer of the male cells to the female cells—occurs. The pollen then

matures into sperm cells and develops a pollen tube that grows toward the egg cells in the ovule. When a sperm cell is carried to the egg cell, the two join and fertilization occurs. The fertilized zygote then develops into the sporophyte embryo that becomes the seed. The seeds grow on the scales of the female cone. Scales are modified types of leaves that protect the forming seeds. Germination occurs when the seeds disperse and have the right conditions, such as proper temperature and amount of water. Seeds then develop seedling roots and begin to grow in the ground.

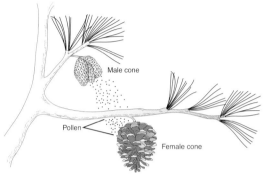

male and female cones

Flowering Plants

In angiosperms, or flowering plants, the flower is the reproductive organ of the plant; this is where seeds are produced. A typical flower is composed of four sets of whorls, or circular arrangements, of modified leaves: sepals, petals, stamens, and carpels; each is specialized for its function in the reproduction of the plant. The outermost structures are the sepals, which form the outermost parts of the flower. They are usually green and they are often thicker than other leaves, probably to protect the young flower while it begins to develop. Within the sepals are petals. These are often brightly colored and scented in order to attract animal pollinators. Some flowering plant species produce both male and female reproductive parts on the same plant. Other species produce only male or female parts on separate plants.

Wind or water may serve to pollinate some plants, but this method is random and is not always successful. Many plants rely on insects and other animals to help with pollination. Animals become inadvertent pollinators when they find food in the flower's nectar—a sugary substance the plant produces. The animals are attracted to the nectar and, as they move from one plant to another, brush against the anthers containing the male pollen and carry it to female flower parts. Many types of insects, including bees, ants, butterflies, and moths, birds (such as hummingbirds), and even some bats are pollinators. Flowering plants that depend on particular animal pollinators tend to have evolved showy petals that are frequently large, brightly colored, and sometimes scented.

The remaining two structures are the only parts that contribute directly to seed formation. The male reproductive structure, the stamen, consists of a thin stalk with a tip called an anther. The anther is responsible for producing pollen grains. The female reproductive structure is known as the carpel or pistil (named for an apothecary's pestle, which it resembles). The top of the carpel is called the stigma. The stigma's surface is sticky in order to capture male pollen grains. The stigma connects to the stalk, into which the maturing pollen tube can pierce.

Teaching Idea

Bring in some natural cones that still have seeds. Invite students to locate seeds in the female cones. Note the structures students observe.

Teaching Idea

Have students dissect a flower to learn the different parts. Observation is easier with large flowers, such as tulips, daylilies, and irises. (Note: Check with a florist or gardener when selecting the flower to dissect. Some flowers, such as orchids, have merged or specialized leaves and petals that can be confused with other parts.) Use a plastic knife to cut a flower in half. Have students circle the parts labeled on Instructional Master 71, *Reproductive Structure of Flowering Plants,* as they locate them in the flower. Have students make a drawing of the dissected flower and label the parts. You may wish to do this activity a second time with a different flower, as each flower is somewhat different.

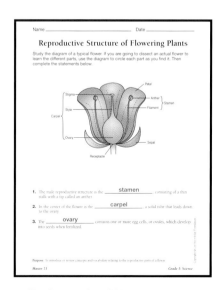

Use Instructional Master 71.

III. Plant Structures and Processes

Cross-curricular Teaching Idea

You may want to have students read *The Secret Garden* while studying this topic. Students can imagine the types of plants that would be growing in the secret garden, or could even invent their own secret garden based upon plants studied in this section.

Teaching Idea

Hold a plant scavenger hunt with the class. Have local field guidebooks about plants available. List different types of plants for students to find. (Some of the most common plants include but are not limited to grasses, dandelions, mosses, and trees.) Invite students to record descriptions of the plants they locate. If possible, have students make drawings or take photographs of their plants. Discourage students from picking plants, for both environmental and safety reasons. If students do wish to bring back specimens, make sure that the plants have been identified as being common and nonirritating, and that you (or landowners) grant permission to remove any plants.

Cross-curricular Teaching Idea

You may want to have students look at the types of plants seen in the landscapes from Japan, which is a Visual Arts topic for Grade 5.

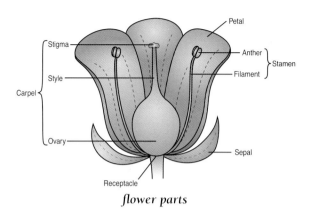

flower parts

The enlarged base of the carpel is the ovary, containing one or more ovules. The ovules are the individual egg cells that, when fertilized, develop into seeds.

A sperm cell developing from the pollen travels down the pollen tube to the ovary. As the cell moves down the tube, it divides into two cells (male gametes). One sperm cell unites with, or fertilizes, the egg cell and forms a zygote. The zygote becomes the embryo, which will develop into the seed. The other sperm cell (gamete) unites with another cell in the ovule to form the endosperm, which will provide the food supply for the seed. This process of forming a zygote and endosperm, called double fertilization, is unique to flowering plants. The outermost layer of the ovule becomes the seed coat and, as the ovary around the ovule matures, the ovary is called a fruit.

As this ovary, or fruit, ripens and the seeds form, other floral parts may fall off. When the ovary matures, the ripened fruit with its seeds may be blown by the wind or water or simply drop to the ground below the parent plant. If an animal eats the fruit, the seeds will pass through the animal's system and be deposited hours later far from the parent plant, where the new plant may have a better chance for survival. When temperature and moisture levels are suitable, water softens the seed coat and enters the seed, allowing the embryo to begin to grow. When the embryo splits the seed coat open, one part grows down into the ground to become the root. Another part grows up to form the shoot, which develops into the stem and leaves. This whole process is called germination. Seed leaves, called cotyledons, are the first leaves to emerge. The cotyledons conduct photosynthesis until the seedling develops its first true, or foliage, leaves. Once this occurs, the plant will continue to make its own food and go through the life cycle again.

Flowering plants are classified into two groupings: monocotyledons and dicotyledons. Monocots (the shortened form of the term) have one cotyledon [kah-tuh-LEE-dun], or seed leaf. It is usually enclosed in a sheath that surrounds and protects the shoot. Grass is an example of a monocot. If you plant a grass seed and water it, in a few days a single seed leaf will break out of the seed and push its way through the soil. Dicots have two cotyledons, both of which photosynthesize for the seedling until the foliage leaves can take over to supply nutrients for the plant. A bean seed is an example of a dicot. If you plant a bean seed and water it, it will send up two seed leaves.

There are other differences between monocots and dicots, too. The total number of flower parts on a monocot is often a multiple of three. So a monocot flower might have three petals, or six, or nine. By contrast, the total number of flower parts on a dicot is often a multiple of four, like eight or 12, or a multiple

one cotyledon

long narrow leaves with parallel veins

flower parts usually in multiples of three

two cotyledons

broader leaves with net-like veins

flower parts usually in multiples of four or five

of five, like 10 or 15. Monocots usually have long narrow leaves, with veins running parallel to one another. Dicots tend to have broader leaves with veins that look like nets.

Grains like wheat, corn, and rice are all monocots, as are some flowers, like lilies and tulips. Most fruits and vegetables are dicots, as are many garden flowers.

Review

Below are some ideas for ongoing assessment and review activities. These are not meant to constitute a comprehensive list.

• Have the class organize and plant a school garden. Based on their study of a variety of plants, have them suggest different plants and flowers for the garden and then have a planting day. This activity might be organized around Earth Day festivities. Have the class prepare to give tours of the garden to school visitors and be able to present a short talk about the plants and flowers in the garden.

• Arrange for a local gardener or plant store owner to come and talk to the class about the variety of plants discussed in this section. After the study of each kind of plant and how it reproduces, you may want to invite this expert back to the class to bring examples and talk about those particular plants and flowers.

• Bring in a bunch of different flowers to class. Using hand lenses, have students work in pairs to dissect a flower and look for the parts that they have studied. Have students draw and label what they observe.

• Have students tour the school grounds or a nearby park with field guidebooks to identify trees, flowers, and other plants. When you return to the class, have students make a field guide for the school property, using large index cards that include

The Big Idea in Review

Plants have structures to take in water and make their own food, and they have several different ways to reproduce.

pictures of the trees, flowers, and other plants they found and a short description of each one, including information on how each species of plant reproduces. Laminate these cards and then make them available in the front office for visitors.

• Using the study of world history from Grade 5, have students study other parts of the world, such as Central and South America, Europe, and Japan, to find plants and flowers that grow there. Have students summarize information they learn in paragraph form, as well as find or draw pictures of these flowers and plants. Post these pictures on a large wall map of the world. Be sure that students are able to identify the plants according to the classifications studied in this section and are able to describe the characteristics of these plants from around the world.

• Plant a garden in your room with a variety of plants from this section, and organize weekly observations of the growth of plants and the blooming of flowers. What do students observe about the plants throughout the year? Students should organize the information that they are observing into graphs and charts to display next to the garden. At the end of the year, have students write a paper describing what the class has observed using the information from the class graphs to support their observations.

• You may wish to grow some plant seedlings with light and others without light. (Use grass, radish, or bean seeds for rapid growth.) Plant several seeds in each of two small pots. Place one pot near a sunny window and the other pot in a dark area, such as a closet. Water both pots as needed for at least two weeks. Then display the pots next to each other for comparison. The seedlings grown in the light will be noticeably greener than those grown in the dark, which will be straggly, spindly, and pale in color. This experiment will help to demonstrate to students that photosynthesis can occur only in the presence of sunlight.

• You may also ask the following questions after completing this section:

1. What is the purpose of photosynthesis?

   Photosynthesis is a plant life process that allows plants to make their own food by trapping sunlight and using carbon dioxide and water to form carbohydrates.

2. Why are nonvascular plants usually small and short?

   Nonvascular plants don't have specialized parts such as stems that could help them grow taller.

3. What are the two groups of tubelike structures that act as the transport system in vascular plants?

   Xylem and phloem are the two tubelike structures.

4. What is in a seed?

   A plant embryo, endosperm to nourish the embryo, and a seed coat to protect the embryo and endosperm are in a seed.

5. Name the male and female reproductive parts of a flower.

   The male stamen and the female carpel (or pistil) are a flower's reproductive parts.

6. What are some ways in which plants can be pollinated?

   The wind can carry pollen from an anther to a carpel, or insects and other animals can carry it.

7. What is the difference between sepals and petals?

Sepals are the outermost leaves around a flower; they are often green and thick; petals are closer to the center of the flower and are often showy and colorful to attract pollinators.

8. What is the difference between sexual and asexual reproduction?

Sexual reproduction involves the union of a male and female gamete, e.g., a sperm and an egg. Asexual reproduction does not. Sexual reproduction can lead to genetic variation; asexual reproduction produces cloned organisms.

More Resources

The titles listed below are offered as a representative sample of materials and not a complete list of everything that is available.

For students —

• *How a Plant Grows*, by Bobbie Kalman (Crabtree Publications, 1996). Straightforward terminology with clear illustrations and photographs. Introduces many terms, such as *biennial, photosynthesis, pistil, spores,* and *carnivorous.* Paperback, 32 pages, ISBN 0865057281.

• *Janice VanCleave's Plants: Mind-Boggling Experiments You Can Turn into Science Fair Projects*, by Janice VanCleave (John Wiley & Sons, 1997). How does water move through moss? What are the first signs of corn seed germination? Does gravity affect plant growth of pinto beans? Paperback, 90 pages, ISBN 0471146870.

• *The Science of Plants (Living Science)*, by Jonathan Bocknek (Gareth Stevens Publishing, 1999). Library binding, 32 pages, ISBN 0836824679.

• *Seeds: Pop, Stick, Glide*, by Patricia Lauber and photography by Jerome Wexler (Knopf Books for Young Readers, 1988). Thoughtful black-and-white photography helps explain the different ways seeds are transported. Hardcover, ISBN 0517541653.

• *Seeds, Stems, and Stamens*, by Susan Goodman (Millbrook Press, 2001). Information on plant adaptation, nutrition, protection, and reproduction through general concepts and specific examples. Hardcover, 48 pages, ISBN 0761318747.

• *Wildflowers, Blooms and Blossoms (Take-Along Guide)*, by Diane L. Burns (NorthWord Press, 1998). A simple, well-illustrated guide for young people. Includes instructions on preserving wildflowers, making a wildflower paperweight, etc. Paperback, 48 pages, ISBN 1559716428. See also in this series *Berries, Nuts and Seeds.*

For teachers —

• *Arthur Harry Church: The Anatomy of Flowers*, by David Mabberley (Merrell, 2000). These drawings by Church (1869–1937) are reminiscent of the detail and beauty of Audubon's artwork. Hardcover, 128 pages, ISBN 1858941164.

• *National Audubon Society Field Guides to North American Trees and Wildflowers* (four separate volumes) (Knopf, 1980, 2001). Simple, first-impression visual cues to identifying hundreds of trees and wildflowers. Four books in all, but purchased individually depending upon your location. Great for beginners, and the turtleback binding makes it outdoor friendly. Since no book can cover all local species native to your area, you may also look for other books specific to local ecosystems. *Trees, Eastern Region:* ISBN 0394507606; *Trees, Western Region:* ISBN 0394507614; *Wildflowers, Eastern Region:* ISBN 0375402322; *Wildflowers, Western Region:* ISBN 0375402330.

• *The Natural History of a Garden*, by Colin Spedding and Geoffrey Spedding (Timber Press, 2003). A wonderful look at plants (and animals) within the garden environment. The last chapter focuses on gardens for children. Hardcover, 246 pages, ISBN 0881925780.

• Science Kit & Boreal Laboratories, www.sciencekit.com or 1-800-828-7777.

• *Trees: Trees Identified by Leaf, Bark, and Seed (Fandex Family Field Guides)*, by Steven M. L. Aronson (Workman Publishing, 1998). Each card on this "fandex" includes a die-cut leaf at the top, the bark pattern, a flower/seed/nut unique to the tree, and a photograph of the full tree. There are 50 trees in the complete set, but if some in your area are not part of the group, consider making your own fandex with the class. Cards, ISBN 0761112049. See also *Wildflowers.*

IV. Life Cycles and Reproduction

The Big Idea

All organisms go through a series of developmental stages called the life cycle. When maturity is reached, the organism is capable of reproduction.

Remember that each subject you study with students expands their vocabulary and introduces new terms, thus making them better listeners and readers. As you study life cycles and reproduction, use read alouds, independent reading, and discussions to build students' vocabularies.

What Students Should Already Know
Students in Core Knowledge schools should be familiar with

Grade 2

▸ cycles in nature: life cycles
  • birth, growth, reproduction, death
  • reproduction in animals: egg to egg with a chicken, frog to frog, butterfly to butterfly (metamorphosis)

What Students Need to Learn
▸ **The life cycle and reproduction**
  • **life cycle: development of an organism from birth to growth, reproduction, death**
    • **example: growth stages of a human (embryo, fetus, newborn, infancy, childhood, adolescence, adulthood, old age)**
  • **All living things reproduce themselves; reproduction may be asexual or sexual.**
    • **examples of asexual reproduction: fission (splitting) of bacteria, spores from mildews, molds, and mushrooms, budding of yeast cells, regeneration and cloning**
    • **Sexual reproduction requires the joining of special male and female cells, called gametes, to form a fertilized egg.**
▸ **Sexual reproduction in animals**
  • **reproductive organs: testes (sperm) and ovaries (eggs)**
  • **external fertilization: spawning**
  • **internal fertilization: birds, mammals**
  • **development of the embryo: egg, zygote, embryo, growth in uterus, fetus, newborn**

What Students Will Learn in Future Grades
In future grades, students will review and extend their learning about life cycles and reproduction. In Grade 7, they will study cell division and genetics.

Vocabulary

Student/Teacher Vocabulary

adolescence: the period from childhood to adulthood, usually between the ages of 12 and 20 (S)

adulthood: the time of being a fully grown person (S)

asexual: having no sex organs, or involving reproduction without the joining of male and female gametes (S)

birth: the act of bringing forth offspring (S)

budding: a small protuberance from a cell or organism that develops into a new individual (S)

childhood: the time of being a child; usually between the ages of 16 months and 12 years old (S)

clone: a living thing that grows from a small amount of material taken from a parent. A clone and its parent are always identical. (S)

death: the end of life (S)

differentiated: having developed differences; having become specialized (T)

egg: a female sex cell (S)

embryo: a stage of development of a fertilized egg (S)

fetus: the stage of development in which an embryo has grown for at least two months and most organs are differentiated (S)

fission: cell division; reproduction by a cell dividing into two or more equal parts, each of which develops into a new individual cell or organism (S)

gametes: mature sex cells, either male (sperm) or female (egg) (S)

growth: development; the process of growing (S)

hermaphroditic: having both male and female characteristics biologically (T)

infancy: the time of early childhood (S)

life cycle: the development of an organism from fertilization to birth, growth, reproduction, and death (S)

newborn: the stage of an offspring from its birth to four weeks of age (S)

offspring: the young, or descendants, of parent organisms (S)

ovary: the female reproductive organ; produces eggs (S)

regeneration: a form of asexual reproduction where missing parts of an organism are regrown; in some species, entire new individuals can develop by regeneration (S)

reproduction: the process by which living things produce offspring (S)

spawning: a method of reproduction in which a very large number of eggs are laid so that some are likely to survive egg-eating predators (S)

spore: a type of reproductive cell that is tough and resistant and capable of developing into a new individual cell or organism (S)

testis: the male reproductive organ that produces sperm (S)

uterus: the womb; part of the female reproductive tract that contains and nourishes a developing embryo (T)

zygote: a fertilized egg (S)

Materials

Instructional Master 72
Stages of Development, p. 603

overhead transparency and projector, p. 603

living plant parts (such as potato with eyes, sweet potato, houseplants, African violet, or others), p. 604

plant pots, p. 604

potting soil, or other growing medium, p. 604

water, p. 604

toothpicks, p. 604

plastic bag(s), clear (with rubber band to secure over stem or leaf cutting), p. 604

photographs of humans and/or other animals in different developmental stages, p. 605

a class set of books about life cycles and reproduction, p. 605

chart paper, p. 605

pictures of various animals, p. 605

sandwich bags containing pictures of the events in a life cycle or the development of an embryo for groups of students to sequence, p. 606

Vocabulary continued

Domain Vocabulary

Life cycles and reproduction and associated words:
reproduce, method, way, alternative, fuse, unite, specialize, simple, complex, stage, phase, cycle, cyclical, develop, immature, mature, characteristic, trait, feature, generate, fertilize, pregnancy, gestation, growth, baby, infant, toddler, puberty, adolescent, teenager, adult, aging, elderly, frail, degenerate, deteriorate, classify, organize, nourish, nourishment, nutrient, food, biology, zoology, botany, DNA, descendant, ancestor, forefather, conditions, surroundings, environment, habitat, survival, fluctuation, variation, resistant, favorable, unfavorable, equal, alike, similar, different, species, specific, change, formation, form, moisture, humid, humidity, weather, climate, adaptation, bacteria, mold, mildew, mushroom, fungus *(and specific names)*, plant *(and specific names)*, animal *(and specific names)*

At a Glance

The most important ideas for you are:

- The life cycle is the development of an organism from fertilization to birth, growth, reproduction, and death.
- All organisms reproduce themselves. Reproduction may be asexual or sexual.
- Sexual reproduction in animals requires the development of reproductive organs: the male testes, which produce sperm, and female ovaries, which produce eggs.
- Female eggs are fertilized either externally, as with most fish and amphibians, or internally, as with reptiles, birds, and mammals.
- A fertilized egg develops into an embryo, which grows and develops through the other life cycle stages.

What Teachers Need to Know
A. The Life Cycle and Reproduction

All organisms pass through a sequence of developmental stages called a life cycle. The four main stages of the cycle are birth, growth, reproduction, and death. An individual organism is born as a newly formed immature member of its species with the potential of becoming a mature adult. Physical maturity is marked by full development and the ability to reproduce. For some species, the adult stage is very brief—it may be only a matter of hours; for others, it may last many years. The adult reproductive stage allows individuals of a species to reproduce themselves in their offspring; in the offspring the cycle begins again. The end of the adult stage for all organisms is death. Death is the final stage of an individual life cycle.

You are probably most familiar with the human life cycle. The growth and developmental stages of a human begin when a male sex cell (sperm) unites with a female sex cell (egg, or ovum) to become a fertilized egg, called a zygote. The zygote grows, begins cell division, and develops into an embryo. The embryo grows inside the mother, nourished in the mother's uterus. After two months, the embryo is generally referred to as a fetus, with most organs differentiated. The fetus continues to grow and develop until birth, an average of 266 days after fertilization. At this point begins the newborn stage, lasting from birth to four weeks, followed by the infant stage, which continues to 15 months after birth. After infancy, the individual is referred to as a child. In general, at around 11–16 years of age the child enters puberty, the stage in which sexual reproductive organs (genitals) mature and secondary sexual traits develop. In females, menstruation also begins. For at least 3–5 years after the onset of puberty, the individual continues to develop physically, mentally, and emotionally (through the stage known as adolescence) to maturity. The mature adult stage is reached at around 18–25 years of age, when growth and bone formation are mostly complete. Changes during the adult stage happen very slowly, until aging (a collective term) occurs, a process by which the body gradually deteriorates as cells lose the capacity to repair themselves. Aging results in the gradual loss of body functions, which eventually leads to the death of the individual.

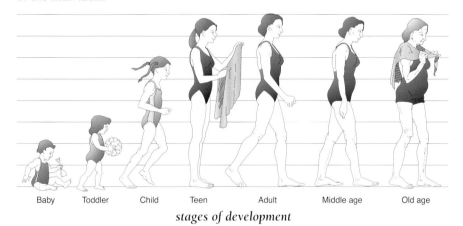

| Baby | Toddler | Child | Teen | Adult | Middle age | Old age |

stages of development

Methods of Reproduction

All organisms have the capacity to reproduce themselves. There are two methods of reproduction: sexual reproduction involves the exchange of reproductive material with another individual, and asexual reproduction does not require the involvement of any other organism. If you have taught Section III, "Plant Structures and Processes," pp. 584–599, your students will already be familiar with these concepts.

Asexual Reproduction

In asexual reproduction, an individual of a species produces a copy of itself by dividing its cells. The result of this division can be two individuals from the original (fission), a complete reproductive cell (spore), or an outgrowth of the original (budding). Single-celled organisms, such as bacteria and protozoa, reproduce primarily by fission. The cell divides into two equal cells, smaller than the original parent cell, and two complete individuals are formed.

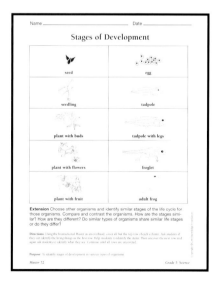

Use Instructional Master 72.

IV. Life Cycles and Reproduction

Teaching Idea

Invite students to try 1 or more of the following methods of regeneration—growing new plants, asexually, from parts:

Cut a piece of potato with at least 1 "eye," or bud. Let the cut piece dry for 24 hours, then plant in soil and keep watered.

Suspend a sweet potato (an enlarged root) with toothpicks over a glass of water, just touching the water. Add water as needed.

Make stem cuttings from house-plants such as geraniums, gardenias, or others. Cut off a growing shoot and plant the stem in soil. At each stem node in contact with the soil, new roots will develop, starting a new plant. New leaves will develop from nodes above the soil level.

Cut off a leaf from an African violet and place the leaf node, where the leaf meets the stem, in contact with soil. Add water and cover with a plastic bag to make a mini-greenhouse.

These and other methods are how plant growers can produce new plants quickly and can continue to grow plants genetically identical to the original plant with which they started.

Teaching Idea

You may want to teach about Ernest Just in conjunction with this section. (See Section VII, "Science Biographies," on pp. 634–646.)

Another method of asexual reproduction is by spore production. A spore is usually a single cell produced by cell division within one single organism. The new cell, or spore, is then released into the wind. When moisture and temperature conditions are favorable, the spore germinates, or begins to sprout and grow into a new organism. Most fungi, including mushrooms, mildew, and most molds, produce spores, as do some plants, especially mosses and ferns.

Some single-celled organisms, such as yeasts, reproduce by budding. In budding, a small outgrowth from the cell called a bud grows and develops into another new organism.

Regeneration is yet another form of asexual reproduction. Regeneration is the regrowth of missing parts of the organism; in some species, entire new individuals can develop by regeneration. For instance, plants can regenerate from fragments of roots, stems, or leaves. Many simple animals (those with simple body structures) can regenerate entire new individuals from fragments, as in such invertebrates as sponges, starfish (also known as sea stars), and worms. If you slice certain kinds of worms in half, each half will develop into an individual organism. Some higher order animals (animals with more complex body structures) can break off parts, such as limbs or a tail, and then regenerate the missing part. In these instances, the broken-off part does not have the capacity to regenerate another individual. For example, lobsters and crabs can break off and regrow a claw, or a lizard may regrow a tail or a leg, but a broken-off claw or tail could not regrow another new individual. Although in organisms with very complex body structures, such as humans, some cells and tissues (e.g., blood cells or skin tissues) may be regenerated, structural systems such as organs cannot be differentiated, or be fitted for a new function. The more complex the organism, generally the less ability it has to regenerate.

Organisms that reproduce asexually are highly adapted to a particular set of environmental conditions. If the conditions are limited and remain fairly consistent, an organism's survival rate is high. However, if there is a change to environmental conditions, especially a drastic change such as flood, drought, or large temperature variation, a population of genetically identical organisms could all die off.

Sexual Reproduction

Sexual reproduction requires the development of special male and female reproductive structures, or sex cells, called gametes. When male and female gametes unite, they produce a fertilized egg with variations of traits, also called characteristics. Sexual reproduction generally produces wider variation, and under changing or variable environmental conditions, generally allows some individuals to survive and reproduce. While asexual reproduction produces clones of the original (identical or with very little variation), sexual reproduction combines DNA from two parents, producing wider variations, which may provide a higher probability that some species members will survive changing environmental conditions.

Some organisms, such as snails and earthworms, are hermaphroditic. These organisms develop both male and female reproductive organs, either at the same time, or as male or female at different stages of development. Most hermaphroditic organisms still cross-fertilize, or fertilize other members of their species, to achieve variation in offspring.

B. Sexual Reproduction in Animals

For animals to reproduce, male and female gametes must unite. In most animals, separate individuals produce either male or female gametes. The primary reproductive organ of males is the testis (plural: testes), which produces sperm cells, the male gametes. The ovary is the female reproductive organ, which produces egg cells, the female gametes. A sperm must unite and fuse with an egg for fertilization to occur and a new individual to develop.

In some animals, such as most fish and amphibians, the egg and sperm cells are fertilized externally, or outside the body. Females produce and lay eggs in the water, usually in large numbers or masses. The process is known as spawning. In spawning, a very large number of eggs are laid so that some are likely to survive egg-eating predators. The male then swims over the eggs and deposits its sperm. The sperm will swim toward the eggs; some sperm will penetrate the eggs, thus fertilizing the eggs.

In other animals, including reptiles, birds, and mammals, gametes are fertilized internally, or inside the body, through sex organs. When a sperm cell fuses with an egg cell, the fertilized egg cell—the zygote—attaches to the uterine wall of the mother, where the cell begins to divide to become a multicellular embryo. Cells continue to divide and groups of cells begin to specialize, differentiating into organs and tissues, and becoming a fetus. The fetus continues to grow and develop, drawing nourishment from the uterus, and develops to the stage where it can survive on its own (i.e., organs are developed and functional so the individual can breathe and maintain a normal body temperature). At this point the mother's uterus begins to contract and birth occurs, expelling the fetus. The newborn then has the capacity to become a mature adult capable of reproduction.

Review

Below are some ideas for ongoing assessment and review activities. These are not meant to constitute a comprehensive list.

• Meet with the media specialist or librarian to collect a class set of books on life cycles and reproduction. You should make sure that you have a variety of books pertaining to humans and animals. Have students create a drawing of life cycle stages based on their reading of one of the books, and then share these with the class.

• Create a chart with the class about sexual reproduction in animals with the headings *external fertilization* and *internal fertilization*. Using books from the class library, brainstorm a list of animals that would fit in either group. You may want to provide pictures of different animals and have students place the pictures under the appropriate heading. Then have students write a paragraph describing the steps in either external fertilization or internal fertilization, using one of the animals as an example.

Teaching Idea

Invite students to find sequences of development in animal pictures from nature magazines, illustrations, online sources, or other resources. Students may also wish to ask an older adult to gather photos of him- or herself through the years, showing that person's developmental stages of the human life cycle, from baby (or earliest picture available) to present. You may also wish to have students write a story and/or collect photos detailing the growth and development of themselves, a sibling, a pet, or some other animal.

Note: Be sure to use consideration if you suggest using family relationships or pets. If students do not live in a traditional home situation, pictures or stories about family may be a sensitive issue.

Teaching Idea

To make the abstract processes described in this section concrete, create a number of "animal profiles." Describe how each animal reproduces. This will help students form a composite idea of sexual reproduction and its varieties. This will also set the stage for a discussion of human reproduction in the next section.

The Big Idea in Review

All organisms go through a series of developmental stages called the life cycle. When maturity is reached, the organism is capable of reproduction.

• Provide groups of students with sandwich bags containing pictures depicting events in the life cycle or the development of an embryo. Have them sequence the pictures and then label each picture correctly. Once the group has sequenced the pictures, have students draw their own depiction of the sequence and write sentences under each picture describing it.

• You may also ask the following questions after completing this section:

1. What are the four main stages of the life cycle?

   Birth, growth, reproduction, and death are the four main life cycle stages.

2. How do all living organisms start?

   All living organisms start as single cells (zygotes).

3. How can some organisms reproduce asexually?

   Asexual reproduction methods include cell division (fission), spore production, budding, and regeneration.

4. What is fertilization?

   Fertilization is the joining of male (sperm) and female (egg) sex cells (gametes) to produce a cell capable of developing into a new individual.

5. What is the difference between external and internal fertilization?

   External fertilization is when male and female gametes unite outside of the body. Internal fertilization is when gametes unite within the body of the mother.

6. What is an advantage of sexual reproduction?

   An advantage of sexual reproduction is producing offspring that have variations from the parents and are not identical to either parent. When a species has a wider genetic range of variation, it is more likely that some members of that species will survive a dramatic change of climate or environment.

More Resources

The titles listed below are offered as a representative sample of materials and not a complete list of everything that is available.

For students —

• *An Extraordinary Life: The Story of a Monarch Butterfly,* by Laurence Pringle, with paintings by Bob Marstall (Orchard Books, 1997). Honored by the Orbis Pictus Awards program for excellence in children's nonfiction. Hardcover, ISBN 0531300021.

• *Nine Month Miracle,* described as "a multimedia journey into the miracle of pregnancy and childbirth," (from the publisher) is available through the award-winning software company A.D.A.M. at www.adam.com. See also *A.D.A.M.: The Inside Story,* which also includes an instructor's CD.

For teachers —

• A.D.A.M. Interactive Anatomy 4. Order through A.D.A.M. Software, at www.adam.com.

• Science Kit & Boreal Laboratories, www.science kit.com or 1-800-828-7777, offers 11 prepared slides depicting the typical stages of development of a baby chick.

V. The Human Body

The Big Idea

Changes that prepare humans for adulthood and reproduction occur in the body during puberty. These changes are controlled by the endocrine system.

Remember that each subject you study with students expands their vocabulary and introduces new terms, thus making them better listeners and readers. As you study the human body, use read alouds, independent reading, and discussions to build students' vocabularies.

What Students Should Already Know

Students in Core Knowledge schools should be familiar with

Kindergarten

▸ the five senses and associated body parts: sight (eyes), hearing (ears), smell (nose), taste (tongue), touch (skin)

▸ taking care of the body: exercise, cleanliness, healthy foods, rest

Grade 1

▸ body systems: skeletal, muscular, digestive, circulatory, nervous

▸ germs, disease, and preventing illness: taking care of your body; vaccinations

Grade 2

▸ cells: all living things are made up of cells, too small to be seen without a microscope

▸ Cells make up tissues; tissues make up organs; organs work in systems.

▸ the digestive and excretory systems

• salivary glands, taste buds

• teeth: incisors, bicuspids, molars

• esophagus, stomach, liver, small intestine, large intestine

• kidneys, urine, bladder, urethra, anus, appendix

▸ taking care of your body: the food pyramid, vitamins and minerals

Grade 3

▸ the muscular system

• involuntary and voluntary muscles

▸ the skeletal system

• skeleton, bones, marrow

• musculo-skeletal connections, including ligaments, tendons (Achilles tendon), cartilage

• skull (or cranium), spinal column (vertebrae), rib cage, sternum, scapula (shoulder blades), pelvis, tibia, fibula

• joints, broken bones, and x-rays

▸ the nervous system

• brain: medulla, cerebellum, cerebrum, cerebral cortex

• spinal cord, nerves, and reflexes

V. The Human Body

Materials

**Instructional Masters
73–75**

Endocrine System Match-up,
p. 612

Female Reproductive System,
p. 616

Male Reproductive System,
p. 617

**index cards for vocabulary
matching game, p. 619**

**a box in the classroom for
anonymous questions,
p. 619**

**information from school
nurse, p. 619**

**information on local
hospital nursery, p. 619**

What Students Should Already Know continued

▸ vision: how the eye works
  - parts of the eye: cornea, iris and pupil, lens, retina
  - optic nerve
  - farsighted and nearsighted
▸ hearing: how the ear works
  - sound as vibration
  - outer ear, ear canal
  - eardrum
  - Three tiny bones (hammer, anvil, and stirrup) pass vibrations to the cochlea.
  - auditory nerve

Grade 4
▸ the circulatory system
  - pioneering work of William Harvey
  - heart: four chambers (auricles and ventricles), aorta
  - blood: red blood cells (corpuscles), white blood cells (corpuscles), platelets, hemoglobin, plasma, antibodies
  - blood vessels: arteries, veins, capillaries
  - blood pressure, pulse
  - coagulation (clotting)
  - filtering function of liver and spleen
  - Fatty deposits can clog blood vessels and cause a heart attack.
  - blood types (four basic types: A, B, AB, O) and transfusions
▸ the respiratory system
  - process of taking in oxygen and getting rid of carbon dioxide
  - nose, throat, voice box, trachea (windpipe)
  - lungs, bronchi, bronchial tubes, diaphragm, ribs, alveoli (air sacs)
  - smoking: damage to lung tissue, lung cancer

What Students Need to Learn

▸ **Changes in human adolescence**
  - **puberty: glands and hormones (see below, The endocrine system), growth spurt, hair growth, breasts, voice change**
▸ **The endocrine system**
  - **The human body has two types of glands: duct glands (such as the salivary glands), and ductless glands, also known as endocrine glands.**
  - **Endocrine glands secrete (give off) chemicals called hormones; different hormones control different body processes.**

What Students Need to Learn continued

- • **pituitary gland:** located at the bottom of the brain, secretes hormones that control other glands and hormones that regulate growth
- • **thyroid gland:** located below the voice box; secretes a hormone that controls the rate at which the body burns and uses food
- • **pancreas:** both a duct and ductless gland; secretes a hormone called insulin that regulates how the body uses and stores sugar; when the pancreas does not produce enough insulin, a person has a sickness called diabetes (which can be controlled)
- • **adrenal glands:** secrete a hormone called adrenaline, especially when a person is frightened or angry, causing rapid heartbeat and breathing
- ‣ The reproductive system
  - • **females:** ovaries, fallopian tubes, uterus, vagina, menstruation
  - • **males:** testes, scrotum, penis, urethra, semen
  - • **sexual reproduction:** intercourse, fertilization, zygote, implantation of zygote in the uterus, pregnancy, embryo, fetus, newborn

Vocabulary

Student/Teacher Vocabulary

adrenal gland: one of a pair of endocrine glands near each kidney; secretes adrenaline (S)

duct gland: a gland that secretes through a duct (S)

ductless gland: a gland that secretes directly onto a surface rather than through a duct (S)

egg: a female sex cell (T)

embryo: a stage of development of a fertilized egg (T)

endocrine glands: a group of organs that release chemicals called hormones (S)

fallopian tube: a tube that connects the ovaries to the uterus and acts as a passageway through which an egg released from an ovary travels to the uterus (S)

fertilization: the process in which a sperm cell and egg join (T)

fetus: the stage of development in which an embryo has grown for at least two months and most organs are differentiated (T)

gland: an organ in the body that makes a substance the body needs; for example, some glands produce sweat or tears (S)

hormones: chemical messengers produced and secreted by glands (S)

implantation: the process in which a fertilized egg enters the uterus and becomes implanted into the uterine lining (T)

insulin: a hormone produced by the pancreas that regulates the way the body uses sugar (S)

intercourse: the act of sexual procreation in which a male inserts his penis into a female's vagina (T)

Vocabulary continued

menstruation: the process in females in which an unfertilized egg and the uterine lining are released from the body through the vagina (S)

newborn: the stage of an offspring from its birth to four weeks of age (S)

ovary: the female reproductive organ that produces egg cells (S)

pancreas: an organ involved in the endocrine system (S)

penis: the male organ for sexual intercourse (S)

pituitary gland: an endocrine gland in the brain that produces hormones that regulate hormone production in other endocrine glands (S)

pregnancy: the implantation and development of a fertilized egg once it enters the uterus and becomes embedded in the uterine lining (S)

puberty: a time in adolescence that prepares humans for adulthood and results in the ability to reproduce, or have children (S)

scrotum: the external pouch that contains the testes in males (S)

secrete: to produce liquid so that it flows (S)

semen: the fluid that contains and transports sperm (T)

sperm: a male sex cell (T)

testis (pl., testes): a male reproductive gland (S)

thyroid gland: the gland responsible for the rate at which cells burn fuel to produce energy; located in the lower neck below the voice box (S)

urethra: the canal that carries off urine from the bladder; in the male, serves as a passageway for semen (S)

uterus: an expandable organ, resembling an inverted pear, where a developing fetus is supported during pregnancy (S)

vagina: a three- to six-inch-long, narrow, muscular structure that serves as the birth canal—the opening through which a baby is born—and as the female organ for sexual intercourse (S)

zygote: the cell that is formed once a sperm cell enters the egg and the nuclei of the sperm and egg fuse (T)

Domain Vocabulary

The human body and associated words:

immature, mature, adult, adulthood, adolescence, teen, teenager, sex, sexual, sex characteristics, male, female, masculine, feminine, pubic hair, follicle, menses, period, cramps, erection, ejaculate, awkward, gawky, develop, fill out, acne, zits, chemical, release, absorb, store, relay, transmit, travel, circulate, bloodstream, signal, immediate, brief, ongoing, continual, receptor, regulate, production, balance, sensitize, desensitize, metabolism, rate, process, energy, increase, decrease, concentration, dilution, dilute, response, respond, trigger, maintenance, life cycle, reproduce, contraceptive, preventative, cells, fuse, trimester, premature, full-term, birth, birth canal, labor pain, contraction, contract, expand, expel, passageway, tube, membrane, placenta, afterbirth, umbilical cord

At a Glance

The most important ideas for you are:

- Puberty begins during adolescence as a result of the production of certain hormones in the body: estrogen and progesterone in females, and testosterone in males.

- Puberty usually begins between the ages of 11 and 16 and is distinguished by changes that result from the development of secondary sex characteristics.

- Hormones are chemical messengers produced and secreted by glands. Hormones and the glands that produce them are part of a body system known as the endocrine system.

- The endocrine system is involved in many body processes and helps to regulate such things as growth and development, metabolism, sexual function, and reproduction.

- The reproductive system includes the organs that enable humans to reproduce sexually via internal fertilization. The reproductive organs of males and females are different from one another.

- The male reproductive organs include the penis, urethra, testes, and scrotum. These organs enable males to produce sperm (male sex cells) and have sexual intercourse.

- The female reproductive organs include the vagina, uterus, fallopian tubes, and ovaries. These organs enable a woman to develop and release eggs (female sex cells), support a developing fetus, give birth, and have sexual intercourse.

What Teachers Need to Know

Background

Note that there is some flexibility in the grade-level placement of the study of topics related to human reproduction, as different schools and districts have differing local requirements, typically introducing these topics in either fifth or sixth grade.

Some teachers prefer to separate classes into girls and boys, and have same-sex teachers discussing these topics with students. Often, parental permission is needed before discussing human sexuality with students. Check with your school administrator for school policies, and inform parents before teaching this topic. Also, check with your school nurse and/or guidance counselor, as they may have a program or materials to support you.

A. Changes in Human Adolescence

Puberty is a time when humans pass from childhood into adulthood. Puberty occurs during adolescence, a stage in the life cycle that prepares humans for adulthood and results in sexual maturation—the ability to reproduce, or have children. Puberty begins when certain hormones, primarily estrogen and

Teaching Idea

You may wish to discuss hormones and the functioning of the endocrine system (part B of this section) with students before teaching them about puberty. As puberty is related to the production of hormones, a working knowledge of these chemical messengers may aid students in their understanding of puberty. You may also wish to discuss and review the stages of the life cycle with your class in introducing puberty.

V. The Human Body

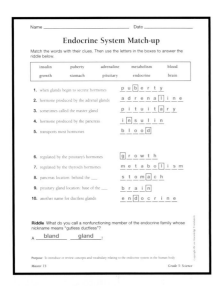

Use Instructional Master 73.

progesterone in females and testosterone in males, begin to be produced by the body and cause secondary sex characteristics to develop. (Hormones will be discussed further in this section.)

Between the ages of 13 and 16, at the onset of puberty, boys experience an enlargement of the testicles, or testes, and a growth of pubic hair as a result of testosterone production. This is followed by a growth spurt. Boys' arms, legs, hands, and feet often grow faster than the rest of their body. Their shoulders broaden and they begin to gain weight and muscle. Hair begins to grow and thicken on their chest, legs, arms, and face. The penis becomes larger. Their voices become deeper.

Girls experience an enlargement of the breasts and a growth of pubic hair as a result of estrogen production at the onset of puberty. For most girls, this usually occurs between the ages of 11 and 14. A year or two later, girls experience a growth spurt, and their arms, legs, hands, and feet get larger. They also experience a growth of hair under their arms and on their legs. They build up fat and their hips widen as they develop the contours of a woman's body. The onset of menstruation is the final stage of puberty in girls.

B. The Endocrine System

As mentioned, puberty begins as a result of the production of certain hormones. To fully understand puberty, it is important to have an understanding of hormones and the endocrine system. Hormones are chemical messengers produced in the body by structures called glands. Together, hormones and the glands that produce and secrete them make up the endocrine system. This important system is involved in almost every body function from metabolism and cell growth to sexual reproduction and human development.

The human body has two types of glands: duct glands and ductless glands. Duct glands, including salivary and sweat glands, have channels through which secretions are carried to specific locations in the body. Ductless glands, or endocrine glands, secrete their products into the bloodstream.

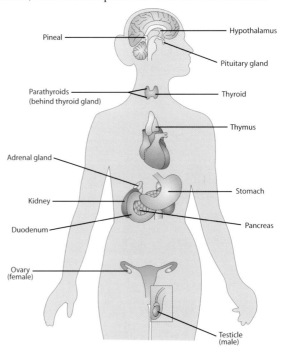

the endocrine system

The main glands of the endocrine system are the pituitary, thyroid, parathyroid, hypothalamus, adrenal, pineal, and reproductive glands. The pancreas, although involved in digestion, is also part of the endocrine system. These glands, which are spread throughout the body, collectively produce more than 20 different hormones. While each hormone has a unique chemical structure and function in the body, all hormones serve as a messaging system between different parts of the body. Most hormones are secreted into the bloodstream and are transported through the blood to target cells, those for which their message is intended. Target cells have hormone-specific receptors that enable the hormone to bond with the cell. (Receptors are specialized, or designed, for specific hormones; this means that hormones can "communicate" with only specific cells in the body.) When a hormone reaches a target cell and "locks" into the receptor on that cell, it sends a chemical signal that causes the cell to act in some particular way.

Students may recall another messaging system that they have already learned about—the nervous system. Explain to students that while the nervous and endocrine systems are similar in that they both relay messages in the body, they are somewhat different with regard to how they relay messages. The nervous system communicates messages through electrical signals that travel along the nerves to the spinal cord and brain, while the endocrine system communicates through chemical signals that travel through the blood. (There is an important parallel, however, that nerve cells have with the endocrine system. Neurotransmitters must cross the space between nerve cells and reach a receptor before the next nerve cell can "fire," or begin its electrochemical enervation.) In addition, point out that the functions of the nervous system are more immediate and finite (you are scared for a brief point of time and then it's over), while the functions of the endocrine system are slower and involve ongoing processes.

The Endocrine Glands

Located at the base of the brain and no bigger than the size of a pea, the pituitary gland is sometimes considered the master gland of the endocrine system. The pituitary produces hormones that regulate hormone production in other endocrine glands and produces hormones for several of the other endocrine glands. The pituitary is divided into an anterior and posterior lobe. The anterior lobe regulates the activity of the thyroid, adrenal, and reproductive glands through the production and secretion of hormones that trigger these glands to produce and secrete hormones of their own. It also produces, among many others, such hormones as growth hormone, responsible for the growth of bone and body tissue, and prolactin, responsible for the production of milk in nursing women. The posterior lobe releases oxytocin, responsible for initiating contractions during labor, and antidiuretic hormone, responsible for regulating a balance of water in the body through its effect on the kidneys. In addition to these and other hormones, the pituitary gland also secretes endorphins, hormones that desensitize us to pain.

The hypothalamus, a structure in the brain that is connected to the pituitary gland, is part of both the nervous and endocrine systems. As part of the nervous system, the hypothalamus controls the body's temperature, blood pressure, and emotions. As part of the endocrine system, the hypothalamus produces hormones that control the pituitary gland.

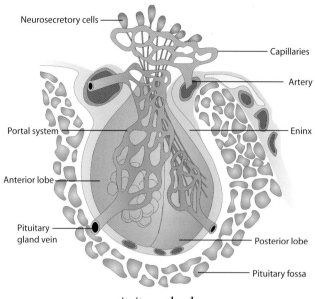

pituitary gland

The thyroid gland, located in the lower neck below the voice box, is responsible for metabolism—the rate at which cells burn fuel to produce energy. Controlled by the pituitary gland, the thyroid gland produces thyroxine and triiodothyronine. The rate at which cells burn fuel increases as the level of these hormones increases in the bloodstream; likewise, the rate at which cells burn fuel decreases as the level of these hormones decreases. Hormones of the thyroid are also involved in growth and development of the brain and nervous system in children.

Explain to students that the thyroid controls how the body uses and stores fuel. Students may better appreciate the functioning of the thyroid by learning about problems associated with thyroid dysfunction. Explain that a condition called hyperthyroidism occurs when the thyroid produces and secretes too high a concentration of hormones. With hyperthyroidism, a person's metabolism is too high and the body burns calories so rapidly that it cannot store fuel. This condition often results in decreased body weight, nervousness, increased heart rate and blood pressure, and excessive sweating. Explain also that a condition called hypothyroidism occurs when the thyroid does not produce and secrete enough hormones. This condition often results in weight gain, fatigue, decrease in heart rate, constipation, dry skin, and delayed puberty. Making students aware of these and many other conditions may help them to be less judgmental of others' appearances.

The pancreas, both a duct and ductless gland, is located behind the stomach and produces insulin and glucogen, hormones that work together to regulate the concentration of glucose in the bloodstream. (Glucose is a simple sugar used as fuel by the body's cells.) When the concentration of glucose in the blood increases, as occurs directly after a meal, insulin is produced and secreted by the pancreas and circulates through the bloodstream signaling the cells to absorb and store the glucose. When the concentration of glucose in the blood decreases, as occurs several hours after a meal has been eaten, glucogen is produced and secreted by the pancreas and circulates through the bloodstream signaling the cells to use stored glucose.

Diabetes, characterized by the body's inability to control blood sugar levels, is one of the most serious and most common endocrine disorders. Dangerously high glucose concentrations can build up in the blood as a result of this disorder, leading to coma and even death. There are two types of diabetes. Type 1 diabetes occurs when a person does not produce enough insulin. This type of diabetes usually develops during childhood and can be controlled with regular injections of insulin and a carefully planned diet. Type 2 diabetes is characterized by a person's cells not properly responding to insulin, and not enough glucose is removed from the bloodstream. This type of diabetes can be controlled with regular exercise, medication, and a carefully planned diet. People with either type of diabetes are recommended to limit their intake of sugary foods.

Teaching Idea

You may want to teach about Percy Lavon Julian in conjunction with this section. (See Section VII, "Science Biographies," on pp. 634–646.)

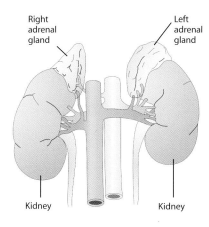

Right adrenal gland

Left adrenal gland

Kidney   Kidney

adrenal glands

Located on top of each kidney (and also controlled by the pituitary) are the adrenal glands. The outer part of the adrenal glands, the adrenal cortex, produces corticosteroids—hormones involved in the immune system, metabolism, sexual function, the regulation of a balance of salt and water in the body, and the body's response to stress. The inner part of the adrenal gland, the adrenal medulla, produces the catecholamines epinephrine, also called adrenaline, and norepinephrine. These hormones cause the heart rate and blood pressure to increase in stressful and frightening situations and help the body to respond to stress.

You read that puberty begins as a result of the release of certain hormones— estrogen and progesterone in females, and testosterone in males. You also read that these hormones are responsible for the changes observed during puberty; in addition to being responsible for the secondary sex characteristics that develop during puberty, these hormones are necessary for the maintenance and functioning of the reproductive system. The reproductive glands—the ovaries in females and testes in males—produce estrogen, progesterone, and testosterone.

The production of estrogen and progesterone in females and testosterone in males is triggered by the release of a hormone known as gonadotropin-releasing hormone (GnRH) from the hypothalamus to the pituitary gland. GnRH signals the pituitary to release luteinizing hormone (LH) and follicle-stimulating hormone (FSH) in both females and males. These two hormones are targeted for the reproductive glands and signal the ovaries and testes to begin production of their respective hormones. (It is not yet known what triggers the hypothalamus to begin production of GnRH.)

C. The Reproductive System

While most of our body systems are designed primarily to keep us healthy and alive as individuals, the reproductive system is responsible primarily for keeping the human species healthy and alive. The reproductive system enables humans to reproduce. Unlike all other body systems, this system is not essential for sustaining an individual's life. The reproductive systems of females and males are unique to one another, but both are designed to support and nourish sex cells, eggs and sperm respectively, which together create new life. (All other body systems are identical in men and women.)

The Female Reproductive System

Unlike the male reproductive organs, the female reproductive organs, consisting mainly of the ovaries, fallopian tubes, uterus, and vagina, are almost entirely concealed inside the pelvis. These organs enable a woman to store and release eggs, have sexual intercourse, support a fertilized egg until it is fully developed, and give birth. The two oval-shaped ovaries are the female reproductive glands. The ovaries produce the hormones estrogen and progesterone, which play a major role in controlling the female reproductive cycle and which are responsible for a female's secondary sex characteristics, such as the development of breasts. In addition, the ovaries store eggs and are the site where eggs are developed and released. The fallopian tubes connect the ovaries to the uterus and act as a passageway through which an egg released from an ovary travels to the uterus. The uterus is an expandable organ, resembling an inverted pear, where a developing fetus is supported during pregnancy. The uterus is only about three inches long and two inches wide in its nonpregnant state. Located at the base of the uterus, the cervix connects the uterus with the vagina. The vagina is a three- to six-inch-long, narrow, muscular structure that extends from the uterus to the vaginal opening. The vagina is lined with a mucous membrane and serves as the birth canal—the opening through which a baby is born—and as the female organ for sexual intercourse.

A major function of the female reproductive system is the development and release of eggs. Eggs are developed and released during the female reproductive cycle. The reproductive cycle lasts approximately 28 days and is controlled by hormones released from the hypothalamus (GnRH), pituitary (FSH and LH), and ovaries (estrogen and progesterone). During the cycle, an egg matures in a special structure in one of the ovaries and is released into the corresponding fallopian tube. The release of an egg from an ovary is called ovulation. The egg travels through the fallopian tubes, where it may be fertilized. The egg usually remains in the fallopian tube for three to five days before reaching the uterus. During this time, tissue builds and lines the walls of the uterus in preparation to support a fertilized egg. If the egg is fertilized, it is implanted in the uterine lining and the reproductive cycle is interrupted. If the egg is not fertilized, it is released into the uterus and the uterine lining begins to disintegrate. The unfertilized egg and the

Teaching Idea

Make copies of Instructional Master 74, *Female Reproductive System*, and distribute them to students. As you discuss the parts of the female reproductive system, invite students to label the parts on the diagram. Students can use this diagram to take notes on the function of each body part.

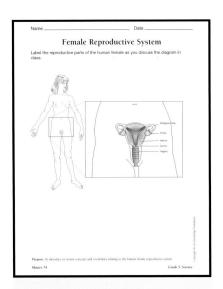

Use Instructional Master 74.

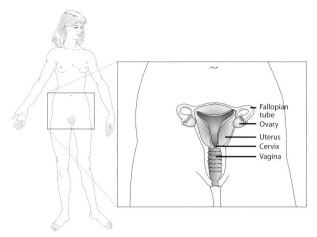

female reproductive system

uterine lining are released from the body through the vagina in a process known as menstruation. Menstruation usually lasts from three to seven days. The first day of menstruation begins the first day of the female reproductive cycle.

Students may find some of the following facts about the female reproductive system interesting and informative:

• It was once believed that a woman was born with all the eggs that she would have. However, recent scientific research seems to indicate that female mammals produce eggs into adulthood.

• A female's body temperature is lowest during ovulation to help ensure that sperm survive long enough in her body to reach the egg in her fallopian tubes.

The Male Reproductive System

Many of the male reproductive organs are external. The male reproductive organs enable a man to produce sperm and have sexual intercourse. The testes are the male reproductive glands. They produce the hormone testosterone, which is responsible for the male secondary sex characteristics, such as the growth of a beard and the production of sperm. These two oval-shaped glands occupy an external sac called the scrotum. The scrotum protects the testes and hangs down from the body slightly in order to keep the testes slightly cooler than body temperature; a lower temperature is important for the proper development of sperm cells. Hanging in the scrotum alongside each testis is the epididymis. The epididymis is a coiled tube that connects the testes to a muscular tube known as the vas deferens. The vas deferens connects to the urethra, a tube that runs through the penis and transports urine and semen (the fluid that contains sperm) out of the body. The penis is the male organ for sexual intercourse. This cylindrical organ is made of a spongy tissue that can expand and contract. When narrow tubes within the tissue fill with blood, the tissue expands and the penis becomes erect.

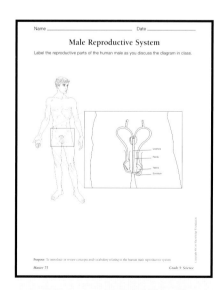

Use Instructional Master 75.

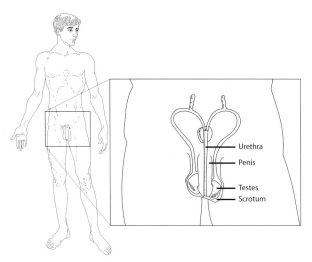

Urethra
Penis
Testes
Scrotum

male reproductive system

Students may find some of the following facts about the male reproductive system interesting and informative:

• Although males are able to have erections as infants, these erections do not result in ejaculations until puberty, when the production of sperm begins.

• Mature males produce millions of sperm every day.

• Semen is the fluid that contains and transports sperm. In addition to sperm, semen also contains several fluids including fructose, which acts as an energy source for sperm cells.

• Testes are kept approximately 3.6°F (2°C) cooler than the rest of the body to ensure production and survival of sperm.

Reproduction

Humans reproduce sexually through internal fertilization. During intercourse, a male inserts his penis into a female's vagina. A male's penis must be erect in order for this to happen. Semen is released from the male's penis and travels through the female's vagina and uterus to the fallopian tubes, where fertilization—the process in which a sperm cell and egg join—may occur. Although millions of sperm are released from the male's penis, only a few thousand will reach the fallopian tubes. Once in the fallopian tube, only one sperm can enter the outer membrane of an egg. Once a sperm cell enters the egg, the nuclei of the sperm and egg fuse and a new cell called a zygote is formed. In rare cases, the zygote will split into two cell masses to form monozygotic, or identical, twins. Twins can also be formed when two eggs are fertilized by two sperm, forming dizygotic, or fraternal, twins. Whatever the type, the zygote now travels through the fallopian tube toward the uterus for approximately one week. During this time the zygote begins to grow from a single cell and develops into what is called a blastocyst—a hollow ball of multiple cells. The blastocyst enters the uterus and becomes implanted in the uterine lining in a process known as implantation. If implantation is successful, a pregnancy will occur.

Once implanted in the uterine lining, the blastocyst continues to grow and develops into a structure known as a gastrula. Three layers of cells—the ectoderm, mesoderm, and endoderm—form in the gastrula. These layers of cells will develop into all the body's tissues and organs. Once the layers have developed, an embryo is formed. Two supporting membranes surround an embryo. These supporting membranes form the amnion, and, with some of the mother's endometrial cells, the placenta. The amnion contains a fluid that surrounds and protects the embryo. The placenta is an organ through which nutrients, oxygen, and waste are transported between the mother and embryo. An embryo is connected to the placenta by the umbilical cord. After about nine weeks, the embryo is referred to as a fetus. The fetus continues to develop in the mother's uterus for approximately seven more months.

About nine months after fertilization, the fetus becomes fully developed and hormones released in the mother signal the birthing process, or labor, to begin. During labor, the uterus contracts strongly and the cervix and vaginal opening begin to widen so that the fetus can pass from the uterus to the vagina and out of the vagina through the vaginal opening. A new human is born, similar to but not exactly like its parents. After labor, the newborn begins to breathe on its own and the umbilical cord is cut.

Review

Below are some ideas for ongoing assessment and review activities. These are not meant to constitute a comprehensive list.

• Make a vocabulary matching game to play in groups so that students become familiar with the endocrine system's different glands and their functions. Make index cards with the names of the different glands and organs of the endocrine system, and then make a matching card with the definition or an example for the term. Mix the cards and have students play a concentration matching game to try and match terms and definitions.

• Since students may not be comfortable asking questions during the study of human adolescence and the reproductive system, provide a box where students can submit questions that they might have. Before arranging a day where all of the questions are addressed as a class, you should read through the questions. You may choose to answer these questions or have a health care professional come to visit the class and answer them.

• If you have a school nurse, this person can be an excellent resource during the study of this unit. Plan a day where the nurse talks with the class, or work collaboratively to plan a culminating activity for review of the material from this unit.

• Take the class to visit the nursery of a hospital to see the newborn babies. During the visit, arrange for one of the nurses or doctors to talk about how they care for the babies after they are born. Before the trip, have students write down questions to ask about the development of the fetus or the delivery of the babies for discussion during the trip.

The Big Idea in Review

Changes that prepare humans for adulthood and reproduction occur in the body during puberty. These changes are controlled by the endocrine system.

• You may also ask the following questions after completing this section:

1. When does puberty typically occur in males and females?

   In males, puberty typically occurs between the ages of 13 and 16, and in females, between the ages of 11 and 14.

2. What are some changes associated with puberty?

   A boy develops pubic hair; he experiences a growth spurt and his hands and feet may grow more rapidly than the rest of his body; his penis and testes tend to enlarge; his shoulders broaden; and his voice deepens. A girl develops breasts and pubic hair; her hips widen; she experiences a growth spurt; and she begins to menstruate.

3. What is the endocrine system?

   The endocrine system is a body system of glands that produce hormones that help regulate a variety of ongoing body processes.

4. What are three of the endocrine glands?

   Answers may include pituitary, pancreas, thyroid, adrenal glands, and reproductive glands.

5. What are the male reproductive organs? What are the female reproductive organs?

   The male reproductive organs are testes, urethra, scrotum, and penis. The female reproductive organs are ovaries, fallopian tubes, uterus, and vagina.

More Resources

The titles listed below are offered as a representative sample of materials and not a complete list of everything that is available.

For students —

• *The Human Body: A Fascinating See-Through View of How Bodies Work,* by Lawrence T. Lorimer and others (Reader's Digest, 1999). Hardcover, 16 pages, ISBN 1575842483.

• *Nine Month Miracle,* described as "a multimedia journey into the miracle of pregnancy and childbirth" (from the publisher), is available through the award-winning software company A.D.A.M. at www.adam.com. See also *A.D.A.M.: The Inside Story,* which also includes an instructor's CD.

• *The 100+ Series: The Human Body,* by Daryl Vriesenga (Instructional Fair • TS Denison, 1990). Reproducible activities, and black-and-white diagrams of the human body. Paperback, 128 pages, ISBN 0880128275. Distributed through School Specialty Children's Publishing, http://elementary-educators.teacherspecialty.com/home.php or 1-800-417-3261.

For teachers —

• *A.D.A.M. Interactive Anatomy 4.* Order through A.D.A.M. Software, at www.adam.com.

• *DK Guide to the Human Body: A Photographic Journey through the Human Body,* by Richard Walker (DK Publishing, 2001). Hardcover, 64 pages, ISBN 0789473887.

VI. Chemistry: Matter and Change

The Big Idea

Everything around you is matter. All matter is made up of elements, the smallest unit of which is the atom, and is described by its properties and composition.

Remember that each subject you study with students expands their vocabulary and introduces new terms, thus making them better listeners and readers. As you study chemistry, use read alouds, independent reading, and discussions to build students' vocabularies.

What Students Should Already Know
Students in Core Knowledge schools should be familiar with

Grade 1

▸ basic concept of atoms

▸ names and common examples of three states of matter: solid (for example, wood, rocks); liquid (for example, water); gas (for example, air, steam)

▸ water as an example of changing states of matter of a single substance

Grade 4

▸ All matter is made up of particles too small for the eye to see, called atoms.

▸ Scientists have developed models of atoms; while these models have changed over time as scientists make new discoveries, the models help us imagine what we cannot see.

▸ Atoms are made up of even tinier particles: protons, neutrons, and electrons.

▸ the concept of electrical charge
  • positive charge (+): proton
  • negative charge (-): electron
  • neutral (neither positive nor negative): neutron
  • "Unlike charges attract, like charges repel" (relate to magnetic attraction and repulsion)

▸ mass: the amount of matter in an object, similar to weight

▸ volume: the amount of space a thing occupies

▸ density: how much matter is packed into the space an object fills

▸ vacuum: the absence of matter

▸ Elements are the basic kinds of matter. There are a little more than 100 elements.
  • There are many different kinds of atoms, but each element is composed of only one kind of atom.
  • familiar elements, such as gold, copper, aluminum, oxygen, iron
  • Most things are made up of a combination of elements.

VI. Chemistry: Matter and Change

What Students Should Already Know continued

- A solution is formed when a substance (the solute) is dissolved in another substance (the solvent), such as when sugar or salt is dissolved in water; the dissolved substance is present in the solution even though you cannot see it.

- concentration and saturation (as demonstrated through simple experiments with crystallization)

What Students Need to Learn

- **Atoms, Molecules, and Compounds**

  - **Basics of atomic structure: nucleus, protons (positive charge), neutrons (neutral), electrons (negative charge)**

  - **Atoms are constantly in motion; electrons move around the nucleus in paths called shells (or energy levels).**

  - **Atoms may join together to form molecules and compounds.**

  - **Common compounds and their formulas:**

    Water: H_2O

    "Table" salt: NaCl

    Carbon dioxide: CO_2

- **Elements**

  - **Elements have atoms of only one kind, having the same number of protons. There are a little more than 100 different elements.**

  - **The periodic table organizes elements with common properties.**

  - **Atomic symbol and atomic number**

  - **Some well-known elements and their symbols:**

Hydrogen	H	Silicon	Si
Helium	He	Chlorine	Cl
Carbon	C	Iron	Fe
Nitrogen	N	Copper	Cu
Oxygen	O	Silver	Ag
Sodium	Na	Gold	Au
Aluminum	Al		

  - **Two important categories of elements: metals and non-metals**

  - **Metals compose about $\frac{2}{3}$ of the known elements.**

  - **Properties of metals: Most are shiny, ductile, malleable, conductive.**

- **Chemical and Physical Change**

  - **Chemical change alters the composition of a molecule and results in a new substance with a new molecular structure. Examples of chemical change are the rusting of iron, the burning of wood, and milk turning sour.**

  - **Physical change alters only the properties or appearance of the substance, but does not change what the substance is made up of. Examples of physical change are cutting wood or paper, breaking glass, and freezing water.**

What Students Will Learn in Future Grades

In future grades, students will review and extend their learning about chemistry, matter, and change.

Grade 6

> ‣ energy, heat, and energy transfer, including states of matter, expansion and contraction, and changing phases

Grade 7

> ‣ chemical bonds and reactions, including ionic, metallic, and covalent bonds, and different types of reactions (oxidation, reduction, acids, bases, and catalysts)

Vocabulary

Student/Teacher Vocabulary

atom: the smallest unit of an element (S)

atomic number: the number of protons in the nucleus of an atom; determines the chemical properties of an element (S)

atomic symbol: one- or two-letter abbreviation used to indicate a specific element (S)

chemical bond: the property of two or more atoms that are chemically combined and essentially share one another's electrons, e.g., nitrogen, hydrogen, and water (T)

chemical change: a change that results in the formation of new substances (S)

compound: a pure substance made of two or more elements (S)

conductive: having the ability to convey or transmit, e.g., metals are conductive when it comes to heat or electricity (S)

ductile: capable of being drawn out into wire or thread (S)

electron: a negatively charged particle that spins around the nucleus of an atom (S)

element: a pure substance that cannot be broken down into simpler substances (S)

formula: the means to represent compounds; made by combining the symbols of the elements from which the compound is made with numbers that represent the ratio of each element within that compound (S)

malleable: capable of being extended or shaped by physical pressure (S)

matter: anything that has mass and occupies space; the material of the universe (S)

metal: a type of element that is a good conductor of heat and electricity (S)

molecule: two or more atoms that are chemically combined (S)

neutron: a neutral particle in the nucleus of an atom (S)

nonmetal: an element that is typically a poor conductor of heat and electricity (S)

nucleus: the center of an atom (T)

periodic table: the table originally created by Mendeleev that organized the elements according to their properties (S)

Vocabulary continued

physical change: a change that does not result in the formation of new substances; a change in the physical properties of matter (S)

property: an attribute or characteristic that is used to describe an object or thing (S)

proton: a positively charged particle in the nucleus of an atom (S)

shell: an energy level containing spinning electrons that surrounds the nucleus of an atom (S)

symbol: the alphabetical letter or letters used to represent an element and/or compound (S)

Domain Vocabulary

Chemistry: matter and change and associated words:
Democritus, Aristotle, Plato, Dalton, particle, indivisible, unit, hypothesis, theory, identical, similar, different, like, unlike, opposite, electric charge, positive, negative, electron cloud, forces, electrostatic forces, orbit, spin, rotate, revolve, sphere, circle, encircle, attract, attractive, repel, repulsion, pull, push, mass, massive, volume, energy, energy shell, pick up, give off, absorb, release, discharge, combine, chemically combined, joined together, share, substance, material, simple, complex, pure, impure, unique, represent, show, characteristic, feature, atomic mass, gas, liquid, solid, change of state, formula, equation, ratio, proportion, combination, mixture, blend, alloy, Dmitri Mendeleev, cycle, groups, rows, periods, columns, arrangement, metalloid, composition, rearrange, interact, conditions, favorable, unfavorable, reaction, product, *plus the names of elements*

Cross-curricular Connections

Language Arts

Writing, Grammar, and Usage
Writing and Research

At a Glance

The most important ideas for you are:

- Matter is everything around you; it is the material of the universe.
- Matter is made of elements. There are a few more than 115 different elements.
- Each element is represented with a symbol.
- Two or more elements can combine to form compounds.
- The smallest unit of an element is an atom. All the atoms of an element are alike; the atoms of one element are unlike the atoms of any other element.
- Atoms are made of smaller subatomic particles—protons, neutrons, and electrons.
- Protons are positively charged particles contained in the nucleus of an atom.

- Neutrons are uncharged particles in the nucleus of an atom.
- Electrons are negatively charged particles that spin around the nucleus of an atom in energy levels called shells.
- Two or more atoms of the same or of different elements can combine to form molecules.

What Teachers Need to Know

Background

Everything around you that you can see and touch is matter. This includes water, soil, and colorful flowers, as well as things you cannot see, such as air and carbon dioxide. Matter is anything that has mass and occupies space. Everything in the universe that has mass and occupies space is matter.

A. Atoms, Molecules, and Compounds

People have been thinking about matter for more than 2,500 years. For a long time, it was widely believed that all matter was composed of four elements—earth, air, fire, and water. In the 5th century BCE, the Greek philosopher Democritus hypothesized that matter was made of very small indivisible units. He used the Greek word *atomos*, meaning "indivisible," to describe a particle that could not be further subdivided. His theory was quickly dismissed by such philosophers as Aristotle and Plato; however, it managed to persist through the ages. In 1803, scientist and schoolteacher John Dalton came up with a precise definition for the indivisible unit we call the atom today. Dalton's theory explained, among other things, that all elements are composed of extremely small particles called atoms; that all atoms of a given element are identical; and that the atoms of one element are different from atoms of any other.

We have continued to study and learn much more about atoms and their structure over the past two centuries. We now know that atoms have an internal structure and are made of even smaller parts known as subatomic particles. These subatomic particles are protons, neutrons, and electrons. Protons are particles in the nucleus of an atom that have a positive (+) electric charge. Neutrons are uncharged (electrically neutral) particles that are also contained in the nucleus of an atom. Electrons are negatively (-) charged particles that spin around the nucleus. Although electrons are often compared to planets, the comparison is imperfect, because planets orbit the sun in very orderly and predictable paths, whereas it is difficult to pinpoint the exact path that electrons travel because they move so quickly. Electrons circle the nucleus, and form what is called an electron cloud.

Teaching Idea

As you teach this section to students, keep a vocabulary list on chart paper on the wall. Include words discussed, as well as definitions and examples. If you generate this list with the class as you are teaching the topic, students are more likely to remember the meanings than if you simply provide them with a list.

Teaching Idea

Demonstrate the concept of atoms with your class by taking one small sample of aluminum foil and cutting it in half. (Use aluminum foil instead of paper because foil is a pure element.) Cut the half in half again and again until you are left with a piece too tiny to cut. Explain that although the aluminum foil has shrunk in size, it is still aluminum. Now invite students to imagine cutting that foil into even tinier and tinier pieces until the pieces are too small to be seen and then into even tinier pieces until cutting it anymore would mean you no longer have aluminum! Explain that, like your actual piece of aluminum foil, at some point the pieces can no longer be cut into smaller pieces. These tiny pieces that can no longer be cut are called atoms—the smallest unit of an element.

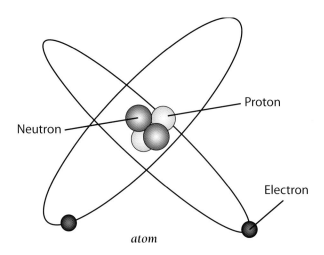

atom

Protons and electrons have exactly equal (but opposite) charges, so an atom tries to stay electrically "neutral" by having the same number of protons and electrons. Protons and neutrons are in the nucleus of an atom and cannot be removed by ordinary chemical reactions. Electrons, however, are in shells around the nucleus, and can be added or removed during chemical reactions.

Electrons are held around the nucleus by electrostatic forces, much as the force of gravity holds the planets in their orbit around the sun. Although atoms can be divided into the parts that make them up, once divided, they no longer represent an element or a complete unit of matter. An atom is the smallest unit of an element that retains the properties of that element. The number of particles (protons and neutrons) in the nucleus and the number of electrons around the nucleus determine the properties of the element. An atom with one proton is an atom of the element hydrogen. An atom with two protons is an atom of helium. An atom with 79 protons is gold. (Note that the number of electrons in any given atom is equal to its number of protons.)

Look at the periodic table of the elements on page 630. The number above each symbol is called the atomic number. This number tells how many protons are in the nucleus of an atom of a particular element. You will see that no two elements have the same atomic number. There is only one kind of atom with 29 protons (copper), and only one kind with 30 (zinc). The atoms of a particular element are unique to that element.

Normally, an atom contains an equal number of electrons and protons, making the whole atom electrically neutral. This means that the negative charges of the electrons balance the positive charges of the protons in the atom. If an atom loses any electrons, though, the atom becomes positively charged, and if it gains more electrons than protons, the atom becomes negatively charged. These positively and negatively charged atoms are called ions. A positively charged atom will be attracted to a negatively charged atom, but repelled from another positively charged atom.

In atoms, as well as in all objects, like charges repel and unlike charges attract. For example, if you have ever combed your hair and had your hair stand up as a result, it was because your hair acquired electrons from the comb. The individual hairs, all being made of the same material, will each acquire the same charge and are repelled from each other, thus making them stand up or stick out.

Teaching Idea

To reinforce the idea of "electronically neutral" atoms, demonstrate using a balance scale and unifix cubes or wooden blocks. Ask students to think of one side as protons, and the other side as electrons. Place an equal number of blocks on each side of the scale to show balance, just as an electronically neutral atom would have the same number of protons and electrons. Take some away from one side and what is the result? Imbalance. Then talk about how if the atom loses electrons (which are negatively charged), it becomes positively charged, and if the atom gains more electrons than protons, it becomes negatively charged.

Since the comb has lost electrons, it has become positively charged and will be attracted to your negatively charged hair. This behavior of attraction and repulsion works in a similar way with magnets. The north poles of two magnets, which are alike, will repel each other, but the north pole of one magnet and the south pole of another magnet will attract one another. In this case, like poles repel and unlike poles attract.

Have you ever walked across a carpet and touched a doorknob, only to receive a shock and see a spark? When your feet rub against the carpet, electrons from the carpet are transferred to you, and this excess of electrons makes you become negatively charged. If you then touch another object, such as a metal doorknob, the electrons move from you to the doorknob, getting rid of the charge. This is called a discharge. When an object discharges, it loses the excess electrons and becomes neutral again.

We can visualize atoms as incredibly small, fuzzy-looking spheres that are held together by the attractive forces between positively charged protons and negatively charged electrons. Nearly 99% of an atom's mass is concentrated in the protons and neutrons making up its nucleus, which are each approximately 1,840 times more massive than an electron. Most of the atom's volume is occupied by the electrons that spin rapidly around the nucleus in defined shells, or energy levels. Each shell contains a set number of electrons and represents a fixed amount of energy that electrons are said to be able to pick up or give off.

Some elements, such as helium, are made up of single atoms that do not attach to any other of its atoms. Other elements, however, such as nitrogen and hydrogen, do not exist as single atoms, and instead exist as molecules—two or more atoms chemically combined. When atoms are chemically combined, they are joined together by a chemical bond, and essentially share one another's electrons. Students will learn more about the various types of bonds in future grades. While the molecules of an element are made up only of that element, molecules may also consist of two or more atoms of different elements chemically combined. (One unit of water is a water molecule. A water molecule consists of two hydrogen atoms that are bonded to an atom of oxygen.) Hydrogen, nitrogen, oxygen, fluorine, chlorine, bromine, and iodine are elements that exist in nature as molecules.

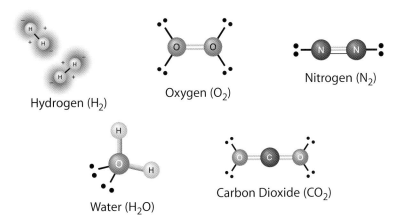

Hydrogen (H_2)

Oxygen (O_2)

Nitrogen (N_2)

Water (H_2O)

Carbon Dioxide (CO_2)

Name _____ Date _____

Common Elements

As you study different elements, fill in the chart below.

Element	Symbol	Properties
Hydrogen	H	a gas; the least dense element; bonds with oxygen to make water
Helium	He	a low-density gas; extremely unreactive in nature (inert)
Carbon	C	a nonmetal; exists in nature as graphite, diamond, and fullerenes (large compounds that resemble soccer balls)
Nitrogen	N	a gas making up 78% of the air we breathe
Oxygen	O	a gas making up 21% of the air we breathe; supports combustion
Sodium	Na	a low-density, soft, highly reactive metal; constitutes 50% of table salt
Aluminum	Al	a common metal used in many everyday items; good conductor of heat and electricity
Silicon	Si	a metalloid; major constituent of sand; used to make glass and computer chips
Chlorine	Cl	a pale green, poisonous, highly reactive gas; constitutes 50% of table salt
Iron	Fe	a strong, hard, magnetic metal; forms the major constituent of steel
Copper	Cu	a metal; good conductor of heat and electricity; often used in wires and cookware
Silver	Ag	an unreactive soft metal; often used in jewelry
Gold	Au	a very unreactive yellow metal; often used in jewelry

Purpose: To introduce or review the symbols and properties of common elements

Master 76a   *Grade 5: Science*

Use Instructional Masters 76a–76b.

B. Elements

Matter is composed of elements. Gold, silver, aluminum, and oxygen are all elements—they are pure substances that cannot be broken down into simpler substances. Each of these elements has its own distinctive kind of atom: an atom of gold has 79 protons, an atom of silver has 47, an atom of aluminum has 13, and an atom of oxygen has 8.

copper, gold, and silver

Students will already be familiar with some of the elements. They may know that they need oxygen to breathe and that helium makes balloons float high in the air. They may have been told they need calcium for strong bones and iron to stay healthy and strong. Explain that these things are examples of elements, the stuff that makes everything around them.

Many elements are metals. Metals are good conductors of heat and electricity, and, with the exception of mercury (Hg), are solids at room temperature. Nonmetals are typically poor conductors of heat and electricity. Nonmetals may be solid (as in carbon, C), liquid (as in bromine, Br_2), or gas (as in helium, He) at room temperature. Metalloids have properties between those of metals and nonmetals; for example, they may be good conductors of electricity, but may be brittle.

Students might find it interesting that over 97% of the human body is composed of different combinations of just six elements—oxygen, carbon, hydrogen, nitrogen, calcium, and phosphorus. In fact, most living things—trees, flowers, dogs, cats, fish, etc.—are largely made of these six elements, too!

Scientists have developed symbols of one to three letters, for the sake of convenience, to represent each of the elements. The first letter of the symbol is always capitalized and the remaining letters are not. Many of the symbols were derived from the first two letters of either the Latin or the English name for the element. Gold, for example, was given the symbol *Au* from its Latin name, *aurum*. Nickel was given the symbol *Ni* from the first two letters of its English name. The table on p. 629 lists some common elements with their symbols and highlights some of these elements' properties.

Some matter is made purely of one element. Diamond and graphite are made solely of the element carbon. Most matter, however, is made of a combination of elements. Elements may combine in different ways—they may combine chemically or physically. When two or more elements combine chemically, they form a compound, a pure substance with properties different from the properties of the elements from which it is made. Water is an example of a compound. It is made by the chemical combination of the elements hydrogen and oxygen. Unlike

Element	Symbol	Properties
Hydrogen	H	A gas; the least dense element; bonds with oxygen to make water
Helium	He	A low-density gas; extremely unreactive in nature (inert)
Carbon	C	A nonmetal; exists in nature as graphite, diamond, and fullerenes (large carbon compounds that resemble soccer balls); the basis for organic compounds
Nitrogen	N	A gas making up 78% of the air we breathe
Oxygen	O	A gas making up 21% of the air we breathe; supports combustion
Sodium	Na	A low-density, soft, highly reactive metal; constitutes 50% of table salt
Aluminum	A1	A common metal used in many everyday items; good conductor of heat and electricity
Silicon	Si	A metalloid; major constituent of sand; used to make glass and computer chips
Chlorine	C1	A pale green, poisonous, highly reactive gas; constitutes 50% of table salt
Iron	Fe	A strong, hard, magnetic metal; is the major constituent of steel
Copper	Cu	A metal; good conductor of heat and electricity; often used in wires and cookware
Silver	Ag	An unreactive soft metal; often used in jewelry
Gold	Au	A very unreactive yellow metal; often used in jewelry

oxygen and hydrogen, which are both colorless gases at room temperature, water is a liquid at room temperature and has its own unique set of properties and characteristics. Carbon dioxide, a compound produced in your body as a waste gas, is made of the elements carbon and oxygen. Table salt is another common compound. It is made of the elements sodium and chlorine.

The elements that make up a compound combine in fixed proportions. Water is always made of two parts hydrogen and one part oxygen; carbon dioxide is always made of one part carbon and two parts oxygen; salt is always made of one part chlorine and one part sodium. In different proportions from those stated above, the combinations of these elements would make different compounds. If two parts hydrogen and two parts oxygen are combined, for example, the compound hydrogen peroxide is formed; if one part carbon and one part oxygen are combined, the poisonous gas carbon monoxide is formed. Both of these compounds, while made from the same elements as water and carbon dioxide, respectively, are unique compounds with properties much different from water and carbon dioxide.

Scientists represent compounds with formulas. Formulas are made by combining the symbols of the elements from which the compound is made with numbers that represent the ratio, or proportion, of each element within that compound. The formula for water is H_2O. The H represents the element hydrogen, and the O represents the element oxygen. The number 2 following the H tells us that for every one part of oxygen there are two parts of hydrogen. The formula for carbon dioxide is CO_2; the formula for salt is NaCl.

Teaching Idea

Based on formulas, challenge students to name which elements these compounds are made of: CO_2 (carbon dioxide), NaCl (sodium chloride, or table salt), NH_3 (ammonia), Fe_2O_3 (iron oxide, or rust), and CH_4 (methane).

Teaching Idea

You may wish to use Instructional Master 77, *Elements and Compounds*, to assess students' mastery of the topics discussed thus far in this section.

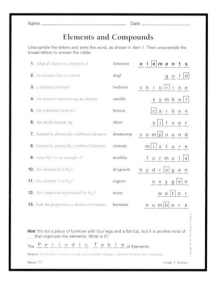

Use Instructional Master 77.

As mentioned, elements can also combine physically. When elements combine physically, they form a mixture; the elements blend together without forming new substances, and the properties of the elements remain unchanged. Unlike compounds, mixtures can be separated back into the pure elements from which they were made. Mixtures can be made by the physical combination of elements, and also by the physical combination of compounds. Brass, steel, most rocks, and even your blood are examples of mixtures—in fact, most matter exists as a mixture of elements or compounds.

The Periodic Table

In the late 1800s, a Russian scientist, Dmitri Mendeleev, discovered that the properties of elements go through repeating cycles. He saw that some elements always combine with other elements in a certain way—lithium, sodium, potassium, and rubidium all combine with chlorine in the same way, for example. Mendeleev created a table that organized the elements according to these observed cyclical properties. The table, called the Periodic Table of Elements, is shown below as we know it today. The elements are listed in the table according to chemical and physical properties they exhibit.

The Periodic Table of Elements

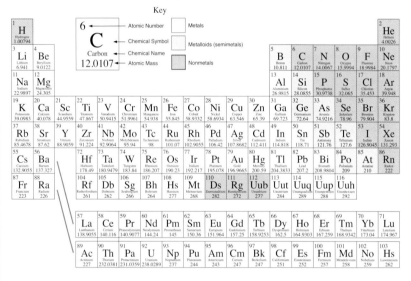

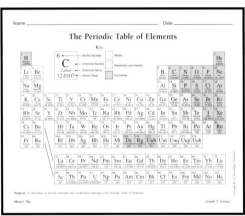

Use Instructional Masters 78a–78b.

As shown in the periodic table, most of the elements are metals. Metals are good conductors of heat and electricity, and, with the exception of mercury (Hg), are solids at room temperature. Nonmetals are typically poor conductors of heat and electricity. Nonmetals may be solid (as in carbon, C), liquid (as in bromine, Br_2), or gas (as in helium, He) at room temperature. Metalloids have properties between those of metals and nonmetals

C. Chemical and Physical Change

When elements and compounds interact with each other and with energy, two types of changes may result: physical changes and chemical changes. Physical

changes occur when the physical properties of an element or compound change without also changing the composition or identity of that element or compound. When a substance changes in size, state, or is combined with other substances to form a mixture, the result is a physical change.

The grinding of salt, breaking of glass, and cutting of wood or paper are some simple examples of physical changes. Salt, glass, wood, and paper do not turn into new substances as a result of the actions described; only the physical appearance of these materials changes.

Water changing from a liquid to a gas or solid is also a physical change. Although water changes form, it does not become a new substance with a new chemical composition. The molecule does not change—it is still the pure substance composed of two parts hydrogen and one part oxygen; only the orientation of the molecules in relation to one another changes.

The dissolving of sugar in tea to form a sweet solution is also an example of a physical change. Both the tea and sugar retain their own properties; atoms do not rearrange and new substances are not formed. The solution can be separated back into the parts that make it up.

Chemical changes occur when two or more substances interact and form new substances. A change occurs in the way atoms are linked or bonded; new substances form, with properties different from the original substances. When hydrogen and oxygen react and form water, a chemical change occurs. Hydrogen gas and oxygen gas—previously two separate, unlinked substances—are now bonded to each other and form a new molecule. (The formula for the reaction is $2 H_2 + O_2 \rightarrow 2 H_2O$)

Chemical changes are also referred to as chemical reactions. The substances that change are called reactants, and the new substances that form are called products. Some common examples of chemical changes include the rusting of iron, the burning of wood, the baking of a cake, and the souring of milk. When iron (Fe) interacts with air and moisture under certain conditions, a new compound, iron oxide (Fe_2O_3), or rust, is formed. As a cake bakes, baking soda ($NaHCO_3$) in the cake dough is changed into sodium carbonate (Na_2CO_3), steam (gaseous water), and carbon dioxide gas (CO_2).

$$2\ NaHCO_3 \rightarrow Na_2CO_3 + H_2O + CO_2$$

The sodium carbonate is a harmless solid that remains in the cake, the steam helps make the cake moist, and the carbon dioxide gas helps make the dough expand and makes the cake light and airy.

Sometimes it may be difficult to detect whether a substance has undergone a chemical or a physical change. If a change results in the evolution of a gas, the formation of light and heat, or a change in color, then in most cases the change is a chemical change. When vinegar is added to baking soda, for example, chemical changes occur and carbon dioxide gas is released. When wood burns, chemical changes occur and light and heat are given off. When iron becomes rusty, chemical changes occur and a color change is observed. Chemical changes are typically more difficult to reverse, or "undo," than physical changes—it is

Science **631**

Teaching Idea

To help students track the difference between chemical and physical changes, use Instructional Master 84, *T-Chart*, to record the 2 types of changes, a definition of each, and examples. This can be an ongoing chart during this topic of study.

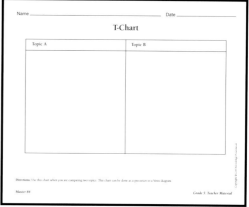

Use Instructional Master 84.

Teaching Idea

You may wish to play a game called "Chemical or Physical Change?" with students. Demonstrate an everyday occurrence, then ask students if they think the change is chemical or physical. Tell them if they are right, and discuss the reasons with the class. For example: cut a piece of paper in half (physical); draw a circle on a piece of paper with a colored marker (physical); pour a teaspoon of baking powder in a half cup of vinegar (chemical); light a candle (chemical); mix salt in a cup of water (physical); cut a piece of wood in half (physical).

VI. Chemistry: Matter and Change

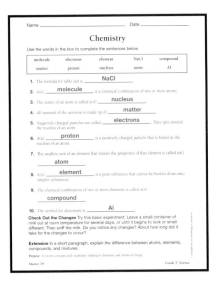

Use Instructional Master 79.

The Big Idea in Review

Everything around you is matter. All matter is made up of elements, the smallest unit of which is the atom, and is described by its properties and composition.

difficult to "unburn" wood or "desour" milk, for example, whereas it is easy to melt ice to regain liquid water. This fact can also be used to predict whether a change is physical or chemical.

Review

Below are some ideas for ongoing assessment and review activities. These are not meant to constitute a comprehensive list.

• To review the elements and the periodic table, give students a copy of the table and review some of the familiar names. Then, provide a variety of magazines and newspapers for students to search. Have students make a collage titled *Elements Around Us*. They should collect pictures that illustrate elements on the periodic table. Have students share their collages and explain why they chose each picture to illustrate an element from the table.

• Have students write diamante poems to illustrate their understanding of the properties of solids, liquids, or gases. Diamante poems are shaped like diamonds and are formed with lines of one noun, two adjectives, three participles, four nouns, three participles, two adjectives, and one noun. Have students choose solid, liquid, or gas to be the subject of their poem and then write the poem to illustrate the properties of that state of matter. Share these with the class.

• Have students rotate through stations set up around the room to see the differences between physical and chemical changes. Each station should have materials so that students can observe the change and then record results. For chemical change stations, make sure that the experiments are simple, and follow safety procedures. If you would prefer, have adult volunteers perform the chemical change, and then have students record what they observe.

• Organize a chemistry fair at the end of this unit, where the students can demonstrate simple experiments, read their poems (mentioned above), or share any other research they have participated in during this unit. Invite other classes to participate.

• In addition to making small models of atoms in class, ask students to make atom models at home from materials that they choose, and then bring them to share with the class. Make sure the models display the basics of atomic structure. Arrange a day to share these with the class.

• You may also ask the following questions after completing this section:

1. What is matter?
   Matter is anything that has mass and occupies space.

2. What are some examples of elements?
   Students may mention gold, silver, oxygen, hydrogen, aluminum, copper, or other elements found in the periodic table.

3. What kinds of things are listed in the periodic table?
   Elements are listed in the periodic table.

4. What is an atom?
   An atom is the smallest unit of an element that has the properties of the element.

5. What particles are found in the nucleus of an atom?
Protons and neutrons are found in the nucleus of an atom.

6. What particle in an atom carries a negative charge? What particle carries a positive charge?
Electrons carry a negative charge, and protons carry a positive charge.

7. What is the difference between a molecule and a compound?
A compound is made of two or more elements that may or may not be chemically combined, while a molecule is made of two or more atoms that are chemically combined.

8. What is an example of a chemical change?
Students may mention the burning of wood, the rusting of iron, or the baking of a cake.

9. What is an example of a physical change?
Students may mention the cutting of wood or the mixing of salt in water.

More Resources

The titles listed below are offered as a representative sample of materials and not a complete list of everything that is available.

For students —

• *Adventures with Atoms and Molecules: Chemistry Experiments for Young People*, by Robert C. Mebane and Thomas R. Rybolt (Enslow, 1991). One of five volumes now available in this series. Paperback, ISBN 0766011224.

• *Atoms (KidHaven Science Library)*, by Don Nardo (KidHaven Press, 2002). Hardcover, 48 pages, ISBN 0737709421.

• *Chemistry (Eyewitness Books)*, by Dr. Ann Newmark (DK Publishing, 1999). Hardcover, 64 pages, ISBN 0789448815.

• *Janice VanCleave's Chemistry for Every Kid: 101 Easy Experiments that Really Work*, by Janice VanCleave (John Wiley & Sons, 1989). Paperback, 256 pages, ISBN 0471620858. See also *Janice VanCleave's Molecules.*

• *Kitchen Chemistry (Revised Edition)*, by Robert Gardner (Enslow, 2002). Library binding, 128 pages, ISBN 0766017060.

• *Matter,* by Christopher Cooper (DK Publishing, 1999). A well-illustrated history of exploration into the material world. Hardcover, 64 pages, ISBN 0789448866.

• *The Nature of the Atom: Great Scientific Questions and the Scientists Who Answered Them*, by Natalie Goldstein (Rosen Publishing Group, 2001). Advanced reading. Library binding, 112 pages, ISBN 0823933857.

• *Potassium (The Elements)*, by Chris Woodford (Benchmark Books, 2003). Library binding, 32 pages, ISBN 0761414630. One of several books in this series.

• *What is the World Made Of? All About Solids, Liquids, and Gases (Let's-Read-and-Find-Out Science, Stage 2)*, by Kathleen Weidner Zoehfeld (Harper Trophy, 1998). An easy-to-read introduction. Paperback, 32 pages, ISBN 0064451631.

For teachers —

• *Hands-On Science*, by John Graham, Peter Mellett, Jack Challoner, and Sarah Angliss (Houghton Mifflin, 2002). Includes several experiments about matter and materials, each designed to take between 5 and 20 minutes to complete. Paperback, 160 pages, ISBN 0753454408.

• Chemicool, www.chemicool.com, offers an online periodic table. Click on any element to learn more about it—the name, atomic number, symbol, atomic weight, year discovered, and much more.

• The American Chemical Society website has a link for "Kids" and a lot of information about simple experiments. See www.chemistry.org.

The Big Idea

Science is built on the careful observations and creative contributions of individuals.

What Students Should Already Know

Students in Core Knowledge schools should be familiar with

Kindergarten

- George Washington Carver: scientist who helped Southern farmers by teaching them to plant new crops and by discovering new uses for peanuts, sweet potatoes, and soybeans
- Wilbur and Orville Wright: invented the first airplane and had the first successful powered flight from a level surface
- Jane Goodall: animal behavior scientist who observed chimpanzees and discovered that they are intelligent, social, and emotional animals

Grade 1

- Rachel Carson: wrote many books and articles about the environment and the harmful effects human actions can have on the environment, revealing the devastating effects of DDT on the environment and setting the stage for the modern environmental movement
- Thomas Edison: one of the most prolific inventors of the past two centuries who invented the electric light and the phonograph and formed the foundation for many of the machines and devices we use today
- Edward Jenner: developed a vaccine for smallpox and essentially began the field of immunology
- Louis Pasteur: established the scientific field of microbiology; developed the process of pasteurization; and discovered the vaccine for rabies

Grade 2

- Anton van Leeuwenhoek: created powerful microscope lenses that allowed him to observe bacteria and protists
- Elijah McCoy: invented the automatic lubricator, which saved time by allowing machines to be lubricated automatically while they continued to run
- Florence Nightingale: worked to make hospitals more sanitary; wrote about the principles of nursing; and opened a school for nurses
- Daniel Hale Williams: performed the first successful open-chest surgery and opened a school for African-American women to study nursing

Grade 3

- Alexander Graham Bell: prolific inventor who invented the telephone and the photophone, which laid the foundation for fiber optic technology today; developed a variety of designs for airplanes, kites, and hydroplane watercrafts; and experimented with early forms of air conditioning

Remember that each subject you study with students expands their vocabulary and introduces new terms, thus making them better listeners and readers. As you study the contributions of individuals to science, use read alouds, independent reading, and discussions to build students' vocabularies.

Text Resources

91 *Galileo Galilei*

92 *Percy Lavon Julian*

93 *Ernest Just*

94 *Carolus Linnaeus*

- Nicolaus Copernicus: astronomer who developed the heliocentric theory that Earth and other planets circled the sun; theorized that Earth completes a daily rotation as it circles the sun; and published a formal work on his theories entitled *De Revolutionibus Orbium Coelestium,* which suggested that the universe was much larger than had previously been believed
- Dr. Mae Jemison: medical and social issues pioneer who was the first African-American woman to go into space; founded companies dedicated to using medicine and technology to improve the lives of people in underdeveloped countries
- John Muir: naturalist and writer who founded the Sierra Club; was instrumental in the creation of several national parks; and influenced President Theodore Roosevelt's conservation programs

Grade 4

- Benjamin Banneker: African-American surveyor, astronomer, and mathematician; published an almanac that predicted weather patterns, tides, and astronomy tables; corresponded with Thomas Jefferson and helped design plans for Washington, D.C.
- Elizabeth Blackwell: first female to graduate from medical school in the U.S.; founded a clinic to serve the poor in New York City that became New York University Downtown Hospital; opened medical schools for women in the United States and England
- Charles Drew: pioneering African-American doctor and blood researcher; discovered that blood plasma could be separated from blood cells and stored more effectively and that, unlike blood types, plasma does not differ from person to person; established blood banks that saved many lives in World War II
- Michael Faraday: chemist and physicist; discovered electromagnetic rotation; proved that gases could be converted to liquids by liquefying chlorine; discovered the First and Second Laws of Electrolysis; established scientific lecture series that continue today

What Students Need to Learn

- **Galileo Galilei: Italian mathematician, scientist, and inventor**
- **Percy Lavon Julian: American chemist and inventor**
- **Ernest Just: American biologist and medical pioneer**
- **Carolus Linnaeus: Swedish botanist and the "Father of Taxonomy"**

VII. Science Biographies

Materials

string, p. 637

pen or small ball, p. 637

stopwatch (optional), p. 637

encyclopedia or Internet access, p. 641

1 piece of poster board per student, pp. 643, 645

index cards for questions to famous scientists, p. 644

newspaper and magazines for collages, p. 645

What Students Will Learn in Future Grades

Students will review and extend their learning about scientists and inventors in each year of the Core Knowledge curriculum.

Grade 6

- Marie Curie
- Lewis Howard Latimer
- Isaac Newton
- Alfred Wegner

Vocabulary

Student/Teacher Vocabulary

arthritis: inflammation of bone joints (T)

binomial: adjective describing the two-word naming of an organism (S)

embryology: the study of embryos and their development (T)

geocentric: adjective describing the belief that the universe revolves around Earth (S)

glaucoma: a disease that occurs when pressure inside the eye rises because fluid cannot be drained (T)

heliocentric: adjective describing the belief that the universe, including Earth, revolves around the sun (S)

Law of Falling Bodies: the motion theory established by Galileo by studying pendulums and inclined planes (T)

patent: government security for an owner's exclusive control and possession of a particular invention (S)

pendulum: a body suspended from a fixed point so as to swing freely to and fro under the action of gravity (S)

supernova: an explosion of a star in which the star becomes extremely luminous (T)

Domain Vocabulary

Science biographies and associated words:
aptitude, discovery, Pisa, Leaning Tower of Pisa, swing, height, period, motion, back-and-forth, regular, irregular, measure, theory, hypothesis, test, experiment, Aristotle, mass, heavy, light, model, rate, invention, inclined plane, simple machine, nova, explosion, astronomy, heavens, celestial bodies, planets, inspire, telescope, magnify, enlarge, details, lens, observe, observation, reinforce, prove, disprove, Copernicus, Copernican, phases, Ptolemy, revolve, orbit, scholar, theologian, theology, navigation, development, relieve, chemist, chemistry, organic, inorganic, Harvard University, graduate, degree, master's degree, doctoral degree, Ph.D., synthesize, produce, manufacture, drug, medicine, hormone, ailment, treat, laboratory, legal, ownership, biology, physiology, cells, tissues, organs, marine biology, marine animal, marine, sea, ocean, embryology, reproduction, classification, classify, organisms, botany, botanist, expedition, journey, species, nomenclature, naming, descriptor, trait, characteristic, feature, similar, different, unique, specimen

Cross-curricular Connections

History and Geography

World: The Renaissance and the Reformation
• Copernicus and Galileo

Mathematics

Geometry

Galileo Galilei

What Teachers Need to Know

Galileo Galilei (1564–1642)

Galileo Galilei was born in Pisa, Italy, in 1564. His family was of the nobility, but they were not wealthy—Galileo's father worked as a merchant and a musician. As a boy, Galileo showed an aptitude for music, painting, and building small toys, but his father hoped that Galileo would become a doctor. In 1581, Galileo enrolled in the University of Pisa, where he began to study medicine and philosophy.

As a student at Pisa, Galileo made his first significant scientific discovery. While visiting the cathedral of Pisa, Galileo watched a large lamp hanging from the ceiling swing back and forth and wondered if the motion of the swinging was as regular as it appeared to the eye. He timed the motion of the lamp by taking his pulse, and discovered that the amount of time for each swing was exactly the same. Galileo later concluded that a pendulum could be used to accurately measure time, and so the idea for the pendulum clock was born. Galileo would continue to experiment with pendulums throughout his life and make further discoveries in later years.

In 1585, Galileo left the university and returned home without earning his degree. He had decided that he would no longer study medicine, but rather would pursue a career in mathematics and physics. Over the next four years, he taught math as a private tutor in Florence and began to conduct mathematical and physics experiments. Galileo returned to the University of Pisa in 1589 to accept an important teaching position as a professor of mathematics.

While at Pisa, Galileo began to test theories of motion. The ancient Greek philosopher Aristotle had developed the theory that heavier objects fall faster than lighter ones; Aristotelians believed that mass determined the speed of motion. The thinkers and scientists of the 1500s still commonly accepted this theory. Galileo, however, did not believe that this model was correct. He conducted a series of experiments and found that objects fall at the same rate regardless of differences in their mass. Galileo published his findings in a small book called *De Motu (On Motion)*.

There is a famous story that Galileo dropped two unequal weights from the top of the Leaning Tower of Pisa to prove his theory of motion. This story is now largely believed to be myth rather than truth. Galileo was, however, known for his use of experimentation, and if the story helps students remember what Galileo found, then it has its uses. Galileo's employment of experimentation was unusual in his time; most people followed the teachings and theories of so-called

Teaching Idea

Ask students to work in pairs to create a pendulum. Provide each pair with a 2-foot piece of string and a small object such as a ball or pen. Have students create the pendulum by securely tying the string around the small object. While 1 student holds the free end of the string, the other student should pull back the object to set the pendulum in a gentle back-and-forth motion. It is very important that the student holding the string keep his or her hands as still as possible, and it may be helpful to have the student press the free end of the string against some rigid support, such as the side of a desk or a door frame. The student then should measure the motion of the swing with his or her pulse, just as Galileo did, or with a stopwatch if one is available. Each student in the pair should take a turn in both roles. Students will discover, as Galileo did, that each swing of the pendulum takes exactly the same time as the others. Explain to students that this discovery led to the development of modern clocks.

Cross-curricular Teaching Idea

You may wish to teach about Galileo in conjunction with World History and Geography Section IV, "The Renaissance and the Reformation." (See pp. 164–188.)

authorities, such as Aristotle, rather than questioning or discovering things about nature on their own. Galileo is sometimes thought of as the father of modern science for his use of experimentation, direct observation of phenomena, and the application of mathematics to explain physical phenomena.

Through his work on the rules of motion, Galileo began to uncover "secrets of the universe," which were still poorly understood. His findings again contradicted Aristotelian theories that were the basis for much of the scientific thought of the time. Galileo would continue to challenge popular beliefs, and his theories would soon cause him significant problems.

Galileo transferred to the University of Padua in 1592, where he worked as a professor of mathematics for the next 18 years. He made a number of important inventions during the late 1590s, including a water pump and a sector, a type of compass still used today. He continued to experiment with motion, now studying pendulums and inclined planes. These new experiments eventually led to the establishment of his Law of Falling Bodies.

In 1604, a supernova appeared in the sky. This exciting event inspired Galileo to turn his attention to astronomy. In 1609, Galileo learned of an invention that allowed you to see faraway things—the telescope—and set out to build one of his own. By 1610, Galileo had developed a telescope that could magnify objects by 20 times—the most powerful telescope of his day. Using his telescope, Galileo began observing the stars, moon, planets, and sun, and made a number of significant discoveries that were in direct contradiction to the accepted theories of the universe supported by the Church.

The geocentric theory of the universe, popular during Galileo's time, held that Earth was the center of the universe and the sun and planets revolved around it. This theory was based on the teachings of Aristotle and the theories of Ptolemy. The Church supported this theory, as it underscored its teachings that God created a perfect universe with humans as the center of the universe. Also, the Bible contained passages that referred to the sun moving, which seemed to imply that the sun moved around Earth. Counter to these theories was the heliocentric theory of the universe developed some time earlier by the Polish astronomer Copernicus and supported by Galileo, which held that the sun was the center of the universe.

Galileo came to his position through a number of discoveries: he observed spots on the sun's surface that moved over time; he discovered four moons of Jupiter; he discovered that Venus had phases similar to the phases of Earth's moon.

All of these discoveries convinced Galileo that the geocentric theory of the universe had to be wrong. The phases of Venus showed him that Venus and by logical extension, Mercury, revolved around the sun rather than Earth. The moons revolving around Jupiter showed him there was more than one center of motion in the universe. Finally, the sunspots challenged the theory of the perfection of the universe that was at the heart of Church teaching. The Church held that the heavens were perfect and incorruptible, yet Galileo's discoveries challenged their interpretation of the cosmos. Through his empirical discoveries, Galileo provided scientific support for the heliocentric theory of Copernicus.

The Copernican Universe

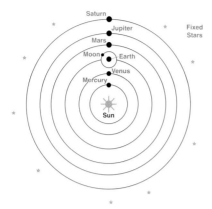

Galileo shared his observations with many scholars and other influential people in Florence and Rome, and in doing so raised the suspicion of the Church. The Roman Catholic Church had recently been stung by Luther and the Protestant Reformation and was very touchy about ideas that seemed to conflict with church doctrines. Galileo was warned by the Church to stay away from matters that threatened theology, so he tried to concentrate on ways that sailors could use his astronomical discoveries. Between 1610 and 1632, Galileo continued to observe the stars and planets, and also began studying the tides—which only further supported his belief in the Copernican model of the universe.

In 1632, Galileo published his *Dialogue Concerning the Two Chief World Systems.* In this book, he tried to treat the Copernican theory of the universe as something to be debated, but when the Church reviewed the material they immediately censored it. Galileo was arrested and the Church sent him before the Inquisition to be tried. Galileo was forced to recant, or take back, his theories, and the Inquisition sentenced him to house arrest. Galileo spent the rest of his life in his home in Florence until his death in 1642. However, Galileo was vindicated by later history and the further development of science. Galileo's discoveries have contributed enormously to the advancement of science and our understanding of the universe. (91)

Percy Lavon Julian (1899–1975)

Percy Lavon Julian was born on April 11, 1899, in Montgomery, Alabama. He was the eldest of six children born to James Sumner, a railroad mail clerk, and Elisabeth, a schoolteacher. Julian's parents emphasized the value of education and encouraged their children to attend school. The children had been told how their grandfather, a slave, had been severely punished when the slave owner found him trying to learn to read and write. Education, they had learned, was a privilege. Despite the fact that in the early 1900s there were few opportunities for black students to pursue an education, all of the Julian children went on to earn advanced degrees.

Julian was a bright child and attended school through the eighth grade—the highest grade black students were allowed to complete. When he was 17, he applied to and was accepted by DePauw University in Greencastle, Indiana. Since he had not been allowed to attend school after the eighth grade, Julian had to take several extra courses in addition to his freshman and sophomore workload to make up for the missing schooling and catch up with his fellow classmates. In

Percy Lavon Julian

spite of this obstacle, Julian graduated in 1920 at the top of his class and as a member of Phi Beta Kappa and Sigma Xi honor societies. He had earned a chemistry degree and hoped to attend graduate school, but was discouraged from continuing his education because of racist sentiments. Julian decided to accept a teaching position at Fisk University in Nashville, Tennessee, but continued to look for opportunities to attend graduate school.

After working at Fisk for two years, Julian was finally given his chance at graduate education—he received the Austin Fellowship in Chemistry in 1923, and enrolled at Harvard University to earn his master's degree. Once again, Julian proved himself academically and graduated at the top of his class. This achievement went unrecognized, however, as he could not secure a teaching position at any major university. Julian finally accepted a position at the West Virginia State College for Negroes, where he worked for one year and then relocated to Howard University as an associate professor of chemistry.

In 1929, Julian received a fellowship from the General Education Board and went to Vienna, Austria, to earn his Ph.D. While in Vienna, Julian developed an interest in plant products, including the Calabar bean and the soybean. In 1931, after receiving a Ph.D. in organic chemistry, he returned to the United States and to Howard University as the head of the chemistry department. Julian then returned to DePauw University, this time as a professor, and taught organic chemistry.

Julian continued to experiment with plants. In 1935, while teaching at DePauw, he worked with Dr. Josef Pikl, a colleague from Vienna, and together they synthesized physostigmine, a drug used to treat glaucoma. Prior to this synthetic (produced in the lab with chemicals) version, physostigmine was made by extracting the compound from Calabar beans, a very time-consuming and tedious process.

This discovery helped propel Julian into international recognition as a chemist. He was considered for the position of chair of the chemistry department at DePauw, but was passed over because of his race. Shortly after, he left academia and joined the Glidden Company in 1936 as the director of the Soya Product Division. Glidden was a paint and varnish manufacturer looking to develop new products out of soybeans. While at Glidden, Julian made a series of new discoveries using soybeans. He discovered that soybeans could be used to inexpensively manufacture testosterone and progesterone hormones. These hormones are helpful in preventing miscarriages and in fighting certain types of cancers as well as other diseases. This discovery allowed chemists to produce large quantities of these hormones (the body makes only small amounts), allowing doctors to treat more ailments less expensively than before.

Julian also developed a foamy substance from soy protein that worked as a flame retardant. This foam was used by the U.S. Navy during World War II and saved the lives of thousands of American sailors. Sailors called it "bean soup."

In 1948, the Mayo Clinic in Minnesota announced that a compound called cortisone relieved the swelling of arthritic joints. Cortisone was taken from the adrenal glands of oxen. This made it both costly and difficult to create large quantities; it took hundreds of oxen to produce enough cortisone for just one person. Julian began working on a synthetic version of cortisone, and by 1949 had developed synthetic cortisone from soybeans. With Julian's discovery, millions of people could enjoy relief from arthritis pain at a significantly lower cost.

Teaching Idea

Glaucoma is a disease that occurs when pressure inside the eye rises because fluid cannot be drained. Glaucoma damages the optic nerve and can lead to blindness. Have students research this disease and present their findings to the class.

Teaching Idea

Review the endocrine system and hormones, taught in Section V, with students. You may wish to discuss hormones and the functioning of the endocrine system with students before teaching them about puberty. As puberty is related to the production of hormones, a working knowledge of these chemical messengers may aid students in their understanding of puberty. You may also wish to discuss and review the stages of the life cycle with your class in introducing puberty. Ask students to explain why hormones are important.

chemical structure of synthetic cortisone

Despite all of his successes, Julian still suffered as a result of racism. His home in Oak Park, Illinois, was set on fire in 1951, and only a year later was firebombed by a stick of dynamite thrown from a moving car. While some did not welcome the black family in their neighborhood, other illustrious residents—including the writer Ernest Hemingway and the architect Frank Lloyd Wright—gathered in defense of Julian's right to live wherever he chose.

Julian left Glidden in 1953 to start the Julian Laboratories, specializing in producing synthetic cortisone from soybeans. Julian continued to experiment and found that yams also had many useful scientific properties. He built a laboratory in Mexico City to grow yams, which were then sent to his laboratory for processing. In 1961, he sold this operation to Smith Kline and French for $2.3 million. Julian also established Julian Associates, Inc., and the Julian Research Institute.

Over the course of his career, Julian was issued more than 100 patents and published articles in a number of scholarly journals. He earned many awards, including the Spingarn Medal from the NAACP. He is recognized as a pioneer in the world of chemistry, and his discoveries have had a positive impact on the lives of millions of people. Dr. Percy Lavon Julian died in 1975 from cancer. (92)

Ernest Just (1883–1941)

Ernest Everett Just was born in Charleston, South Carolina, in 1883. When his father died four years later, Ernest was forced to work as a field hand to help earn money for the family. Despite his difficult childhood, Ernest was a bright and curious child. His mother, a teacher, taught Ernest at home until he was 13 years old. With limited opportunities in South Carolina for blacks to receive a more advanced education, Ernest worked hard and was accepted to the exclusive Kimball Academy in New Hampshire. At Kimball, he distinguished himself by completing the four-year program in only three years. He also led the debate team, was editor of the school newspaper, and graduated at the top of his class.

In 1903, Just enrolled in Dartmouth College and began his studies in biology, specializing in the study of cells. He studied under the famous zoologist William Patten and excelled at his coursework. Just graduated in 1907 with degrees in biology and history. He was the class valedictorian and the only student to graduate magna cum laude. After graduation, Just was hired at Howard University, where he worked as a professor in the biology and physiology departments and at the medical school as well. During the summer months, he would go to the famous Marine Biological Laboratory in Woods Hole, Massachusetts, where he worked as a research assistant to Frank Lillie. It was here that Just began experimenting with marine animal cells and reproduction. His research was well received, and in 1915 he was awarded the NAACP's first Spingarn Medal.

Ernest Just

VII. Science Biographies

Teaching Idea

Explain to students that Just spent his career looking at ways in which the sperm and egg cells of marine animals join together to create offspring. This research was performed in order to gain insights into how cells work and how diseases that affect cells, such as cancer and sickle cell anemia, might be stopped.

Teaching Idea

You may want to teach about Ernest Everett Just in connection with your study of cells and reproduction. (See Section II, "Cells: Structures and Processes," pp. 573–583, and Section IV, "Life Cycles and Reproduction," pp. 600–606.)

Teaching Idea

Review reproduction and the different phases of development, taught in Section IV, with students. Explain that the early stages of development in simple marine animals are similar to the early stages of development in humans, and that studying marine animals is a good way to learn about human development.

Carolus Linnaeus

Assisted by Lillie, who was the head of the zoology department at the University of Chicago, Just returned to school and in 1916 earned his Ph.D. in experimental embryology from the University of Chicago—the first black man to do so. Throughout the remainder of his career, he would focus his research on the reproduction, fertilization, cell division, and cell structure of marine animals, with particular interest in parthenogenesis, the ability of some types of marine eggs to reproduce without sperm.

Just believed that understanding cell development and the functioning of healthy cells would lead to the discovery of cures for cell irregularities. His research on marine animals revealed many new insights about cells and their properties. Just earned broad recognition for his precise experiments and for his expertise in marine animal fertilization. He wrote many articles for journals and other scientific publications, which he compiled into a book titled *Basic Methods for Experiments on Eggs of Marine Mammals.*

Despite the fact the Just was considered a leader in the field of marine biology, he experienced considerable racial discrimination in the United States. However, his expertise was well respected throughout Europe, and he traveled there often, working and lecturing in Germany, Russia, Italy, and France. Just published his second book, *The Biology of the Cell Surface,* while in Europe.

Just was living in France in 1939 when World War II erupted. Although the French government advised all foreign scientists to leave France, Just remained in Paris. When the Germans invaded Paris, Just was detained and held in a prisoner of war camp for a short period of time before being allowed to return to the United States. He went back to Howard University, but had become very ill and was unable to teach. In 1941, Just died of cancer.

Although Dr. Ernest Just suffered racial discrimination throughout his life, he worked hard to overcome this obstacle and to distinguish himself as a scientist and scholar. His work in the field of marine biology contributed to the wider body of scientific knowledge and helped lay the groundwork for important medical discoveries. Ernest Just is considered one of the most influential scientists of our time. **(93)**

Carolus Linnaeus (1707–1778)

Carolus (Carl) Linnaeus is often called the "Father of Taxonomy." The system for classifying organisms that he developed in the 1700s is accepted as the international standard by scientists today.

Carl Linnaeus was born in Stenbrohult, Sweden, in 1707. His father, Nils Ingemarsson Linnaeus, a Lutheran clergyman and an amateur botanist, passed on his love for plants to Carl. From a very early age, Linnaeus tended his own little garden and knew the names of many plants. His parents had hoped that Linnaeus would become a priest, and were disappointed when he showed little interest and poor academic preparation for the priesthood. The local doctor, however, recognizing Linnaeus's fascination with plants, suggested he attend medical school, where botany was part of the curriculum. Doctors in the 1700s relied on their knowledge of the natural healing substances in plants to prepare medications; medical school would provide Linnaeus with an opportunity to study his beloved plants.

Linnaeus entered the University of Lund in 1727, and then transferred one year later to the University of Uppsala—the most prestigious university in Sweden. Although he struggled financially, he was able to secure some money to take a botanical expedition to Lapland in 1731. During his five-month expedition of this unexplored wilderness, he discovered and collected many botanical species and distinguished himself as a botanist.

Throughout his life, Linnaeus would experience ongoing financial instability. With his engaging personality, however, he always managed to find wealthy patrons to support his work. In 1734, Linnaeus mounted another expedition, this time to central Sweden. During this expedition, he met Sara Elisabeth Moraeus and asked her to marry him. Sara's father was a doctor who had studied in the Netherlands, and he asked that Carl do the same before marrying his daughter. Linnaeus moved to the Netherlands in 1735 and earned his medical degree from the University of Harderwijk. He married his fiancée in 1739.

After completing his medical studies, Linnaeus moved to the University of Leiden (also in the Netherlands) in 1737 to continue his studies. While at Leiden, he published his first edition of *System Naturae (The System of Nature)*, a book of his classifications for all living things. Over the course of his study of plants, Linnaeus had developed a unique system for classifying them. Since Aristotle's time, scientists had used the word *genera* (singular, *genus*) to describe a group of similar organisms; however, until the mid-1700s there was no standard system for grouping genera together. Linnaeus was the first to create a hierarchical system that grouped genera into orders, orders into classes, classes into phyla, and phyla into kingdoms based on shared traits. (See Section I for a more complete discussion of the classification of organisms.)

Linnaeus's classification system was based on the number and arrangement of a plant's reproductive organs; a plant's class was determined by its stamen, and its order by the pistils. Linnaeus's system was very controversial at the time because of its sexual nature and because it did not always accurately classify organisms. Today Linnaeus's idea of classifying organisms by common traits, rather than his specific groupings according to reproductive organs, remains as the basis for scientific classification systems. However, scientists have been able to develop more accurate classification based on recent science, including DNA-based science.

In addition to his classification system, Linnaeus also developed a system for naming organisms. Scientists of the time made up often long, unwieldy names for species, which were often subject to change, making communication and the sharing of information difficult. As more new species were discovered, the need for a conventional naming system increased. Linnaeus came up with the binomial system of nomenclature that we use today to name organisms. The word *binomial* means that an organism is given a two-word name; in Linnaeus's system the first word is the organism's genus and the second word is a short descriptor name for the organism's species.

Although Carl Linnaeus was not the first botanist to use the binomial system, he was the first to use it consistently. As such, the oldest plant and animal names commonly accepted in the scientific community today were published by

Teaching Idea

You may want to teach about Carl Linnaeus in conjunction with Section I, "Classifying Living Things." (See pp. 554–572.) Share with students that under Linnaeus's system the classification of human beings is as follows: kingdom *Animalia*, phylum *Chordata*, class *Vertebrata*, order *Primates*, genus *Homo*, and species *sapiens*. Humans are generally referred to by their binomial classification of *Homo sapiens*.

Teaching Idea

If you have not yet studied Section I, "Classifying Living Things," invite students to collect different plants from their surrounding environment. Challenge students to classify the plants they collect into groups that share similar traits. They may classify plants according to the types of leaves they exhibit, or whether or not they produce flowers, etc. Have students create a poster to show the plants they have collected and to show and describe the classification system they have developed. It is important to reiterate that there is a universal system of classification used.

Linnaeus in his 1758 edition of *Systema Naturae,* and in his 1753 edition of *Species Plantarum.* Today, his system of taxonomy is accepted as the international standard for naming organisms.

In 1738, Linnaeus returned to Sweden to practice medicine and then moved to the University of Uppsala to serve as a professor of medicine and botany. He refurbished the school's botanical garden and arranged the plants according to his new system. He continued to update his *Systema Naturae* and published other articles on botany and classification. He encouraged his students to make botanical expeditions to collect new specimens. (He had made arrangements with the Swedish East India Company to allow his students to periodically travel for free to wherever the company may have been trading.) Under his guidance, a number of his students traveled around the world collecting plants from the South Pacific, Australia, the Americas, and Asia.

Linnaeus also continued to work as a doctor and secured a position as the senior physician to the Swedish royal family. He became very involved in developing new ways to stimulate the Swedish economy and believed that by growing important plants such as rice, tea, and cacao in Sweden, the country would become more self sufficient. Unfortunately his attempts in this area failed.

Throughout his life, Linnaeus anchored his research to his religious beliefs, believing that the study of plants and animals would allow people to gain insight into the divine order set forth by God. Carl Linnaeus died in 1778. After his death, his collection of plant species and his manuscripts were sold to Sir James Edward Smith, who founded the Linnean Society of London, still in operation today. (94)

The Big Idea in Review

Science is built on the careful observations and creative contributions of individuals.

Review

Below are some ideas for ongoing assessment and review activities. These are not meant to constitute a comprehensive list.

• You may teach each of these scientists within the context of specific sections in the science unit. You may find that the class makes connections between the unit material and the individual scientist.

• This section provides an opportunity for students to complete short research reports on any of these scientists. Using the Language Arts section, provide the class with topics for short reports to write in formal style. Each day of a week, provide a mini-lesson on different aspects of report writing, such as correct paragraph form or bibliographies. Share these reports when completed.

• After the study of each scientist, have the class write interview questions to illustrate what they have learned about each scientist. For example, they might ask where that person was from and why he was famous. Then, ask the class to write each interview question on an index card and write the answer on the back of the card. Have pairs of students perform the interview for the class, with one student playing the role of interviewer and one playing the role of the scientist.

- During the study of each scientist, make a poster to illustrate that person's accomplishments. For example, take a piece of poster board and post the name of the scientist and that person's picture. Then, have the class find pictures or words related to the scientist's work from magazines and newspapers and add them to the poster. When you have completed the study of each individual, select a student to stand and talk about that scientist, explaining the significance of the words and pictures from the poster.

- Ask students to write a journal page as if they were one of these scientists, writing in the first person. Students should pick one of these men and then write a journal page describing their scientific discovery. Have students share their journal entries with the class. You may be able to have students act out their writing, as if they were explaining the scientific discovery for the first time.

- You may also ask the following questions after completing this section:

1. What discovery did Galileo make that supported the Copernican theory that the sun is the center of the universe?

   Galileo's discovery of the phases of Venus supported the Copernican theory that the sun is the center of the universe.

2. What did Percy Lavon Julian develop that helped millions of people with arthritis pain?

   Julian developed synthetic cortisone to treat arthritis pain.

3. Ernest Just explored the fertilization process of what types of animals?

   Just explored the fertilization process of marine animals.

4. What is Carl Linnaeus credited with standardizing?

   Linnaeus is credited with standardizing the system for naming and classifying organisms.

More Resources

The titles listed below are offered as a representative sample of materials and not a complete list of everything that is available.

For students —

- *Black Pioneers of Science and Invention*, by Louis Haber (Odyssey Classics, 1992). First published in 1970. Tells the story of 14 African-American scientists and inventors, including Percy Lavon Julian and Ernest Just. Paperback, 288 pages, ISBN 0152085661.

- *Carl Linnaeus: Father of Classification (Great Minds of Science)*, by Margaret J. Anderson (Enslow, 2001). Paperback, 128 pages, ISBN 0766018679.

- *Five Brilliant Scientists (Hello Reader, Level 4)*, by Lynda Jones (Scholastic, 2000). Contains easy-to-read biographies of Percy Lavon Julian and Ernest Just. Paperback, 48 pages, ISBN 0590480316.

- *Galileo and the Stargazers*, an audio recording by Jim Weiss (Greathall Productions, www.greathall.com or 1-800-477-6234).

For teachers —

- *Black Apollo of Science: The Life of Ernest Everett Just*, by Kenneth R. Manning (Oxford University Press, 1984). Paperback, 416 pages, ISBN 0195034988.

- *Galileo Galilei: First Physicist (Oxford Portraits in Science)*, by James MacLachlan (Oxford University Press Children's Books, 1999). May also be used as an advanced text for interested students. Paperback, 128 pages, ISBN 0195131703.

- Project Linnaeus, www.c18.rutgers.edu/pr/lc/proj.lin.html, a part of the c18project at Rutgers, is an online collection of Linnaeus's writings.

More Resources continued

• The Starry Messenger Project, www.masters.ab.ca/bdyck/Galileo, is self-described as "an online collaborative project for middle school students from around the globe. The focus of our project is learning about Space (the movement in the skies) and using what we've learned in a simulation experience surrounding the 1633 trial of Galileo."